Niels Steensgaard

The Asian Trade Revolution of the Seventeenth Century

The East India Companies and the
Decline of the Caravan Trade

The University of Chicago Press
Chicago and London

The Asian Trade Revolution of the Seventeenth Century was originally published as
Carracks, Caravans, and Companies, volume 17 in the Scandinavian Institute of Asian
Studies Monograph Series, Copenhagen, Denmark, in 1973.

NIELS STEENSGAARD is a professor of history at the University of Copenhagen in
Denmark. He is the author of several articles in the fields of European and Asian
history.
[1974]

The University of Chicago Press, Chicago 60637
The University of Chicago Press, Ltd., London

© 1973 Studentlitteratur, Niels Steensgaard. All rights reserved
Published 1973. The University of Chicago Press edition 1974
Printed in the United States of America
78 77 76 75 74   987654321

Library of Congress Cataloging in Publication Data

Steensgaard, Niels, 1932-
    The Asian Trade Revolution of the Seventeenth Century

    Originally presented as the author's thesis,
Copenhagen.
    Bibliography: p.
    1. Commerce—History. 2. Europe—Commerce—
Asia—History. 3. Asia—Commerce—Europe——History.
I. Title.
HF495.S83   1975   382'.094'05   74-16397
ISBN 0-226-77138-5   ISBN 0-226-77139-3 (pbk.)

Contents

3

Tables

Maps

Diagram

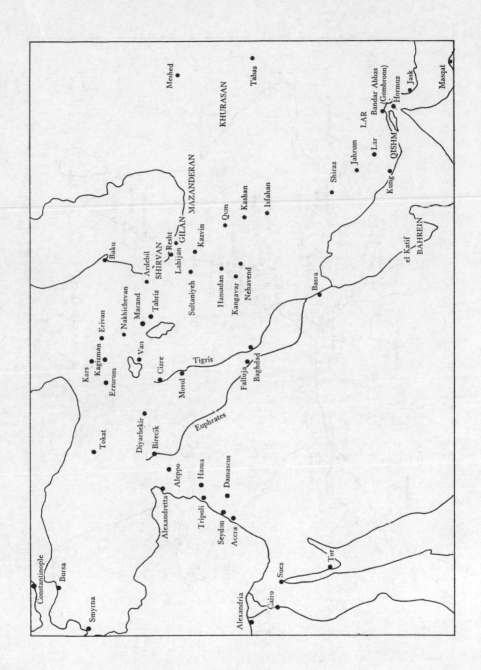

5

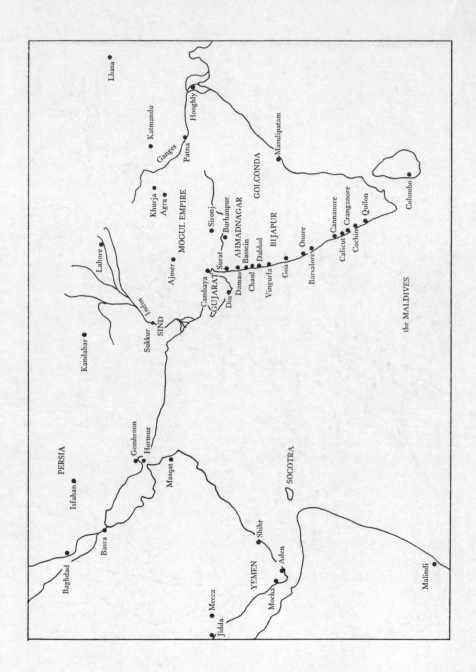

Preface

The dramatic shift of balance in the European-Asian trade in the decades following 1600 has fascinated me for several years. It appeared to me that the decline of the Portuguese Empire in Asia, the decline of the intercontinental caravan trade and the triumph of the Dutch and English East India Companies – the confrontation of the *carracks*, the *caravans* and the *companies* – was more than a tale of triumph and disaster, but also constituted a decisive moment in world history, pointing towards that distribution of wealth and power which characterized later centuries and the world in which we live.

My point of departure was a study of the victorious companies, but I soon found that the shift in balance could not be accounted for by looking at the victorious side only. A satisfactory study would have to be made on a comparative basis, taking into account what evidence might be unearthed concerning the losers – the Portuguese Empire and the caravan merchants – as well as the evidence contained in the company records. An early working hypothesis based upon a simple comparison of the costs born by the merchants on the various routes proved insufficient; the composition of the costs revealed that the outcome was determined neither by size nor by technical and managerial efficiency alone, but rather by deep-rooted structural differences between the institutions concerned. I found that the shift in balance might best be conceived of as the outcome of a confrontation of structures or a *structural crisis* and that the comparative analysis should be focused on key institutional features. This approach implies a high level of abstraction. I hope, however, that I have nor broken what I consider a basic rule for the historian, and lost sight of the men who acted and the reality in which they found themselves.

The work on this book was begun in 1961–62 when I was a *British Council* scholar. I divided my time in London between the School of Oriental and African Studies and the archive of the Commonwealth Relations Office. It is with pleasure and gratitude I think of the hospitality and kindness extended to me by these institutions and by the British Council. On my return to Copenhagen I was more or less submerged in teaching in the difficult years when the number of students swelled without a corresponding increase in staff and facilities. A grant from *Statens almindelige Videnskabsfond* enabled me, however, to continue the collection of material in

7

France and Venice. In 1967 I became a research fellow at the University of Copenhagen, a further grant from the University enabling me to visit archives in Spain, Portugal and Rome. In all essentials the manuscript was finished in October 1971.

There are still a few languages I ought to know in order to master all the evidence relevant to the subject, and there are archives I have not yet visited in which I suspect more data might be uncovered. The comparative approach has necessarily brought me into specialized fields and led me to conclusions that are in conflict with national historiographical traditions. I can only hope that I have substantiated my conclusions or, if I have erred, that my errors may prove useful.

One of the pleasures of this study has been the quest for material, which brought me to a large number of archives and libraries all over Europe. Everywhere I have met with kindness and efficiency and I am very glad to have this opportunity of expressing my gratitude to the staffs of the archives and libraries in which I have worked. I am also greatly indebted to *the Scandinavian Institute of Asian Studies,* which did me the honour of including this volume in their monograph series, to Karl Reinhold Haellquist, fil. lic., of the Institute, who saw the volume through the press, and not least to Mrs Paula Hostrup-Jessen, who heroically undertook to translate my convoluted Danish into English.

Numerous friends, colleagues and students have a share in this book. *The Institute of History at the University of Copenhagen* offers a lively and stimulating *milieu* for the study and teaching of history, and I am happy to acknowledge my debt to my friends and students at the Institute as well as to the many other Danish and foreign historians with whom I have discussed subjects bearing upon the problems of this book. I would especially like to mention the advice and guidance I have drawn from conversations with Professor C. R. Boxer, Professor Kristof Glamann, Professor Bernard Lewis, Professor Erling Ladewig Petersen and the late Professor Maurice Lombard.

I have a special debt of gratitude to Professor Aksel E. Christensen, who was the director of the Institute in its (and my) formative years, and to Professor Svend Ellehøj, the ideal superviser, who encouraged, but never interfered. Finally, I wish to acknowledge my debt of gratitude to the late Professor Astrid Friis who first introduced me to the study of the history of international trade, and who taught me that historical subjects should be studied, not in the safe hinterland of established categories, but in the unpleasant regions where one may have to revise one's ideas on being confronted with the sources.

The Institute of History at the
University of Copenhagen

January 1973
Niels Steensgaard

Introduction

The destructive effects of the discovery of the sea route to Asia upon the traditional intercontinental trade routes were not felt until after the elapse of an entire century. After a set-back at the beginning of the 16th century the trade routes through the Middle East regained their former importance, and at the end of the 16th century the transcontinental caravan trade reached dimensions which must presumably be regarded as its historical culmination. No decisive blow was struck at the caravan trade until the establishment of the North-West European trading companies, the Dutch *voorkompagnieën* from 1595, the East India Company in 1600, and the Dutch United East India Company (VOC) in 1602. During the first few decades of the 17th century the most important Asian commodities disappeared from the west-bound caravans to the Levant towns; in some cases the west-bound stream of goods was replaced by an east-bound stream, the ocean having triumphed over the mainland.

This sequence of events, which may be regarded as established, raises a problem which the historical literature has so far only touched upon to a limited extent. How were the Companies able to triumph, where the Portuguese had failed? Why did the transcontinental trade, which had resisted Portuguese competition and attempted blockade throughout a whole century, have to retire in favour of the Companies?

No direct investigations of the problem are available, but although the question cannot be said to have been finally formulated or satisfactorily answered, several historians have dealt with it within a wider context. For Braudel, the problem is the survival of the caravan trade in the 16th century, not its downfall in the 17th century, the date of which, moreover, he does not regard as finally established. Braudel sees the explanation in the Portuguese ruthlessness and negligence and in the rise of alternative routes from the pepper-producing areas in South-East Asia to the Red Sea and the Persian Gulf, primarily based upon the Sultanate of Achin in North Sumatra. This development he places within a wider context: the relative abundance of silver in the Mediterranean region in the second half of the 16th century.[1] Ralph Davis emphasizes the relative power of

1. BRAUDEL I p. 514–16.

9

the European nations: the Portuguese had not been able to avoid or control the wars hindering the free transport of goods, but the newcomers were able to carry on trade without regard to the political conditions.[2] Meilink-Roelofsz connects the decline of the transit trade with the North-West European Companies' activities in South-East Asia, activities in this context implying both the purchase of spices and the blockade of the production areas.[3] For all three historians the problems may be said to lie in the periphery of their spheres of interest; the explanations they have produced cannot very well be rejected, but cannot on the other hand claim to be exhaustive.

It is astonishing to find that the available literature scarcely seems to have mentioned such an important problem of discontinuity. Part of the explanation must be sought in the fact that it has only been possible to raise the question on the basis of the last generation's research, but in addition the problem, even though on the surface it may be a simple breach of continuity, is particularly unwieldy. The answer is not hidden somewhere on the road between the Banda Islands and Amsterdam, but must be sought in the global, political and economic context. The downfall of the caravan trade, the defeat of the Portuguese and the triumph of the Companies was an episode in the historical process during which the Middle East and the Mediterranean region relinquished the economic leadership in favour of the Atlantic regions. It was part of the clash between the Catholic Iberian powers and the Protestant Channel powers, and it was part of the confrontation between older and newer entrepreneurial forms – a step towards the development of modern economy. If the problem of the downfall of the caravan trade is isolated from this context it is simultaneously cut off from the fields in which a relevant explanation may be sought. On the other hand, if it is viewed in its full context, what appears to be a concrete problem is lost in global confusion.

This dilemma is naturally none other than that which the historian so frequently encounters when attempting to delimit the problem in the face of the indivisibility of reality, and an attempt has been made in this book to overcome the dilemma in several ways. Firstly, attention has been concentrated on Hormuz, the Portuguese fortress at the entrance to the Persian Gulf, which fell in 1622 as the result of a combined Persian and English attack. A different town could have been chosen, such as Baghdad, Aleppo or Alexandria – towns we know more about – but the fate of Hormuz dramatizes the breach of continuity, because its very existence depended on the transit trade, and because its fall was so definitive and so clearly connected with the larger confrontation. If we know why Hormuz

2. DAVIS p. 191–194.
3. MEILINK-ROELOFSZ p. 222–225.

fell we are well on the way towards knowing why the Companies not only ousted the Portuguese, but also took over most of the trade which by the end of the 16th century still passed along the traditional transcontinental trade routes.

Secondly, two different methodological procedures have been chosen when investigating the problem: the comparative approach and the procedure of following the sequence of events leading up to the fall of Hormuz. In the comparative study the institutions concerned are compared, assuming that their institutional structures contain features able to explain their advance or decline. The question, why did the Companies triumph and why did the Portuguese fail, may thereby be reformulated as follows: did the structure of the Companies present features capable of explaining their success as compared with those of the competing institutions?

When employing the second method of investigation, i.e. following the sequence of events, the problem is reformulated correspondingly: were there any features in the sequence of events prior to the fall of Hormuz and in the actions and motives of the persons involved which might be able to explain the loss of Hormuz? The result of this investigation is negative, in so far as there turns out to be an astonishingly poor connection between the intentions of those involved and the actual chain of events. However, the very negativity of the result supports the thesis that is formulated on the basis of the comparative investigation: the conflict about Hormuz was not a conflict between contestants on an equal footing, but a structural crisis, in other words, a confrontation of fundamentally different institutional complexes. The Companies were victorious over the transit trade of the pedlars and the redistributive institutions because, by virtue of their greater control of the market and the internalization of protection costs, i.e. by subordinating the production of protection to the market mechanism, they utilized the resources more economically than the older institutions.

This thesis is substantiated and its limitations explored in the shorter, third book, which follows the adaptation of the parties concerned to the new situation that arose after the fall of Hormuz. The institutional innovations of the Companies are conspicuous, despite the differences between the two Companies, but there were limits to the extent of the innovation. The Companies represented a new entrepreneurial form as far as Asia was concerned, but they did not revolutionize the Asian market. The Company became an element in "the early Asian trade".

Part I: The Fall of Hormuz

A comparative study

The intention in the first book is to represent by means of a comparative study the fall of Hormuz as a structural crisis, the latter being defined as a confrontation of fundamentally different institutional complexes. It endeavours by this means to furnish the structural description with a dynamic element, but it goes without saying that it does not thereby aim at an absolute distinction between a "before" and an "after": "before" is not a state of rest, unaffected by things to come, "afterwards" is not a new era lacking all connection with the past. The demonstration of the structural crisis may be regarded as accomplished if it can be proved that the institutions controlling the scene at the end of the period were not victorious as the result of chance events or individual decisions, but because they belonged to a structural complex dominated by institutional innovations which, in the defeated structure, played a smaller part.

The comparative method presupposes an organization of the material on the basis of theoretical concepts which are not necessarily explicit in the sources. An early working hypothesis, which was based on a comparison of the costs met by the various competitors in the trade between Europe and Asia, turned out to be insufficient in the light of the cost structure ascertained. Important elements, first and foremost the cost of protection, made the comparative calculation to a great extent unrealistic. The comparison therefore concentrates on the institutional variables that distorted the simple cost analysis: the relationship to the market and the "production" and "sale" of protection.

The question of the universal validity of the "theoretical" market has been energetically raised by Polanyi and his associates. According to Polanyi the self-regulating market is an historical phenomenon characteristic of the Western World in the 19th and the beginning of the 20th centuries, whereas the concrete historical and empirical market is not necessarily governed by the same laws as the market of the economists. Not least, his demonstration that the roles of buyers and sellers were fixed in the concrete historical market is relevant here: "In the modern market there is a price level at which bears turn bulls, and another price level at which the miracle is reversed. This has induced many to overlook the fact that buyers and sellers are separate in any other than the modern type of market."[1] In continuation of Polyani's ideas Walter C. Neale has characterized the European situation between the 15th and the 19th centuries as "a stage between non-supply-demand-price Market Places and a supply-demand-price Self-Regulating-Market.[2]

The incongruencies between the empirical *markets* and the theoretical *Market* to which Polanyi and his associates have drawn attention are of fundamental interest in the present context. If the market institution itself and its elements, the supply and demand "crowds" and the price formation, are variables, the market and the relationship of the relevant institutions to the market must be incorporated in the comparative analysis. In 1931 van der Kooy published a thesis in which he sought to formulate a market theory that would explain the unique position of Dutch trade in international economy throughout the 17th century and its retrogression in the 18th and 19th centuries. In van der Kooy's analysis the concrete nature and hierarchial construction of the pre-industrial market is emphasized. The goods are literally carried to local markets, and from there to regional and national markets, in a hierarchy the concrete capstone of which was the world market in the Netherlands.[3] In his description of the Dutch market van der Kooy emphasized first and foremost the distinction between three market functions: imports, which were taken care of by geographically specialized "zeehandelaars", storing, which was taken care of by "kooplieden van de tweede hand", who specialized in certain types of commodities, and the export trade, which was taken care of by geographically specialized "exportgrossiers".[4]

The description both of the hierarchical structure of the world market and of the triple nature of the Dutch market was schematic, and it has not been difficult for van der Kooy's critics among historians to show that in practice the three functions were not separated. A more positive criticism of van der Kooy's theory has been put forward by Klein in his entrepreneurial study of the family Tripp in the 17th century. He, too, criticises the all too rigid distinctions in van der Kooy's scheme, but he emphasizes the justification of the distinction between various market functions, even if the three functions could quite well be executed by the same persons or by the same groups. Klein's special contribution in this connection, however, is his attempt to replace van der Kooy's static market description by a dynamic market theory, which was to explain why a market form like the Dutch attracted trade at the expense of other markets. Van der Kooy had fastened upon the price levelling effects of storing, and

1. POLANYI p. 268.
2. *Ibid.* p. 370.
3. Van der KOOY, *hoofdstuk* 1, especially pp. 3–5.
4. *Ibid.* pp. 18–19.

13

it is this aspect that especially interests Klein, who combines it with his own observations of the monopolist tendencies in the Dutch market.

In the past, historiography has as a rule implicitly regarded monopolies as damaging under all circumstances, this being in accordance with the conception of that time as expressed in the pamphlet literature as well as with the classical economic theory. Referring to Schumpeter's theory of monopoly.[5] Klein on the contrary maintains that under certain circumstances attempts at monopolization serve a productive purpose as far as social economy is concerned: namely, a reduction of the risks connected with stock formation. Schumpeter's theory of monopoly has been elaborated with the "creative destructions" of industrial capitalism in mind, but van der Kooy's results already showed that the same need for reduction of risk was present in the pre-industrial market. Here it was not the steady stream of new products and new production methods that made the entrepreneurs seek to protect their investments with the aid of monopoly, but on the contrary the imperfections of the technical apparatus. The demand for commodities was more or less predictable, but the supply was irregular and unpredictable. It is as intermediary or "shock-absorber" between supply and demand that van der Kooy places his "koopman van de tweede hand". Klein goes a step further. In his opinion the risks attached to stock formation would discourage the entrepreneurs under the non-transparent conditions of the market if they did not have the possibility of controlling the market by means of a monopoly or a quasi-monopoly. The monopolistic tendencies reduced the risk and thereby the transaction costs, and thus, far from being disturbing elements, they fulfilled an important function in the concrete, pre-industrial market.

Whereas van der Kooy had solely characterized the market in relation to modern economy and had demonstrated its connection with an imperfect communication and transport technique, Klein, through his incorporation of monopolistic tendencies and his overall dynamic view, was able to determine the advantages of the Dutch market over more primitive market forms. The market's concentration of supply and demand gave both the buyers and the sellers a greater chance of carrying out a planned transaction at the planned time. Furthermore, the conditions under which the transaction could be carried out became more predictable and information

---

5. Schumpeter Part II, Ch. 7–8. As late as 1947 Hamilton wrote (p. 52): "The monopolistic trading companies depressed the prices of exports and raised those of imports in Europe and the Eastern colonies. In the short run producers suffered, and consumers were permanently oppressed." The concept of monopoly has been avoided in this book in favour of concepts like oligopoly, quasi-monopoly and monopolistic competition in accordance both with modern theory and with the observations regarding the Dutch market made by Klein and Glamann.

concerning prices and quantities became more easily accessible, i.e. the market became more transparent. Thereby not only were the risks attached to the acts of God and Man reduced, but also the risk of ruinous price fluctuations. Thus Klein is justified in emphasizing the correlation between the rational, calculating entrepreneur and this market form.[6]

On the basis of Weber's theories, but with a mass of concrete details, van Leur has described the Asian market, or rather the Asian markets around 1600, as an institutional complex which appears in direct contradistinction to the market described by van der Kooy and Klein. It is difficult to summarize what van Leur describes as the characteristics of "the early Asian trade"; it is more like an impressionist picture than a systematic analysis. The central element is the pedlar, that humble servant of world trade who, with his small stock of goods, is for ever travelling from market to market. He is dependent upon the rhythm of the monsoons and employs routes and methods used by generations before him. He can follow the commodity from producer to consumer, but the commodity may also have changed hands many times before it reaches the last buyer. For van Leur it is a structure radically different from modern capitalism. The fundamental difference is not altered by the circumstance that some individuals may have an unusually large amount of capital at their disposal; van Leur classifies this phenomenon as "political capitalism", a universal concept that must not be confused with "modern capitalism".

To this entrepreneurial structure corresponds a market structure which is characterized by its lack of cohesion and by the large number of concrete markets: "as many as there are towns or ports". He illustrates his description of "the early Asian trade" with a number of quotations obtained from descriptions of Asian markets from Arabia to Japan; the quotations substantiate his description convincingly, and for those who are familiar with the sources there can be no doubt that they are representative and that their number could be multiplied.[7]

For van Leur it is a matter of exposing a sociological structure, "a historical constant", not of describing a dynamic system, and he goes so far in this respect as to place European activity in Asia before 1650 within this context. The sharp distinction between political capitalism and modern capitalism provides the basis for his placing the Portuguese expansion convincingly within the Asian context[8], but it gets him into difficulties regarding the activity of the Companies, in which case he appears to contradict himself. On the one hand he draws a sharp line between Portuguese imperialism and the later (undated) colonialism, but on the

6. KLEIN pp. 3–15 and *passim.*
7. Van LEUR pp. 214–219 and *passim.*
8. *Ibid.* pp. 118, 169–170.

15

other hand he maintains that around 1650 the Dutch East India Company had not yet contributed anything to the Asian economic structure.[9] Although he does not in any place make himself clear, it must be assumed that van Leur feels himself bound, when faced with this question, by his (and Max Weber's) definition of modern capitalism: "exploitation of a rationalized organization for the mechanized mass production of goods built up with free labour and based on a free, specifically peaceful market for sales".[10] Van Leur's way of presenting and tackling the problem excludes a dynamic analysis: there is no room for qualitative alterations or institutional innovations prior to "modern capitalism".

The institutional features alone present decisive differences between the Asian market, as described by van Leur, and the concrete world market, as described by van der Kooy and Klein. But the contrast appears even stronger if we consider the problem which for Klein, with his dynamic approach, is the central problem (whereas for van Leur, whose aim was sociological, it was peripheral), i.e., price formation under the respective market forms. A trend in the direction of greater transparency and greater price stability is for Klein the greatest advantage the Dutch market has to offer compared with other forms of market. The material produced by van Leur clearly shows that the market form he described precisely distinguishes itself by its poor transparency and extremely unstable prices. Ninety bahars of pepper can knock the bottom out of the pepper market in Aracan for a whole season. Too great supplies of pepper to Shihr and Aden can inflict a loss of up to 40%–50% on the merchants during one monsoon; another year the big ship from Suez to Mocha fails to arrive, and the Indian merchants have to return home with their goods unsold if they do not wish to suffer the great losses incurred by an immediate sale.[11]

The examples could be multiplied on the basis of van Leur's material alone, but the question will be discussed in more detail later on. At this point we need only draw attention to the fact that the asumption that the market is not a constant, but subjected to institutional change, is supported by that difference in price formation which may be observed within the two market forms. If some European entrepreneurs based their activities on a superior market form this is a relevant moment of decisive importance which ought to be incorporated in any further investigation.

A theoretical framework for analysing the economic role played by

9. *Ibid.* pp. 188–190, 233–234: "The history of the development of modern capitalism ... has very little directly to do with the history of the Company as an entrepeneurial form, unless it would be in the fields of financial and banking affairs in later Company times."
10. *Ibid.* p. 17.
11. *Ibid.* pp. 214–219.

16

protection has been elaborated by Frederick C. Lane.[12] In Lane's opinion the use of violence, at least in some cases, may be regarded as a productive activity, the service produced being protection. In its most primitive form the only result of the exercise of violence is the transfer of income, as for example in highway robbery, but in cases where violence is exercised in permanent and organized forms protection is produced, i.e. the roads and countryside are kept free of other agents of violence. The highwayman's momentary and localized monopoly is replaced by a permanent and extensive, and thereby far more predictable, protection monopoly.

It is on this basis that Lane develops the concepts of tribute and protection rent. Tribute is defined as the transferred income that exceeds the production costs of the protection. Protection rent is defined as the difference between the profits made by the entrepreneur with the smaller protection costs and the entrepreneur with greater protection costs. Lane goes so far as to compare protection rent with land rent, interest and wages. The reason why the concepts of tribute and protection rent have largely been ignored in modern economy is that protection is implicitly regarded as a free service in modern Western societies, and the price is assumed to be identical with the production costs. The production of protection in modern society is controlled by the consumers of protection, but this is an unusual situation when seen in a historical light; protection rent and tribute are natural and necessary concepts when we are dealing with the pre-industrial period.[13]

Lane's analysis presents certain logical difficulties: on the one hand Lane endeavours to place the protection producer within the context of market economy by regarding him as a producer of a service, on the other hand we must admit that the analysis of price, supply and demand with regard to protection cannot easily be carried out within the ordinary theoretical framework of a market economy. The supply and demand of protection are identical, and the price is determined by the seller. Exceptions may be found, but the general rule will be that it is not the demand but conditions within the protection-producing institution that determine the size, quality and price of the supply. The problem confronting us is precisely the problem that creates a barrier between theoretical economy and what economists call political policy.[14]

The logical problem may be overcome in two ways: we may decide to concentrate on the limited validity of the market model like Polanyi, who

12. LANE developed his theory in four articles published between 1941 and 1958; they have subsequently been collected in *Venice and History* pp. 373–428.
13. LANE, *Venice and History*, pp. 412–420.
14. See for example NORTH & THOMAS, pp. 8–10.

finds three "main patterns" in empirical economies, i.e. "reciprocity", "redistribution" and "exchange". Exchange corresponds to a market mechanism that is in accordance with the theoretical market of the economists, but the theoretical market has no relevance to the remaining patterns.[15] If we follow this line of reasoning we must abandon the idea of the protector as producer of a service and regard him instead as entrepreneur in an economic pattern that is subjected to other laws than those of the market.

We can also solve the logical problem by regarding the protector as a monopolist who, in his transactions, has full freedom of movement within the limits determined by the marginal rate of substitution. He can expand his production apparatus without regard to the cost, for the buyers are sure to pay. He can also put up his prices and increase his tribute. But in the final instance his freedom of movement will be limited by the marginal rate of substitution. The ceiling may be high, with emigration, revolt, revolution or conquest from without as the only possible substitutes, but in certain cases the ceiling is not so high, as for example in the international transit trade in which the closest substitute is the choice of a different route.

The two solutions described above do not exclude one another. The first concentrates attention on what, seen from a theoretical point of view, is an irrational margin between production costs and prices, and on the redistribution of the available goods that takes place within that margin. In the second solution we fasten upon the circumstance that even the producer of protection is bound in the end by the laws of the market; the price of the services delivered can be so high or the quality so poor that emigration, revolt or, in the case of the transit merchant, the desertion of the usual routes, becomes an economically rational choice. The following has been based on both points of view. The producers of protection are regarded and described as redistributive entrepreneurs assuming that the primary aim of the institutions concerned was not to increase the total satisfaction of demand by the production of protection, but to carry out a redistribution of the available goods by means of armed force. At the same time it will be possible to show that the existence of substitution possibilities contributes a dynamic element to the structure; in several cases, but first and foremost as far as the Companies are concerned, entrepreneurial behaviour may be observed that aims at

---

15. POLANYI pp. 250–256. Independently of POLANYI, HICKS has pointed out from a theoretical point of view the nature of the market institution as a historical variable. HICKS also distinluishes between three "stages" or "models": "customary economy", "command economy" and "exchange economy". HICKS pp. 7–15.

reducing the transaction costs by evading the existing protection institutions.

In theory the last possibility should have been ruled out. The tribute having left a wide margin above the production costs of protection, we should expect that the protector threatened with an evasion of his territory would lower his prices to compete with the alternative route. In practice, however, this was not the case. It can partly be explained as normal, rigid entrepreneurial behaviour: the protector had investments tied up in his production apparatus which he could not very well write off, and a large staff he could scarcely dismiss on the spot. Furthermore, the protecting institutions we are concerned with in this period were not monoliths. By this we are not referring to the all too frequently forthcoming generalizations such as "the Arab trade monopoly in the Indian Ocean" or "the Venetian trade monopoly in the Eastern Mediterranean", but to the State's incapability of acting with one will. Nobody familiar with pre-industrial society can be in any doubt that decisions taken centrally are often carried out with limited effectiveness, and that corruption in its widest sense constitutes an elementary component of the social, political and economic structure. The problem has caused contemporary historians great difficulties; it is embarassing to see personages in history, great or small, habitually devoting themselves to actions we regard as both criminal and morally reprehensible. A characteristic example is Hurstfield's analysis of corruption in 17th century England. He takes the following definition as starting-point: "If we assume that the object of the state is the welfare of all its members we may define corruption as the subversion of that object for other ends."[16] In his subsequent analysis of the problem Hurstfield finds that corruption must be seen as a result of the rise of bureaucracy, its tasks and extent, that characterizes all West European states from the close of the Middle Ages, combined with the insufficient state revenue that prevented the payment of suitable wages. Hurstfield concludes that the concept of corruption is in reality an anachronism concealing more than it discloses if we are concerned with the period before the middle of the 18th century; the concept of corruption is of no value as a tool of analysis before a proper system of taxation is in force, as well as reasonable payment for civil servants and a feeling of responsibility in those occupying public positions.

We may follow Hurtsfield's conclusion, but it should be added that the conclusion eradicates the definition he took as his starting-point. If essential parts of the national income are regularly transferred from some social groups to others as a result of corruption, the assumption "that the object of the state was the welfare of all its members" falls away. One cannot

16. HURSTFIELD p. 19.

have it both ways, one cannot decriminalize corruption and at the same time maintain that the state and the civil servants were working for the general welfare.

Van Klaveren's analysis of the phenomenon is far more penetrating.[17] His basis, though implicit, is the conception of *ancien regime* as a political system lying mid-way between the out-and-out Absolute Monarchy and the out-and-out Sovereignty of the People. The corruption that interests him is not the accidental criminal corruption, but the corruption that is built into the constitution, as it were. Every civil servant finds himself in a position of monopoly; if he regards his office as "a maximizing unit", and he constitutionally adopts an independent position as regards his "customers", there will be no relation between the receipts of the office and its social utility value; his income will be determined by his ability to find the point of maximum gain under the current conditions of the "market".

Corruption as a component of the constitution presupposes that the development towards a money economy has commenced and, furthermore, that the official classes and other intermediary groups have a certain amount of independence within the constitutional framework. The Prince might be able to limit corruption; in isolated cases (e.g. Louis XIV) the Absolute Princes even managed to overcome it. When a limited interference on the part of the Prince constituted the usual practice the cause might well be the Prince's weakness, but another possibility was the fact that he, too, regarded corruption as constitutionally substantiated. The people served not only the Prince, but also the officials. Strangely enough van Klaveren does not take the same consequence as Lane in regarding the Prince's income as the greatest of all the gains of corruption, but he indicates that corruption creates a vertical division of the governmental apparatus as opposed to the horizontal division of feudal society. New institutions or persons appointed to control the Establishment would more likely than not become monopolists seeking merely to reap the benefits of their office. Under a monarchy the corruption would be organized in hierarchial form, the senior officials seeking to thwart their inferiors with regard to such practice, not in order to protect the Prince or the People, but in order to maximize their own income. The struggle for corruption gains is gradually converted into political struggle for power, the right of patronage and higher incomes serves to secure the political position, which in turn secures the right of patronage and the higher incomes, and so on – a *perpetuum mobile*. Corruption may be the downfall of a politician,

17. Van KLAVEREN elaborated his theory in two articles published in 1957–60. The following is chiefly based upon "Die historische Erscheinung der Korruption". (1957).

but the downfall is political, the corruption continues. A further consequence of this connection between corruption and political influence is that the system is cumulative and unstable.

The elements of a theory referred to above are not easily assembled to form a finished model for pre-industrial institutional innovation, but they can be assembled into a rough sketch, which has served as a heuristic guiding-line and as a basis for the organisation of the material in the comparitive section of the book. We assume with Polanyi, that empirical markets do not necessarily behave in accordance with the market of economic theory, and with Klein, that the creation of a concrete market or markets with a large degree of transparency and consequent price stability was an important step towards the development of modern economy. Furthermore, we assume with Lane, that protection was an appreciable expense for the pre-industrial entrepreneur, and that the administration of organized violence was an important source of income and formed the basis of the redistribution of the available goods. In accordance with van Klaveren this is extended not only to apply to the formal agents of organized violence, the states, but also to the states' local representatives.

The implicated institutions are grouped according to these theoretical guiding-lines. Both the pedlars and the redistributive enterprises may be regarded as entrepreneurs within the early Asian trade, but with different functions. The pedlars were immediately attached to the market institutions; they were dependent for their survival on a correct calculation of prices, costs and possibilities for gain in a distant market. The redistributive institutions were sellers of a service, protection, but they normally found themselves in a position of monopoly and therefore possessed considerable freedom of movement within the framework determined by the marginal rate of substitution. Formally speaking, the Company was a new element in Asian trade; the analysis of the Companies seeks to determine whether they were in fact an institutional innovation. The first book concludes with an attempt to date and determine the extent of both the Companies' victory and of the losses of the peddling trade and the redistributive institutions.

Chapter I: The Peddling Trade

Van Leur has provided the classical description of "the early Asian trade" – the peddling trade – in the following: "The international trade of southeast Asia was a small-scale peddling trade. The traders, shipping out with their goods by dozens on long voyages the periodicity of which was governed by the semi-annual monsoon winds, were pedlars with valuable high-quality products. They went out either as independent pedlars, perhaps in companies, or as traders on *commenda*."[1] The criticism that has been levelled at van Leur has scarcely invalidated this description as a sociological model, and it will be used as the starting-point for discussion in this chapter. However, the question will be handled in a slightly different way than van Leur handled it. What interested the latter was the peddling trade viewed as a sociological concept, whereas it is the validity of the concept from the point of view of economic theory that is of interest here. The following discussion will therefore be concentrated on exploring those features that presumably would be decisive when the peddling trade was confronted with an entrepreneurial form built on entirely different institutional lines, i.e. on cost structure and price formation.

The Pedlars

Van Leur based his description on indirect evidence, and first and foremost on the descriptions and reports of actual market conditions provided by the employees of the Dutch East India Company. The caravan merchants themselves seldom left any source material; among the hundreds of accounts of journeys in Asia published in the 16th–18th centuries, only a handful have been written by merchants.[2] This secrecy was probably intentional, the routes and market conditions constituting part of the merchants' *misterio,* but there must be other sources for the activities of the caravan merchants that have not yet been brought to light – accounts

1. Van Leur p. 133.
2. Federici, Balbi, Texeira and Tavernier are the only examples of importance from the period treated here. To these, of course, should be added the reports published by Hakluyt and Purchas, but they were originally prepared for private use and were not published until the information they contained had lost its economic usefulness.

and letter books still lying unnoticed. A valuable source, at present unique, is the journal of the Armenian merchant, Hovhannes, which was unearthed and analysed by Khachikian a few years ago.[3]

Hovhannes's journal provides a penetrating close-up of the work of a pedlar, but we know nothing of his person other than what the journal reveals. The journal describes his journeys between 19th December 1682 and 6th December 1693. We know from a single reference in the journal that he had previously made at least one journey to Smyrna. We may furthermore conclude from the journal that he had received a thorough education, but that he himself was scarcely wealthy, at least not at the beginning of his travels. He was the factor of two brothers, who may presumably be identified with two prominent Armenian merchants from the Isfahan suburb of Nor Jougha.

During the eleven years in which we can follow Hovhannes he travelled far afield. In 1682 he left Isfahan and travelled via Bandar Abbas (Gombroon) to Surat. From there he continued inland to Agra. In 1684 he again went to Surat and from there he returned to Agra. He spent the greatest part of the following year travelling in the neighbourhood of Agra, to which he returned at the end of the year. In 1686 he left for Tibet, arriving at the capital, Lhasa, in September. He remained in Lhasa for nearly six years until June 1692. Thereafter he retraced his steps as far as Patna, but from there he journeyed to Bengal, to Hooghli and Calcutta, where his journal comes to an abrupt end.

Hovhannes was not an isolated adventurer. He followed roads which other Armenian merchants had followed before him,[4] and everywhere he went, even in Lhasa, there was an Armenian "nation", which he endeavoured to contact. We are scarcely entitled to conclude from this that he was none other than a "typical" Armenian caravan merchant, but there is nothing to indicate that he in any way differed from his contemporaries on the Asian caravan routes. That is, apart from the circumstance that his journal has been preserved.

3. Lvon KHACHIKIAN, "Le registre d'un marchand arménien er Perse, en Inde et au Tibet (1682–93)", *Annales E. S. C.* 22, pp. 231–78. The journal and the journey originate from a half to a whole century after the period dealt with here and particularly concern journeys in India and Tibet. It is not quite as irrelevant as it might appear at first glance, however. There is scarcely any reason for believing that the Armenians employed different organizational forms in India and Tibet from what they might have used in Persia and Turkey, and although Armenian trade was under development in the 17th century it is not likely to have undergone any revolutionary changes as far as organization and technique is concerned. On the other hand the journal naturally does not permit any conclusions regarding prices, etc.

4. An Armenian merchant's manual from the 17th century gave instructions for trading in all the areas Hovhannes visited. KHACHIKIAN p. 235.

At first glance Hovhannes's journeys appear to have been quite aimless, but on closer inspection they show a certain pattern. They can be divided into a preliminary journey from Isfahan to India, two business trips to the densely populated central Indian region around Agra, the great journey to Lhasa and, finally, the return journey from Lhasa to Bengal. For we must presume that it was the return journey he had begun at that time, and that it was his intention to seek a passage home to Persia on an English ship. The rhythm of these journeys corresponded with Hovhannes's business transactions. At his departure from Isfahan in December 1682 his capital was nominally 250 tomans – well over 3,000 piastres,[5] including 18 English cloths at a total value of 217 tomans and the remainder as a bill of exchange drawn on Shiraz. The whole of that capital was given him on *commenda,* his own share being fixed by contract at 25% of the profit. He sold the cloth in India and bought indigo with the proceeds. The whole of the transaction – the conversion of three camel-loads of cloth into approximately as many loads of indigo – took nearly a year, and characteristic of Hovhannes's activity was the slow wandering from town to town following upon his arrival in India. He was in Surat from 23rd March to 15th May, in Aurungabad from 29th May to 15th July; he arrived at Burhanpur on 21st July and continued after some time to Sironj, where he stayed from 11th August to 24th November. He was in Agra from 2nd December to 6th January 1684. From Agra he made a detour to Khurja in order to buy indigo, and on 13th March he was back in Agra. Eight days later, on 21st March, he again left Agra, and this time the journey was without interruption and detours, for he was in Surat already on 12th April. The contrast between the outward and return journeys is revealing: the eighteen English cloths were retailed, piece by piece and yard by yard until it was time to purchase the indigo.

Hovhannes did not himself accompany the indigo all the way back to his principals, but he left it in Surat in the charge of another Armenian, who was commissioned to take part of it to Isfahan, presumably to the principals, and the rest to Basra to be sold. It is probable that he had received a new supply of commodities from Persia in the meantime, because on 29th May he left Surat once more in order to repeat the lengthy inland journey of the previous year, and this time he purchased cotton cloth, which he forwarded to Isfahan through his Armenian connections at the end of the season.

In 1686 he set off for Lhasa. Before leaving Agra he concluded an

---

5. Here and throughout the following a rough conversion into piastres at approximately 25.5 grm. fine silver has been made. This form of conversion has been preferred in favour of a conversion into grm. fine silver so as not to give the impression of an exactitude the material seldom permits. The toman in Hovhannes's time was 306.4 grm. fine silver. KHACHIKIAN p. 267.

agreement with an Armenian business acquaintance; he apparently still considered himself as being dependent upon his principals in Persia, but after the journeys of the past three years he possessed some capital himself, since he contributed half of the 9,370 rupees, i.e. more than 2,000 piastres, which constituted his working capital in Tibet throughout the next six years. In Tibet he sold the commodities he had brought with him in small quantities, at the same time purchasing gold and musk. But he also carried on a considerable amount of passive business, lending or selling on credit to merchants of Armenian or other nationality, who were following the almost 1,250 mile long route from Lhasa to Sining on the Chinese border in order to buy tea and gold.

Hovhannes was not a specialist, neither as regards the areas he frequented nor as regards the commodities that passed through his hands. During the first years his biggest transactions were in cloth, indigo and cotton, but this did not deter him from also interesting himself in other commodities, and on the eve of his departure to Lhasa he possessed an extremely varied assortment of goods. Khachikian has identified 174 articles of trade in Hovhannes's journal, and in addition there are a number of items it has not been possible to identify with certainty. Van Leur's description: "pedlars with valuable high-quality products" appears appropriate. Hovhannes's capital is modest – 3,000 piastres on his departure from Isfahan; this was sufficient for him and his principals and his three camels.[6] 4,000 piastres on his departure to Lhasa was sufficient to keep his business going for more than six years and, as far as we can judge, to ensure him a renumerative journey.

But this peddling trade should not be characterized as primitive.[7] The technique may well be primitive, but the organization does not lack sophistication. Hovhannes acts a factor, as a partner in a company partnership, contributing his own capital, and he himself places capital at the disposal of other merchants. He does not have to accompany his goods to their destination, but can hand on part of the transport to others, at least on such frequented routes as Surat-Isfahan and Surat-Basra. He transfers money by means of bills of exchange, and some of the exchanges registered are pretty complicated. He does not use double-entry bookkeep-

6. One camel-load of cloth corresponds to two bales each containing three cloths, *Letters Received* V p. 281 f.
7. See MEILINK-ROELOFSZ p. 5: "Moreover, the great stress he lays on the peddling – that is to say, rather primitive – character of Asian commerce, brings Van Leur into conflict with one of his own most important theses, namely, that up to the beginning of the 19th century, Asian and European trade were on an equal footing in Asia." But Van Leur himself has in no place characterized the peddling trade as primitive.

ing, but his accounts are meticulously kept, and he handles complicated calculations involving coins and measures with the greatest of ease.

Hovhannes is an Armenian, and his relations with the local Armenian communities, the Armenian "nations", are vitally important for his business. Everywhere he goes he makes contact with local Armenians, and he contributes to Armenian churches and institutions. He participates with Armenians in credit transactions and concludes important business deals using Armenians as witnesses. It is only with reluctance that legal disputes are referred to local authorities, usually they are settled among the Armenian merchants themselves. Even in far away Lhasa legal disputes are settled by a body of Armenians supplemented with merchants from Kashmir, rather than being brought before the local authorities.[8] To belong to a "nation" was at once a protection and an organizational advantage; in the eyes of the local authorities the possession of a distinct law and nationality ensured the merchant extra-territorial rights, at any rate as far as internal disputes were concerned.

It is possible with regard to some transactions to calculate Hovhannes's gross profits; they were between 50–130% for those transactions that are identifiable. The lowest profit registered is on the large consignment of indigo he sent to Basra, this being at a gross profit of approximately 50%. The remainder of the identified transactions involved smaller sums, ranging from 17 to about 100 rupies.

Two rates of interest were charged for loans. When the lender and the borrower were staying in the same town, the customary interest was $3/4$ % per month. When the borrower obtained a loan in connection with a journey the lender seems to have participated in the risk and has accordingly demanded a higher rate of interest.

At present Hovhannes's journal is our only source of direct information; and both as regards time and space it lies outside the sphere of greatest interest in the present context: transcontinental trade in the years around 1600. It is now necessary to determine whether the indirect evidence obtained from Western sources supports the assumption that he is none the less a representative of a peddling trade that carried the Asian commodities all the way to the trading towns on the Mediterranean.

Six English merchants, who travelled from Aleppo to Hormuz in 1583, had a working capital of £2,000 or approximately 9,000 piastres.[9] Four

8. Precisely Hovhannes's experiences in Tibet illustrated the advantages of internal jurisdiction. In one case it proved impossible to settle a dispute by mediation, and the matter was brought before the local magistrate, who determined the outcome by throwing dice. Hovhannes lost and even had to pay costs. KHACHIKIAN p. 266.
9. Eldred in PURCHAS IX pp. 496–497.

Venetians on their way from Hormuz to Aleppo, whom the merchants met in Basra, were carrying 20 bales of cloves, long pepper, cinnamon, musk and ostrich feathers.[10] In 1608 the Carmelite, Paul Simon, travelled from Isfahan to Baghdad together with some Armenian merchants who were on their way to Aleppo to sell four loads of silk.[11] In 1613 a factor in the service of the East India Company, William Finch, who had great experience of trade in the Levant, left the Company's service in India in order to return home over land at his own expense. At the time of his death in Baghdad his estate comprised eleven mule loads of indigo and a few curiosities of lesser value.[12] The many merchants, each with his small lot of bales and chests, became a feature of the carrying trade developed by the Companies between Surat and Gombroon following the fall of Hormuz. Thus in 1626/27 the *Blessing* carried six merchants with altogether 65 bales and chests from Surat to Gombroon,[13] and on a similar journey in 1630/31 the *Royal James* brought 100 passengers with 689 bales to Gombroon and 70 passengers with 800 bales to Surat on the return journey.[14] When in 1642 the Augustinian, Sebastian Manrique, wished to travel from India to Persia by way of Kandahar without attracting attention, his Indian friends advised him to disguise himself as a merchant. But if the disguise was to be foolproof "it was essential to purchase at least two thousand rupees' worth of the usual wares and load them on two camels . . ."[15] Anything less would be suspicious, but two camel loads on the six to eight months' long march between Lahore and Isfahan was obviously nothing unusual.

Hovhannes penetrates right to the production areas when purchasing his indigo and cotton cloth, and he frequently deals in small quantities. We cannot with any certainty find parallel features in the European source material, but it may be said with some justice to be the same tendency that manifests itself when English, Venetian and French merchants travel farther along the caravan routes to more distant markets in times of hard competition in Aleppo. For the Armenians the tendency to get as close to both producer and buyer as possible seems to have been characteristic. The Armenians used to buy up raw silk in the production areas by the Caspian Sea,[16] but it is also said of the Armenians when they were

10. Newbery *ibid.* p. 495.
11. *Chronicle* p. 135.
12. *Letters Received* I p. 273.
13. C. R. O. Factory Records, Surat 102 p. 498.
14. James Barry, a/b the *Royal James*, to Co. 22/3 1631, *English Factories* 1630/33 p. 143.
15. MANRIQUE II p. 248.
16. "met bondelkens wert alle de zyde van dorp tot dorp en huys tot huys ingecocht, "Verantwoordinge . . . Overschie, 15/12 1638, DUNLOP p. 670.

purchasing indigo in North India that they rushed from one village to the other, "running and racing about like hungry folk".[17] In his commentary on the Surat factors' plan to establish trade with Persia, the English Ambassador to the court of the Great Mogul, Sir Thomas Roe, draws comparison to these merchants: "to travel in an out like the merchants of Persia will neither become nor advantage them..."[18] And especially hard is the comment in Marseilles: "In order to earn a little bit more they are willing to run to the end of the world, and they live so miserably (si porque), that for the most part they only eat herbs."[19]

However indirect and fragmentary our knowledge, there can scarcely be any doubt that van Leur's model is also valid for the Middle Eastern caravan routes. It is a prosperous trade plied by small people – a trade carried on by pedlars, buying and selling small quantities on continuous travels from market to market. The European material provides a large amount of evidence to this effect, and further confirmation is provided by the very silence of the sources as far as itinerant merchants carrying large quantities of merchandise are concerned. The only caravan merchants mentioned with more than a dozen loads in their charge are those the Shah of Persia occasionaly sent to Europe in order to sell silk (see below p. 103 ff).

But it would be wrong to characterize the peddling trade as primitive; the organizational sophistication documented in Hovhannes's journal is confirmed by the indirect evidence. Based on his observations in Goa in the 1580s Sassetti declares that 6–700 ducats were sufficient for that merchant who wished to undertake a journey, but that over and above their own capital they usually took 8, 10 or 20 thousand ducats with them as bills of exchange at 2% per month. The high level of interest is explained by the great risk.[20] The second journey of the English merchant, Mildenhall, provides a concrete example of trade employing foreign capital. Following his arrival home from his first journey to India in 1609 Mildenhall applied for an appointment in the East India Company, but was rejected, presumably because his demands were too great.[21] Instead he set out on a new journey along the caravan routes, at least part of his capital being placed at his disposal by four London merchants with great experience and interests in both Levant and Asian trade: Morris Abbot, Nicholas Leate, Richard Staper and Robert Offley.[22] As time passed and

17. PELSAERT p. 16.
18. Sir Thomas Roe to Robbins, Isfahan, 17/1 1616/17, Letters Received V p. 51.
19. Memorandum of 14/7 1623 from Marseilles Town Council to the King, quoted in BERGASSE and RAMBERT pp. 65–67.
20. SASSETTI pp. 360–361.
21. Court Minutes 30/5–17/11 1609 passim, Calendar S. P. East Indies 1513/1616 pp. 184–196.
22. Letters Received II pp. 98, 169; V p. 91.

nothing was heard from him the consortium grew uneasy, and in 1613 Richard Steele was sent out from Aleppo on Mildenhall's tracks in order to contact him and demand settlement. Steele found Mildenhall in "Tombaz, near the confines", presumably Tabas, three weeks' journey east of Isfahan, and took over on behalf of the consortium money and goods to the value of 9,000 piastres. No explanation as to the year-long stay in Persia is forthcoming, but we are informed that upon his death he left a wife and two children in Persia. He died in Lahore the following year, and his estate was estimated at about £500 or over 2,000 piastres. Mildenhall's year-long journey seems thus to have been undertaken with a capital of less than 10,000 piastres, and his own business capital at his death was little more than 2,000 piastres.[23]

Also extremely informative is Sir Thomas Roe's mention of a package of letters which came into his hands by way of his contact in Isfahan in 1616. These letters revealed that merchants of various nations in Aleppo, amongst others the English consul, had formed a company for the purpose of trading with Lahore, with a certain Bonelli as factor or active partner. However, the company had been informed that Bonelli had been killed by bandits in India, and addressed themselves in these letters to another Italian, who was supposed to be staying in Lahore – Jeronimo Galicia by name – or in his absence to a Jesuit priest also mentioned by name, in order to try to rescue the company's assets. Enclosed were powers of attorney, copies of invoices for goods and ready cash, and bills of exchange confirmed by transcripts from the chancellery register of the Venetian consulate in Aleppo.[24] Unfortunately, the letter from Roe to the governor of the East India Company, Sir Thomas Smith, does not contain the precise details; Roe noted these down on a separate sheet of paper, which he urged Smith to burn.[25]

The use of letters of credit and bills of exchange is well documented. During his year-long stay in the East the Italian traveller, Pietro della Valle, was able to supplement his travelling funds by means of letters of credit sent him by his agent.[26] In 1598 Anthony Sherley drew 800 piastres on the English nation in Aleppo from Baghdad. As it happens the bill of exchange was not honoured, but the very fact that a foreigner placed in Sherley a confidence not shared by those who knew him ought to be an illustration of the commonplace nature of the transaction.[27] The English

23. *Letters Received* II pp. 98, 105.
24. Roe, Ajmer, to Sir Thomas Smith 27/11 1616, *Letters Leceived* IV p. 248; cf. Roe pp. 300–301.
25. Roe was afraid that his encroachment upon the secrecy of the mails might affect the dispatch of the Company's mail through Aleppo.
26. della Valle, *India* p. 333.
27. B. M., London, Sloane Ms. 867, ff. 33–34.

merchants who in 1583 investigated the possibilities of the Aleppo-Hormuz route were not least interested in the rates of exchange. Newbery, the most enthusiastic of the pioneers, maintained that with an eye on the sale of commodities and remittance of the proceeds to Aleppo by means of bills of exchange alone it would be advantageous to establish factories in Baghdad, Basra and Hormuz, because the difference in exchange between Hormuz and Aleppo was 60%.[28] The mechanism is illustrated very well by a business transaction the English concluded in Basra with the above mentioned Venetians, who had arrived with their goods from Hormuz: "(they) had taken up ten thousand Ducketts, by exchange to bee payed heere in Balsara, this money their credits will not serve to take up for Babylon." They were therefore interested in striking a bargain with the English, by which they received half English goods, half ready cash, in return for their Asian commodities.[29]

This interesting way of financing purchases for export is lengthily described by the French merchant, Tavernier. He maintains that it was possible to pay in Surat, for example, with bills of exchange drawn on Gombroon. Bills of exchange in Gombroon might be paid with bills of exchange drawn on Erzurum or Baghdad, the final cash reckoning taking place in Leghorn or Venice. The costs of this type of combined credit and transfer transaction were naturally great, though not prohibitive, if we are to believe Tavernier. From Golconda to Leghorn or Venice – bill of exchange against bill of exchange – the money cost 95% at the cheapest, but more frequently 100%.[30]

A peddling trade: buying and selling in small quantities on continuous travels from market to market. But if Hovhannes's journal and the indirect evidence does not deceive us, a peddling trade that makes use of very sophisticated organizational forms such as commenda,[31] bottomry, partnerships and combined credit and tranfer transactions by means of bills of exchange. Nevertheless the ordinary entrepreneur operates on the pedlar level, and there is nothing in the sources to indicate the existence of comprehensive coordinated organizations – of an Armenian, Turkish or Persian version of a Fugger, Cranfield or Tripp.

This negative feature is emphasized so strongly because the fact that trade was distributed among so many individual entrepreneurs contrasts sharply with that form of organization introduced by the East India Companies into Asian trade, and because this spreading of the trade, as will be

28. Newbery in PURCHAS IX p. 495.
29. Eldred *ibid.* p. 499.
30. TAVERNIER I p. 624.
31. It may be noted that Hovhannes's share according to the agreement on his departure from Isfahan was precisely that 25 % which in fact characterized commenda, ARUP p. 9.

shown later, was of decisive importance for the price formation on the markets of the caravan trade. However, before investigating the question of price formation there is another problem demanding closer examination, namely, the costs of the caravan transport.

The Economy of the Peddling Trade

Information concerning the costs of caravan transport is unfortunately extremely scanty. This is hardly an accident, since it was one of the pedlar's business secrets just like routes and prices. The information at our disposal is scattered and difficult to interpret precisely; conversions of coins and measures can only be made with considerable margins of error and it would be a hazardous business to draw general conclusions from the scattered information available. Just as hazardous as for a caravan merchant to calculate his costs before the journey had come to an end. The seasons and the weather conditions changed, the safety of the roads was unpredictable, tax-gatherers came and tax-gatherers went, and some journeys were lucky, others unlucky.

Despite everything it is possible to form an idea of the magnitude of the costs the merchant had to reckon with on the journey. Two questions are of special interest in this connection: how did the true transport costs compare with the protection costs? And how did the predictable costs, i.e. purchase prices and true transport costs, compare with the sales price?

The silk routes from Persia occupied a special position among caravan routes because they retained their importance in this period in competition with the ocean transport of the Companies. The oldest description containing information about costs originates from the English merchant, Newbery, who in 1581–82 followed the route from Kashan to Bursa as part of a more extensive journey through the Levant and Eastern Europe.[32] He left Kashan on November 4th 1581 and arrived at Bursa on February 23rd of the following year, i.e. after less than four months' journey. The trip comprised 79 marching days with short stops in the towns of Tabriz, Erivan, Erzurum, Erzincan and Tokat. As regards transport costs he informs us that the stretch Kashan-Tabriz, i.e. 20 marching days, cost 120 shahi per 100 man Tabriz, i.e. 7 piastres per camel load of 36 man-i shah.[33] In addition he quotes the transport costs on the stretch Erzurum-Erzincan as being 12 shahi per mule load and on the stretch

32. Concerning Newbery, see FOSTER pp. 79–89 and PARKER pp. 132, 137. His account of the journey Kashan-Bursa printed in PURCHAS VIII pp. 465–475.
33. The size of a camel-load varied with the terrain and with the size of the animals, but about 200 kg. seems to have been the norm. Conventionally, a load of silk in Persia was reckoned at 36 man-i shah of 12½ lb. or approximately 5.575 kg.. 1 man-i Tabriz was ½ man-i shah. HINZ passim, DUNLOP p. 799. There were about 13 shahis to 1 piastre, see appendix.

Erzincan-Tokat as being 3 ducats per mule load. Converted into piastres per camel load this is approximately 8 piastres for 15 marching days.[34] This information comprises 35 of the journey's altogether 79 marching days; we may then by means of extrapolation obtain the total transport cost of 30–35 piastres per camel load for the stretch Kashan-Bursa.

Between Kashan and Tabriz Newbery paid a quite inconsiderable sum in convoy money, i.e. four times one kasbek per load. In Tabriz, on the other hand, he had to pay 12 shahi and 2 bisteg in "tribute", i.e. approximately 1 piastre, as well as 10 shahi or ³/₄ piastre in "safe conduct" from Kashan to Tabriz. These were apparently personal expenses unconnected with the bulk or value of the goods he brought with him. In Erivan a duty of 5 sequins (approx. 7–8 piastres) was charged on every load of silk. In Echmiadzin he had to pay a bribe of 22 shahi or almost 2 piastres. At the Persian-Turkish frontier 5⁰/₀ was demanded on the goods which were not going to pass through Erzurum on their way elsewhere. He does not mention any customs in connection with Erzurum, but on the contrary a duty of 2⁰/₀ on the goods sold in the town. Thus it is possible that the duty of 5⁰/₀ was not a general transit duty, but a special duty that was intended to force the trade in through Erzurum. From Erzurum to Bursa there were no customs stations of importance, it being merely necessary to pay some inconsiderable convoy duties. In Bursa foreign merchants payed 3⁰/₀.

To sum up, without forgetting the reservations we have made above: 30–35 piastres for the transport, possibly 5 piastres in personal duties, charges and bribes, 7–8 piastres in export duties, possibly 5⁰/₀ on entering Turkey and, finally, 3⁰/₀ in Bursa. A load of silk at this time cost somewhat less then 600 piastres in Persia and could be sold on the Levant markets for nearly 1200 piastres.[35] The astonishing conclusion is that the

34. The approximate relationship between mule, donkey and camel loads appears from a letter from the English factory in Persia, in which it is recommended that all the goods to Persia should be packed in bales of 130 lb., two such bales making up a donkey-load, three, a mule-load and four, a camel-load. Barker to Roe, April 1618, C. R. O., London, O. C. 792. Generally speaking, however, the animals do not seem to have been so heavily loaded, cf. the Dutch invoices quoted below p. 35.

35. In 1565–68 the Muscovy Company's agents quoted prices of 60–70 shahis per man-i Tabriz in Tabriz and Shamakhi, i. e. 330–400 piastres per load of 36 man-i shah. *Early Voyages and Travels* pp. 388, 391, 400, 414.
In 1618 the prices in Isfahan were 200–260 shahis per man-i shah for the preferred export qualities, *legia* and *ardasse,* i. e. 540–720 piastres per load. Monox, Isfahan, to East India Co. 18/4 1618, C. R. O., London, O. C. 586:2; Pettus, Isfahan, to East India Co. 27/9 1618, *ibid.* O. C. 699; Barker, Isfahan, to Roe, April 1618, *ibid.* O. C. 792. Between 1585 and 1636 prices fluctuated from 10 to 13 piastres per rotolo of 2,000 grm. in Aleppo. HERMITE; DUNLOP; B. M., London, Sloane Ms. 867; P. R. O., London, S. P. 110/10.

transport costs for a commodity as valuable as silk was quite insignificant, apparently not more than 3% of the sales price. Somewhat heavier, though not exhorbitant, however, were the customs duties. If there were 600 piastres to be earnt on that route, it was at any rate not the camel that got the money, not even the tax-gatherers. Even if we increase the uncertain figures that may be derived from Newbery's account by 100 or 200% there will still be a very considerable margin between costs and sales price for the valuable commodities.

Newbery's information, however, can be substantiated with the help of other material. In 1618 the English agent in Persia, Monox, sent the Court of the East India Company an estimate which he had "procured from a Venetian merchant, that hath ofttymes carried sylck that way."[36] The estimate concerned a load of silk of 36 man-i shah, the object being to provide a comparison with the transport costs on the route to the Persian Gulf; it is thus fairly safe to assume that the costs are more likely to be reckoned too high than too low. The entries concerning the transport between the terminal towns, Kazvin and Aleppo, are relevant for comparison with Newbery.

Table 1. *Monox's estimate of the costs on the route Kazvin-Aleppo 1618.*[37]

Convoy money	7	abasi	approx.	2	piastres
Transport Kazvin-Tabriz	17	–	–	5	–
Customs Tabriz-Aleppo............	97	–	–	30	–
Transport Tabriz-Aleppo	58½	–	–	18	–
Presents on the journey............	24	–	–	7	–
Presents to the Pasha in Aleppo	18	–	–	5	–
	221½	abasi	approx.	67	piastres

The figures supplied by Newbery are confirmed by this estimate. The true transport costs on this route are estimated at a mere 23 piastres; the customs duties, etc., are considerably heavier, about 44 piastres in all, the total expenses, however, only comprising a small percentage of the sales price of the silk.

Monox's estimate can be supplemented with some further vague statements about expenses in connection with the transport of silk. An English estimate from approximately the same time reckons with 25 piastres in

36. Monox, Isfahan, to East India Co., 18/4 1618, C. R. O., London, O. C. 586.
37. *Ibid.*

camel hire and 30 piastres in customs before Aleppo. To this may be added the consulage, etc., in Aleppo at altogether 25 piastres, approximately, and a profit of 25–50% to the Armenian merchant.[38] Some years later the head of the Dutch Factory, Overschie, estimated the expenses somewhat higher, assessing them at 13–14 tomans or about 200–215 piastres; these expenses he associated with a sales price of 85 tomans or approx. 1300 piastres in Aleppo.[39]

Probably no Europeans have known the caravan routes as well as the French merchant, Jean Baptiste Tavernier; his big book of travels contains an abundance of details about routes and customs stations, but unfortunately he never reveals the transport rates. The route between Smyrna and Persia won increasing popularity in the 17th century in spite of its length – about 100 marching days to Kashan or Isfahan.[40] The shortest routes started from Aleppo: in 32 days a man on horseback could reach Tabriz via Cizre or Isfahan through "The Little Desert" and via Kangavar,[41] but these routes were considered unsafe and were not used by the merchants. The same applied to the route via Mosul and Hamadan to Isfahan, which would take a caravan about 58 days.[42] The most popular route from Aleppo to Persia in Tavernier's time was the route via Birecik, Diyarbekir and Van to Tabriz, which took about 42 marching days; if the traveller wanted to go as far as Kashan or Isfahan it would take as much as 66 marching days.[43]

The growing popularity of the Smyrna route during the 17th century was not due to its being a short cut, nor was it on account of its convenience, the stretch Smyrna-Tokat being sparsely furnished with caravanserais; the advantage of this route was its relative safety and the comparatively low customs duties on the way and in Smyrna itself. 1/2 piastre per camel load and 1/4 piastre per horse load was paid in Tokat and Ezbider, whereas 1/2 piastre per camel or horse load in the direction of Persia and 1/4 piastre in the direction of Turkey was paid in Hassan Kela. The most important customs station on the Turkish side of the border, however, was Erzurum, where the merchants paid 24 piastres per load of silk in the direction of Turkey, whereas a duty of up till 100 piastres per load was charged on Indian materials. 6% was paid on other commodities. In the direction of Persia the duty on ready money was apparently only 2%, but this was demanded with such great laxity, however, that in practice the merchants got away with 1%. In Kagizman on the Persian side of the border 4 piastres per camel load and 2 piastres per horse load were paid, but if the

38. Barker, Isfahan, to Roe, April 1618, C. R. O., London, O. C. 792.
39. DUNLOP p. 547.
40. TAVERNIER I Book I, Ch. 2–7.
41. ibid. pp. 255, 259.
42. ibid. p. 160.
43. ibid. Book III, Ch. 3 .

caravan took the 7-day longer route via Kars, it got away with 2 piastres per camel load and 1 per horse. A duty was also demanded in Erivan. Tavernier does not reveal how much, but in Nakhichevan 10 abasi per camel were paid and in Marand, 13.[44] According to this information the total duty on a load of silk between Tabriz and Smyrna in Tavernier's time amounted to 36–37 piastres excluding the duty in Erivan.

The shorter route between Aleppo and Tabriz had many more customs stations. Before the Turkish frontier-town was reached duties had to be paid eight times, 22 piastres per load in all. In Van 2 tomans 4 abasi were paid, or nearly 35 piastres, in Nuchar 16 abasi were paid and the same in Marand, about 67 piastres in all between Aleppo and Tabriz.[45] There was some uncertainty concerning the customs duties in Nuchar, however, which had to be supplemented with an extra gift, and then there was the risk of further extortion on the part of the local Kurdish Chief. But apart from this, says Tavernier, the merchants liked this route. It was short and the customs duties were moderate.[46]

These estimates of the costs on the caravan routes to Persia may be supplemented with information concerning the costs on the route Ispahan-Gombroon. Here we have unusually solid ground under our feet, since we can take as our starting-point three invoices concerning silk dispatched by the Dutch East India Company's Factory in Persia, the information being contained in the following table:

Table 2. *Dutch invoices for silk exported from Persia 1634/35–1636/37.*[47]

	1634/35	1635/36	1636/37
Number of packs ..	420	621	500
Gross weight	6971 7/8 ma. T.	10331 5/8 ma. T.	8602 1/2 ma. T.
Transport charges per 100 man-i Tabriz	100 mah.	110 mah.	150 mah.
Purchase price ..	?	508584 fl.	416855 fl.
Packing	4448 fl.	7165 fl.	6865 fl.
Transport	5476 fl.	9223 fl.	10592 fl.
Gifts and dues	330 fl.	9568 fl.	3435 fl.
Sundries	262 fl.	1911 fl.	
	?	536,451 fl.	(437747) fl.

44. *ibid.* Book I, Ch. 2–7.
45. *ibid.* Book III, Ch. 3.
46. *ibid*, pp. 251–253.
47. DUNLOP pp. 496, 543–545, 629.

3*

The transport costs stated in the invoices are confirmed by additional scattered information to be obtained about transport charges on this route. Thus in 1652 110 mah. per 100 man-i Tabriz was paid for the transport of 300 loads from Isfahan to Gombroon within 65 days. 50 tomans were paid in advance, the caravan left Isfahan on June 5th and arrived in Gombroon on August 13th.[48] We have some information from English sources regarding the transport costs on parts of the stretch. In 1620 120 camels were hired for the stretch Shiraz-Isfahan for 18 mah. per 100 man-i Tabriz.[49] The same year 30 mah. per 100 man-i Tabriz was paid on the stretch Lar-Isfahan, it being noted that "camelhire is grown much deerer than it was by reason there is some merchants lately gone to Ormuz".[50] On the other hand the same camel men obtained only 20 mah. per 100 man-i Tabriz for the return journey Isfahan-Lar.[51] During the siege of Hormuz in 1622 the transport charges rose, the English having to pay 25 mah. per 100 man-i Tabriz for the stretch Gombroon-Lar.[52] The year afterwards the Dutch paid only 31 mah. per 100 man-i Tabriz for the stretch right up to Shiraz.[53] Thus the quotations from the beginning of the 1620s show quite considerable fluctuations in the sum spent on camel hire in accordance with the fluctuating demand. They seem also to indicate a somewhat lower level of transport costs than what we know from the Dutch invoices from the middle of the 1630s. It is reasonable to suppose that this development reflects the increased importance gained by the route Gombroon-Isfahan after the fall of Hormuz, but it is necessary to add that there are references to an epidemic among the camels in 1631/32, which led to a doubling of the transport costs, at any rate for a time.[54]

A load of silk was 72 man-i Tabriz and there were about 6¹/₂ mah to one piastre. The rates for the route Isfahan-Gombroon in the Dutch invoices thus correspond to approximately 12–18 piastres per load. Since it may be assumed that the general price level was lower the further one moved towards the east, this result supports the calculations mentioned above, which have been worked out on a less satisfactory basis for the transport to the towns on the Mediterranean. Without making any claims to exactitude we may assume that, disregarding protection costs, the transport of one

48. van DAM II³ p. 301, cf. CUNAEUS pp. 308, 363.
49. C. R. O., London, O. C. 869.
50. C. R. O., London, O. C. 864.
51. C. R. O., London, O. C. 872.
52. C. R. O., London, Factory Records, Persia I, 107, 114.
53. Visnich's journal and ledger, DUNLOP pp. 70, 102.
54. "Transport of goods from port to Spahan is so extreame dear, double the rates of former times, by scarcity of camels through mortality happening amongst them", Heynes, Gombroon, to Surat, 26/2 1632, C. R. O., London, O. C. 1423.

camel load around 1600 cost 10–20 piastres from Gombroon to Isfahan and 20–35 piastres from Isfahan to one of the Levant towns.

The connection between the Indian Ocean and the Mediterranean could be maintained by means of this route through Persia as evidenced by the travels of Newbery, but at the end of the 16th century, in the best years of the Aleppo trade, the most popular route was without doubt that of Aleppo-Baghdad-Basra-Hormuz. We possess some information from the years around 1580 which provides a little insight into the question of costs along the stretch. The English Levant merchant, Newbery, mentioned above, followed the route which seems to have been the most used at the end of the 16th century and the beginning of the 17th century. He arrived at Birecik on the Euphrates with a camel caravan after having left Aleppo three days previously. In Birecik the goods were loaded on to a barge and the caravan continued down the Euphrates to al Falluja on a level with Baghdad. From al Falluja it was only 1–2 days' transport over land to Baghdad, but from Baghdad the goods were once more conveyed on barges, this time down the Tigris to Basra. From Basra he took another ship and continued to Hormuz, where he arrived after a journey of over three months.[55]

Newbery gives some account of his expenses concerning transport, etc. on the way, but he is not consistent. He only quotes the transport costs proper in connection with the stretches Baghdad-Basra as 6 shahi per load, and Basra-Hormuz as 20 larins per 100 vessens. Converted into piastres per camel load this corresponds to about 1 piastre per load from Baghdad to Basra and somewhat less from Basra to Hormuz.[56] As was to be expected

55. PURCHAS VIII, pp. 452–459. Federici followed the same route in 1563, *Nuovo Ramusio* pp. 3–7; Rauwolf in 1574, RAUWOLF pp. 137–209; Balbi in 1579–80, *Nuovo Ramusio* pp. 71–108; Eldred in 1583, HAKLUYT VI pp. 3–7; Feynes de Monfart in 1608, FEYNES de MONFART *passim* and the Carmelites, Redempt and Benignus, in 1609, *Chronicle* pp. 172–173. But before the middle of the 17th century the river route along the Euphrates from Bir to Felugia was no longer in use; according to Tavernier, because the many water-wheels lifting water from the river for artificial irrigation made navigation difficult. Only once, in 1638, when the Sultan's army was advancing on Baghdad, had Tavernier seen much shipping on the Euphrates, TAVERNIER I p. 125. This closure of a previously important route is interesting. It may possibly be connected with the Persian occupation of Baghdad from 1623, since one of the Persians' problems was that, unlike the Ottomans, they were unable to supply the town from the upper course of the Euphrates and the Tigris, TAVERNIER I p. 169. But it is not impossible that the closure of the route also reflects a decreased interest in river navigation coincident with the recession in the transit trade.
56. Calculated according to Barret in HAKLUYT VI pp. 10–11: 1 shahi = 5 maidins, 33 maidins = 1 piastre, 1 larin = 1¹⁄₃ shahi and 16 vessens = 1 quintal Aleppo, i. e. approximately 200 kg. Cf. Balbi in *Nuovo Ramusio* p. 97.

the transport costs on the return journey from Hormuz to Basra were the same, but they were somewhat higher on the way up the Tigris than on the way down, namely 32 maidins per load, i.e. almost 1 piastre.[57] Regarding customs and other duties he states that in Birecik a charge of 1 maidin or shahi per load or bale was paid. In Baghdad he attempted to bribe himself free of being searched for ready money; it cost him four shahi for the searcher and the scribe in al Falluja and 33 maidins to the officer who accompanied him to Baghdad, but the money was discovered just the same. Unfortunately he does not reveal what he subsequently had to pay.[58] In Basra 3³/₄ maidins per load was paid on arrival. The customs amounted to ¹/₁₄ on money, glassware, etc., whereas spices and European textiles were taxed with no less than 20%, tare, however, being fixed at 30%.

Somewhat more detailed information regarding the costs of the journey through Iraq is to be found in an approximately contemporary source, which has been handed down in 2 practically identical versions through the English consul in Aleppo, Barrett,[59] and through the Italian traveller, Balbi.[60]

Between Aleppo and Baghdad Balbi mentions a few expenses which are partly specified per load and are partly general. As he counts on the hire of a boat accommodating 30–35 loads between Birecik and al Falluja the general entries are distributed on the assumption that the goods altogether totalled 30 loads. If this assumption holds the total expenses per load from when the caravan left Aleppo until it came to rest outside Baghdad consisted of 176¹/₂ maidins for transport and "household expenses", i.e. 5¹/₃ piastres, and 88¹/₂ maidin or approximately 2²/₃ piastres for customs, presents and bribes. The transport expenses from Baghdad to Basra are not mentioned; on the other hand it is revealed that between Basra and Hormuz 18 larins per carra of 4 Basra cantara was paid, i.e. slightly less than 1 piastre per load. Finally it is mentioned that the transport costs from Hormuz to Goa were 6–14 larins per bale or chest, presumably fixed with regard to both the size of the pack and the value of the goods. In 1622 it was stated that the normal transport costs between Hormuz and Surat were 12 larins per load.[61] We are thus able to estimate the probable transport costs between Hormuz and Goa at 2–3 piastres per load. In relation to the

57. The boats were hauled up the stream by bargemen "like our Westerne bargemen upon the Thames", Eldred in HAKLUYT VI p. 7.
58. At a somewhat later date (1609) all travellers passing through Baghdad were obliged to change their ready cash into the Pasha's coinage. *Chronicle* p. 173.
59. HAKLUYT VI pp. 10–24.
60. *Nuovo Ramusio* pp. 71–108. The information given by Barret and Balbi is identical, although a direct connection seems to be ruled out on account of the publication dates. There was probably a common Italian source, *Nuovo Ramusio* intr. pp. XXX–XXXI.
61. See below, p. 400.

transport costs the customs duties must have been a great deal heavier. It is mentioned that 5–6% was paid in Baghdad, 6% in Basra as well as 11% + 3% extra for non-Christian merchants in Hormuz.

If we tabulate the information it is possible to derive from Newbery and Barrett/Balbi concerning the transport costs we obtain the following result:

	Newbery	Barrett/Balbi
Aleppo – Baghdad		approx. $5^1/_3$ piastres
Baghdad – Basra	almost 1 piastre	
Basra — Hormuz	almost 1 piastre	almost 1 piastre
Hormuz – Goa		2–3 piastres

Thus, all in all, it should be possible to bring a load from Aleppo to Goa for 9–10 piastres in pure transport costs. Compared with the calculations made above and in the light of the great use made of river transport and ships this result does not appear improbable.

The return journey to Europe was necessarily more expensive, however. On the way to Baghdad the merchants could make use of lighters on the Tigris at a somewhat greater expense than on the down river journey; but from Baghdad onwards there was no possibility of water transport; from here it was the rule that the merchants used the caravan route through "The Little Desert" in an approximately straight line from Baghdad to Aleppo. Regarding this route Federici, who followed it in 1579/80, reveals that from Baghdad to Aleppo he paid 7 ducats per camel, in that for every 10 camels he and his companions hired the camel men added an eleventh gratis. To this must be added the expenses for riding animals, supplies, etc.,[62] According to this, the expenses on the return journey from Baghdad to Aleppo should be twice as much as those on the outward journey, i.c. approximately 10–11 piastres per load. With the customary reservations we can estimate the cost of the transport of a camel load from Goa to Aleppo to be 14–16 piastres per load.

As mentioned before everything is extremely fragmentary and uncertain, but all the available information is alike in indicating that a camel cannot have been so terribly expensive to keep, and that the transport costs, as far as the goods entering into the transcontinental trade were concerned, cannot have been especially onerous. Of course, for cheaper goods, it was quite a different matter. The Dutch purchase of wheat in Jahrum between Lar

---

62. This route was used, amongst others, by Eldred in 1584, HAKLUYT VI pp. 7–8; Fitch in 1590, FOSTER, *Early Travels* p. 47; Texeira in 1604–05, TEXEIRA pp. 32–50; Coverte in 1610 (His description is somewhat obscure, however; possibly he has travelled from Baghdad to Aleppo via Mosul), COVERTE *passim;* and by Manrique in 1643, MANRIQUE II p. 364 ff.

and Shiraz in 1636 provides an extreme example of this.[63] It concerned about 17,108 man-i Tabriz of wheat, the purchase price of which was 10,264 mahmudi. The transport costs to Gombroon, scarcely more that 20–25 marching days, were 50 mahmudi per man-i Tabriz, in all 8,554 mahmudi, i.e. nearly as much as the purchase price of the wheat.

But if the transport costs calculated here are compared with the shipping costs of the East India Companies, the direct voyage to Asia does not immediately appear to be a convincing technological advantage. If the calculations above are correct, at the end of the 16th century it should have been possible to bring a load of approximately 200 kg from Aleppo to Goa and back again for about 25 piastres in pure transport costs. The English Company's freight costs for a round trip to Asia and back in the beginning of the 17th century can be estimated at about £30–£32 per ton.[64] or about 135–145 piastres. If the commodity was pepper, for example, a ship's ton amounted to about 1200–1500 lb. or about three camel loads. Thus we reach the paradoxical result that the transport by ship was more expensive than the caravan transport. And on top of this we must assume that the route through the Red Sea, for which there is no available information concerning transport costs, was cheaper than the route through Iraq.

Part of the explanation is to be sought in the protection costs. From the above survey of the expenses connected with caravan journeys it will already become apparent that in every single case the customs duties undoubtedly exceeded the true transport costs. A further example may be obtained from Hovhannes's journal. We know that his export through Gombroon consisted of eighteen pieces of cloth, i.e. three camel loads. If the transport charges applicable in the 1630s and 1650s had not radically altered, the transport of these cloths from Isfahan to Gombroon can scarcely have cost him more that 60 piastres. But he had to pay 24 tomans or about 300 piastres in export duty in Gombroon.[65]

In the peddling trade the protection costs normally exceeded the transport costs. This observation has far-reaching consequences. It may already at this point be advanced that one reason why the Companies were superior to the peddling trade was the fact that they internalized the protection costs.

Another question raised above in connection with the transport costs was the relationship between the predictable expenses, such as the purchase price and the transport costs proper, and the sales prices. Pepper was the cheapest of the goods regularly entering into the transcontinental trade routes. The purchase price of 1 bahar of pepper on the Malabar coast in

63. Invoice in DUNLOP p. 572.
64. STEENSGAARD, *Freight Costs* p. 148.
65. KHACHIKIAN p. 255.

the 1580s was about 25–30 piastres, one bahar more or less corresponding to a camel load and a quintal of Aleppo.[66] If the above calculations are correct it could be brought to Aleppo for 15 piastres – ignoring the fact that it was officially forbidden to export pepper by this route. In the last few years of the 16th century a quintal of pepper could be sold in Aleppo for 300–350 piastres, but this was likely to have been a higher price than usual, the normal having probably been 200 piastres.[67] The most expensive of the goods regularly entering into the pedlar trade was silk. In 1600 a load of silk in Persia presumably cost somewhat under 600 piastres; it could be brought to Aleppo for 25–30 piastres in pure transport costs and sold for about 1200 piastres. Not such a good business in percentage as the cheaper pepper, but a greater profit per load.

The calculation may be wrong; let us suppose for example that the transport costs were double as much as we have reckoned. Even so, if it cost 30 piastres to bring a load from Goa to Aleppo and 50–60 piastres to bring a load from Persia to one of the Levant markets, there would still be a striking disparity between the predictable expences, the purchase price and transport cost proper, on the one hand and the sales price on the other. From a modern point of view a profit margin of this magnitude seems monstrous, and presumably this is the reason why the question of monopolies has always been raised in connection with the East India trade. But there can be no doubt that the East India trade was always competitive and never more competitive than when it took the form of a peddling trade. If the competition did not succeed in forcing down the prices still further, this must have been due to the unpredictable costs – protection and risk.

It has already been pointed out that the protection costs in the form of customs on the routes investigated here in all probability exceeded the true transport costs. In favourable periods and on good routes they would nevertheless be predictable, and this certainly applies to the route from Isfahan to Surat in Hovhannes's time, for example. We must assume that, as well as his information allowed, the caravan merchant had before every journey to try and weigh up the expected transport costs, protection costs and risk on alternate routes against the expected sales prices on the final market. Tavernier's discussion of the advantages and disadvantages of the various routes are indicative in this respect: the road via Smyrna was long and uncomfortable, but safe and without many customs stations. The route from Aleppo via Diyarbekir and Van had numerous customs stations but was shorter. The routes across "The Little Desert" and via Hamadan were even shorter, had still fewer customs stations, but were unsafe.

The peddling trade always had an element of risk, but to the risk that

66. Magalhâes-Godinho p. 639 cf. p. 505.
67. Mun, *East Indies*, printed in McCulloch, p. 11.

may be ascribed to robbers and rapacious tax-gatherers, must be added yet another element of risk: namely, the risk that was attached to the non-transparency of the market. It has been shown above that trade was distributed among many hands, and that there is no evidence of the existence of entrepreneurs, who have to a greater extent coordinated the trade in individual markets or in individual commodities. The following investigation seeks to discover how these institutional conditions affected price formation on the peddling market.

The Peddling Market

The towns of the Levant were the meeting ground of European and Asian market institutions. In certain respects we must expect to find these towns characterized by European organizational forms; thus trade on commission was widespread among the European merchants and was for them possibly the most usual entrepreneurial form,[68] whereas trade on commission, if practised at all by Asian merchants, is at any rate not demonstrable in the sources. Also State interference in the shape of the formal organization of merchants into "nations" headed by a consul seems to have been a specially European feature.[69] But in spite of these differences the Levant towns in the first half of the 17th century must still be characterized as peddling markets, i.e. predominantly characterized by the many entrepreneurs and the numerous purchases and sales in small lots.

This claim may be substantiated especially where Aleppo is concerned, thanks to a number of merchants' letter-books preserved from the middle of the 16th to the middle of he 17th century. Only with reservations does this material admit conclusions regarding the long term trends – each of them only covers a short period of time; on the other hand they are so much the more interesting as sources for the short-term fluctuations of the peddling market. Despite their differences they all bear evidence of an unrest and wariness that is difficult to document with isolated quotations, but which is expressed by the rapid changes of mood from letter to letter and in the attention paid to rumours. What they express is not the restlessness of the capitalist, but a nervous consciousness of the unpredictability of the market. Part of this worried tone may naturally be explained by the nature of the source material: in these letters the merchant would try to explain his less fortunate decisions to his partners, or the commission agent or apprentice

68. STEENSGAARD, *Consuls and Nations* p. 47.
69. The organization into nations is a phenomenon to be found everywhere in Asia; on the other hand, attempts to provide the privileges of the nations with a basis in international law is, as far as one can judge, a specially European phenomenon.

would try to justify his blunders. After all, having made a good purchase it is not always necessary to draw the principal's attention to the fact that anybody could have bought that particular commodity for a song. On the other hand we must reckon that the information contained in these letters about the market is fairly reliable, because the supply of accurate information must have been one of the first things one expected of a clever merchant, and the information contained in many of the letters regarding prices is a sure corrective of a possible bias. There can be no doubt about the rapid and unforeseeable fluctuations of the market.

The preserved letter-books bear each other out in so far as the merchants are all subject to the same basic conditions, but each one is also characteristic of the person and the time. The oldest letter-book, kept by the Venetian merchant, Andrea Berengo, covers a comparatively short period of time, from October 1555 to June 1556. On the other hand this period is especially well documented: the letters are composed at intervals of one to two weeks and under each date there are various versions of the same letter addressed to a number of different correspondents in Cyprus or Venice.[70]

On Andrea Berengo's arrival in Aleppo the Venetian nation was at loggerheads with the local authorities; following the imposition of new customs rates the nations had *batellated* the spices, i.e. declared a buyers' strike.[71] Since he was primarily interested in purchasing silk, this would not have concerned him had not the spice merchants, barred from making their assustomed purchases, now begun to interest themselves in silk. To this a further complication was added: Berengo, like all Venetian merchants in the Levant, was both importer and exporter, and the *batellation* of the spices indirectly hit the sale of Venetian commodities. Already here we encounter two characteristic features of the peddling trade: easy substitution (if one commodity became inaccessible demand was transferred to another one) and high price responsiveness to changes in demand.

On 3rd November Berengo sighed: "Here we live as if dead, without doing business".[72] A caravan with silk had been expected, but it had gone up in smoke, i.e. had turned out to be a false rumour. Little by little silk trickled into the town, and between October and November about 50 loads arrived in small lots.[73] The buyers were hesitant, however, in the hope of greater quantities to come; Berengo considered investing in leather, but he postponed the decision, knowing that it would never be a really lucrative business. For a time he considered buying spices as soon as the

---

70. Ugo Tucci (ed.), *Lettres d'un marchand vénetien, Andrea Berengo* (1553–1556) Paris 1957.
71. BERENGO p. 27.
72. *Ibid.* p. 76.
73. *Ibid.* p. 176.

batellation was over, but when he heard what was being paid for spices in Alexandria he found also that possibility disadvantageous.[74]

Around the turn of the year the *batellation* was raised, but the buyers held back because the caravan from Mecca was on its way and a fall in prices might be expected on its arrival. But the Mecca caravan, which arrived at the beginning of January, was a disappointment. It consisted of 800 loads – scarely 100 loads more than what was needed locally, including 200 loads of pepper, 50–60 of cloves, 30–40 of ginger, 10–12 of mace, as well as indigo, lacquer and cotton material. It had been difficult to obtain transport from Mecca because an epidemic had broken out among the camels, and that was why the caravan was so small. Many merchants had remained behind and were now sending their goods in small lots via Tor to Cairo. A good season was therefore expected in Alexandria, but for Aleppo the prospects were anything but cheerful. If the Basra caravan doesn't help, we're in a fine pickle, says Berengo, because the silk routes are still closed.[75] The news from Venice was not encouraging: a letter sent at the end of October reported very few sales and low prices. Berengo was indignant about the topsy-turvy state of affairs: "I don't know what to say. Here silk is at a premium and there is very little of it, and at home there is plenty to be had at low prices. Here there are spices in plenty but the prices are exhorbitant, even higher than I have written in my previous letters, and at home there are no spices and the prices have reached the bottom".[76] But as Tucci, who published Berengo's letters, has correctly remarked, it is not quite so extraordinary as one might expect at first glance: the prices in Aleppo were not only a function of the supply of Asian goods, but also of the supply of European goods. Another Venetian merchant had stated the problem a few years previously: "This trade will quite definitely not pick up again so long as so many commodities are sent, and it would pick up by itself on the other hand if less was sent; that is to say, the evil originates from the excellent principals and not from the merchants in this country who, seeing so many of our commodities, seek with good reason to keep the prices down."[77]

In spite of all these complaints Berengo and the other Venetian merchants managed to do some business. During the spring some Persian silk seems to have arrived in the town, and some combined cash and barter trade was done in silk. "The price quotations" at the beginning of May give as good an impression of the peddling market as can be found anywhere: "Two loads of canary silk at 5¼ veneziani per rotolo have been bought for 70

74. *Ibid*. p. 115.
75. *Ibid*. p. 189.
76. *Ibid*.
77. *Ibid*. pp. 15–16.

veneziani in cash, the remainder, kersey, at 12 veneziani per piece. Further-more 12 cantars nutmegs at 25,000 dirhams, 5¹/₂ cantars cloves at 24,000 dirhams and 2 loads of cinnamon at 20,000 dirhams for 4 pieces of purple cloth at 70 maidins per pico, 10 pieces of kersey at 10 veneziani per piece, the rest in cash ... etc., etc."[78] One can imagine the haggling that must have preceded the completion of such business. But what is just as important, one can imagine the market in which combined transactions of this nature might serve as price quotations. Towards the end of the 16th century cash transactions came to play a greater part in the Levant trade, but in Berengo's time combined transactions seem to have been the rule.

Yet another feature in Berengo's correspondence deserves attention: his interest for the conditions in other markets. His comments upon the condi-tions in Venice are already mentioned, but he also receives and forwards reports about prices, stores and realized transactions from Mecca[79] and Alexandria.[80] Before 29th June 1556 it is known in Aleppo that a caravan on its way to Cairo has arrived from Tor with 1200 camels, including 350 – some say 450 – with pepper, 750 with ginger, 22 with nutmeg, 35 – some say 350 – with cloves, the remainder with indigo and lacquer, and that yet another caravan of the same size was expected on its way to Cairo. This gave cause to much optimism among the Venetian merchants in Alexandria; they reckoned on being able to make some good purchases if no Frenchmen turned up, for there were already 7–8,000 cantars of pepper and ginger in the town.[81] That Berengo passes on this information is not merely of academic interest, because it formed part of what he and his principals based their decisions on regarding purchase. Thus it is also important that in June a swarm of grasshoppers ravaged the area around Hama, and that the cotton rose immediately afterwards from 20 to 30 veneziani per cantar.[82]

We find the same problems in the correspondence of the Marsilian brothers Hermite from the last decades of the 16th century, the same un-certainty with regard to supplies and stores, the same indecision with re-gard to the best objects of investment. In April 1578 Gilles Hermite, like Berengo 23 years earlier, had almost decided to buy leather when he put off the ultimate decision in order to see how the market would develop after the arrival of the caravans from Basra and Mecca, which were expected to arrive at approximately the same time. According to report the caravans were big, but on the other hand all sorts of goods were in demand except nutmeg, in which nobody is interested, there being a lot of nutmeg

78. *Ibid.* p. 255.
79. *Ibid.* p. 203.
80. *Ibid.* p. 318.
81. *Ibid.*
82. *Ibid.* p. 309.

in Alexandria, his brother reports from Marseilles.[83] The caravans arrive, but are not up to expectation and Hermite is not satisfied: "everything is so dear that I don't know what I shall do."[84]

But how seriously should one take these eternal complaints that everything is dear and that no investments are lucrative? Five years later Gilles Hermite is in Aleppo again, and his complaints are just as heartrending: "In brief, the country is in such a state that I do not think either profit, satisfaction or honour are to be found."[85] The prices of Asian commodities are always higher than they should be, the sale of European commodities is always more sluggish than it ought to be, but there is always the hope of improvement.[86] The silk purchases are postponed for a couple of months because a caravan of Kurdish merchants carrying silk is expected; they are people who are always in a hurry to return home and the price of silk usually drops when they are in town.[87] Did the price of silk fall? This we are not told. The merchants' letters do not contain much in the way of glad tidings.

The letter-book of the English Levant merchant, Clark,[88] is especially interesting since it covers precisely those years when, in the middle of a boom, the merchants of Aleppo were informed about the first Dutch returns from Asia, i.e. 1598–1600 and 1602. But in spite of these particular circumstances the tone is the same as with the Venetian Berengo and the Marsilian Hermite. He awaits the caravans, which are always smaller and always turn up later than rumour has it. He weighs up the investment possibilities against one another while trying to form an estimate of the price development in Aleppo and in the European markets: "I never had more trouble to make imployments than have had this year chiefly by reason commodities were here at such uncertainties espetially silke, which commodity in july was bought up by Venetians and French that we were not able to buy any, they gave such extreame prices, so then in August understanding that noe certainty of another to come of 2 or 3 months I was then forced to buy then some 12 coles [bales] for all accounts as time advized at 12 rials of eight pr Rl [rotolo] and in mydle September came another carravan which was but 9 somes [loads] and given out that noe more would come of two months soe then was forced again to give 11$\frac{1}{2}$, 12$\frac{1}{4}$ 7 maidins, 12$\frac{1}{2}$ and soe bought 4 bales. Yet the 10th October came in some 200 somes, the which noe sooner entered but presently the Vene-

83. Micheline Baulant (ed.), *Lettres de négociants marseillais, les Frères Hermite* (1570–1612) p. 18.
84. *Ibid.* p. 19.
85. *Ibid.* p. 50.
86. *Ibid.* p. 49.
87. *Ibid.* p. 51.
88. B. M. London, Sloane Ms. 867.

tians gave 12³/₄ and 13 rials of eight. After 5 or 6 days it began to fall a lytle so I bought ... 13 coles very excellent good silk at 12¹/₄ 7 m and 12¹/₂ and some at 12 soe here hath been a great dyfference in times."[89]

The problem concerns not so much high prices, but their instability and the non-transparency of the market. Price fluctuations of up to 10% within a few months or weeks were nerve-racking: the day or hour of the purchase could determine whether the investment was a success or a fiasco. But there were no middlemen to avert the violent fluctuations in prices: in the busy months when the ships lay outside Alexandretta waiting, the silk was bought "as soon as it was off the camels' back."[90] The English imports were also hit by the unpredictability of the market, but here we encounter something unusual: an attempt to limit by means of a cartel agreement the competition between members of the nation and to fix minimum prices for the English goods.[91] Unusual, because the Venetian nation, which was just as well aware of the problem, if not more so, apparently never attempted anything similar. It did also cause the English a lot of trouble: it was not easy to make sure that the minimum prices were observed as far as barter or combined barter and cash trade was concerned, but the cartel agreements concerning the prices of cloth, tin and kersey nevertheless remained a recurrent feature of the English trade in Aleppo.[92]

Another feature already discussed, which may be illustrated by means of Clark's letter-book, is the fact that prices were interrelated. The unusual demand for silk in the year 1600 can be traced to the guardedness of the European merchants as regards spices after they had been informed about the safe return of the Dutch ships.[93] Another remark serves to show the complex relations within the market: "with spices durst not meddle with any, finding indigo soe reasonable, neither would I have bought soe much wool but for the scarcity of galls."[94]

The glorious peddling trade demanded good health. It was not for nothing that Alexandria was called "the Churchyard of the Franks", and in Alexandretta only a few tough characters survived the dangerous climate. But the trade also demanded strong nerves, a sure eye for the trends of the market and the patience to postpone buying and selling until the right

89. *loc. cit.* f. 113.
90. *Ibid.* f. 107.
91. *Ibid.* ff. 9, 20, 43; STEENSGAARD, *Consuls and Nations* p. 46; ARUP p. 112; it is interesting when Arup points out that it was the unpredictability of the prices more than their absolute level that worried the factors: "Thus on the whole it is probably more justifiable to say that the factors were more bent on maintaining *stable* prices than on maintaining *high* prices."
92. ARUP p. 111 ff.
93. B. M. London, Sloane Ms. 867 ff. 61–62, 95–96.
94. *Ibid.* f. 125.

moment. An anonymous letter-book of an English Levant merchant from 1634–36 illustrates the problems in quite a dramatic manner.[95] We meet him for the first time in December 1634, presumably when he has just arrived in Aleppo with the annual fleet of Company ships that usually called at Alexandretta in November and December, and he has in all probability been young and inexperienced.[96] He is at once full of the usual complaints about the market for return goods, especially silk. "Returns for England are difficult to be obtained, noe Persia silk cometh in ... the like scarcety of commodities in this place scarce ever knowne."[97] As usual, what was wrong was not so much the shortage of return goods, but the disparity between supply and demand, which he immediately points out: "And here is wayting a great estate to be ymployed and must wayt for future fortunes."[98]

But the market is rapidly on the turn. Already a week afterwards he reports: "Pertia silk comes peddling in",[99] and from the end of December to the end of January silk falls about 1 piastre per rotolo. Shortly afterwards he is able to report with relief: "The French and Venetian money are all invested and all their shipping provided for."[100] The fall in silk prices continues in February: "if 2 or 3 French ships shortly looked for hindereth not, both ledgee and ardasse wilbe hadd very reasonable and that happeninge gauls must answerably declyne for when sylke is cheape they most commonly fall lowe ..."[101] Not only were regular supplies of Persian silk contributing to the price fall, but also a widespread fear that the plague would break out again that summer as in the previous year; for his own part the English merchant declares: "I think I will to the mountains".[102] From 15th April to 18th June there is a gap in his correspondence, and he was not back in Aleppo until 4th July. A few Englishmen had been holding the fort, however, having locked themselves in

95. P. R. O. London, S. P. 110/10.
96. "I am beholden unto you for directing mee to the widowe whose husbands death I pitty – butt that you should thinke me fitt for such an honor is mutche out of the way, and untill have gott more monies in my Purse, I must nott without any disparedgment entertayne any thought of maredge, although in God Almyghties tyme I should be glad to arryve into itt – as Indico declineth with you so here it is falling . . ." *loc. cit.* ff. 446–47. Of course this remark to a business friend does not prove youth or inexperience, but it nevertheless points very strongly in that direction.
97. *Ibid.* f. 8.
98. *Ibid.* f. 32.
99. *Ibid.* f. 24.
100. *Ibid.* f. 46.
101. *Ibid.* f. 67.
102. *Ibid.* f. 91.

their houses, "but some of them by meanes of a bell and trustie servants have procured lardge sayles of clothe . . ."[103]

In the meantime the price of silk had risen once more. After the defeat of Fakhr al-Din, Murad IV had launched a new offensive against Persia, and now, in 1635, although Persian silk was still arriving by way of the northern routes, uncertainty ruled as regards the fate awaiting the caravan from Baghdad. The following months are marked by great uncertainty and many rumours; in August a caravan was expected from Erzurum, and in September the report once again is: "Rumours again afoot that shortly we shall be served with great supplies from divers places, heatherto noe truth appeareth."[104] Rumours about reasonable supplies of silk, partly via the northern routes, partly via Baghdad when the summer campaign is over, are persistent. On the other hand there is also the risk of increasing demand. "From Marcellis dayly expected a bark and some pretend an English ship and the Venetians doe shortly look for a ship from Venis."[105] The silk prices are high and there are only about 100 bales of Persian silk and 60 quintals of Syrian silk in the town. It is heads or tails: if the caravans arrive the prices will fall, if the ships arrive the prices will increase still further.

Rumours only make things more difficult. On 1st October are reported "dayly rumours of greater quantities . . .", and on 10th October "appearance that some caravan of importe is at hand, but as yet not confirmed."[106] On 13th November the situation improves: 240 bales have arrived in the town by way of the northern route and 400 bales are still expected via Baghdad, but the prices are not yet determined. "Men that have parcells doe look at shipping here expected and wayghte their arryvall before they enter into sayles."[107] In December the long awaited Baghdad caravan arrived with 400 bales and with the message that there were still considerable stocks in Baghdad that could be expected to arrive in Aleppo the following April at the latest.[108]

But at the same time as the supply increased so did the demand. There had not been any European ship in Alexandretta since April, but on 13th November the English ship *Hercules* arrived together with a Dutch ship which, according to reports, carried considerable supplies on Marsilian account. Furthermore, in December a Venetian and a Marsilian *pollacra* arrived. The factor's deliberations clearly reflect the new situation. He balances the supply against the demand: "In town may be to sell not

103. *Ibid.* ff. 122–23.
104. *Ibid.* f. 169.
105. *Ibid.* f. 168.
106. *Ibid.* ff. 188, 192.
107. *Ibid.* f. 199.
108. *Ibid.* f. 228.

much above then 300 in 350 coles, but of white silk, if it were cheape, is at leaste 60 kintals: with the Hercules came a great flemmine thought to have broughte down upwards of 60,000 $ and besides in our nations hands cannot be soe littel as 100,000 $ how will be invested God above best knoweth, now galls have deceived all men's expectations."[109] The English nation made its purchases between 5th and 29th December, on which latter date the merchant declares: "the Hercules will goe away very rich".[110] The cargo comprises among other things 270 bales of Persian silk, most of which is legia, i.e. the majority of the Persian silk the letter-writer had estimated to be in the town. It was now known that the French and Venetian ships carried 6–700 Venetian cloths, 70–80,000 piastres and other commodities to the value of a further 40,000 piastres.[111] But they will find difficulty in making their purchases, thinks our informer, "our Nation have swept Aleppo clean of Percya silke", and this has taken place at a price of 12–13 piastres per rotolo.[112]

Then follows a month without letters, but suddenly in February 1636 a new subject crops up: "As a young man my sufficiency in pinte of a factor hath met averse and evill times such as worse could not well happen and therefore I must request you among all the rest to pass by all wants and my yielded fruitless successes ... All nations heire save us Inglish are butt on poor terms and their force to buy silk although thought great prooveth very small."[113] The reason behind these self-reproaches and melancholy concerning the competitors' lack of spending power is soon revealed. In December our factor has bought 4 quintals over and above what he needed for the returns, confident that the price would increase still further after the English had completed their purchases and the French and Venetian imports were brought to the town. But he has miscalculated. The two *pollacras* leave Alexandretta without silk and the supplies they have landed have not been immediately invested, but await better times, i.e. lower silk prices. "And if the Marcillians late losses keepe hence store of moneys – and the quantity of silk cometh that is spoken of – it must needs abate lustily."[114] It will be good for the trade, but bad luck for the letter writer who has expected a rising market; it is this dilemma that characterizes the letters of the subsequent months.

The factor's misgivings come true. On 10th February he still reckons on there being only about 40 bales of silk in the town, including 6 bales of legia. On 15th February a caravan arrives via Diyarbekir with 43 quintals,

109. *Ibid.* f. 226.
110. *Ibid.* f. 233.
111. *Ibid.* f. 239.
112. *Ibid.* ff. 233, 238.
113. *Ibid.* f. 263.
114. *Ibid.* f. 267.

including 23 ardasse and the remainder legia. On 25th February 400 bales arrive from Baghdad, on 1st March he thinks there are only 550 bales for sale in the town, and 16th March he has to confirm that the French and the Venetians have now invested nearly all their money, and that they have only bought 20 bales of silk. He still has his own lot: "By 4 kintalls [400 rotolos] Ledgee on my hands I would cheerfully loose 1 $ per Rl to have my money back, but in all likelihood I shall not come off under $1^1/_2$"[115] – 600 piastres. It was a serious matter for a young factor, and merely because what appeared to be a dead certain boom turned out to be a slump. The prices of silk continued to drop throughout April and May, but the rumours about several arrivals from Baghdad continued at the same time as appreciable quantities of the new harvest of Syrian silk arrived. And the buyers still failed to show up. A Venetian ship went on to Alexandria in order to load there, and no French ships at all called at Alexandretta. On 2nd July a long expected caravan arrived from Baghdad with 300 bales of silk and the message that more was on the way. Later on in July 12 bales arrive from Van, and on 5th August 80–100 bales arrive from Van and Erzurum. A single French ship touches at Alexandretta in September, but it only carries few commodities and still less money and is loaded with heavy goods and only 40 bales of silk.[116]

In the middle of September there were still 450 bales of silk for sale in Aleppo, but the factor was still on the look-out for signs of rising silk prices, because the Ottoman army at Baghdad had confiscated all the beasts of burden, and on 14th September a heavily loaded Venetian ship arrived with woollen and silk materials and various wares to the value of about 350,000 piastres, but very little money. "English, French and Venetian shipping in port must needs do harme to cheap investments", he says hopefully.[117] But silk still arrives in the town: as late as September 24 bales of ardasse arrived, and at the end of the month he reckoned on there being about 500 bales for sale in the town. The Venetians preferred to buy white, i.e. Syrian silk, of which there was also a good supply, whereas the French were so heavily in debt that they made practically no investments.[118] A ship arrived from Marseilles carrying only a few commodities, and the same was the case with the French and Venetian ships that arrived at the end of October.

On 4th November 1636 the correspondence abruptly ceases. We do not know whether the factor has been called home as the result of his unfortunate transactions or whether he has been taken ill while busy pre-

115. *Ibid.* f. 304.
116. *Ibid.* f. 374.
117. *Ibid.* f. 402.
118. *Ibid.* f. 428.

paring his share of the cargo of the *London*, which was expected in Alexandretta in November. The fact that his letter-book has been preserved in the Levant Company archives indicates that his homeward journey cannot have taken place in the normal peaceful manner. Like his name, his subsequent fate must remain unknown, but his letter-book illustrates convincingly the conditions of the peddling trade, and especially the risk the non-transparency of the market created for the merchant who wished to carry out the function of "the second hand". If the price quotations contained in the letter-book (piastres per rotolo) are tabulated, the trap into which the factor fell in December 1635 is revealed:

Table 3. *Silk prices in Aleppo 1635–36.*

	Jan.	Feb.	Mar.	Apr.	May	June	July	Aug.	Sept.	Oct.	Nov.	Dec.
1635..	13	12		$12^{1}/_{2}$			$12^{3}/_{4}$	13	13	$12^{3}/_{4}$		$12^{3}/_{4}$
1636..		12	$11^{1}/_{2}$	11		11	$10^{1}/_{2}$	11	$10^{3}/_{4}$		11	

Yet another episode from the anonymous merchant's letter-book deserves mention. In the beginning of June 1636 the factor received a certain sum of ready money from Alexandretta, but his correspondent in the harbour, Mr Hexte, had packed the money inside bales of cloth in order to avoid paying customs. The factor loudly expressed his indignation: "Mr Hexte contrary to my order sending of itt most naughtely packed upp in 8 clothes of his owne ..." But when the bales went through the customs "they spoke Spaynish soe clearly and did soe rattel that the Agaws jewes and all else admired att the madness of him that tooke noe better care in packing of itt." The episode naturally caused great indignation and cost the nation an *avania,* at the same time as the customs control on English goods was intensified;[119] it is apparent that the factor wished to disclaim responsibility for the attempted smuggling. But he was scarcely innocent. His letter to Mr Hexte containing instructions for the dispatch of the money is cryptic, but there can be no doubt as to its meaning. It concludes: "As before I am bould uppon you and doe presume you will assuredly stand my friend in seeing this business discreetly and faithfully carried. I meane soe that the consull hath noe notice thereof for prevention thereof your experience needeth not any further advice, therein I rest referred to your good discretions."[120]

The fifth and last letter-book from Aleppo adds nothing to the impression gleaned above.[121] During these years the silk prices were low

119. *Ibid.* f. 343.
120. *Ibid.* f. 333.
121. P. R. O. London, S. P. 110/11.

in Aleppo, i.e. 9–10 piastres per rotolo, but there is insufficient basis for deciding whether the price fall was permanent or only a passing fluctuation. Perhaps because trade was slack at this time the correspondent manifests more personal features than are usual in merchants' letters. Not only did he have time to write letters to his friends, but even letters to his mother are entered in the letter-book; however, there were not many commissions. Perhaps the hard times were the cause, supplies in 1659 being hindered by political unrest. But trade in galls and cotton was apparently flourishing, so it was possibly the reputation of the merchant himself that was the greatest difficulty. "My deare Brother wee have both lived long enough to see the vanitics of this age wee live in and both have had our share of these vanities, wittness now the conditions wee are brought to pr our own fopperies. But I hope wee have seen our errors, for my own part shall trule endeavour to raise my fortunes ..."[122] Totally reformed he was not, however. He mentioned with longing the fair Lady Ann, who perhaps was more fair than she was lady: "Were she nott in your ill deserving island, I should say England was the worst place under the heavens, nay worse than Gombrone in India, where Mr Wm. Garraway is now dead, but her presence being there, she is easily the flower of England's garden, and forces me to allow it precedence from Rome or Florence or any the Grand Duke's territories."[123]

Yet another of the letter-books investigated is relevant in this context. Although it does not originate from a Levant town it is chiefly concerned with the Levant business, first and foremost the Venetian import of pepper from Alexandria, and it thus gives us the opportunity of viewing the Levant trade from the importing town. The sender of this series of letters, which cover the period from August 1587 to May 1590, is Paolo Dandolo, and the recipient in almost every case is his brother, Vincenzo Dandolo, who was the Venetian consul in Alexandria until 1591.[124] It appears from the letters that the two brothers were jointly concerned with the sale of Venetian goods in Alexandria and the import of pepper in Venice. Paolo's letters first and foremost contain information about the state of the business in Venice as well as information concerning the European market of interest to the pepper trade.

Without doubt the most important thing in this connection was the account of the imports of pepper in Lisbon. On 1st October 1587 Paolo Dandolo was thus able to say that this year's total import in Lisbon was 10,000 cantars, a modest amount that gave reason for optimism, even if the prices in Alexandria were high at the moment.[125] Dandolo's infor-

122. *Loc. cit.* f. 51.
123. *Ibid.* f. 39.
124. Museo Civico-Correr, Venezia, Ms. Cicogna 2698.
125. Paolo Dandolo to Vincenzo Dandolo, *loc. cit.*

mants have received accurate accounts: in 1587 the actual import in Lisbon is given as 9,722 quintals.[126] The year afterwards the question returned at the time when the merchants expected to hear some news from Lisbon: on 2nd September still nothing had been heard about Portuguese returns to Lisbon. This gave rise to some optimism, because at the same time – it was in 1588 – merchants in Venice had heard about "Drago inglese havendo in certo modo maltratata l'armata spagnola", and had therefore hoped that the returns to Lisbon would either fail to arrive or be greatly delayed. But the hope was in vain, because already two weeks later it is revealed that the Indian fleet had arrived with 22,000 cantars of pepper. It was feared that such a large amount would bring about a fall in prices, even though Venice had not much in stock.[127] Once again the spies had got hold of the correct figures, the Venetian import of pepper in 1588 being given as 21,819 quintals.[128]

In November 1588 it was reported through the Venetian Ambassador in Spain that the contractors for the European sales, Welser and Rovellasco, were planning to set up an agency in Venice and transfer 6,000 cantars of pepper to the town. Paolo Dandolo feared this might lead to the total ruin of the Venetian pepper trade and advised his brother to exercise the greatest care in the purchase of pepper: "piu presto vorrei qualche altra cosa".[129] The rumour turned out to be an exaggeration, however: no proper agency was set up, and of the transfers of Portuguese pepper to the Mediterranean only the transfer of 500 quintals to Venice and 2,000 quintals to Leghorn are mentioned in the following.[130]

In the summer of 1589 the reports from the Atlantic once again gave reason for optimism in Venice: it was rumoured that Drake was blockading Lisbon, but on 26th August it was reported that the blockade had been raised. The European contractors still had some of the previous year's import of pepper in stock and planned to send a consignment to Hamburg, while that year's import from India was, according to report, as much as 30,000 quintals. This time the spies estimated too high: the of-

126. FALCAO p. 61, cf. KELLENBENZ, Poivre p. 3, where the import in 1587 on the basis of information obtained from the Fugger Archives is given as 10,386 quintals.
127. Museo Civico-Correr, Venezia, Ms. Cicogna 2698.
128. FALCAO p. 62; according to the Fugger Archives 22,963 quintals, KELLENBENZ, Poivre p. 3. In this case the Fugger Archives give the gross amount as loaded in India without taking wastage into account, cf. FALCAO loc. cit.
129. Museo Civico-Correr, Venezia, Ms. Cicogna 2698.
130. The Europe contract comprised more than just the Houses of Welser and Rovellaschi; it included also the brothers Philip-Edward and Octavian the second, Fugger, who corresponded regularly with the House of Ott in Venice. In 1592 the Fugger brothers disposed of approximately 500 quintals in Venice through that House. KELLENBENZ op. cit. pp. 13, 10.

ficial figure for the Portuguese import in 1589 is 24,840 quintals.[131] In any case the European pepper stocks were now so considerable that there were serious grounds for anxiety. On 6th September Paolo Dandolo declared that the pepper market in Venice was now at a complete standstill: no buyers and no sellers. "I bid you be cautious in sales, in purchase and in barter ... it is necessary, with pen in hand, that you calculate bearing in mind the price that might be expected in Venice." The fear turned out to be justified, since within three months the price in Venice fell by 20%, and in January Paolo declared: "All is ruined". During the autumn 2,500 cantars of pepper were transferred to Venice from Portugal, and Paolo Dandolo declares that there are no prospects of better prices; he will sell when he can, despite the low prices, because keeping the pepper in stock will only increase the loss.[132]

The low prices were maintained throughout the spring and the summer, and the accounts of the annual fleet to Lisbon that were received in Venice before 2nd August gave no reason to hope for an improvement. It was said to be carrying 30,000 quintals – the official figure was 22,270 quintals.[133] Furthermore, there were said to be 25,000 quintals of the previous year's import of pepper left in stock in Lisbon. Paolo Dandolo consequently sold the rest of his and his brother's pepper in Venice for the best prices he could obtain: 120–128 ducats per cargo. This should have been a good price in the light of the most recent accounts, but it was nevertheless a mistake. In a postscript to the letter he relates that after his sales the prices have increased "contrary to all reason" up to 130–134 and that they were expected to increase to as much as 140 ducats per cargo.[134]

On the basis of the Dandolo correspondence the price fluctuations in pepper in Venice from 1587–90 (ducats per cargo) have been tabulated in the following:

Table 4. *Pepper prices in Venice 1587–1590.*

	Jan.	Feb.	Mar.	Apr.	May	June	July	Aug.	Sept.	Oct.	Nov.	Dec.
1587							150		172–75			
1588	140–60	154		147		148	148–55	160	168	160		140–4
1589	140–45	140–46	146	140–44	140–44		143	150	144	137–38	134–40	127–2
1590	120–23			120–24	120		120	125–27	130–34			

131. FALCAO p. 63; KELLENBENZ, *Poivre*, p. 3: 20,258 quintals.
132. Museo Civico-Correr, Venezia, Ms. Cicogna 2698.
133. FALCAO p. 64; KELLENBENZ, *Poivre*, p. 3: 23,682 quintals.
134. Museo Civico-Correr, Venezia, Ms. Cicogna 2698.

The see-saw of the Levant prices is repeated on the European market. In Venice as in the Levant towns there is no sign of "the second hand"; on the contrary the price fluctuations seem to be even more violent on account of the distribution of the pepper among so many sellers. In January 1589 Paolo Dandolo writes as follows: "Pepper has for many days been priced at 140 ducats per cargo, it has been sold at that price by those who needed to sell some big lots, but now they are used up and there are buyers at 145 ducats . . ."[135]

What conclusions does the material presented above allow us to draw with regard to the peddling market? Firstly, it may safely be established that the impression of a competitive market is overwhelming. Considered in isolation the Levant market is an almost clinical example of the classical market: a certain quantity of European commodities and money demanded a certain quantity of Asian commodities within a limited period of time, many buyers were confronted with many sellers, no single entrepreneur had sufficient resources to determine the price and prices had to be fixed at the level at which supply and demand balanced each other. The merchants are well aware of this state of affairs. The first questions they ask are always: how big a capital has been brought in by the European nations? How big are the stocks of Asian goods?

Cartels related to the buying and selling of specific commodities could do nothing to alter the general conditions: the maintenance of prices under conditions of falling demand would only lead to decreased sales or to the prices or sales of other commodities being affected. There cannot be any doubt, however, that a price cartel such as the one put in force by the English nation must have been a considerable advantage to the English merchants. They were unable to force up the prices of their goods appreciably, since the substitution possibilities were near at hand, but throughout periods extending over several years they were able to make sure of stable prices for those goods they sold, a stability that cannot entirely have been offset by the increased instability with regard to the prices of the commodities they bought. There is no evidence of this procedure having been employed by other nations, however; on the contrary, the available price quotations rule out the possibility that it should have been general practice as regards the sale of Asian goods.

Generally speaking, the most important stabilizing factor must be stock formation. Voluntary speculative stock formation, "the second hand", was apparently only an exceptional occurrence; transactions were concluded directly between the caravan merchants and the European merchants. The same apparently applies, at least as far as the pepper trade is concerned,

135. *Ibid.*

to the Venetian market: the Dandolo Company sold the pepper import in Fondaco dei Tedeschi directly to the exporters.[136] We find an isolated attempt at speculative stock formation in the anonymous SP 110/10 – merchant, but his fate merely illustrates the risk the isolated entrepreneur ran in making such an attempt under the non-transparent conditions of the market. In this case the merchant merely contributed to the see-saw of the prices by buying during a boom and selling during a slump; we may presume of course that others, more ingeniously, have carried out similar speculations with greater success and have thereby contributed to the stabilization of prices. But the speculator was forced to trust his own judgement alone; we have no evidence of speculators possessing resources that enabled them to secure price leadership until the business was wound up. Under these conditions the most important stock formation was that practised by the importing and exporting merchants themselves. A merchant might postpone buying and selling for shorter or longer periods in the hope of a more favourable market. This involved increased risk and increased loss of interest, although it helped to limit the reaction to especially violent fluctuations of supply and demand. – That the merchants were aware of this, too, their correspondence makes plain. Side by side with their comments regarding the stocks in town we find their forecasts with regard to coming supplies for both the Asian and the European side of the market.

The market lacked buffers in the shape of middlemen, but there was also another condition that contributed to the particularly marked short-term fluctuations: namely, the imperfect communication between market and consumer, and in particular between market and producer. In the letters of the European Levant merchants we clearly note their endeavours to establish a connection between market, consumer and producer. The factor would not only take into consideration the conditions on the Levant market. He would try to form an idea of the expected demand on the European market and keep his correspondents in the European towns informed about the price development in the Levant. The transaction costs on the European side of the market: transport, insurance and customs, were to a large degree predictable, even though there were differences between the conditions under which the merchants of the various European nations laboured in this respect. But the most important variables for the European entrepreneur were the prices, and we must regard the industri-

136. Museo Civico Correr, Venezia, Ms. P. D. 1480, Paolo Dandolo's journal. The journal is difficult to interpret, and no attempt has been made to analyse it systematically, but a cursory reading of its entries shows a clear repetition of the pedlar pattern: numerous sales in small lots to different buyers and a wide range of goods (cloves, nutmeg, aloes, turmeric, ginger, etc.).

ous merchant correspondence as evidence of the efforts made to create a comprehensive view of these variables.

It is obvious, however, that these endeavours cannot have been carried out with the same consistency on the Asian side of the market or in the Asian peddling trade over long distances. The letter-books show that the Venetian and English factors corresponded with their principals within the trade year and at intervals of a few weeks. The rhythm of the monsoon excluded a similar regular correspondence on most of the Asian routes of international importance. The caravan merchants would try to obtain information about price conditions in the Levant towns when they reached Baghdad or Mecca, for example, but they had no recent information regarding prices in the distant market at the time they or their suppliers made their purchases in the producing area. In addition the costs of carrying the goods to the market was even more unpredictable than on the European side. In these circumstances information about the latest prices on the Levant market was a rather unimportant variable for the Asian entrepreneur who wished to make purchases with a view to exporting to Europe.

In the long run a shift in demand would necessarily be felt in the peddling trade and ultimately by the producers. In Venetian cloth and in English cloth and kersey we have examples of long-term reorientation of European production in accordance with Asian demand in the 16th century. It is probable that an expanding silk production in Persia and Syria in the 16th and 17th centuries represented a corresponding adaptation to a sustained demand on the European side of the market. But in the short run there could scarcely have been much connection between the price fluctuations on the one hand and the quantities of a given commodity brought to the market on the other hand. In other words: in the short run very considerable price elasticity corresponded with very poor elasticity of demand and, above all, of supply.

The peddling trade is just as much an economic concept as it is a sociological one. It was subject to the same laws that governed price formation as every other market, but it possessed institutional peculiarities that made violent short-term fluctuations unavoidable. These factors also help to explain why the big profits to be found in the peddling trade did not entice sufficient entrepreneurs, who might be able to force the prices down, and why the supplies arriving at the Levant markets never seemed to keep pace with the European demand. The peddling merchant who had to make a decision with regard to investments in a distant market had to make a calculation involving many unknowns. The known data would comprise the purchase price of the commodity, his own wages, the loss of interest and, to a certain degree, the transport costs. To this he had to add his forecast regarding protection costs and the risk of complete or partial loss of stock resulting from the attack of robbers or from extortion. He had to balance these figures against a sales price he could only estimate with a considerable margin of uncertainty, and with the knowledge that the fluctuations could be as much as 20% or more within the same year. The pedlar could often manage with less profit than what he actually received, but he did not set out unless he was reasonably certain of making a profit.

All this presupposes a rational attitude. But why not? In the literature on modern capitalism great emphasis has been laid on "the spirit of capitalism": the rational calculation of the possibilities of making a profit or a loss. But perhaps this emphasis upon a mental attitude is putting the cart before the horse. The pedlar might well have possessed the habit of thinking rationally, but he had no possibility of making a rational calculation of his costs in the modern sense so long as the protection costs and the risk remained unpredictable and the market non-transparent.

Chapter II: The Redistributive Enterprises

In Chapter I it was established that an important role in the peddling trade was played by protection costs, partly because customs duties and the risk of attack by robbers as well as extortion on the part of local authorities constituted some of the most important items among the pedlar's expenses, and partly because these expenses were more or less unpredictable, thereby hindering the organization of a rational business strategy.

Protection costs are generally considered a "non-market factor" and, as such, are customarily excluded from economic analysis. Considering the fact that in the present context they are one of the most important variables, if not the most important, this isolation of the field of investigation appears unsatisfactory. The political institutions are therefore placed in the economic context by regarding them, in extension of Lane's and van Klaveren's train of thought, as enterprises using organized violence in order to "produce" and "sell" a special kind of service, i.e. protection, or with the phrase used as title of this chapter: as redistributive enterprises.

In order to prevent misunderstandings I must at once emphasize that I do not hereby mean to say that the early modern state in Europe or the Middle East was nothing else but this, and neither do I wish to decide whether these states were bearers of religious, cultural or national values. I shall leave it to others to decide whether this was indeed the case. Here it is a question of investigating the possible variations within the older trade structure and the differences between the older and the newer structures.

"Publicans and Thieves"

Robbery was a very real risk for the caravan merchant, but it was not the lonely desperado he feared, since the organization of the caravan itself was an insurance against him. If the caravan expected to pass through an especially notorious area, extra precautions might be taken under the leadership of the head of the caravan without any appreciable interference with the travel plans. In the case of a large caravan it was a matter of the careful positioning of those travellers who were armed at regular intervals along the procession. In 1609, between Baghdad and the Persian frontier, the two Carmelite friars, Redempt and Benignus, were able to observe the defence precautions taken by the caravan. Most of the 100 travellers possessed bows and arrows, fifteen of them had arquebuses ..." all the same, the road being dangerous, more so than any other highroad in the land of the Turks, and as we had news that here a few days previously a large caravan had been plundered, we proceded apprehensively and with a caution beyond measure noteworthy. The two headmen of the caravan divided all those fit for fighting into several separate groups: so marching in good order from place to place they made the arquebuse-men go on ahead and hold the more perilous passes on the road."[1] A smaller caravan could take extra precautions by employing additional guards. On part of the stretch between Katmandu and Patna, the Armenian merchant, Hovhannes, joined forces with some Jewish merchants in employing twelve extra guards.[2]

Taking such precautions the caravan was able to protect itself against the chance bandit, but the transition from highway robbers to sovereign princes with a right to transit duties was not always easy to determine. Especially in three areas: the Syrian Desert, the mountainous regions between the Ottoman Empire and Persia and the mountains between Persia and India, the Ottoman, Safavid and Mogul administration was never fully effective. When in 1610 Coverte left Sukkur in order to travel to Kandahar, the land was said to be full of "theeves and rebels". On the border between the territories of the Baluchis and the Pathans his caravan encountered ten or twelve men "playing on fiddles". Despite this harmless passtime they turned out to be robbers, but not of the uncompromising type. After threats on both sides and subsequent negotiations they agreed to escort the caravan for the rest of the day. "Though we had a caffilae convoy of 200 strong we were glad to intreate the Captaine of that unruly crew to stand our friend and both to bribe him privately and to pay openly in the name of custom besides, twenty checkeenes in gold ..."[3]

Thieves or customs officers? How big must a band of robbers be in order to call itself an army? How extensive in time and space must the power of a robber chief be before he may be regarded a prince? In the trackless areas in between the organized states it was to the merchant immaterial whether he was a victim of a Sovereign Prince or of a private criminal, the price being determined by whoever happened to be in power. The shortest route from Aleppo to Tabriz was via Cizre and Salmastre through the

1. *Chronicle* p. 174.
2. KHACHIKIAN p. 245.
3. COVERTE n.p.

Kurdish area. But the merchants were reluctant to use it because they did not trust the Kurdish beys who controlled this area. If they should be robbed they did not know to whom they should address their complaints, and the beys were just as liable to condone the robbery as to inflict punishment for it. There was only one consolation: the west-bound caravans travelled with greater safety than the east-bound ones, which generally carried ready money.[4] As for the bey in Nuchar, between the Ottoman Van and the Persian Tabriz, was he a robber or a tax-gatherer? In addition to a fixed customs rate he demanded a personal gift, and if he did not obtain it he came to fetch it himself. In 1671 Tavernier lost one camel with English cloth and two with supplies in this fashion.[5]

The Syrian Desert was another frontier region which was never entirely brought under control. Formally speaking, the Sultan's domains stretched over the whole of Syria and Iraq; in the years between 1534 and 1547 the Ottoman forces had driven the Persians out and defeated the local rulers in the five provinces of Mosul, Baghdad, Basra, al Ahsa and Shahrizor. From the protection point of view this constituted a widespread "rationalization" of a previously confused situation, and the Ottoman expansion along the Euphrates and the Tigris was presumably the chief cause of the increased importance of that trade route in the second half of the 16th century.[6] But even in the towns the Ottoman position was never quite secure, and on the desert routes the local rulers, the Beduin tribes, were still able to demand transit duties from the caravans, either on the formal authority of the Porte, or in the confidence of their own invulnerability in these inaccessible areas. The situation is just as confused for the historian as it must have been unpredictable for the traveller. In some periods all important routes have been controlled by a single tribe under strong leadership, in other periods anarchy reigned, the rival tribes fighting among themselves, each one attempting to squeeze as much as possible out of the merchants. Under such conditions the costs were unpredictable: if the caravan were to meet a tribal chief on the way it might mean total disaster, whereas on another occasion it might be able to slip through without paying any duties at all.

Under these conditions an interesting practice was developed, which is once again a striking illustration of the gradual transition from free-lance criminality to the regulated world of international law, i.e. the traveller attempted to safeguard himself in advance by contacting in his town of departure representatives of the tribes through whose territory he was

4. TAVERNIER I p. 255. Cf. the English traveller, Parry's, harsh description of the Kurds: "... the Courdes' country, which is by interpretation the thieves' country. The people whereof are altogether addicted to thieving, not much unlike the wild Irish ..." Ross p. 115.
5. TAVERNIER p. 251–252.
6. STRIPLING pp. 81–82; HOLT pp. 56–57.

about to venture. "... the caravan always keep in pay, as ours did, some Arabs, of such tribes as they may meet, to secure good usage, and as guides of the ways and the watering places."[7] It is presumably an example of a similar kind of practice when Texeira and, fifty years after him, Carré both agreed with their Arab guide on an all-inclusive price – i.e. including customs duties.[8] Bugnon, who is scarcely reliable, however, maintains that the Beduin sheiks drew up actual treaties with important merchants, and cites as an example the case of an Armenian merchant prince who, against an annual tribute of 52,000 piastres, obtained a safe conduct and guarantee against the pilfering of other tribes.[9] At any rate, by the middle of he 18th century this system of safe conduct was fully developed into an institution, which in fact is remarkably similar to the Portuguese issue of *cartazes* for ships in Asian waters. At that time a single Beduin tribe, the Agail, had acquired the mastery of all caravan transport through the Syrian desert. The relationship with the other tribes was arranged by agents in all the important towns of exit, who issued a safe conduct to the caravan *bashi* against a suitable payment. This payment was distributed between the tribes whose territories the caravan was to pass through; the Beduins on their side respected the immunity the safe conduct guaranteed.[10]

From the merchant's point of view the tax-gatherer had one advantage when compared with the robber: he was to a larger degree predictable. In a state of anarchy a rational calculation was impossible. It was not a question of a "spirit of capitalism", since the necessary preconditions for predicting the final result of business transaction on the basis of a rational calculation were simply not present when the equation contained so many unknowns. Complete certainly with regard to protection cost and risk could not be obtained in a fully organized state either, but there would nevertheless be greater possibilities for forecasting the profit or loss.

Within the Islamic area there was apparently a tendency to maintain customs rates once they were agreed upon. Thus it is interesting to compare the customs rates in the Portuguese Hormuz with those in Gombroon after the town came under Persian administration. The Portuguese demanded 11% in royal customs, 1% as an extra duty for naval defence and 3 % in special duties for non-Christian merchants. (see page 198) When in 1637/

7. TEXEIRA p. 39. Cf. also the English merchant and pilgrim, Timberlake's, experience when travelling from Jerusalem to Cairo accompanied only by a Moroccan and two "Wild Arabs". At one point, when Timberlake and the Moroccan were alone, they were in danger of being robbed; but when the Moroccan mentioned the names of the two Arab guides the robbers refrained from molesting them. TIMBERLAKE p. 43–44.
8. TEXERIA p. 33; CARRÉ pp. 78–79.
9. BUGNON pp. 98–100.
10. GRANT pp. 138–139, 172.

38 the Persian authorities demanded customs from the Dutch East India Company the rates were fixed at 13½ %.[11] From Hovhannes's journal we can obtain the customs rates in Gombroon in 1682/83. He paid 10.75% in *oushour*, i.e. customs. To this was added a duty or *khoorooch* of 3.6 %. Khachikian translates *khoorooch* as "export tax", but although this may be linguistically correct there can scarcely be any doubt that we are here concerned with *koruja*, the special duty imposed on non-Christian merchants during the Portuguese administration. Finally, Hovhannes paid a duty or *eresoom* of 1.22%, and it is natural to see in this an extention of the 1% to the galley fleet demanded by the Portuguese. Over and above the fixed percentages Hovhannes paid 100 dinars on every bale for his travel permit and 650 dinars in gifts to *shahbandar* and scribes. In all, these payments amounted to 16% of the total value of his goods.[12]

It tallies, but not quite. Hovhannes paid more than he should have done according to the old Portuguese rates, and also more than he vas obliged to according to the Armenian merchant's book of rules with Khachikian has compared his information.[13] We do not know what lies hidden behind the increases: they may have been legally imposed, but there may also have been a question of illegal commissions to the officials.

But for the merchants an even greater moment of uncertainty than these irregularities was the valuation of the exported goods. In Hovhannes's case his eighteen cloths were valued at 148.5 tomans, but at the time he had taken possession of them their value was fixed by contract at nearly 217 tomans. There may be more than one explanation of this disparity. The passive partners may have forced Hovhannes to credit them for a larger amount than he had actually obtained. But it may also have been a case of deliberate moderation on the part of the customs officials.

The tax-gatherers in the widest sense of the word, i.e. any local magnate, did not necessarily abide by the law, or rather, the merchant and he might have different conceptions as to what was legal. The so-called *avanias* are well-known from the Levant trade. Masson defines *avanias* as "sums demanded by the pashas from merchants on the Levant markets on various pretexts – pretexts, that as a rule were unjust and at times extraordinarily bizarre."[14] I have tried elsewhere to show that *avanias* were never so completely arbitrary as assumed by Masson, and that the conflict often reflected the European merchants' and the Ottoman officials' different conception of the law.[15] On the other hand it is undeniable that fines or special duties were often imposed, which hit the individual merchant, the

11. DUNLOP p. 654.
12. KHACHIKIAN p. 255.
13. *Ibid.* pp. 234–235.
14. MASSON p. 1.
15. STEENSGAARD, *Consuls and Nations* p. 15 ff.

individual nation or all the merchants in the town; they were unpredictable expenses that could be extremely burdensome. The organization into nations and the consular institution functioned as a kind of "insurance", which could spread the losses and ward off the worst effects, but they could not guarantee the merchants against unforeseen losses. No example is typical, but an embargo on pepper in Cairo in 1586 illustrates very well what might happen. The tax-gatherers in Cairo charged 10% in customs on all spices, and they apparently received it in kind, for suddenly they let it be known that no more pepper would be cleared before the Sultan's warehouses were empty. "But the two consulls went up to show their priviledges, that all men were at liberty to buy where they could." No attention was paid to this abstract right, however, and the negotiations were in fact concerned with how much should be paid for the tax-gatherers' pepper. The parties could not agree upon the price, and the pepper trade came to a standstill for the next two months. "At last Venturin a Venis merchant, secretly went and agreed with the Bassa for all his pepper at 25½ with condition that none might buy any pepper for the space of ten days except Venetians. Nowe in this ten days the caravan was to depart for the Mecca; and all the Venetians furnished themselves at dts 23½ and 24 per quintall. The French weare faine to buy of the Venetians perforce." In ten days' time the embargo was lifted and immediately, in less than eight days, 3,000 quintals of pepper for export to Constantinople and Salonika and other places were bought by Turkish and Jewish merchants for prices of between 24½ and 27 ducats per quintal.[16]

This was only a small incident: the Venetians apparently made a profit on the embargo while others made a loss. "L'affaire de Cecy" was a big affair: to start with, it cost the French merchants in Aleppo 12% of their stocks and cash balance and it invalidated French trade in Aleppo for a whole generation.[17] The risk of such ruinous extortion was always present, and no actuary would have been able to calculate the risk.

On the other hand it was definitely the exception. There were differences between robbers and tax-gatherers: the tax-gatherer was interested in the continuation of the trade, whereas one might say that the robber, as soon as he had established himself and acquired a corresponding interest, was no longer a robber, but had become a tax-gatherer. This interest in the continuation of the trade implied that the tax-gatherer did not necessarily press his claim to the limit set by the law. Tavernier provides an interesting example of this. In Erzurum a distinction was made between the silk from Shirvan, on which a higher duty was paid, and the silk from Gilan, which was let off more cheaply although it was the more expensive. The reason

16. SANDERSON p. 135.
17. STEENSGAARD, Consuls and Nations pp. 39–41

was that the silk from Shirvan, if it was not transported by way of Erzurum, would have to make a long detour in order to reach the good markets, whereas the silk from Gilan could follow routes which were just as good. If the tax-gatherer in Erzurum was not obliging towards the merchants from Gilan they would choose another route next time in order to punish him. "But if the tax-gatherer had no revenue he had to call them back to Erzurum by depositing a considerable sum with the Khan of Erivan as guarantee, in order to satisfy the merchants that he would not treat them so harshly in future."[18] The example is so informative because it demonstrates that protection was a commodity and that even the use of force was not a monopoly, but a case of monopolist competition. The tax-gatherer who maximized his revenue would place his future profits in jeopardy, because there were always other routes. If the customs was too high in Erzurum the merchants could travel via Van; if the customs was too high in Gombroon the merchants could travel via Kandahar. One might add that if the customs was too high on the caravan routes the merchants could sail around Africa.

The merchants were aware of the strength of their position, and apparently used it to procure other advantages. A merchant could avoid being searched by the customs officials in Erzurum, and thus transport money and jewels in unlimited quantities by paying a lump sum of 80 piastres, presumably per bale. If he had made sure of the camel men's help beforehand, this redemption might be further reduced by repacking the bales before arrival in the town, making two camel loads out of every three. The merchants also took care to put "light" coins aside for the tax-gatherer in Erzurum, "and sometimes the tax-gatherer is not so impudent as to refuse them: he takes them as if they were good and full weight." And even at the final customs examination on the departure of the merchants from the town, which was supposed to reveal whether any of them had hidden their cash while staying in the town, the tax-gatherers' respect for the merchants as "customers" came to light: "The tax-gatherer himself comes together with his men: but as he does not want to offend the merchants who, as I have said, can take another route, he often closes his eyes to many things, and the most he takes is 1 %". After the examination the tax-gatherer held a banquet for the merchants, and the party concluded with the formal cry: "Merchants, you may proceed!"[19]

The accommodating attitude towards the merchant described above is not an isolated phenomenon. In Basra the customs is 5%, says Tavernier, but the tax-gatherer and the pasha often make certain concessions, so that in

18. TAVERNIER I pp. 17–18.
19. *Ibid.* p. 19.

practice one pays only 4%.[20] The most touching example of a local ruler's PR activity was nevertheless that of the Khan of Salmastre on the little frequented route between Cizre and Tabriz, who was so eager to attract merchants to the town that he presented each of the travellers on departure with a robe of honour.[21]

More important for the merchant than a robe of honour, however, was doubtless whether the local ruler offered good protection in return for the customs. The very high customs in Gombroon corresponded to a very much higher degree of safety on the route Isfahan-Gombroon-Surat than on the route Isfahan-Kandahar-Lahore. Again it is Tavernier who offers the best illustration of the connection between customs and protection and the tax-gatherer's recognition of the merchants' possibilities of choice. When the bey in Nuchar mentioned above exceeded his usual role as tax-gatherer, and carried out an attack on a caravan, the Turkish pasha in Van and the Persian khan in Tabriz joined forces in sending a punitive force: "in particular the Pasha of Van who, when he saw that the merchants were tired of being treated in this fashion and had decided to abandon the route, determined to force the Bey to deliver up a part of what was stolen and in future to let two of his subjects remain in Tabriz and just as many in Van, as persons responsible for any attack that might be made on the caravans."[22]

It has been indicated above that the moderation of the tax-gatherers and their zeal with regard to the protection of the caravans must chiefly be referred to their consciousness of the fact that they themselves were in a competitive business. But this naturally presupposed that the tax-gatherer had an interest in the continuation of the trade. It raised a problem where the offices were filled for a limited period; all important offices throughout the Portuguese Empire were occupied for three years, whereas the Levant trading towns were characterized from the end of the 16th century by a still quicker changeover of officials. In such cases where an official only had a shortish time of function before he retired or moved on to the next post, the only factor restricting the misuse of an office would be the fear of sanctions from a higher level of the hierarchy, which had a permanent interest in the continuation of the trade. In other words, the economic behaviour of the tax-gatherer was determined not only by his interest in the continuation of the trade, but also by the entire political system of the state concerned.

20. *Ibid.* p. 200.
21. *Ibid.* p. 255.
22. *Ibid.* p. 252.

Persia

Among the relevant political bodies Persia affords the clearest example of control through a hierarchy. From the time of Abbas and throughout the 17th century one traveller after another expresses his admiration for the safe conditions on the Persian caravan routes, whereas there are no complaints of those extortions on the part of local rulers so familiar from travels in the Ottoman Empire. In 1609 the Carmelite friars, Redempt and Benignus, crossed over the river forming the boundary between Turkey and Persia with a caravan, "and those Moslems made many signs of delight at finding themselves on Persian soil, where robbers in particular are rigorously pursued ..."[23] In 1612 Coverte writes: "And there a man may travell without danger of robbing, for it is there a strange thing to hear of a thief.[24] In 1618 the English agent in Persia, Barker, said about the route between Isfahan and Jask: "(we are) confident that these parts are so free from any theeves and robbers, that in this particular it is hardly paralelled by any of our Christian governments and exceeded by none, insomuch that Banyans (Whoe carry neyther weapon offensive nor defensive) goe about freely and frequently passe with their ready money throughout the whole Persian territory."[25] This early impression is confirmed by the later experiences of the Companies; throughout the whole of the first half of the 17th century we hear nothing about any plunderous attacks on the numerous Company caravans travelling between Gombroon and the interior of the country. After many years' experience on travels in the Orient Tavernier maintains: "On garde sur tout en Perse un tres-bon ordre pour la sécurité des chemins." And still in 1675 this impression is confirmed by the Dutch traveller, Leeuwenson.[26]

It was the local governors and the special "highway police", or *rahdari*, who were responsible for the good order on the Persian roads. The *rahdaris* were stationed at regular intervals along the route, chiefly by bridges and fords, so that they were able to keep a truly effective watch on the entire traffic. They were paid by the travellers in the form of a fixed duty per beast of burden, also referred to by the Europeans as *rahdari*, usually a fairly modest sum.[27] The Dutch and the English East India Companies

---

23. *Chronicle* p. 174.
24. COVERTE n.p.
25. C.R.O. London, O.C. 792, Barker to Roe, April 1618.
26. TAVERNIER I p. 554; LEEUWENSON pp. 106–107.
27. TAVERNIER I p. 556, at the end of the 17th century the *rahdari* was increased until it constituted an important item on the Persian State budget, but until then the country was practically speaking devoid of internal customs boundaries, MINORSKY p. 180.

were by privilege exempted from these tolls.[28] If, despite all this control, some travellers should be robbed, the local governor was made responsible and was obliged to pay compensation if the stolen goods could not be recovered.[29]

Why did this control over the local authorities operate in Persia whereas it was lacking in the Ottoman and the Portuguese Empires? We cannot give any clear answer to this question; we can only enumerate some factors that are customarily considered significant, namely, the personality of the prince and the so-called despotic form of government, and seek to throw further light on the concept we have termed the redistributive enterprises by comparing the three relevant political bodies.

It is usual when discussing the early modern state, particularly the early modern state outside Europe, to draw attention to the personality of the prince: there is in fact a striking contrast evident in the sources between the bureaucratic anonymity of the European decision-makers and the personal participation of the Shah, particularly Abbas, in important matters of state as well as everyday business affairs. Philip III and Philip IV, although formally heads of one of the states involved, do not feature in this account. We very seldom encounter them in the sources; occasional questions or critical comments in the margin of a memorandum indicate that they kept an eye on the business, but we are unable, at least not without a very detailed analysis, to form any idea of the role they or any of their chief ministers played.

The impression we have of Abbas is quite different, and he himself was well aware of that difference and flirted with it. "He says that is how to be a king, and that the king of Spain and other Christians do not get any pleasure out of ruling, because they are obliged to comport themselves with so much pomp and majesty as they do."[30] One is inclined to believe he enjoyed himself. In many of the European accounts he makes his entrance with a charm and spontaneity that takes both friends and opponents unawares and helps to throw light on the magic aura surrounding Persia at the beginning of the 17th century. He persuades the Portuguese Augustinian, Gouvea, together with his travelling companions, to sing psalms to him in his tent one evening, a glass of cool wine within reach, and he returns the compliment by seizing his lute and playing it himself.[31] He receives the Carmelite envoys of the Pope in the scorching mid-day sun outside his bath and continues the conversation for over an hour, while he

28. Barker to Roe, April 1618, C.R.O., London, O.C. 792; Visnich, Gombroon, to Gov. Gen., Batavia, 9/2 1625, DUNLOP p. 137.
29. FEYNES de MONFART p. 8; TAVERNIER I pp. 556–557.
30. Paul Simon's report of 1608, *Chronicle* p. 158.
31. GOUVEA p. 67.

carelessly shoots arrows in the direction of anyone who tries to approach.[32] He punches the Indian ambassador in the stomach and calls the Spanish ambassador 'Uncle'.[33]

But does this charming image really tell us anything about Abbas the statesman? He took delight in being in the limelight and loved the handsome gesture or dramatic exit, but his audiences are no less theatrical than are the ceremonies of the Spanish Court. The difference, though at the same time the fundamental similarity, in the political use of such theatricals is possibly illustrated most vividly in connection with the initial reception of Figueroa, the Spanish Ambassador, at the Persian Court in June 1618. Figueroa brought with him many gifts, which, after being unpacked, were immediately inspected by the Persian master of ceremonies, the *mihmandar*. Figueroa suggested sending the gifts in advance, so that he might avoid this practical problem at his reception, but this was vehemently rejected by the *mihmandar* as being contrary to Persian custom. On the day of Figueroa's reception the *mihmandar* turned up together with 600 men who were to carry the gifts, each of them bearing one item only. The procession wound its way along some of the busiest streets in Kazvin and eventually reached the street outside the Royal Palace. There everything came to a standstill. For half an hour, says Figueroa, or for two hours, if we are to believe della Valle, he had to wait in the sun while nothing further took place. "The Ambassador felt very tired and ill at ease in the court dress which he had not been wearing for so long, and summoned the master of ceremonies and said to him that he should go to the King and inform him that he felt very tired and uncomfortable in the youthful dress he had donned that day to show the King an honour and that the King might see how Spaniards were clad when they celebrated their Kings' birthdays or weddings ..." Figueroa therefore requested to be let in, otherwise he would return to his house.[34]

The request was complied with, and the reception was begun and continued in the form of a magnificent banquet that nevertheless came to an end earlier than usual, as the Spanish Ambassador soon excused himself as being tired and withdrew. The Shah had seated himself in a pavilion in the garden with the Turkish and Spanish Ambassadors as sole company, but one has a suspicion that the atmosphere, despite the magnificent illumination and the numerous courses that were brought in, had been somewhat cool therein.[35]

Figueroa thought that the delay at the gates of the Palace was staged for the benefit of the Turkish Ambassador, and he was probably right.

32. Redempt's and Benignus's report of 1609, *Chronicle* pp. 175–79.
33. della VALLE, *Persia* II:2 p. 30.
34. FIGUEROA II p. 84.
35. FIGUEROA II pp. 92–94; della VALLE, *Persia* II:1 p. 326–332.

Delays in a programme of that nature are hardly accidental, however unpredictable and impulsive the Shah might appear. The impression of the Shah gained from European sources may be misleading when they depicted the decisions as being taken impulsively and theatrically. The Europeans obtained the impression they were intended to obtain, but they had no or only little chance of seeing below the surface. Linguistic and cultural barriers made it even more difficult than under European conditions to determine what was really going on in Abbas's immediate vicinity or behind the scenes, let alone form an idea of Abbas's personal motives. Della Valle, who was not only a sophisticated observer, but also possessed the advantage of having acces to the harem gossip through his beloved Ma'ani, is certainly among the European observers the one whose description of Abbas is most fitting. He had personal acquaintances and friends among the representatives of all the implicated European nations, and he was an attentive observer of the political scene in Persia throughout a number of years. Abbas, according to della Valle, is primarily the crafty *realpolitiker*. In order to maintain and expand his power he makes use of the actual and potential means at his disposal. He is anxious for information about everything under the sun; his religious tolerance is an expression of his wish to acquire the Georgians and the Armenians as allies.[36]

If the Augustinians, Belchior dos Anjos and João de S. Joseph, have quoted Abbas correctly this corresponded to his own idea of himself: "He says that there can be two reasons for Kings to be friends, either on account of belief (la ley), if they both profess to the same faith, or for reason of state (por razon de estado), and that the first of these reasons cannot be applied to Your Majesty and himself, because there is such great difference in belief, and that if the other reason was not present either there was no basis for friendship."[37]

In Abbas, too, we find examples of the cruelty and apparent arbitrariness that have nourished the Western ideas of an Oriental despotism in which everything is dependent on the whim of the ruler.[38] But if the above is correct it would be extremely risky to conclude from the apparent capri-

36. Della VALLE, *Delle conditioni passim*, pp. 31, 80–81.
37. Arch. Simancas, Estado, leg. 495. Cf. *Bewindhebbers*, Amsterdam, to Visnich, Isfahan, Dec. 1624: "Wy verstaen, ... dat Syn Mat aldaer en seer verstandich prins is, meest lettende op 't woordeel van sijn eygen landt en ondersaten," DUNLOP p. 126.
38. At the welcome audience for the remainder of the Imperial embassy in 1603 Abbas personally executed a Turkish prisoner, TECTANDER pp. 57–58; when the Persian Ambassador, Janghiz Beg, was in audience in 1613, and about to kiss the Shah's foot, he was greeted with a kick, and some days later he was executed, *Chronicle* p. 203. But both these examples and the more notorious episodes such as the deportation of the Armenian nation and his rough treatment of his own family must clearly be seen in a political context.

ciousness and the stage effects to the actual distribution of power. Also despotism is a political system, and also the despot must be a politician. Della Valle provides some interesting observations, which presumably may be regarded as a reflection of Abbas's manipulation of important groups at Court and among his entourage. In June 1618 Abbas received a Turkish Ambassador at a public audience in Isfahan – very public indeed, as the reception took place in the square, the *meidan*, and Abbas spoke so loudly that the many thousands who were present could hear every word he said. He refused to accept the letter the Ambassador wished to give him, and which contained an offer of peace, declaring that whatever was his, was his, and that whatever was the Turks', was the Turks'. With this he referred to his demand for a restoration of the borders to the situation before the outbreak of war in 1578. The Ambassador's answer was less audible, but those present nevertheless understood that the Turks were unable to accept Abbas's conditions, because for them it would mean a recognition of the Persian conquests in the years succeeding 1603. The audience was concluded abruptly, since Abbas turned his horse and galloped off "in un modo assai fantastico e bizarro", while the crowd, who regarded the episode as an open challenge to Turkey, broke out into cheers.[39] But already the next evening Abbas received the Ambassador again, this time in a secret audience, and rumour has it that on this occasion realistic negotiations for peace took place.[40]

In August-September of the same year a new and higher-ranking Turkish Ambassador arrived and the peace negotiations continued. If at the audience on the *meidan* we encountered the hawks, this time we catch a glimpse of the doves. At the Ambassador's farewell audience Abbas points towards his mullahs, declaring: "here are the men who pester me to make peace, but if they plague me more I'll chop their heads off."[41] There is no evidence in the sources of his having carried out his threats; it is probably best to regard the episode, not as an expression of Abbas's arbitrary power, but rather as an expression of the fact that he, too, knew what opposition was, and as evidence of the means he employed to counteract this opposition, i.e. threats and appeals to a wider public.

We have attempted above to show that the most prominent of the Safavid Shahs could not be made solely responsible for the law and order of the country; he, too, acted within a political framework in accordance with norms for political action that must have been understandable for his entourage, even if they appeared "fantastic and bizarre" to the European observer. The problem can be tackled from a different angle. A quick

39. della VALLE, *Persia* II:I pp. 320–322.
40. *ibid.* pp. 325–326.
41. *ibid.* p. 409.

glance at the internal history of the Safavid Empire will show that the label "oriental despotism" is a cliché that conceals more than it reveals.

Safavid Persia was created in the years following 1500 from the ruins of the Turcoman tribal confederacies. The core of the new state was a religious brotherhood of Shiite observance, and the rapid advance of the movement must to a great extent be accredited to its leader, Ismail, who enjoyed both religious and secular authority. During a series of campaigns between 1500 and 1513 Ismail amassed the greatest part of present day Iran and Iraq, until the chain of victories was broken by the Ottomans at Chaldiran in 1514.

Ismail's soldiers, the *quizilbash*, belonged to a number of tribes of Turkish origin, and it was around their chieftains, as feudatories or military governors, that the new State was built up. Ismail took over a civil administration from the White Horde, however, whose personnel were predominantly of Iranian nationality. Tension between the tribal chieftains' attempts to decentralize and the Shah's endeavours at centralization with the help of the Iranian bureaucracy, which became a constant feature in the history of the Safavid Empire, is already in evidence under Ismail, but it was not until the reign of his successor, Tahmasp (1524–76) that the contrasts stand out clearly. Under Tahmasp's sons, Ismail II (1576–77) and Muhammad Khudabanda (1577–88), the tendencies towards disintegration culminated. The Ottomans made successful attacks in the west and northwest, while the *quizilbash* emirs were intriguing around the throne or making themselves independent in their provinces. It was thus under extremely unfavourable circumstances that Abbas I took over the government in 1588 following a state coup in which Muhammad Khudabanda was deposed, and his internal policy must necessarily be seen in this light.

Under Abbas the *quizilbash* were forced into the background, partly by a more widespread application of Iranian bureaucracy in the administration, partly by the establishment of a new military force, the *qullar,* which, like the Ottoman janissaries, were recruited among the conquered non-Islamic peoples who were outside the tribal organization. The balanced system Abbas built up manifested its strength after his death. His successor, Safi, was scarcely a striking personality, but after a few years of uncertainty stable conditions were established within the framework created under Abbas.[42]

This development will not be followed up here. What has been mentioned will be sufficient to show that Safavid Persia housed a number of

---

42. A satisfactory history of Safavid Persia does still not exist in any western language. The brief account by BRAUN and the older, though more comprehensive, accounts by SYKES and BROCKELMANN must be supplemented with a number of monographs, amongst which the most important is MINORSKY. See also the bibliography in BRAUN pp. 172–176.

the same fundamental conflicts that marked the 16th and 17th century European states: the contrast between bureaucracy and military caste, between mercenaries and "feudal" levy, between prince and feudatory.

It is confusing to find the problems of the European renaissance state outside Europe, but it is a circumstance that deserves attention, because among European historians there has been, and still is, a marked tendency to ignore the similarities and emphasize the differences in the history of the European and the non-European states. A characteristic example is the analysis undertaken by Mousnier and Hartung in 1955 of European absolutism, which has been the starting-point for all recent research on European absolutism. They maintain here a division between European absolutism and Oriental despotism that cannot easily be defended.[43] If by the concept of despotism we understand a political system in which all decisions and all initiative issue from one man alone, it is obviously not applicable. If, as Mousnier, we associate the concept of Oriental despotism with legal arbitrariness and independence of natural or divine law, this is likewise inapplicable. For how in such a case are we to understand the order and security on the Persian caravan routes and in the Persian towns?

The section on Persia as a redistributive enterprise must remain without a conclusion, or rather we cannot in the conclusion get any further than in the opening words: in Persia control of local personnel was carried out through the hierarchy. Persian merchants, or merchants travelling in Persia, could reckon with a high degree of predictability regarding protection costs and risk. The personality of the ruler alone cannot explain this state of affairs; on the contrary, the discussion of Abbas's role reveals that what to Europeans has often appeared to be despotism may conceal a complicated political system. We cannot throw any further light on the problem with the information about Persian conditions at our disposal, but there is a possibility that a comparison with other redistributive enterprises will provide additional enlightenment.

The Ottoman Empire

In 1525 the Venetian Bailo in Constantinople, Piero Bragadin, wrote to his son at home in Venice: "I know of no State which is happier than this one

43. HARTUNG & MOUSNIER pp. 49–55. The points of view advanced were already criticized when they were presented at the Xth International Congress for Historical Sciences, *Atti* pp. 436–40, but might still be regarded as representative of the views of western historians. Cf. also MOUSNIER, *XVIe et XVIIe siècles* p. 511: "L'exercise du pouvoir est, pour le Chah et ses fidèles, comme pour tout l'Orient, un moyen de se procurer des avantages personelles, non un service que l'on doit à la société."

(Turkey), it is furnished with all God's gifts. It controls war and peace with all, it is rich in gold, in people, in ships and in obedience; no State can be compared with it. May God long preserve the most just of all Emperors . . ."[44]

In 1626 the Dutch Vice-Consul in Aleppo, de Willem, wrote to the Court of Directors of the East India Company in Amsterdam: "It has reached such a pitch here that every person does what he likes, especially the powerful, and that is what accounts for the state of the realm. It is not just one pillar that is broken or weakened, but all four pillars of State: religion, justice, politics (den raet) and finances, and besides that the Grand Turk's reputation is now so weakened that all Archimedes's discoveries and all Archimedes's instruments and all Architas's instruments would not be able to raise them up and repair them; one must ask oneself whether it can continue thus."[45]

A hundred and one years separates these two passages. They do not reflect superficial changes of mood or short-term fluctuations, but a decline and fall from the political heyday of the Ottoman Empire, which troubled and confused contemporary observers. Territorially speaking, no great losses were suffered in the intervening period; on the contrary, despite the Persian occupation of Baghdad a few years previously, the extent of the Empire was greater in 1626 than it had been a century before. No hostile army had penetrated deeply into the Ottoman territory, but about the decline all the European observers were in agreement from the first years of the 17th century. This is the background for the sudden resurgence of the idea of Crusade, whose most famous fruits are "le Grand Dessein" and the Duke of Nevers' and Père Joseph's project. But Sully, Charles di Gonzaga and Père Joseph were not alone in thinking along these lines: the weakness of Turkey and the hopes of Christendom are a constant theme in the diplomatic correspondence and pamphlet literature of the time. "From the beginning of the 17th century Europe discounted the inheritance of "the sick man", but the hot-heads were wrong: the sick man did not die so readily. He lived for a long time still, but he never regained his former strength."[46]

The decline of the Ottoman Empire was just as confusing at the time as it is for the historians. At the time when it first set in it cannot be put down to a decline in the relative international position of the Empire; the Ottoman Empire was not overrun by powerful or technologically superior enemies. With the exception of a few years it always managed to avoid the war on two fronts that could have been fatal for the continued

44. BRAUDEL, Réalités économiques p. 733.
45. DUNLOP, p. 204.
46. BRAUDEL II, p. 47.

existence of he Empire. There is of course some connection with external pressure, but that alone cannot explain the sick man's sickness: the decline came from within.

The problem was naturally as obvious to the Turks themselves as it was to the foreign observers. An interesting monument to the endeavours to get the ship of state on to even keel again, and which from the last years of Murad IV's reign was effective for a while, is the memorandum which Murad IV's advisor, Koja Beg, submitted in 1630.[47] Koja Beg's memorandum has rightly attracted the attention of historians: he is ruthless in his historical analysis and dauntless in his criticism of the existing state of affairs; he does not mention the names of any of his contemporaries, but he is not afraid of pointing out and attacking shortcomings as regards the execution of the office of Grand Vizier and the faults committed by Murad IV's own ancestors.

In Koja Beg's analysis the heart of the matter is the dissolution of the feudal system. Again and again he returns to the disappearance of the large and small feudatories and the increase in the number of mercenaries. The fiefs are no longer given away locally to promising sons of deserving soldiers and feudatories, but by the Grand Vizier himself to courtiers and other favoured people. The soldiers have thereby been deprived of their fiefs; on the other hand the number of mercenaries has increased enormously, and outsiders, i.e. people who are not sons of deserving corps members or recruited through *devshirme*, have gained access to the illustrious corps of janissaries. Corruption and venality has spread to all branches of public life. Undeserving people can procure a fief or a salary by means of bribes. Many who have been put down on the army pay lists simply draw their salaries without ever dreaming of serving in the war. Corruption has also spread to the *Ulema*: judges buy their offices and sell their decisions, and nobody is interested in he acquisition of learning any longer because that is not the way to gain advancement or respect. The weakening of the army has led to the loss of rich provinces, whereas other provinces are ravaged by revolts and banditry, and the steadily increasing need of funds with which to pay the soldiers and officials has multiplied the taxes at the expense of the ordinary population.

It is a vicious circle of State dissolution Koja Beg describes. The need for ready cash has forced the leading officials into a policy that solves the immediate problems, but which in the long run only increases the need for ready cash and at the same time undermines the capacity of the population for bearing new burdens. His understanding of the circular pro-

---

47. 'Kogabegs Abhandlund über den Vervall des osmanischen Staatsgebäudes seit Sultan Suleiman dem Grossen", transl. W. F. Behrnauer, *Zeitschrift der Deutschen morgenländischen Gesellschaft* XV, 1861.

cess is clearly expressed in the following: "The Sublime Porte's might and power is the army, the army's existence is dependent upon the state taxes, these are procured by the subjects and the subjects' existence depends upon justice and equity."[48] But what has set off the vicious circle? Koja Beg answers the question like a true conservative: there is nothing wrong with the system, the faults are human faults and these must be corrected so that the system may be reinstated in all its pristine purity. The Sultans have erred. Since Suleiman they have not been present in person at the divans, and they have to far too great an extent tended to listen to the slander of their intimates, so that no Grand Vizier could feel himself safe in his office. The Grand Viziers have had to procure a party at Court, and they have therefore shown that indulgence concerning demands for favours that has set the avalanche going.

The historian cannot be satisfied with this explanation. To be sure there is scarcely any doubt that the personal ability of the Sultans was declining: Mohammed III (1595–1603) was the last Sultan to receive a practical administrative training as *sanjakbey,* whereas his successors were brought up in the harem and even after their accession were subjected to harem intrigues. But it appears unsatisfactory to explain the social and political decay of a great Empire as being due to harem intrigues.

In his famous synthesis Braudel compares the Ottoman with the Spanish decadence at the beginning of the 17th century; the time of the Empires was past, the future belonged to the medium-sized states: "En fait, la roue a tourné. The beginning of the century favoured the big States, those which economists would say represented the political enterprises of optimum size. The century has passed, and for reasons we cannot determine with as much precision as we should like, these big organisms are gradually betrayed by circumstances."[49] In this place Braudel is cautious, but in another context he expresses himself with greater precision: "La thèse que sera la nôtre établit une correlation entre la renversement de la tendance séculaire et les difficultés en chaîne que connaîtront les grands ensembles politiques des Habsbourgs comme des Osmanlis."[50] It has proved to be an extremely inspiring thesis for the last generation's researches into early modern history, but it cannot be maintained in the light of that research. It is not so easy to fix the date for the change in the secular trend. In the second edition of his book Braudel has himself taken the consequence: "J'en avait placé le terme, lors de la première édition de ce livre, au delà de 1600, ou même de 1610–1620. Volontiers je reculerais ce terme d'une trentaine d'années."[51]

48. KOGABEG p. 308.
49. BRAUDEL II p. 47.
50. *ibid.* p. 26.
51. *ibid.* p. 215.

A correlation with a secular movement the nature of which we do not know and cannot date is just as unsatisfactory as an explanation that merely builds upon some men's human failings. Bernard Lewis is far more concrete in his placing of the Ottoman decline in the context of world history. He emphasizes three factors: firstly, the closing of the European "frontier", secondly, the discoveries with their effects on transcontinental trade and in the form of price revolution and depreciation of the Turkish money and thirdly, the reorganization of the army from feudal cavalry to mercenaries.[52] There will not be any objections raised against this interpretation in the following, but the question as to whether the factors that Lewis treats as being isolated from one another can be thought of as being interconnected will be investigated.

The reorganization of the European-Asiatic trade cannot have affected the first phases of the decline of the Empire – there can scarcely be any doubt that the transit trade in the last decades of the century flourished to an extent that makes it reasonable to regard precisely these years as the historical culmination of the caravan trade. It is also a fair assumption that the arrival of American silver in Turkey fell within a period of flourishing foreign trade rather than within a period of stagnation. It is in the years after Lepanto that we first hear about a large-scale French import of coin into Turkey – to the disgust of the Venetians who both before and afterwards tried to stick to the traditional barter trade: goods for goods.[53] In his historical account Koja Beg circles around the year 1584; the Grand Vizier's position was undisputed until 1584;[54] but from 1584 onwards he began to give fiefs to outsiders and unworthies;[55] since 1584 the number of mercenaries increased enormously[56] and since 1582 the taxes multiplied.[57] But there is one event from 1584 he does not mention: the depreciation of the asper, and he also leaves unmentioned the problems of liquidity which afflicted the Sublime Porte that year and the following ones.

The development can be followed in the Venetian Bailo's dispatches. An early uncertainty with regard to the stability of the currency is hinted at in 1578, though the problem remains unmentioned in the following years; quite possibly it has only been a question of difficulties in maintaining the traditional ratio between gold and silver.[58] But in 1584 silver coin dropped

52. LEWIS pp. 116–121.
53. BERCHET, *Soria* p. 61.
54. KOGABEG p. 286.
55. *ibid.* p. 294.
56. *ibid.* p. 298.
57. *ibid.* p. 304.
58. A. d. S. Venezia, Rubricari Constantinopoli, D2 f. 11.

to half its previous value[59], and from that time on the Porte's financial difficulties became a main topic in the Bailo's accounts. In Tripoli an increase in the evaluation of the commodities in the customs house is attempted,[60] and the tax-gatherers in Constantinople also try to force up their profits.[61] Shortly after a failed attempt in that direction they are replaced by other customs farmers who have promised to procure a greater revenue.[62] In January 1585 there is for the first time talk of unrest among the soldiers because they have not obtained their pay;[63] this is a phenomenon that repeats itself with increasing frequency and violence during the following years. At the same time there is an outcry against the high prices, not only in Constantinople, but also on the road to Persia.[64] In February 1586, in words that reveal the soldiers' merciless dilemma, it is said: "It is deemed true that it is impossible for a soldier, even though he may take up money on the security of his fief for many years into the future, to procure all the equipment he needs for this campagin."[65]

The chronology of the development sketched here is important: increased liquidity in connection with increased silver import, thereafter depreciation of the money and finally, *after* the depreciation, increase in prices. At first glance the coincidence between increased liquidity and depreciation appears paradoxical: Lewis explains it by referring to the fact that scarcity was the problem the Ottoman authorities were normally confronted with in their monetary policy, and that they therefore sought to control the abundance of silver with the same medicine they had used for scarcity.[66] Such a gross miscalculation of the situation is scarcely credible, however, since debasement of small coin is a phenomenon to be met with almost universally in that period. The motive for a debasement of the coinage is scarcity, though it does not have to be scarcity for the society as a whole, but only for the public treasury that brings it about. A more complicated connection between the arrival of the American silver and the debasement of the Ottoman coinage seems to be indicated than a mere misunderstanding of the situation.

We know that the Turkish treasury was in liquidity difficulties some years after the American silver had begun to make itself felt, but we cannot in view of the available information account for these liquidity dif-

59. BRAUDEL II p. 447.
60. A. d. S. Venezia, Rubricari Constantinopoli, D2 f. 125.
61. *ibid.* f. 224.
62. *ibid.* f. 228.
63. *ibid.* f. 176.
64. *ibid.* f. 225 and *passim*, Rubricari Constantinopoli, D3 f. 2 and *passim*.
65. A. d. S. Venezia, Senato, Disp. Amb. Constantinopoli, vol. 22 f. 545.
66. LEWIS pp. 119–120.

ficulties by referring to rising prices because, as mentioned, it is not until the debasement of the coinage that the rise in prices becomes a recurrent theme in the Bailo's dispatches. The switch-over from feudal cavalry to mercenaries also seems a more obvious explanation. This reorganization is usually regarded as a technological response, but in fact this explanation is untenable if, with Koja Beg, we regard the 1580s as a turning-point, or if we at all regard the reorganization as having been begun in the second half of the 16th century. This period is dominated by wars against the technically less developed Persia, wars in which the *sipahi* cavalry was more useful than foot soldiers and artillery. A different interpretation is possible: the reorganization came about not as a result of a technical need but because of the increased liquidity.

This reasoning is theoretical and cannot be substantiated without a more detailed knowledge of the internal history of the Ottoman Empire than we have at present.[67] But it is highly probable that increased liquidity in the Ottoman society derived from increasing export and transit trade would in the first place benefit rather narrow circles, in particular the local magnates in the ports of disembarkation and in the more important transit towns. Part of the increased liquidity would be neutralized by increased "hoarding", part would be swallowed up by possible increase in prices and part, as in the West European countries, would be absorbed by an increase in the number of economic transactions involving payment in cash. But for the latter theoretical possibility, the T of the Irving Fisher equation, a special condition becomes applicable in an economy like that of the Ottoman Empire. The first beginnings of a capitalistic economy were fragile: the social structure pointed first and foremost towards a pattern of investment favouring investment in redistributive enterprises at the expense of the productive investment. Farming of state revenues, bribery, and purchase of offices and fiefs would be the most attractive objects of investment.

If this process is once started we find ourselves in van Klaveren's world of constitutional corruption, only grotesquely magnified in relation to the examples on which he has based the construction of his model, because the increased liquidity from without has hit a society whose social dynamics are directed towards redistributive activity. The cumulative tendency of the model will make itself felt all the more strongly because the change has occurred so abruptly that the central authorities have only with considerable

67. The development in the Levant trading towns at the end of the 16th and beginning of the 17th centuries, however, supports the viewpoints presented here, see below p. xx. Cf. also INALCIK p. 139, n. 94: "During the second half of the sixteenth century the new conditions called for the growing use of currency in paying soldiers, taxes and making waqfs. Then one might speak of a development of the Ottoman economy into a money economy."

delay discovered the means of restricting the local corruption and have even been involved in the process themselves. The fact that alternative investment objects will become less attractive in a system of constitutional corruption will also contribute to the cumultative effect.

The theory sketched here in fact only differs from Lewis's by its connecting two phenomena which for Lewis are separate: the increased liquidity and the switch over from a feudal army to mercenaries. Is there also a connection with the reorganization of the transcontinental trade? The answer must be positive, even if it would be incorrect to seek the explanation of the revolution of the international trade routes in this connection alone. But the points of contact between the crisis in the Ottoman Empire and the revolution of the transcontinental trade is obvious. Revolt and banditry struck at all important trade routes and trade centres in the Ottoman Empire in the first decade of the 17th century on more than one occasion. Long before then complaints about extortion and corruption and about frequent replacement of the local officials became louder and more frequent. And on the other hand Lewis is doubtless right as far as the 17th century is concerned when he maintains that the reorganization of the trade routes contributed towards the fall of the Empire; the loss of the transit trade must have meant a loss to the local officials and revenue farmers who had invested in their offices and farms in the hope of a continued or expanding trade. Perhaps that is precisely why the revolts within the Ottoman Empire after 1600 are especially concentrated around the great trade routes.

Estado da India

To rule over a kingdom in which the sun never sets involves not only almost insurmountable problems of communication, but also so widespread interests that any policy followed could only with difficulty avoid being paradoxical. It was not at all certain that the atitude of the Spanish Empire to the Ottoman Empire would be the same in the Mediterranean as in the Indian Ocean. After the union with Portugal in 1580 the Spanish Crown had guaranteed the Portuguese nation the sole right to offices in *Estado da India,* and neither was there any decisive attempt on the part of Spain to integrate the Portuguese possessions with the Spanish Empire nor to carry out a reorganization of *Estado da India* that could make a co-ordination of the interests of the two Empires possible. The Council of State doubtless regarded itself as ultimately responsible for the policy followed, but on the other hand it had to accept the fact that its decisions were executed through *Estado da India*'s autonomous bureaucracy.

The Spanish network of councils and juntas is always difficult to disentangle; as far as *Estado da India* is concerned it is far from easy to decide what was the ordinary chain of command. Thus it cannot even be determined with certainty, who drafted the Royal letters to the Viceroy in Goa. A register has been preserved exclusively concerned with the Indian matters dealt with between January 1608 and December 1609 in the Council of Portugal residing at Court. The matters were considered in *consultas* addressed to the King, but occasioned by approaches from various sides: from the Viceroy in Lisbon, from the King through the Council of State, from the Ambassadors or even from subordinate officers in Lisbon.[68] The executive organ seems, however, at that time to have been the Council of India resident in Lisbon. Thus in March 1608 the reception of dispatches from the Viceroy in Lisbon is mentioned, which formally are to be directed from the King to the Viceroy in Goa and the General of the Malaccan fleet, with the comment that the letters concerned have been recognized by the Council of India and by the Viceroy in Lisbon. The Council of Portugal at the Court reviews the letters and forwards them to the King for signature, but receives them again by return for further consideration, especially with regard to the risk of a juridical conflict between the Viceroy and the General of the Fleet.[69] The shrewd lawyers in the juntas and the councils have no doubt solved the juridical problems in a satisfactory way, but the complicated and dilatory business routine seriously reduced the central organs' capability of controlling political development.

The supreme political body in the Spanish-Portuguese Empire was *consejo de estado,* and several preserved *consultas* show that the Council of State really thought it possible to control the political developments in Asia by means of the Royal letters to the Viceroy in Goa. But it is extremely doubtful whether this view was realistic. Even when really vital interests were at stake, as in the question of Hormuz's state of defence, an order might be repeated year after year without noticeable effect. Possibly the distance between the Council of State's view of the situation and its possibilities and the situation as it was in reality becomes most apparent on the occasions when the Council of State attempted to intervene in Persia and the Persian Gulf by circumventing the hierarchy of *Estado da India.* The guarantee against the appointment of Spaniards to offices within *Estado da India* did not of course include diplomats, and Figueroa, the Ambassador appointed to Persia, became, as a Spaniard directly instructed by the Council of State, the most prominent example of an attempt to circumvent *Estado da India*'s hierarchy. He succeeded, though not without difficulty, in overcoming the obstacles the Portuguese put in his way, but only to

68. Arch. Simancas, Secr. Prov., Libr. 1479.
69. *Loc. cit.* f. 106.

ascertain after his arrival in Persia the unrealistic nature of the mission that was entrusted him. He closely followed his instructions, which were the result of careful considerations, but was thereby unprepared to intervene in the threatening political situation that was building up around him. The supplementary instructions he received from Europe while resident in Persia did not help him: there was too great a distance between reality as pictured by the Council of State and the reality in which their local representative found himself. (See p. 312 ff).

The role of the Portuguese Admiral, Ruy Freire, previous to the final fight for Hormuz reflects the same problem: the difficulty of making realistic decisions in Spain with the information available. His establishment of a fortress at Qishm, in accordance with his instructions though against the advice of local Portuguese officials, gave the Persians a good excuse for starting war at the most unfortunate time imaginable. It is the irony of fate that the execution by Ruy Freire of his allotted task is one of the few instances in which an order with far-reaching consequences is executed precisely in accordance with the intentions of the Council of State. (See p. 336 ff).

The Spanish Crown directly intervened, or attempted to do so, in the Persian question by the instruction of its representatives, such as Figueroa and Ruy Freire, as well as by its reception of Persian envoys and its instructions to the Viceroy in Goa and the Captain in Hormuz, but the distance between the intentions and the realization of them was so great that only a part of *Estado da India*'s policy, and the smallest part at that, was arranged at Court. This discrepancy naturally to a great extent reflects the ambiguous situation that had arisen with the integration of the Spanish and Portuguese Crowns. But the lack of co-ordination between the intentions of the central authority and the actions of the local officials must also be seen from a different angle: namely, as an expression of the nature of *Estado da India* as a political system based on constitutional corruption.

"The Portuguese became tax-gatherers", says Braudel. Did they? Or had they ever been anything else? The question is important in this context because it concerns *Estado da India*'s position as regards the concept of redistributive enterprises, and it also concerns the debate about the modernity and decadence of the Portuguese Empire.

The problem presented itself at the very same moment the sea route to Asia was discovered. The Portuguese Empire has often enough been characterized in the light of the famous dialogue between the first of da Gama's people to go ashore in Calicut and two Moors from Tunis who bade him welcome with the words: "May the Devil take thee! What brought you hither? They asked what he sought so far away from home, and we told them that we came in search of Christians and spices." But the immediate continuation of the conversation is seldom quoted: "They said: "Why does not the King of Castile, the King of France or the Signoria of Venice send hither?" He said that the King of Portugal would not consent to their doing so."[70] From the very first the idea of the discovery's redistributive possibilities carried far more weight than that of its productive ones. "If you wish to trade you do not rob competitors' ships", declared a Venetian factor on Cabral's voyage.[71] But it was a futile remark; already in the Royal letter to the Cardinal Protector of 28th August 1499 we find the title: "Lord over conquests, navigation and trade with Ethiopia, Arabia, Persia and India",[72] and already Cabral was instructed to blockade the Red Sea trade.[73] This important decision has customarily been regarded by modern historians as an historical necessity. "The Portuguese immediately realized that they could only break it [the Muslim monopoly of trade in the Indian Ocean] by brute force and not by peaceful competition", writes C. R. Boxer.[74] Meilink-Roelofsz is just as definitive: "As soon as the Portuguese arrived on the scene Islam took up arms against the intruder."[75] It is possible that there was an historical necessity, but there was never any opportunity of investigating it: the Portuguese decided upon the blockade of the Red Sea trade and the exclusion of other European nations from the Cape route *before* they tried to make use of their discovery in peaceful competition. Lane has also demonstrated quite convincingly that the Portuguese did not regard the Cape route as a technical innovation enabling them to compete with their rivals, but as a monopoly based upon brute force.[76]

Magalhães-Godinho has painted the background of this choice between the use of force or peaceful competition. There were moments in the 15th century Portuguese expansion along the African coast in which the interests of commerce took precedence, but in the long run the warrior, not the merchant, became the dominating figure in *Estado da India*. The Portuguese were aware of the contrast between warrior and merchant early on. "An anti-mercantile ideological system was confronted with the wish for gain and the striving for material goods. The desire for gain also inspired the knights; the King himself became the greatest of all merchants, but no revolution took place in the social structure nor in the basic ideology." The State was mercantilized, but it was not organized as a business. The knight let himself be persuaded by the desire for gain, but he did not be-

70. RAVENSTEIN pp. 48–49.
71. MAGALHAES-GODINHO p. 563.
72. RAVENSTEIN p. 115.
73. GREENLEE p. 180.
74. BOXER, *Empire* p. 46.
75. MEILINK-ROELOFSZ, p. 118.
76. LANE, *Venice and History*, pp. 376–77.

come a merchant; he was enticed by the material goods that lay within his reach, but he was ruined by his expenses. The merchant wished to become a knight or felt himself forced to adopt knightly ambitions, and the hypertrophy of the merchant state prevented the development of a strongly mercantile and industrial bourgeoisie.[77] This description of *Estado da India* as a social system in which the ambitions are archaic although the situation is dynamic appears convincing. An illustration which, although it may not be a proof in itself, reveals quite dicisively that the Portuguese choice was integrated within a complete normative system, a whole culture, is Linschoten's description of Goan society. At first glance it merely appears ludicrous, but it is necessary to suppress one's anachronistic amusement on encountering this world where everyone only strove to gain rank or honours, where 6–7 ferocious soldiers shared a gala dress or two, where a meeting in church or in the street was like a formal dance or a game and an infringement of the rules was not merely boorishness but an insult that could not be forgotten until it was revenged.[78]

This view of *Estado da India* very closely approaches that advanced by van Leur. Although recent research has attacked his views on the basis of more comprehensive material, I do not find any evidence has been produced that would shake his fundamental assertion: "... the commercial and economic forms of the Portuguese colonial regime were the same as those of Asian trade and Asian authority: a trade relatively small in volume conducted by the government as a private enterprize, and all further exercize of authority existing only to ensure the financial, fiscal exploitation of trade, shipping and port traffic, with the higher officials and religious dignitaries recruited from the Portuguese aristocracy ..." and further: "The Portuguese colonial regime, then, did not introduce a single new element into the commerce of southern Asia."[79]

77. MAGALHAES-GODINHO, *Descobrimentos* I pp. 51–63.
78. LINSCHOTEN I pp. 145–152, cf. MOCQUET pp. 305–313.
79. van Leur p. 118; van Leur's judgement has been particularly sharply criticized by Meilink Roelofsz, *op. cit.* pp. 119–120 and *passim*, but her arguments are not very convincing. That the mission was successful is hardly certain and not at all relevant, and that the Portuguese were not able to enforce the spice monopoly is scarcely in itself an argument for their modernity. That the Portuguese should have been the Companies' teachers with regard to diplomatic connections with Asiatic States is an unverified statement; there is not yet any evidence of the Companies having had detailed knowledge of the Portuguese negotiations or of any treaty concluded by the Portuguese. On the contrary, as far as the English Company is concerned, it is evident that on entering into diplomatic connection with the Asian Princes it was building upon diplomatic experience gained in the Levant. The argumentation falls most short, however, when M-R draws

Despite the explicit interest of the explorers in spices *Estado da India* should not be placed in a line of evolution towards capitalist entrepreneurial forms. With the terminology employed here it may be expressed thus: *Estado da India* was a dynamic system, but the innovations were kept within the pattern of redistribution and the profit was consumed in a seigneurial way of life or reinvested in redistributive enterprises, not in productive or productivity-increasing enterprises. The Portuguese were tax-gatherers and *Estado da India* was a redistributive institution.

The historical literature covering the Portuguese Empire in Asia has as a rule been concentrated on the Cape route and the Royal pepper monopoly. But this point of view has been taken in analogy with the North-West European trading companies; it does not correspond to the ideas the Portuguese themselves had about *Estado da India* and conceals its characteristic economic and political organization. The pepper trade was big business, and the import of other Asian goods via Lisbon was not inconsiderable either, but the profit from this trade would never have been able to maintain the Portuguese garrisons and the Portuguese administrational apparatus in Asia.

This view can be substantiated by an investigation of the two available budgets for *Estado* from circa 1584 and circa 1607, respectively.[80] It is immediately noticeable that the relationship between the parent state and *Estado da India* is not viewed as a whole. As regards the accounts *Estado* is isolated to an even greater extent than was later the case in the relationsship between the European and Asian sides of the Companies; even the import of pepper was financed by the annual export of cash earmarked for this purpose.[81] To be sure, the budgets for *Estado da India* showed a profit, but there is nothing to indicate that such a profit should ever have been transferred from *Estado* to the parent state. On the con-

attention to the Portuguese personnel lists and the issue of *cartazes*, as examples of the Portuguese role as model for the North-West Europeans, because it is probably first and foremost in relation to the employees and in the question of sovereign rights on the open sea that the pre-capitalist nature of the Portuguese Empire is most clearly reflected, and where the discontinuity in relation to the North-West European Companies is most marked. Nor is Meilink-Roelofsz's sharp criticism of van Leur always consistent with her own conclusions. *Op. cit.* p. 179 says: "The inter-Asian trade of the Portuguese still lacked the capitalistic structure which was a distinguishing feature of the trade of the northern Europeans." Although it is not quite clear what is meant here by capitalistic structure, this seems to be precisely what van Leur is trying to prove.

80. Don Duart de Meneses the Vice-roy, his tractate of the Portugall Indies... PURCHAS IX pp. 160–166; FALCAO pp. 75–116.
81. MAGALHAES-GODINHO p. 693.

trary, in many critical situations the Crown had to send extraordinary contributions in support of *Estado da India*.[82]

But not even the European side of the balance sheet is regarded as a totality: it is divided up into various accounts that do not provide any all-round survey of profit and loss. If we insist on judging the available material from the point of view of "modern" accountancy, i.e. just as modern as that of the trading companies, we must put the annual equipment of the fleet to Asia and the silver for the purchase of pepper returns on the expenditure side. The profits from the pepper monopoly and the freight and customs for privately imported goods as well as the income from certain minor monopolies will figure on the income side. We can form some idea of the size of these items. From 1588–92 five ships were fitted out annually with a total annual expenditure of somewhat less than 250,000 cruzados.[83] The silver export for the projected pepper purchase at the end of the 16th century lay at 150–200,000 cruzados per annum.[84] The Crown's gross income from the pepper monopoly in 1587–98 was about 535,000 cruzados per annum.[85] The duties on other articles imported into Lisbon from 1586–98 were over 165,000 cruzados per annum.[86] The immediate impression is of a sizeable though not excessive profit, even in those years at the end of the 16th century when so many ships were lost at sea. But there is reason to regard the figures with the greatest caution: behind their apparent precision, as detailed by Falcão, considerable elements of uncertainty lie hidden; everything was farmed out, and part of the farms was paid in advance as loans whereas part was paid with bonds. To the visible income and expenses should be added the hidden ones: expenses for convoys, income from the sale of offices, etc. But

---

82. Thus in 1588 in aid of the fight against Achin, *Archivo Portuguez-Oriental* III p. 131, and in 1608 the fight against the Dutch, Arch. Simancas, Secr. Prov., Libr. 1479 ff. 126, 130; in 1612 Spain considered financing the purchase of pepper out of the income of *Estado da India,* since experienced people maintained that this would be possible providing the accounts were in order. The matter was placed before the Viceroy and was then apparently lost sight of, *Documentos Remettidos* II p. 237. Regularly the means of deceased persons were transferred to Portugal from Goa by means of bills of exchange drawn on Casa da India, Federici in *Nuovo Ramusio* pp. 66–67, Meneses in PURCHAS IX pp. 149–150, MAGALHAES-GODINHO p. 648; this money was partly used for advance payment on pepper in India, but it is not possible to see whether the sums transferred from Portugal were reduced accordingly. In 1605 it was ordered that the fitting out of the return ships should be financed with the means of deceased persons which were to be transferred to Portugal. *Documentos Remettidos* I p. 45.
83. FALCAO pp. 201–204.
84. MAGALHAES-GODINHO pp. 688, 693.
85. FALCAO p. 59–69.
86. *ibid.* pp. 46–55.

the main thing was that the Crown and the Royal officials apparently did not think along these lines at all; no survey of profit and loss was tabulated, any more than a survey of profit and loss was tabulated for the towns and provinces in the parent state.[87]

If we inspect *Estado da India*'s budget it is also immediately apparent that we are faced here with an enterprise of quite a different nature than that of the trading companies, and with quite a different function than that of carrying on trade. *Estado da India*'s income consisted predominantly of customs from a fairly restricted number of ports besides the income from a number of less important customs houses and the duties from the territorial possessions proper, especially Goa.

Table 5. *Main items on the revenue budget of Estado da India 1584 and 1607.*[88]

	1584	1607
Goa and Cochin	150,000 xer.	226,666 xer.
Hormuz	170,000 xer.	192,000 xer.
Malacca	72,000 xer.	88,800 xer.
Diu	120,000 xer.	215,550 xer.
Damao	51,520 xer.	60,000 xer.
Baçaim	138,400 xer.	123,600 xer.
	701,920 xer.	906,616 xer.
Other revenue	124,285 xer.	278,584 xer.
In all	826,205 xer.	1,185,200 xer.

Against this background it is scarcely surprising that the dominating items on the expenditure side of the budget were personnel expenses for the garrisons, patrolling ships and administration.

As mentioned, *Estado da India* was self-sufficient; the basis of its existence was not the route around Africa, but *Estado*'s own "production" of protection and "the sale" of this production, i.e. the tribute that was demanded from the Asian trade. As a redistributive enterprise *Estado da*

87. A critic of the existing system like Duarte Gomes Solis was aware of the difference between the Companies, which were run as business enterprises, and *Estado da India*. Throughout his verbose *Alegacion* it is repeated again and again that the King did not have any ministers who understood business, and he complains that offices are not filled according to ability, but to rank, and suggests that Casa da India's difficulties are simply due to the absence of any proper bookkeeping. SOLIS pp. 42–43.

88. *loc. cit.* above n. 80.

India did not depend upon a territory, but upon the mastery of the open seas and the resulting claim to sovereignty. In principle every Asian trading ship should be equipped with a Portuguese pass, a *cartaze*. This was not only a source of income in itself, but also provided the possibility of diverting an important part of the trade through the Portuguese controlled towns, first and foremost Goa, Hormuz and the ports on the Gulf of Cambay.

The legal justification of the *cartaze* institution was given by Freitas, the Portuguese authority on international law, in his polemics against Grotius's *Mare Liberum*. He conceded the Portuguese Crown *quasi possessio* over the Asian waters, understanding by this a right to protection and jurisdiction. This right was again derived out of regard for the safeguarding of the Portuguese territories and of Portugal's responsibility for certain international tasks: the combating of piracy and the spreading of Christianity according to the Papal mandate.[89] This viewpoint was amplified a few years ago by Alexandrowitz: "The claim to free access to the East Indies for spreading the Christian faith must therefore be understood against the background of the primary objective of the Portuguese, to undercut the vital supply lines of Islam in the East and to weaken the military potential of the Ottoman Empire threatening the centres of Christian Europe."[90]

But it is doubtful whether the *cartaze* institution deserves the profound justifications given it by lawyers and historians. The real political usefulness of the *cartazes* when dealing with the Asian Princes is immediately obvious. The connection between *cartazes*, staple rights and customs demands becomes clearly apparent from the correspondence between the King and the Viceroy.[91] But the connection with an ideologically motivated fight against the common enemies of Christendom is very difficult to discern in the sources. Magalhães-Godinho has irrefutably demonstrated that the route through the Red Sea remained open during the second half of the 16th century, not merely because the Asian ships circumvented the Portuguese blockade, but rather because the Portuguese had in reality abandoned the attempt to hinder navigation in the Red Sea by means of force.[92] *Cartazes* permitting navigation in the Red Sea were issued both to Muslims and Hindus. Thus before 1613 Ahmadnagar had obtained the right to send two ships per annum from Chaul to Mocha,[93] Bijapur had

---

89. ALEXANDROWITZ p. 50 ff.
90. *ibid.* p. 54.
91. See for example *Documentos Remettidos* II pp. 38–39, III pp. 167, 267; *Assentos* I p. 182.
92. MAGALHAES-GODINHO pp. 774–780.
93. *Documentos Remettidos* I p. 290.

89

had corresponding rights with regard to Dabhol since 1548[94] and in 1613 Bijapur obtained *cartazes* for six ships "to Mecca, Hormuz and other places."[95] Before 1613 the Grand Mogul had had the right to send at least one ship per year from the Red Sea to Surat.[96] From the beginning of the 17th century *cartazes* were also issued to the South Indian ports and in 1605 or 1606 Calicut requested the Portuguese to refrain from issuing *cartazes* for the Mocha voyage to Cannanore and Cochin as had taken place under Ayres de Saldanha (Viceroy 1600–1603).[97] Calicut's request was supported in Spain, but apparently without effect, because *cartazes* issued to Cochin are still mentioned in 1613.[98] The issue of *cartazes* to the Maldives is mentioned in 1612.[99]

It is interesting in this connection to take a look at the ports of origin of the ships that passed Bab-el Mandeb in three years in the second decade of the 17th century.

Table 6. *Ports of origin of ships passing Bab-el Mandeb 1611, 1612 and 1616.*[100]

	1611	1612	1616
Sind (several ports)		4	14
Surat		3	1
Goga			1
Dabhol	2	2	2
Chaul		1	1
Barsalore	1		
Cannanore	2	1	1
Cranganore			1
Calicut	1	2	1
The Maldives	2		
Achin	1	2	1
Diu	1	3	7
Goa	1	1	1
East Africa	1	2	7
Shihr		2	
The Red Sea	1	1	3
Unknown	4		3

94. *Assentos* I p. 6 n. 2; MAGALHAES-GODINHO p. 776.
95. *Assentos* p. 7, cf. ALEXANDROWITZ pp. 71–72.
96. *Documentos Remettidos* III p. 162.
97. *Ibid.* I p. 35.
98. *Ibid.* II p. 307.
99. *Ibid.* II p. 259.
100. 1611: Middleton in PURCHAS III pp. 151–170; 1612: Middleton *ibid.* pp.

The lists are hardly complete, but one must nevertheless assume that they provide a more or less representative picture of the navigation from India to the Red Sea during these years. The immediate impression is that very little of this navigation circumvented the Portuguese control. There can scarcely be any doubt that the ships from Surat, Goga, Dabhol, Chaul, Cannanore, Calicut and the Maldives had Portuguese *cartazes*, the same probably applying to the towns of Cranganore and Barsalore in which Portuguese forts and factories were to be found. Two Portuguese towns, Goa and Diu, were ports of origin for a fair proportion of the ships to the Red Sea. In 1606 the authorities in Goa had applied for *cartazes* for sailing the Red Sea; the answer to this application is not known,[101] but both in 1611 and in 1612 we are informed that the ships from Goa had called at Shihr or Socotra on the way. Regarding the ships from Diu, van der Broecke informs us that the majority of the merchants on board were Banyans, a few were Moors or Armenians, but as regards one of the ships he adds that most of the goods were Portuguese owned.[102] The important role played by Diu as a port of embarkation seems to be explained in the peace treaty between the Portuguese and the Mogul Empire of 1615. It appears from this that the Grand Mogul had the right to *cartaze* for one ship per year to the Red Sea without paying customs to the Portuguese, whereas the remaining exports were to be cleared in Diu.[103] Only the ships from Achin lay with certainty outside Portuguese control, whereas ships from the ports around the mouth of the Indus constitute an unsolved problem. Despite these exceptions and uncertainties we can be sure that the Portuguese control of navigation in the Red Sea at the beginning of the 17th century was effective, but that it was indeed a matter of control, not blockade.

We cannot exclude the possibility that the situation in the second decade of the 17th century signifies a final abandonment of every hope of blockade after the arrival of the Companies, but on the other hand we have no evidence of such a decisive reversal in the Portuguese *cartaze* policy. On the contrary there are indications in the sources that the theory presented here is in agreement with what the Portuguese themselves thought:

190–192, Downton *ibid.* 281 ff., Saris *ibid.* 389–90, JOURDAIN pp. 205 ff., 1616: van der BROECKE I pp. 82–87, 100–103. Cf. also 1609: "It [Mocha] hath in it very fair buildings (after their manner) of lime and stone, and very populous, as well of Arabs as stranger merchants, and espetially Banians of Gujarat, Dabul, Chaul, Bassein, Daman and Sinda as alsoe of Ormus and Mascat with all the coast of Melinda." JOURDAIN p. 103.

101. *Documentos Remettidos* I p. 133.
102. van der BROECKE I p. 102.
103. BOCARRO pp. 395–397. The importance of the Mecca trade for the Captain in Diu is referred to already in 1582. SILVA, *Elementos* p. 30.

i.e. that the blockade policy had already been abandoned during the 16th century in favour of a policy that may well in principle have maintained the right of the Portuguese Crown to blockade the Red Sea, but which in practice made use of this right in order to guide the European-Asian transit trade through the Portuguese custom houses or to procure friends among the princes on the west coast of India.

The question was brought up during Robert Sherley's first term of office in Spain. Robert Sherley declared that a blockade of the Red Sea was one of the Shah's dearest wishes; the Council of State's immediate answer – possibly in good faith – was that the Royal armadas had already been carrying out such a blockade for several years.[104] In August 1611, however, the Council of Portugal residing in Lisbon was asked to comment upon the proposal. After a joint meeting with the Council of Portugal the Council of India strongly opposed the plan for an effective blockade, with the interesting reason that it was only friends who used the route through the Red Sea – the Turks used the route via Hormuz. "... apart from the first fleets that were sent to India, at the time this Crown began the conquest thereof they [the fleets] have only returned thither one single time, it was in '86 when the galleys that were sent thither were destroyed on the coast by Malindi." The trade from Diu to the Red Sea took place on board ships that were furnished with Portuguese *cartazes* from the Captain in Diu in accordance with the Viceroy's orders. If this traffic were stopped the Royal treasury would lose 200,000 cruzados per annum. Apart from the ships from the Portuguese Diu, only the ships that had obtained permission from the King and possessed *cartazes* were sailing. It was a question of one ship from the Grand Mogul and others from the Kings of Calicut, Cochin and Cannanore – all friends and allies. The Council concluded that an effective blockade would simply mean the ruin of *Estado da India*.[105]

There is no doubt that the blockade policy was undermined long before 1600, and it is reasonable to connect this development with the information that may be derived from *Estado da India*'s budget. The financial basis of *Estado* was not the Cape route and the blockade policy, but customs obtained from the Indian *alfandegas*. An effective blockade would have been the ruin of *Estado*.

In the above *Estado da India* is regarded as a unit, as an enterprise, but it is necessary to determine whether the views presented are valid if we extend the investigation to include the separate individuals or groups in *Estado*. It is doubtful whether the trade carried on by the Portuguese

104. Torro do Tombo, Lisboa, Misc. Ms. do Convento da Graça de Lisboa, Cx. 6, tomo 2e pp. 442–444.
105. Arch. Simancas, Estado, leg. 494.

in Asia can modify the picture we have sketched here.[106] Unfortunately we know extremely little about the private Portuguese trade, but what we do know seems to indicate that the most important entrepreneurs were the officials, and it never reveals a trade that deviated from the Asian pattern.

For the individual Portuguese as well as for *Estado da India* as a whole, the official budgets comprise only that part of the iceberg that is visible above the surface. *Estado da India* was a means of livelihood for thousands of soldiers and officials through the salaries that showed up on the ordinary balance sheets, but to this should be added the income an official might expect over and above his salary. *Estado da India*'s bureaucracy must be regarded as one of the purest examples in history of constitutionally determined corruption. For all important posts the path of office led through the Court, either by means of connections and noble descent or by virtue of the services the applicant had rendered *Estado da India* as a soldier. After 8–10 years of active service a soldier could seek an office by sending in the recommendations and certificates he had obtained from his superiors. Normally he did not acquire an office instantaneously, but obtained the reversion of an office, which might be bought and sold and even passed on. There are examples of up to 30 persons on the waiting-list for a captaincy.[107] When the applicant was finally installed in his office he had three years in which to make sure of the rewards for his services and his patience, this three year limit to the period of tenure apparently being observed with great punctiliousness. That officials attempted to procure incomes over and above their official salaries does not only appear from the adverse comments and complaints, but is plainly revealed in Falcão's description of the offices in connection with his survey of Portugal's and *Estado da India*'s finances. Under the title "Fortresses, forts and offices given away by the King in *Estado da India* and approximately what they yield to those appointed" he gives us a survey of the incomes derived from a long list of offices.[108] A comparison with the expense budget immediately reveals that considerably greater incomes than the official salaries were foreseen. According to Falcão the annual revenue of office-holders amounted to 1,015,772 xerafims, including 518,420 xerafims to the captains in the various towns and fortresses,

---

106. I have a lower opinion of Portuguese private trade in Asia than Meilinck-Roelofsz. She maintains that "Portuguese commercial traffic was organized on a higher level than its Asian counterpart" and furthermore, that the Portuguese merchants "undoubtedly left some trace behind them of their European extraction." *op. cit.* pp. 9–10, but the argumentation for this judgement appears weak, see, for example, *ibid.* p. 178.
107. BOXER, *Empire* p. 299.
108. FALCAO pp. 119–136.

230,000 xerafims to those who obtained a voyage on one of the monopoly routes and 267,352 xerafims to other officials. This survey far from comprises all the income transferred through the Portuguese redistributive system; in addition to the offices listed comes the post of Viceroy and a number of other important offices in Goa (about which we are informed that they are not allocated as payment for services rendered) the offices to which the Viceroy or the Captain in Hormuz had the right of appointment and the church offices.

Falcão's information about the value of the offices could be unrealistic, but we have an interesting possibility for checking his figures. In 1615 an extraordinary "auction" was held in Goa for all the offices under royal patronage in order to obtain extra revenue for the campaign against the Dutch. The offices were sold for a three-year period and the sales brought in altogether 742,806 xerafims.[109] The total amount cannot be compared directly with Falcão's figures, since not all offices were made available for sale. But if we compare the sums paid for the captaincies with Falcão's figures there is pretty exact agreement, if we make allowances for the fact that the purchase prices must leave the buyers a certain margin for discounting their investments and for profits. Furthermore, the income from the offices was doubtless depreciated from the first to the second decade of the 17th century.

Table 7. *Estimated and sales value of captaincies in Estado da India 1607 and 1615.*

	Falcão	Sale 1615
Cannanore	8,000 xer.	5,030 xer.
Damao	66,100 xer.	37,000 xer.
Malacca	173,160 xer.	32,200 xer.
Masqat	40,000 xer.	30,000 xer.
Hormuz	240,000 xer.	145,500 xer.
Chaul	105,760 xer.	30,300 xer.
Diu	80,000 xer.	53,000 xer.
Colombo	25,000 xer.	8,050 xer.
Onore	16,000 xer.	8,000 xer.

"The auction of the offices" in 1615 is revealing. The nearly 750,000 xerafims that could be raised in Goa after a number of difficult years bears comparison with the capital the English East India Company was able to

109. Arquivo Hist. Ultramarino, Lisboa, Papeis avulsos, Cx. 5 5/2 1618; *Documentos Remettidos* III p. 29; the Royal order concerning the sale printed in PYRARD I:1 pp. XXX–XXXII.

muster in the same years. The important difference was not the presence of the capital, but that form of enterprise in which it was invested.

The characteristics we have drawn attention to here provide a clue towards the understanding of a great portion of the Spanish-Portuguese policy in Asia and its internal contradictions: the lack of co-ordination between intentions and results, the eternal complaints about misuse of office, which never resulted in anything else but ineffective reprimands, and the inconsistency between the blockade policy in principle and the actual permissive attitude towards Asian navigation. The central bodies – after the amalgamation of Spain and Portugal primarily the Council of State – worked in order to protect and extend the territory and interests of the Empire, employing means that in principle were no different from the means employed in contemporary European policy. But in Asian affairs the Council had to operate through a special form of political body, an organism that derived its nourishment from its grip on Asian oceanic trade, and which for that reason alone could not be co-ordinated strategically with the interests of the Empire as a whole. Furthermore, *Estado da India* largely delegated not only the execution of power but also its fruits to its local representatives. This state of affairs placed insurmountable difficulties in the way of an integration of the Imperial policy. A clean-up of the constitutionally determined corruption would have torn assunder the bonds that held *Estado da India* together.[110]

The Redistributive Institutions and the Market

It was shown above that the peddling market, even if it was subject to general economic laws, was characterized by institutional peculiarities that were instrumental in creating a situation in which there was poor transparency of the market, weak elasticity of supply over the short term period and thereby considerable price fluctuations. In the following the question as to how far this market was modified by the entrepreneurial activity practised by the redistributive institutions will be investigated.

In a short passage van Leur has considered this question. He quotes Coen in the following address to *Heeren XVII* (the Board of Directors of the Dutch East India Company): "... for in all the Indies there cannot be more turned over than is retailed every day, which is the cause of the extraordinary rising and falling in the prices of merchandize, for there are nowhere great or rich, daring merchants to be found such as one

---

110. Cf. ELLIOTT p. 547: „In fact, it may have been precisely because the Spanish Monarchy was *not* centralized, uniform and closely integrated in the way Olivares desired, that it managed to survive for so long."

encounters in Europe who at the same time have the power and the right to buy up an excellent portion and reserve it for retailing ..." And van Leur continues: "The last part of this quotation is definitely painted too darkly. But it is true, that neither merchant gentlemen, lords nor princes played a continuous, dominant rôle in trade. The power they had over market, weigh-house and boom may have been firmly established; it was the pedlar who carried the wares trading on adventure."[111]

In so far as van Leur is correct in stating that the Princes' interference in trade was not continuous or dominant, we can straightway conclude that their entrepreneurial activity did not modify the peddling market. The immediate and short term monopolization of a particular commodity or its arbitrary confiscation might be provoked by the market conditions, but their only result would be an unpredictable increase in the merchants' expenses, and actions of this kind would therefore only lead to an increase in the non-transparency of the market and an augmentation of the price fluctuations – and thereby the profit margin necessary to maintain the supply to the peddling market.

However, it is not correct to maintain that the official entrepreneurial activity was never dominant or continuous, since a large number of cases can be pointed out in which the redistributive institutions took part in the trade on a particular market, by a particular route or in a particular commodity either continuously or throughout a number of years. Such continuous participation in trade could be found both centrally and locally; one might mention as examples of local economic activity the official or semi-official navigation between Surat and the Red Sea or the private trade of the Portuguese captains in Hormuz. Unfortunately there is insufficient information concerning these activities for a closer analysis. In the following, attention will be focused upon the two great examples of centrally directed state trade within the area investigated: the Portuguese pepper trade and the Persian silk trade.

"First for the Portingal, we know that like a good simple man he sailed every year full hungerly (god wot) about three parts of the earth almost for spices, and when he brought them home, the great rich purses of the Antwerpians, subjects of the King of Spain, engrossed them all into their own hands, yea oftentimes gave money for them beforehand, making thereof a plain Monopoly; whereby they only gained and all other Nations lost. For that the spices, being in few men's hands, were sold at such rates as they listed, to their own private lucre and gain, and to the hurt and damage of all others."[112] This is Coen's "great or rich, daring merchants" seen from the reverse. Wheeler's description of the pepper trade is part

111. van LEUR p. 220.
112. John Wheeler, *A Treatise of Commerce*, quoted by LACH I p. 126.

of a long tradition, which has continued right up until our own age with its bitter accusations against "monopolists and engrossers" and with its simultaneous absolvement of the Portuguese Crown from the responsibility for the high level of prices. In Wheeler's eyes it is the Antwerpians who overstep the just price by virtue of their control of the market, to the detriment of both the consumers and of the good, simple Portuguese. It is both shattering and shocking, but is it correct?

We can consider the question with the aid of the information available about the Portuguese Crown trade, even if it is in many respects incomplete and difficult to interpret. The archives of *Casa da India* have been lost, but material has been preserved in other places that has made it possible to reconstruct the main features of the Portuguese Crown trade.[113] Until 1570 it was the rule that the Crown's own people looked after the Asian side of the pepper trade, whereas the European side was organized as contract sales based on Antwerp in the first half of the century, thereafter on Lisbon. Presumably, in 1584 the Venetian Consul in Lisbon, dall'Olmo, calculated the costs of the Crown pepper trade as it had taken shape before 1570[114]

	Reis per quintal
Purchase price in Asia	1,050
Freight	1,000
Insurance both ways, 14%	150
Interest, 10% in 1½ years	160
Costs of discharge	40
Wastage	60

According to this calculation the pepper cost the King 2,460 reis or 6 cruzados 40 reis per quintal; he sold it to the European contractors for 34 cruzados per quintal, thus making a profit of 27 cruzados 340 reis per quintal, or 557,000 cruzados on the expected import of 20,000 quintals per annum.

Dall'Olmo was promoter of the plan to transfer the pepper contracts to Venice, and there is no doubt that in this table he has tried to show up the profits in as promising a light as possible,[115] but quite unrealistic the calculation is not. Until the beginning of the 1560s the Portuguese were able to keep the purchase price of pepper down to approximately 1,000 reis per quintal,[116] though in the following year prices doubled.

113. The most detailed treatments of the Portuguese Crown monopoly in LACH I pp. 92–150 and MAGALHAES-GODINHO pp. 683–98. But see also KELLENBENZ, *Poivre* and BRAUDEL I p. 503 ff.
114. Museo Civico-Correr, Venezia, Ms. Cicogna 3036/6–10 f. 245.
115. dall'OLMO *passim.*
116. MAGALHAES-GODINHO pp. 637–638.

A freight of 1,000 reis also seems somewhat low: a freight of 4 cruzados per quintal was already reckoned with in 1558, and this sum became the conventional figure in connection with pepper contracts later in the century.[117] The insurance premium corresponds quite well with the frequency of shipwreck at the middle of the 16th century, and neither does the interest allowed for deviate from what must have been the norm. A sales price of 34 cruzados in Europe is also realistic: from 1576–78 wholesale prices of 27–38 cruzados per quintal were noted in Lisbon, which varied not only with the market, but also with the quality and conditions of payment,[118] and 32 cruzados was the Crown's traditional minimum price.[119] That dall'Olmo's report, although very optimistic, did not lack foundations in reality, is finally confirmed by a Portuguese calculation from 1558–59. This operates with purchase expenses in Asia of 2,200 reis per quintal and freight costs of 1,600 reis per quintal, in all 3,800 reis or 9^{1}/$_{2}$ cruzados, and a sales price from Casa da India of 34 cruzados per quintal. Thus even under these conditions there should remain a profit for the Crown of 24^{1}/$_{2}$ cruzados.[120]

It is probable that wastage and corruption have in practice reduced the profits of the Crown; this would be the most obvious explanation for the radical reorganization of the pepper trade carried out in 1570. The trade with pepper from Asia to Europe was made open to all under the condition that the pepper was conveyed to Lisbon and a duty of 18 cruzados per quintal paid there.[121] It was probably less than the Crown had previously been able to reckon with as theoretical profit on every imported quintal, but still a very high duty. None the less the liberalization was followed by a fall in prices that endangered the commodity's "reputation",[122] and after the death of King Sebastian in 1578 the pepper trade was again reorganized, the Asian contract being taken over by a German merchant, Konrad Rott, who had previously contracted for Europe. Rott's contract of 1578 was a "sharecropper's" contract, *partido do meio,* on its arrival in Lisbon half of the pepper bought on Rott's and his associates' account was transferred to the Crown free of charge.[123] Apparently this share system had previously been used in connection with short term pepper contracts, but involved a risk that the King and the contractors might compete with one another on the European markets. Rott attempted to

---

117. *Ibid.* pp. 637, 693.
118. da SILVA, *Lettres de Lisbonne, passim.*
119. MAGALHAES-GODINHO p. 693.
120. *Ibid.* p. 637.
121. VASQUEZ de PRADA p. 90.
122. Museo Civico-Correr, Venezia, Ms. Cicogna 3036/6–10, f. 248.
123. *Documentação Ultramarina Portuguesa* III p. 314; MAGALHAES-GODINHO p. 692.

overcome this problem, however, and obtain control of both the European and the Asian side of the pepper trade, committing himself as European contractor to buy back the King's share at 32 cruzados per quintal. Immediately after this contract was signed the price of pepper in Lisbon rose steeply,[124] but it was soon revealed that Rott had not managed to secure such perfect control over the supplies that he could safeguard himself against an unforeseen drop in prices. Throughout 1579 the European pepper price kept falling, amongst other things owing to considerable supplies (20,000 quintals) to Venice from Alexandria. Rott's pepper syndicate collapsed and he himself had to go into hiding.[125] The syndicate was carried on by Rott's associates, first and foremost the Milanese Rovellasco and the Welsers, and the principle of sharing the import from Asia between the syndicate and the Crown was maintained until 1585; on the other hand it is not sure that the syndicate retained the contract for Europe.[126] A piquant sequel to the collapse of Rott's project was in all probability the Spanish attempts to get Venice to take over the pepper contracts in 1581 and again in 1585.[127] Rott's project demanded the absence of loopholes.

In 1586 the Asian contract was taken over by a new syndicate, the most prominent members of which were Rovellasco, the Welsers and the Fuggers. This time it was not a question of a share contract, since the syndicate was to carry the pepper to Lisbon at its own expense and thereafter hand over the entire lot to the Crown at the price of 12 cruzados plus 4 cruzados for freight.[128] With a normal price of 32 cruzados the result would be the same as with the share contract, but the 1586 contract like Rott's project of 1578 possessed the organizational advantage that all the pepper was gathered in one spot, on this occasion by the Crown. Apparently in 1587 the Crown tried to exploit this advantage by putting up its sales prices to 60 cruzados per quintal, which hardly not without reason made the Fuggers fear that the buyers would make for Venice.[129] In 1592 the Asian contract was taken over by a new syndicate to which a Portuguese house, Ximenes, was admitted in addition to the previous members. The details of the 1592 contract are not known, but according to Falcão there is no doubt that the basis, as in 1586, was the duty of the contractors to hand over the imported pepper to the Crown at a price of 12 + 4 cruzados.[130]

124. da SILVA, Lettres de Lisbonne passim, p. 189.
125. HAEBLER p. 180 ff.
126. HAEBLER, Fuggerschen Handlung pp. 227–229; LACH I p. 136; MAGALHAES-GODINHO pp. 692–693.
127. BRAUDEL I pp. 506–508.
128. The contract in PESCHEL p. 220 n.l., cf. DOBEL pp. 125–126; FITZLER p. 249.
129. FITZLER p. 265.
130. FALCAO p. 59 ff.

The apparently simple equivalents of the contracts in reality conceal far more complicated relations; as intimated by Wheeler, the contracts were closely tied up with the Portuguese and later the Spanish State finances. Thus the Fuggers only entered into the contract of 1592 because they saw a possibility therein of covering part of their advances to the Spanish Crown, and they wound up their interests in this syndicate as quickly as possible.[131] On the other hand the syndicate of 1586 was partly financed by the issue of *juros,* thereby obtaining, as it were, a State guarantee for the foreign capital that had to be taken up in order to finance the business.[132] But although these credit transactions conceal the precise exchange relations there is such a wide margin between the prices paid to the Asian contractors and the prices paid by the European contractors that we may safely say that the Portuguese deserve to be called neither good nor simple. As far as the latter two contracts of 1586 and 1592 are concerned Falcão estimates the expenses of the Crown (the 16 cruzados to the contractors plus wastage and some losses at sea) to be 1,278,828,641 reis and the income from the sale of pepper to be 2,572,805,523 reis. The pepper contracts thus provided a revenue to the Royal *fazenda* of 1,293, 976,882 reis or about 3,225,000 cruzados nett, an annual average for this not particularly flourishing period of approximately 268,750 cruzados.[133] From this expenses must be deducted for the administration and the handling of the pepper, but in view of the fact that the Crown's contribution in this transaction was limited to that of receiving the pepper in Casa da India's warehouses and handing it over again, it cannot have been a matter of large sums.

The nature of the Crown revenue is most noticeable in connection with the contract trade, but in principle it was the same, no matter whether it was a question of direct Royal trade, free trade subjected to the payment of customs or contract trade. Only superficially is it relevant to speak of a merchant's profit earned by "the merchant king". The Portuguese pepper monopoly was not a business but a custom house. Herein lies the key to understanding the price policy carried out by the Portuguese Crown. The prices were not fixed at the optimum level according to long term business considerations, but determined by the quantities most recently supplied to the Levant markets (or by the latest forecasts regarding supplies). The Portuguese pepper trade was that rare phenomenon, a true monopoly, but it was a monopoly on a route that was guarded by armed force, not on a commodity. Like the holder of a patent enabling him to produce his goods cheaper than his competitors the Portuguese King might choose whether he

131. KELLENBENZ, *Poivre* p. 5.
132. MAGALHAES-GODINHO p. 694.
133. FALCAO p. 61.

would monopolize the market by reducing his prices to below the level of his competitors, or whether he would have the greatest profit from a smaller production by letting his prices be determined by the competitors' production costs.

Here in all simplicity we have the secret behind the survival of the caravan routes in the 16th century. As previously shown it is not quite certain that the ocean transport was a technological improvement in the sense that it led to a saving with regard to the transport costs proper; the saving was first and foremost to be made by the avoidance of robbers and tax-gatherers through the internalization and centralization of the protection costs. But the Portuguese takeover of the pepper trade only became a takeover within the existing structure; the protection costs were increased rather than reduced so long as the price was determined by the costs on the caravan routes. Concerning the part of the pepper trade that was diverted to the ocean route, the protection rent and tribute was expropriated by the Portuguese King, but as an economic innovation the discovery of the sea route to India did not during the first century have any effects over and above this transfer.

Was the Portuguese monopoly then a "creative monopoly" in Schumpeter's sense of a monopoly in which gains are reinvested in other productive projects? The question must be answered in the negative. Indeed price rigidity in the Portuguese Crown trade is conspicuous: prices fluctuated passively in pace with the fluctuations of the European market, but did not influence supplies: in fact it was never possible to carry out the intentions of bringing the supplies up in the region of the European consumption at the end of the 16th century. Not in one single year did the supplies reach the 30,000 quintal mark that from 1578 onwards was regarded as desirable.[134] The rigidity in the entrepreneurial activity of the Portuguese Crown becomes no less apparent if we consider the isolation of the pepper trade. An attempt was also made to create a contract trade in ginger and nutmeg, but without much success,[135] and there was no question of co-ordinating this trade with the pepper trade. The equipment of the ships was undertaken, at any rate in periods, by private contractors, but neither in this case was there a question of co-ordinating trade with shipping.[136] Finally we notice the rigidity in the bilateral conception of the pepper trade constantly maintained. The pepper purchases were never co-ordinated with the general Asian trade pattern. No matter whether the trade was conducted by the Crown directly or by contractors, the pepper purchases

134. DOBEL p. 125.
135. da SILVA, Contratos, passim.
136. MAGALHAES-GODINHO pp. 694–695.

were financed by the export of strictly ear-marked capitals.[137] Neither political necessity nor the opportunity for a profitable business transaction was an excuse for using the pepper capital for other purposes. Consequently, neither in Europe nor in Asia is there any trace of a consolidation of the Portuguese Crown trade in the form of the accumulation of a business capital; on the contrary, there is no doubt that *Casa da India*'s freedom of action was hampered by the fact that the contractors frequently were Crown creditors paid with assignments upon the revenue of *Casa da India*.[138]

Strangely enough the latter circumstance constituted the only possibility for a shift from parasitic monopoly to creative monopoly. There were times, in 1578 and possibly also in 1592, when one syndicate controlled both the Asian and the European contracts. But the contractors were not free to co-ordinate prices and supplies: the Portuguese Crown's share in the business tied the contractors to a price policy that would continue to keep the caravan routes open, and they had no control over the navigation or over the political decisions in Asia, and were thus unable to organize a policy that would ensure predictable supplies. On the other hand there is no doubt that the contractors could make use of their leading position as the biggest sellers on the European market in order to increase and stabilize their prices by means of cartel agreements regulating both supplies and prices. This tendency is clearly apparent in Rott's agreements with the Elector of Saxony and the Thuringian Society – an agreement he himself had to break, however, when he found himself short of cash.[139] Thanks to Kellenbenz's analysis of the Fugger papers we may follow even more closely the policy of the European contractors in the years after 1591. The Syndicate of 1591 was constituted by the Ximenes (Lisbon and Antwerp) houses (12 parts), the Fuggers and the Welsers (12 parts), Rovellasco of Italy (4 parts) and Malvenda of Spain (4 parts). This cosmopolitan syndicate took over the pepper at 36 cruzados per quintal and agreed upon a sales price of 40–42 cruzados per quintal according to quality. The contracting houses elegantly and effectively utilized their network of branches, agents and correspondents in Hamburg, Lübeck, Middelburg, Amsterdam, Leghorn, Venice, etc., and placed their shares on the European market after carefully weighing up the relative prices and the rates of exchange. But the contractors did not have complete control of the market: the prices fluctuated rapidly with the supplies or expected supplies to

---

137. The inviolability of the pepper capital is a recurring theme in the letters from Europe to the Viceroy, see for example *Archivo Portuguez-Oriental* IV pp. 881–882, *Documentos Remettidos* I pp. 15, 45.
138. Solis p. 42.
139. Haebler p. 180 ff.

Europe, and even the contractors occasionally ignored the agreed minimum price.[140]

Despite these shortcomings it was possibly in the organization of the European contract that the Portuguese Crown trade made the deepest impression on the economic institutions. The big lump sales created a "counter-vailing power" in the shape of the cosmopolitan merchant syndicates. Though their existence as quasi-monopolistic enterprises was short-lived, the achievements of the syndicates in promoting international co-ordination and in the sophisticated use of a business organization covering most of Europe were impressive.

In Persia just as in Portugal there was a tradition for political capitalism. In 1513 silk was sold in Bursa on Shah Ismail's account.[141] Ismail's successor, Tahmasp, is described as an eager businessman: "He buys and sells with as much cunning as a base merchant", he tries to accumulate riches with "thousands and thousands of tricks that are unworthy of men, not to speak of kings." He orders the purchase of cotton materials in Kandahar, of velvet and silk in Khurasan and of cloth in Aleppo, and from these materials he has clothes made with which to pay his soldiers, pricing them at ten times their true value.[142] In connection with the devaluation of the Persian coin in 1555 he buys 500 loads of silk which he sends to India – at any rate according to what was rumoured in Aleppo.[143] The envoy of the English Muscovy Company also did business with Tahmasp.[144]

From the time of Abbas we are acquainted with a number of Persian business expeditions which, taken singly, are not particularly interesting, but together give an impression of the Shah's entrepreneurial activity before the Companies began to trade directly with Persia. On 8th June 1600 a Persian envoy, Efet Beg, presented himself at the Venetian Senate. It appeared from his conversation with the Doge that it was his task to sell various commodities on the Shah's account and purchase others for the Shah's personal use. He handed over a letter from the Shah containing a personal recommendation of Efet Beg, "agent and merchant of our High Court, who is sent to that part of he world in order to carry out various tasks for your Royal Person" but apart from this the letter contained only empty assurances of friendship. Efet Beg had no special wishes to make known to the Venetian authorities other than a petition for exemption from current regulations with regard to the dyeing of some materials he wished to take home with him, and the request for a letter of recommendation to the

140. KELLENBENZ, Poivre.
141. INALCIK p. 111.
142. BERCHET, Persia pp. 173–175.
143. BERENGO p. 78 and passim.
144. HAKLUYT III p. 58; Early Voyages p. 426.

brokers he intended to use in Venice. The Venetians gave Efet Beg a letter to take home to the Shah, but neither did this contain anything other than polite phrases.[145]

Efet Beg died in Baghdad on the way home. His purchases, or a part of them: six cloths and two arquebusses, were brought to the Shah in Isfahan by a young Venetian, Angelo Gradenigo, who was received in audience by Abbas in March 1601.[146] Presumably on this occasion Abbas gave the young man a quantity of silk, which he was to sell in Europe on the Shah's account. However, Gradenigo was in no hurry to wind up the business – even if, according to what is reported, he had to pledge one of his good friends in Persia.[147] What happened to the friend we do not know, but Gradenigo never returned to Persia. When Robert Sherley passed through Prague as Persian envoy in 1609 he met Gradenigo at the Imperial Court. He had him arrested and confiscated his possessions – which he sold to the Emperor – and took Gradenigo to Rome with him, where, as the result of Venetian pressure, he eventually let him go.[148]

In March 1603, a few months before the resumption of the war between Persia and Turkey, the Venetian Senate again received an envoy from the Shah, Fathi Beg. He brought far costlier gifts with him than did Efet Beg, and was granted a more ceremonial reception – immortalized by G. Caliari as a part of the decoration in the newly constructed *Sale delle quattro porte* in the Palace of the Doge.[149] Not on this occasion either does the envoy seem to have had any other tasks than buying and selling on he Shah's account; there is nothing, neither in a letter from the Shah which Fathi Beg handed over, nor in the account of the conversations that took place in connection with his reception, to suggest that he might have had a political mission. In view of the subsequent political development, however, it is interesting to note that amongst the goods he was commissioned to buy in Venice were weapons.[150]

While Fathi Beg was on his way home war broke out, and part of his goods were confiscated by the Ottoman authorities. When a new agent for the Shah arrived in Venice in 1608 it was an Armenian, and in his letter of recommendation it was emphasized that the roads were closed to people from the Court of the Shah, and that was the reason why he had sent an Armenian from Julfa. The task was the same as for the previous ones, however: to undertake various purchases and sales on behalf of the Shah.[151]

145. BERCHET, *Persia* pp. 192–195.
146. BERCHET, *Nuovi Documenti* pp. 14–16.
147. LUZ p. 589; BERCHET, *Persia* p. 204.
148. PENROSE pp. 174–176.
149. BERCHET, *Persia* p. 47.
150. BERCHET, *Persia* p. 196.
151. *Ibid.* pp. 200–201; BERCHET, *Nuovi Documenti* pp. 17–18.

As will be described later, Abbas sent 50 loads of silk to Europe via Hormuz the same year. In Spain the silk was regarded as a present, but it is highly probable that Abbas took the same view of this consignment as of those he had previously sent with trustworthy people to Venice. The silk was intended to be sold.[152]

In August-September 1609 an Armenian merchant, Hogia Seffer, passed through Aleppo with 50 loads of silk, said to be the property of Abbas. He applied to the Venetian Consul, who received him kindly, advanced him cash and gave him a letter of recommendation to the Venetian authorities.[153] But Hogia Seffer had another task beyond that of selling the 50 loads of silk and the purchase of various commodities on the Shah's account. Some of the goods Fathi had had in his safekeeping at the outbreak of war in 1603 had been rescued by the Venetian consulate in Aleppo; Hogia now wished these goods to be handed over. The Doge remembered nothing of the matter,[154] but it is excellent evidence, not only of the Venetians' sound business principles, but also of the orderliness with which they conducted their affairs that, three weeks afterwards, *Cinque Savi* was able to hand over the goods concerned: various types of hardware, partly of martial character, and eight oil paintings including a "madonna" and a "salvador".[155]

In 1613 two Persian merchants, Sassuar and Alredin, arrived in Venice with 50 loads of silk on Abbas's account. Their journey must be regarded as an expression of the current friendlier relations between Persia and the Ottoman Empire; they had travelled via Constantinople and brought with them a letter of recommendation from the Grand Vizier, at that time the most distinguished representative of the "doves" at the Porte.[156] It was probably this mission, coupled with some Persian merchants' import of silk via Spalato into Venice later on, which in 1614 occasioned *Cinque Savi* and the Senate to discuss the problems of the silk trade together with the possibility of alleviating the conditions under which foreign merchants imported silk.[157]

Sassuar visited Venice again in 1621, once again bringing goods on the Shah's account, but he also had some presents, which he handed over together with a letter of recommendation from the Shah. It was stated herein that he had been sent out not only to confirm the friendly relations but to procure various articles that were "necessary for use in our own Court".[158]

152. See below, p. 269 f.
153. Printed by Favaro pp. 399–401.
154. Berchet, *Persia* p. 206.
155. *Ibid.* pp. 208–209; *Chronicle* p. 192.
156. Hammer iv p. 474.
157. A. d. S., Venezia, Cinque Savi, Nouva Seria 154/19; Berchet, *Nuovi Documenti*, pp. 23–28.
158. Berchet, *Persia* p. 214.

The same Sassuar undertook yet another journey to Europe. In 1624–25, after the resumption of the war against Turkey, and after the two northwest European East India companies had started trading with Persia in earnest, Abbas sent ambassadors to England and the Netherlands; accompanying each of these ambassadors he sent at the same time 50 loads of silk in the safe-keeping of a merchant. To England he sent the above mentioned Sassuar, who was to bring home "commodities and toys" for the proceeds.[159] The silk in his custody amounted to 94 bales, but the prices in London were not quite up to Sassuar's expectations, and at a certain point Sassuar contacted an Armenian who was staying in Venice in order to find out the possibilities of selling the silk there. The Armenian, Simon, contacted *Cinque Savi* and obtained a positive answer: the silk would be welcome.[160] Nothing came out of these plans, however, and the silk was sold to one of the big silk merchants in London, Captain Milward. By order of the Privy Council there was a sheriff present at the weighing in order to safeguard "the King's Peace", with reference to "the violent disposition of these people".[161] Also the Court of the East India Company found that Sassuar was "a little cracked". Whether the confusion surrounding this transaction was due to the Court's pronouncement on the mental condition of the merchant being correct, or whether it was a little difficult for Londoners to understand the Persian way of conducting business discussions, is left open.[162]

The silk consignment that was dispatched in a similar manner to Amsterdam the same year was sold together with the Company's own imports, with the exception of three bales, the sale of which was seen to by the Persian himself. In Amsterdam, too, the sale of the Shah's silk gave rise to discussions, even to the point where the Persian merchant accused *Heeren XVII* of having quoted too low a price in order to make hay with the profits themselves.[163]

At approximately the same time, in 1625 or in the beginning of 1626, official Persian envoys once more arrived in Venice with silk. In a letter from *Cinque Savi* of 26th February 1626 the Consul in Aleppo was instructed to inform the Shah of their safe arrival.[164]

Finally, there is indirect evidence that Abbas had also had merchants in France around that time. In several communications the Persian Ambassador to the Netherlands requested the States General to intervene on behalf of

159. Court Minute 8/4 1626, *Calendar S. P. East Indies* 1625/29 p. 184.
160. A. d. S., Venezia, Cinque Savi, Nuova Seria 4, 22/5 1626.
161. *Calendar S. P. East Indies* 1625/29 pp. 224–226.
162. Court Minutes 8/4 and 19/4 1626, *Calendar S. P. East Indies* 1625/29 pp. 183–184, 187–188.
163. Dunlop pp. 207, 705–706, 711–712.
164. A. d. S. Venezia, Dispacci Console, Soria II.

a Persian merchant, Mahmud Beg Tabresi, who was supposed to have lost 6,000 écus as the result of extortions on the part of the Duke of Guise[165] and when the French Capucine Mission arrived in Isfahan in 1628 the two brothers were lodged in the house of an Armenian merchant, about whom we are informed that they had helped him four years previously when he was in Paris. During his first audience with the Shah Pacifique de Provence reminded him that the Armenians, who had been in Paris three years previously, had taken a message back with them concerning the appointment of a French ambassador to Persia.[166]

Thus we are acquainted with altogether 12 trade missions to Europe on Abbas's account: 8 to Venice, 1 to Spain, 1 to England, 1 to the Netherlands and 1 to France. In each of the five cases in which we have information respecting the quantities of silk concerned, it is a question of approximately 50 loads, a fact which strongly indicates the presence of an established procedure. Unfortunately we have not a single piece of evidence concerning similar trade expeditions to the Levant towns on the Shah's account. Of course we cannot conclude from this that none have taken place, but we may be certain that there would have been traces in the sources if a considerable amount of the Persian silk was exported to the Levant towns on the Shah's account. Before the Companies' establishment of direct trade with Persia the Royal silk trade was neither dominating nor continuous.

We must conclude that the Persian silk monopoly in its origin was fundamentally different from the Portuguese pepper monopoly. The trading activities of the Portuguese Crown were an extension of its tribute levying activity, a case of the tax-gatherer turned merchant in order to maximize his revenue. The information available concerning the Persian silk trade indicates on the other hand that the Royal trade before 1619 must almost be characterized as a Royal peddling trade aimed at the disposal of tribute paid in kind and the purchase of weapons and curiosities, to some extent commodities that might be used for paying soldiers and officials. Additionally there may be yet another point: it is probable that the silk merchants played a role in Abbas's "intelligence service". In several cases there is a chronological coincidence between the dispatching of Persian merchants and Persian ambassadors, even when they were not destined for the same places. The dispatch of Efet Beg coincides with Hussein's embassy; Fathi Beg must have left Persia at approximately the same time as the dispatch of at least four ambassadors to various European courts. Hogia Seffer's expedition coincided with the dispatch of Janghiz Beg and Robert Sherley, and the three Persian representatives even had the pleasure of meeting each other at the Spanish Court. In 1625 Abbas seems to have had both mer-

165. DUNLOP pp. 701–702 and passim.
166. PACIFIQUE de PROVINS pp. 341–342, 365.

chants and ambassadors in the Netherlands and England as well as merchants in Venice and in France.

An intermittant trade, like that conducted by the Shah before 1619, might dislocate the market for a month or a season, but did not modify the market structure; on the contrary, it increased the non-transparency of the market and the tendency to violent price fluctuations. Of greater interest in the present context is the monopolization of the Persian silk trade that began in 1619. A detailed account of the Royal Persian silk trade will be given later,[167] and we shall restrict ourselves here to a discussion of the position of this trade within the market structure.

Unfortunately there are many unknown features in the organization and implications of this trade. There is no doubt that the silk monopoly did not lead to a total diversion of trade from the caravan routes to the route through the Persian Gulf; the import of silk from the Levant to Europe continued throughout the whole of this period, and the caravan route retained its competitive power. From the information available, however, we cannot decide whether the monopoly trade led to increased prices on the Levant markets, or whether the export duty was borne by the Persian producers and/or the export merchants. Closely connected with this problem is the question whether the acquisition of silk by the Persian Crown had the character of tribute levying, or whether it was a question of buying at enforced prices. Finally, we lack reliable information about the stock formation of the Persian Crown; there were considerable stocks left when Abbas died, and it is possible that the silk had been hoarded, had so to speak constituted the Shah's financial reserves. But we cannot decide whether it was the movements of the market, i.e. demand and alternative supply, or whether it was the Shah's need for liquidity that determined the sales and the stock formation.

There are nevertheless some features, which clearly indicate that the adaptation of the Persian Crown to the market was weak, and that even here the behaviour of the redistributive institutions in the market was only to a very limited extent dictated by the desire to be led by or to control the market. As long as Abbas was alive the Royal trade functioned very efficiently on the export side, the quantities desired by the Companies being delivered at the time agreed upon. On the other hand there were clearly difficulties on the import side. The Royal factor contracted for and received considerable consignments of goods from the Companies, which would be extremely difficult to place on the Persian market. There were several reasons for this, the most important of these probably being the fact that it was not possible to "nationalize" a considerable part of the Persian foreign trade from one day to the next without running into extraordinary difficul-

167. See below, p. 377 ff.

ties: nobody could have a clear view of the quantities of various import goods in Persia that were demanded annually. But besides this, the demands of the moment, including not least the corruptibility of the leading Persian officials, but possibly also the Shah's need for instant liquidity, might be a determining factor regarding the acceptance of an import of dubious value on the Persian market.

Neither did the placing of the import on the Persian market demonstrate any utilization of the possibilities the Royal trade possessed by virtue of its quantitively unique position. No attempts can be discerned on the part of the Royal factors to organize a market strategy by virtue of the considerable stocks they had at their disposal; a short term view was taken also as regards sales. Characteristic in this respect was the use of imported goods for paying the soldiers. This ensured an immediately profitable disposal of the stocks, thus solving a possible liquidity problem, but led on the other hand to an immediate fall in prices for the goods concerned to the detriment of the sales af the remaining stocks or later imports.

After the death of Abbas the export monopoly collapsed; it was no longer possible to carry out the restrictions it had been possible to enforce so long as Abbas was alive, and the organizational apparatus that had been built up in order to procure silk fell apart. Once again the Royal agents traded on equal footing with private merchants. Under these conditions it was more advantageous for the Companies to cut down their trade connections with the Crown and take advantage of the competitive conditions on the Persian market by means of the diversification of import and market control. The English Company was the last one to come to this conclusion; the English continued for a long time to view Persian trade as a bilateral business only – English cloth and tin for Persian silk – whereas the Dutch went over to a diversified, largely Asian import specially composed for the Persian market. The Persian reaction to this development is interesting, because it clearly reveals that the Crown trade was determined by fiscal, not by economic motives. The English exemption from paying customs in Gombroon was never questioned, partly because its legal basis – the agreement made before the conquest of Hormuz – was solid, though not invulnerable (the agreements mentioned Hormuz, but not Gombroon), and partly – probably the most important point – because the English, so long as their trade was appreciable, concentrated on doing business with the Royal agents. On the other hand the Dutch exemption from customs in Gombroon came under fire in the 1630s. The legal basis as far as the Dutch Company was concerned was less solid than for the English Company, but of more importance was doubtless the fact that during that period the Dutch trade won its independence from the Royal trade. From 1637–38 the Dutch trade was presented with a clear alternative: either the Company had to buy up the Royal silk in the quantity and at the price offered, or else it had to pay customs in Gombroon on equal footing with other merchants, i.e. 13¹/₂ %. The result was a compromise: the Dutch had to invest part of their proceeds in the Royal silk at a price above the market price, but in return they avoided paying customs in Gombroon. The Persian silk monopoly, which Abbas had tried to create, was thereby reduced to a redemption duty.[168]

In the introduction to this section we raised the question whether the peddling trade was modified by the entrepreneurial activity carried on by the redistributive institutions. The answer to this question must remain negative: the examples investigated provide no reason for assuming that the market conditions described were modified by these activities. The tax-gatherers might enter the market as pedlars on a grand scale, their role might be dominating and continuous, but their behaviour did not modify the market pattern in which they operated. Their attitude was expressed in a supply and price fixing policy that was only affected by the market in so far as their prices could not exceed the price of the closest alternative. On the other hand there was no question of a long term adaptation to the market, no trace of attempts to diversify or co-ordinate the economic activities and only faint traces of speculative stock formation. Because the prices were ultimately determined by external factors, first and foremost the prices of the closest substitutes, the entrepreneurial activity of the redistributive institutions did not lead to any short term stabilization of the prices or increased transparency of the market. On the other hand the maximizing of the tribute on a commodity that was subject to monopoly might in the long run be an advantage to other producers who, in a transition period, would be able to calculate with a protection rent.[169] The market conditions were not affected by the entrepreneurial activity of the redistributive institutions, but these in turn did not exploit the opportunities offered by the market.

Indirectly, however, a certain importance must be attributed to the redistributive institutions regarding the development of new entrepreneurial and market forms. As far as the Portuguese pepper trade is concerned the Crown monopoly formed the basis for international syndicates, which as regards the invested capital, the international communications network and actual market control were among the 16th century's most advanced entrepreneurial groups. The case of the Persian silk monopoly is fundamentally different. The Royal trade was originally intermittent and marginal; in the 1620s it became dominating and continuous under the influence of the Companies, but the Companies on their part would scarcely have been

168. GLAMANN pp. 119–120.
169. Concerning the concept protection rent, see LANE p. 386.

able within such a short space of time to divert a considerable part of the Persian foreign trade if the Persian authorities had not been co-operative. The redistributive enterprises were unable to revolutionize the market conditions, but they were instrumental in creating the quantitative basis for such a revolution.

The Redistributive Enterprises

Although the investigation of the redistributive enterprises in the above has been restricted to a fairly narrow field – the exchange of goods between Asia and Europe – the institutions investigated manifest extremely varied and partly contradictory features.

Of primary interest in the present context, however, is the conclusion that any analysis of long distance trade that ignores the question of protection and its price in favour of the conventional market factors will be incomplete. Protection was a service that was necessary for the maintenance of trade; it was not a free service – protection had its price just as well as a camel.

It may also be considered established that the use of the concept, redistributive enterprise, although paradoxical, is justified. There was normally a greater quantity of protection for sale than the customer required; on the other hand the commodity was not always of the desired quality. Furthermore, at times there was a considerable margin between the production costs of the protection and its price. In so far as the production of protection did not satisfy any social need and the price of protection contained an element of tribute, its producer added nothing to the total satisfaction of demand, but merely carried out a redistribution of the available goods.

The ruler has a commodity, protection, which he sells. He has a territorial monopoly on its output, and can therefore to a large extent omit considering demand when he plans his production and fixes his prices. As far as the international transit trade is concerned, however, it is demonstrable that in this case monopolistic competition is the rule rather than monopoly. The price of protection is limited by the marginal rate of substitution: if the price rises above this level the merchant will seek other routes. This situation is not modified by the direct appearance of the redistributive enterprise in the market; whether the protector appears as tax-gatherer or as merchant there is the same upper limit for the tribute.

Within this general framework there are considerable possibilities of variation, determined first and foremost by the particular ruler's interest in the maintenance of trade. On one end of the scale we can place the isolated robber who totally plunders his victims, and on the other, the

111

zealous and moderate among the Ottoman tax-gatherers or the system of tolls and protection in the Safavid Empire as a whole.

The variable emphasized here, i.e. the permanent interest in the maintenance of trade, is not sufficient, however, even if we take the scant information available regarding possibilities for substitution into account, to explain the differences in behaviour of the three Empires. One would not expect an official appointed for a short period to be greatly interested in the maintenance of trade, but the Empires would in principle always be interested. It can be ascertained nevertheless that an effective control of the local magnates by the central government was only possible in Persia, whereas the short-term interests of the local officials and magnates in *Estado da India,* and in many cases in the Ottoman Empire, took precedence over the long-term interests of the Empire. To this we may add that it is possible, at least as far as *Estado da India* is concerned, to discern a tendency also on the central level to let short-term interests take precedence over the interest in the maintenance of trade, so that the price of protection was forced up to a level that kept the traffic along the caravan routes going and ultimately made it economically attractive to break the Portuguese monopoly of the Ocean route.

This paradoxical behaviour constitutes a problem that is insoluble within the above context. Reluctantly one seizes the traditional way out in maintaining that the politician, unlike the merchant, does not behave rationally. A possible explanation is hinted at above in connection with the mention of the Ottoman Empire, and it will be repeated here in the form of a general hypothesis. Van Klaveren has already demonstrated that, historically speaking, corruption goes hand in hand with a money economy; we can try to adapt this observation, which was derived from a static situation, to a dynamic view with special regard to the 16th century. The effects of the increased amounts of silver circulating in the 16th century has in general been analysed on the assumption that the increased amounts of money appeared in a Europe with an already well-developed market economy. In the first instance attention has primarily been directed at the price level, but particularly in the last few decades a number of historians have drawn attention to the fact that the number of cash transactions and the velocity of the circulation of money are also variables that can be affected by the amount of silver.

Extending the argument in this chapter it will now be possible to maintain that increased economic activity as a result of increased liquidity does not necessarily have to take place within the sector traditionally regarded as dynamic, i.e. the market sector, but can also take place within what is designated as redistributive activity. The money used for bribes, for the purchase of offices, for weapons or the payment of soldiers will naturally reach the market sector sooner or later, so long as it is not hoarded. But on its way it will have had considerable effects on the social and political balance of the society, and under the conditions characterized as constitutional corruption, it can set off a cumulative and ultimately a self-destructive process, because everyone – in order to preserve his status – must surpass his predecessor. This will particularly apply to a society with a poorly developed market economy, where increased liquidity will in the first instance especially benefit the exponents of organized violence, and where the production of protection or redistributive activity is the most important path leading to the acquisition of considerable income and status, and is thereby the most attractive opening for investment.

Chapter III: The Companies

It has been established above that the protection costs played a very great role in the trade between Europe and Asia, partly by virtue of their absolute size and partly because they were unpredictable, thereby having a restrictive effect upon the Asian supply to the Levant markets. The first century following the discovery of the sea route to Asia had not ushered in any changes in this condition. *Estado da India* existed on the strength of the tribute it could levy on this trade over and above or instead of existing redistributive institutions, not by virtue of its own productive activity. Even the pepper trade, which was carried on by the Crown or in the Crown's name, had the character of tribute levying, in so far as the European pepper price was maintained at the level fixed by supplies through the Levant.

Not until the arrival of the Companies does an institutional innovation take place. Simplifying greatly, one might say that here the relationship between "profit" and "power" is reversed. *Estado da India* was a redistributive enterprise, which traded in order itself to obtain the full benefit of its use of violence, whereas the Companies were associations of merchants, which themselves used violence and thereby internalized the protection costs. That the factors were not interchangeable was manifested in the Companies' relation to the market; in their flexible planning they turned out, in contrast to the redistributive enterprises, to be sensitive to the movements of the market at the same time as they sought to control the market by virtue of their quasi-monopolistic position.

The early history of the Companies is well-known, and there is no point in repeating that story in the following pages. It is the intention in this Chapter to elaborate further the above assertion regarding the Companies' character of institutional innovation, partly by a discussion of the Companies' relation to the State authorities in their country of origin and their own view of the relationship between power and profit, and partly by an account of the Companies' relation to the market.

The East India Company and the English Crown

The East India Company was an association of merchants, not a "department of State". Formally, State control of the Company was excluded by Charter, which without reservation established the Company members' right by means of an annual election to choose the Governor and the 24 members of the Court of Committees according to the principle, one man one vote, and by simple majority. The Company's independence was furthermore secured by its right to decide for itself upon future membership.[1]

This naturally did not exclude the possibility of the Company being made a tool in the service of the Crown by means of pressure exerted on the Court of Committees or by infiltration among its members or employees. Already on 3rd October 1600, during the preparations for the Company's first voyage and before the granting of the Charter, the Court of the Company dealt with a request from Lord Treasurer Brockhurst, in which he recommended a gentleman with privateering experience, Sir Edward Michelbourne, as "principall commaunder". The reaction of the Committees was bluntly negative and couched in phrases that established most precisely the merchants' assessment of the risk attached to indulgence towards the Court: ". . . which motion this assemblie have noe lykin of for that they purpose not to imploy anie gent in eny place of charge or commaundement in the said viage for that besides ther owne mislike of the imployment of suche they knowe the generalyty will not indure to hear of such a motion . . . therfore this assembly do intreat mr. Garway to move his Lordship to be pleased noe further to urge the imployment of this gent to the Companie, and to Geave them leave to sort ther business with men of ther owne qualety . . ."[2]

The firm attitude of the Court of Committees at this early stage was symptomatic of the group that took the initiative in setting up the Company,[3] but also anticipated a policy that was maintained throughout the whole of the 17th and most of the 18th centuries. The Company not only emphasized its formal independence of the English Crown, but also avoided indirect political infiltration through the right of patronage.[4]

1. The Charter printed *First Letter Book* pp. 163–189. The Company's form resembled in many respects that of the Regulated Companies, but it was from the very first a capital association. It is thus incorrect when Meilink-Roelofsz asserts that the English merchants traded individually in Asia during the first years, MEILINK-ROELOFSZ p. 192.
2. Court Minute 3/10 1600, STEVENS p. 28.
3. There were no noblemen nor members of the gentry among "the founding members", and the only nobleman admitted to the Company before 1609 was the Earl of Cumberland, who received a share in the first Separate Voyage as part payment for his ship, the *Mare Scourge*, STEVENS p. 45. Not until 1609 do the nobility or the gentry appear in any great numbers among the Company's members. CHAUDHURI p. 35 ff.
4. The only exceptions to the rule were the Ambassadorial posts; of the two Royal Ambassadors dispatched to Asia during the period we are concerned with, one, Sir Thomas Roe, clearly managed to win the confidence of the Court of Committees, whereas, when Dodmore Cotton was appointed to Persia in 1626, the Court took care to ensure that his commission expressly forbade him to interfere in the Company's business transactions. See below, 363.

After 1609 some members of the nobility and the gentry were admitted to the Company; a certain tension between the passive gentlemen shareholders and the active merchant shareholders may be discerned at any rate from 1620,[5] but the aristocratic wing did not bring any great official influence with it. It was doubtless this same attitude that in 1624 determined the Court's polite but firm refusal of James I's offer to become a member of the Company.[6]

It is also obvious that the East India Company did not follow the official English foreign policy with regard to the European rivals, the Portuguese and the Dutch. Without regard to the details of James I's and Charles I's foreign policy the Company, from its foundation right until the Goa agreement of 1635, was in a state of undeclared war with *Estado da India* and thereby with the Spanish-Portuguese Empire. Neither were the frequent clashes with the Dutch East India Company and the open war from 1618 to 1620 in accordance with the official English foreign policy. From the very first the Company's policy was dictated by its own, not by England's place in the international system.

Although it may thus be denied that the Company was created and functioned in extension of English State interests, it is nevertheless possible that the Company's political freedom of movement was restricted by the English Crown. Formally, the Charter created such restrictions; it established explicitly that the Company's trading rights did not include places under a friendly prince who refused the English entry.[7] The seemingly clearly worded restriction contained an insoluble dilemma, in that *Estado da India*, as we know, claimed sovereignty over Asian waters, a claim which on the part of Spain-Portugal was regarded as valid in international law, but which was rejected by the English. An observance of the English interpretation of the concept, i.e. places in the possession of a foreign prince, was therefore, as was already well-known to the English, no guarantee against armed clashes with *Estado da India*. For practical reasons there was no question of an infringement of the English interpretation of the situation according to international law; in contrast to what was the case in Spanish America, local interests in the Portuguese possessions in Asia were for a long time opposed to trade connections with the North-West Europeans. When the Spanish-Portuguese claim to sovereignty over the seas was infringed, the English Government chose to condone the Company's armed defence of the right to free navigation to places under the rule of a third power.

The English Crown's acceptance of the Company's freedom of action

5. CHAUDHURI pp. 56 ff.
6. CHAUDHURI p. 31.
7. *First Letter Book* pp. 174, 188; CLARK pp. 29–30.

underwent a hard test when the defence was extended to include the English-Persian conquest of Hormuz in 1622, at a time when one of the most cherished aims of English foreign policy was the creation of a Spanish-English *entente*. That the Crown's sanctions against the Company were as moderate as was actually the case – substantial, but not crushing shares of the presumed booty to the King and the Lord Admiral – appears significant.[8] The outcome of this case raises the question of the Crown's freedom of action in relation to the Company rather than that of the Company's freedom of action in relation to the Crown.

For the fact that the Company cannot be regarded as a foreign political instrument in the hands of the English Crown immediately raises the additional question as to whether the Crown then managed the Company's foreign policy or was restricted in its freedom of action out of regard for the Company's interests. The Company's urge for independence did not go so far that it might not desire the support of the Crown in a critical situation. Shortly after the so-called Amboyna massacre became known in Europe, the Company beseeched James I "to apply the strength of his favour in severing the two companies that cannot hold together, and in righting this company by the power of his arm ..."[9] – in other words the Company asked the Crown to manage the protection problem.

In later times it became commonplace to see the English Government protect English business interests in far-off regions, but the English East India Company could not expect any help from James I or Charles I; the Company's interests had a low priority in the foreign policy of the first Stuarts, as illustrated by the Crown's treatment of the relations with the Dutch Company. It is known that the Dutch East India Company, the VOC, laid claim to a number of territorial monopolies in the spice-producing areas already in the first decade of the 17th century. There was no question of formal Dutch possessions – in that event it would obviously have come under the restrictions in the Company's Charter mentioned above – but of areas where the Dutch Company had achieved the more or less voluntary acceptance of monopoly contracts by the local princes in connection with the fight against the Portuguese. The English Company demanded free trading rights – ironically enough, with reference to the Netherlands' own Grotius – and both in 1613 and in 1615 attempts were made to solve the conflict by means of negotiations conducted with the co-operation of the States General and James I. The negotiations were unsuccessful in settling the conflict, however, at any rate not before it had had disastrous consequences for the English in Asia. In

8. CHAUDHURI p. 64, cf. James I's well-known retort: "Did I deliver you from the complaint of the Spaniard, and do you return me nothing?" *Calendar S. P. East Indies* 1622/24 p. 125: "Minutes touching the business of Ormus."
9. Court Minute 28/7 1624, *Calendar S. P. East Indies* 1622/24 p. 335.

1618 the negotiations were resumed. The Netherlands now abstained from what had been their chief aim during the previous negotiations – a total merger of the two Companies – and aimed instead at collaboration for defence purposes within a framework that continued to secure the Dutch Company's strategic superiority. The negotiations, which took place in London, dragged on, but although a postponement of the decision was clearly to the Netherlands' advantage within the given balance of power, James I does not seem at any time to have attempted to exert pressure on the Dutch delegation or on the States General. His most active contribution was "a kind message" to the Dutch plenipotentiaries at a time when they threatened to break off the negotiations.[10]

When the negotiations finally reached a deadlock with regard to the important question concerning the control of fortresses and forts (article 24 of the Treaty) James offered his good offices, declaring that "their association being a matter that so nearly and highly concerns the weal of both countries, his Majesty will neither spare any travail to effect it, nor be in any thing more partial to either side than if they were both his own subjects."[11] The offer was accepted both by the Dutch plenipotentiaries and by the English Company, the King's decision following shortly afterwards: a confirmation of the formula proposed by the Dutch plenipotentiaries.[12]

It is difficult to see what can have moved James I to set aside the interests of his own subjects in this manner. The thought of bribery, if not of the King, then of his entourage, cannot be excluded,[13] but the possibility that James I really felt convinced he was thus serving the cause of peace and the best interests of his people cannot be excluded either. One thing is clear: the East India Company itself was unable to dictate terms to James I in respect of what it wanted done in the Company's interests. The decision obviously did not satisfy the Company; at the General Court shortly afterwards there was considerable unrest among the ordinary members, and the King felt obliged to send a personal message through Lord Digby: "that upon complaint of my Lords, His Majesty's Commissioners and the rest of the English commissioners, that they found too great advantage against them in this treaty with the Dutch, they being

10. Sir Gerard Herbert to Carleton 16/3 1619, *op. cit.* 1617/21 p. 261.
11. Viscount Doncaster to Carleton 12/5 1619, *ibid.* p. 273.
12. The crucial point was the garrisonning and command of the fortresses in those areas where the Companies had reached agreement about a quota arrangement. The Dutch point of view: that *status quo* was to be maintained so far as the command of the fortresses was concerned, whereas the expenses were to be shared proportional to the trade, was clearly against the interests of the English, since at the conclusion of the negotiations they only commanded one fort in the Moluccas, the well known fort of Pulorun.
13. *Calendar S. P. East Indies* 1617/21 pp. XVI–XVII.

some of them the States themselves, who are interested in the action, have the best furtherance and assistance of the States General, who make it a matter of state, and therefore stand so earnestly in defence thereof, authorizing and maintaining whatsoever have been done by them; and the English that oppose them are but private merchants, and too unequal a match (in that respect) to contend against them. Whereunto his Majesty's gracious answer was, that he esteems the East India Company a great ornament and strength unto his kingdoms, whom he hath and will maintain, wishing them to proceed comfortably in their trade, which only increaseth when all other trades decay; and doubteth not to procure them in some convenient time their own desires in the Indies, which, if the Dutch should deny, that quarrel should be no longer the Company's but of the State; and if the Dutch hold not good correspondency with his subjects beyond the line, he will not hold any with them here, willing the Lords of his Majesty's Council to take knowledge of his resolution, and to cause an act of Council to be entered to make it appear to be his act, . . ."[14]

Digby's message is worth quoting at this length because it not only aptly establishes the difference between the relations of the English and the Dutch Companies to the respective States but voices a Royal manifesto, which, if it had been put into practice, would have speeded up the development of the English foreign policy by a generation. But the disputes in the East Indies did not become "a matter of state", neither under James I nor under his son. A few years later the Amboyna massacre presented an opportunity of putting the Royal promise to the test. Although massacre is probably a rather strong word for the occurrences in Amboyna in 1623 there is no doubt that the English Crown had a *prima facie* case against the Dutch for a breach of the Defence Treaty of 1619. But the Royal reaction to the Company's and the public's demand for retribution, manifested by the demand for the arrest of the outward-bound Dutch East India fleet, appeared particularly weak and to be playing for time. The report of the Amboyna massacre reached Europe in May 1624; in September of the same year the King ordered the arrest of the outward-bound Dutch ships, but the order was not executed, on the pretext that there were only two serviceable English men-of-war in the Channel, whereas the Dutch totalled 7–8 ships.[15] But there is scarcely any doubt that the real explanation was that the general foreign political interests took precedence over those of the Company. At the end of 1623 it was

14. General Court Minute 2/7 1619, *ibid.* pp. XV–XVI.
15. Court Minute 24/11 1624, *Calendar S. P. East Indies* 1622/24 pp. 449–450. The attitude of the English Crown in this situation is so much the more remarkable, since Carleton had reported from the Hague on 15/11 that for once the States General did not support VOC in this matter, Carleton to Conway 15/11 1624, *ibid.* p. 443.

obvious that the Spanish matrimonial negotiations had broken down and that the Spanish *entente* had been abandoned. Buckingham was fully occupied with the reorientation of the English foreign policy, and an English-Dutch *rapprochement* was confirmed with the defensive alliance of June 1624. After the death of James I the relations between England and the Netherlands became even more cordial. In the Southampton Treaty of September 1625 the English King promised to let the matter rest for 18 months; this would give the Dutch time to find a suitable compensation for the damages inflicted. This they did not, however, and after the time-limit had expired, in September 1627, three Dutch East Indian ships sheltering in Portsmouth were arrested.[16] At first the arrest aroused great enthusiasm in the East India Company, but there is no reason to believe it brought the members any material advantages. On the contrary there are signs that Charles I himself benefited from the episode. A memorandum from Josias de Vosberghen and a letter to him from Charles I gives the impression that the release of the ships was not gratis for the Dutch Company, but that it was the King himself who pocketed the proceeds.[17]

Its relations with the Dutch Company was so decidedly the English Company's most pressing political problem in this period, that any argument derived therefrom must be regarded as conclusive. The East India Company's influence on English foreign policy under the first Stuarts was no greater than the Crown's influence on the Company's policy.

What is the significance of this statement? From its very foundation the East India Company was organized as a Sovereign Power in Asia on a par with *Estado da India* and VOC. But when compared with the other two European institutions the East India Company was unique in that it operated independently of existing political institutions, took its place in the international system under the management of its Court of merchants and preserved restricted economic goals. The East India Company played its part in international politics independent of reason of state in the traditional sense and with what, sociologically speaking, was an atypical body of supreme decision-makers.

The East India Company in the International System

An institution of this nature was unique within the international system. It was independent of the State's immediate interests – territorial defence and expansion – because, with the exception of the short-lived occupation

16. CHAUDHURI pp. 66–69.
17. Memorandum, Josias de Vosberghen to Coke, undated; Charles I to Vosberghen 2/5 1628, *Calendar S. P. East Indies* 1625/29 pp. 493–494.

of Pulorun, there was no question of territorial occupations within the period with which we are concerned.

Instead there was another immediate interest: the preservation and increase of the Company's capital. The Company was established and maintained with an eye to the profits. Decreased profits and thereby decreased payment of dividends would not only constitute an immediate economic loss to the shareholders and the members of the Court, but would also put the very existence of the Company at stake. Under the system of separate and short-term capital issues that was general during the first half of the 17th century the Company would only be able to carry on if the economic results proved satisfactory to the shareholders.

However, it does not necessarily follow from this that the Company should have concentrated on trade and desisted from the use of force as an income-creating activity. Even piracy might be undertaken as a business on a joint stock basis. The Company possessed physical means of power, which in itself could bring in revenue, just as was the case with *Estado da India*. Whether the Company's profits were to be derived from tribute levying or as a mercantile profit had to depend on a conscious choice on the part of the Company's management.

The Company's official policy as far as the use of the annual fleets is concerned is expressed in the commissions and instructions issued to the Commanders. In these documents the regulations regarding the Commanders' employment of the armed force that was placed at their disposal were laid down, both in respect of the English authorities and of their employers and the providers of these arms: the shareholders. As concerned the first separate voyage the matter was simple. It embarked in 1601, while England was still at war with Spain, and the expedition was equipped with a conventional letter of marque directed against the subjects of the Spanish King, of which good use was made, incidentally.[18] When the second separate voyage set out in 1604 the situation had already changed. In the meantime peace had been made with Spain, and the English King's commission to the leader of the expedition, Henry Middleton, now contained a distinct ban on the use of armed force, except in the case of self-defence: "unlesse you shall first by them theareunto iustlie be provoked or driven in the iust defence of your owne persons your shipps vessels goodes or merchandizes as you will Aunsweare to the Contrarie at your

---

18. The letter of marque printed in *First Letter Book* pp. 191–195. When the question of the distribution of the prize money was raised before departure, the Court observed: "ther is noe intension to make anie attempte for reprisalls but onlie to pursue the voyage in a merchauntlike course." Stevens p. 118.

uttermost perills."[19] The Company Court had nothing to add to this; Middleton's instructions did not intimate that he might need his guns.[20]

In the Royal commission for the Commander of the third separate voyage[21] the wording had been purposely altered. To the above permission to use arms in self-defence the following was added: ". . . or for recompense or recovery of any the persons, goodes or merchandizes, of any our subjects that are alreadie in or neare the East Indies as you will Aunsweare . . . etc". The alteration was important because the East India Company was thereby authorized to undertake privateering in time of peace, in so far as it could document attack against or loss of English subjects or property on the way to or from Asia or in Asia itself – very wide limits. In practice this wording recognized the Company's independent foreign policy, and it was repeated in the commissions issued to the following years' commanders and in the patent of 1615, which allowed the Company, without further permission of the King, to furnish its commanders with the authority as regards jurisdiction, self-defence and retribution that previously was allotted them in the Royal commissions.[22]

Attention must hereafter be drawn to the way in which the Company interpreted its authority. This problem first presented itself in the case of the instructions for the third separate voyage in 1607: the journey in which the Commander's authority was extended by virtue of the Royal commission to include retribution. It was pointed out herein that Sir Edward Michelbourne's expedition[23] possibly had resulted in the confiscation of the Company's ships or goods. If this should be the case the Commander was ordered first of all to seek compensation with the local King or the local officials. Only if this did not give any result was the following course recommended: "Then our will is, that you use the benefitt of our Kinges ma^ties commission given you in that behalfe.[24] This formula was repeated in the instructions for the fourth and fifth separate voyages, but after that it was left out. The question was not touched upon in the following years' instructions and it first appears again in the standard commission, which was elaborated after the rights to issue commissions to the Commanders independently was taken over by the Com-

19. *First Letter Book* pp. 50–51.
20. *Ibid.* pp. 51–56.
21. *Ibid.* p. 113.
22. *Ibid.* p. 473.
23. Sir Edward Michelbourne, who had in vain sought an appointment in the Company (see above, p. 115), obtained James I's permission in 1604 to undertake an expedition to Asia, disregarding the Company's Charter. He returned home in the summer of 1606, and the Company's Court obtained the impression – scarcely incorrectly – that he had financed his voyage by means of piracy.
24. *First Letter Book* p. 135.

pany in 1615. The wording used here was the one that had been used in the Royal commissions ever since 1607.[25]

Unfortunately the Company instructions are not preserved from any voyage later than the eighth separate voyage, so that we are unable to pursue the problem any further along this route. The limited material available is unambiguous, however. The Company regarded itself as legally authorized to undertake privateering to the extent that could be justified by past attacks, but did not intend to make this right its economic basis. In contrast to *Estado da India* the Company did not seek tribute, but commercial profit.

This attitude may be illustrated by many pronouncements made in situations that seem to exclude hypocrisy. Possibly the most explicit is the letter written by the English factor, George Cokayne, to the Governor of the Company, Sir Thomas Smith, after a visit to the Moluccas: "They [the Dutch] have not enough to do with the Spaniardes and Portingales, but they will make wars with all inhabitants where they come, which ere long they will not find profit but much sorrow and grief, for that their actions are without reason or honesty, and all countries where they come doth hate them, but what fear compels them unto. The trade that comes by compulsion is not profitable; and if it pleases God your Honours continue as you have begun you will have good and happy success in all your trading in these parts, holding peace and friendship with the inhabitants of all countries; for enemies, Portingales and Spayniardes is sufficient ... They [the Dutch] have many castles with much trouble and little profit."[26] As a source of information concerning the Dutch policy in general, and in the Moluccas in particular, Cokayne's letter is naturally greatly biassed, but there is reason to pin on his unsentimental deprecation of power politics. He did not think it would pay.

Negatively the attitude of the East India Company is revealed in the almost total lack of appeal to national glory in the Company's papers and in the relevant pamphlet literature, in contrast with other contemporary English joint stock companies such as the Virginia Company.[27] Also indicative are the Company's deliberations concerning the rejection of the Dutch offer in 1615 of a fusion of the two Companies. It was stated that the Dutch were to all appearances primarily interested in obtaining English support in covering the expenses they were incurring during the war against the Spaniards and the Portuguese in Asia. But it was the Court's opinion that the war was superfluous from a business point of view. Patience and tolerance were needed in order to ensure that the

25. *Ibid.* p. 495.
26. *Letters Received* III p. 146. Cf. Roe p. 303.
27. Rabb pp. 39–40.

Spaniards abandoned their position in the Moluccas; fighting only aroused the Spaniards' pride and made them fight on in order to preserve what they otherwise would have resigned voluntarily: "The English Company would be well satisfied that the Hollanders should surcease from all war there and leave the English to the trial of their fortunes, being confident that in time they will eat the Spaniard out of that trade only by underselling him in all parts of Christendom."[28]

But the decisive criterion of the Company's intentions must nevertheless be the particular course chosen in cases where a choice between tribute and profit existed. Thus the attitude towards the mastery of the caravan route outlets on the Red Sea and the Persian Gulf was important in this respect. As shown above the control of these routes in all probability formed the basis of Estado da India, at least towards the end of the 16th century. From the English victory over the Portuguese fleet outside Surat in 1612 to the opening of trade with North-West India and Persia by the Dutch in the beginning of the 1620s, the control of both the classic routes lay within reach of the English Company. But the opportunity was not exploited. On the contrary, the commercial attitude of the Company was reflected in the halfhearted attempts at blockade.

From 1607 the outgoing English fleets were instructed to call at Mocha on the way to India, hoping that by virtue of the then friendly relations between England and the Ottoman Empire it would turn out possible to trade there. It was emphasized in the instructions that trade was the aim, and that factors and captains should ensure that no cause was given for conflicts with the local population or the local authorities, even if they should be on guard against ambush.[29] Attempts to open peaceful trade were not at first successful, however, the English being regarded with the greatest suspicion. There could be no question of establishing a permanent factory, and the sixth separate voyage spent the monsoon of 1610–11 in fruitless negotiations.

The sixth separate voyage was on the whole unlucky, and the attempts made in 1611 to open trade with Surat and Dabhol also proved to be in vain. Especial hopes had been pinned on this voyage in England; its flagship, the Trade's Increase, was the biggest merchant vessel ever launched in England, but two years after embarkation the ships were lying idle off the coast of India, both cargo and ships were damaged by the many months at sea and still nothing had been accomplished in the way of procuring profits for the shareholders. The situation must have been extremely depressing for the leaders of the voyage, and in a very personal letter,

28. Court Minute 18/8 1615, Calendar S. P. East Indies 1513/1616 p. 424.
29. Instructions for the fourth Separate Voyage, First Letter Book pp. 248–50; for the sixth Separate Voyage, ibid. pp. 334–335.

which begins with the sorrowful words: "Environed with swarms of perplexed thoughts by present view or likelihood of the ruin or overthrow of this our journey begun with glory ..." the next-in-command, Nicholas Downton, summed up the events of the voyage in order to justify a plan he had conceived against the three nations who had hindered the success of the voyage: the Turks, the Portuguese and the Surat merchants. The losses suffered on the voyage up to date he estimated at £30,000, and what according to Downton made the losses still more serious was that the holds of the ships were still filled with European goods like kersey, cloth and tin, which under no circumstances could be sold in other places in Asia than India or the Red Sea. Downton's plan was that the fleet should now return to the Red Sea, where it would obtain compensation for the losses by forcing a barter trade on the enemy ships. In this way the Turks, too, would be hit, since they would lose the income from customs. By carrying out the action as a barter deal it would be possible to get rid of the worthless goods and at the same time to maintain the illusion of a regular trade.[30]

Downton's plan was accepted in the General's Council, and in March 1612 the ships once more set course for the Red Sea. On the way they met the fleet of the eighth separate voyage under Saris, which, furnished with a pass from Constantinople procured by the Company from the English Ambassador,[31] had called at Mocha. The pass had not been able to change the hostile attitude of the Turkish officials, however, and so the two fleets joined forces and, from April to August 1612, they carried out a blockade of the entrance to the Red Sea. Ships from Surat and from what were regarded as Portuguese-dominated harbours, were seized and forced to exchange their goods for the English ones at a price laid down by the English. The prices that had been current in Surat at the beginning of the year were followed, though with an additional 10–20% for freight from India to the Red Sea.[32]

Although the sixth separate voyage had suffered great losses in the first years of the voyage,[33] and despite the fact that the flagship never returned home to England, the voyage brought the shareholders a dividend of 121²/₃ %.[34] There is scarcely any doubt that this profit primarily originated from the barter trade in the Red Sea. When the action became known in England the Levant Company protested on seeing the good relations with Turkey endangered. The Court of the East India Company denied that anything had been committed against "the law of God or

30. *Letters Received* I pp. 155–161.
31. Pass printed in Purchas iii pp. 383–385.
32. Saris's journal in Purchas iii, p. 398.
33. Downton's journal, *ibid.* p. 291.
34. Scott ii p. 124.

nations",[35] but in order to settle the matter it instructed the Governor of the Company, Sir Thomas Smith, to reach a compromise with the Governor of the Levant Company without too much publicity. The two gentlemen agreed upon a compensation of £900.[36] To those responsible for the action the Court of the Company did not seem to have raised any objections; the Commander, Sir Henry Middleton, died on the voyage, but the next-in-command, Downton, was appointed leader of several subsequent voyages.

In the given circumstances the Court condoned the aggressive behaviour, but the interesting thing about the episode, and that which makes it relevant in this connection, is its isolation. Technically speaking, the English were able in these years to effect a blockade of the Red Sea, which the Portuguese had never been able to do, or they could have taken over the role as tax-gatherer, but the Company did not utilize this technical possibility and maintained its mercantile goal. As will be shown later, it was the same attitude that came to light in connection with the conquest of Hormuz and the utilization of this conquest. It was a custom house the English conquered, but neither on a local level nor on the part of the Court of Committees were there any serious attempts to dispute the right of the Persian King to exercise the sovereign rights that followed from the conquest – first and foremost the collection of customs – or to make use of the maritime superiority to blockade or monopolize the trade on the Persian Gulf.

The difference between the East India Company's and *Estado da India*'s conception of the economic basis of the institutions is of fundamental interest. They represent essentially different structures, whose clash makes the breach of continuity in the European expansion at the beginning of the 17th century more than a takeover of one nation from another.

The United East India Company and the Dutch Republic

The organizational form of the Dutch United East India Company, the VOC, has been the object of interest for a number of prominent historians. None the less there is far from being any clarity or agreement concerning the problem dealt with here: the relations between the Company and the domestic political authorities.

---

35. Court Minute 16/7 1614, *Calendar S. P. East Indies* 1513/1616 p. 306.
36. This was not a bad bargain. In October 1613 the Levant Company instructed the Ambassador in Constantinople to employ bribery with discrimination in order to avoid any unpleasantnesses. Pindar paid out altogether £ 1,800 in this matter. P. R. O. London, S. P. 105/110, ff. 75, 78.

It is unnecessary here to summarize the shrewd contributions to the extensive debate about the origin of limited liability and the early forms of the joint stock companies.[37] The debate had for a long time the character of a formal juridical argument and, what perhaps appears even more strange today, it was characterized by attempts to place the Dutch United East India Company (VOC) in a lineal evolutionary model, the end result of which was the modern limited company and the anonymous share capital. The first to abandon this line of approach was Mansvelt, who was interested in function, not origin.[38] One might add, however, that van Brakel had in many respects anticipated Mansvelt's results, and that there is often only a very small shade of difference between Mansvelt's and van Brakel's concept of the *voorcompagnieën* and VOC.

The *voorcompagnieën* must be regarded as true capital associations, divested of political interests, and probably the first organizations of that kind in the European expansion in Asia. There is no evidence of their having aimed at anything other than making a profit on the capital invested, and the commanders of the fleets were instructed to avoid any encounter, let alone a clash, with the Portuguese ships.[39] The *voorcompagnieën* were not incorporated, but were run by a number of *bewindhebbers*, who were joined together like partners in a simple company, i.e. traded on joint account. At the same time the *bewindhebbers* were factors to the stockholders who invested money in the Company through the individual *bewindhebber*. Thus between the Company and the stockholder there was no direct relationship; the stockholder was represented in every respect by his factor, the *bewindhebber*. On the other hand the stockholder's investment and responsibility were limited: before the voyage began, by his contract with the *bewindhebber*, and after embarkation, by common sea law.[40] The stockholder had no influence as regards the running of the business; his guarantee that the capital was administered in accordance with his interests was the *bewindhebber*'s credit and good repute and the fact that, after the voyage was wound up, he was free to place his capital elsewhere.

In the Charter of 1602, by which the *voorcompagnieën* became united in VOC, many of the formal characteristics from the earlier capital associations continued. Nevertheless VOC cannot be regarded as a further development of the *voorcompagnieën;* what took place in 1602 was not an evolution, but a metamorphosis. There were two considerations that precipitated the merger, the most important for the *bewindhebbers* being the

37. Surveys of the debate in MANSVELT pp. 17–19 and van DILLEN pp. 21–22.
38. MANSVELT p. 37.
39. van BRAKEL p. 18.
40. MANSVELT pp. 33–45; van BRAKEL pp. 93–120.

realization that cooperation would be more advantageous than continued competition between the *voorcompagnieën*. The opening up of the direct trade between the Netherlands and South-East Asia provided an innovation premium, which, if the unrestricted competition continued, would benefit the Asian sellers and the European buyers, but not the Dutch middlemen. To this, political considerations were added; referring to the experience of the Dutch – and perhaps even more so, the English – during the war with Spain, it was easy to see the trade with East India as an instrument that might be used in the fight against Spain-Portugal.[41] Oldenbarnevelt's achievement was to combine these two interests in the monopoly company; the negotiating parties were the States General and the *bewind-hebbers* of the *voorcompagnieën*, the Charter being an expression of the state of accord and compromise between the two interested parties. In 1602 the Dutch East Indian trade departed from its hitherto line of development towards capitalist organizationalist forms, VOC from the very first being closely attached to the political authorities at home.[42]

It was the form of the *voorcompagnie*, with modifications, that continued in VOC. Mansvelt maintains[43] that the merger was entirely without legal consequences for the stockholders, their liability continuing to be limited by sea law. On the other hand he finds it significant that the Charter unquestionably places the *bewindhebbers* on equal footing with the stockholders as regards liability. Van Dillen points out two more features, which he considers more important from the point of view of the stockholder: the capital was invested directly in the Company, not through a

---

41. van BRAKEL pp. 18–20. Although MASSELMANN will see a defensive feature in the association, it is very badly supported by the quotation from Oldenbarnevelt he himself produces in support of the statement: "The great East India Company, with four years of hard work, public and private, I have helped establish in order to inflict damage on the Spaniards and Portuguese." MASSELMANN p. 150 n. 12.

42. Thus also GLAMANN p. 7. Much of the lack of clarity in the older accounts of VOC seems to originate from the difficulty in accepting what from a laissez faire point of view must be a retrogression. This appears clearly in HECK-SCHER I p. 336; he finds the character of the Company "difficult to explain", because he completely ignores the mixture of political and economic interests represented by the Charter. He touches upon the possibility that the Company's peculiar constitution might have something to do with the war against Spain, but sees the final explanation in the lack of medieval models for capital associations of a corporate nature in the Netherlands. Cf. also RIEMERSMA pp. 32, 36–37, who equates a priori the State and use of force on the one hand and merchants and entrepreneurial activity on the other; but the significance of the Charter is hereby concealed. Riemersma even finds that the stockholders' lack of influence was a reflection of the fact that the Company "was more an association of capitals than an association of persons."

43. MANSVELT p. 50.

bewindhebber, and the capital association, unlike the *voorcompagnieën*, was not limited to a voyage, but to a number of years.[44]

But if we wish to know how the establishment of VOC effected Dutch foreign policy in Asia there is one very important feature: the effect of the monopoly the Charter allotted the Company together with the maintenance of the *voorcompagnieën*'s rules regarding the influence of the stockholders. As mentioned, the stockholders had no influence on the management of the business so long as the *bewindhebber* abided by his contract; the stockholder's guarantee that his interests were being looked after lay in the contractual freedom and in the fact that every voyage was a separate venture. The subscription of a new capital was, so to speak, an election of a new management. In VOC the powerlessness of the stockholders and the omnipotence of the *bewindhebbers* was maintained, but the stockholder's guarantee disappeared with the introduction of the monopoly and – as it later transpired – the permanence of the capital. In relation to VOC the stockholder was like the owner of a government bond: he could dispose of his claim at whatever price he could obtain, but he could no more influence the Company's policy than the owner of the bond can influence the State's policy.

Thus after 1602 the ultimate authority did not lie with the stockholders, but with the *bewindhebbers* and their joint committee, the *Heeren XVII*. The *bewindhebbers* were no longer responsible to the stockholders; on the contrary, rules of election ensured a considerable degree of integration between the *bewindhebbers* and the Dutch oligarchy. In the first instance the *bewindhebbers* were the managers of existing *voorcompagnieën*, but in the event of any future vacancies every Chamber had to submit on its own behalf three names, from among which the burgomasters of the towns where the Chambers lay might make their choice.[45] Scarcely very many could foresee the consequences of the Charter; at any rate capital was subscribed in VOC without any difficulty. But before the renewal of the Charter in 1623 the *bewindhebbers* suffered an extremely sharp attack on the part of the stockholders. A number of pamphlets were issued demanding that the accounts be made public, the democratization of the electoral rules, etc. The *Heeren XVII* defended themselves by referring to reason of state: concern for the security of the Republic demanded secrecy and an

44. van DILLEN pp. 26–27. As is well-known, no winding up of the capital as presupposed in the Charter took place; the share capital remained the same throughout the whole of the Company's life-time, excepting that in 1691 it was rounded off to 6,440,200 fl., KLERK de REUS pp. 176–178.

45. These election rules were not incorporated in the Charter, which conferred the ultimate right of appointment on the Provinces, but already in 1602 the States General resolved that the right of appointment, if requested, might be transferred to the burgomasters. KLERK de REUS p. 26.

oligarchical management. The authorities of the Republic came to the aid of the Company in this dispute. The States General declared the most critical of the pamphlets to be treasonable and promised a reward to whosoever could disclose the anonymous author. The Estates of Holland issued a prohibition against receiving complaints against the Court of Directors in court;[46] without this support, which was contributed both by Oldenbarnevelt and by Maurice, Prince of Orange, the *bewindhebbers* could scarcely have survived the storm, declares Mansvelt.[47] The protests of the stockholders were suppressed by the coalition between the *bewindhebbers* and the political leaders in the Netherlands; the new Charter of 1623 contained only admittances of a formal nature.[48]

Against this background it is clear that a discussion of the relation between the foreign policies of the Dutch Republic and of VOC cannot reach the same unequivocal result as in the case of the East India Company. After a few years there was no longer any clear division between the interests of the *Heeren XVII* and those of the Dutch oligarchy. But it is interesting to note that clauses were incorporated in the Charter, which, in the event of a conflict concerning Asian policy, would have given the States General the formal authority. The *Heeren XVII* could install governors and commanders, but those appointed were bound by oath to the States General as far as political affairs were concerned. That the intention was to make sure that the States General was able to control the Company's policy appears from the attitude of the States General at the appointment of the first Governor General, Pieter Both, in 1609. In the resolution concerned the States General speaks of "those lands, fortresses and settlements we and ours possess in India", and in the formal oath taken by Both it is emphasized that the States General was his true superior and that his only duty towards the *Heeren XVII* was to take care of the trade and the proper conduct of business. Although the *Heeren XVII* drew up Both's instructions, they were submitted to the States General for approval. The same applied to Reijnst's (1613) and Coen's (1617) instructions. But before the issue of Brouwer's instructions in 1632 and, what is even more important, before the issue of the general instructions in 1650, the situation had changed: both these instructions were issued without the participation of the States General.[49] To the view expressed by the States General in 1609, the *Heeren XVII's* oft quoted words of 1644 are in clear contrast: "The places and strongholds which they have

---

46. LANNOY & van der LINDEN II pp. 166–168.
47. MANSVELT p. 85.
48. van BRAKEL p. 134.
49. KLERK de REUS pp. 81–82; Mac LEOD p. 100; *Plakaatboek* I, pp. 3–22, 23, 28–52, 263–276, II, pp. 135–157.

captured in the East Indies should not be regarded as national conquests but as the property of private merchants, who were entitled to sell these places to whomsoever they wished, even if it was to the King of Spain or to some other enemy of the United Provinces".[50]

No one will take this development as indicating that the Netherlands had undergone political disintegration in the meantime; on the contrary, this gradual transition from control to negligence on the part of the Government authorities most likely implies that the integration between the Dutch oligarchy and the Court of Directors had in the meantime been carried out. Control on the formal level was superfluous; the Company had become a part of the ordinary political system of the Republic. There were so many bonds uniting the Company and the Regents that the Company could no longer be regarded as a sovereign concern, but had more in common with *Estado da India* than with the East India Company.

It must be emphasized, however, that this merger of the Company's and the Republic's interests did not lead to a state of unambiguous subordination on the part of the Company. That the relations with the States General could be antagonistic appears from the Company's reaction to the English-Dutch reparations agreement concluded on 23rd January 1623, at a time when the political leaders of the Republic were extremely interested in maintaining good relations with James I. The Dutch delegates agreed to reparations amounting to 290,000 fl. and at the same time distributed gifts in England to a value of 100,000 fl. The *Heeren XVII*, who had to pay, and who at the same time had been presented with a bill for 200,000 fl. from the Admiralties, (and were negotiating about the renewal of the Charter), felt themselves unfairly treated. The States General backed the negotiations up, but admitted that "in some cases one had had to exceed what was right and reasonable for the Company for reasons of state." To this the *Heeren XVII* retorted, that if this was the case, one ought to investigate how much the Company had paid in order to obtain its rights, and how much the country should forfeit for reasons of state. But the *Heeren XVII* had to give in.[51]

Power and Profit in the Policy of the United East India Company

As a result of the Dutch Company's relations with the political authorities in the Netherlands it is impossible to carry out the same clear-cut analysis of its policy, as based on the Company's own interests and resulting from

50. Boxer, *Empire* p. 46.
51. Mac Leod I pp. 280–281.

decisions made by a well-defined circle of decision-makers in accordance with a clearly defined policy, as was the case with the English Company. The policy it followed must necessarily reflect many different interests, some of them conflicting. Moreover both the instructions and the actual policy followed manifest such inconsistencies as to necessitate a detailed analysis of every single decision.

There can be no doubt, however, that the merger of the East India Companies in 1602 immediately resulted in a change of policy as regards aims and means. Whereas the admirals of the *voorcompagnieën* were instructed to avoid armed conflict, van der Hagen's instructions of 1603, the first to be drawn up by the *Heeren XVII*, has been characterized as "definitely offensive and militant".[52] Both this fleet and the following one under Matelief were instructed to undertake a military cruise before seeking a return cargo for the ships.[53] We do not know the details connected with this alteration in policy, but there is no doubt that those circles, who, in the establishment of the United Company, had seen the creation of an instrument of power for use in the fight against Spain-Portugal immediately took the initiative.[54]

The reversal is illustrated by an interesting protest, which five merchants with interests in the *voorcompagnieën* registered with a notary in 1608.[55] They referred to the dispatch of fleets under the old Amsterdam Company, which, according to the information they supplied, were equipped with goods, money and merchants "with explicit orders, injunctions and instructions for trading like honest merchants, as is their wont. And the fleets or ships mentioned were not equipped with soldiers or warriors for attacking the Spanish King's towns, fortresses or troops or for seizing carracks or other Portuguese or Spanish ships or goods ..." In addition the protest states that at the departure of the fleet in 1601 pressure was exerted on the Company on the part of the Amsterdam burgomasters to order the ships to attack the Portuguese in the Moluccas, but that the *bewindhebbers* had rejected the request for the following reason: "They had on their own initiative as merchants established the Company solely for the purpose of doing honest business and trading in peace and not from hostility or maliciousness, and that many of the stockholders had invested their money under these conditions and rather would withdraw from the Company than agree to such a thing." Those protesting conclude

52. van BRAKEL p. 21; *Opkomst* III, 28–29, 146–47.
53. Mac LEOD pp. 19, 59.
54. This, in contrast to LANNOY & van der LINDEN II pp. 54 ff., and 331, where it is asserted that the commercial aims were maintained until 1609, and to MEILINK-ROELOFSZ, *Aspects* p. 70, in which a continuity is postulated from the *voorcompagnieën* to the General Instructions of 1650.
55. printed in van DILLEN pp. 98–99; cf. GLAMANN pp. 7–8.

by saying that they now wished to break with the Company "since the conditions are now changed, and decisions are now being made concerning hostility and the use of force on account of the merger with the various other Chambers and the Charter issued thereafter . . ."

The difference in attitude, not only when compared with the *voorcompagnieën*, but also when compared with the English Company, also appears in the notes that were exchanged by the English and the Dutch during the negotiations concerning a merger of the two Companies in 1613 and in 1615. The Dutch aimed at a union of the two Companies, in fact an extension of the setting up of VOC in 1602, whereas the English only desired the right to free trade with the Moluccas, also within the areas where the Dutch maintained that they had acquired contractual rights of monopoly. In reality there was no question of a compromise between the two attitudes, which was also manifested in the years following the conclusion of the Defence Treaty of 1619.[56] The lack of agreement was not a question of degree, but of an either/or. The parties could agree about the legal and opportune nature of defending themselves against the attack of a third party and in procuring compensation for losses incurred as the result of a Spanish-Portuguese attack, but the English Company would not commit itself to a systematic campaign against the Spanish Crown. The Dutch view went a stage further, and is clearly expressed in the memorandum the Dutch delegates handed the English on 6th April 1615: "Or, ceste defence se doit faire non pas par le bouclier seul, mais auusi par l'espée. Il ne se defend pas bien, qui ne faict estat de se defendre. On ne peut mettre en seureté ses amis sans faire peur à son ennemy, et sans luy oster les moyens de mal faire."[57]

The drastic effects of this policy on the Banda Islands and the Moluccas is well-known. During the first half of the 17th century the Dutch East India Company gradually gained control of the islands producing the fine spices: cloves, nutmeg and mace. The legal formalities were always in order: the Company more often acted as protectors than attackers, but the result was as complete a subordination of the economy of the spice-producing areas as was technically possible. One may therefore raise the question as to whether the Dutch East India Company ought not to be considered a redistributive enterprise using organized violence with a view to the acquisition of income.

That a part of the Company's income was contained within this defini-

---

56. CLARK probably contains the most balanced account of the English-Dutch conflict and the attempt to overcome the friction by means of the Defence Treaty of 1619. In HUNTER and Mac LEOD the problem is seen from the English and the Dutch angle respectively.
57. EYSINGA p. 223.

tion there cannot be any doubt, particularly as regards the relations with the Banda Islands and the Moluccas, where the hostility between the Dutch and the Portuguese led to an unmitigated policy of force and extortion with regard to the local population on the part of the Dutch. But the Dutch Company's policy was not unambiguous; it is known that the *Heeren XVII*, despite the fact that they accepted and supported Coen's policy based on conquest, were not wholeheartedly behind it, and the same hesitation appears in their relations with Persia. When the *bewindhebbers* in Amsterdam in 1625 heard reports that their agent in Persia, Visnich, should have received Hormuz from the Shah and had promised in return to protect the coasts of the Persian Gulf, they were anything but enthusiastic. In an express letter to Visnich they expressed their profound hope that the rumour might turn out to be incorrect – which it was – and that he would keep away from affairs of state and solely concern himself with the business with which he was entrusted. If the rumour should happen to be true, Visnich was ordered as diplomatically as possible to withdraw from his commitment; only if he had already taken possession of the fortress was he to keep it and defend it, but with as little cost as possible, "and with the least possible neglect of and inconvenience to our trade and without undertaking unnecessary or expensive cruises that might cause us harm."[58]

It is conspicuous that it was frequently the Governor General and his Council, "the supreme government" in Batavia, who went in for an active policy as regards the Asian powers, whereas the *Heeren XVII* held back. This clash of interests appears very clearly in connection with the conflict about customs and the export of the Persian silk in the years following 1638. Already in December 1643 the Governor General hinted that it might be necessary to make a show of force,[59] but the final decision was not taken until the following year. Justifying their decision to the *Heeren XVII*, the Government in Batavia added up all the injustices they thought the Dutch Company had been subjected to in Persia. The details are less important in this context; briefly, it concerned a demand on the part of Persia that the Company either invested the proceeds of its sales in Persia in the Royal silk or paid customs in Gombroon on equal footing with other merchants. The Dutch appreciated that the trade with the King was the necessary condition for acquiring exemption from customs, but it disputed the right of the King to fix his own prices completely arbitrarily. That this view was correct according to the agreements is more than doubtful, but it was not the legal side of the affair that interested the Governor

58. *Bewindhebbers*, Amsterdam, to Visnich, Isfahan, 24/4 1625, DUNLOP pp. 157–159.
59. *Generale Missiven* II p. 203.

General and his Council. The conclusion – that the policy they intended to put into operation as regards Persia – pointed at far more than a mere show of force in order to protect the contractual or legal rights. Batavia had decided "to offer resistance in order to bring the Persian to a better knowledge and understanding, so that we can obtain free trade everywhere in Persia without being bothered and without having to pay customs." Free trade under guns. This was what a later day has termed "the imperialism of free trade". But Batavia aimed still higher: "We must organize conditions in the Persian Gulf so that we no longer need to reside under Moorish rule, but can rest in our own and demand customs ..."[60] With such an aim the Supreme Government had boxed the compass from trade to trade under its own protection, and from trade under its own protection to tribute-levying on the trade of others.

The *Heeren XVII* opposed these plans, however. They reprimanded the Governor General and the Council in Batavia severely for taking such important decisions as the discontinuation of an important factory and declaring war on a great Asian power on their own initiative. The Company's affairs were not so mysterious that an order could not be given in the Netherlands without its meeting a lot of opposition before being put into operation in Asia. The Governor General and his Council gave no less sharp a reply. If they were to comply with the orders from home in detail on every occasion it would have important consequences for the Company. They were not small children in Batavia. If things had to be arranged in that way the Company did not need such a costly General and Council in Asia; the work could quite well be performed by lesser men.[61]

The clash left its traces in the Company's general instructions of 1650. It was asserted herein that the good relations with Persia should be maintained, and at the same time the Court of Directors dissociated itself from an active imperialist policy: "Company trade over the whole of the Indies (must) be based on the common right of all peoples [i.e. international law] consisting in freedom of commerce, the which being granted in neutral places by free nations where we find laws and do not have to bring them, we may not appropriate the aforesaid trade according to our own ideas and constrain such nations thereto by force, just as the Company could not consider it that other nations would desire to prescribe law for the way of trading in places under its territory ..."[62] With this quotation van Leur illustrated the Company's still comparatively weak

60. *ibid.* pp. 248–249.
61. *ibid.* p. 378.
62. quoted from van LEUR p. 243; in van DAM II³ p. 295 the same passage appears in connection with the discussion of conditions in Persia. The expression used here, "het gemene regt der volckeren" really ought to be translated by "international law", not as in van LEUR by "the common right of all peoples".

position in Asia at the middle of the 17th century. But it may illustrate to an even greater extent a different matter: the disparity between the wish for stability characterizing the policy of the *Heeren XVII* and the Batavia Government's wish for a more active policy with regard to the Asian powers. After his return to the Netherlands in 1655 van Goens handed in a report to the *Heeren XVII,* which undoubtedly must be regarded as veiled criticism of the general instructions of 1650. The picture of the state of the trade he paints herein is deplorable, but he found it most sorrowful of all that the Company's Christian wish to live in peace and friendship with the Asian Princes should be so cruelly misused. The Asian Princes knew that the Batavia government was ordered to show moderation, and they made use of that knowledge "such that matters sooner or later must be decided by war, since most Asian people are not inclined by nature to do good by the love of virtue, but they can easily be prevented from doing something bad by fear of punishment."[63]

However, statements of this nature cannot give us a clear answer to the question raised above as to whether the Dutch Company deserved to be called a redistributive enterprise; the moderation indicated could always be put down to the Company's appreciation of its own limited resources. We have a better clue to the problem in the Company's view of profit and loss as the ultimate measure of success or failure. As far as *Estado da India* is concerned it is emphasized above that this institution cannot entirely have been regarded as an economic enterprise. The Empire may certainly have been regarded as a profitable asset, but it was atomized in a number of separate enterprises in continuation of the ordinary activity of the Crown, analogous with the viewpoints on which the administration of any other possession was based at that time. The question as to whether it would ultimately give any profit was simply not raised.

We are now straightaway able to point out a difference between *Estado da India* and the Dutch Company in the fact that, despite the integration between the Court of Directors and the political authorities of the Republic, and despite the at times very extensive co-operation as regards ships, etc., between the Admiralties and the Company, there was never at any time a question of confusing the Company's and the Republic's separate economies. The *Heeren XVII* did not, like the *feitor* in *Casa da India,* risk the returns being pawned or sold before they were docked.

The Company remained economically defined, even if its aims following the merger were ambiguous. Strangely enough it was precisely this ambiguity, that rendered one of the most important stages in the early history of the Company easier to accomplish: the accumulation of reserves in the form of a capital that was permanently circulating in Asia. The

63. van GOENS pp. 177–178.

voorcompagnieën had stuck to the principle of the winding up of the capital at the end of each voyage, even if, like the English separate voyages, they had soon discovered that assets had often in practice to be transferred from one voyage to the next. The United Company's Charter professed the same view of the capital, but the *bewindhebbers* did not follow this principle in practice, and were furthermore very reticent with regard to the payment of dividends throughout a number of years. The capital was never liquidated; a dividend was paid for the first time in 1611, a total of 200% being paid out up to and including 1622.[64] It was not a staggering profit for those days, scarcely any more than the stockholders would have achieved by lending their money on good security in the Netherlands. Moreover, there were times during the first twenty years of the Company's history in which the picture had appeared still bleaker. Both the stockholders' protests and the Republic's support of the *bewindhebbers* shows that the conservative dividend policy was tied up on both sides with the political role of the Company: the partners felt that they had been cheated into financing a war and not a business, whereas the States General on its part went very far in its support of the *bewindhebbers'* policy.

The important factor, however, is that the merging of the Republic's and the stockholders' interests that took place at the union of the Companies in 1602 as a consequence of the pressure of the Republic, made possible a conservative dividend policy as well as the accumulation of reserves in Asia, but it did not on the other hand alter the Company's fundamental nature of a business. The yardstick of success was not victory or conquest, but the financial results.

To wish to build such a wide generalization upon balance-sheets of which only isolated fragments remain and which have often been characterized as primitive may appear daring. However, the same appears here as elsewhere: in order to understand the innovatory character of the Companies it is irrelevant to compare them with fully developed capital associations of a later age. What is interesting is a comparison with older or contemporary institutions. The imperfections in the accounts are easy enough to demonstrate, but to criticize the Company for not having made use of modern bookkeeping methods is scarcely more relevant than to criticize it for not having made use of steamships. They never attained to a central bookkeeping permitting a general survey of the state of the Company's affairs, but the time factor, at any rate in the early days of

---

64. Not until 1625 did the payments of dividends become somewhat regular; from then on there were very few years in which the stockholders received as little as 12$^{1}/_{2}$ % of the nominal value of their shares. KLERK de REUS pp. 179–180, Beilage VI; van DILLEN p. 31 n. 1.

the Company, made such centralization impossible,[65] – the accounts would only be of historical interest by the time all the material had been collected and revised. A distinction between running costs and investment would only have provided the *bewindhebbers* with some hypothetical figures the actual significance of which only time could show. How was one to enter into the books a defeat inflicted on the Portuguese, a map of difficult waters acquired on an otherwise unsuccessful voyage or bribes used for making sure of a preferential business agreement?

Mansvelt's survey of the accounts was used by van Leur in support of his view that "the Company as a commercial enterprise represented an old-fashioned, extremely conservative type."[66] There is no doubt, however, that this conception must be revised in the light of Glamann's results. The Court of Directors attentively observed the gross profit on every single commodity and kept a close eye on the profitability of every single factory.[67] In addition, despite the fact that they did not achieve a fully centralized bookkeeping, the Dutch took a big step in that direction when they assembled all the Asian activities in the annual balance-sheets from Batavia. The accounting system initiated by Hans de Hase and Coen in 1613–14 was kept up for 194 years. It might certainly have been improved during this time, but in the "heroic age" of the Company it provided a clear answer to the questions the *bewindhebbers* asked, and its structure contained within it the nucleus of the idea of a permanent circulating capital in Asia. It is important to emphasize that the balance-sheets from Batavia[68] partly referred to a given time, partly to the whole of the Asian business activity from the moment bookkeeping was initiated. Batavia's relation to *Patria*, the factory *Nederland*, was that of a factor obliged to give an account of the means entrusted him. On the debit side he enters the *reëlle effecten* (the stocks, cash-in-hand and good debts), the buildings, etc., as well as the expenses he has incurred on the principal's account since the accounts were opened. On the credit side he enters the *winsten*, i.e. the profit from the sales of commodities and, in the case of Batavia, also from any transaction between the factories themselves, from prizes captured from the enemy and eventually certain customs duties. Transfers between the factor and his principal are registered under the heading *reëlle effecten*. A comparison between the two sides will show the factor's credit or debt to his principal. If the stocks plus the cumulated expenses

---

65. GLAMANN p. 247.
66. van LEUR p. 233; cf. GLAMANN p. 251.
67. GLAMANN pp. 258–261.
68. The establishment of the accounting system: Coen to *Heeren XVII* 10/11 1614, *Coen* I p. 54; Batavia balances 1623, 1626 and 1632 in DUNLOP pp. 772–781; 1627: KLERK de REUS Beilage XI, summarized and analysed by GLAMANN pp. 245–247.

exceed the receipts the difference must have been financed by the principal. If on the other hand the cumulated income exceeds the stocks and the expenses it means that the factor has returned more than he has received and the surplus belongs on the debit side.

The cumulation of the items: expenses and income, *ongelden* and *winsten*, replaced to some extent the distinction between the capital expenses and the running costs. The fact that all expenses, which cannot be entered as stocks or fixtures, are entered under "ongelden" does not imply that every investment was immediately written off – on the contrary. Cumulation, which was also employed in respect of the relations between each separate factory and Batavia, made it possible to ascertain at a single glance what it had cost to open up and carry on trade throughout a number of years as well as the profit and loss of the factory. With the help of the balance sheets the factory could be placed in a wider context (or Batavia in relation to Patria), and it could be determined whether the factory had received more than it had delivered or vice versa. Comparisons between the balance-sheets over several years would reveal fluctuations in the factory's profitability.[69]

The isolation of the item *reëlle effecten* reflects the tendency of the merchant to focus on liquidity. Interesting, however, is the fact that in time this item changed character from being the surplus that could be called in at short notice when the factor's accounts had to be terminated into being "the Indian capital": the goods or money that were permanently circulating between the Asian factories and were not returned. This change of viewpoint may be detected in Coen's correspondence. In nearly every one of his letters home Coen pleaded for an increase in the Indian capital, whereas the *Heeren XVII* were only with difficulty able to divest themselves of the idea of the stocks as something on their way home. Already when drawing up the first balance-sheet in 1614 Coen remarked that still another 700,000 piastres might be needed for building up the Asian trade, whereas according to his estimate 1.2 million piastres annually was needed to finance the purchase of the returns.[70] The distinction between a permanently circulating capital and the capital needed for the annual returns must have appeared confusing in the Netherlands, because as late as in January 1618 he protests against a misinformed criticism of this proposal, which has been regarded at home as an order of 1.9 million piastres per annum. What he meant, he says, was that there had already for several years, as it appears

69. For an account of profit and loss for the individual factories, see "Confrontatie van de generale ongelden tegen de generale winst, incompsten tollen ende prinsen op den vyandt van tijt tot tijt op d'ondergeschreven plaetsen in Indiën gedaen, 1st January 1625–7th January 1626" DUNLOP pp. 776–778; cf. Brouwer et al. to *Heeren XVII* 15/12 1633, *Generale Missiven* I p. 426.
70. Coen to *Heeren XVII*, 10/11 1614, *Coen* I p. 95.

from the books, been a constant circulation of between 2.5 and 3.5 million fl. between the Asian factories. The purpose of his proposal had merely been to increase this circulating capital to 4.5 million fl.[71]

If one did not know *Estado da India*'s and the English East India Company's attitude towards permanent investments there would be nothing surprising about the sum he was aiming at. Coen himself compared it with alleged Spanish-Portuguese investments in Asian trade of 500 tons of gold or 50 million fl.,[72] a comparison that has been taken by several historians as a measure of the Company's relative insignificance in the time of Coen.[73] But it was naturally a piece of propaganda on the part of Coen staged precisely in order to stimulate the *Heeren XVII* to make an increase in the circulating capital. We have no possibility of judging the extent of the Spanish-Portuguese private investments in Asian trade, but we can with certainty maintain that the only centrally controlled capital, the pepper money, did not exceed 200.000 piastres, and that this capital was not meant to circulate in Asia, but was to be returned immediately. As far as the East India Company was concerned the maintenance of the temporary capital associations throughout the first half of the 17th century excluded in principle every establishment of a permanent circulating capital. In practice this principle was modified at the moment trade was opened up between the factories themselves, but in the English material there are only faint traces of a distinction between capitals issued with returns in mind and a permanent circulating capital, and no traces of any conscious endeavour to build up a permanent circulating capital.

In the Dutch Company Coen's policy was victorious. The scattered details about the balances in the general missives are dangerous to compare, because their interpretation presupposes knowledge of the most recent returns or of the most recent receipts from *Patria*, but the increase in the item, *reëlle effecten* throughout the 1620s and the 30s is unmistakable.[74] Around 1630 the point was reached when the income in Asia regularly exceeded the expenses, so that the returns to *Patria* exceeded the funds sent out

71. Coen to *Heeren XVII*, 10/1 1618, *Coen* I p. 316 f.
72. Coen to *Heeren XVII*, 21/1 1622, *Coen* I p. 700.
73. van LEUR p. 229; MEILINK-ROELOFSZ pp. 182–183. Surprisingly the latter estimates a ton of gold as equal to 10,000 fl., not 100,000 fl.; since the same error of conversion appears in connection with Coen's evaluation of the Dutch capital in Asia, it does not affect Meilink-Roelofsz's estimate of the relative strength of the two nations, but it undeniably results in a somewhat distorted picture of the Dutch East India Company's absolute size. It was a large jump from 290,000 fl. to 2.9 million fl.
74. 1614: *Coen* I p. 54; 1618: *ibid.* p. 318; 1620: *ibid.* p. 663; 1622: *ibid.* pp. 699–700; 1623: *ibid.* p. 802, cf. DUNLOP p. 772; 1626: DUNLOP p. 774; 1627: KLERK de REUS Beilage XI; 1632: DUNLOP p. 780; 1633: *Generale Missiven* I pp. 426–427; 1636: *ibid.* pp. 580–582; 1637: *ibid.* pp. 653–655.

at the same time as the building up of the Asian reserves continued. In January 1636 Batavia could praise itself that the income throughout three years had exceeded the expenses by more than 3 million fl., of which 2 million were used for the purchase of returns, whereas 1 million was added to reëlle effecten, these thereby having been brought up from 4.6 to 5.6 million fl.[75] In 1636 the earnings in Asia were 1.8 million fl.[76] and in December 1637 the year's net profit was estimated at 2.3 million fl. In connection with the last mentioned statement reëlle effecten were estimated at 9.2 million fl., minus the cargo of some return ships in the process of being cleared.[77]

The Dutch East India Company was not a "pure" type: it contained features in its constitution, in its structure and its policy, more reminiscent of a redistributive enterprise than of a business. But for the final understanding of the Company's ability to win over its antagonists the testimony of the balance-sheets is important. As regards the details and the individual transactions it will often be difficult to demonstrate the difference between the Portuguese and the Dutch policy. The difference is manifested in the comprehensive view and in the maintenance of a quantitive measure of success and failure. The Dutch never forgot to take their economic pulse, no matter how high feelings might run.

The Companies and the Market

It is the intention in the following to discuss the Companies' market policy and the market's reaction to this policy. A discussion of this problem has been considerably lightened by the existence of Glamann's and Chauduri's basic works on the Dutch and the English Companies, respectively, and the answer to the question raised here will already be known to those readers who are familiar with these two works. Glamann's exposure of the myth about the Dutch East India Company as a monopoly without history is important in this connection. The flexibility and vitality that characterize the Company, at any rate as far as the 17th century is concerned, reflects a conscious interaction between institution and market, which is in clear contrast to the entrepreneurial activity of the redistributive institutions as it comes to light in the Portuguese pepper trade, for instance.

The key words are flexibility and planning. Quite fundamental in this connection is naturally the connection between price development and orders placed. But the Companies' adaptation to and attempts to stabilize

75. Brouwer et al. to Heeren XVII 4/1 1636, Generale Missiven I p. 550.
76. van Diemen et al. to Heeren XVII, 28/12 1626, ibid. p. 582.
77. van Diemen et al. to Heeren XVII, 9/12 1637, ibid. p. 652 ff.

the market went much further than an automatic raising and lowering of the orders according to the fluctuations of the European demand. Through a number of measures they sought to influence price development not only in order to maximize their immediate income, but also in order to reduce price fluctuations and thereby the non-transparency of the market. One of the ways of controlling the market was by the accumulation of stocks. In its simplest form it might be a question of the short-term postponement of sales in the hope that reticence might provide better prices: "The governor then gives notice that the Court of Sales put off on account of the fall of the price of pepper in Holland, which has now risen again, will be held next Friday."[78] This was the kind of decision a merchant was always having to take – bull or bear? If there was anything new in the situation it was the fact that the decision here had been taken for the whole of the English pepper trade and for a good proportion of the European pepper trade by one enterprise, instead of by a number of individual entrepreneurs. But stock formation could be much more extensive and stretched over a longer period. In 1625 the Dutch Company had a stock of 3.85 million ponds of pepper, which was cautiously sold together with the new arrivals over the following years.[79] A still more striking example of market control by means of stock formation is the Dutch Company's reaction to a fall in the price of cloves in 1623. As the result of English competition in the years following the Defence Treaty of 1619 the market price had fallen to a level that lay below the dividend price, which had already been fixed as low as 3 fl. per pond. In the three following years the Dutch Company refrained from selling or distributing pepper. Since the Company was at the same time practically the sole importer of cloves into Europe during these years following the Amboyna massacre it succeeded in forcing the prices up to the double: in October 1626 a price of 5.10 fl. per pond was achieved by contract sale and in August of the following year the contract price was up to 6 fl. per pond. Since in 1628 the prices showed a tendency to decrease again, the Company initiated an interesting form of cartel, in that it drew up an agreement concerning minimum prices with the previous clove contractors who still had considerable stocks. Apparently it succeeded by those means in maintaining the price at 5.40 fl. per pond in the following years.[80]

Stock formation could be utilized to maximize profits over a short term, as the previous examples have shown, but there are also examples of price fixing having been used as a means of increasing the Company's control of the market over a long term. The further development of the clove

78. *Court Minutes* 1635/39 p. 223.
79. GLAMANN pp. 77–78.
80. *Ibid.* pp. 94–95, cf. p. 37.

142

trade is a good illustration of this. The high prices at the end of the 1620s encouraged the competitors, first and foremost the English, to break through the attempted Dutch blockade of the Moluccas: In 1633 London was supplied with more than 150,000 lb. cloves from Asia, for instance. Faced with this threat to the Dutch control of the clove trade, in 1635 the *Heeren XVII* reverted to a policy of lower prices, at the same time as the use of cloves in dividend payments was resumed. The effects were immediate: in 1635 the price of cloves fell from 5.40 to 3.28 fl. per pond and the same year the price fall was felt in London. The Dutch dumping turned out to be effective, in so far as the English Company in 1638 instructed the factory in Masulipatam to decrease investments in Macassar because the Dutch Company had fixed the clove prices at such a low level. On the other hand the circumvention of the Dutch attempt at blockade had clearly demonstrated that there was a ceiling for the economic monopoly price, a demonstration that was not lost upon the Dutch. Despite the still more effective control of the clove-producing areas throughout the rest of the 17th century it was only seldom that the Dutch clove prices rose to the level that had been reached in the years around 1630.[81]

On the whole, the Companies, though naturally pleased with good prices, were not interested in excessive prices: "They created unstable marketing conditions and, as it were, invited the competitors to start a new buying offensive".[82] Characteristic of this attitude is the *Heeren XVII's* reaction towards the rapidly increasing pepper prices at the end of the 1630s. Instead of trying to make the best of the existing stocks, the Dutch Court of Directors tried to offset the price increases by putting its stocks on sale at fixed prices, at the same time as the pepper orders were greatly increased.[83]

The Companies were able to control the market not only by fixing the prices and planning the supplies, but also by their chosen method of sale. There were four possibilities: dividend payment in kind, sale in small lots at fixed prices, sale by auction and contract sale. In practice dividend in kind meant that the Company desisted from market control: the one seller, the Company, was replaced by many – the Company's members. Accordingly the use of dividend payments in the form of cloves by the VOC was for a number of years part of a low price policy; on the other hand there was scarcely anything planned about the dividend payment in pepper in 1603 in connection with the first separate voyage of the English Company,

81. GLAMANN pp. 95–96; CHAUDHURI p. 171. At the same time the factories in Asia were called upon to reduce the clove prices in order to increase the sales and deprive the competitors of the wish to deal in these commodities. *Bewindhebbers*, Amsterdam, to Gov. Gen., Batavia, 21/4 1635, DUNLOP p. 539; Brouwer et al. to *Heeren XVII*, 4/1 1636, *Generale Missiven* I p. 524.
82. GLAMANN pp. 73–74.
83. *Ibid.* pp. 78–80.

which was followed by an immediate price slump. This episode should rather be taken as an expression of lack of experience on being faced with the new situation, which, as emphasized by Chauduri, demanded the establishment of a re-export system alien to traditional English foreign trade.[84] The price fall in 1603 was long remembered; 20 years afterwards it was said at a General Court: "To divide upon stocks to sell in England will destroie the Trade of Calicoes as had happened to the Co. in the beginning of the Trade into thindies when a dividend was made of pepper to sell here which bredd such confusion in the Trade as some of the underwriters had of that pepper in their handes 6 or 7 years after."[85] And a few weeks later it was said in a similar context, "that this would breed distraction in the Co. and so bringe downe the value of that commoditie that it would be worth nothing as was instanced in pepper brought home by Sir James Lancaster which was divided upon stock to be sold in town at 2 s. per lb. but every man striving to put off his pepper it came by that meanes to 14 d per lb."[86] But as the discussion in 1623 shows, the Company did not forget this lesson. It still continued dividend payments in kind – for pepper this was the normal sales method until 1627 – but the re-export of the dividend payment was favoured, since a distinction was made when fixing the price of the pepper that was taken out with regard to the Home market as opposed to the pepper that was taken out with a view to export.[87] In certain cases the stockholders were even forbidden to sell their dividend payment themselves or through a middleman on the home market – it was to be exported.[88]

Dividend payment in kind had its strong supporters among those stockholders who were themselves active merchants, and who regarded their share in the Companies as a part of their own working capital; for them liquidity was more important than the ultimate gain, or rather, they could make sure of a greater ultimate profit by taking over the marketing themselves. But in opposition to this group were the other shareholders: partly the growing circle of passive investors who wanted their dividend in the form of cash, and partly the influential circle of stockholders who, amongst other things, dominated the Court of Committees, and who preferred to see the Company's imports disposed of in big lots by contract sales or by public auction. In the Dutch Company dividend payment in kind remained an exception directed by the marketing policy of the *Heeren XVII* as a whole, as in the case of the cloves mentioned above, whereas the structure

84. CHAUDHURI pp. 5, 141–143.
85. General Court, 29/8 1623, C. R. O., London, Court Books, vol. 6, f. 93.
86. Court Minute 8/10 1623. C. R. O., London, Court Books vol. 6 f. 165.
87. CHAUDHURI p. 155 ff.
88. This applied to the dividends in cotton cloth in 1623. General Court 17/10 1623, C. R. O., London, Court Books vol. 6 ff. 191–193.

of the English Company allowed the stockholders far greater influence. The East India Company's standing orders stated, however: "The Custome which hath beene used heretofore in selling the Wares of this Company at a generall Court, and the remnants of small value in the Warehouses by the light of a candle, (i.e. by auction) shall be continued; onely in some cases excepted, where the Governour, Deputy, and Committees shall conceive it needfull to take some other course for the good of the Company."[89] It is not necessary to be a lawyer to see that this ruling allowed considerable possibilities of interpretation, and that in reality the sales policy lay in the hands of the Court of Directors, even though they must stand responsible for the chosen policy at the frequent General Courts and the annual Court of election. This is the background of the detailed and often acrimonious discussions about sales procedure characterizing the General Courts, expecially in the 1620s. But the tendency, despite the marked discrepancies, is unmistakable; presumably the Dutch Company's price leadership was the only factor which, throughout so many years, counteracted a price fall resulting from the distribution of the pepper among so many hands with the dividend payments. From 1627 contract sales, also of pepper, remained the rule in the English Company.[90]

With other sales procedures the Company managements preserved far greater control of supplies and prices. The sale of small lots at fixed prices naturally involved the risk that the commodity would be divided up among many hands and that the price might be driven down during a panic, but faced with this risk the Company safeguarded itself to a certain extent by guaranteeing to maintain the prices for a given period, which, if there were ample stocks available, would naturally have a price-levelling effect.[91] But sale in bulk consignments, either after secret negotiations between a syndicate of buyers and the Directors or following public auction, was undoubtedly the form of sales preferred by the managements. Contract sale was the characteristic form of marketing in the Dutch Company until 1642;[92] in England sale by auction was more frequent, because the English Company's Court had to take heed of the shareholders' distrust of secrecy, but this did not prevent the sales, as in the Netherlands, being accompanied by guarantees on the Company's part against sale within an agreed period, a stilstand.[93] Both parties had something to gain from these agreements

89. *Lawes and Standing Orders* p. 59.
90. CHAUDHURI p. 151.
91. Court Minute 5/4 1622 and 26/6 1622, C. R. O., London, Court Books, vol. 5 f. 386, 462.
92. GLAMANN p. 33.
93. This applied, for example, to the sale of the East India Company's indigo import in 1618 and 1619, Court Minute 25/2 1618 and 4/5 1619, C. R. O., London, Court Books, vol. 4, f. 130, 344.

in restraint of trade. The Companies were safeguarded against the panic-like rise and fall in prices that might easily result if a commodity was distributed among many hands; the contractors on their part acquired for a time a corner in the commodity concerned. They were running a risk, because supply and demand on the European market was not predictable, but, by virtue of their quasi-monopoly, they had a considerable chance of profit.

The previous pages do not do justice to the wealth of details and the conflict of interests covered by the Company's marketing policy, but they will be sufficient to show that in their relations to the market the Companies represented an innovation as opposed to traditionel entrepreneurial forms. The investment policy was planned in accordance with the fluctuations of the market, but the latter were also controlled by means of an investment and marketing policy. By reducing or increasing orders, by building up stocks, by price fixation and in the chosen method of sales the companies were able to influence the European market, and they used this power, not for an immediate maximization of the profits, but as an integral part of their long-range policy. It must not be thought that this flexible planning or planned flexibility was immediately felt with each of the Companies' fields of activity – intentions were often very far removed from reality. The important thing here is the innovation as compared with older entrepreneurial forms, not their clumsiness as compared with the corporations of the 19th and 20th centuries.

A number of circumstances prevented the coincidence of intentions and reality. First of all it must be stressed that the competition of the peddling market was not succeeded by monopolization, but by monopolistic competition and oligopoly. Under exceptional circumstances a Company might control the total European stocks of a given commodity at a given moment, but as the Dutch clove trade illustrates, they were well aware that this was not the same as controlling supplies to Europe over a longer period of time. Thus every business decision, without regard to the immediate market situation, must take into account the competitors' reactions as well as the present or potential subsitutes.[94] But normally in the period under review the market situation was a case of oligopoly under Dutch price leadership.

To this was added a fundamental, if banal, factor: the technical difficulties connected with the collection of data and the realization of the Companies' aims. The factors scarcely ever complied to the letter with the instructions that were sent out from Europe. Shipwreck or surprise deals on the part of competitors could throw the prognoses overboard as far as the European supply was concerned; harvest failure or war could have the

94. GLAMANN pp. 10–11 and *passim.*

146

same effect on the European demand. Some of these technical difficulties were not overcome until the introduction of telegraph and steamships, some of the difficulties are hardly overcome even today. In these respects it is the Companies' endeavours and their results when compared to older entrepreneurial forms more than their perfection that attracts attention.

The concentration also carried with it problems of an institutional or ethical nature. Indeed it is remarkable that the monopolist tendencies of the Companies raised so few protests in the contemporary English and Dutch opinion. Both in England and in the Netherlands the giants were accepted regardless of the contemporary aversion to monopolism; the vulnerable point in both countries was the marketing. In the Netherlands the protests of the stockholders had no effect; it was more effectual that the *Heeren XVII*'s right to manage the sales on behalf of all the Chambers was attacked by the Zeeland Chamber in 1629. The States General supported the *Heeren XVII*, but decided at the same time that the Directors themselves were not to operate as buyers. There is scarcely any reason for believing that such a ban was practicable, however. On the other hand it is probable that it was this criticism, combined with the contractors' growing tendency to form monopsonistic combinations, that was responsible for the Dutch Company going over to sale by public auction after the pepper panic around 1640.[95]

From the very beginning the constitution of the English Company gave the Court of Committees less fredom of movement in the market, although formally, as mentioned above, it was free to dispose of the Company's imports at closed Committee meetings. As in the Netherlands it was primarily the Committees' own purchases that gave cause for criticism, and in 1619 it was suggested at a General Court – after the new Court of Committees had been elected – that in the future the Committees should be forbidden to undertake purchases. The proposal was indignantly rejected by the Directors: "To have their hands tied it will be disgraceful and prejudicial", and was not carried.[96] Whether the Directors used to feather their own nests under cover of the contract sales cannot be determined from the sources; we can only draw our conclusions from our view of human nature as those malicious people "... who have noe other ground for what they say than that it were unlikely the committees would serve with such diligence as they do without recompense if they did not find gain in their imployment, ..."[97] It would have been inhuman if the Directors had not used their advance knowledge and their key position to better their own position. But it is worth noticing that the General Court did *not* deprive

95. Glamann p. 38.
96. General Court 2/7 1619, C. R. O., London, Court Books, vol. 4 f. 378.
97. Court Minute 12/10 1621, C. R. O., London, Court Books, vol. 5 f. 121.

10*

the Directors of their right to undertake the purchasing of the Company's imports, whereas when discussing sales the Directors frequently cast a sidelong glance at the reaction that might be expected in "the generality". In 1619, for instance, a syndicate offered to take the Company's entire silk import and pay 6d more per lb. than was expected to be offered at an auction, providing the price was kept secret. The Committees discussed the offer, but although they were reminded that they could act at their discretion they decided to sell the silk by public auction in two lots and with a minimum price that was determined beforehand, so as not to cause any unrest amongst the Company's ordinary members.[98]

Perhaps the most important obstacle in the way of a long-range policy, that which the Dutch Company specially contributed towards overcoming, was the demand for a quick turnover of capital. It is well known that the Dutch Company in theory and the English Company in practice operated with terminable stocks; the idea of a permanent capital occupies just as little place in the Company Charters as it does in their bookkeeping. The English Company did not succeed in solving this problem in the first half of the century; the dividend payments literally took the form of payment of "capitals", and the necessity of procuring whole and half capitals for the impatient shareholders time and time again determined the English Company's investment and marketing policy.[99] For the English the question of the building up of stocks or the postponement of sales over long periods could only be the exception. Characteristic in this connection is a discussion in 1623. At a General Court on 22nd August it was proposed to distribute $1^{1}/_{2}$ capitals to the partners. Immediate objections were raised against this proposal, it being emphasized "that the Co. must be careful of 3 things, first to maintain the trade, secondly to pay their debts, 3 to provide money to divide to those that take not out upon stock...[100] These were clever words, and it is especially interesting to see the concern for the maintenance of trade taking first place, but they were spoken in vain. At the General Court a week later the Committees proposed to distribute one half capital in cloves or pepper and 2–3 half capitals in cottons. The Court's proposal was accepted.[101] Also characteristic of the English Company's preference for "quick returns" is the Court's attitude in 1632, when it was debated as to whether more tonnage was sent out than was needed in relation to the capital remaining in the East, or vice versa. The Court concluded that it was better to send out too many ships than too few.[102]

98. Court Minute 13/9 1619, C. R. O., London, Court Books, vol. 4 f. 414.
99. CHAUDHURI pp. 56–58.
100. Court Minute 22/8 1623, C. R. O., London, Court Books, vol. 6 f. 82.
101. General Court 29/8 1623, C. R. O., London, Court Books, vol. 6 f. 93 ff.
102. STEENSGAARD, *Freight Costs* pp. 155–156.

The Dutch Company broke through this barrier already a few years after its establishment; although it neither left any traces in its constitution nor in its accounts, in fact during the first decades of the Company's existence considerable reserves were built up in Asia, these being tabulated in the Batavia balance-sheets either as *reëlle* or *inreëlle effecten,* bur also under *onkosten.* This very lack of formal adaptation reveals the fundamentally new aspects in this situation, and the significance of these reserves, which in reality could probably only have been built up by virtue of the ambivalent relations between the *bewindhebbers* and the stockholders after 1602, can hardly be overestimated. The Dutch Company's activity in Asia was consolidated to an extent that could never of course satisfy a Coen, but which far exceeded what *Estado da India* in the past or the East India Company of that time could have achieved. The consolidation meant more than security; it made possible a widespread diversification and co-ordination of trading activities. One of the features in the planning of the Dutch Company most strongly emphasized by Glamann was the constant endeavour not to see the individual commodity or the individual market in isolation, but to see it in relation to the Company's total interests. This was only possible because in certain cases the Court could let the returns remain in the background in favour of the most profitable investment, no matter whether it was on an Asian or a European market.[103] A more detailed account will be given below of the Company trade on the Persian market, but already here it may be mentioned that the English trade only with difficulty detached itself later on from the bilateral pattern, whereas right from its beginning the Dutch trade with Persia was integrated into a whole: a polygon whose corners were the Dutch trading offices in Asia and Patria.

Both Glamann and Chaudhuri have commented upon the violent fluctuations of the prices both in Amsterdam and in London, and Chaudhuri has in particular emphasized the considerable risk the Company ran with regard to unforeseen price fluctuations.[104] But if the previous argument is correct the Companies' quasi-monopolistic or oligopolistic position should ensure them a certain measure of control over the prices and thereby reduce the unpredictability of the market, if not entirely eliminate it. In addition, the concentration of the East India trade in the intimately connected London and Amsterdam markets must have meant a greater transparency of the market for the individual merchant than for the buyer in Aleppo or in any other peddling market.

Unfortunately it has not been possible to localize any letter-book material from London and Amsterdam in the relevant period of the same character

103. GLAMANN p. 103 and *passim* cf. p. 316.
104. CHAUDHURI pp. 149–150.

as that employed above in describing the short-term fluctuations on the peddling market.[105] But in the *bourse* price lists published by Aeckerle from 1624–26 we are able to follow the short-term fluctuations from the same viewpoint as the merchants' letters, i.e. the bulk sale chiefly with export in view.[106]

Table 8. *Prices of pepper, indigo and cloves in Amsterdam 1624–26.*

	Small-grained pepper			Lahore-indigo			Cloves		
	1624	1625	1626	1624	1625	1626	1624	1625	1626
Jan			16–26	11–12			96		134–56
Feb	32		26	12	11–12				
Mar			16–26	11–12					154
Apr									
May	32			12–13			76–100		
June	32	32		13–14	12–13		106–08	110–12	
July		32			12–13			110–12	
Aug	32	32	26	14–15	13	10–11	110	110–12	168–70
Sept	32	32		13–14	13		112	110–12	
Oct		32			11–12		114		
Nov			29			11–11½			
Dec	32	32	28–28½	12	11½–12	11–12	116	126	192

The above hypothesis concerning the stabilization through market control seems clearly to be confirmed as far as pepper is concerned. Throughout two years there is perfect stability, but towards the end of 1625 and the beginning of 1626 the large-grained qualities disappear from the records, at the same time as a fall in prices of small-grained pepper occurs which, even if we desregard the 16 d that must presumably be either an error or due to especially poor qualities, is almost 20%. The price is apparently maintained at this level for some time until, at the end of the year, a rise in prise occurs once more. What happened between 1st December and 5th January we do not know; it may have been the effects of an English dividend payment in pepper that made itself felt on the Dutch market,[107] but it is also possible that a new syndicate has taken over a new Dutch import of pepper or that a price limiting agreement has expired and been replaced by a newer one.

The price curve for indigo shows less stability, but some of the price

---

105. Cranfield's correspondence contains isolated data from Amsterdam and Hamburg, but not sufficient to create the basis for a total picture.
106. *d. Vl.* per pond. ACKLERLEE *passim.*
107. The payment of two half capitals in pepper was decided at a General Court in London 30th November 1625. C. R. O., London, Court Books, vol. 8 f. 163.

fluctuations can be isolated as characteristic seasonal price fluctuations. As is emphasized time and time again in the English material, summer was the time for dyeing with indigo; thus the rising prices in the early summer culminating in the late summer were only to be expected. Even if the seasonal fluctuations are isolated, the indigo price is less stable than the pepper price – a condition probably reflecting the fact that in these years it was not the Dutch, but the English Company, that was the biggest importer of indigo, and that the English-imported indigo was sold in consignments of varying size at a fixed price.[108]

Cloves demonstrate yet a third pattern characterized by considerable fluctuations, nearly all of them tending upwards, however. The background for this particular price trend has been described previously; it was without doubt the result of the restrictive policy regarding the marketing of imported cloves carried out by the Dutch Company during these years, the object of which was to force the price up. Thus, despite the fluctuations, the price development for cloves during these years must also be regarded as a consequence of market control.

The material available regarding short-term prices is too scanty to possess any evidential weight of its own, but in conjunction with the information available about the Companies' marketing policy it illustrates strikingly the difference between the peddling market and the international market for Asian wares that arose in Amsterdam and London in the 17th century.

The Companies as Institutional Innovation

In the previous chapter the peddling trade was characterized by the importance that must be attached to the unpredictable costs, and the protection costs in particular, as well as to the non-transparency of the peddling market. The Companies not only went a long way towards solving these problems, but turned them, so to speak, to their own advantage.

The factors precipitating this decisive break-through are far from simple, even if, as here, we consider the problem isolated from the general European market development, but the important item, as far as one can judge, is the internalization of the protection costs. If the Portuguese King became the world's biggest tax-gatherer, the Companies became the world's biggest smugglers. The comparison is not merely a joke, but reflects quite well the Spanish-Portuguese Crown's view of the legal position. The Companies themselves produced the protection they needed; this meant that,

108. CHAUDHURI pp. 185–186. Finally, it is of importance that Amsterdam was also supplied with South American (Guatemala) indigo. ACKERLEE passim.

in contrast to the peddling trade and the contractors of the Portuguese Crown, they could obtain their protection at cost price. The merchants expropriated the tribute, so to speak. It also meant that they were largely able to foresee their protection costs and could to a great extent co-ordinate their political and economic activities.

Apart from the internalization of the protection costs the Companies' relations to the market also constitutes an innovation, even if in this respect it is undoubtedly a question of an extension of entrepreneurial forms and methods already developed on the European markets before the establishment of the Companies – amongst other things in connection with the marketing of the Portuguese Crown's pepper. Characteristic of the Companies' relations to the market is the quasi-monopolistic regulation of supplies and prices, which, just like the internalization of the protection costs, serves to reduce the number of unknowns in the Companies' calculations. In evaluating the Companies' market policy, however, it is important to remember that they never had the monopoly, but that their position was quasi-monopolistic or oligopolistic. It meant that, on the one hand they were unable to fix their prices just as they pleased, but always had to take the marginal rate of substitution into account, though on the other hand, by virtue of the quantities they had at their disposal, they were able to control the prices and supplies within the limits determined by the marginal rate of substitution. There were technical and institutional difficulties connected with putting such a market policy into full operation, but the market policy of both Companies clearly indicates that they were aware of this margin of freedom and that they used it, not for an immediate maximizing of the profit, but as an integral part of a long-range commercial policy or as a guarantee for stable prices, i.e. increased transparency of the market. The Companies could safeguard themselves not only against the unpredictable protection costs, but also against the unforeseeable price fluctuations that the peddlar had had to take into account in his calculations.

It is trivial, but none the less important in this connection, to emphasize once again the fact that after the Companies had been set up there was always more than one entrepreneur in the Asian trade. If the proposed characteristic of the Companies as an institutional innovation is correct, this break-through should give repercussions in a more economic utilization of resources, which again should lead to falling consumer prices and/ or rising producer prices. Although the present price information is far from conclusive, it seems to indicate such a trend. We are best informed about the price development for that commodity which dominated the East Indian trade at the time the Companies were established, i.e. pepper. According to the evidence available there can be no doubt that the European pepper prices dropped after 1600 to a level considerably lower than what had been the norm in the 16th century,[109] and that the fall in prices, despite interruptions, continued throughout the 17th century.[110] At the same time pepper prices rose in the Indonesian production areas in the first decades of the 17th century.[111]

For Oriental saltpetre and for Guatemala indigo, which, as a close substitute, may be used as indicator in this connection, there are price series showing a considerable fall throughout the 17th century.[112] As far as indigo is concerned this evidence can be substantiated by the information given about English dumping of indigo in the Mediterranean region. (see p. 173 f.). The Companies would only be able to maintain this market so long as the price was kept below that for which the commodity could be transported over land.

For the fine spices – cloves, nutmeg, mace and cinnamon – the production areas of which were brought under Dutch control so far as was technically possible, the picture was another. There was for these commodities a question of a monopoly price maintenance, reflected in a price stability on the Amsterdam *bourse* that was something approaching a world record. But it must be stressed that the risk of an evasion of the monopoly fixed a ceiling for the Company's price, and that the Company's Court of Directors was well aware of this state of affairs.[113] Precisely this feature once more reveals the fundamental difference between *Estado da India*'s and the Company's relations to the market. The risk of an evasion of the monopoly had not prevented the Portuguese Crown from letting the pepper prices rise to a level at which it was not only possible to maintain the alternative route over land, but at which it ultimately became a temptation to invest in an evasion of the Portuguese monopoly.

With the material available it is impossible to base any argument on other than a rough estimate, as far as the remaining Asian commodities, particularly cottons, are concerned. The price development on the Asian markets in the 17th century is by and large unknown; however, the available price series for Byana[114] and Lahore[115] indigo, respectively show marked price increases in the first half of the 17th century. The ultimate proof must await the elaboration of Asian price series, but the information to be gained from available price series is that the gap between the buyers' and the producers' prices was reduced after the rise of the Companies.

109. See diagram p. 423.
110. POSTHUMUS I diagram V cf. pp. 174–175 and 505.
111. GLAMANN pp. 76–77.
112. POSTHUMUS I pp. 415–416, 462–463.
113. GLAMANN p. 99 ff.
114. HAZAN pp. 857–858.
115. MORELAND, *Aurangzeb* p. 161.

Chapter IV: The Fall of Hormuz

Lane, Braudel, Meylink-Roelofsz, Mahalhães-Godinho and other historians have irrevocably proved that the intercontinental trade between Asia and Europe throughout the 16th century continued along the traditional routes. Year after year the peddlars' bundles and bales kept up the exchange of goods between East and West, from market to market, from hand to hand.

The attempt has been made in the first two chapters of this book to demonstrate the structural conditions under which the trade continued. The establishment of *Estado da India* was a revolution, but it was a revolution within the system. Part of the proceeds of the exchange of goods between Europe and Asia went into other pockets after the discovery of the sea route to India and the establishment of *Estado da India,* but it led to no structural changes in the Asian trade or in the traditional relations between the protector and the protected, between the merchant and the producer of organized violence. The Portuguese carracks did not obtain any great economic significance as a connecting link between Europe and Asia. After the first years of vigorous expansion the Portuguese shippings were stabilized at a level that did not undergo great changes in the 16th century.[1] Probably the Portuguese return cargoes, after a boom in the 1580s, were less at the close of the century than at its beginning. The increase that took place in the 16th century in the European consumption of Asian goods: pepper, spices, drugs and silk, was channelled through the Levant.

The paradoxical ineffectiveness of the Cape route ceased with the first decades of the 17th century. The establishment of the Companies led in a few years to an increase in the number of ships sent out and returned per annum, and a number of goods disappeared from the intercontinental caravan routes. From the first decades of the 17th century Asian goods were conveyed from the Atlantic to the Mediterranean and to the Levant towns that previously had been exporting the same goods.

The downfall of *Estado da India* and the collapse of the peddling trade on the intercontinental routes are two aspects of the same structural crisis, the crisis represented here as the fall of Hormuz. In this Chapter an

1. STEENSGAARD, *European Shipping,* tables 1 and 3.

154

attempt is made to find an answer to the questions, how much? and when? The material does not permit a simple and direct analysis of the quantities, prices and profits. It will be necessary to circle around the problems and attack them indirectly in the hope that the details revealed may be able to replace the lack of statistical data.

The Cape Route and the Caravan Routes around 1600

"Le commerce des épices sera encore le premier de tous les trafics mondiaux au XVIIe, si ce n'est au XVIIIe siècle."[2] We might well make some reservations regarding silver, which Braudel perhaps does not consider to be a commodity, but with this single reservation we must agree with Braudel, at any rate as far as the 17th century is concerned. The next commodity in order of preference may also be identified: this was raw silk. Pepper, fine spices and raw silk: these were the goods in the limelight at the beginning of the 17th century; they were the most important goods in intercontinental trade. But what were the quantities, and how great a part of the trade in these goods was already diverted to the Cape route by the Portuguese?

From about 1620 we have both an English and a Dutch estimate concerning the European consumption of Asian goods; they are scarcely independent of each other, however.

Table 9. *Estimates of European consumption of Asian goods circa 1620.*[3]

	MUN	VOC
Pepper	6,000,000 lb.	7,000,000 pd.
Cloves	450,000 –	490,000 –
Mace	150,000 –	180,000 –
Nutmeg	400,000 –	450,000 –
Indigo	350,000 –	–
Persian raw silk	1,000,000 –	–

2. BRAUDEL I p. 500.
3. MUN, *East Indies*, printed in McCULLOCH, p. 11; *Heeren XVII* to Coen, Batavia, 4/3 1621, COEN IV p. 490; this letter directly refers to the partitive agreement between the English and the Dutch Companies; since Mun was one of the leading members of the East India Company's Court of Directors, an interconnection between the two sources is probable. It is remarkable that the Dutch estimate lies roughly 10–20 % above the English one; a mistake regarding the conversion rate between the English lb. and the Dutch pond cannot be ruled out.

These estimates were worked out by experienced merchants, but even for the most experienced it was impossible to survey the European market. A comparison with the actual imports, to the extent they can be ascertained, is necessary in order to assess the reliability of the estimates.

Pepper. The North-West European estimates of the total European pepper consumption lay considerably higher than the figures mentioned in connection with the Portuguese pepper contracts. Thus in 1580 an annual European consumption of 28,000 quintals was anticipated; in 1611, 30,000 quintals, i.e. 3–3^1/$_2$ million lbs.[4] It is also probable that even Mun's conservative estimate was too high. The average Dutch pepper import from 1620–1638 is estimated by Horst at about 2,5 million pond per annum, a figure Glamann has not found cause to dipute.[5] Chaudhuri's survey of the English Company's pepper import shows an annual average of a little over 1 million lbs. for the same period.[6] From 1611–1626 the Portuguese ships loaded an average of 10.266 quintals of pepper per annum in Asia;[7] thus, taking into regard wastage and losses at sea, the Portuguese pepper import in that period cannot on the average have been more than a million lbs. per annum. For the following years we do not know the extent of the Portuguese pepper trade; it is probable, however, that the decline continued. Thus in 1628 Lisbon received only 1,981 quintals of pepper from Asia.[8] An average of 5 million lbs. per annum thus seems rather on the liberal side for the European pepper import after 1620.

Spices. Possibilities for comparing the estimate from around 1620 with the actual imports are very limited as far as spices are concerned. Most probably the South-East Asian spices had largely disappeared from the Portuguese return cargoes after 1600,[9] whereas the English Company's import of spices was so irregular that the little data available does not provide any basis for an estimate of the average extent of the trade.[10] The best control material is therefore the information available about the

---

4. KELLENBENZ, *Poivre* pp. 7–8.
5. HORST p. 98 cf. GLAMANN p. 78. According to Horst, in 1625 VOC had a stock of pepper amounting to 11,000 bales of 315 pond net, while the annual import was 8,000 bales. Since in 1625 only 2,000 bales were sold it was decided the following year to reduce the price and to sell 6,000 bales per annum at the lower price, at the same time reducing the annual import. Thereafter the stock was reduced by 2,000 bales per annum until in 1636 it was exhausted. Horst's intention is not quite clear, but the main impression is that the annual sales were rather below than above 2^1/$_2$ million pond.
6. CHAUDHURI, table V p. 148.
7. MAGALHAES-GODINHO p. 706.
8. *ibid.*
9. *ibid.*
10. CHAUDHURI pp. 167–169.

Dutch Company's imports at the middle of the 17th century. This information largely confirms the order of magnitude in Muns's estimate.[11]

Indigo. Nor in this case does the material permit a conclusive control of Mun's figures. Only in isolated years does indigo play a role in the Dutch return cargoes;[12] on the other hand it is probable that the Portuguese still imported indigo in the 17th century.[13] We know the extent of the English indigo import in 1618 and 1619, since in these years sales constituting the whole of the year's import of 255,000 lb. and 300,000 lb. respectively were registered in London. These consignments, which closely approximate Mun's estimate of the total European consumption, seem to have threatened to overload the market;[14] amongst other things there were complaints that indigo, in contrast to pepper, was still conveyed to the Levant markets by the caravan routes, and from 1624 the Levant Company's merchants attempted by means of deliberate dumping to drive the indigo of the caravan trade away from the Levant market.[15] This policy succeeded to a certain extent; in 1626 and 1627 the English export of indigo to the Mediterranean area was 268,889 lb. and 145,735 lb. respectively.[16] Pelsaert's description of the state of the trade in the Mogul Empire from 1626 illustrates extremely well the unstable balance that still characterized this trade. He noted that the most important indigo market was no longer Lahore, but Agra, because the English now played a greater role as buyers than the buyers for the caravans. On the other hand he stated that the Armenians and the Indians still exported indigo to Isfahan "whence some of it goes to Aleppo".[17] At any rate in the years 1634–36 indigo was regularly quoted as an English import to Aleppo[18] but during the same years the East Indian indigo met competition from a new quarter: from Guatemala. The prices of "Indigo-Guattimalo" were quoted regularly in Amsterdam in 1624–26;[19] in 1633 Guatemalan indigo was offered for sale in London, and in 1645 the competition from the West Indies was said to be the cause of the reduction in the Company's orders to Surat.[20] It must on the available information be regarded as probable that Mun's estimation of the European consumption is too low, or perhaps rather that

11. GLAMANN pp. 93–102.
12. CHAUDHURI pp. 174–175; GLAMANN pp. 17–18.
13. Portuguese purchases were still mentioned in 1630: Wylde et al. to E. I. Co. 13/4 1630, *English Factories* 1630/33 p. 20.
14. CHAUDHURI pp. 179, 182–183.
15. *ibid.* p. 175.
16. See below, p. 174.
17. PELSAERT pp. 18, 30.
18. P. R. O. London, S. P. 110/10 *passim.*
19. ACKERLEE *passim.*
20. MORELAND, *Aurangzeb* p. 113.

the consumption of East Indian indigo rose considerably in the first decades of the 17th century.[21]

Silk. Whereas silk material regularly constituted part of the cargo of Portuguese ships to Europe, the Portuguese only seem to have carried insignificant amounts of raw silk around the Cape. In 1514–19 small consignments are mentioned of from 5 to 160 quintals; thereafter no import of raw silk to Lisbon can be demonstrated before 1610, and the consignment imported in that year is undoubtedly the trial lot that Abbas sent to Europe with his ambassador, Janghiz Beg.[22] Since there are no accounts of any import of Bengal or Chinese silk to the Levant either, and no qualities of raw silk are mentioned on the Levant markets which cannot be identified as Persian or Syrian, among the Asian production areas at the end of the 16th and beginning of the 17th centuries solely Persia and Syria, and particularly the former, may be regarded as deliverers to the European market. Before the North-West European attempt at diversion in the third and fourth decades of the 17th century the whole of the trade took place exclusively along the caravan routes.

It cannot entirely be ruled out, however, that Chinese raw silk found its way to the European market via Acapulco and Seville. The import of raw silk from Manila to Mexico and from Mexico to Seville was not inconsiderable, but it cannot in the latter case be determined whether the silk was Mexican or Chinese, although Chaunu tends to believe that the import of Chinese silk to Mexico had already ousted the Mexican production by this time.[23] The Dutch East India Company discovered already with the capture of the Portuguese Macao ship, *S. Catharina*, in 1603 that the Chinese silk could be a remunerative commodity on the European market.[24] It was several years, however, before Chinese silk came to play any great part in the returns to the Netherlands. This was partly because the Dutch were only able to procure Chinese goods indirectly by capturing ships or through Chinese middlemen, and partly because in the Company's orders Chinese silk was always reserved for the Japan factory, where it could be sold for silver.[25] In 1617 the *Heeren XVII* put

---

21. The latter possibility is supported by MORELAND, who estimates the Company export at 5–600,000 lb. annually when the indigo trade was at its peak, *Aurangzeb* p. 116.
22. MAGALHAES-GODINHO p. 708. Magalhães-Godinho puts forward the case for a regular Portuguese import of raw silk, referring to Balbi's surveys of the *San Salvador's* cargo in 1587, but this was doubtless a matter of woven cloths, *Nuovo Ramusio* p. 220. Cf. below, p. 167.
23. SCHURZ pp. 32, 72–73, 365; CHAUNU, *Galion* p. 456 n. 3; CHAUNU, *Seville* t. 8:1 pp. 742–744.
24. GLAMANN p. 114.
25. *ibid.*

their annual order for Chinese silk at 72,000 ponds, but it is improbable that the supplies reached this level before the second half of the century.[26] How great was the Persian export of raw silk to Europe? In 1623 during his negotiations in England Sir Robert Sherley estimated the Persian silk export at an annual 34,000 bales, with a purchase price of £5,000,000 – incidentally, the fact that he could propose to James I that he should venture upon a business of this magnitude was a pathetic example of his economic innocence. The Court of the East India Company also found "a wonderful mistake" in this estimate, both as regards quantities and price. They imagined that 7,500 bales purchased for £650,000, i.e. well over 2,000,000 lb., at 280 lb. per bale would correspond better with reality. But the Company, too, has certainly exaggerated a bit in order not to appear too mean by the side of the magnificent Sherley.[27] A few years earlier, in connection with the negotiations with the Dutch East India Company respecting co-operation in the trade with Persian silk, the following estimate of the annual import of Persian silk to Europe was tabulated, presumably on the part of the English:[28]

Netherlands	500 bales
England	600 –
Venice	1,500 –
Marseilles	3,000 –
Genoa, Lucca, Messina, Florence	400 –
	6,000 bales

Reckoned at 280 lb. per bale this table thus estimates the total European import to be 1,680,000 lb.

Other contemporary estimates calculate with even smaller figures, however. In an estimate which can be accredited to Sir John Wolstenholme, together with a contemporary estimate that presumable builds upon Wolstenholme's figures, the total European import of Persian silk is put at 4,000 bales of 280 lb., i.e. 1,120,000 lb. per annum.[29] As noted above, Mun estimated the import at 1,000,000 lb. per annum.

There is a great jump from the Company's over 2 million lb. to Mun's one million, and it is not even sure that the truth should be sought between these two extremes; the information available concerning the actual size of the import suggests that Mun, too, overestimated the import of Persian

26. *ibid.*
27. Sir Robert Sherley, the Persian Ambassador's Propositions . . . East India Company's answer, *Calendar S. P. East Indies* 1622/24 p. 370.
28. *Bewindhebbers,* Amsterdam, to Batavia 4/3 1621, DUNLOP p. 11.
29. P. R. O. London, C. O. 77/1 no. 88 and 77/2 no. 23, cf. CHAUDHURI p. 120.

silk to Europe. From Venice there are some interesting import statistics regarding Levant silk comprising the years 1590/91–1612/13. Until 1603/04 the import hovered around 1,500 bales per annum, with 559 bales in 1594/95 and 2,427 bales in 1595/96 as extreme points.[30] If we take the consul, Giorgio Emo's period of office in Aleppo, 1596–99, as a triennium we obtain an average per annum of 1,574 bales. Sella, who has published the Venetian import statistics, thinks the bales concerned must be of 300 *libbre sottile*, i.e. about 90 kg.; thus the average import for the triennium must be a little over 140,000 kg. Emo estimated that, with an annual import to the value of 1½ million ducats, the Venetians in his time controlled half the European trade with Aleppo.[31] Towards the end of the century the price of silk was about 7–8 ducats per rotolo;[32] i.e. the purchase price of 140,000 kg. raw silk would be about half a million ducats and thus correspond to about one third of the Venetian turnover in Aleppo – which sounds quite reasonable. In those years Aleppo was far the most important silk-exporting market in the Levant, but other European nations than the Venetians were trading with Aleppo. If we assume that the silk import was relatively as important to the English and the French as to the Venetians we will reach a total European import of Persian and Syrian raw silk of about 280,000 kg., or approximately 600,000 lb. per annum.

It is probable that even this figure was too high, however. The English nation scarcely invested such a great proportion of its capital in silk as the Venetians. In the English Levant Company's order list of 3/6 1586[33] raw silk appears far down on the list, underneath goods like raw cotton, indigo, nutmeg, mace and galls. In 1588, a year in which we know the English import from the Levant, there are only small amounts of silk among the imported goods,[34] and even in 1598 the English silk import from the Levant was scarcely more than 25–30 bales.[35] It was probably the Dutch and English direct imports of spices from Asia that first turned the attention of the English and Dutch Levant merchants to silk as a possible substitute.[36] Well over two decades later, in the Dutch estimate of the silk import to Europe quoted above, the annual import into Eng-

30. SELLA pp. 111–112.
31. BERCHET, *Siria* p. 103.
32. MUN, *East Indies* p. 11.
33. SANDERSON p. 130.
34. WILLAN pp. 407–408, 9,133 lb. in the year that ended at Michelmas 1588.
35. B. M. London, Sloane Ms. 867 ff. 19, 26.
36. "The truth is all men have such cold advice out of England, of the glut of indigo and spices there, that noe man dare as yet venture upon anything. But all men's orders are for raw silk which commodity at present not here to be had for any money..." *ibid.* 22/7 1958, f. 13.

land was put at 600 bales, whereas Mun's contemporary estimate was only 300 bales[37] – certainly a more realistic figure. On the basis of the chancellery register from the English consulate in Aleppo we can estimate the English silk export from this town in the years 1619/20, 1620/21 and 1622/23 at 352, 223 and 295 bales respectively, the latter figure probably not constituting the whole of the English export for the year, however. According to the same source the English silk export from Aleppo in 1629 was at least 358 bales.[38]

Similarly, as regards the French nation, it is unlikely that silk achieved any great importance until the first years of the 17th century. In 1623, in a memorandum addressed to the King, the Marseilles merchants declared: "Comme l'on ne voyait venir à Marseille par le passé, en tout un an, plus haut de 100 ou 200 balles de soie, on en tira depuis, arrivées sur en seul vaisseau, 1,000 ou 2,000 balles."[39] "On a single ship" is doubtless an exaggeration, because it was a characteristic of the French that they employed small, fast vessels when sailing to the Levant, in contrast to the big Venetian and North-West European ships. The Marseilles merchants would never have loaded such a consignment on a single ship. But if we alter this to "in a single year", we are possibly not very far from the truth. We are able to reconstruct the French export from the Levant for the year 1621/22 on the basis of a series of ship's manifests, that have been preserved in the archives of the Chamber of Commerce.[40] Altogether 44 vessels are concerned, which sailed from Alexandria, Alexandretta, Smyrna, Accra, Seydon, Tripoli and Constantinople, and they carried a total of approximately 338,833 Marseilles lb. silk, i.e. approximately 137,000 kg., or roughly the Venetian average import at the end of the 16th century.

But in the meantime the Venetians had lost their share in the Levant silk trade. There is a striking similarity between the memorandum from the Marseilles merchants quoted above and the Venetian trade commission, Cinque Savi's statement from the same year: "Si come nel anni passati solevano venire in questa citta fino 2,000 et piu colli di seda all'anno, cosi in quest'ultimi anni per l'informazione che tenimo non ne sono giunti piu di 300 in circa ..."[41] This dismal statement is confirmed by the accessible statistical information; in the series published by Sella the import after 1603/04 is only 200–400 bales per annum. After 1612/13 we have

37. PURCHAS V pp. 268–69.
38. P. R. O. London, S. P. 110/54: The cargoes of silk on the ships *Hector* (1619/20), *Saphire* and *Eagle* (1620/21) and *Saphire* and *London Merchant* (1621/22) cf. *ibid.* f. 204.
39. COLLIER & BILLOUD p. 476.
40. Arch. Chambre de Commerce, Marseille, J. 921–922.
41. A. d. S. Venezia, Cinque Savi, nuova serie 154 no. 19[1].

only a little scattered information at our disposal, but this indicates nevertheless that the recession was permanent. *Cinque Savi* estimated as mentioned the annual import at about 300 bales in 1623; in 1624–26 the average import was 87 bales per annum, but of these three years the last two were exceptionally difficult for the Levant trade.[42] In the autumn of 1629 the Venetian galleys loaded 650 bales of silk in Alexandretta, but this was after navigation had been interrupted for more than a year.[43] In 1636 a silk import of over 300 bales is mentioned.[44]

A table constructed on the basis of the information concerning the European import of silk from the Levant extracted here would give the impression of a certainty that cannot be established. But certain tendencies do nevertheless appear. Between 1600 and 1630 Venice and Marseilles changed places in the Levant silk trade; at the beginning of the period the lion's share of the imported silk – we might hazard a figure of 140,000 kg. – is handled by the Italian merchants, whereas at the end of the period it is handled by the French. The quantity handled by the smaller importers is even more difficult to determine. According to the wording of the Marseilles memorandum of 1623, 100–200 bales to Marseilles would be the norm before the French took over Venice's position. Until the beginning of the 17th century the English import has presumably been less; on the other hand it is probable that silk has to a certain extent been transported in English and Dutch ships to other harbours, such as Leghorn. If we cautiously estimate the non-Venetian export of silk from the Levant towns at the end of the 16th century at 400 bales per annum, the total export becomes 180–190,000 kg. At the beginning of the 1620s the export seems to lie at a corresponding level, or possibly a bit higher. The approximately 140,000 kg. have now been claimed by Marseilles, whereas Venice's import lies around 27,000 kg. The English export from the Levant is apparently quite stable at about 300 bales of 280 lb. or about 38,000 kg. – in all approximately 200,000 kg. The end result of this discussion of the European import of silk from the Levant harbours must therefore be that even Mun's estimate is excessive: the European consumption of Asian silk must at the most have been in the region of 500,000 lbs.[45]

The next problem is to ascertain the way in which the European con-

42. SELLA p. 112.
43. A. d. S. Venezia, Senato, Dispacci Console, Siria III no. 22.
44. SELLA p. 112.
45. By far the majority of the Levant silk export originated from the Persian production areas. In the merchant's letter books the Persian qualities, *legia* and *ardasse*, are mentioned 5–10 times more frequently than *bianco* and *chauf*. There is scarcely any doubt, however, that the Syrian, or rather the Lebanese, silk came to the fore at the end of the 16th and beginning of the 17th centuries. In the French export of silk from the Levant 1621/22, 86 % of the silk export is of Persian origin *(stravatine, ardasse* and *legia)*, whereas 14 %

sumption of imported goods in the years before 1600 was distributed between the two routes: the overland route and the route around Africa. As far as silk is concerned the answer is simple: as mentioned above there are no grounds for assuming that raw silk regularly formed part of the Portuguese return cargoes; throughout the 16th century the European consumption of Persian silk was imported along the caravan routes.

As regards pepper, we know the extent of the Portuguese import from 1587–99; it averaged 10,731 quintals, i.e. well over a million lb. There is no doubt that this import represented a decline compared to earlier results, but information regarding the extent of the Portuguese pepper import before the introduction of the Asian contracts is extremely scanty. In 1547 and 1548 36,000 and 24,000 quintals respectively were shipped from India; in 1558 the import of pepper into Lisbon was over 30,000 quintals, but hereafter there is no reliable information as regards quantities until 1587.[46] In the three years under the first contract, from 1588–90, the pepper import into Lisbon reached record heights: in each of the three years no less than 20,000 quintals; but the available price historical information indicates that these amounts also exceeded the previous years' imports.[47] Despite all, as will be shown below, it is probable that the average Portuguese pepper import in the 1570s and '80s lay around 20,000 quintals, but in the '90s it fell to a half. This would imply that 3–4 million lbs. per annum were imported along the caravan routes, which seems to be confirmed by the few available estimates concerning the extent of the pepper trade through the Levant. In 1585 a well-informed Portuguese estimated the annual transport of spices to Jidda from Gujarat and Achin at 40–50,000 quintals.[48] In 1593 it is mentioned that the caravan from Suez had brought 30,000 kantara of pepper, i.e. over 3 million lbs.,[49]

is of Syrian (Lebanese) origin (chauf, blanc, jaune, beyrouth), Arch. Chambre de Commerce, Marseille J. 921–922. This development, which was followed up by the French merchants in particular (MASSON pp. 381–90), is of interest respecting the special role played by the Lebanon within the Ottoman Empire in this period. Under the Emir, Fakhr al-Din (1593–1633), the Lebanon was the only bright spot in an economically disconsolate Syria. Fakhr al-Din entered into contact with several European states; in the diplomatic negotiations as well as in the bribes which, in difficult situations, ensured his independent position within the Ottoman Empire, gifts of silk played a considerable part. He also pursued a conscious "silk-promoting" policy, both by ensuring the silk-producing Maronites a home among the Druses in the Lebanon and by planting mulberry trees around Tripoli. CARALI pp. 38–39, 47–49; ISMAIL p. 132 f.

46. MAGALHAES-GODINHO p. 704 f.
47. LACH I p. 146 sums up in convenient table the Austrian, Spanish and Flemish price historical data concerning pepper in the 16th century.
48. BOXER, Portuguese Empire p. 59.
49. KELLENBENZ, Poivre p. 5.

and in 1601 it was maintained that the same caravan had brought 40,000 quintals to Cairo.[50]

For the remaining relevant groups of commodities the material is not sufficient to permit anything approaching a reliable determination of the distribution between the routes. We can, however, gain an impression of the total extent of the Portuguese import trade. The number of Portuguese return ships is known, whereas there has been some uncertainty as regards the capacity of the Portuguese carracks. However, it has been possible to determine the cargo on 21 Portuguese ships, which returned from Asia in the period 1587–1609.[51] The provenance of the material is heterogeneous: as far as three ships are concerned it is a matter of official reports from Goa to Lisbon; we know the cargo of six ships from the consular reports from Lisbon to England, five from a news letter in the Fugger archives, six from a news letter to Venice and one from Florence, probably also in this case from a news letter. But it is precisely the varied provenance of the material, compared with the conspicuous homogeneity which not only comprises the composition of the cargoes, but also the sequence in which the items are listed, that provides a reason for trusting the material.

However, it will be reasonable to raise the question as to how far the lists comprise the total cargo of the ships, including the privately-owned commodities, or merely the official, Royal part of the cargo. According to the available information there is scarcely any doubt that the lists comprise the whole cargo, first and foremost because there are no grounds for assuming that there was any Royal trade in non-enumerated goods; consequently the appearance of these goods on the list clearly indicates that it must include private trade. In addition, the lists, with the exception of the first three mentioned, appear in a context in which the informant has chiefly been interested in their commercial aspects. Thus the list entered under g) and h) begins: "A nott of al thuch marchandises and commoditis which cam from the easte India in these 2 ships and now unladen hiere in Lisbourne this august of a. 1602"; a reservation would be most probable if it was not a matter of the entire cargo. Naturally this does not exclude smuggling; much more could have been hidden in the bales and chests than *roupas e sedas;* on the other hand, it has not been possible to practice any large-scale deceits regarding the numbers of bales and chests!

The question as to whether the cargoes are representative must also be raised. In the three relevant decades 83 Portuguese ships returned; we possess knowledge of the cargoes of 21 of them, i.e. over one quarter. Furthermore, of the 83 ships we know the cargo of pepper only on the 32

50. SANDERSON p. 219.
51. See table 10, p. 166.

164

ships returned in the years 1587–98.[52] If we compare the average cargo of pepper in the 32 ships with the average load of pepper in the 21 ships, the full cargo of which is known, we obtain the results, 4,743 and 4,834 quintals respectively. Although 8 of the ships are repeated in the two columns compared, the coincidence is so striking that we need not hesitate to regard the 21 ships as representative. On the other hand the variations in the amounts of drugs and spices listed are so considerable that it is scarcely advisable on this basis to draw any conclusions with regard to the average annual import of individual goods other than pepper.

Apart from the 4,834 quintals of pepper the 21 ships carried on the average 1,436 quintals of other goods, the quantities of which are given in weight, altogether 6,270 quintals. In addition there are a number of chests and bales without weight specification, an average of about 672 bales and chests in all. Thus, if we reckon with such a high average weight as 2 quintals per pack, we only reach an average capacity per ship of about 7,600 quintals. A direct conversion from quintals to tonnage is not possible, but 12 quintals per ton, considering the dominating position of pepper, will scarcely be very far short of the mark. By this route we reach a calculated average capacity for the Portuguese carrack of 6–700 English tons of that time, or 300–350 Dutch lasts.

On the face of it this figure appears very modest when one considers the reputation of the carracks as the biggest ships sailing the oceans at that time. Beyond doubt a lack of distinction between the size of the ships and their capacity has led to exaggerated ideas about the extent of the Portuguese import trade. The significance of the distinction appears clearly in Hakluyt's description of the *Madre de Dios*, which, on its last journey in 1592 when it was seized by the English, was carrying 7,101 quintals of pepper,[53] and thus was really one of the giants in *carreira da India*. According to Hakluyt, English experts estimated the *Madre de Dios* at 1,600 tons, but of these only 900 tons were used for freight goods, the remainder being occupied by 32 brass guns, 6–700 passengers and provisions and water for the passengers and crew.[54] The latter circumstance provides us with a clue to the discrepancy between size and capacity: the ships in *carreira da India* were to just as great, if not greater, extent passenger ships as freight ships.

The calculations made here about the average capacity of the Portuguese East Indian ships lead us to a very important conclusion: the Portuguese import of Asian goods must have been considerably smaller than ordinarily

52. FALCAO p. 59.
53. KELLENBENZ, *Poivre* p. 3.
54. HAKLUYT, (Everyman ed.) V pp. 66–67.

Table 10. *Known Portuguese return cargoes, 1587–1609*

	a) 1587 1 ship	b) 1587 1 ship	c) 1587 1 ship	d) 1588 5 ships	e) 1600 5 ships	f) 1600 1 ship	g) 1602 1 ship	h) 1602 1 ship	i) 1603 4 ships	j) 1610 1 ship
Pepper (quintals)	2,586	6,259	4,109	22,963	30,300	2,185	4,350	3,248	21,349	4,170
Indigo (quintals)	1,223	1,077	530	1,627		?	7½	10	309	521
Indigo (bales)					1,918					
Cinnamon (quintals)	658	683	257	1,735	3,934	574	331	420	3,008	478
Cloves (quintals)	137	62	21	162	3,114	62	50	11½	1,214½	6
Nutmeg (quintals)	137	22	17	212	20	2	0	18	0	0
Mace (quintals)	50	0	21	28	204	2	0	20	11	0
Ginger (quintals)	401	93	5	1,750	899	200	1,126	151	0	101
Drugs* (quintals)	87	67	19	?	340	?	155½	187½	0	141
Lac (quintals)	0	26	0	?	978	411	0	0	0	114
Roupas & sedas (chests)	141	198	33	2,004	414	15	271	118	931	145
Roupas & sedas (bales)	188	188	25		151	63	150	123	959	149
Roupas & sedas (small bales)					442			16	5,314	95

* Under the group "drugs" a number of goods specified in the sources are collected: galanga, benzoin, borax, campher, aloes, incense, wax, etc. Apart from the goods mentioned here the lists comprises smaller lots of porcelain, furniture, musk and the undoubtedly extremely important, but indeterminate category: precious stones and pearls.

supposed. The most conservative estimate reckons with 25–35,000 quintals at the end of the century, with a preference for the lowest of these figures.[55] Magalhães-Godhinho, the most recent historian to investigate the problem, reckons with somewhat greater figures: 40–50,000 quintals or more per annum in the first third of the century, increasing to 60–75,000 quintals. But if we combine the average calculated above with Magal-

Authorities for Table 10.

a) b) and c) Arch. Simancas, Secr. Prov., Libr. 1551 ff. 213–215, bills of lading for the ships, Salvador, "Não Capitania" and Concepcão preserved with the correspondence from Goa from the end of 1586.

d) DOBEL p. 133.

e) "Portata delle nave d'India di Portogallo ent[e] a Lisbona a 23 di agosto 1600", Museo Civico-Correr, Venezia, P. D. 988.

f) "Portata della nave che resta a dietro", ibid.

g) h) i) P. R. O. London, S. P. 89/3 ff. 39–40.

j) BRAUDEL & ROMANO p. 68, cf. BRAUDEL I p. 572. Most of these ships can be identified by other means. b) and c) must be identical with São Tome and Concepcão, which arrived in Lisbon in 1587 with altogether 10,378 quintals of pepper, FALCAO p. 61. (Bills of lading in all 10,368 quintals.) It is even more amusing that the third ship in this fleet, a) the Salvador, must be the San Salvador, which the Italian traveller Balbi saw arrive in Hormuz in damaged condition in June 1587, Nuovo Ramusio p. 220. Balbi relates that goods to the value of 300,000 ducats were thrown into the sea while the ship was in distress; nevertheless, the following goods were landed in Hormuz: 4–5,000 cantaras of pepper, 1,500 bales of indigo, 500 cantaras of cinnamon, 100–150 cantaras of ginger, about 40 chests of "Seta della China", 80 small chests of various piece goods, 200 cantaras of nutmeg. It is this list together with Linschoten's even more liberal estimate that have often been taken as the standard cargo of the Portuguese East Indian ships, see, for instance, MAGALHAES-GODINHO p. 700. But Balbi's reliability is dubious; of course there was smuggling, but it is not easy to smuggle 1500–2500 quintals of pepper. If we compare Balbi's information with the bill of lading, moreover, other important discrepancies are that Balbi only has half of the amount of ginger recorded in the bill of lading and only 120 small and big chests of silks and cloths as against the bill of lading's total of 329 chests and bales. The difference is presumably accounted for by the goods thrown overboard during rough weather; presumably ginger, which was the cheapest of the spices, and chests and bales that were deck cargo belonging to individual sailors and passengers have been the first to be sacrificed. Lamentations from the owners of these chests there certainily must have been, but it is doubtful that the value of these goods should have been 300,000 ducats, however.

Braudel leaves the question of j)'s nationality open, but there is scarcely any doubt that Nostra Signora de Pieta ven' dalla India orientale 14. august 1610 must be Falcão's N. S. da Piedade, which he states as having arrived in Lisbon on 14th August 1610. FALCAO p. 188. Thus it is doubtful whether the ship concerned, as assumed by Braudel, really touched at Leghorn; more probably the cargo list published by Braudel was a report of the same nature as those found in Venice and London.

55. LANE, Venice and History, p. 31, n. 27; cf. MEILINK-ROELOFSZ p. 363, n. 140.

hães-Godinho's information concerning the number of returned ships, we reach considerably lower results.[56]

Table 11. *Estimate of tonnage returned to Portugal from Asia 1571–1610*

	return per annum	pepper	spices, drugs, etc.	in all
		quin.	quin.	quin.
1 ship, calculated average		4,834	1,436	7,600
1571–80	4.3	20,786	6,174	32,680
1581–90	4.1	19,819	5,887	31,160
1591–1600	2.3	11,018	3,302	17,480
1601–1610	2.5*	12,085	3,590	19,000

* I follow here Magalhães-Godinho's count. According to my own calculations only 21 Portuguese ships returned in the decade 1601–10.

Naturally a calculation of this nature is encumbered with a considerable degree of uncertainty, but a sample of 25% cannot be ignored, and the verification undertaken by a comparison of the pepper imports contains a certain guarantee that the preserved bills of lading are representative. We may therefore tabulate a revised estimate of the presumed European consumption of Asian goods around 1600, distributed along the two routes.

Table 12. *Estimate of European consumption of Asian goods around 1600*

	the Cape route	the caravan route	in all
Pepper	1–2,000,000 lb.	3–4,000,000 lb.	5,000,000 lb.
Cloves Indigo Drugs Mace Nutmeg	350,000 – 650,000 lb.	700,000 – 1,000,000 lb.	1,350,000 lb.
Textiles	?	?	?
Raw silk	0	500,000 lb.	500,000 lb.

56. MAGALHAES-GODINHO p. 700; cf. BOXER, *Portuguese Empire* p. 59.

Despite all the reservations made above this calculation can scarcely be very far from the truth. The greatest uncertainty is attached to the groups of drugs and textiles, whereas the uncertainty regarding spices and pepper is much less. "Le premier de tous les trafics mondiaux" at the end of the 16th century comprised about 6–7,000,000 lbs. or about 3,000–3,500 metric tons per annum. Only in the case of a few years was as much as half brought to Europe by the route around Africa.

The Triumph of the Companies

Throughout the whole of the 16th century the Portuguese had in practice been alone in utilizing the route around Africa to Asia; hardly a single ship of a different nationality had carried out the voyage with a cargo of market value before the first Dutch ship returned in 1597. It was the remains of a fleet sent out in 1594; throughout the following years Northwest European shipping and trade to Asia expanded enormously. Before 1602 the Dutch *voorcompagnieën* sent 61 ships to Asia, in 1600 the English East India Company was set up, which sent out its first fleet in 1601, and in 1602 the *voorcompagnieën* were united to form VOC, the Dutch United East India Company.

The events leading to the establishment of the two Companies and their early history is well-known, and an account of their institutional structure is given elsewhere. Here our concern is merely to place the immediate triumph of the Companies into its context both chronologically and quantitatively, especially in relation to the caravan trade that continued throughout the 16th century despite the discovery of the sea route to Asia around Africa. No material exists, and it will scarcely be possible to reconstruct any material able to provide a detailed and quantitative account of the Company trade in the first decades of the 17th century. In one respect, however, it is possible to create a survey showing the rhythm of the Companies' infiltration into the older structure, i.e. with the help of the numbers of ships returned per annum to European harbours from Asia. At first glance it appears from table 13 that there is a reduction in the number of returned Portuguese ships demonstrable in the beginning of the 1590s, which therefore provides a background both for the boom in the Levant trade in the last years of the century and for the setting up of the Companies. Behind this reduction in the number of returned ships lies a tremendous increase in the frequency of shipwreck. Of the 33 ships sent out from Lisbon in 1590–96 only 8 returned after having completed a normal voyage, 5 returned after a year's delay, 4 remained in Asia, there is one whose fate is unknown, but which presumably also remained in Asia, and,

Table 13. *Ships returned to European harbour from Asia 1581–1630*[57]

	Portugal	Netherlands	England	Denmark	France	Total		Portugal	Netherlands	England	Denmark	France	Total
1581	3					3	1606	1	7	2			10
1582	4					4	1607	1	3	0			4
1583	4					4	1608	2	6	0			8
1584	6					6	1609	0	4	2			6
1585	4					4	1610	3	1	1			5
1586	3					3	1611	2	4	1			7
1587	2					2	1612	3	1	0			4
1588	5					5	1613	3	7	2			12
1589	6					6	1614	1	2	5			8
1590	4					4	1615	1	5	2			8
1591	0					0	1616	3	5	3			11
1592	1					1	1617	2	4	5			11
1593	1					1	1618	4	8	2		2	16
1594	2					2	1619	3	5	3			11
1595	3					3	1620	2	6	2			10
1596	1					1	1621	1	6	1			8
1597	4	3				7	1622	1	8	5	2	1	17
1598	3	0				3	1623	3	8	5		0	16
1599	0	4				4	1624	2	6	3		1	12
1600	6	8				14	1625	3	4	4		0	11
1601	2	7				9	1626	0	10	6		1	17
1602	2	10				12	1627	3	7	3		0	13
1603	4	13	4		1	22	1628	0	7	4		0	11
1604	6	8	0			14	1629	2	7	5		0	14
1605	0	8	1			9	1630	1	9	4		0	14

57. Compiled on the basis of the following:
Portugal: FALCAO pp. 176–190; B. N. Paris, Fonds Portugais, no. 1 and 36; Arquivo Hist. Ultramarino, Lisboa, Cx. 7.
Netherlands: VALENTIJN I p. 211 ff. Apart from the ships he has listed Valentijn reveals that yet another 12–13 ships, the names of which he does not know, returned before 1613. 6 of these ships may be identified with the help of TERPSTRA, *Voorcompagnieën*; to the Dutch returns listed here must therefore be added another 6–7 ships, which arrived home between 1604 and 1613.
Denmark: OLSEN pp. 89–90.
France: BARASSIN pp. 376–81.
England: CHAUDHURI pp. 91 and 230 ff., cf. STEENSGAARD, *Freight Costs* pp. 161–162.

finally, 16 were wrecked or captured. It is a percentage of losses of nearly 50 against a risk that, for the century as a whole, lay below 20%.[58]

The decline in the number of returned Portuguese ships left its traces in the pepper prices and thus became an important factor behind the establishment of the North-West European East India Companies. But within a few years the Companies' shipping greatly surpassed the Portuguese decline. The average number of returned ships per annum in the 1580s was 4.1 and in the 1590s, 3.6, but it rose to 9.9 and 9.8 in the first two decades of the 17th century and to 13.3 in the 1620s, i.e. three times as much as in the 1580s and four times as much as in the 1590s. Whether the tonnage available for the transport of goods from Asia to Europe increased correspondingly is doubtful, however. We do not at the moment possess any material on which to base a reliable calculation of the Company ships' average capacity in this period. We know they were smaller than the Portuguese carracks, but they carried also far fewer passengers, and the difference between the size and the capacity must have been correspondingly less.

There seems, however, to be a fairly good correspondence between the quantity of goods attributed in the previous section to the caravan routes and the increased number of return ships after 1600. We have already estimated the total European consumption of Asian goods at 6–7,000,000 lb. per annum, of which the Portuguese still freighted approximately 2,000,000 lb. in the 1590s. The transport of the remaining 4–5,000,000 lb. would necessitate a tonnage of 3,000–3,700 tons per annum, i.e. immediately after 1600 the Company ships, with an average capacity of 4–500 tons, would have handled a quantity of goods equal to that which used to pass along the caravan routes.

To all appearances such a switch over from the caravan routes is more likely than the assumption that the return goods on the Company ships represented an increase in the European consumption of Asian goods: such an explosive development would be unique in the history of pre-industrial economy. Moreover, it seems to be fully confirmed by the information available about the Levant trade. Naturally it is impossible to determine the exact date when the transit trade ceased; strictly speaking it never did cease, and Asian goods were occasionally conveyed to Europe through the Levant well into the 17th century. But the broad stream that had characterized the 16th century, particularly its last decade, ceased abruptly at the beginning of the 17th century. As mentioned elsewhere there were still considerable supplies of pepper to Alexandria in 1601. The information concerning the following years is sparse and ambiguous; in

58. FALCAO pp. 179–182; MAGALHAES-GODINHO pp. 670–673.

1609 the Venetians were still buying pepper in Alexandria,[59] though not in very great quantities, however, and this may possibly have been a consignment the Pasha forced on the merchants out of his own stocks.[60] In the same year 35 Asian ships called at Mocha, but among the goods the following had first place: "All kinds of commodities made of cotton wool, many sorts of gums, pretious stones of all sorts, store of indicoe;"[61] When the English blockaded Mocha in 1612 only three of the sixteen ships – from Achin, Cannanore and Calcutta respectively, had pepper on board, and only in the case of the ship from Achin does the cargo seem mainly to have consisted of pepper.[62] In 1616 33 Asian ships called at Mocha, some of these having pepper on board, but only the ships from Achin and two of the Malabar ships carried larger amounts.[63]

But even previously there were signs that the trade was about to change course. The first reports from around 1610 are still somewhat unreliable; the English traveller, Sandys, declares that "spices brought out of the Levant are now with profit brought thither by our merchants."[64] If Braudel is right in his suspicion that the two ships *N. S. de Pieta* and *N. S. do Monte del Carmine* touched at Leghorn in 1610 with Goa as port of embarkation,[65] there is no doubt about what it implies: if in Lisbon in time of peace East Indian ships were redirected to Leghorn, the import of spices must obviously have shifted from the Mediterranean to the Atlantic. Anyway a few years later there is no longer any doubt. In 1614 the Venetian agent in Florence reported that pepper was being supplied from England to Leghorn, and the following year the whole of the English Company's import into London was bought up in the course of one day, amongst other things with the re-export to Constantinople, the Levant and Naples in view.[66] In January 1617 the Court of the Levant Company wrote to the Ambassador in Constantinople: "For our bringing in of spice into the G.S. dominions it is a matter of that consequence, as you must know their mindes fully in that point, that we fall not hereafter into danger, when we think ourselves secure, for either we must have that freedome, or our trade in Turkey wilbe little worth."[67] In 1618 a Dutch ship touched at Constantinople with a cargo consisting for the most part of spices,[68] and in 1620 accounts appear for the import of pepper, nutmeg

59. Museo Civico-Correr, Venezia, P. D. 2329/xi f. 64.
60. A. d. S. Venezia, Relazioni Collegio Cinque 31, Relation from Cairo 1609.
61. JOURDAIN p. 103.
62. *ibid.* p. 205 ff.
63. van den BROECKE I p. 84 ff.
64. quoted by WOOD p. 78.
65. BRAUDEL I p. 572, cf. BRAUDEL & ROMANO p. 68.
66. CHAUDHURI pp. 156–159.
67. P. R. O. London, S. P. 105/110 f. 92.
68. The *Bailo* to the Doge 24/5 1618, *Calendar S. P. Venetian* p. 219.

and cloves from the Netherlands in the ledger of the Dutch Leghorn merchant, ten Broeck.[69] In 1625 the diversion was commented upon by a learned Turk: "Now the Europeans have learnt to know the whole world; they send their ships everywhere and seize important ports. Formerly the goods of India, Sind and China used to come to Suez, and were distributed by Muslims to all the world. But now these goods are carried on Portuguese, Dutch and English ships to Frangistan, and are spread all over the world from there. What they do not need themselves they bring to Istanbul and other Islamic lands, and sell it for five times the price, thus earning much money. For this reason gold and silver are becoming scarce in the lands of Islam."[70]

Nothing illustrates so convincingly the abrupt manner in which diversion took place than the fact that the Levant towns that previously exported Asian goods to the European markets now imported the same goods from the same markets. Pepper and spices were the first goods to change direction, indigo following somewhat later. The first consignment of any size conveyed by the North-West European Companies to Europe was sent from Surat to London in 1615. Already in 1617 a reduction in the Company sales price was proposed, "to divert the sale of indico from Turkey as hath been of spices."[71] Apparently the Company nevertheless preferred to maintain a price that did not immediately oust the import via Aleppo, even if it meant the accumulation of considerable stocks; at any rate it is maintained in November 1623 that it could still pay to import indigo from the Levant for the Company's price of 5s. per lb.[72] Shortly afterwards, and possibly even prompted by that observation, the Court changed its policy, deciding to enforce price discrimination: exporters to the Mediterranean region were thus offered especially favourable prices and credit facilities.[73] This policy was maintained throughout the following

---

69. HEERINGA pp. 100–105.
70. Omar Talib, quoted by LEWIS p. 118.
71. Court Minute 30/9 1617, C. R. O., London, Court Books vol. IV f. 17.
72. Court Minute 7/11 1623, C. R. O., London, Court Books vol. VI f. 232.
73. Court Minute 26/11 1623, C. R. O., London, Court Books vol. VI f. 281. The initiative came from the Levant merchants, Morris Abbott, who was also the Vice-Governor of the East India Company, and William Garraway. Abbott went out while the case was being heard, but the proposal was received kindly: "It was then agreed that by bringing down the price they shall gaine the Trade and so the Co. shall have the honour to add unto Trade. That 5 for 1 will be gotten at 4 sh. towards charges wheras they are content with a far less gaine in their calicoes. In the end it was agreed and so ordered that Mr. Deputy and Mr. William Garraway shall have 100 barrells of indico at the rate of 4 sh. 9 d. pr lb. at 4 · 6 mo. to be shipt out for the streightes". This decision was extended immediately afterwards to apply to all those willing to take out 100 barrels under the same conditions.

Table 14. *English re-export of Asian goods 1626–1627.*[75]

	Pepper (lb.)		Indigo (lb.)		Calico (pieces)	
	1626	1627	1626	1627	1626	1627
Mediterranean .	801,347	1,799,693	268,889	145,735	3,709	24,232
Netherlands ...	62,926	210,603	23,697	37,550	66	6,348
NW Germany .	145,775	414,214	23,340	8,224	0	927
West France ..	89,705	37,684	19,055	3,050	2,084	0
Baltic area	11,379	33,476	0	0	0	0
Other areas	7,198	1,945	1,050	3,453	1,295	277
Uncertain dest.	46,207	16,780	4,150	0	0	1,724
In all	1,164,537	2,514,395	340,181	198,012	7,154	33,508

years, and there cannot be any doubt about its purpose. In 1625 it was said at a Court meeting: "In the beginning to the East India trade the transportation of pepper into Turkey and other parts adjoining diverted the trade of pepper and it was hoped the same might be brought to pass by sending indigo into Italy and Turkey, which would hinder the bringing of that commodity into those parts."[74] There is no doubt that the trial was a success. As mentioned above indigo was among the regularly quoted English import goods in Aleppo in 1634–36, but it is probable that the stream had already turned at the end of the 1620s. It is possible to tabulate the re-export of Asian goods from London for the years 1626 and 1627, and it seems quite clear from this table that pepper and indigo were by far the most important East Indian re-export articles and that the Mediterranean area was at that time by far the most important re-export market. (see table 14)

At this point the battle about pepper and indigo was won; that cloves and nutmeg were already controlled by the Dutch Company is well-known.[76] The only important commodity remaining from the caravan trade was Persian raw silk. The battle of the silk trade routes became long and hard; in the 1630s, as will be described elsewhere, perhaps half of the Persian silk was directed to the ocean route, but nevertheless the victory in the first instance belonged to the peddlars.

74. Quoted in CHAUDHURI p. 175.
75. P. R. O. London, Port-books E 190/29/4 and E 190/31/1.
76. This was not synonymous with a Dutch monopoly in the sense that VOC could fix their prices at will; some spices evaded the Dutch blokade by means of smuggling, GLAMANN pp. 91–92. But the blockade combined with the Dutch price policy seems to have kept competitors away from the caravan trade.

The Reversal on the Levant Markets

What did the loss of the transit trade mean for the Levant markets? In money it was a matter of about 3–4 million piastres, judging from the above estimate (p. 168) of the extent of the trade and Mun's estimates of Asian prices in Aleppo.[77] In a contemporary context this was a considerable sum, but it does not immediately follow that the loss of the transit trade was disastrous for the Levant economy. The capital that was tied up in the peddling trade could easily be transferred to other investments, since it mainly consisted of stocks of commodities. The service sector that had nourished the transit trade, first and foremost transport, was not very important: those few thousand tons of goods did not require many camels. Curiously enough, it must have been the protectors of the trade, the "publicans and thieves", who suffered the greatest losses. Their investments could not so easily be transferred to other fields.

In addition, the reversal of the transit trade might very well bring about an expansion of the export of commodities produced in the Levant when the European Levant merchants began to seek new investments to replace the vanished goods. That there were in fact such paradoxical effects seems apparent from a closer investigation of trade development in the Levant towns in the years around 1600. The description of the economic fluctuations over a course of years in these towns is full of pitfalls, because, as shown elsewhere, the market conditions were also characterized by short-term fluctuations and non-transparency under normal conditions. A natural tendency to exaggerate the risks and possibilities further distorts the impression created by isolated sources. Thus, as a basis for the following survey of the fluctuations in the terminal towns, a more or less homogeneous material is chosen, which also reflects the market conditions as they developed throughout a number of years: the relations of the Venetian Consuls. On their return home from their three-yearly period of office the Venetian consuls were obliged to present the Senate with an account of the conditions in the places where they had been resident, as well as of the general development within their period of tenure.[78] None of the series is complete, but they are nevertheless sufficiently representative to enable us to follow the development in Aleppo and Alexandria through Venetian eyes in the important decades around 1600. The information contained

77. Mun was adressing a public that knew the Levant prices partly from own experience; thus there is no reason to doubt that the prices he quotes were normal prices, in so far as there is any question at all of normal prices on a market with such great short-term fluctuations as the Levant market. MUN, *East Indies* p. 11.
78. Over and above the current reports, *dispacci*, since 1268 all Venetian representatives were obliged to make a complete report, or *relazione*, on their return, BERCHET, *Siria* p. 22.

in the series is only supplemented from other sources to the extent that they appear to throw light on the long-term development rather than reflecting the immediate situation.

1574–78.[79] Navagero's description of the town of Aleppo during these years is quite rapt: "It lies in an extraordinarily beautiful situation amid many hills in a very fertile and pleasant landscape." The town is about the size of Padua, but more densely populated; he estimates the population to be 400,000. The three leading officials are the Pasha, the *defterdar* (leader of the finance administration) and the *kadi*. In their administration of law and justice they are all corrupt, though everyone nevertheless manages to live in peace and friendship. The Venetian trade had its problems: the Turkish-Persian war, which had begun in 1578, had prevented the free passage of the caravans and created difficulties regarding the supply of Persian silk and the sale of the Venetian goods normally re-exported to Persia. However, with their accustomed flexibility, the caravan merchants had already found new routes, and even before Navagero's departure Persian silk had begun to arrive in the town again. A problem that caused Navagero great anxiety – and justly so, as became apparent later – was the growing French competition in Aleppo. This was something new; the French had not been in evidence before the war (Navagero means the Venetian-Turkish War of 1570–73), but the interruption in the Venetian trade during those years had been their chance,[80] and they had now become irritating competitors who forced up the prices to the detriment of all (that is to say, the Venetians). But in spite of the problems Navagero concludes: "Despite all these difficulties the state of this trade is still very good."

1581–83.[81] Pietro Michele's relation almost exclusively concerns the continued war between Turkey and Persia, and he has very little to say about the state of the trade. He provides one interesting piece of information, however: the number of Turkish officials is rising, thereby creating further expenses to be met by the Venetian nation's common chest, *il cottimo*. Moreover, apart from the officials already haunting the port of embarkation, Tripoli, a *defterdar* sent out directly from Constantinople had arrived, and the new man had tried to increase the evaluation of the goods

79. Andrea Navagero's relation, BERCHET, *Siria* pp. 59–65.
80. COLLIER & BILLIOUD do not regard the war with Cyprus as having any important bearing on the Marseilles trade with the Levant. But see ZELLER p. 130. In the Venetian sources it is only from this date that the French are taken seriously as competitors on the Levant markets.
81. Pietro Michele's relation, read in the Senate 18/12 1584, BERCHET, *Siria* pp. 65–73.

in the customs. It had nevertheless been possible to win him over by means of a modest gift.

1590–93.[82] This turned out to be a problem of growing importance. When Tomaso Contarini took over the consulate in 1590 *il cottimo* had had to pay out 80,000 ducats in extraordinary payments to the officials in Tripoli. The main cause of these irregular extortions, it is maintained, was Tripoli's relative independence of the Porte; in Tripoli, as in the Lebanon on the whole, the traditional rulers continued to play a considerable political role; formally speaking they acknowledged the sovereignty of Constantinople of course, but an order from Constantinople did not carry the same weight against an Emir supported by his armed local tribesmen as against a *beglerbeg* of the regular "civil service".[83] The Venetians found a temporary solution to the problem by transferring the port of embarkation from Tripoli to the little harbour, or rather the little fishing hamlet, of Alexandretta. Apart from a short period from 1609–13[84] Alexandretta became from now on the port of Aleppo. The advantage seen from the European point of view was primarily political; the harbour was bad and the climate unhealthy, but the town, unlike Tripoli, did not have its own Pasha, it belonged administratively under Aleppo, and the only local representative for the Ottoman Empire was an aga of the janissaries.[85]

As for the Venetian trade with Aleppo, during his period of office Contarini maintained briefly that it was "of great importance"; he estimated its extent at one million ducats per annum, chiefly in the form of cloth and silken materials, and states that it was distributed among sixteen "houses".[86]

1593–96[87] Malipiero's relation indicates clearly that the trade in Aleppo was particularly prosperous in the last years of the century, an impression that is also confirmed by other sources.[88] The Venetians were still the most important European nation, with an annual import of about 2 million ducats distributed among sixteen houses as in 1593. The export chiefly

---

82. Tomaso Contarini's relation, read in the Senate 11/12 1593, *ibid.* pp. 74–78.
83. HOLT pp. 103–105, 113–115.
84. WOOD p. 76; cf. P. R. O. London, S. P. 105/110 f. 47, 80.
85. BERCHET, *Siria*, pp. 123–125.
86. In 1557 the Venetian import to Aleppo was estimated at about 350,000 ducats per annum, the French at about 80–100,000 ducats. BERENGO p. 16 n. 2.
87. Alessandro Malipiero's relation, read in the Senate 16/2 1596/97, BERCHET, *Siria* pp. 79–100.
88. See, for example, Dorrington, Aleppo, to Sanderson, Constantinople, 23/6 1596, ". . . hear are 5 Venetian ships in port which have brought in money and commodities above 2 millions . . ." B. M. London, Lansdowne 241 f. 401.

consisted of silk, spices, cotton material and indigo, but the most important part of the Aleppo trade for the Venetian economy was the sale of cloth and silk materials. In Malipiero's time 20,000 cloths were imported annually and 200,000 *braccio* silk cloth. The debt that had burdened the nation was all paid off, and it had been possible to reduce the consular duty to the ordinary 2% as against 5% or more in recent years.

There is no doubt that these were years of boom. There was peace on the Persian border and the route via Basra and Hormuz was also open. The only threat came from the Turkish officials. Their ingenuity, as far as extorting the European merchants was concerned, was inexhaustibile it is maintained. The most dangerous attack had been the attempt to bring the customs evaluation of the import goods in line with the market price, "with a certain right", Malipiero admits; a more realistic customs evaluation would have cost the Venetian nation more than 20,000 ducats per annum. Malipiero nevertheless succeeded in fencing off the Turkish demand once again, though not until he had made a costly appeal to Constantinople.

The boom in the international trading town of Aleppo presented a striking contrast with the screaming poverty in the upland of the town, however. Of the Syrian towns only two prospered: Damascus, which was an administrative centre, and Aleppo. Also the villages lay for the most part deserted, the fields were uncultivated and the country thinly populated. Many had fled, and even the Islamic part of the population wished to be under Christian rule. The main cause of the misery, it is asserted once more, was the extortions of the Turkish officials,[89] again due to the venality of offices. The office of Pasha in Damascus, Aleppo or Tripoli cost 80–100,000 ducats, a *defterdar* paid 40–50,000 and a *kadi* a little less, but they were expert in covering the initial investment with the aid of extortions from their subordinates. These latter in their turn took it out of their subordinates, until the final burden came to rest on "il misero popolo", who not only had to pay the purchase price of the offices, but had to satisfy all the cruel and avaricious demands of the officials. In addition Syria had to maintain an important Ottoman garrison, and every year 460,000 ducats were sent in tribute to Constantinople, of which 300,000 came from Aleppo.

1596–99.[90] The boom in Aleppo continued. According to Emo's estimate,

89. The decline in taxation receipts from Syria as a result of the despotic government and chaotic situation was already mentioned under Selim II (1566–74), HEYD, *Documents*, pp. 117–18. Cf. Filippo Pigafetta from Jerusalem 27/4 1587: ". . . la maledizione data da Dio a questi paesi é cosi terribile, che a poco a poco saranno abbandonati dai Christiani Latini." PIGAFETTA p. 8.

90. Giorgio Emo's relation, read in the Senate 12/12 1599, BERCHET, *Siria*, pp. 100–109.

the Christian nations imported 3 million ducats worth per annum, of which about half was imported by the Venetians, whereas the French and the English each imported about half a million worth of goods per annum, chiefly in the form of coin and woollen materials. In 1599 a Dutch ship had imported goods to the value of 100,000 ducats.[91] As in the time of Malipiero the wiles of the officials constituted the greatest setback; it had cost many thousands of ducats to obtain commands from the Porte prohibiting their extortions, but it had nevertheless been possible to hold them at bay. The merchants had no grounds for complaint, but apparently the population did not have the same possibilities of procuring support in Constantinople. The countryside lay waste and furnished neither the same taxes nor the same surplus of corn as before, and the sole cause, it is repeated, was the ruthless extortions of the officials. 300,000 sequins had to be sent to Constantinople per annum, but the officials were always 100,000 sequins in arrears.

As mentioned, the boom in the transcontinental trade continued, but for the Venetians the competition from the North-West Europeans and the French became steadily more noticeable. Ironically enough, Emo saw a faint hope in the reports about the dispatch of a number of Dutch ships to Asia, however, because with a direct connection to the Asian market it was possible they might give up trading with the Levant. The English Consul himself had said that if the new trade continued he would go home, because 3–4 English merchants in Aleppo would be quite sufficient to take care of the purchases of silk and cotton.

1599–1602.[92] But the peak had already been reached. Although in Dandolo's time the Venetian imports still amounted to 1¹/₂ millions per annum, the investments were only undertaken in order to maintain trade connections while waiting for better times; the momentary prospect was quite unpromising. Here one instinctively expects to find a reference to the effect of the Dutch trade with Asia on the Levant trade, but Dandolo does not mention this matter. The main cause of the difficulties he traces to the extortions of the officials and to the increasing political unrest. The caravans had to pass through many towns and countries, and everywhere the Turkish rulers demanded heavy duties over and above the customary ones, the desert Bedouins did the same, and before the unhappy merchants had reached Aleppo they were so impoverished that none who had once

91. It was not spices that drove the Dutch to the Levant: "The flemysh shippe make account will depart home some 15 days hence she ladeth all galls and cotton-wool and some little indicoe, but not any spices." 29/9 1599, B. M. London, Sloane Ms. 867 f. 64.
92. Vencenzo Dandolo's relation, read in the Senate 27/2 1602/03, BERCHET, Siria, pp. 110–130.

made the journey attempted to do so again. In Aleppo itself the conditions were no better: all the officials, from the most subordinate to the Pasha, the *defterdar* and the *kadi,* extorted money from the merchants, and no one would raise a finger to help them. The source of the trouble, it was maintained yet again, was the venality of offices. In Dandolo's time there had been nine Pashas in Aleppo, and all of them were only interested in recovering the cost of the initial outlay on acquiring the office and accumulating new capital for the purchase of new offices. The *Bailo*'s endeavours in Constantinople and his complaints about the behaviour of the Pashas in office had certainly been able to protect the Venetian nation from the hardest knocks, but had not been able to bring about a radical improvement.

1605. [93] At this point we can interpolate a description of Aleppo from another source: that of the Spanish-Portuguese traveller, Texeira. Though Aleppo, as Texeira saw it, was marked by the war and by political unrest, it was definitely still a prosperous trading town. The year before his visit the customs had brought in 200,000 sequins, which was less than normal, and during his stay the prices in the town were abnormally high, because the Pasha had been obliged to blockade the town in order to drive his predecessor out. Apart from the Consul's house the Venetians still had 14 houses. The value of their annual imports lay between one and 1½ million ducats, and these included 5–6,000 cloths and as much in silks. The French had only five houses in the town, but there were more Frenchmen than Venetians trading in the town because, unlike the latter, they did not live there permanently, but came and went. He estimates the annual French import at 800,000 ducats, chiefly in the form of silver coin. The three houses owned by the English imported goods to the value of 300,000 ducats per annum, chiefly kersey, whereas the Dutch had two houses and an annual import of approximately 150,000 ducats. Every year Alexandretta was visited by 4–5 Venetian ships, 2–3 English and over 20 French.

1608–11.[94] Before and during Sagredo's time of office the situation had become catastrophic for the Venetians, and his relation is first and foremost an attempt to account for the decline in the Venetian trade with Syria. It is remarkable that he is less concerned with the absolute decline in the Syrian trade than with the Venetians' position in relation to other European nations on the Syrian market. According to Sagredo the French annual

93. TEXEIRA pp. 113–122.
94. Gio. Francesco Sagredo's relation, read in *Cinque Savi* 4/7 1611, and his relation, read in the Senate 15/5 1612, BERCHET, *Siria* pp. 130–156.

import was now on a level with that of the Venetians in their best years: 1¹/₂ million ducats. The French Consul, who previously had admitted the Venetian Consul pride of place, now demanded to be recognized as the most distinguished Christian representative in Aleppo. Sagredo saw the causes of the Venetian recession first and foremost in the great losses resulting from shipwreck and piracy, which had raised the insurance premiums to 20–25%. Finally the French, English and Dutch competitors were better supplied with coin than the Venetians, and with their cash purchases forced up the prices. They even made the best buys, whereas the Venetians, who preferred barter, or a combination of cash and barter, had to be content with the poorest quality commodities. This was not quite the kind of crisis one might have expected; the threat was the competition from the other European nations, not the failing supplies of marketable goods. The impression is confirmed by the decision of the *Cinque Savi* in 10/7 1614 to exempt silk exported overland from Venice from the customs duty of 2% that had hitherto been demanded, on the grounds that the Dutch and other merchants previously competed in purchasing silk in Venice, but that they now preferred to seek it elsewhere.[95]

1612–15.[96] The same complaints are repeated in Morosini's relation of 1615. "The trade in Aleppo is as flourishing as ever, because there still come caravans from different places with valuable goods, especially silk ..." Trade in Aleppo prospers, but the Venetian trade with Aleppo has fallen behind, especially compared with the French. The Venetian import was now down to 800–900,000 ducats per annum, including approximately 150,000 ducats in cash. The French imported the equivalent of 3 million „di reali" (presumably piastres) in cash and 500,000 in cloth and tobacco. (This is the first time the latter is mentioned as imported into the Levant). The English imports are estimated to be worth half a million, chiefly in cloth and kersey.

From 1615 to 1625 no consular relations have been preserved, but the lacuna may partly be breached with the aid of the consular dispatches. In the beginning of 1615 the Venetian galley *Balbi* was seized by pirates outside Limasol. In this connection Morosini's successor, Foscarini, spoke about "the evident destruction of this market and especially of this our poor trade ... all the Venetian merchants here are so downhearted and have to that degree lost courage that some think of returning home to Venice, whereas others will travel to India or to Persia. And in August of the same year he repeats: "The main cause of the loss we have suffered

95. A. d. S. Venezia, Cinque Savi, Nuova seria 154, no. 19–19¹.
96. Girolamo Morosini's relation, read 9/2 1615, Berchet, *Siria* pp. 157–60.

is, as I have previously written, the Corsair activity around Cyprus."[97]

It is probable that the resumption of the Turkish-Persian war the following year also caused the merchants worry, since in the beginning of 1620 the Venetian Consul expressed a foreboding that the cease-fire between Persia and Turkey would now be reflected in increased supplies from the East to the Syrian market.[98] His premonitions turned out to be justified. In October he writes: "The trade has increased and improved every day; after my arrival here more than 4,000 bales of silk have been supplied." Because of the great supplies, silk has fallen in price, even though within the last two months more than 500,000 piastres have arrived in Alexandretta from Marseilles.[99] The ample supplies from Persia continue throughout the following year. On 17th October 1621 the Consul writes: "There is plenty of silk here, and considerable amounts are still expected ..."[100] And the following January 1622: "Here the trade is as usual, everyone lacks money, and there are plenty of commodities, especially silk."[101]

But the fresh outbreak of war around Baghdad in the winter of 1622/23 put a stop to the good supplies. Already in May 1623 mention is made of the shortage of goods in the town.[102] In June the French Consul declared: "Alep est battu de tant d'orages que je prevoy grand meconte a ceulx qui l'estimeront a l'esgal du passé. Les guerres du Roy de Perse avec ce prince l'affaiblissent beaucoup en son commerce, d'aultant que les caravannes de soye n'y peuvent plus aborder."[103] In August 1624 the arrival of the caravans was still awaited with impatience;[104] in January and March 1625 the Dutch Consul's letter speaks of the shortage of silk in Aleppo.[105]

The tone in the Venetian relation for the years 1622–25[106] is also in accordance with this development. There were now only 5 Venetian houses in Aleppo, but it is no longer only the Venetians who experience difficult-

---

97. A. d. S. Venezia, Senato, Dispacci Console, I 5/5 1615; *ibid* 1/8 1615.
98. *ibid.* 29/1 1620.
99. *ibid.* 17/10 1620.
100. *ibid.* 17/10 1621.
101. *ibid.* 13/1 1622.
102. P. R. O. London, S. P. 110/54 f. 52.
103. Arch., Chambre de Commerce, Marseille, J 890.
104. Bardier, Aleppo, to Cecy, Constantinople, 4/8 1624, B. N. Paris, Fonds Franc. 16161 f. 62.
105. Laurens de Croy, Aleppo, to *Bewindhebbers*, Amsterdam, 27/1 and 6/3 1625, Dunlop pp. 133, 149; cf. also the French consular dispatch of 25/1 1625: "le commerce ici est maintenant en fort pauvre estat attendue la division de ceste Empire." Archive, Chambre de Commerce, Marseille, J 891.
106. Giuseppe Civran's relation, read in the Senate 21/8 1625, Berchet, *Siria* pp. 161–164.

ies: the whole of Aleppo's existence as an international market is threatened. The extortions of the officials are now worse than ever. The difficulty in selling Venetian textiles is no longer put down to the European competitors alone, but also to the country's impoverished state resulting from the continuous wars and disturbances. Finally, the fighting around Baghdad meant that the caravans did not arrive, especially the Persian caravans, which, for Aleppo's trade, were the richest and the most important. In Aleppo there were rumours about the Dutch contract with the Shah concerning the export of Persian silk through the Persian Gulf, and Civran feared that it might have serious consequences for the town in the long run.

In 1626 there are still complaints about the failing supplies of goods to Aleppo,[107] and there is no better news to be found in the relation that concludes the series of preserved Venetian relations from this period: Pesaro's from 1628.[108] Its very brevity is symptomatic; it concerns merely the continued difficulties caused by the passage of troops, the extortions of the officials and the war that puts a stop to the caravans. The dispatches present a somewhat more detailed picture of the development. In 1627 the caravans come through from Baghdad again despite the continued state of war, and throughout 1627 and 1628 they give the impression of renewed activity and moderate prosperity in the Venetian nation. But it is not really like earlier times: "Veramente, questa piazza non ha di bisogno piu all'anno di doi millia panni di lana..."[109]

In Alexandria, as in Aleppo, the relations of the Venetian consuls provide the best basis for a description of the trade development over a longer period of years. In Dandolo's relation from 1591 the tone is not optimistic.[110] The extortions of the officials are the worst source of grievance, and Dandolo declares that if conditions do not improve it will be necessary to give up the trade with Alexandria and seek the spices elsewhere. However, he had scarcely imagined such a drastic solution to the problem as the one the Dutch and the English discovered a decade later.

---

107. de Willem, Aleppo, to *Bewindhebbers*, Amsterdam, 15/9 1626, DUNLOP p. 204; on the other hand the English Levant Company seems to have increased its activity in Aleppo considerably in 1626, see below, p. 188, cf. Levant Co. to Kirkham, Aleppo, 3/4 1626, P. R. O. London, S. P. 105/110 f. 217: "We are now come for the dispatch of our ships for Turke, the Samson for Const and the Rainbow and Margret for your part, on all which are more goods then ever were sent in one year..."
108. Alvise Pesaro's relation, read in the Senate 1628, BERCHET, *Siria*, pp. 165–166.
109. A. d. S. Venezia, Senato, Dispacci Console II no. 46 and *passim*.
110. Vencenzo Dandolo's relation of 9/8 1591, A. d. S. Venezia, Collegio Cinque, Relazioni Alessandria.

Business picked up in the next few years. Dandolo's successor declared in 1596[111] that in his time of office trade had been better than he had hoped – undoubtedly a result of the failing Portuguese returns in the same years. Only in 1596 had the supplies of spices to Alexandretta been so small that serious price increases were the result, but at the same time it was reported that the supplies of spices to Lisbon had failed,[112] so there was reason to hope that the sales prices would be high there, too.[113] Incidentally, this relation, like the following one from 1599[114], was chiefly filled with complaints about the extortions of the officials, explained as in Aleppo by the venality of offices.

Thus before 1600 there was no indication of any crisis; on the contrary, the main impression is that the boom that characterized Aleppo in the last year of the century also included Alexandria. A gap in the relations until 1615 prevents us from following the development in the decisive years, but there is no doubt that the supplies of spices failed during this period. In 1612 it says in a relation from the Venetian Ambassador in Constantinople, the *Bailo:* "In Alexandria the spices are dearer than in Venice, the trade there has declined considerably."[115] The Consul's relation of 1615 makes sorrowful reading. The difficulties suffered by the Venetian trade in Aleppo, such as shipwreck, capture by pirates and competition from the French, had also struck the nation in Alexandria. But apart from the French competition, what hit the Venetians hardest of all was the fact that spices were no longer supplied to the Egyptian market. "Against pirates Your Serenity will protect us with means that exceed my poor experience. Against shipwreck God will protect us with His loving kindness. But against the new western route of the spices, which has ruined the trade here, and against the large amounts of capital that are conveyed here from different places, in particular from Marseilles, I cannot see any protection, although I realize that it is to our detriment and destruction ..."[116]

This same theme is repeated in the following Venetian relations from Egypt. In 1623 it is stated that the number of Venetian merchants trading

---

111. Tadio Morosini's relation, read in *Cinque Savi* 22/1 1596/97, A. d. S. Venezia, Collegio Cinque, Relazioni Alessandria.
112. According to Portuguese information the import of only 2,642 quintals of pepper in 1596 was the lowest on record, FALCAO p. 67.
113. He was probably right; the retail prices for 1598 show a considerable increase everywhere in Europe in comparison with the level of the previous year, LACH I p. 146.
114. Andrea Paruta's relation, 16/12 1599, A. d. S. Venezia, Collegio Cinque, Relazioni Alessandria.
115. The *Bailo* Contarini's relation 1612, BAROZZI 234.
116. Anon. relation of 1615, A. d. S. Venezia. Collegio Cinque, Relazioni 31.

with the Levant has fallen greatly in recent years, the cause being "the lack of spices from Asia, which have chosen another route after the Dutch have found the new sailing route, and no longer arrive in Cairo, or at least only in small quantities." Trade still continues with the local products, however, just as Venetian cloth still sells well.[117] Again in 1628 the Dutch East Indian trade is blamed for being the most important cause of the difficulties confronting the Venetian trade in Alexandria. "There are various reasons why trade everywhere in the Levant, but especially in Alexandria, has now been declining for many years. The first of these is without doubt the rediscovery by the Dutch of the sea route to Asia, because by travelling to Asia and from there conveying the spices to all parts of the world they have affected our interests in two vital ways at the same time . . ." In addition there are the other problems of piracy and the French competition. In Foscarini's time of office alone, the Venetians have lost eleven ships in connection with Corsair attacks between Alexandria and Venice or Crete. The French have to an increasing extent begun to import cloth, which, though it certainly cannot be compared with the Venetian in quality, is nevertheless in demand on account of its low price, not least by magnates who buy up big lots in order to be able to clothe their men. And, finally, the Venetian silk materials meet competition from local silk materials both in Alexandria and in Aleppo.[118]

In addition to the difficulties already mentioned, in the middle of the 1620s the revolt in the Yemen began, which placed difficulties in the way of the Red Sea route. César Lambert, who was in Egypt from 1627-32, maintained that the revolt closed the route so completely that Egypt had to import cloves, cinnamon, nutmeg, pepper, ginger and indigo from Europe.[119] This revolt is also emphasized in Donado's relation of 1635. The Red Sea trade has now practically ceased, and the cause is the unrest and extortions in Mocha, Jedda and Cairo. The only export commodity of value is sugar, but an embargo is placed on this export by the Pasha in order to collect revenue from the sale of export licenses.[120]

In the 16th century Aleppo and Alexandria were by far the most important trading towns in the Levant as far as the transit trade between Asia and Europe was concerned. But a sketch of the development of the trade in these decades would be incomplete without considering Smyrna. With re-

---

117. Antonio Capello's relation is undated, but according to internal evidence can be referred to 1623, A. d. S. Venezia, Collegio Cinque, Relazioni Alessandria.
118. Gieronimo Foscarini's relation of 13/3 1628, A. d. S. Venezia, Collegio Cinque, Relazioni Alessandria.
119. LAMBERT pp. 6–7.
120. Zuanneo Donado's relation of 20/11 1635, A. d. S. Venezia, Collegio Cinque, Relazioni Alessandria.

gard to sources, however, we are not standing on so firm ground as compared to the older centres. Characteristically, the decline of the old markets is better illuminated in the material preserved in the archives than is the rise of the new star; it was with some delay that the European States appreciated Smyrna's rapidly growing importance and sent out consuls to the town.

At the close of the 16th century Smyrna played no part in the transcontinental trade, even though it occupied a not insignificant position as exporter of local products. In 1603 it is said contemptuously in a letter from Smyrna: "Here is not any news worth writing from this barren place."[121] Lithgow, who visited the town a few years later is more positive: "They have great traffick with all Nations especially for the fine silk, cotton woolle and Dimmetie brought to it by the country peasants, which strangers buy from them."[122] In 1624 it is still said about Smyrna: "La ville ... est a demi-ruinée et de peu de consideration aujourd'hui."[123] But half a century later Tavernier wrote about Smyrna: "Smyrne est aujourd'-huy pour le négoce, soit par mer, soit par terre la ville la plus célèbre de tout le Levant, et le plus grand abord de toutes les marchandises qui passent de l'Europe en Asie, et de l'Asie en Europe ..."[124]

The beginning of this astonishing development must be placed in the 1620s. The first mention of supplies of Persian silk to Smyrna dates from 1621,[125] but it was in the years following the resumption of the Persian-Turkish war in the winter of 1622–23 that Smyrna became a serious competitor to Aleppo as the terminus for the Persian silk caravans. In July 1623 the Venetian *Bailo* reported from Constantinople: "Many Persian merchants have begun to arrive in Smyrna with silk and other commodities from those areas."[126] Some of these merchants had continued to Marseilles, and the *Bailo* pointed out that it would be an advantage if they could be persuaded to go to Venice with their silk instead.[127] *Cinque Savi* discussed the Bailo's recommendation in a joint session with the Senate; it was appreciated that a Persian-Armenian import to Venice via Smyrna, as the trade had developed, would be desirable, and it was therefore decided to relieve the Armenians of their ordinary import duties: 2% *bailaggio* and 1% *cottimo*.[128]

At approximately the same time the first mention of the silk trade via

121. B. M. London, Lansdowne Ms. 241, f. 151.
122. Lithgow K 2 v.
123. Gédouyn p. 145.
124. Tavernier I p. 79.
125. Masson p. 372 n. 4.
126. A. d. S. Venezia, Rubricari Konstantinopoli, D 14 f. 78.
127. *ibid.*
128. A. d. S. Venezia, Cinque Savi, Nuova seria 4, 7/9 1623.

Smyrna appears in the French material. Vieuville's special envoy to the Levant, Sanson Napollon, endeavoured immediately on his arrival in Smyrna in January 1624 – against the French merchants' wishes[129] – to persuade the Armenians to freight on French rather than on Venetian or Dutch ships,[130] and later the same year he writes from Constantinople: "There are reliable reports here that 300 loads of silk are on their way to Smyrna and are fifteen days from the town".[131]

Presumably the supplies have been irregular and conditioned by the political situation in the first years – the Armenians' interest in continuing to a European harbour from Smyrna indicates that it has taken time to build up a regular buyers' market – but the interrelationship between the new market and Aleppo very soon became apparent to those interested. The greater the extortions the trade was exposed to on the route between Persia and Aleppo and in Aleppo itself, the more reason there was to take the longer, but peaceful and less overburdened northern route. This connection appears quite clearly in a dispatch from the Venetian consul in Aleppo from the end of 1626. He had tried in vain to get the hated farmer of the customs, Bedick, dismissed, but the attempt had not succeeded, and he now predicted the total ruin of the Aleppo trade in the most gloomy phrases: "Already the scourge is felt, since many big caravans with silk and other costly goods expected from Emit, Erzurum and Basra have now already dispersed, and most of them have made for Smyrna."[132]

From this account of the conditions in the individual terminal towns we can return to the general problem: how and when did the transit trade disappear and what did its disappearance mean to the Levant economy, or perhaps even for the economy of the Mediterranean as a whole?

The answer to the first two questions ought to be provided by a comparison between this section and the previous one, even if the material does not provide any possibility of following the development quantitatively from year to year. The abrupt increase in the number of ships re-

129. Archive, Chambre de Commerce, Marseille, J 1565, 24/1 1624.
130. Already in November 1622 the Marseilles town government had complained to the King about the silk trade carried on by Armenian merchants through Toulon. The transport had taken place on a Dutch ship. Archive, Chambre de Commerce Marseille, J. 889, 16/6 1623. The complaint was repeated in a memorandum of 14/7 1623, in the form of a bitter attack against the merchants' activities in France. If this traffic continued, it said, one might just as well abolish the consulates in the Levant and let the Armenians open up a consulate in Marseilles. – The King resolved that it would be a sufficient countermeasure to order the Armenians to take home the profits from the silk sales in the form of goods. BERGASSE & RAMBERT pp. 65–67.
131. Archive, Chambre de Commerce, Marseille, J 1565 10/6 1624.
132. A. d. S. Venezia, Senato, Dispacci Console, Siria II no. 18.

turned to Europe from Asia after the establishment of the Companies around the turn of the century did not merely mean that the European consumption was increased by so many tons of Asian goods, but marked a definitive change from one trading route to another. The very last years of the 16th century were years of prosperity in the Levant trade; it follows that the cause must be sought in the North-West European activity, not in the Levant.

The question concerning the effects of the loss of the transit trade is more difficult and eludes a simple answer. There was no question of the balance of trade merely becoming re-established at a lower level; matters were much more complicated than that. The most important observation in this connection is that the recession did not effect all the nations equally; in fact only the Venetian nation showed definite signs of recession within the first three decades of the 17th century. The Dutch did not enter the Levant trade until 1597, and their activity in this area reached its temporary culmination in 1614 with the shipping of goods and money to the value of well over half a million piastres from Alexandretta.[133] Regarding the English Levant Company the scattered evidence indicates progress rather than stagnation or regression. A very rough estimate of the English trade with Aleppo may be established on the basis of the attendance at the meetings of the English nation in Aleppo in the

Table 15. *Attendance at the meetings of the English nation in Aleppo 1616–1629.* [134]

	No. of meetings	Names mentioned	New names
1616	5	22	
1617	9	25	13
1618	6	21	6
1619	15	26	5
1620	5	21	4
1621	11	19	3
1622	5	23	8
1623	7	23	8
1624	9	17	3
1625	8	19	3
1626	6	28	12
1627	6	22	1
1628	22	35	15
1629	9	22	0

133. BRAUDEL I p. 569; HEERINGA pp. 486–487; WÄTJEN pp. 138–145.
134. P. R. O. London, S. P. 110/54 *passim.*

years 1616–1629. At every meeting the names of those attending were registered, and the number of those absent was modest; these lists should thus provide a reliable impression of the number of English merchants who arrived and worked in Aleppo.

The scattered information available about the English import in these years also supports the impression of continued prosperity in the English Levant trade.[135] Finally, the French Levant trade also seems to have been prospering at any rate until the beginning of the 1620s, and there are no sure signs of serious difficulties before the outbreak of the French-Spanish war in 1636. The time-honoured conception of the disastrous decline of the French Levant trade following the good times under Henry IV[136] rests upon a very slender foundation: a comparison between Seguiran's estimate of the extent of the trade in 1633 and an estimate of the extent of the trade at the beginning of the century accredited to the French Ambassador in Constantinople, de Brèves. Whereas Seguiran's estimate is authentic and is apparently worked out on the basis of carefully collected material, it is even doubtful whether de Brèves' evaluation exists, and, if so, whether it can be regarded as a reliable source.[137] The Venetian Consul's statement concerning French advance in the years after 1600 is supported by the small amount of statistical material available, as, for example, the number of French ships to the Levant. For the years 1614–18 Bergasse and Rambert provide the following figures for ships from Marseilles with the Levant as destination:

Table 16. *Ships leaving Marseilles for Levantine ports 1614–18.*[138]

	Egypt	Syria	Greece	In all
1614	26	26	15	67
1615	17	25	8	50
1616	19	26	13	58
1617	20	19	18	57
1618	7	23	10	40

135. MILLARD table B (Countries from which goods were imported into London) gives the following figures for the import from the Levant and the East Indies respectively, calculated on the basis of the preserved port-books:

	The Levant	The East Indies
1620–21	£ 181,997	£ 87,040
1625–26 (10 months)	£ 73,570	£ 171,274
1629–30	£ 352,263	£ 164,206
1633–34	£ 207,057	£ 205,734

136. MASSON pp. 118–130.
137. COLLIER & BILLIOUD pp. 549–550.
138. BERGASSE & RAMBERT pp. 95–97.

The correspondence of the consuls provides a few supplementary figures. In 1625 Alexandretta was visited by 21 French ships, in 1626 by 18, in 1627 by 18, and in 1628 by 16.[139] The import of ready money registered in the consulate, i.e. with reservations regarding smuggling, constituted well over a million piastres between 23rd April 1620 and 4th March 1621.[140] In 1633 Seguiran still estimated the annual navigation to the Levant from Marseilles at about 70 vessels: 15 to Alexandria, 8 to Seidon, 20 to Alexandretta, 12 to Smyrna, 10 to Constantinople, 4–5 to Satalia and a few to the islands.[141] On the other hand there is no doubt that the outbreak of war in 1635 and 1636 was a serious blow to the French Levant trade.[142]

The incongruity between the fate of the Venetian merchants and the other European nations reveals that more was at stake than mere supplies of Asian goods to Aleppo and Alexandretta. If we take our starting-point, not in the establishment of the North-West European East India Companies, but some decades earlier, both the Venetian catastrophe and the establishment of the Companies may be placed within a wider context. The most important new factor was the interest of the North and West Europeans in a trade they had not previously been concerned with to any great extent, and their success with this trade. In the 16th century the French, the English and the Dutch entered the scene as competitors in a market the Venetians had largely had for themselves until then. They proved to be able competitors by virtue of three factors: their cheaper textiles, their ready money and their safer navigation.

The Venetian economy did not adapt itself to this challenge. We know, thanks to Cipolla and Stella,[143] that it was what we might call the socio-economic barrier, primarily the rigidity of the guilds, that prevented a reorganization of the textile industry. The question of silver appears at first glance more mysterious. Braudel in particular has emphasized the importance of the inflow of American bullion; the stream of silver from

139. Archive, Chambre de Commerce, Marseille, J. 969.
140. *Ibid.* (comptes de la nation).
141. MASSON p. 131 n. 1.
142. "Vous apprendera . . . le miserable estat auquel le négosse est reduit, la ruine de toutes les échelles du Levant, et particulierement celle d'Alep . . ." Viguier, Marseille, 26/5 1636, Arch. Affaires Étr., Paris Corr. Pol., Turquie I f. 484. – ". . . de toutes les afflictions et calamités dont elle [Marseille] a esté accuelli depuis douze ou quinze ans en ça rien ne la tant desolée que l'interruption ou plutost suppression entière dudit negoce, car appres que par la rupture des deux couronnes toute sorte de commerce leur a esté interdit avec les estats du Roy d'Espagne, il ne leur rien rien est resté que celuy du Levant a la ruine duquel toutes choses ont conspirés . . ." Archive, Chambre de Commerce, Marseille, J 1729, memorandum undated, but can from the context be referred to 1641. – Cf. also the *Bailo* Contarini's relation of 1640, BAROZZI p. 388.
143. CIPOLLA pp. 137–139; SELLA *Woollen Industry* pp. 120–124.

Potosi followed a new course.[144] But this interpretation does not appear satisfactory: a dollar does not choose its own fate, but must travel wherever its owner sends it. If the money circumvented Venice but passed through Marseilles and Amsterdam, it was because its owners expected the largest profit on their investment through these towns. The Venetians knew that. "Li capitali che concorrono in Marsiglia (siccome corre la voce) sono per 300,000 ducati di Genovesi, 500,000 di Lionesi e 100,000 delle altre citta circonvicine."[145] If money did not arrive in Venice we cannot blame a natural catastrophe for having altered its course, the cause must be sought in the Venetians' failing competitive power. The money had not left the Mediterranean; that is proved by the hectic activity in the Levant markets of the 90s, when the Portuguese *carreiras* failed.

A North and West European trade initiative in the Levant was the first phase in the battle. The Venetians did not adapt themselves to the new situation, but by relying upon their well-oiled trade machinery they joined in the boom that reached its culmination in the 1590s. In the years following 1600 the situation became even less favourable for the Venetians, still without any adaptation taking place. The spices disappeared from the Levant markets – this must have happened during the first decade of the century – and the competition concerning other objects of investment was thereby increased, first and foremost as regards silk. This shift in the interest of the buyers can be observed directly after the reception of the news of the arrival of the first Dutch East Indian ships (see page 47), and is very apparent in the report of the Dutch Ambassador in Constantinople in 1615 of the discussions concerned with the introduction of the new customs charges on silk in Aleppo: "Since on account of the great navigation to India the trade with spices has thus declined in the Levant and has in recent years, as it were, become nothing, whereas on the other hand trade with silk has increased considerably on account of the passion for display that is daily becoming greater in Christendom, so that Frenchmen in particular load their ships with it ..."[146]

Additionally there are other difficulties that particularly decreased the

144. "Or si, de 1550 à 1620, dates grossièrement fixées, le poivre et les épices passent par la Méditerranée, n'est ce pas par ce que l'argent d'Amérique finit par y aboutir et pendant de longues années?" Braudel i p. 516.
145. Sagredo in 1612, Berchet, *Siria* p. 149.
146. Haga to the States General 2/5 1615 Dunlop p. 451; cf. also the memorandum from Marseille Town Council to the King of 14/7 1623, quoted by Masson p. XXXII: "Les marchands reprirent leur premier train [sous Henri IV] auqel néanmoins ils reconnurent un grand changement; car de ce que le fonds principal du négoce consistait en épicerie, ils trouvèrent qu'il était entièrement diverti et transféré du côté du Ponant par l'ouverture que les flamands avait faite d'aller quérir les épiceries aux Moluqes ..., Les marchands de Marseille s'adonnèrent alors a porter des soies ..."

Venetians' competitive power. The wars against Persia and the many other disturbances in the Ottoman Empire in the first half of the 17th century created difficulties for the sale of the luxury goods in which the Venetians specialized. Under the harsh conditions it was not silk material and fine cloth that were needed, but coarse cloth and ready money. But it is probable that the political situation, too, was part of the general strucural crisis. It is argued above (p. 79 ff.) that the increased liquidity in the Ottoman Empire in the last quarter of the 16th century was an important element in the political instability of the period. But, as Haga's account illustrates, the redirection of the intercontinental trade moved the basis for imposing customs. Thereby not only was the fiscal basis for important parts of the Ottoman administration disturbed, but also a shift must have occurred in the balance between the separate organisms of the redistributive institution.[147] And, finally, the attacks of pirates on the merchant vessels, which particularly affected the Venetians, may be placed in the same context. In the words of Braudel, the Empires had turned their backs on the Mediterranean,[148] and in the years around 1600 the Corsair activity underwent no less than a technological revolution. The North-West Europeans were, quite literally, armed to take up this challenge, and the small ships of the French also had a good chance of being able to defend themselves against the Corsairs – at any rate they spread the risk, but the Venetians did not adapt themselves to the new security problem until after a long period of deliberation.[149]

All these factors were self-increasing in their effects; every blow decreased the victim's ability to repel or avoid a new blow, and it was those best established that were the hardest hit; a reorganization required the immediate writing off of the existing investments.[150] On the other hand, for those who adapted themselves there was not merely an immediate profit to make, but a world market to conquer.

The spices disappeared from the caravan trade in the first decade of the 17th century, but this decisive shift was not an isolated event: it belonged within a wider context. The battle about the Asian goods in the

147. DUNLOP p. 451 ff.
148. BRAUDEL II p. 190 n. 3; cf. DERMIGNY I p. 92 ff.
149. TENENTI pp. 136–144.
150. A good example of the fact that the most consolidated merchants could have the greatest difficulties in a period demanding adjustments is the Venetians' unwillingness to transfer the chief market to Tripoli in order to avoid the extortions in Aleppo and the transport inland. The English desired such a transfer, but they were well aware that it could only be put into effect if the European nations were in agreement: "we wish withall, that the Venetian factors of Aleppo might be brought to inhabit in Tripolis and make that their mart-towne ... which the Venetians will hardly be drawn unto, by reason of the extraordinary charges bestowed upon their houses in Aleppo." P. R. O. London, S. P. 105/110 f. 47.

Levant markets had already been initiated several decades previously, and the battle about the Levant goods continued after the spices had definitively disappeared from the transcontinental routes. The cessation of the transit trade was an integral part of a comprehensive structural confrontation.

The Fall of Hormuz

In this book the fall of Hormuz has been chosen as a symbol of the structural crisis because Hormuz, with its peculiar unnaturalness, was only able to survive within the old structure and had to perish on confrontation with the new. It was an island of salt and sulphur, a barren volcanic island beneath skies whose climate must be reckoned among the most unpleasant in the world. It had no vegetation, not even any drinking water, and yet throughout centuries it was one of the centres of world trade. And the fall of the town was just as strange as its life; when Hormuz fell in 1622 it was deserted by its inhabitants, never to rise again.

Hormuz was a trading centre and the heart of a Maritime Empire in the Persian Gulf when the Portuguese made their entry into Asian waters. Apart from Hormuz itself the Empire included some of the neighbouring islands, several points on both the Arabian and the Persian sides of the Gulf and the island of Bahrein, whose pearl-fishing was one of the Empire's main sources of income.[151] By virtue of its strategic position Hormuz was one of the first points to attract the attention of the Portuguese. In 1507 Albuquerque occupied the island; he began the establishment of a fortress, but withdrew shortly afterwards after having imposed a tribute to the Portuguese King on the King of Hormuz. During a subsequent visit in 1515 Albuquerque strengthened his grasp on the island, which was relieved of all effective possibilities of defence and equipped with a Portuguese garrison.[152] The Kingdom retained its formal independence, however, in vassalage to Portugal, and not until 1543 did the Portuguese authorities take over the control of the *alfandega,* or custom house, in Hormuz. The official justification was that the King of Hormuz was in arrears with the tribute, (he owed 500,000 ducats),[153] but it seems probable that the Portuguese takeover of the custom house in Hormuz also reflects the increasing interest in the Gulf route after the Turkish conquest of Basra.[154]

With the takeover of the *alfandega* the real political power in Hormuz

151. Hormuz in the years immediately preceding the arrival of the Portuguese is described by Ludovico de Varthema, HAMMOND pp. 107–111.
152. FAROUGHY pp. 53–69.
153. DANVERS I pp. 461–462; *Documentação Ultramarina Portuguesa* II pp. 83–84.
154. STRIPLING pp. 79–81; BRAUDEL I pp. 496, 498–99; HOLT p. 56.

was transferred to the Portuguese Crown's representatives on the spot. The Italian traveller, Federici, who passed through the town in 1563 or 1564, was present at the enthroning of a new King. The old King was dead, and the Portuguese Captain appointed a new one from among the relatives of the deceased at a ceremony in the Portuguese fortress. The new King swore allegiance to the King of Portugal and received thereafter the Royal insignia from the hands of the Portuguese Captain, whereupon everyone accompanied the new King to his palace, which lay outside the fortified area in the town itself. Federici adds that the Captain saw to it that the King was well looked after and showed him the respect befitting his Royal rank whenever they rode out together. But the King was not allowed to ride out with his train without first having informed the Captain.[155]

If the world was a ring Hormuz would be its jewel.[156] Presumably it was under the Portuguese rule in the second half of the 16th century and the beginning of the 17th that this strange town experienced its heyday. At the beginning of the 17th century the population of the town was estimated to be about 40,000, distributed in 2500–3000 houses.[157] 300 of these houses were in reality only mud-built huts occupied by the poorest people, but the majority, those which constituted the town proper, were well-built 2–3 storey houses with many windows covered with venetian blinds. The streets were so narrow that two pedestrians could scarcely pass each other, and on the roofs of the houses were the characteristic cowls described in detail by Figueroa, which drew fresh air down into the houses through an ingeneous system of air channels. From May to Sep-

155. *Nuovo Ramusio* p. 8.
156. "Si terrarum orbis, quaqua patet, annulus esset, Illius Ormusium gemma decusque foret." Thus Thomas Herbert. But the island is described in similar terms by nearly all the travellers who visited it. See, for example, ALEXANDRE de RHODES p. 52: "Si le monde estoit une bague, Ormus en seroit la pierre precieuse." Pyrard has a somewhat different and almost better version: "If the world was an egg, Hormuz would be its yolk," PYRARD de LAVAL II:I p. 240.
157. Hormuz is exhaustively described by a number of European travellers: Circa 1500, Ludovico de Varthema, HAMMOND pp. 107–111; 1549–50, Gaspar Barzaeus, WICKI I pp. 646–647, II pp. 77–79; 1563 or 1564, Federici, *Nuovo Ramusio* pp. 7–8; 1580, Balbi, *Nuovo Ramusio* pp. 118–124; 1583, Newbery, PURCHAS VIII p. 452 ff.; 1583, Fitch, HAKLUYT V pp. 468–469, PURCHAS X p. 165 ff.; 1586–87, Giovan Battista Vechietti, VECHIETTI pp. 158–160; circa 1590, Augustinho Dazevedo, SILVA p. 62; 1587, 1593–97, 1604, Texeira, TEXEIRA pp. 19–24, 164–168; 1601–02, Gouvea, GOUVEA f. 15–16; 1605–06, Gaspar de San Bernardino, GASPAR de S. BERNARDINO pp. 109–95; Garcia de Silva y Figueroa, FIGUEROA I pp. 256–272, II pp. 452–474; Anon., B. N. Lisboa, Ms. F. G. 580, f. 33; – Finally, second-hand descriptions of considerable value by LINSCHOTEN and PYRARD de LAVAL.

tember the entire population of Hormuz: men, women, children and cats, spent the night in négligé on the roof terraces of the houses. And although, as Figueroa says, there were bridges between all the houses, and there thus was ample opportunity for committing theft or other crimes, not least because the inhabitants were of so many different nationalities, nothing like this took place; on the contrary, they all behaved towards each other with great consideration and tolerance.

The atmosphere of the town was cosmopolitan. The nucleus was Persian-speaking, some of them Christians "da tierra", the majority Muslims. In addition there were Hindus from Sind and the Cambaya towns, a small colony of 100-150 Jewish houses, whose religious ceremonies were strongly influenced by Hindu and Muslim rituals, but which were saved for orthodoxy in the 16th century by the immigration of Spanish-speaking Jews who arrived in Hormuz via Constantinople, Aleppo and Tripoli.[158] There were about 200 Portuguese households at the beginning of the 17th century. To this should be added the garrison of the fortress, nominally 500, later 800 men, but in practice scarcely ever up to the specified number. This mixed gathering was joined by people travelling through: merchants and seamen of all the religions and nations of Europe and Asia. Newbury's companions on his arrival in Hormuz in 1581 provide an excellent illustration of the motley assortment: "One Turk, and one Moore of Lahore, and one Moore of Fez in Barbarie, and five Persians, and twelve Moores of Aleppo, Aman and other places, and one Nostrane, a Christian, and my man, who was a Greeke."[159]

Hormuz, the island of Hormuz, was in itself worth nothing: "A barren rock, inhabited by some two hundred souls, who eke out a precarious existence by the sale of the salt which forms the main staple of commerce and by mining red oxide for export to Europe."[160] That was how the island was described at the beginning of this century. No vegetation apart from some puny thorn bushes and a modest garden surrounding the island's only freshwater well on the east side of the island, established by the Kings of Hormuz. The water supply was secured with the help of cisterns for catching the rainwater, which fell at times with great violence. The wealthier people, however, preferred the water that was sailed across from the neighbouring island of Qishm or from the mainland; in longer periods of drought all the water had to be brought to the island in that way. When Figueroa, the Spanish Ambassador to Persia, passed through Hormuz in 1619, it had not rained for two years and the cisterns were empty. Some days after his arrival it rained for a quarter of an hour,

---

158. WICKI II p. 78, cf. FIGUEROA I p. 263.
159. PURCHAS VIII p. 459. "There are people of so many nations on this island that it is asserted by some to be the centre of the world." WICKI II p. 77.
160. WILSON p. 151.

though only enough to lay the dust. But on the night of the 2nd January 1620 Figueroa experienced a proper cloudburst in Hormuz. For two hours the rain streamed down, the cisterns filled to the brink, and all over the island the rain was lying in puddles and waterholes. The next morning the entire population of the town: people and animals – camels, oxen, pigs, goats, donkeys and dogs, streamed out in order to drink the water and bathe in the water-holes. For several weeks afterwards water was gratis for the poor.[161]

The wealth of Hormuz was its position: sooner a cork in a bottle than a jewel in a ring. There had to be a trading town in the mouth of the Gulf, the strange thing was merely its site on the least habitable of all the islands in the Gulf. But this site obviously possessed strategic advantages for whichever power happened to rule over the sea. Even if the attacker should manage to transport invasion forces across to the island he would soon meet insurmountable difficulties with regard to supplies. The town and the fortress possessed their own supplies and cisterns; the besieged could starve out the besiegers. But the command of the seas was the precondition, and it was by virtue hereof that the Portuguese managed to retain the fortress throughout more than a century with a garrison of less than 500 men, and grew accustomed to regarding Hormuz as invincible.

A certain production of hand-made luxury articles took place in Hormuz, but most people lived from trading. In view of this it is remarkable that merchants from Hormuz are practically never mentioned on any other of the great international trading markets in Asia. The role of the Hormuzians seems to have been to mediate between the merchants of the various nations who brought their goods to the town. Following the rhythm of the monsoons, from Hormuz there were regular connections with Persia via Lar and Shiraz, with Bahrein, with Basra and Baghdad and from there on to the Syrian trading towns, with the towns along the west coast of India, including Goa, and via Goa with East and South-East Asia. The goods exchanged in Hormuz were characteristic of the glorious peddling trade. From Basra came European textiles, coral and haberdashery, Venetian mirrors, glass and paper, but primarily coined and uncoined silver; from Arabia, horses; from Persia, carpets and silken materials; from India, cotton materials; from South-East Asia, spices and drugs; from China, porcelain. In Hormuz the routes converged, and from Hormuz they also started. To Basra went cotton materials, drugs and spices and even pepper, on which the Portuguese officials usually turned a blind eye against payment of bribes;[162] to Arabia and Persia, similar goods; to India and

161. FIGUEROA II p. 452 f.
162. *Documentação Ultramarina Portuguesa* II p. 43.

196

thence to East and South-East Asia, money and horses, European haberdashery and Persian materials. In addition there was the local trade: food
and drink for as many as 40.000 people, water and fodder for their
domestic animals and supplies for the ships. Everything had to be brought
to the island from outside and more than one traveller remarked on the
high cost of living in the town.

How extensive was the trade through Hormuz? Information regarding
the number of ships calling there does not provide any clear impression.
In 1619 one of the best observers, a Portuguese, estimated 20–30 ships per
annum on the Asian side of the town.[163] It is probable that this estimate
was more realistic at the time concerned than the information the Dutch
agent, Visnich, was able to procure in 1623 concerning the regular calls
before the fall of the town.

Table 17. *Visnich's estimate of the annual arrivals to Hormuz before
1622.*[164]

Towns	No. of ships	Loaded with
Mouth of the Indus	8	white and couloured materials
Nagena	3	calico and coarse baftas
Diu	5	precious goods from Cambaya, Ahmadabad, Agra, etc.
Damao	3	materials, rice, cardamom, tobacco
Bassein	3	materials, rice, cardamom, tobacco
Chaul	8	many kinds of materials
Dabhol	4	precious linens from Deccan
Goa	12	many kinds of commodities
Cochin	2	pepper, cinnamon, materials, etc.
Malacca	2	different articles of value
Bengal	2	sugar, lac, wax, etc.
Malindi	2	drugs, gums, etc.
	54	

With the aid of some scattered information concerning customs revenue
available from the town's *alfandega* we can throw a little more light on the
problem of the extent of the trade through Hormuz, although it is insufficient to illuminate the fluctuations or reveal the absolute extent of the
trade with certainty. The first tribute Albuquerque imposed on the town
was of 15,000 xerafims; after a few years it was raised to 25,000 xerafims

163. Belchior dos Anjos, Luz pp. 594–595.
164. Terpstra p. 285 ff.

and in 1523 to 60,000 xerafims per annum.[165] In the years between 1524 and 1543 the annual income from the custom house must have been about 90,000 xerafims per annum; after the Portuguese took over the customs a fall occurred, but already in the end of the 1540s the annual income was well over 100,000 xerafims.[166] Around 1585 the annual income from the Royal customs in Hormuz was estimated at 170,000 pardaos of 300 reis.[167] In 1594 the proceeds were transferred to Goa after subtracting the local expenses; it was a matter of 30,000 pardaos, which was regarded as unusually little and resulted in some questioning in the King's letter to the Viceroy the following year.[168] The permanent local expenses in the 1590s were estimated at 60,000 cruzados per annum, i.e. the income in the bad year must have been 110,000 pardaos. In an undated source which, according to internal criteria, may be traced to the 1590s[169] and, according to the author, builds on observation during an eleven-year stay in Hormuz, it is maintained that 200,000 cruzados or about 270,000 pardaos was demanded in Royal customs in Hormuz per annum, but it is added that the proceeds could be as much as 350,000 cruzados if the officials were honest. If to the existing duties there was added a 5% duty on the import of silver, which was duty-free under the current regulations, and an export duty on textiles, on which there was only a small duty, the sum would amount to 500,000 cruzados. Despite these possibilities, the Viceroy had planned to farm out the customs for 100,000 cruzados per annum "either because he had no better information concerning India, or for other secret reasons."[170] In 1602 a certain Vencente Henrique Depaz took over the farm of the *alfandega* in Hormuz against an annual payment of 250,000 pardaos.[171] In 1607 Falcão estimated the Crown's annual income from customs in Hormuz at 144,000 cruzados, or 192,000 xerafims.[172]

The rates of duty, according to the Italian traveller, Balbi, in *circa* 1580, were 11% in Royal customs and 1% for the maintenance of the defence fleet. In addition, for Jews, Armenians and Muslims there was an extra duty of 3%.[173] In 1619 a duty of 14% in Hormuz is mentioned, and since it appears from the context to be non-Portuguese merchants the author has in mind, it may be regarded as a confirmation of Balbi's infor-

165. FAROUGHY p. 75.
166. MAGALHAES-GODINHO, *Crises* p. 5.
167. PURCHAS ix p. 162.
168. *Archivo Portuguez-Oriental* IV p. 574.
169. *Documentação Ultramarina Portuguesa* II p. 43, p. 79 ff.
170. *Ibid.* pp. 91–92.
171. C. R. O. London, Hague Transcripts I, no. XI a.
172. FALCAO p. 77.
173. *Nuovo Ramusio* p. 124. Concerning 1 % to the defence fleet see also *Archivo Potuguez-Oriental* III p. 89, *carte real* of 6/2 1587.

mation.[174] Unfortunately it does not seem clear whether it is merely a transit duty. Assuming the latter, which would be in accordance with Asian practice, and reckoning $1/8$ as an average duty on the turnover, we reach a turnover that, after the middle of the 16th century, has seldom been less than one million pardaos, usually nearer two millions. But these figures must be regarded as the absolute minimum; there is no reason to doubt the frequent statements confirming the existence of large-scale, officially aided and abetted smuggling in Hormuz, and to this must be added the fact that such an important part of the import as silver was not taxed. In the 1590s the export of silver alone was estimated at two million (cruzados?) per annum.[175]

Some fragmentary information may supplement the impression of the extent of the transit trade through Hormuz. Shortly before 1600 the annual export of horses to India via Hormuz was estimated at 1500. At embarkation every horse had cost the exporter 40,000 reis, of which 19,500 was customs for the King.[176] Reckoned at 300 reis = 1 pardao, the annual export of horses alone could thus be valued at 200,000 pardaos, of which 97,500 pardaos, or nearly half, were duties to the King. In 1589 the Superintendent of the Royal finances in Hormuz thinks that a 6% duty on drugs like indigo, cloves, cinnamon, nutmeg, lac, ginger, long pepper and sugar, which were exported by Arabian merchants to Basra, would be able to fetch 25,000 cruzados per annum, i.e. he reckoned with an annual export of these commodities to the value of 400,000 cruzados.[177]

The official posts in Hormuz were much in demand, and the attitude to the offices is very well illustrated by the anecdote concerning Alvaro de Noronha, who, as Captain in Hormuz in 1551, declared that since his predecessor, who was a Lima, had been able to make 140,000 pardaos in his three years, he himself, who was a Noronha, ought to be able to do even better.[178] In *circa* 1580 the positions of Factor and Captain in Hormuz were reckoned among the most lucrative of their kind in the Portuguese Empire.[179] Diogo do Couto maintains that a Captain in Hormuz could make about 2–300,000 pardaos in three years;[180] in 1619 a Captain's income for the three-year period in Hormuz is still estimated at 300,000 cruzados, and it is said in this connection that a single ship from Dabhol had paid 40,000 ducats in customs, but that it was taken for granted that

174. Belchior dos Anjos, Luz pp. 594–595, cf. also C. R. O. London, O. C. 792 (1618): "14 per cent which is the custom they pay at Ormuz."
175. *Documentação Ultramarina Portuguesa* II, p. 43.
176. *Ibid.* p. 113.
177. Arch. Simancas, Secr. Prov., Libr. 1479, f. 718.
178. Boxer, *Portuguese Empire* pp. 323–324.
179. Silva, p. 30.
180. Faroughy p. 121.

just as much had been derived in addition from unofficial payments to the officials.[181] That these statements were not entirely unfounded appears from the price the interested parties at least in one case were willing to pay for the offices. As mentioned above, in 1615 by Royal decree all the offices in *Estado da India* were sold by public auction for three years. The proceeds from this unusual sale were to go towards the fight against the Dutch.[182] In Hormuz the following offices were sold:[183]

Table 18. *Proceeds from sales of offices in Hormuz 1615.*

Capitão	145,500 xer.
Feitor	11,550 -
Xabandar	6,500 -
Escrivaninha gr^d d'alfandega	2,810 -
Escrivaninha peq^{na} d'alfandega	2,200 -
Escrivão do feitoria	2,110 -
Escrivaninha do feitoria	2,180 -
Portero d'alfandega	1,250 -
Alcaide do Mar	1,200 -
Escrivaninha dos almazens	150 -
	175,450 xer.

This amount obtains its right perspective when compared with the total proceeds of the sale of the offices, 742,806 xerafins, i.e. nearly one quarter of the total income from the offices in Portuguese India was still expected in 1615 to come from Hormuz.

The officials did not obtain this income merely by sitting down and waiting to draw their salary in the three years allotted them. Not least from Hormuz we have a long series of spoken evidence concerning the means those appointed employed in order to get the most out of their offices. Thus the situation in the 1580s is described by Linschoten: "The captaincy of Hormuz is regarded next after Sofala and Mozambique as one of the best and most lucrative posts in India ... They [the Captains] have their own ships, which they send to Goa, Chaul, Bengal, Masqat and other places, and no man must buy or sell, load or unload any goods before the Captain has sold, shipped, freighted and sent off his goods, not that he has any such authority from the King who on the contrary forbids it, but they take upon themselves this authority."[184] In 1589 Luis Leita Coutinho,

181. B. N. Lisboa, Ms. F. G. 580, f. 33.
182. BOCARRO pp. 363–366.
183. Arquivo Hist. Ultramarina, Lisboa, Papeis avulsos, India Cx. 5.
184. LINSCHOTEN I pp. 40–41.

superintendente da fazenda in Hormuz, writes to the King: "There is nothing to do on behalf of the King here, for the Captains in this fortress desire to be Gods, and to be worshipped and recognized accordingly." The Captains buy from the merchants with bad coin and at the price they themselves dictate to the great detriment of the custom house. Contrary to the current ban, all kinds of drugs are exported to Basra free of export duty, only on paying the Captains for a license, who moreover force the exporters to buy from their own stocks at a premium. The stipulated garrison of 560 men including the Captain's personal servants, etc., is not maintained; there are at most 300 men in the garrison.[185] In 1596 it is reported that the armadas do not patrol so frequently as they should, and that they are poorly equipped. Of the garrison of 500 men 100 are ill or invalids.[186] The same year there are complaints that the horse exporters are forced to use boats that are too small, and to trade with the Captain.[187] In 1601 the complaints about the treatment of Persian subjects in Hormuz are the most concrete of the matters the Persian Ambassador, Husain Beg, has to make known in Europe. Customs is demanded of the Persians over and above the customary; they are forced to buy goods they do not want and they waste time because they are prevented in doing business, etc.[188] In 1602 the Augustine missionary, Gouvea, remarks on Hormuz's big turnover, but the adds that the trade was even more considerable previously. "I do not know whether this decline is due to the Captains, but since they all wish to retire with great riches, this must necessarily happen at the expense of the third estate."[189] From the 1590s we have the very detailed anonymous account of Hormuz quoted above: according to law, it says here, the Turks were forbidden to trade in Hormuz, but the Turks pose formally as Persians, and on embarkation a Persian destination is inserted pro forma into their *cartaze*. This is not performed without payment of course, and the Captain furthermore compels merchants from Basra to purchase to the value of 100 cruzados in his own factory at prices 15% above the market price for every 1,000 cruzados they invest. Finally, the Captain claims 450 reis for every bale of indigo or quintal of cloves or other drugs they export. And, adds the author, this is something the Captains in Hormuz have introduced on their own initiative many years ago.[190]

The stream of complaints and accusations continues, but after 1601 all

185. Arch. Simancas, Secr. Prov. Libr. 1551, ff. 718–719.
186. Rodrigo de Mouro, Ormuz, to the King, 19/7 1596, Torre de Tombo, Lisboa, Corpo Chronoligico, Iª parte, maç. 113, no. 87.
187. *Arquivo Portuguez-Oriental* III, pp. 711–14.
188. Arch. Simancas, Estado, leg. 1856, draft reply.
189. GOUVEA ff. 15–16.
190. *Documentação Ultramarina Portuguesa* II, pp. 43–44.

the complaints contain the additional information that the extortions in Hormuz have been laid before Abbas, and that they have repeatedly aroused his anger against the Portuguese and made him declare that he doubted whether there could be friendship between the Persians and the Portuguese so long as such extortions continued. A sharp and penetrating letter from Andre Furtado de Mendonça from 1607 not only criticises the persons concerned, but extends the attack to include the general practice of giving offices to people who had neither the ability nor the interest to occupy them to the Crown's advantage, and the farming out of custom houses "por respectos particulares" at much too low rates and to people who were only interested in squeezing as much as possible out of their farms. [191] In 1608 the Superintendent and brothers of Hormuz's *Casa di Misericordia* write to the King with a humble request that the Captains in Hormuz might be instructed not to use their own people *(criados)* on the patrol ships, but people from the town instead, because the Captain's people are responsible for many attacks and robberies.[192] The same year the *ouvidor,* Francisco de Gouvea, while acting as Captain during a vacancy in the office, writes that the garrison did not usually contain the prescribed 500 men, but frequently only 200 men "because it is to the advantage of the Captains." The Captains were also responsible for supplying the town arsenal, and they themselves determined the prices, i.e. two or three times above the market price.[193] The year after, in 1609, the Carmelite missionary, Paul Simon, made known the Shah's complaints during his journey to Spain as the Pope's special envoy. They concerned the shameless treatment of Persian envoys passing through Hormuz, the Shah having even been called names in the presence of his envoys, but there was also the matter of the Persian merchants having been forced to buy goods they were not interested in with a 60% surcharge, or of their horses being bought off them at too low a price. These violations had resulted, maintained Paul Simon, in the Persian merchants giving up travelling to Hormuz entirely, and awaiting instead the arrival of the caravans in Basra or Shiraz. The Captain in Hormuz had promised to make amends, but when the merchants ventured to Hormuz thereafter he did not keep his word.[194]

From the years immediately preceding the fall of Hormuz, 1617–20, we have Figueroa's and his companions' descriptions of the conditions in Hormuz. The Portuguese citizens all lived from trading with Persia or Basra, but their capital was modest, and their profits became smaller and smaller every year because the Captains took over the entire profits of the

191. Arch. Simancas, Secr. Prov., Libr. 1479, ff. 210–218.
192. *Ibid.* f. 444.
193. *Ibid.* f. 425.
194. *Ibid.* f. 419.

trade.[195] The King paid for 700 soldiers in Hormuz, but most of the money went into the pockets of the Captain and the other leading officials, and most of the soldiers who obtained their pay were not to be found in Hormuz, despite the threatening situation, but on board the Captain's ships that were sailing to Basra, Sind, Goa and Califa. It was a practice that was already introduced by previous Captains, adds Figueroa.[196]

In a letter dated 12th February 1621 and preserved in a roundabout way, Hormuz's own marionette King repeats similar complaints to the Spanish King.[197] He blames the representatives of the Spanish-Portuguese Crown: "The losse and overthrow of this Kingdom of Ormuz proceedeth althogether from the Captaines your Majestie placeth therein ... if that your Majestie be pleased, that this Kingdome and Fort shall enjoy either peace or means to subsist, you must send such Captaines as are no Merchants, because the Mariners, which might serve in your Majesties Navie to keepe this Streit are all imployed in the Captaine's Ship and Frigats." Previously the Captains had been satisfied with earning 50,000 cruzados in the three years, but now they were not satisfied with 200,000. Before they possessed at the most two ships, but the present Captain possessed four and just as many frigates. The letter is only preserved in an English translation by Purchas, who does not reveal anything about its source; there can be no doubt, however, that it is sent in connection with Ruy Freire's arrival in Hormuz and in compliance with him, since we have a letter of the same date and with a similar content in his own hand.[198] He avoids blaming any particular person, but maintains that the town lacks everything in the way of defence. Ships and men are only occupied with trading and nobody bothers about the defence of the town. So long as His Majesty does not punish the guilty ones there is no hope of improvement. It was the year preceding the fall of Hormuz. Three months before the fall the Bishop of Cochin is still repeating the same complaints: the officials in Hormuz are endangering Estado da India by acting contrary to the King's interests.[199]

The unending stream of complaints and accusations did not disappear on the long journey from Asia to the Spanish-Portuguese administrative offices. Time and time again the problem is dealt with in the Council of State and the Council of Portugal, and to the broad stream of complaints there is a correspondingly broad stream of Royal orders and regulations,

195. FIGUEROA I p. 264.
196. FIGUEROA II p. 471. The Garrison was increased to 700 men with carte real of 31/1 1612, CORDEIRO p. 11.
197. PURCHAS x pp. 365–367.
198. Documentação Ultramarina Portuguesa II p. 274.
199. B. N. Madrid, Ms. 2352, ff. 147–148.

all equally ineffective.[200] The monotony of the complaints and the equally monotonous stream of ineffective Royal orders has prompted the historians to raise the question of moral decadence in the Portuguese Empire or even the insidious pollution of European blood as the result of the tolerant attitude of the Portuguese towards marriage between Europeans and Asians. But the complaints constitute more than evidence of personal negligence or avariciousness; they reveal the innermost core of *Estado da India*'s political system, referred to above as constitutionally determined corruption. The complaints do not originate from an individual pressure group or a single injured party, but all take part: laymen and clergy, officials and merchants, Carmelites and Augustinians, Hormuz's own citizens and citizens of other towns in *Estado da India*, Persians, Portuguese, the Castillian Figueroa and the Dutch Linschoten. The complaints not only concern the extortion of the merchants, but also the neglect of the King's interests: the defence fleet is sent on trading voyages, the garrison is sent with it as crew, the defence precautions are undermined by the private business of the Captains and that most dangerous neighbour, Persia, is provoked by the ruthless treatment of the Persian subjects. The King has known about these conditions for several decades, yet he can do nothing about it because the redistributive system, the triennial periods of office, the patronage and the venality of offices, in short: those institutions that safeguarded the practice of offices being used as sources of personal income, *were* in fact *Estado da India*. Should these institutions be abolished there would no longer be any reason for remaining faithful to the hierarchy in the distant outposts along the Asian coasts.

It is probable that Hormuz was an extreme example of the effects of this system, and that the effects were less undermining, or even advantageous wherever a Portuguese town corporation acted as counterweight against the Royal officials, as was the case in Goa, Malacca and Macao.[201] But Hormuz had no corporative existence; although Barbosa describes a strong

200. *Archivo Portuguez-Oriental* and *Documentos Remettidos* have copious examples of repetitions of almost identically sounding orders. The normal tenure of office in most cases was three years, – i. e., precisely the time it took to send a complaint to Europe, to reply to the complaint with an order to make good the abuse and to return some kind of excuse as to why it was not at present possible to comply with the order. It was possible to bring a case against an official afterwards; the documents from a *residencia* over Henrique de Noronha, former Captain in Hormuz, is to be found in Arquivo Hist. Ultramarina, Lisboa, Papeis avulsos, Cx. 3; Cordeiro has published documents from the case brought against those responsible for the capitulation of Hormuz, cf. also Meneses in Purchas ix p. 139, but the preventive effect of this threat seems to have been slight.
201. Boxer, *Society* pp. 142–143 and *passim*.

mercantile influence upon the government of the town before the Portuguese conquest,[202] every trace of civic influence disappeared under Portuguese rule. The special rights won by citizens in town corporations: staple rights, right of pre-emption, the sole right of transport along certain routes, etc., had in Hormuz reverted to the Captain. In the rare event that a circle of citizens addressed themselves to the Spanish-Portuguese Crown, it was the superintendent and the brothers from *Casa di Misericordia* who spoke on behalf of the citizens.[203]

The only counterbalance for the Captain was the convivial roof-top congregation described by Figueroa, but was it a well-adjusted bourgeoisie, or was it merely a gypsy population that encamped in the sultry, summer nights on the roof terraces above the glowing town? The clue to understanding is provided by the peddling trade – the magnificent though insignificant trade, distributed among many hands, bound up with the monsoons and the limits they imposed on the trade year, cosmopolitan, sensitive to the fluctuations of the market and political movements, a trade whose entrepreneurs were at home everywhere on the Asian market. They were people on the move, people taking a short rest from the journey, which, in a couple of years or a couple of generations, might lead them from one end of the Old World to the other. It was a trade well-adapted to the redistributive institutions, a merchant congregation whose corporative organization did not, as became the case in Europe, coincide with the frontiers of the town; the dividing lines, both in the home town and on the foreign market, did not follow "the nations" but "the law", i.e. the religious affiliation.

Therefore Hormuz was the most extreme and the most vulnerable example of the institutional structure that came under attack when the East India Companies were established. It was not merely that the military defences were ridiculously insufficient in relation to the fortress's economic potential and strategic importance, whereas Persia was militarily reinforced. Della Valle, who visited Hormuz the year after the fall of the fortress, was dismayed to see how poor the defences were. The fort on Qishm did not even deserve the name of "casa forte", it was "una colombaia", a dove-cot. The guns of the fortress of Hormuz were new, but they were badly mounted and pointed towards the town. According to Valle it was a wonder the fortress could hold out so long as it did, and he concludes: "Hormuz se perdé, quando tanti anni prima se perdé Lar."[204] But this loss alone was not decisive; it was more important that the trade during the same

---

202. STRIPLING p. 25.
203. Arch. Simancas, Secr. Prov., Libr. 1479, ff. 210–218; *Documentação Ultramarina Portuguesa* II p. 333.
204. della VALLE, *Persia* II:2 p. 527 ff.

years began to desert the town and seek new outlets. The repeated Persian blockades of the town, in 1602, in 1607–08 and in 1614–15, and the loss of Bahrein in 1601 and Gombroon in 1614 isolated the Portuguese outpost from the areas from which it obtained its daily necessities and inflicted losses on the merchants.[205] In addition there was in all probability a general decline in the trade through the Persian Gulf in the first decades after the establishment of the Dutch and the English East India Companies. But the most decisive factor was that these external difficulties initiated a vicious circle, which created an incongruity between the protection afforded by the Portuguese fortress and the Portuguese armadas on the one hand and the protection duties paid by the merchants in Hormuz on the other. For the merchants the costs rose to a level at which it became advantageous to seek other routes.

The problem is touched upon for the first time by Texeira, who in 1604 was passing through Hormuz on his way to Europe, but who had some basis for comparison from his earlier visits to Hormuz in 1587 and in 1593–97. On his last journey through the Persian Gulf he noticed that Qishm had a smaller population than before and was unable, as previously, to deliver ample supplies of wheat, barley, fruit and vegetables to the barren neighbouring island. This was caused by the incessant plundering and pirateering of the coastal Arabs, the Niquilus, who were allowed to continue year after year, unchecked, on account of the indifference of the Hormuz Captains. On the other hand the ship he boarded on his way from Hormuz to Basra was unable to take in supplies on its way through the Gulf because the Portuguese armadas had ravaged the coast everywhere. After the Persian conquest of Bahrein the conditions in the Persian Gulf seem already to have been characterized by a permanent war, a *guerre de course* – or perhaps rather *guerilla*. The Portuguese ships preferred to sail in convoy and the Persian and Arab ships were captured and treated like pirates if they were discovered without *cartaze*.[206]

But the turning-point seems to have been the conquest of Gombroon and the simultaneous blockade of Hormuz in 1614–15, which hit the town hard. Redempt, who was passing through Hormuz in 1615, maintains that there was not enough money to pay the soldiers with, and that they therefore were in state of permanent mutiny.[207] The two first clashes between the Persians and the Portuguese had also resulted in a temporary blockade, but trade had been reinstated as soon as there was peace along the routes again. Around 1614, or perhaps a few years earlier, an important new development is mentioned, however: the goods from North-West India had

205. GOUVEA ff. 15–16; *Chronicle* p. 1049.
206. TEXEIRA pp. 19–24.
207. *Chronicle* p. 1049.

begun to follow a new route to the Persian market, i.e. the long and difficult caravan route via Kandahar. The Englishman, Steele, who followed this route on his way out in 1614 and home again in 1615, draws particular attention to this in his reports to the Company: "By reason of frequent passage of caravans [Kandahar] is much enlarged lately, that the suburbs are bigger than the city."[208] "At this present the Merchants of India assemble at Lahore, and invest a great part of their monies in Commodities, and joyne themselves in Caravans to passe the Mountaines of Kandahar into Persia, by which way is generally reported to passe twelve or fourteen thousand Camels lading, whereas heretofore scarcely passed three thousand, the rest going by the way of Ormuz."[209] This important diversion of the trade route between India and Persia is confirmed in the same year by Portuguese sources. The Bishop of Cyrene (Gouvea) writes from Hormuz to Spain that, as a result of the uneasy situation some merchants had taken the route from Lahore via Kandahar to Persia. Cyrene hopes, however, that by allowing them concessions, such as permission to sail from Hormuz to other Portuguese harbours in Portuguese ships, it would be possible to entice them back to the Hormuz route.[210] The same year (1614) the Captain in Dabhol obtained formal permission to load a ship and send it to Persia on the pretext that there was a risk that the entire trade might otherwise be taken over by the Persians themselves, who had opened a new trade route overland to Cambaia. This can scarcely refer to anything other than the Kandahar route.[211]

Already before the fall of Hormuz the merchants were about to give up the town as a trading centre, since the protection costs were too high and the conditions too unsafe. In addition the Portuguese no longer had the means with which to force the trade into the desired channels. In an anonymous memorandum dated 14th February 1619 the causes of the decline in the Portuguese customs revenue in Hormuz were analysed. As point no. 1, it is mentioned that the big ships from Dabhol used to pay 45,000 pardaos in customs, but that in recent years they had only paid 7–10,000, because the goods circumvented Hormuz. The same applied to ships from Sind, Goa and Chaul. Avoiding Hormuz, the goods were sailed to the Persian Gulf, partly on ships that had obtained *cartaze* for this express purpose and partly on smuggling ships from Goa. An additional cause was contributed by the caravans, which now travelled between

208. PURCHAS IV p. 272.
209. *Ibid.* pp. 268–269.
210. *Documentos Remettidos* III p. 185. Gouvea had mentioned the new route already in 1611 during his stay in Spain. Arch. Simancas, Estado, leg. 2864 ff. 89–90.
211. LUZ p. 352.

India and Persia on account of the insults, extortions and bad treatment the merchants were subjected to in the customs house in Hormuz.[212]

The competitors could not avoid noticing the weakened position of the Portuguese. "They are now so weak in shipping and men through their many losses lately (and chiefly by us and the Hollanders) sustained, that these passages are molested by small frigates of sea robbers, which they cannot, or at least doe not, remedy: (which?) doth discomfit strangers merchants, and they themselves through want of shipping necessitated, so that in no measure is that quantity of spice hither brought as in former times, is cause that all sorts of spices are here very much improved in price and will yield almost as much profit as by their transport into England."[213] Thus write the English factors from the South Persian port of Jask in 1617. In 1619 the same features are emphasized: "... all India Commodities we hope will vend to good profitt, both this year and also the ensewing year by reason fewe ships or none is this year arrived by the last monsoon what will come with this monsoon we know not, but doubtless not soe many will come as in former time, for as we increase so doth Hormuz decrease."[214]

Not least is it important to observe the high prices and the high margin of profit on the Persian market during these years. During this time the Companies' import of Asian commodities competed successfully on the Levant market with the commodities supplied by the traditional channels. But on the South Persian market, the starting-point for one of the two important caravan routes, it was the supply, not the demand, that failed. Not as a result of a systematic North-West European blockade, but as a result of the collapse of the Portuguese system of protection. Extortion was acceptable if it was accompanied by protection against robbery. The merchant was likewise unafraid of meeting robbers, if only he could avoid paying protection money. But, faced with the combination of extortion and lawlessness, the merchants sought new routes. The structure Hormuz represented was already in a state of collapse before the fortress fell.

212. Arquivo Hist. Ultramarina, Lisboa, Papeis avulsos, India Cx. 6.
213. *Letters received* V p. 65, cf. Connock et al., Jask, to Co. 19/1 1617, *ibid.* p. 57. Meilink-Roelofsz (p. 190) interprets this passage as an indication that the Portuguese were no longer able to obstruct foreign shipping, but the way in which the information about higher prices is worded leaves no doubt as to the state of affairs: "[the Portuguese] are now unable to defend the stranger merchant trading to and from Indus, India and Ormuz; they are now catched up by theves and searobbers living and inhabiting the coasts of these ther passages."
214. C. R. O., London, O. C. 835.

Part II: The Loss of Hormuz.
People and Events

In Part I Hormuz was placed within its structural context, and the fall of the town was portrayed as the result of a confrontation between fundamentally different institutional complexes. The internal dynamics of the redistributive institutions undermined productive activity and inhibited its organizational development until a point was reached when the merchants, organized in Companies, found new routes that circumvented the Ottoman Empire and *Estado da India*. The Companies were much more dangerous than any enemy within the system itself could be because they diverted the stream of goods that formed the basis of the redistributive institutions. The Ottoman Empire was shaken, but was nevertheless able to regain its balance; the income from the transit trade was despite everything only of regional or personal importance. *Estado da India,* whose entire political and economic position was based on the protection – or exploitation – of the intercontinental and Asian trade, collapsed.

But there is more than one way of relating a story. The confrontation was not only a clash between structures, it was also a clash between people. The loss of Hormuz had been feared and predicted by many people in the Spanish-Portuguese Empire throughout a number of years; Spanish diplomacy had been concerned with a Persian problem at least since the loss of Bahrein in 1601. This awareness of a latent Persian threat to Hormuz was bound up with an essentially different problem – the desire on the part of the Christian powers to see Persia involved in a struggle with the Ottoman Empire that would safeguard Europe against the threat of Islam. This idea was centuries old, but the endeavours to realize it culminated in the years preceding the fall of Hormuz.

"Events are dust" says Braudel, but they are the dust that, for the living, constitutes historical reality. In Part II the story of the fall of Hormuz is to be related once more, but from another angle and using a different approach. The object of this investigation is not structures, but people and events; the method is that of traditional diplomatic history. The aim of this unorthodox change of viewpoint is serious. If the argument in the first part is correct, the actors on the diplomatic and military scene were only players in a drama they themselves were unable to shape. They were the prisoners

14 Carracks, Caravans and Companies

of a structural confrontation the outcome of which they could not control. What we may observe is the actors' attempt to grasp the meaning of the development taking place around them, and the attempt to change the course of the development. It is not history created by men, because the final decisions were improvised and parenthetical, but men's attempt to comprehend and to mould historical development.

Chapter V: The Dream of the Great Alliance

The enormous interest surrounding the Persian Embassy from 1599–1601 is reflected in pamphlets, news letters, diplomatic dispatches and diaries from one end of Europe to the other. The galley war in the Mediterranean was endemic, and ever since 1593 there had been open war on the Hungarian frontier – a war that had attracted adventurers and pious crusaders from all over Europe, and which in its ferocity and ruthlessness became a model for several of the army leaders and regimental officers during the Thirty Years' War. In the light of ordinary European consciousness the Turks and the Grand Turk himself were more than mere rivals or enemies in the political struggle for interests and positions; they were the forces of darkness, they were devils, and the Grand Turk was the Evil One himself. The offer of co-operation that appeared to be forthcoming with the Persian Embassy must for the simple believer have seemed like the fulfilment of the dream about Prester John: now must be the time for the final destruction of the Evil One.

Simplified ideas about power in the service of Good and Evil have nourished the European States and the European political system during its historical infancy, but in the Council Chambers, in the Chancelleries and in the Princes' Cabinets, wherever the decisions were taken, the ideas were less simple. There, the fear of the Turk and the idea of Crusade were contained by other issues; they were perhaps a vision, a dream to be indulged in when the daily tasks allowed a breathing-space, but more often than not a mere catchword, a weapon employed in the general pushing and shoving around the individual throne or between the thrones themselves. Just as true as it is that the idea of Crusade, the dream about this the most just of all wars, the ultimate struggle with Islam, was still alive at the beginning of the 17th century, it is equally true that none of those politically responsible were willing to set aside other interests in order to realize this dream. The relations with the Ottoman Empire may well have had their peculiarities, but in practice they were subjected to the same rules as were the relations with every other state. The Turk was a part of the European political system; the Persian initiative was not the fanfare that started off a Crusade, but only an isolated factor among many in the political game.

14*

The Persian Initiative and Anthony Sherley

It has been contended that one of the main reasons why the route via Hormuz was not included in the Portuguese blockade of transcontinental trade was regard for political friendship with Persia.[1] Although diplomatic contact between Persia on the one hand and Goa and Lisbon on the other cannot be excluded, it is highly probable that the Persian-Portuguese *entente* is a geo-political post-rationalization; after 1532 there is no trace in the sources of Persian-Portuguese contact. The relations throughout the 16th century seem to be characterized by the apathy of distance: no co-operation, but no conflicts either. It is worth while remarking in this connection that in practice Persia and Hormuz were not neighbouring states. The Persian coastal region facing Hormuz – the province of Lar – was, until it was conquered in 1601 by Abbas's faithful vassal, Allah Verdi Khan, under a hereditary governor who had in fact won his independence.

In the 16th century there were other European powers who had approached Persia regarding an alliance against the Ottoman Empire, but the attempts were isolated and lacked far-reaching consequences. After the union between Spain and Portugal, Spanish interests in the Mediterranean were united with the Portuguese connections in Asia. This situation was exploited in the attempt made once again in the middle of the 1580s to co-ordinate Persian and Western policy as regards the Ottoman Empire – or perhaps rather to incite Persia, who was at war with Turkey at that time, to greater exertions, which might ensure Spain coverage in the Mediterranean during the preparations for the conflict with the Netherlands and England. A letter from Philip II to the Persian Shah, which was dispatched in the beginning of 1584,[2] seems to have been answered immediately by a return embassy, which left Goa for Lisbon in February 1585[3] and reached Madrid in 1586.[4] At the same time the Florentine Vecchietti travelled overland to Persia as Papal envoy.[5] The practical significance of these approaches was slight. The defeat of the Armada in 1588 and the Persian-Turkish peace treaty in 1590 safeguarded Turkey for the time being on both the eastern border and in the Mediterranean, and opened up the possibility for the attack that was begun a few years later towards the north. On the European side no attempt was made to follow up the contact; Vecchietti sought on behalf of the Pope to interest Philip II in a new initiative while he was resident in Madrid in 1593–94, but the reaction of the Spanish King was negative. It is interesting to note in this

1. MAGALHAES-GODINHO p. 768; BOXER, *Portuguese Empire* p. 59.
2. *Archivo Portuguez-Oriental* III p. 42.
3. SASSETTI p. 301.
4. PALOMBINI p. 110.
5. *Ibid.* pp. 108–111; VECCHIETTI *passim.*

connection that Philip II expressed to Vecchietti his fears that possible military aid to Persia might be used against Hormuz.[6] Already at this point we encounter a theme that was repeated time and time again throughout the following decades: the conflict between Spanish interests in the Mediterranean and Portuguese interests in the Persian Gulf.

The Englishman, Anthony Sherley, became the catalyst that set off further attempts to establish contact and precipitated intensive efforts to create the great alliance with Persia. Whatever his role may have been in the eyes of the Persians, there is no doubt that his endeavours and those of his brother, Robert, determined for a number of years the way in which the Christian States evaluated the Persian policy. It will therefore be necessary to investigate in detail the circumstances under which the brothers Sherley became involved in Persian policy.

Anthony Sherley arrived in North Italy at the beginning of 1598 at the head of 24 English gentlemen belonging to Essex's train who wished to offer their aid to Cesare d'Este, who had quarrelled with the Pope over the hereditary right to Ferrara after Alfons II's death the previous year. He was at that time 33 years old, of good but "declining" family; he had earned a certain reputation as a soldier, amongst other things by his participation in Essex's cruise to the Azores and as leader of an English raid on Jamaica. When the Englishmen reached Italy, however, the Ferrara conflict had already been settled; they continued further to Venice, possibly in order to offer the Republic their services, but the very same summer they embarked rather surprisingly for the Levant.

After an adventurous journey via Aleppo and Baghdad Anthony Sherley and his companions, who now also included the Syrian interpreter, Michelangelo Coray, alias Fathulla, arrived in Kasvin in December 1598, just as the Persian Shah, Abbas I, returned home from Khurasan, where he had gained a considerable victory over the Uzbegs. He presented himself to the Shah as a private person who had been attracted to Persia by the rumour of the Shah's greatness, and he was well received, thanks to the presents he brought with him and the exaggerated information about his own aristocratic birth, together with the ability, apparently so natural for his family, of making others believe in their importance. During the following months he had various conversations with Abbas, and during these talks he succeeded in convincing the Persian Shah, who since 1590 had carried on an appeasement policy with Turkey, that the moment had come to launch an attack against the common enemy of Persia and Christendom, the Sultan in Constantinople, and to create the great alliance between Persia and the Christian Princes that would mean the downfall of the Ottoman Empire. In the middle of 1599 he began the return journey in company with

6. PALOMBINI p. 113.

a distinguished Persian, Husain Ali Beg; together, as Ambassadors to a number of European Courts, they were to work for the league proposed by Anthony, while Anthony's younger brother, Robert, together with other members of the English company remained in Persia as military advisers. They stopped on the way in Moscow, to which Court another Persian was accredited, and where the winter and the Russian suspiciousness forced the company to stay for some months. In the summer of 1600 the Ambassadors continued to Archangel, from whence they sailed to Stade at the mouth of the Elbe, and after the final stage through Germany they reached Prague in October, where the Emperor, Rudolph, gave them an unusually warm welcome. From Prague the journey continued via Tuscany to Rome, where Clement VIII welcomed the Persian Ambassadors with just as great enthusiasm as the Emperor.

A disagreement between Anthony Sherley and Husain, which had already been smouldering on the journey, flared up in Rome. In May 1601 Anthony suddenly left the embassy and allowed Husain to continue the journey through Spain and Portugal alone, from whence the Persian eventually reached home via Goa. Although for Anthony Sherley the journey had thus ended in an anti-climax, his initiative had been instrumental in establishing a connection that was maintained throughout the following years by means of the exchange of a number of Ambassadors, but which never manifested itself in the form of a planned co-operation against the arch-enemy, primarily on account of the lack of unity between the European Princes.

This in the main, though without the numerous bizarre details, is the generally accepted version of the account of the first Persian embassy to Europe under Abbas.[7] A critical examination of the material, however,

7. Although much has been written about the adventurous Sherley brothers, the tendency has been to concentrate on the picturesque aspects of the subject and to amass anecdotes rather than to place their contribution within a general historical context and to make a critical analysis of the sources. The most thoroughly documented, and at the same time the best written, narrative of Anthony Sherley's journey is to be found in CHEW pp. 239–298. Anthony Sherley's career is furthermore described in Ross pp. 3–91, and by Xavier-A. Flores in his introduction to *Peso Politico* pp. 19–34. BABINGER establishes the route of the embassy through Germany and Italy. Both brothers, or rather all three brothers – Anthony and Robert also had an elder brother who only managed to become a Captain of Corsairs in the Mediterranean – are described by PENROSE: From the Persian side the negotiations have been dealt with by BAYANI and SIYASSI. However, both the latter may be characterized as largely uncritical and incomplete. Some documents have been published in SHIRLEY; *Chronicle* also deals with the Sherley brothers in the service of Persia, and the two volumes contain some interesting and relevant sources. For the sake of completeness it must be mentioned that Rev. S. F. SURTEES in his work, *William Shakespere of Stratford-on-Avon: His epitaph unearthed, and the author of the plays (Sir A. Sherley) run to*

gives cause for scepsis regarding several important points, first and foremost Anthony Sherley's formal status and titles and, behind this formal problem, the Shah's object in dispatching the embassy. That Anthony Sherley was a pretty unreliable person with a tendency to exaggerate his own importance even his admirers are agreed upon, but this evaluation has not left its trace in the attitude to the source material. With few exceptions both the accounts and the documentary material preserved in Europe are an expression of Anthony Sherley's and his interpreter's view of the embassy; Husain did not bring any interpreter,[8] and even Anthony's enemies were therefore obliged to trust his information.

Anthony Sherley's most detailed account of the events preceding the dispatch of the embassy is the relation he composed in 1611. In this he describes his long talks with the Shah and his advisers and stresses his own diplomatic adroitness in the long dialogues during which he managed to win over the Shah for the fight against Turkey. He explains convincingly, moreover, how there were both doves and hawks at Court: men who desired peace with Turkey and men who desired war. Eventually the Shah was convinced by Anthony's eloquence: "Well said the King you would then have me to write to as many of the Christian Princes as are greatest amongst them, who if they will apply themselves to our purpose may draw all other lesser unto it, by the example of their authoritie; or at the least (if they will not consent in that point) will command their Marchants to repair to our Dominions: so that we and they may have some good friendly use the one of the other. The letters you shall appoint to be written to as many and to whom, you will; with priviledge for Marchants, and the

ground, Hertford 1888, has proved that Anthony Sherley, among his other accomplishments, was also the author of the plays generally ascribed to William Shakespeare. The author has unfortunately not had the opportunity of consulting this latter work.

The chief sources for Anthony Sherley's journey are his own accounts and those of several of his travelling companions, supplemented with information from documentary material in almost every European archive of importance. The very amount of relevant material preserved constitutes documentation of the attention this exotic embassy aroused all over Europe. Among eye-witness accounts are the following: ANTHONY SHERLEY, *His Relation of his Travel into Persia*, London 1613, in abridged edition also in PURCHAS VIII pp. 375–441; Anon., *A True Report of Sir Anthony Shierlie's Iourney* ... London 1600; WILLIAM PARRY, *A New and Large Discourse of the Travels of Sir Anthony Sherley*..., London 1601; ABEL PINÇON, *Relation d'un Voyage de Perse* ..., Paris 1651; and GEORGE MANWARING, *A True Discourse of Sir Anthony Sherley's Travel into Persia*, The four latter are reprinted in Ross. In addition there is the account published in 1604 by the Persian "defector", Uruch Beg, alias Don Juan. The edition of his *Relaciones* used here is the English edition of G. le STRANGE, *Don Juan of Persia*, London 1926.

8. Arch. Vaticano, Fondo Borghese III:106 e.

secure posession of their Religion, and peaceable posession of their goods, and persons, in as ample sort as your selfe will devise; and not onely for them but for all Christians whatsoever, which for curiositie to see, or love to me, will take pains to come hither; or for any purpose soever; being impossible their purpose can at anie time be ill towards us, which wish them in all things so well. And because you have been the Mover and Perswader of this businesse, you also shalbe the Actor of it, assuring my selfe that my Honour cannot be more securely reposed in any mans hands, then your own: both in that I judge of your owne disposition; and more, in that which I know of your obligation to me; besides, *There is none so proper an Executor of any enterprise, as hee which is the first deviser of it.*" (Sherley's italics). Sherley goes on to report how he himself, in order to emphasize the embassy's importance, requested the company of a distinguished Persian, to which the Shah graciously gave his consent. Before the Court had finished celebrating the great decision – according to Sherley the festivities lasted for 30 days – a Portuguese friar, Nicolo de Melo, arrived on a journey from Asia to Europe; Sherley does not reveal much else about him in his relation than that he found his behaviour unfitting for a cleric. Finally, Anthony relates that the constitution of the embassy underwent a deplorable change before departure, in that the Shah gave away the distinguished Prince, whom he had originally chosen to be Sherley's companion, in marriage to one of his aunts, thus preventing the yong man's departure. As nobody else in the inner circle wished to undertake the task the post was applied for by one Husain Ali Beg "a Courtchie of six Thomans Stipend by the Year, and in disgrace also..." The Shah, again according to Sherley, was very much against sending him off in such low company, but eventually gave in. Anthony left the Court and journeyed to the Caspian Sea, leaving Husain to follow with the presents and the letters to the Christian Princes, which had been drawn up, but not yet sealed. This last event Anthony makes appear as if Husain was a kind of messenger-boy; to put it mildly, however, it is peculiar for an Ambassador to be so nonchalant about the delivery of his credentials.[9]

The narrative of these events is repeated with minor variations in all the accounts given by other members of Sherley's company; even Pinçon, who quite obviously is not one of Sherley's admirers, supports it, but, as previously mentioned, this agreement hardly proves anything, because it is more than likely that members of his company obtained the information from Anthony himself or through his interpreter. Thus it is interesting that the only independent witness to the events preceding the embassy's departure, Don Juan of Persia, differs from the above tradition in some essential points. Firstly, he maintains that the Shah had planned to send an

9. SHERLEY pp. 118–127.

Ambassador to Spain via Hormuz and Goa already before Sherley's arrival. Secondly, he says that Sherley posed in Persia as the cousin of the English King, and "that all the kings of Christendom has recognized him as such, and had now empowered him as their ambassador to treat with the King of Persia, who should make a confederacy with them in order to wage war against the Turk." Thirdly, this is the only place where Don Juan refers to Anthony as Ambassador; in his account of the Persian embassy only one Ambassador is mentioned: Husain.[10]

The discrepancies between the two traditions is important, because they would imply essentially different intentions behind the dispatch of the Persian embassy in 1599. If Anthony Sherley's version is the correct one the embassy was dispatched with the object of assembling the Christian Princes in one big alliance against Turkey. But if Don Juan's version is correct, on the dispatch of the embassy Abbas must have presumed that there already existed an offer on the part of the Christians concerning an alliance, and it was Husain's and not Sherley's task to investigate and discuss this.

Is there any possibility of deciding between the two traditions? The European documentary material from the embassy's visits to the various European Courts cannot solve the problem, for even there we must expect to find Anthony Sherley's version. Two groups of documents provide the possibility of checking the accounts, however: the letters Sherley and de Melo sent to Europe before their departure from Persia and the Persian documents preserved in translation.

In the correspondance from the Spanish Ambassador in Rome in the Simancas archives four letters from Sherley and de Melo, sent while they were still in Persia, are preserved.[11] Two of the letters are addressed to the Spanish King from de Melo and Sherley, respectively, and dated 24th May 1599. None of these letters describes the appointment of an Ambassador of Persian nationality. Anthony Sherley expresses his heartfelt joy at having been permitted to be instrumental in a matter so significant as that he had negotiated with Persian Shah, "who sends me to your Majesty and to all the Princes mentioned above in order to negotiate and come to an agreement about the best means by which one can strike a sucessful blow at the common enemy." He dares not express himself any more clearly in the letters. Concerning de Melo he says that he can confirm the negotiations, since he had been present at some of them, that he has helped as well as he was able, and that he also will bring a kind of greeting, "algun recaudo"

10. Don JUAN p. 232.
11. Arch. Simancas, Estado, leg. 972. According to the tradition of the Augustinian Order de Melo was sent to Persia by the Archbishop of Goa in 1598, LUZ p. 310. It appears from his letters from Persia, however, that he was on his way to Rome to negotiate on the part of the Philippines province of the Augustinian Order.

to the Spanish King. The tone of condescension in the description of de Melo is unmistakable. De Melo confirms that the negotiatiaons whith the Shah were carried out by Sherley before he himself had a chance to do so, but that he was received by the Shah together with Sherley and that the tasks were divided between them: "This King has appointed me as agent (comisario) to Your Majesty and to His Holiness and sends his formal message with gifts." De Melo is to travel to Europe together with Anthony Sherley, whereas the latter's younger brother, Robert is to remain in Persia "como en peñor de la respuesta", as hostage while the answer is awaited. The two final letters in this group are written by de Melo barely three weeks later, on 12th June, to the Spanish Ambassador in Rome and to the Portuguese Viceroy, Castel Rodrigo, respectively. In the meantime the Shah had decided to send an Ambassador of Persian nationality: "enviar su embaxador con un mui magco presente y al uno destos segnores llamado Don Antonio que es el mas viejo, avia echo su comisario para con todos los principes Cristianos y despues de yo venido par assi gustar este cavellero me a hecho su comisario particularmente con su Santidad y su Magestad ... envio con nosotros un Parcio de su casa aunque no de mucha autoridad ..."

These letters were undoubtedly brought to Europe by Anthony's interpreter, Michelangelo, who in November 1599 handed over a letter from Anthony Sherley to the Venetian Doge, also dated 24th May. This letter is couched in very vague terms, Sherley referring to Michelangelo, "who is well informed about the instructions and credentials (autorita e potere) with which His Majesty sends me to Your Serenitá and all the other Christian Princes." When received by the Senate Michelangelo reported that he had travelled six days before the rest of the company's expected departure, and that the remainder of the company, apart from Anthony Sherley, consisted of one Assan (Husain) Beg, "but this man has no say in the matter, because everything is decided by the said Antonio and a Portuguese friar, Nicolo Damego, and even the latter obeys the said Antonio's orders and commands."[12]

It is worth noting that nowhere in the correspondence from Persia does it say that Sherley was appointed Persian Ambassador alone or in company with Husain, but that only Husain is described as Ambassador. On the other hand it is obvious that both Sherley, Michelangelo and de Melo are eager to belittle Husain's rank and importance, whereas Sherley and Michelangelo are just as eager to represent de Melo as unimportant. Although it is impossible to draw any final conclusion from the silence of the letters, they strengthen our suspicions regarding Sherley's title as Persian Ambassador.

12. BERCHET, *Nuovi Documenti* pp. 7–14.

The final proof is provided by yet another group of documents: the translations of the Persian documents carried by the envoys. The problem must have been made an object of investigation during the Embassy's stay in Rome, because in a separate bundle in the Vatican archives a number of relevant documents have been collected:[13] Husain's and Anthony Sherley's arguments concerning their respective dignity, Anthony's alleged verbal instructions from the Shah and the Italian and Latin translations of four Persian documents attested by the Armenian, Tomasso di Angelis and Leonardo Abel, Bishop of Sidonia. Naturally the form in which these documents have been preserved excludes a formal diplomatic analysis, but together with the arguments of the various parties the documents nevertheless provide the possibility of reaching a final decision regarding the question of Sherley's status.

The formal basis of the embassy, according to Anthony's reply to Husain's complaint, consists of two patents and two letters. The first patent, which is in his own possession, he regards as the embassy's credentials; he says it is "commune per negotiare con tutti i principi." The other is more specifically on behalf of the Christian religion. As for the letters, Husain has obtained one of them from the Shah "et e solamente di compimento"; it is merely a greeting. Regarding the other letter, Anthony says that it has been in his possession, but that he entrusted it to Husain by the shores of the Caspian Sea. Anthony concludes: "The four together provide the entire authority for negotiating and the knowledge of the secrets to the said Antonio without bestowing any rights to negotiate or make agreements on the Persian whom the King sent Don Antonio so that he might be of use to him, to be sure also with the title of Ambassador." In contrast to this is Husain's statement that he has regarded Anthony as a helpful travelling companion, but that, before the departure from Persia, he had never heard anything to the effect that there should be more than one Ambassador: Husain himself.

However, there is no doubt that Anthony's description of the documents is incorrect; of the four documents it was not the first, but the third – the one Anthony describes as merely a greeting – that was the embassy's credentials. This document corresponds in style and construction to the credentials sent with the Persian Ambassadors in the following years.[14] Anthony Sherley's name is mentioned, but this is in accordance with the

13. Arch. Vaticano, Fondo Borghese III: 106 e.
14. The best published examples are *Chronicle* pp. 94–96 and PONTECORVO pp. 160–162; but there is an even closer correspondence with the Shah's letter to the King of Spain with the Ambassador Paquesa (1605), Torre do Tombo, Lisboa, Misc. Ms. 1104 f. 117, cf. Arch. Simancas, Secr. Prov., Libr. 1479 ff. 8–9, and the Shah to the King of Spain with Belchior dos Anjos, (1613) Arch. Simancas, Estado, leg. 495.

practice to be found in other Persian letters: after a number of fragrant compliments reference is made to the latest message received, in this case Anthony Sherley's arrival in Persia, after which is mentioned the name of the Ambassador who is sent with the letter in answer to the message received, Husain Ali Beg.[15] The actual Persian Ambassador must have been the man who was mentioned in the Ambassador's place in the credentials and who also handed them over: Husain Beg.

After the credentials are identified the remaining documents lose part of their interest and especially the importance Sherley attributes to them. The patent, about which he says that it authorizes him to "negotiate with all the Princes", diverges both in form and content from all the other known Persian credentials; from Husain we even have the interesting comment that it only bore the seal at the top of the front page, which showed that it was an epistle of lesser importance, since all important official documents bore the seal at the bottom and on the back.[16] This statement is confirmed by our knowledge of Persian diplomas of this time.[17] The patent did not contain the flowery compliments so characteristic of credentials; it confined itself to a short account of Sherley's arrival in Persia, his task with regard to informing the Shah about the disposition of the Christian Princes, which had prompted the Shah's decision to express his own friendly feelings, and his return to Europe in company with a Persian ambassador. The nearest parallel in form and content is the epistle given to the Carmelite, Redempt, by the Shah when, in 1615 he left

15. Since credentials are only preserved in translation the problem cannot be solved in the simplest manner. The available translations seem, however, to support the assumption that Husain alone was accredited to the Christian Princes. In a translation of the credentials to Spain undertaken by the Imperial interpreter, Negroni, while the embassy was in Prague, the crucial passage is worded as follows: "..... Habiamo espediti da queste parte per Ambasciatore il nostro stimatissimo et considerato personaggio Cusimali Bag in compagnia del sopradetto Signor Antonio ..." But in Negroni's translation of the presumably identical letter to the Pope it says: "l'havemo fatto tornare [Anthony Sherley] in quelle parte et per il mezzo suo l'havemo accompagnato con un Imbasciatore aggiunto ad elle, il nostro honorato Cussein Aalebeg ..." Leonardo Abel's translation of the same passage is as follows:" [Anthony Sherley] poi al ritorno al suo paese e stato licentiato, et con l'occasione del sudetto da parte nostra con lettere in forma di imbasciatore honorato, il grande delli magnati et magnifici Assein Aalibeg il fidate e charo delli miei huomini al sudetto nato Principe congionto...." – The first of the quoted translations in Arch. Simancas, Estado, leg. 707; the latter two in Arch. Vaticano, Fondo Borghese III: 106 e.
16. Arch. Vaticano, Fondo Borghese III: 106 e.
17. Persian diplomas are reproduced in *Chronicle* p. 94–95, p. 217; BERCHET, *Persia* p. 46, 55; JOZEFOWITZ pl. IV. On the other hand JOZEFOWITZ plates III, V and VI have the seal on top and on the front. Cf. BUSSE p. 53.

Persia in order to accompany Robert Sherley on his second embassy.[18] Sherley's second patent is a general assurance with regard to the rights that were granted Christians in Persia; this epistle also has parallels.[19] The fourth and last document is simply a letter of recommendation to the Grand Duke in Moscow for use during the journey through the latter's country.[20]

A final argument in support of Husain's claim is that both Husain and Anthony offered to travel back to Persia or to be imprisoned in a fortress in Italy until information was obtained from Persia. Anthony never returned to Persia, however. Husain returned and is mentioned in a letter from the Shah to the King of Spain in 1605;[21] there is no hint of his having suffered any unpleasantness after his homecoming.

Was Sherley an imposter who bluffed his way through as Christendom's envoy in Persia and as Persian Ambassador in Europe, or was he in good faith when he maintained that he returned home from Persia as a diplomat in the service of the Persian King? The latter possibility cannot quite be ruled out; his knowledge of Oriental languages and Oriental diplomatic practice was slight; he was dependent upon his interpreter, Michelangelo, who on a later occasion made known his opinion (either genuine or simulated), that is was solely Cardinal San Giorgio's mistrust of Sherley that had destroyed the great possibilities of the first embassy.[22] But the question is merely shifted to another quarter hereby: could Michelangelo be in good faith? If we return to the summer of 1599 there does not seem any doubt, however, that the verdict cannot be in favour of Sherley and Michelangelo; it is conspicuous that at this time, while de Melo was still attached to the

18. *Chronicle* p. 217. The original for Anthony Sherley's so-called patent has disappeared, but the Spanish Ambassador in Prague has given a description that exactly corresponds to the diploma illustrated in *Chronicle*, Arch. Simancas, Estado, leg. 707.
19. BERCHET, *Persia*, pp. 255–256.
20. At least two editions of Anthony Sherley's alleged Persian credentials were in circulation before the Ambassador reached Rome. The first was printed in the anonymous *True Report* under the title: "The Copy of Sir Anthony Sherley's letters of credence from the great sophi to the christian Princes." This is a version of the letter of recommendation to Moscow particularly flattering to Sherley. The other is to be found without commentaries and with an anonymous translator as an enclosure in a report from the Papal nuncio in Prague of 8th January 1601. This does not correspond with any of the authorized translations, but seems to be composed of fragments, partly from the letter of recommendation to Moscow, partly from Anthony Sherley's letter of recommendation. Arch. Vaticano, Principe 54, f. 142.
21. Torre do Tombo, Lisboa, Misc. Ms. 1104, f. 117.
22. MEYER p. 187; the conversation referred to here only makes sense if one bears in mind that it was Michelangelo who functioned as interpreter.

Mission, they do not describe Sherley as Ambassador, and it is conspicuous that Anthony left it to Husain to receive the Shah's letters and presents.

Some of the more adventurous and enigmatic events connected with the famous embassy may be explained on the basis of Anthony Sherley's freebooter morals and doubtful diplomatic status. De Melo was arrested by Sherley on a somewhat shady pretext as soon as the embassy had gone ashore on Russian territory in Astrakhan; he was released by the authorities in Moscow, but he was arrested again, deprived of money and papers and ended his days as a prisoner in a monastery in Archangel.[23] His fate obtains a sinister perspective in the light of what is mentioned above: he was the only possible rival who knew the truth of the matter. The negative attitude of the Russian authorities is also explained; in Moscow people were familiar with Persian diplomatic practice, and to Sherley's indignation both of the Persian Ambassadors were given precedence before him.[24] The mystery of the vanished presents is also more understandable in that light. From the Shah's treasury Husain brought with him 63 presents to each of the eight European Princes the embassy was to visit.[25] In Archangel Sherley had the presents put on board an English ship, maintaining that it was safer to send them direct to Rome by sea. The presents never turned up, and Husain thought later that Sherley had sold them; Sherley was unable to explain away the disappearance of the chests, but maintained that he had found the presents too trifling and had therefore sent them back to Persia.[26]

Rather more important is the fact that the re-appraisal of Sherley must involve a re-appraisal of the part played by the famous embassy in Persian politics. In Prague and in Rome it was Sherley who presented the Shah's offer of a great alliance on the basis of secret verbal instructions given him by the Shah in his capacity as Ambassador. Since he was not recognized by the Shah as Ambassador, it can at the most be a question of messages the Shah urged him to bring back in the belief that he was sent out by the Christian powers, but if we consider Anthony's whole, somewhat doubtful performance we have no possibility at all of deciding how openly Abbas had expressed himself in 1599 in respect of the coming war against Turkey. It is quite certain, however, that the letters sent with Husain to the Pope and the Emperor, in contrast to corresponding later letters, contained no direct reference to the possibility of military co-operation.

23. Ross pp. 130–132; *Chronicle* pp. 70–71. A doubtful tradition permits him to regain his freedom only to perish at the stake as a martyr in Astrakhan in 1613, Luz p. 314.
24. Ross p. 130.
25. Don Juan's information regarding this point, Don JUAN pp. 261–262 and pp. 283–284, is confirmed by Husain's complaint against Sherley, Arch. Vaticano, Fondo Borghese III: 106 e.
26. Ross p. 53.

An investigation of Persian policy in the interval between the Ambassador's departure in 1599 and the outbreak of the Persian-Turkish war in 1603 also shows that Abbas has not been so sure of his case as Anthony Sherley asserts. True enough, Don Juan of Persia relates that a Turkish Ambassador who was at the Persian Court at the same time as Anthony Sherley, as a punishment for his exorbitant demands, was bereaved of his long beard, which Abbas thereupon sent to the Grand Turk.[27] This delightful anecdote seems to be confirmed by a letter from the Venetian Ambassador in Prague, Pietro Duodo, of 8th December 1600, i.e. while the embassy was still at the Imperial Court.[28] That it was put into circulation is significant, but it cannot be true. At approximately the same time as Husain's and Anthony Sherley's departure from Persia another Persian Ambassador left the Persian Court for Constantinople; he arrived at the Turkish capital on 10th July 1599 and was in audience on 24th July. On this occasion he handed over 12 golden keys and 12 silver keys to the towns the Shah had conquered from "the tartars"; presumably what is referred to here is the victory over the Uzbegs the previous year.[29] In October 1599 there was still an official Persian agent in Constantinople, who informed the Venetian *Bailo* about the dispatch of the letter from the Shah to the Christian Princes,[30] and in April 1600 a new Persian Ambassador arrived at Constantinople. A cut off beard would have constituted a declaration of war, but the connections between Persia and Turkey were still outwardly friendly, even though the new Ambassador's task was to complain about the Turkish governor in Tabriz.[31] Throughout the following two years there were many rumours in Constantinople, but few reliable accounts about the relation with Persia. As late as between March and September 1602 there was a Persian Ambassador at the Porte, but there is no reliable information available about his task or the negotiations he carried on.[32] Not until August 1603 can the *Bailo* report that the war between Persia and Turkey is a fact; most significantly it occurs in connection with an "agreement for military aid" between Turkey and the Uzbegs, according to which the latter obtained 20 guns and 200 arquebuses for use against the Persians.[33]

Persian policy during the four years between 1599 and 1603 thus clearly indicates that Anthony Sherley's visit had not led to any immediate change

27. Don JUAN p. 232.
28. PENROSE p. 19.
29. A. d. S. Venezia, Rubricari Konstantinopoli, D 6, ff. 261, 263.
30. *Ibid.* f. 271.
31. A. d. S. Venezia, Rubricari Konstantinopoli, D 7 f. 10.
32. *Ibid.* ff. 116–129.
33. *Ibid.* f, 185.

of aims; in these years Abbas's main political interests lay in quite a different direction. The Uzbegs continued to give cause for anxiety, and in 1602 Abbas directed a large-scale attack against Bukhara, which ended in one of the most serious defeats in his career. Ironically enough, on his eastern borders that year he made precisely the mistakes that were later repeated by the Turks on *their* eastern border during the fight against himself. He led his newly-created regular army into thinly populated areas, where the difficulties as regards supplies and the hardships associated with a summer campaign enervated the troops and forced him into a costly retreat before he had made contact with the main forces of the enemy.[34] A modernization of the army in the Middle East was not only a question of gun founders and loyal infantrymen. Without overcoming the technical problems regarding supplies the modernized army was unable to face the mounted units in the frontier regions.

It is impossible to decide from the information available whether the concurrent events by the Persian Gulf were a part of Abbas's policy or whether they represented an independent initiative on the part of the Governor of Shiraz, Allah Verdi Khan, but considering the friendly relations between Abbas and Allah Verdi Khan and later the latter's son, Imam Quli Khan, it must be assumed that these have not been against the Shah's will. In 1601–02 Allah Verdi Khan took possession of the province of Lar on the Persian coast opposite Hormuz and of the island of Bahrein which belonged to Hormuz. Although in Persia it was maintained that Hormuz was under Persian suzerainty and that the Shah consequently had a right to let Allah Verdi Khan take Bahrein, the Shah cannot have been in any doubt that this step would not help to promote co-operation with the Christian Princes.

Both Anthony Sherley's influence upon Persian policy and the importance attached to the famous embassy on the part of Persia must be reduced in the light of the above. Anthony's contribution obtained significance first and foremost as a grand-scale advertisement for Persia. If he exaggerated the Shah's friendly feelings for the Christian Princes and his desire for a common action against the Ottoman Empire it could only serve to increase European interest in a closer contact with Persia. But at the same time it paved the way for misunderstandings that proved in the long run to be detrimental.

34. BELLAN pp. 114–118.

The Christian Princes' Reply

As Sherley formulated the aims of the Persian Embassy in 1600,[35] it was not merely a greeting and an application to join the "club", it was an offer of an alliance against the Turks, a proposal to co-operate in the most just of all wars. "The thought of a reconciliation between special interests and religious denominations at the expense of the Turks was unable to alter the course of events, but it was not therefore less honest or less widespread; it was a matter of course for the most varied persons, for Gustav-Adolf as for Tilly, for Wallenstein as for Maximilian; it was incorporated, so to speak, in the style of writing of the chancelleries."[36] But in the workaday reality of power politics there was no place for such great thoughts. Already in Prague there were visible signs of dispute and intrigues between the diplomatic representatives. "It is known that the English Queen has friendly relations with Turkey, and that she is not kindly disposed towards the Hapsburgs; what then does she intend with this embassy?" asks the Venetian Ambassador, Pietro Duodo[37] "Anthony Sherley's confessor is a Jesuit by the name of Buyza, a man who consorts with the French Ambassador", reports the Spanish Ambassador, Guillen de St. Clemente.[38] The Ambassadors spy on one another; they seek by means of rumours and confidential reports to survey the new situation; their job is not to run straight into the arms of a beautiful project, but to evaluate the significance of the new element in a European context.

Anthony had more or less taken it upon himself to assemble all the Christian Princes for a crusade, but already between Prague and Rome an open quarrel broke out between Anthony and Husain, and in Sienna it came to blows. In a letter to Henry IV Cardinal d'Ossat commented cynically from Rome: "It could happen that someone will tell them that since they, who are only two and are sent out by the same Prince on the same errand, cannot themselves agree, they will find it even more difficult to create unity between so many Christian Princes and others with regard to overthrowing the Turkish Empire."[39] The embassy was accredited to eight European powers: the Emperor, the Pope, England, Scotland, France, Spain, Poland, and Venice. The embassy avoided Poland, presumably under

---

35. Anthony Sherley's note to the Emperor is summarized in Arch. Simancas, Estado, leg. 707, cf. Arch. Vaticano, Fondo Borghese III: 106 e.
36. FAGNIEZ p. 180. But see, for example, DELACROIX p. 89: "L'opinion générale, que se fut dans l'Église, la cour ou la nation, persistait à penser que la délivrance de la Terre Sainte était l'oeuvre par excellence de la France royale et chrétienne.
37. Ross p. 43.
38. Arch. Simancas, Estado, leg. 707.
39. PENROSE p. 101.

pressure on the part of Russia, neither were England nor Scotland contacted formally; Anthony assured Cecil in a letter from Archangel that it was only Husain's obstinacy that forced him, in accordance with the Shah's instructions, to travel to the Emperor before he travelled to England, and he humbly requested Cecil to send a messenger to Prague about his wishes concerning the embassy.[40] If Cecil had deigned to answer it it would scarcely have been a friendly letter; in Rome Sherley informed d'Ossat that the Queen had forbidden him to travel to England.[41] Venice declined the honour of a visit: the Republic had no mind to destroy the neighbourly relations with Turkey for the sake of a Holy League,[42] and France adopted the same attitude.[43] The only three powers remaining were those already at war with Turkey: the Emperor, the Pope and Spain. No Holy League was formed, but each in turn sent a gracious reply to the Persian letter; moreover they immediately replied with return embassies, through which they ordered their envoys to convey their intentions to fight against Turkey. If, as we assume, Anthony Sherley greatly exaggerated the embassy's anti-Turkish aims these answers were bound to make a very strong impression in Persia.

In Prague the answer was not composed until after fairly lengthy negotiations. Anthony Sherley insisted that the Emperor should promise not to make peace prior to a consultation with the Shah. The Emperor was unwilling to go as far as this, however; the reply, dated 12th December 1600, handed to the Ambassadors – Husain and Sherley each obtained a copy – was of a general nature. The Emperor expressed his pleasure in receiving the embassy; he accepted the offer of friendship and co-operation, though without specifying it in concrete terms, and promised on his part to pursue the war against the Ottomans with great vigour. Everything was expressed in very general terms, the question of the terminability of the co-operation or of a separate peace was thus unmentioned.[44]

The replies from Rome are dated 2nd May 1601 and have as little content as that of the Emperor; the little there is is expressed very beautifully, however. The offer of friendship was received in heartfelt phrases; the Pope promised to work for the co-operation of the Christian Princes, such as he had already supported his dear son Rudolph – both in full

40. Ross p. 245.
41. *Ibid.* p. 49.
42. Chew p. 272. Since 1594 Venice had rejected every attempt by the Pope to persuade the Republic, openly or in secret, to support the Emperor's war against Turkey. Pastor xi pp. 204–205.
43. Ross p. 23.
44. Arch. Simancas, Estado, leg. 707.

accordance with the actual Papal policy of these years.[45] To this was added a special word of thanks for the concessions the Shah had guaranteed the Christians in his countries and a promise to send missionaries and learned doctors to Persia very soon.[46]

In Rome Anthony Sherley left the Persian embassy abruptly; it will therefore be necessary to make a small diversion in order to see how he wound up his relations with his self-appointed embassy. His sudden disappearance has often been taken as an indication of the fiasco in which the Shah's and his magnificent project had resulted.[47] But, as already mentioned, the replies sent to the Shah were cordial, and in Rome, too, Anthony had managed to cope with the attacks on his person; the Papal reply was completed in two examples, of which he received one.[48] In a memorandum dated May 1601 (considering that the Papal reply is dated 2nd May, this is most likely to be after the reply had been received), Anthony Sherley declared it was his intention to return immediately to Persia accompanied only by an interpreter and two servants.[49] On 25th May the Pope issued a letter of recommendation to Anthony Sherley addressed to the Portuguese Captain in Hormuz.[50] On 28th May Clement VIII received Sherley in an extraordinary audience and handed him a present of money in addition to what he had received at the farewell audience on 10th May.[51] On 29th May he left Rome and on 6th June he arrived in Ancona.[52] It is more than probable that the extra gift of money had been prompted by his intention to return to Persia, while he left it to Husain to continue to Spain.

From that time on, however, Anthony Sherley's wanderings remain obscure; we possess many rumours but few certain clues in the following years. A letter from an anonymous Hessian agent in Verona, produced by Babinger, is nevertheless so detailed that it appears reliable. According to this informant, in 1601 Sherley should have reached as far as Ragusa, but from there he turned about and travelled to Venice.[53] Another clue is provided by the dispatch from Lello, the English Ambassador in Constantinople, of August 1601. According to Lello, the reply the Emperor sent with Sherley should already have been in the hands of the Turks by this

45. Pastor XI p. 201 ff.
46. *Chronicle* pp. 82–84.
47. Thus Babinger p. 30; Penrose pp. 111–112; Chew pp. 277–278.
48. *Chronicle* pp. 78–79.
49. Arch. Vaticano, Fondo Borghese III: 106 e.
50. *Chronicle* p. 79.
51. Ross p. 50.
52. Anthony Sherley, Ancona, to Cardinal Aldobrandini, 6/6 1601, Arch. Vaticano, Fondo Borghese III: 106 e.
53. Babinger p. 32 n. 3.

time; one of his servants was said to have stolen it while he was staying in Rome and sold it to a Turkish agent.[54] Whether it was this theft, fear of the Turkish authorities or something as banal as lack of money that checked Sherley in Ragusa must be left open. His movements during the following years are irrelevant to the main theme of this book, but it may be noted that up till 1604 he stayed in Venice, where he divided his time between alchemist experiments and political intrigues.[55]

In the meantime Husain had continued from Rome to Spain with the remainder of the Persian company; on 30th August his embassy was up for discussion in the Spanish Council of State.[56] According to the Council's *consulta* the offer of friendship was of a more general nature than Sherley's verbal notes in Prague and Rome; on the other hand Husain had a concrete point to put forward: a request that the Captain in Hormuz should be ordered to treat Persian subjects with greater respect than had previously been the case. In particular he requested that the Persian merchants who came to Hormuz to sell slaves or horses should not be forced to accept half of their payment in kind from the Captains' stocks, but the complaints also included the levying of extraordinary customs dues and chicanery in general. In the Spanish answer that was completed in October 1601 the Shah's offer of friendship was accepted, and the Spanish King gave his assurances that it was his intention as previously to fight the Turks with all the means at his disposal. With regard to Hormuz it was emphasized that care would be taken to ensure that extortions would not take place in future.[57] The Spanish willingness to take an active part in the fight against the Turks may appear surprising in view of what modest interests Spain really had in the Eastern Mediterranean, but surprise diminishes on remembering the practical consequences of the Spanish promises. The idea of a staunchly Catholic King as the Defender of Christendom was probably still alive under Philip III, but it cannot pass unnoticed that the Council of State had its eye upon Spain's two uncertain allies in a hostile Europe when it answered the Persian Ambassador. The Spanish Ambassador in Rome was reminded that important concessions had been made, that the Persian embassy had been expensive, but that it had been done for the sake of the Emperor and of the Christian cause,[58] and steps were also taken to ensure that the Spanish Ambassador at the

---

54. Ross p. 55.
55. Anthony Sherley was arrested in Venice in March 1603 after he had forced his way into the house of a Persian merchant with armed men in order to take over the merchant's stocks on the plea of his Ambassadorial rank. *Peso Politico* p. 26–28.
56. Arch. Simancas, Estado, leg. 493.
57. Arch. Simancas, Estado, leg. 1856.
58. *Ibid.*

Court of the Emperor was informed of all the details in the reply to Persia.[59]

On the other hand it may be observed already in connection with this embassy that the Council of State was responsible on two counts. The Spanish Government was able at this time to co-ordinate its policy of being the foe of Islam and Defender of Christendom within its general European policy. But as supreme authority, also for the Portuguese Empire, the Council of State was faced with other problems and other interests, and there can scarcely be any doubt that both the Council of State and the Portuguese leaders were aware of this. Already in October 1601 an Ambassador was appointed at the Court who was to accompany Husain back to Persia. This decision aroused opposition in Lisbon, however. On 27th October the Viceroy, Castel Rodrigo, wrote to the King saying that he found the Ambassador, Antonio de Scovar, to be of too humble lineage; in his opinion it would be more opportune to let the Viceroy in Goa appoint a suitable diplomatic representative.[60] Just over a week later de Scovar had already discovered that he was in fact too old and weak to undertake the demanding task, and applied for his release. The Council of State graciously consented to his request and resolved that the case should be laid before Castel Rodrigo;[61] Husain was not accompanied by any Spanish Ambassador on his return from Europe.

From the Court Husain continued to Lisbon, where he arrived in the middle of November 1601. He and his company were "slightly intractable" for the first few days, but only because the company had partaken too liberally of the Portuguese wine; once the visits were under way everyone found Husain amiable.[62] A particular problem troubled the Portuguese authorities. The Persians wished to invest the King's parting gift in various weapons, including lances, swords and arquebuses, but the export of arms to Islamic regions was forbidden of course. The problem was referred to the Spanish Council of State, which, after due consideration and having consulted theological authorities, resolved that in the present case, in which there was reason to believe that the weapons would be used against infidels, it might be allowed.[63]

We have no direct information concerning Husain's return journey, but it is known that it was planned for the ordinary *carreira* in the spring of 1602.[64] Theoretically he should thus have been able to be back in Persia

59. Arch. Simancas, *Estado*, leg. 707.
60. Marquese del Castel Rodrigo, Lisbon, to Philip III, 27/10 1601, Arch. Simancas, Estado, leg. 493.
61. Arch. Simancas, leg. 493.
62. Arch. Simancas, leg. 618, f. 90.
63. *Ibid.*
64. Arch. Simancas, Estado, leg. 1856.

in the winter of 1602/3, i.e. before or at the same time as the resumption of the Turkish-Persian war, but since Gouvea, who was at the Persian Court at that time, does not mention his homecoming, it most probably did not take place until the following monsoon in 1603/4.[65] Thus the replies Husain brought with him scarcely had any direct significance for the outbreak of war, but they must have considerably strengthened Abbas's hopes with regard to a Christian offensive against the Ottoman Empire. The Emperor, Pope and King of Spain had accepted his offer of friendship and promised to make war on his arch-enemy.

The Replies Come in, War Begins

Already before Husain's return, however, Abbas had begun to receive answers to the letters he had sent with Husain in 1599. Everyone responded quickly, but even under the most favourable circumstances the postal service was slow. Husain and Anthony Sherley left Persia in the summer of 1599, in the autumn of 1600 they were in Prague, and a few months later reliable reports of the mission were available in Valladolid. Before the next departing fleet, in the spring of 1601, letters were prepared for the Shah; they were sent to Goa with orders to forward them with a cleric. They must have been received in Goa towards the end of 1601, and in February 1602 a Mission of Augustinians left Goa with Gouvea at its head in order to perform this errand. In September 1602 they were received in audience by Abbas in Meshed; it could not have been quicker – it had taken three years.

Gouvea, who was always anxious to exaggerate the part played by the Augustinians, is unfortunately our only source for the significant phase, 1602–03, the period when replies from Europe came in and during which the breach between Persia and Turkey took place. The central problem in this period is of course the correlation between the receipt of the European reactions to the Shah's communication as formulated by Sherley and the change in Persian foreign policy in 1603. The available sources provide no possibility of obtaining a deeper understanding of Abbas's deliberations and possible discussions at the Persian Court; however, a determination of the chronology, as far as the diplomatic communications and the outbreak of war are concerned, provides fairly certain indications with regard to the correlation.

On his arrival in Hormuz in April 1602 Gouvea did not find the situa-

---

65. The earliest mention of Husain's arrival home is to be found in Abbas's letter with Paquesa, which was completed by February 1605 at the latest. Torre do Tombo, Lisboa, Misc. Ms. 1104 f. 117.

tion very promising for the envisaged co-operation. In 1601 the Khan of Shiraz, Allah Verdi Khan, had occupied Bahrein, which, as a part of Hormuz, was indirectly a Portuguese possession. From Hormuz an *armada* was sent to the island in order to attempt to regain it, but the Persians on their part had begun a siege of the Portuguese bridgehead on the mainland, Gombroon, and blockaded the caravan routes. With Gouvea as mediator, however, it was possible to bring about a cease-fire fairly quickly. The Persians raised the siege of Gombroon, while the Portuguese refrained for the time being from attempting to reconquer Bahrein.[66]

From Hormuz Gouvea travelled through Lar, where he remarked upon the widespread destruction caused by the war of the previous year; on his further travels he met Allah Verdi Khan, who nourished particularly unfriendly feelings towards the Portuguese, because he regarded the Mission as dispatched by the Captain in Hormuz with the purpose of lodging a complaint against him with the Shah because of his attack on the possessions of Hormuz. In September 1602 he eventually reached Meshed, where the Shah was in residence following the disastrous summer campaign against the Uzbegs. Both in Meshed itself and on the journey from Meshed to Isfahan, where they arrived on 10th November, Gouvea was several times received in audience by the Shah. Gouvea emphasizes very strongly in his account of these conversations that he stuck to his original instructions, which were drawn up before the conflict concerning Bahrein was known in Goa, and that he consequently only negotiated about the possibilities for co-operation against Turkey. Abbas, too, seems tacitly to have regarded the matter of Bahrein as being merely of local interest.

According to his own narrative Gouvea's talks mainly consisted of heavy propaganda for the European intention of fighting the Ottoman Empire. Gouvea reproduces his long talks, in which he states that the relations between the European states are for once fairly peaceful, and he intimates strongly that both the Pope, the Emperor, Poland, Moscow, Savoy, Tuscany and Spain will be united in a Holy League. The Shah's reaction is at first evasive; he will await his Ambassador's (Husain's) return from Europe before he determines upon war, winter is on its way, etc., but, when pressed, he admits that it is his secret wish to start war with Turkey.[67] Gouvea's account cannot be regarded as a word-for-word summary of the negotiations, but there is no reason to doubt the main points of view exchanged. Abbas did not hide his own feelings against the Turks, who had forced him into a humiliating peace in 1590, but on the other hand he had not taken the final decision, which was to give the signal

---

66. GOUVEA f. 17.
67. *Ibid.* f. 51.

for the next generation's almost continuous fight between the Ottoman and the Safavid Empires.

A relevant factor in this connection is probably the arrival of Fathi Beg (see p. 104) in Venice in March 1603. He was treated like an Ambassador in Venice, but there is nothing, neither in the letter he brought from the Shah, nor in the talks that took place in connection with his reception, to suggest that the war was impending.[68] On the contrary, on his return journey the Persian envoy took with him some goods he had bought on the Shah's account, and which were confiscated in Aleppo on the outbreak of war in 1603. Abbas regarded this loss as sufficiently serious for him to send an Armenian to Venice five years later in order to rescue what had been taken into custody by the Venetian consulate and carried off to Venice.[69] Fathi Beg must have left Persia in the summer or autumn of 1602 and had not been informed of the approach of war.

Before Abbas, with Gouvea among his company, reached Isfahan on 10th November 1602 yet another European embassy arrived, a Papal Mission under Diogo de Miranda and Francesco da Costa. In order to see how this embassy had come about it will be necessary to retrace our steps to the summer of 1600, when the rumours flew ahead of Husain and Anthony Sherley who were on their way through Germany to Prague.

It has already been mentioned that Anthony Sherley and Nicolo de Melo had sent the interpreter, Michelangelo Coray, on ahead from Persia through Turkey to Europe in order to bring tidings of the embassy. He arrived in Venice in November 1599 and delivered the letters to Rome the following December. The letters from de Melo, who emphasized the possibilities for a Christian Mission at the Court of the Shah, aroused some interest; apparently information was obtained about de Melo, because enclosed with the Spanish Ambassador's account about the letters is a copy of a personal testimony concerning de Melo from Friar Tomas Marquez, the procurator of his Order for the province of the Philippines in Rome, who knew him well. In this he declared that de Melo had always behaved "virtuously and like a good religious, but that he was regarded as a man of little substance and content."[70] If there was a certain amount of scepsis in Rome concerning de Melo's information regarding the Shah's wish to co-operate against the Turks, his love of the Christian religion and his promises of guarantees for Christian subjects and travellers, it was only natural. But during the following year, 1600, his information was confirmed by two apparently independent sources.

In August 1600 a Portuguese religious, Francesco da Costa, presumably

68. BERCHET, *Persia* p. 196.
69. *Ibid.* p. 206.
70. Arch. Simancas, Estado, leg. 972.

a Jesuit who had left the Society, arrived in Rome from Persia, which he had passed through a few months after Husain's and Anthony Sherley's departure. He had heard about the embassy and about the Shah's protestations of his warm feelings for the Christians from the Europeans who had remained at the Persian Court. He hurried off to Rome immediately, arriving eight months in advance of the embassy, and handed a report to Cardinal Aldobrandini about the great news.[71] Not least his tremendous optimism with regard to the impending conversion of the Shah and his entire household must have aroused both interest and scepsis in Rome, but his account was substantiated shortly afterwards by a Portuguese soldier, Diogo de Miranda, from Hormuz. Miranda, like da Costa, had travelled through Persia from Hormuz. In Venice he had met a Persian envoy, "Asad Beg", who was posing as a merchant, though recognized as Ambassador "dalla Piazza e dall'universale". Miranda maintained that this Persian had confided in him that his business was merely a cover-up; his real job was to obtain information about the Persian Ambassadors, and help them if they were short of money. During subsequent talks the Persian should have disclosed the fact that he was really a Christian, and that the Shah, too, had leanings in that direction. He was supposed to have said that the Shah's two dearest wishes were to create a Grand League against the Ottoman Empire and to obtain a Papal nuntius to Persia who would be able to negotiate on behalf of the Pope and to look after the Shah's Christian subjects. Reportedly Miranda and an anonymous cleric eventually persuaded the Persian to travel to Rome, assuring him that the year of jubilee was his guarantee for a magnificent and heartfelt reception – this event excludes any doubt as regards the dating – but before he could set off, Michelangelo Coray disclosed the plans to the Venetian authorities, which latter took immediate steps to have him put on board ship and sent to the Levant.[72]

It is a strange story. There is undoubtedly some truth in it. There was a Persian envoy in Venice in the summer of 1600, (see p. 103) though his name was not Asad Beg, but Efet Beg. Other parts of the account also have a certain ring of authenticity; it is quite possible to imagine Michelangelo Coray in the role of informer, so as not to destroy the market for the awaited Sherley embassy in which he himself had a share, and it is extremely likely that the Venetian authorities would get rid of a Persian negotiator quickly and discretely if he threatened in 1600 to travel to Rome and work for the Crusade against Turkey. But if we can

71. Arch. Vaticano, Fondo Borghese II:20 f. 158–60.
72. *Ibid.* ff. 192–197, cf. I:965 f. 96 ff. Gouvea, who has known of this account, follows it minutely in his own account of the dispatch of da Costa and Miranda, which discloses the anonymous cleric to be Bishop of Pistoia. GOUVEA f. 56.

imagine that, interested contemporaries might well have imagined the same. How much truth there is in Miranda's story must be left open; in Rome it appeared plausible in conjunction with the reports received in the same year from de Melo and da Costa. The part of the story that received most attention in Rome was the most unlikely statement about the Shah's accessibility for Christian conversion. Already on 4th September Spain was informed of the promising outlook for a mission, and February 1601, still some months before Anthony Sherley and Husain had reached Rome, Miranda and da Costa were sent as Papal Ambassadors to the Shah. Their instructions and credentials were in accordance with the information available in Rome before their departure; they contained a liberal offer of support from Rome for the Christian missionary work in Persia, a promise to dispatch promptly many able missionaries and a friendly description in general terms of the plans for a war against Turkey.[73] In addition the Ambassadors brought a letter to one of the Shah's wives, who was reported to be a Christian. It must have aroused some consternation in the harem if the letter got as far.[74]

This was rush work. Not only had Rome let itself be deceived by the apparently tallying accounts of the Shah's religious turn of mind, but the men who had been allotted the task by virtue of their supposed local knowledge were not worthy of it. The intention was that, in disguise, they should have followed the shortest route through Turkey, but this plan had been spoilt before they reached Venice on account of their lack of discretion. Consequently they had to follow the longer route through Poland and Russia; before long they fell out, and although the nuntius in Poland managed to reconcile them temporarily, on their arrival in Persia in the beginning of 1602 they had finally broken off relations. Miranda confiscated a Venetian merchant's stocks, maintaining that he had Papal authority for this action, and travelled on ahead in order to be able to make his entry at Court before his fellow Ambassador. He did not create a good impression there either, however; he is said to have arrived at the audience with the Shah with the Pope's letter in his back pocket. The Augustinians and the Carmelites seldom agree, but their opinion of Miranda is quite unanimous.[75] For once we even seem to possess a Persian statement that substantiates the European one. In October 1605 the Papal nuntius reports concerning a conversation with the Persian Ambassadors in Prague that, as proof of the Shah's interest in establishing diplomatic contact between

73. Arch. Vaticano, Fondo Borghese II:20 ff. 199–205; *Chronicle* pp. 84–87.
74. *Chronicle* pp. 88–89.
75. Arch. Vaticano, Fondo Borghese II:20 ff. 208–211 cf. *Chronicle* p. 90 ff. GOUVEA f. 50 and *passim*. After Clement VIII's death, if not earlier, the dispatch of the two adventurers was regretted also in Rome. Arch. Vaticano, Nunziature Spagna 333 f. 259–262.

Persia and the Holy See, they had stated that Clement VIII's Ambassadors had been kindly received, despite their low rank.[76]

Neither the Papal nor, for that matter, the Spanish envoys, the Augustinians, were particularly representative; furthermore the Papal envoys made things worse with their continual quarrelling amongst themselves. There is scarcely any reason to doubt Gouvea's statement that the Shah's deliberations concerning a decisive break with Turkey were influenced by a religious faction at the Court.[77] The opponents of the war against the Islamic neighbour must have been strengthened when, in the beginning of 1602, it was rumoured that a relief fleet had been sent from Goa to Hormuz, and that its ultimate goal was Bahrein.[78] Gouvea likes to give the impression that his Mission had been a determining factor behind the Shah's decision; he maintains that his departure from Court was delayed until February 1603 because the Shah wished him to take the message about the first Persian victory with him,[79] but on the other hand he discloses a few pages further on that it was not until his stay in Shiraz on the way to Hormuz that he heard that Nahavand had submitted to the Persian Governor in Hamadan.[80] Another indication that the final decision had not yet been made when Gouvea left the Court is the letter the Shah gave Allah Verdi Beg, who accompanied Gouvea on the return journey as Persian Ambassador to Spain. There is no direct reference in this letter to the approaching war with the Ottoman Empire; although it is sent by the safe route via Hormuz it is only a greeting and an assurance of friendship expressed in general terms.[81] But the decision about the war must have been definitive during the spring of 1603, as the reception of Nahavand's surrender indicates. Shortly afterwards the Kurdish commander of the Turkish frontier stronghold of Salmas revolted in order to place himself under the protection of the Shah. With these events the great Ottoman-Safavid war, which with few exceptions was to continue until 1638, began.

An accurate estimate of the influence of the European envoys on Abbas's decision cannot be made, amongst other reasons because information concerning the negotiations Abbas simultaneously conducted elsewhere, especially with the Georgian Princes, is too fragmentary to form a total picture. Subsequently Abbas liked to maintain, and especially after the peace in Sitva-Torok, that it was the Christian Princes who had inveigled

76. MEYER p. 552.
77. GOUVEA f. 62.
78. Ibid. f. 63 ff.
79. Ibid. f. 68.
80. Ibid. f. 79.
81. Ibid. ff. 71–72.

him into starting the war by means of empty promises;[82] in the light of the preceding events this is unlikely, but the chronological coincidence between the Papal and the Spanish communications and the outbreak of war is too precise for their significance to be totally rejected. The turning-point in Persian foreign policy is not coincident with Anthony Sherley's and Husain's departure in 1599, but must be placed in the beginning of 1603. That Abbas at this time attached great importance to the diplomatic connections with the Christian powers is apparent from the diplomatic activity of the following years. As mentioned, a Persian Ambassador to Spain, *Allah Verdi Beg*, left the Persian Court in the beginning of 1603, accompanied by Gouvea. Before November 1603 an Ambassador, *Zainal Khan*, was sent to the Imperial Court; he arrived in Prague in July 1604.[83] At approximately the same time *Bastam Quli Beg*, accompanied by Miranda, was dispatched via Hormuz to the Pope.[84] In November 1603 an Imperial embassy, or rather the remains of it was received at the Persian Court; it had been sent in reply to Husain's and Anthony Sherley's mission, but the company had been beset with misfortunes, the Ambassador had died on the way and only a subordinate member of the mission reached the Court of the Shah.[85] From the Persian point of view the Emperor's dispatch must have been clear proof of the Christian Princes' interest in co-operation with Persia, and the Imperial mission was answered immediately by the dispatch of yet another embassy to the Imperial Court under *Mahdi Quli Beg*, who arrived in Prague via Moscow in December 1604.[86] At approximately the same time, i.e. during the winter of 1603–04, another Ambassador, *Ali Quli Beg*, was sent to Rome accompanied by da Costa and an envoy to Poland.[87] who may possibly be identified as that *Mechter Lubik Turchwana* who in 1605 brought Sigismund III a letter from Abbas.[88] For the sake of completion it should finally be mentioned that Abbas sent an Ambassador by the name of *Hasan Beg* to France in the company of Zainal Khan.[89]

We cannot determine the influence of the communications of the Christians on the Persian decision, but there can be no doubt that Abbas was

82. Gouvea, Isfahan, to Philip III, 27/12 1607, Arch. Simancas, Secr. Prov., Libr. 1479, f. 556.
83. MEYER p. 181.
84. Bastam Quli Beg's credentials in English translation, *Chronicle* pp. 94–95.
85. TECTANDER p. 53.
86. TECTANDER pp. 53, 68; MEYER pp. 264–265.
87. *Chronicle* p. 92. The Persian Ambassador's name is not mentioned in this context; it appears, however, in the Papal reply, Arch. Vaticano, Arm. 45, vol. 5, f. 47.
88. JOZEFOWITZ p. 331.
89. Arch. Simancas, Secr. Prov., Libr. 1479, ff. 269–70.

greatly interested in the co-operation in 1603–04. Six or seven Persian Ambassadors were sent to Europe within a single year; it was an initiative without precedence in the history of European-Persian relations.

Seven Persian Ambassadors

If there ever was to be a Holy War against the Ottoman Empire then this was the moment. In December 1603 Sultan Muhammed III died; the Asian provinces were in revolt; the war on two fronts had become a fact in the summer of 1603. But if Abbas had expected a Christian offensive against the tottering Ottoman Empire he was disappointed. No intensification of the Christian States' conduct of the war in the East ensued, let alone a Holy League; on the contrary, the Imperial participation in the war decreased on account of the increasing unrest in the Hapsburg countries from 1604. The embassies sent out by Abbas had to fight against distances and the trials of the journey, and they were pursued by misfortune. But even the greatest good fortune would not have been able to conceal the harsh truth: for the Christian powers the Holy War was only one of many problems, and not the most urgent. It was not the diplomatic envoys, but experience that, in the years after 1603, informed Abbas of the concrete possibilities of Persian-European co-operation.

If the historical significance of the embassies is consequently very limited, it is nevertheless of some importance to sketch briefly the fate of the individual missions, not only because they reflect the Persian optimism on the outbreak of war, but also because their reception in Europe reveals the political reality that made the realization of the Crusade impossible.

Allah Verdi Beg, who left the Persian Court in February 1603, still before the war with Turkey was a fact, was accredited to the Spanish Court, but he did not reach any further than Goa. From here he returned already in the following year accompanied by Lacerda, an envoy from the Viceroy (see p. 242). The Viceroy's wilfulness in this matter earned him a rebuke;[90] there is scarcely any doubt that in this the Portuguese in *Estado da India* were serving their own cause. There was no interest in Goa in the Turkish question; on the other hand it was of the utmost importance to re-establish friendly relations with Persia after the war of 1601–02 as quickly and cheaply as possible, even if it meant having to give up the idea of reconquering Bahrein for the time being. This is the background against which the Viceroy's decision to accept the Persian offer of friendship unconditionally, and without delaying the issue by sending the Ambassador on to Spain, must be seen.

90. *Documentos Remittidos* I p. 11 f.

Bastam Quli Beg was sent via Hormuz to the Pope in the middle of 1603 accompanied by Miranda. He died on the journey to Europe, and the leadership of the embassy had to be taken over by one of the Persian secretaries.[91] The Secretary and his company were well received in Spain, but while they were staying at the Court in May 1605 the Secretary was attacked and killed by a fellow countryman, Husain's nephew, who during the previous Ambassador's residence in Spain had been baptized under the name of Phelipe.[92] The Shah's letter eventually reached Rome, however. It was a repetition of the promises from 1599 regarding the treatment of the Christians, whether these were the Shah's subjects or were passing through Persia on their travels. The letter contained no direct mention of the war, but it ends with a phrase that seems to indicate that, at the dispatch of Bastam Quli Beg, Abbas expected Husain to return with concrete proposals for co-operation: "If God Almighty wills, as soon as the ambassador, whom We have formerly sent, returns, We shall carry out whatever You may have written and recommended by him; and after learning the true facts of the situation and conditions there and of the resolution arrived at by their Highnesses the European monarchs, We shall do whatever may be expedient in every respect, and dispatch the aforementioned priest (da Costa) to You."[93]

As mentioned, the Pope's reply in 1601 had not contained anything concrete, and in 1605 Paul V was still less prepared to put forward definite offers; the Hungarian front was crumbling, the Papal finances were exhausted after several years' fruitless subsidies to Rudolph, and the Papal attempts to join the Christian Princes in co-operation against Turkey gained no response anywhere.[94] The answer to the letter that had been sent with Bastam could hardly seem very satisfactory from the Persian point of view; it was an almost condescending recognition of the Shah's good treatment of the Christians and a promise that the Pope would pray for the Shah's greater wisdom and future victory – a hint that the Shah, as Muslim, was not quite acceptable.[95] The letter was dated October 1605, but did not come into Abbas's hands until it was handed him by the Carmelite Mission in the beginning of 1608, i.e. nearly five years after Bastam left Persia; none of Bastam's companions seems to have reached home alive.[96]

Hasan Beg, who was sent to France in the middle of 1603, was refused

91. *Ibid.* p. 115.
92. Arch. Simancas, Estado, leg. 493.
93. According to the translation in *Chronicle* p. 95.
94. Pastor xii p. 500 f.
95. *Chronicle* pp. 109–110.
96. Arch. Simancas, Secr. Prov., Libr. 1479, f. 64. Miranda accompanied the Ambassador to Portugal; he appears again in 1606 as applicant for an office in Lisbon. Arch. Hist. Ultramar., Lisboa, India Cx. 1.

admission on his arrival at Marseilles in 1604; Henry IV did not wish to receive a representative of the enemy of the Sultan.[97] Already Husain had been turned away when he tried to contact Henry IV; with this second attempt France was out of the Persian question for several years and it was with bitterness that Abbas later remembered the insulting French rejection.

On the other hand, *Zainal Khan*, Ambassador to the Imperial Court, had a magnificent reception when he and his train entered Prague in July 1604, and he was received in audience by the Emperor on 26th July. According to the Papal nuncio, on this occasion a couple of the Persian servants ran swiftly up to the Emperor on all fours and kissed his foot, "this form of respect raised a smile from His Majesty, who hadn't been seen to smile in public for twenty years." Regarding the war, the letter Zainal handed to the Emperor was similar to the letter sent to the Pope with Bastam, and Zainal himself stressed that the only reason why he was sent was to negotiate about the war.[98] He was in a hurry to get home; already before 9th August he begged to be allowed to take leave of the Court; he wished to return home before the winter made the journey through Russia too difficult.[99] At the Imperial Court matters did not move so fast, however; the Ambassador was entertained in all manner of ways and there was even a special parade of troops for his benefit, but the truth was that the question of the continuation of the war against the Ottoman Empire was already under debate. During 1604 the first tentative offer of peace had been received from Constantinople, where it was well known that also the Emperor had domestic problems to cope with. The Imperial ministers were strongly divided on the question of war or peace, and Rudolph himself felt hesitant and uncertain. Thus the question of Zainal's departure was continually put off; it was now so late in the year that the return journey could only be accomplished with difficulty, and in October a report was received that a new Persian Ambassador was on his way to the Imperial Court. It was undoubtedly with great relief that the decision was taken to postpone sending a reply with Zainal until the new Ambassador had been received.[100]

Mahdi Beg, who entered Prague in December 1604, was sent out after the reception of the remainder of the Imperial Embassy in the end of 1603. No copy or translation of his credentials seem to have been preserved; there are indirect reports, however, to the effect that they contained nothing new in comparison to previous letters apart from the report about the conquest of Tabriz and 57 other places.[101] It was now so late in the

97. BARBICHE p. 781.
98. MEYER p. 186; Arch. Vaticano, Fondo Borghese II: 152 f. 60.
99. MEYER p. 197.
100. *Ibid.* p. 236.
101. *Ibid.* pp. 264–265.

year that the departure could be postponed without complications; the new Ambassador was therefore lodged together with Zainal Khan and Hasan Beg, who had reached Prague after his wasted journey to France, so that in the following year the Imperial Court could boast of no less than three Persian Ambassadors. In accordance with his instructions the nuncio tried to make their stay as pleasant as possible. He entertained them to dinner and obtained permission for them to witness a Mass in the town's Jesuit church, unobserved. He enjoyed their company, and shortly after Zainal's arrival he noted with satisfaction that, as opposed to the preceding one (Husain), this Ambassador was willing to make do with fish on Fridays – he had been instructed from home to observe the customs of the country.[102]

This incident, as well as the Ambassadors' express wish to learn something about the Christian religion, could possibly be regarded as mere politeness towards the ecclesiastical diplomat; however, there is another feature which can only be interpreted as springing from Abbas's wish to strengthen by a show of friendship the basis of that co-operation with the Christian Princes which was so important for Persia. During the first Persian campaign in the summer and autumn of 1603 Abbas had conquered the Armenian centre, Three Churches, and Mahdi Beg assured the nuntius that the Shah wished this important church office to be filled by ecclesiastics who were under the Pope.[103] He likewise emphasized that, after the conquest, the Shah had bestowed rich gifts on the Church in order to demonstrate his friendship with the Christians. This information was confirmed by the Armenians in the Ambassador's train.[104]

The atmosphere was friendly enough, but the realities were embarrassing; the Ambassadors' farewell audience was repeatedly postponed, and there were rumours in Prague in the beginning of 1605 that they planned to make off without formal leave. In June the Emperor summoned Anthony Sherley to the Court from Messina, so that he could act as adviser regarding the composition of the reply to Persia. Not until 31st October 1605 did the nuntius report that the Ambassadors had received their farewell audience. The reply they were handed contained the Emperor's promises to continue the war against Turkey and to send an Ambassador to Persia the following year.[105]

It was double-dealing. The same day the Emperor gave instructions for

---

102. Cf. that, in 1620, della Valle reports concerning the Persian Ambassador in Constantinople, that he was instructed from home to avoid drinking wine while resident in the Ottoman Empire, della VALLE, *Persia* II: 2 p. 87.
103. MEYER pp. 264–265.
104. *Ibid.* p. 317.
105. *Ibid.* p. 552. Copy of the Emperor's reply in Arch. Vaticano, Fondo Borghese II: 152 ff. 61–62.

peace negotiations to be initiated with Turkey.[106] At first the nuncio thought that this step was merely a concession to the Court "doves", and that the Emperor was in reality determined to carry on the war. The Emperor's true wishes are difficult to determine, but the defeats on all fronts during the campaigns of 1605 and the domestic political troubles in the Hapsburg countries were real enough. The peace in Sitva Torok, moreover, was a fact before the Ambassadors had reached Persia with the Emperor's promises. Rudolph scarcely violated the international norms of the times; he had explicitly rejected a proposal for irrevocable co-operation during Husain's and Anthony Sherley's stay in Prague in 1600. But his behaviour must greatly have shaken Abbas's confidence in the vague promises contained in the Christian Princes' letters.

There was no question of the Emperor's letter arousing false hopes in the Shah, however, because the Ambassadors did not arrive home in Persia until after the news of the peace in Sitva Torok had been received. The political unrest following Boris Godunov's death in April 1605 complicated the return journey; from April to July the Ambassadors were couped up in Kazan together with the Carmelite envoys from the Pope, they spent the winter in Tsaritsin on the lower Volga and not until August 1607 did the company reach Astrakhan. Whereas the Carmelites continued from there to Baku, Zainal seems to have fallen out with the people of one of the false Dimitris, who detained him in Astrakhan.[107] The next time we hear about Zainal was when he arrived in Holland in June 1608; from there he sent a messenger to the Shah overland, whereas he himself took the route via France so that he could take ship in Lisbon for Goa.[108] In September 1608 he arrived in Portugal accompanied by Hasan Beg; the Portuguese authorities were willing to see to their transport home, and presumably they departed with the spring fleet in 1609. There is no available information regarding their subsequent fate.[109] The third Ambassador from Prague, Mahdi Beg, followed another route; he is known to have arrived in Persia before May 1609, but scarcely very much earlier.[110]

Concerning *Ali Quli Beg*, the Ambassador who was sent to the Pope accompanied by da Costa, there is very little information available. Presumably they left Persia early in 1604, i.e. shortly after Mahdi Beg, but for reasons unknown they did not get any further than Astrakhan. The Governor is reported to have forbidden them to continue their journey, on the other hand da Costa was on excellent terms with the local authorities when the Carmelite Mission encountered him on the Lower Volga in the

106. MEYER p. 555.
107. *Chronicle* pp. 111–112.
108. *Ibid.* p. 170.
109. Arch. Simancas, Secr. Prov., Libr. 1479, ff. 267–270, f. 406.
110. *Chronicle* p. 169.

end of 1607.[111] Ali Quli Beg is not mentioned on this occasion, but probably he too remained in Astrakhan, because it was there that Robert Sherley met him one year later, in 1609, when the latter was passing through from Persia on his way to Rome; from there Ali Quli Beg accompanied him as far as the Papal Court, from whence he returned home in September 1609.[112] There is no information about his further travels or his homecoming, which cannot have taken place before 1610 at the earliest.

Even more scant and uncertain is our knowledge about the messenger or Ambassador to Poland, who should have left Persia together with da Costa and Ali Quli Beg. In the end of 1607 he was still supposed to have been together with da Costa.[113] If this was the case he cannot have been identical with the above mentioned Mechter Lubik Turchvana, who handed Sigismund III a letter from Abbas in 1605.[114]

The Ambassadors travelled slower than the news. Apart from Allah Verdi Beg, who returned directly from Goa and thereby failed to carry out his mission, Abbas did not see anything of the Ambassadors he sent out in 1603–04 until the years 1608–10. The only official message the Shah received from the Europeans during these important years was with Lacerda, the Ambassador who accompanied Allah Verdi Beg back to Persia from Goa in 1604, and of course the communication from Goa had little relevance to the matter of primary interest to Abbas: the war with the Ottoman Empire. As already mentioned this question could not greatly interest the authorities in Goa; *Estado da India*'s primary interest was to reopen the caravan routes and secure peace in the Persian Gulf; they were willing to sacrifice Bahrein in order to achieve that goal, but had no wish to see their relations with Persia subordinated to Spanish world politics.[115] In Lacerda's instructions he was ordered to establish friendly relations with the Shah and warn him not to contact other European nations; Bahrein, on the other hand, remained unmentioned.[116]

Lacerda visited Abbas at the head of his army, where in October 1604 he was received with great kindness, but he left the camp already one week afterwards in order to settle in Kazvin together with two Augustinians, one of whom, Belchior dos Anjos, had accompanied him from Goa. In the beginning of 1605 Belchior was sent to the Shah in Tabriz in order to request the dispatch of the Ambassador, but Abbas's attitude was now more

111. *Ibid.* p. 92.
112. Arch. Vaticano, Arm. 45, vol. 5. ff. 47–49.
113. *Chronicle* p. 92.
114. JOZEFOWITZ p. 331.
115. GOUVEA f. 66.
116. LUZ p. 319. Of course the reason why Bahrein is not mentioned in Lacerda's instructions cannot, as suggested by Luz, be that Bahrein had not yet fallen at the time the instructions were issued.

reserved, if not downright unfriendly. Spain had not yet undertaken anything which might indicate that any realities lay behind the Spanish promises to co-operate against Turkey, said the Shah, and when Belchior tried to raise the question of Bahrein, he was sent away.[117] In March 1605 the Ambassador obtained the desired dismissal and was sent home with a new Persian Ambassador to Spain, Paquesa Eman Quli Beg.[118] From Goa Paquesa continued to Lisbon, but Lacerda never reported to Spain concerning his embassy; the Council of State had to be content with the information they obtained through Belchior dos Anjos; this circumstance, which undoubtedly reflects Goa's wish to reserve diplomatic contact with Persia, was criticized sharply in a letter from the King to the Viceroy in January 1607.[119]

The letter that was dispatched with Paquesa is interesting, because Abbas in this case departs from the assurances of general friendship and not only gives a factual description of the course of the war, but also expresses his impatience with the Spanish war effort. After the initial compliments Abbas refers to Husain's embassy to Spain and maintains (which can hardly be true) that *after* Husain's homecoming he assembled his army and went to war, since he had heard from the latter that the King of Spain wished him to start the war against the Ottoman Empire. Then a long description of the fortresses Abbas has since taken from the Turks follows: "Since I have now commenced operations against the Turks as promised, and there is now a bloody war between me and Turkey, Your Majesty also ought to do what he has promised me . . ."[120]

Paquesa arrived in Lisbon in November 1607; he appeared to be of higher rank than the Ambassadors hitherto received, i.e. Husain and the remnant of Bastam's embassy, and he was treated with great respect before he was sent on to the Court. During the negotiations concerning the answer he should take back to Persia it was proposed in the Council of Portugal that the demand for the return of Bahrein should be repeated; this proposal was not carried, however, and it was decided not to mention Bahrein.[121] This recommendation was supported by the Council of State, which decided that the letter should take the form of a repetition of general promises and compliments, with a special account of the Spanish galleys' attacks on the Turkish fleet in the Mediterranean.[122] The actual content of the Spanish

---

117. Luz p. 321.
118. Relacion del proceder que Luis Pereira de Lacerda huvo ... Arch. Simancas, Secr. Prov., Libr. 1479 f. 6–7. This relation is without doubt composed by Belchior dos Anjos.
119. *Documentos Remettidos* I p. 108.
120. Torre do Tombo, Lisboa, Misc. Ms. 1104, f. 117.
121. Arch. Simancas, Secr. Prov., Libr. 1479, f. 4.
122. *Ibid.* ff. 47–48 and Estado, leg. 435 ff. 192–193.

answer is not known, but it is extremely probable that this was the form that was chosen, since Paquesa returned to Lisbon already in March 1608 in order to take ship with the *carreira* to Goa.[123] The return journey was difficult, however; his ship sank outside Malindi and he did not reach Goa until 1610. His subsequent fate is unknown.[124]

If the diplomatic offensive of 1603–04 had not brought Abbas other advantages, it had at least illustrated the problems of communication. It was a long way from Persia to the European capitals. But in the light of the political events of the same years there is scarcely any doubt that Abbas came to a further conclusion; there was a long way between the declared anti-Ottoman policy of the Christian Princes and the political reality.

The Course of the War and the Crisis of Confidence 1607–08

It may be considered established that the hope of co-operation with the Christian powers was in Abbas's mind when he commenced war with Turkey in 1603. While in the following years his Ambassadors spread out over Europe and Asia he himself fought at the head of his army on the Turkish frontier. Although he received nothing in the way of European help, the campaigns nevertheless proved favourable to the Persians.

There cannot be any doubt that the Ottoman Empire was in extremely great difficulties in these years; if at any time the Ottoman Empire was threatened with downfall and disintegration it was in the decade after 1600. The Emperor alone was not a formidable enemy, neither was Persia, but a war on both fronts such as Turkey was faced with after 1603 was precisely the situation the Turkish leaders had always tried to avoid at almost any price. In addition, after 1599 the Empire was shaken by a number of serious revolts. In Aleppo, in Baghdad, in Lebanon and in Anatolia the provincial governors revolted, while in Constantinople the *spahis* revolted on several occasions. The finances of the Empire were strained and a ruthless depreciation of small coin, which not least affected the janissaries, weakened the army's loyalty towards the Ottoman dynasty still further.[125]

Abbas's fortunes of war in the first years after 1603 must be seen against this background; it was not the consolidated power of the Ottoman Empire that stood behind the armies that were sent against him. Already in 1603 he took Tabriz, in September he defeated a Turkish army at Sofia and in

---

123. Arch. Hist. Ultramar. Lisboa, India Cx. 1.
124. MOCQUET pp. 267–269.
125. HAMMER IV pp. 309–396.

the same year the siege of Erivan was begun, which fell in June 1604. In the beginning of 1604 the Turks began to assemble an army in Constantinople under the veteran, Cigala. In June the army broke camp, but the advance through Asia Minor was delayed by those rebels Cigala either was forced to fight or attempted to co-operate with during his advance; he did not reach Kars until 1604. In the meantime Abbas had withdrawn to Tabriz, having laid waste the countryside behind him and taken the greatest part of the chiefly Armenian population with him during his retreat. In the beginning of 1605 Cigala initiated the campaign with a siege of Van, but he was beaten by a relieving force under Allah Verdi Khan, and in November of the same year he suffered a new defeat against the Persians when he attempted to advance against Tabriz. The Ottoman counterattack was thereby brought to a standstill for the time being; Cigala died in the end of 1605 and his army disintegrated. In 1606 Abbas was able to concentrate on the problems of the politically complicated borderland between Azerbaijan and Georgia. In Constantinople a new army was assembled against Persia, but the conditions in Asia Minor were now so difficult that in June it had to abandon its advance and retire to Constantinople. The revolts and the continued fighting in Hungary had given Abbas a breathing-space, and in particular safeguarded him from being exposed to the full force of the Ottoman Empire before he had strengthened his position: strategically, by occupying also the smaller frontier strongholds, and politically, by consolidating his relations to the Kurdish and Georgian Princes.[126]

But it was the correctly chosen moment, not European participation, that procured Abbas these advantages; the Hapsburg army was crumbling and the Papal attempt to create a united Christian front behind the Hapsburgs was in vain. In the summer of 1605 the Pope wrote to Tuscany and Venice in order to encourage them to co-operate in the war against Turkey at sea; he himself could only afford to offer encouragement and prayers, however.[127] In October and November of the same year Papal letters were dispatched to the Emperor, the Kings of Spain and Poland, the Duke of Bavaria, the three spiritual Electoral Princes and to Savoy, Genoa, Lucca, Tuscany, Mantua, Urbino and Modena, requesting them to form a league for the defence of the Catholic faith. It was a good cause nobody should be able to refuse, but the replies were a long time coming; they were

126. *Ibid.*, BELLAN pp. 120–147. An interesting source for the events in Persia 1603–05 is an anonymous report, presumably composed by one of the Augustinians who remained in Persia after Gouvea returned home, Torre do Tombo, Lisboa, Misc. Ms. 1113 ff. 120–128. This is the report on which Gouvea bases his own account.
127. MEYER pp. 410–411.

characterized by general good will, but contained no concrete offers.[128] At the same time Rudolph's authority in the Hapsburg countries was seriously weakened. In 1605 Stefan Bocskai, as vassal of the Sultan, was crowned King of Hungary and Siebenbürgen, and the Protestant movement in Austria was about to take on disturbing proportions. The latter event was perhaps even more disturbing to Rome than the negative results of the campaigns; in the summer of 1605 the Papal nuntius in Prague was instructed not to oppose any possible attempts to make peace: the reason given was that the war, if it continued with the insufficient means at the Emperor's disposal, would only lead to the loss of more important fortresses.[129]

The diplomatic reports from both Prague and Constantinople reflect the disunity that was prevalent among the leaders in both capitals. Both were perfectly clear that the opponent was on the brink of total collapse, but in both places they were just as clear about their own weakness. Already at the beginning of the campaign in 1605 the Grand Vizier was instructed to initiate peace negotiations side by side with the continuation of the fight.[130] The political and military defeats during 1605 strengthened the cause of the doves at the Imperial Court, too, and while the Persian Ambassadors were still residing in Prague the Emperor instructed his envoys to initiate proper peace talks.[131] The negotiations continued throughout most of 1606 with several interruptions, but by November 11th the Imperial and the Turkish representatives had reached agreement with respect to the seventeen articles that constitute the Peace of Sitva Torok.[132]

Already some days previously it was rumoured in Constantinople that a peace treaty was imminent; on 3rd December the news was official, and the Spanish Ambassador in Venice, with his permanent secret agent in Constantinople as source, was able to report that the news had been received with great satisfaction in the Turkish capital.[133] The position was not yet quite stable, however; preparations for a campaign against Persia the following year were delayed by persistent rumours of the Emperor's treacherous intentions,[134] and not until June was it sufficiently sure that no Imperial offensive was pending so that the risk of sending the whole of the assembled army towards the east might be taken. Shortly afterwards a Persian Ambassador arrived in Contantinople with offers of peace. He was kept carefully isolated by the Turkish authorities so that he should

128. *Ibid.* p. 555 n. 2, p. 635 f.
129. *Ibid.* p. 501.
130. HAMMER IV p. 366.
131. MEYER p. 555.
132. HAMMER IV p. 393.
133. Arch. Simancas, Estado, leg. 1352, f. 21, f. 35.
134. *Ibid.* f. 71.

not obtain contact with persons who might inform him about the weakened state of the Ottoman Empire.[135] The Ambassador did not come in order to capitulate; there had already been several attempts to commence peace negotiations with Persia, and the demands the Persian envoy now presented on behalf of the Shah were not modest.[136] But his arrival reflects a change in Persian foreign policy, which it is reasonable to associate with the reports about the Peace of Sitva Torok. With the commencement of negotiations in 1607, as with the outbreak of war in 1603, the European policy, or rather – the information the Shah had at his disposal regarding the European policy – was of vital importance for his decisions.

This assumption is confirmed if we regard Abbas's attitude to the Christians in the period during which peace was concluded. Since 1603 Abbas had conducted a friendly policy in two fields in which the possibility for conflict was latent; this applies, despite the transfer of population, to the relations with the Armenians, who after the campaigns of 1603–04 had once more come under Persian rule, and also to the problems concerning Hormuz and the Persian Gulf, where there had been no disturbances since 1603.

Abbas's attitude to the Armenians was from the very first ambiguous – a reflection of the difficult legal situation the incorporation of the big non-Islamic minority confronted him with. During his retreat in the winter of 1604–05 he put into operation that transfer of population which is regarded as one of the greatest catastrophes in the history of the Armenian people.[137] Robert Sherley, who can scarcely be called delicate, was shaken; in May 1605 he writes to Anthony: "... in all his actions, he publisheth to the world the hatred he bears to the name of Christians, for evy daie he maketh slaves of the poor Armenyans, wch are daile brought like Sheepe into evy mkett, burnying and pulling downe all Churches..."[138] But it was doubtful whether there lay any religious bigotry behind these actions; as mentioned above it was important for Abbas to give the Christian powers the impression that he was intent on protecting the Armenians and their religion, even if for strategic reasons he had to ravage their land. This protective attitude towards the Armenians is confirmed by the Armenian chronicles: Abbas respected the Armenian leaders with whom he was on

135. *Ibid.* f. 90, f. 100.
136. Turkish messengers to Persia were sent in the winter of 1604–05, Torre do Tombo, Lisboa, Misc. Ms. 1105, f. 117, and again in 1606, BELLAN p. 156 f. Paulo Simon maintains that there had been three Turkish Ambassadors in Persia between the outbreak of war and 1607, *Chronicle* p. 161. Abbas's envoy demanded that the frontier should be fixed at Diarbekir, but the Turks insisted on those frontiers established at the Peace of Amasia following the conquests of Suleiman. Arch. Simancas, Estado, leg. 1352, f. 109.
137. PASDERMADJIAN pp. 276–277.
138. PENROSE p. 163.

friendly footing, he reduced the taxes incumbent upon the Christians, he favoured the Christians in legal cases between Christians and Muslims, he found homes for the refugees from Julfa in New Julfa near Isfahan at the expense of the Muslims, he supported the erection of churches and often witnessed the religious ceremonies on feast days himself and he made no attempts to hinder the practice of the Christian religion.[139]

The Portuguese seem to have become very rapidly aware of the opportunities offered by the new political status and immediate difficulties of the Armenians, both for the Catholic Church and for Portuguese influence in Persia. Presumably already during or immediately after the deportations in the winter of 1604–05 the Armenian leaders and the Augustinians in Isfahan discussed the possibility of an affiliation of the Armenian Church with Rome. The initial discussions, which met no opposition from the Persians, were so promising that the Archbishop of Goa, Aleixo de Meneses, who was also the functioning Governor, decided in 1606 to send a special envoy, the Augustinian Diogo de Santa Anna, to the Shah with a present and with a definite proposal regarding the Armenians.[140] The Shah was in Shirvan with the army when Diogo arrived in Isfahan at the beginning of 1607, but the Augustinian put forward his proposal to recognize the Pope as the head of the Armenian Church to representatives of the Armenians in Julfa, and he succeeded in getting a request for union of the churches signed by a bishop and some of the monks, priests and laymen.[141] Thereafter Diogo left Isfahan to visit Abbas in Shirvan at the end of July 1607. The proposals he put forward in the name of the Archbishop were possibly well-intentioned, but they were not tactful: firstly, Abbas was requested to order the liberation of those Christian Armenians who were enslaved, secondly, he was asked to command his Armenian subjects to recognize the Pope as "loro capo e vicario di Christo nostro Signore in tutta la sua chiesa", thirdly, he was asked to donate the Armenians in Julfa a ground where they could erect churches, a monastery, and a school.

In his answer Abbas expressed first and foremost his indignation about the Peace of Sitva Torok, and he did not forget to remind the Augustinians that he had won his many victories alone and without the help of the Christian Princes. His reply to the three points was negative: "To the first point he made no reply at all, to the second he said that„ I had attempted to convert the Armenians to my religion by ringing for them with bells, "and concerning the third point he merely said: churches with bells, churches with bells, churches with bells, at the same time biting his fingers." Abbas had not quite lost his sense of humor, however, in spite

139. Arakel de Tauritz in Brosset I pp. 300–301.
140. Arch. Vaticano, Fondo Borghese II: 68, ff. 95–108.
141. *Chronicle* pp. 100–101.

of the disappointing Peace of Sitva Torok, because he added that the Christians could build all the churches they liked in the countries they had conquered from the Turks.[142]

Diogo had to leave the Shah's camp without having obtained other than "rotten treatment and bad answers", and on his return to Isfahan he found that the Armenians were already informed of the Shah's change of attitude and that they now rejected every thought of co-operation with the Augustinians.[143] By the end of 1607 the Augustinian Mission in Isfahan felt itself painfully isolated. It is possible that they had acted clumsily concerning the question of the union of the churches – that was at any rate what the Carmelites thought –[144] and in letters to the Spanish Ambassador in Rome and to the Spanish King in February 1608 they attempted to protect themselves in advance from any possible criticism of their clumsy diplomacy. If they had become "odiosos" in Persia it was solely due to their zeal in defending the faith and serving the Spanish King.[145] It is doubtful whether their clumsiness and Abbas's temperament was all-important, however. The chronological coincidence with the Peace of Sitva Torok is so close that a connection cannot be excluded; until 1607 Abbas had not received other than empty promises from the Christian powers, and in his eyes the first Christian communication after the Imperial-Turkish peace treaty was an arrogant intervention in the relations between himself and his Armenian subjects. All things considered he treated the Augustinian Mission with astonishing moderation, and there is no sign of the Armenian nation having suffered from his possible indignation.

The other point of issue, which had been slumbering since 1603, was the situation around Hormuz. The Persians had kept Bahrein and there had been no attempt on the part of the Portuguese to re-conquer the island; on the other hand a formal peace had never been concluded either, and the Portuguese, as was later apparent, had not forgotten their claim to Bahrein. But the Persians on their part had not forgotten their irritation over the Portuguese administration of the entrance of the Persian Gulf. After the conquest of Lar the Persians had tacitly accepted the fact that the Portuguese refrained from paying the protection money, or *mocarrerias*, for the free passage of the caravans, which Hormuz had paid the Sultan of Lar right from olden times, and which now rightfully belonged to the Khan of Shiraz. In 1606 the demand was raised again, however; on 24th December 1606 the Archbishop-Governor, de Meneses, informed the King of this new demand together with other demands raised simultaneously

142. Arch. Vaticano, Fondo Borghese II: 68, f. 98.
143. *Ibid.* f. 101.
144. *Chronicle* p. 101.
145. Diogo de Santa Anna, Isfahan, to Aytona, Rom, 8/2 1608 and to the King of the same date, Arch. Simancas, Estado, leg. 493.

on the part of Persia: the demand for a ban on the confiscation and baptism of young slaves passing through Hormuz as merchandize, and the demand that the Shah's own goods should be exempted from paying customs in Hormuz's *alfandega*. Already at this time the Archbishop regarded the matter with anxiety, since in his opinion it involved a real risk of war.[146] It is interesting to compare de Meneses' opinion with the comment made by the Captain in Hormuz, Pedro Coutinho, in March 1607. Coutinho was far more confident about the friendly relations with Persia: "This fort lives in peace and quiet", he declared. The threat to *Estado da India* lay in quite a different quarter: in the relations with the Netherlands, and therefore he recommends the establishment of a permanent postal connection through Hormuz to the Venetian Consul in Aleppo.[147] Coutinho, who had been responsible for Hormuz's relations with Persia during these years, and whose period of office had now expired, undoubtedly wished to minimize the Persian threat as far as possible, also by diverting attention towards difficulties in other parts of the Empire. A less interested observer, Andre Furtado Mendonça, felt less happy about the situation in the Persian Gulf. In a lengthy memorandum to the King, dated 29th September in Malacca, he warned him in very condemnatory phrases against the consequences of the violation of Persian subjects that took place in Hormuz and said that the arrogance of the Captains might very likely lead to war with Persia.[148]

The pessimists were right. In 1607 the demand for *mocarrerias* was repeated with greater vehemence by the Khan of Shiraz's local representative, Camber Beg. At first the Portuguese in Hormuz attempted to postpone the decision by declaring that they could not settle the matter without authority from Goa, but when Camber Beg threatened to blockade the caravan routes around Hormuz, the farmer of the customs himself decided to advance the money – it was a matter of such a relatively moderate sum as 2,000 cruzados.[149] It was not without cause that the Portuguese would

146. *Documentos Remettidos* I p. 218.
147. Concerning the question of a Portuguese mail route through the Ottoman Empire, see KELLENBENZ, *Le front Hispano-portugais* and FERREIRA.
148. Arch. Simancas. Secr. Prov., Libr. 1479, f. 210 ff.
149. Francesco de Gouvea, Ormuz, to the King, 3/5 1608, *ibid.* f. 425 f. Antonio de Gouvea, Isfahan, to the King, 27/12 1608, *ibid.* ff. 556–560. The way in which the question of the payment of *mocarrerias* was dealt with is a good example of the difficulties that arose if cases could not be settled locally and promptly. Goa had forwarded an inquiry from Hormuz in December 1606; the inquiry was answered in Spain in a letter to the Viceroy of 15/3 1608, *Documentos Remettidos* I pp. 218–219. Out of concern for the friendly relations with the Shah an exception was made regarding the payment of the tribute-like duty. This answer cannot have arrived in Hormuz before the beginning of 1609 at the earliest. A great deal had happened in the meantime.

rather pay than risk a breach on this question. A blockade of the caravan routes would under all circumstances affect the leading officials, who occupied the offices for three years, economically. Moreover, the defences of the fortress were disturbingly poor. In 1608 the *provedor* and brothers of Hormuz's *Casa di Misericordia* appealed directly to Philip II for help for the town, with a sharp, though indirect criticism of the rule of the Captains.[150] A new *ouvidor*, Francesco de Gouvea, who arrived in Hormuz in 1608, was more direct in his criticism. The fortress lay in ruins, the vital cisterns were defective, the revenue was diminishing because the customs were farmed out, the enemy was so close at hand that he could be before the fortress walls within an hour; and he knew all about the wretched state of the fortress itself: 500 soldiers were prescribed for Hormuz's defence, but there were seldom more than 200 in the town. Where the responsibility lay de Gouveà was not in any doubt: it was the Captains who were responsible for the appalling condition of the fortress and the lack of supplies, for they undertook the deliveries themselves, and that at prices twice or three times as much as the market prices.[151] The town council in Goa repeated the same complaints: Hormuz was in a highly dangerous situation after the Emperor had made peace with the Turks, the Shah wished to take possession of the fortress and threatened to negotiate with the Dutch in order to obtain the aid of their ships, the state of the town defences was appalling and the prescribed number of soldiers was not maintained.[152]

In 1608 the Persians again demanded *mocarrerias*. The Portuguese refused to pay – their compliance the previous year had been sharply criticized in Goa – and Camber Beg thereafter moved down to the coast with a small force and occupied Qishm, from which Hormuz normally fetched part of its drinking water. At the same time be began to erect a Persian fortress on the mainland. The Augustinian, Antonio de Gouvea, who arrived at the Persian Court in the middle of the year on his second Mission to Persia, tried to settle the dispute by negotiating directly with the Khan of Shiraz. According to what he himself maintains he was about to conclude a favourable settlement when the report arrived that the authorities in Hormuz had once again decided to pay up rather than see the town blockaded by Persian troops.[153] The Shah promised Gouvea shortly afterwards – still according to Gouvea's own statement – that Camber Beg would be punished, and that the partly completed fortress would be demolished,[154] but at the end of the year Francesco de Gouvea reported

150. Arch. Simancas. Secr. Prov., libr. 1479, f. 444.
151. *Ibid.* f. 425.
152. Camara, Goa, to the King, 8/1 1609, CORDEIRO p. 11.
153. Arch Simancas, Secr. Prov., libr. 1479, f. 558.
154. *Ibid.* f. 559.

from Hormuz that the Persians were still manning the newly begun fortress, and had not withdrawn their soldiers from Qishm.[155]

Goa's town council were undoubtedly correct when they declared that Hormuz was in danger after the Peace of Sitva Torok, but the final conflict did not come in 1607–08. A new European initiative and a number of coincidences rekindled the Shah's hopes for co-operation with the Christian powers and, from 1608, concentrated attention upon the route from Persia via Hormuz to Europe in the European-Persian negotiations.

155. *Ibid.* f. 446.

Chapter VI: Hormuz is the Question

The time factor was continually responsible for upsetting the calculations in the diplomatic contact between Persia and the Christian States. The messages were outdated before they reached their destination, while instructions were drawn up under conditions that had completely altered by the time the negotiations finally took place. At times this factor makes the chain of events seem like a caricature of diplomatic history: the events rolled relentlessly on while the matters were up for discussion in the Councils or being communicated from one part of the world to the other.

But there are other aspects in this caricature, this "play at diplomacy", than just the practical problem of communications. The obscurity surrounding the reciprocal relations meant that every decision had to be taken on the basis of slender or distorted information and implemented outside the control of the formal decision-makers. Under these conditions the envoy's or the informant's private interests might easily carry more weight than regard to the political institutions they were supposed to represent.

In the years immediately preceding Sitva Torok the plans for a cooperation with the Ottoman Empire had been in the foreground; in the years following the peace the question of Hormuz became more and more pressing. From being a diplomatic question concerning the three Catholic world powers the relations with Persia became to an increasing extent a Spanish Matter. In the Spanish Council of State and in the Council of Portugal a serious attempt was made to determine upon a Persian policy. The importance of the problem was recognized, but the difficulties and the indecision uncover yet a third aspect in the political masque: in reality the politically responsible Spaniards were unable to appreciate the nature of the problem and decide from which quarter the danger threatened because the forces ultimately responsible for the fate of Hormuz were set loose in a context without any demonstrable bearing on the Persian policy. Only a man as mad as Anthony Sherley could perceive the connection with the new tendencies in intercontinental trade and devise a project that could utilize these tendencies to the advantage of the Spanish Crown. Anthony Sherley's project had only one fault: it was no easier to realize than it would be for an express train to turn in its tracks and drive in the opposite direction should there be a red light ahead.

The Carmelite Mission of 1608

In the beginning of 1607 the outlook as regards co-operation between Persia and the Christians appeared gloomy: the Peace of Sitva Torok and the Augustinians' clumsy handling of the Armenian question had, to put it mildly, created a cool atmosphere. It was sheer accident that re-opened the dialogue; after having been nearly four years on the way the first barefoot Carmelites reached the Persian Court with a message from the Pope. It was Clement VIII who in 1604 had decided to dispatch the Carmelites. The immediate background for this decision is not quite clear. It is possible that information about the unfortunate impression made by the first Papal embassy under da Costa and Miranda had reached Rome, and that it was considered desirable to re-establish the lost prestige now that the war between Persia and Turkey was a fact and while the Persian Ambassador was at the Imperial Court. It cannot altogether be excluded, however, that in dispatching the Carmelites the Pope was attempting to win part of the initiative in the Persian question. The Persian Mission touched on the delicate matter of the Spanish and Portuguese right of patronage outside Europe, and is undoubtedly correctly regarded as an important stage in the history of the founding of *Congregatio de propaganda fide*. It is significant in this context that the Pope chose to use the Carmelites for this task. In 1597 the barefoot Carmelites were divided into a Spanish and a Papal branch, and until the Order was re-unified in 1876 it was the Papal congregation that was responsible for the Persian Mission.[1] No matter whether the dispatch of the Carmelites should be regarded as a counter-move against the Spanish policy or not, from the very first there were antagonisms and friction between the Papal Carmelites and the Spanish Augustinians at the Persian Court.

The first Carmelite Mission had a particularly difficult outward journey. They dared not use the Aleppo route because of the Persian-Turkish war, and the route through Portuguese India was presumably to be avoided for political reasons.[2] The journey through the Empire, Poland and Russia was also difficult on account of the political situation, however, and it was not until September 1607 that the Mission reached Baku, which had been

---

1. *Chronicle* pp. 7–8.
2. In 1605 the Augustinians in Rome sought the Spanish Ambassador's support for a complaint about the Carmelite Mission to Persia, referring to the ban on travelling to the Portuguese "conquistas" for all others than the Portuguese. The Augustinians intended to submit their complaint to the Pope, but there is no mention as to whether this intention was put into practice. Arch. Simancas, Estado, leg. 981, Escalona, Rome, to Philip III, 19/9 1605. The reason why the matter was raised at this time has presumably to do with the change, or rather changes, of Pope in 1605.

conquered by the Persians a few months before.[3] The local officials received the Fathers with great hospitality and, ignoring their desire to be regarded as mendicant friars, treated them like ambassadors during the rest of their journey. They arrived in Isfahan where the Shah was in residence on 2nd December; they were received outside the town by a representative of the Shah, and accompanied during their entrance by the Augustinians and by two Venetian laymen, but contrary to the usual practice they were not at once summoned to an audience.[4] The reason for this was the Shah's immediate resentment towards the Christians; the Armenians had informed them about this after their arrival in Persia and the Augustinians had since been able to amplify it after their arrival in Isfahan. The Carmelites were not received in audience before 3rd January. The circumstances were not promising: the Shah received them in his stables while he was inspecting the horses that were to take part in the coming campaign, but his tone was not cold; he questioned them with his customary curiosity about the European political situation, and the Fathers took the opportunity of excusing the Christian powers' lack of initiative regarding the Turks as being due to the death of Clement VIII and Leo XI,[5] and of requesting a confidential audience under more suitable conditions so that they might discuss their secret mission. At the same time they handed over their letters from the Pope and from various Christian Princes together with a modest present.

Two days afterwards they were summoned to a confidential audience. Its confidential character was not conspicuous, however, because the audience took place on the *meidan,* where bull and goat fights had been arranged in honour of the Carmelites. The leader of the Carmelite Mission, Paulo Simon, presented the main points in his secret instructions nevertheless, and when he came to the second point (the first was a formal declaration of friendship), which concerned the Pope's wish to unite the Christian Princes in a league against Turkey, particularly as regards war

---

3. From Moscow to Astrakhan they travelled in company with the Persian Ambassadors, Zainal and Hasan. See above, p. 241.
4. All accounts of the first Carmelite Mission's journey and its reception in Persia build in all essentials on the very detailed report of the Mission's leader, Paulo Simon. This report is published in extract in English translation in *Chronicle* (pp. 113–141) based on copies obtained from the Carmelite Order's archives and from Arch. Vaticano (Fondo Borghese II:20). The following builds upon *Chronicle,* compared with the copy in the Vatican archives.
5. Clement VIII died on 3/3 1605. Leo XI, who succeeded him on 1/4, died on the 27th of the same month. After violent clashes of opinion in the College of Cardinals he was succeeded by Paul V on 17th May 1605. PASTOR XII pp. 21–30.

at sea, Abbas stopped watching the animal fights in order to listen to the Carmelites. None of the parties seems to have become wise to the fact that the message was somewhat outdated, the Fathers having left Rome in the summer of 1604 while Clement VIII was still alive and before the Peace of Sitva Torok. When Abbas heard about the Pope's desire for a campaign against Turkey he immediately began to take the initiative in the conversation. He declared he was a staunch friend of the Holy See and that he intended to pursue the war the very same winter with a campaign against Baghdad followed by a march on Constantinople. In this connection he requested that the Pope might send a Latin bishop to Echmiadzin (Three Churches), since this patriarchy was vacant after Abbas had deposed its previous occupier.

This turn of events apparently took Paulo Simon by surprise. He had been advised to avoid mentioning the Armenian question, which, reasonably enough, the Augustinians regarded as dangerous following their fiasco in the summer of 1607; he was therefore afraid that the Shah's offer might be a trap and avoided answering it directly.

A few days afterwards Paul Simon was received in a third audience together with the other Carmelites.[6] On this occasion he handed over a signed note that largely repeated the points he had already presented verbally; the Pope assured the Shah of his friendly feelings and his desire to create a Holy League against Turkey; he offered military aid in the form of advisers – in fact this offer had already been put into practice, a military adviser having been attached to the Mission on its departure. The expert had died on the way, however. It was furthermore suggested that the Pope and the Shah should exchange permanent Ambassadors. Finally the note contained a request that the Shah would demonstrate his willingness to co-operate with the Christians by his treatment of the Armenians and other Christians either resident in Persia or travelling through the country, and this became the main topic of conversation during this audience. The Shah protested his good will towards the Christians in general and the Armenians in particular, but the request prompted him to launch into a bitter attack on the Portuguese treatment of Persian subjects in Hormuz. Thereafter he raised two further questions, which help to throw light on his attitude to the Armenians and to religious questions in general. He asked whether it was true that the Pope had entrusted the Augustinian Fathers with the task of converting the Armenians from a belief they had held for more than a thousand years. Paulo Simon denied this, adding somewhat disingenuously that this would not be possible

6. "He granted them three audiences: the first in his stables, the second in the square, the third in the park beside his house." Diogo di Santa Anna to the King, Isfahan 13/1 1608, Arch. Simancas, Estado, leg. 493.

because the Armenians' and the Pope's faith was the same. If the Armenians had maintained anything of this nature to the Shah, they must have misunderstood the aims of the Augustinians. The other question Abbas asked was, who was to punish the Latin Christian lawbreakers in his countries? Paulo Simon replied that he and his companions were prevented from doing so on account of their calling, but that the Pope could send someone else able to do this, such as had already been the case with various European Courts (i.e. a nuncio). The Shah expressed his satisfaction with such an arrangement and asked Paulo Simon to communicate this to the Pope.

It seems clearly apparent from this conversation that Abbas must be absolved from religious bigotry in the Armenian question. When in 1607 he opposed the Augustinians' attempts to unify the Churches he must at any rate have been supported by some of the Armenians who were against a union with the Church of Rome, because they were afraid of the Portuguese and of their own position in Persia, or else for dogmatic reasons.

After the third audience Paulo Simon was sent back to Rome with the Persian answer. The Shah's reply to Paulo Simon's note and to the Pope's letter is only known in a doubtful version;[7] the construction and contents would appear to vouch for the genuineness of the document, however, without there being any reason to pay too much attention to detail. The most interesting feature of Abbas's answer is that he regarded the proposed military co-operation as something definite that was to be put into practice immediately. He advises the Pope to direct his attack against Aleppo; as soon as he receives the news of such an attack he will himself march against Diyarbekir. He declares himself interested in every kind of military aid, but he also takes the opportunity of emphasizing that it is not essential in order for him to continue the war. "I have ready such an army that I am able to take action against the enemy at my convenience. Do you also attack them, as I am already in movement with it: and, even should you fail to give me assistance with your troops, with mine I am sufficiently able not only to assault and drive back the enemy, but to break, kill and destroy them."[8] The request for protection of the Christians was answered with the assurance that they were already being treated with the greatest consideration and that none of them had been coerced on account of their faith. And most appropriately these assurances were combined with a bitter attack on the Portuguese in Hormuz and a request that the Pope would

7. The reply to the Carmelites' note is only known by me in *Chronicle's* English translation from a copy in Fr. Eusebius ab Omnibus Sancti's unpublished history of the Mission in the Carmelite Order's archives, compiled *circa* 1730. The letter from the Shah to the Pope is quoted without naming the source in FLORENCIO del NINO JESUS, *A Persia* II, p. 129; cf. *Chronicle* pp. 131–132.
8. *Chronicle* p. 131.

forbid them to plunder the Persian merchants passing through the island or to convert the young slaves by force. With these answers Paulo Simon left Isfahan for Rome in the end of February 1608.

Robert Sherley

The answer Paulo Simon brought with him, however, was not Abbas's only reaction to the message the Carmelites brought from the Pope. The Shah determined to follow the answer up by sending yet another embassy to the Christian Princes; the man to whom the embassy was entrusted was Robert Sherley, Anthony Sherley's younger brother.

Of Robert Sherley's stay in Persia from 1599–1607 we know practically nothing. At the time there were the most fabulous rumours about the honours the Shah bestowed on him and about his incredible performance during the fights against the Turks – rumours which Anthony was surely willing to corroborate.[9] For instance, in 1607 it was reported in an English news-sheet how Robert, as supreme Commander of the Persian army, had been personally responsible for capturing 30 Turkish generals. When the Turks refused to receive them in exchange for his brother Thomas, who was imprisoned as a corsair in Constantinople (the last detail was in fact true) Robert executed the generals, taking 60 other generals prisoner at the first opportunity.[10] An English play from the same year, "The Travailes of Three English Brothers", was no less imaginative in its glowing account of the part Robert Sherley played at the Persian Court.[11] These absurd exaggerations were most likely intended for "the groundlings", but they help to account for the respect Robert Sherley was shown when he came to Europe as Persian Ambassador – and the credit he was offered. He had been a myth for years before he presented himself at the European Courts. Even the serious Samuel Purchas fell for the myth about Sherley. "The prevailing Persian hath learned Sherleian Arts of War, and he which before knew not the use of Ordnance, hath now 500 peeces of Brasse, and 6000 Musketiers; so that they which at hand with the sword were before dreadfull to the Turkes, now also in remoter blowes and sulfurian Arts are growne terrible."[12]

9. I would long since haue sollicited my frends in England for my deliury, but that I knowe you haue extolled the kings name and my usadge heare, even unto the skies, and my deerest love towards you hath eur ben such that I would rather chose to die coupped up in my myseries, then make a contrarie report, ..." Robert Sherley to Anthony Sherley, May 1605, PENROSE p. 163.
10. PENROSE p. 162.
11. CHEW pp. 504–509.
12. PURCHAS X p. 376. Purchas's source was Robert Sherley's own table talk.

The myth that it should have been the brothers Sherley and their companions who introduced firearms into Persia has been astonishingly tenacious,[13] despite the fact that Purchas's flourishing picture seems to have provided its only source. There is plenty of evidence that the Persians were familiar with firearms before the Sherleys entered the scene, and furthermore that, throughout the whole of Abbas's time of government, they played a subordinate role in the military operations. In 1596 the Venetian Consul in Aleppo reported that Abbas, following the Turkish example, had established a corps of arquebusiers,[14] and in 1599 Anthony Sherley's interpreter declared to the Venetian Senate that: "Previously the King did not use arquebuses, but now he is very pleased with them and makes speed to procure them; he also has artillery, because he has taken many guns from the tartars, just as he does not lack founders to make him new ones; these gun-founders have fled from Turkey and come to serve the King of Persia."[15] It is possible that the brothers and their companions have placed their knowledge at his disposal, but it cannot have contributed greatly to the Persian military development; at any rate it is not mentioned in any of the first-hand accounts, but only in the literature, which, imaginatively and probably affected by the Sherley brothers' self-advertisement, exaggerated at safe distance their contribution in Persia.

Why did Robert Sherley, who at that time was scarcely more than eighteen years old, remain in Persia on his brother's departure in 1599? According to Anthony the decision that Robert should remain while he and Husain went on the round trip of the European Courts was not taken until the very last moment. Anthony relates how Abbas visited him for the last time on the morning of their departure in order to beg him to let his brother remain behind at the Persian Court so that he might teach the Persians something more about European affairs, that the young man might be spared the hardships of the journey and, for a third reason, "more particularly his infinite desire of my returne; which he thought would be more assured by so deare a pawne."[16] The last reason given was probably the most weighty: Robert Sherley remained in Persia as a hostage for his brother, "pro obside" says the German envoy.[17] He was apparently well-treated during his stay of nearly nine years, and he was on the Shah's pay

---

13. See, for example ROEMER p. 38; ALLEN p. 63; TERPSTRA p. 140; LUZ p. 311 and Encyclopedia of Islam s. v. Abbas. Already several years ago, however, Minorsky proved that firearms were already known in Persia in the 16th century, MINORSKY p. 31.

14. BERCHET, Siria p. 93.

15. BERCHET, Nuovi Documenti, p. 12.

16. SHERLEY p.127.

17. TECTANDER p. 49.

roll,[18] but there is no evidence as to the capacity in which he served the Shah.[19] Some letters to his brother Anthony from Robert Sherley, whose childish hand and original orthography is quite exceptional for a man with his career, testify that he very far from enjoyed his stay in Persia. In May 1605 he writes: "Deere brother, I am soe besids myself with the travailes and wants I am in, and the little hope I have of yor retorne or of anie helpe from my delivry out of this Countrie, . . ." Already at this time he threatens to flee from Persia without regard to his brother's plans. In another letter of September 1606 his tone is still more critical towards his brother: "Your often promisinge to send presents, Artiffisers, and Signr. Angele, and I know not how many els, hathe made me estimed a common lyar; brother for Gods sake, eather performe, or not promis any thinge, because in this fassion you make me discreditt myselfe, by reportinge things wch you care not to effecte."[20] In all their awkwardness these letters reveal the role Anthony must have intended his brother to play as his most valuable contact at the Persian Court during those years.

At the end of 1607, when the Carmelites passed through Kazvin on their way from Baku to Isfahan, Robert Sherley visited them. He complained that the Shah paid him his salary accompanied by many protests and with great irregularity – from the Augustinians we know he was in economic difficulties and had to borrow money at a usurious interest –[21] and he also intimated to the Carmelites that his relations with the Shah had gradually become strained on account of the pressure laid upon him to renounce his faith. When the Carmelites left Kazvin shortly afterwards Robert Sherley followed after, and he was in constant contact with them during their stay at the Court in Isfahan. Possibly he saw in the Carmelite Mission his opportunity to return to Europe, whereas the Carmelites on their part not only realized how they might profit from his connections and knowledge of local conditions, but were also aware of the damage he could do them if he became their opponent.[22]

It is probable, moreover, that the Carmelites were instructed from home

18. della VALLE *Persia* I:I p. 46.
19. PENROSE ch. IX. An anonymous account, composed in connection with his first visit to Rome, apparently by a cleric with detailed knowledge about his adventures in Persia, says: "The King treated him respectfully in public, but he never made use of his services, and kept him almost as hostage while awaiting his brother Don Antonio's return. Arch. Vaticano, Fondo Borghese IV:52, f. 347.
20. These two letters have presumably been intercepted on the way by Salisbury's agents and by that means have found their way to the Public Record Office, London. Here quoted according to PENROSE pp. 162–166.
21. Diogo di Santa Anna, Isfahan, to the Pope, 3/12 1607, Arch. Vaticano, Fondo Gonfalonieri 22, f. 281.
22. *Chronicle* p. 119 ff.

to put in a word for Robert, since in Paulo Simon's note there was a request that the young Sherley might obtain permission to travel home to Europe. The reason given for the Emperor and the Pope expressing such a wish was that Robert Sherley had powerful friends in England who might at his bidding be influential in causing England to abandon her friendly relations with Turkey. This reason could scarcely have been believed in Rome or Prague; the request is more likely to have sprung from kindness towards Anthony Sherley who attempted in that way to help his hard-pressed brother. In this communication there was no question of wishing to have Robert sent home as official Persian Ambassador, however.[23] Apparently the Carmelites were very astonished at the appearance of the following passage in the Shah's answer to their note: "I now send you, in the guise of an 'ambassador extraordinary' Don Robert Sherley, an English gentleman, very dear to me for his having served me faithfully many years, a man endowed with much sagacity and worth... I should have sent one of my own subjects, if the aforesaid had not been desired and asked of me by the Sovereign Pontiff and the Emperor."[24]

If the Carmelites' astonishment over this appointment is genuine, Robert Sherley has successfully carried out an intrigue through his connections with the Court, making it appear to the Shah as if the Pope and the Emperor had wished him, and him alone, to be dispatched as Persian Ambassador. But their astonishment could equally well have been feigned and his posting a result of an intrigue between him and the Carmelites; in this event his appointment was the payment for the services he had rendered them. Whatever the explanation may have been, just at this very time Robert Sherley had come into possession of information that must have strengthened his position at the Persian Court. He had received a letter from his English relations stating that his brother Anthony had been placed in command of a considerable armada in the Mediterranean in the service of the Spanish King.[25] On request both the Augustinians and the Carmelites confirmed that the letter was genuine; the information it contained, as will be described later, was even true. The Sherley brothers were on their way back into the limelight.

The connection between the Carmelite Mission and Robert Sherley's posting is obvious, judging from his credentials to Rome, since these are clearly influenced by the points put forward by Paulo Simon: "The fathers have informed me that His Holiness desires to know in which direction it will be most advantageous to attack the Turks, our common enemy. As far as this is concerned I cannot say anything other than that I for my part

23. *Chronicle* pp. 127–129.
24. *Ibid.* p. 131 cf. p. 126.
25. Arch. Vaticano, Fondo Borghese IV:52 f. 347.

have previously exerted all my energy and neither will I omit to do so in the future, I have in fact already a large army prepared ... But if I should give my opinion, I think it will be best to march against Aleppo with one army and send another wherever His Holiness thinks fit. For my part I intend to launch an attack with two armies; with one of them I will ravage the country around Diyarbekir, with the other the Anatolian country."[26]

The Carmelite Mission and possibly also the report of Anthony Sherley's appointment as Spanish Admiral had given back the Shah his faith in the Christian alliance as something concrete and impending.

Anthony Sherley's Projects

His appointment as Admiral was not Anthony Sherley's only contribution of significance affecting the Persian negotiations in 1608, however. It will therefore be necessary at this point to go back a little in time in order to take a closer look at his travels following his first mission to Europe in the company of Husain.

After the unsuccessful attempt to return to Persia through Turkey in 1601 Anthony Sherley travelled to Venice, which in the following years until December 1604 was his permanent residence. Anthony's English patron, Essex, had been executed in February 1601, so there could be no question of returning to England. How he earned his living in these years we do not know; his attempts to make capital of his pretended ambassadorial rank is described above, he seems also to have toyed with gold or rather silver-making and worked as a free-lance intelligence agent and political adviser, without the slightest regard to nation or religion.[27] From Venice he travelled to Messina where he entered Spanish service; it was from there he was summoned to Prague in 1605 in order to function as adviser during the negotiations with the Persian Ambassador.[28] During his stay in Prague he succeeded in winning the Emperor's support for a new project – a diplomatic mission to Morocco with the object of creating an anti-Turkish movement in the Maghreb. The project received support from both the Emperor and Spain, and even James I seems to have granted a certain amount of aid, but in the given circumstances there was no possibility of realizing it. After eleven months' stay in Morocco

---

26. *Ibid.* f. 333.
27. CHEW pp. 280–284; PENROSE pp. 117–127 and app. C pp. 252–262; Ross pp. 56–59.
28. MEYER p. 378 and n. 6.

Anthony Sherley arrived in Lisbon in the beginning of September 1606, and from there he travelled to the Spanish Court.[29]

At the Spanish Court Anthony came into close contact with the English Jesuit, Creswell (Cresuelo), with whose help he launched into a veritable orgy of projects stretching from "a secret method for the refinement of silver-containing metals without the use of quicksilver" to "the closing of the Sound in agreement with Duke Charles of Sweden".[30] Of all his projects there was only one, however, which found favour with the Spanish ministers: his offer to create a high sea fleet in the Mediterranean without State expense. In February 1607 he was appointed to "capitan general de los navios de alto bordo del mar mediterraneo" and member of the Council of the Viceroy in Naples.[31]

Such an important appointment may appear somewhat surprising in view of the fact that Anthony Sherley's naval qualifications were largely limited to his participation in a not particularly successful privateering cruise to Jamaica in 1596 and in Essex's no less unfortunate expedition to the Azores in 1597 – both of which cruises could scarcely be qualifying in Spanish eyes. But Creswell guaranteed Anthony's loyalty to the true Church, and Anthony's offer to provide a fleet was not so unrealistic as one might believe. The peace between England and Spain in 1604 had put many privateers out of business, and this was followed in subsequent years by a tremendous increase in piracy based in the Barbary States. Sherley's plan was to contact his privateer connections in England as well as the great pirate captains, Ward and Dantzer, in order to organize with their aid a privateering fleet which could be financed with the help of Dutch and Turkish prizes. It was an attempt to transfer Elizabethan warfare on a business basis to Spain.[32]

With the new patent Sherley travelled to Naples, but left shortly afterwards for Prague in order to report on the Moroccan mission. He came

29. BABINGER, *Sherleiana* II.
30. Arch. Simancas, Estado, leg. 1171, ff. 60–64 and ff. 7–15. Leg. 1171, consisting of 232 sheets, deals exclusively with Anthony Sherley and his projects in the years from 1606–1612. This bundle, which has not previously been investigated as regards Sherley, deserves a closer analysis. Even if Sherley was equipped with a fertile imagination, he cannot possibly have been the originator of all his proposals; he must have acted as a channel for all the projects circulating at the time. A few of them were to some extent realistic, some were even put into practice; this applies, for instance, to the establishment of a mail route through the Middle East to Portuguese India and the division of *Estado da India* into two provinces as regards administration. His most fascinating project is certainly his wish to obtain Capri as a personal fief, with a view to converting the island into a trading centre for the Levant trade. *Ibid.* f. 207.
31. *Ibid.* ff. 17–22.
32. CHEW pp. 290–292; PENROSE pp. 146–152.

to the Imperial Court "full of ideas and incredible suggestions for the defeat of the Turks." He also had some proposals regarding alchemy and the occult arts, which seem to have interested Emperor Rudolph quite considerably, as well as a plan about centralizing the whole of the Levant trade in Trieste.[33] His eagerness for new projects is easily explained, because during 1607 the basis for his fleet project was altered quite considerably. In April the Spanish Atlantic fleet suffered a crushing defeat against the Dutch in the Straits of Gibraltar, and the following month a cease-fire was declared while negotiations took place between the Netherlands and Spain; thus the economic basis for his privateering fleet no longer existed.[34] In 1608 he was back at the Spanish Court with his pocket full of new projects and once again he succeeded in winning over the Council of State. In recognition of the diminished economic possibilities, since now there could only be a question of Turkish prizes, Anthony Sherley was granted the revenue from some legal dues he himself had proposed introducing in Sicily.[35] On this basis a fleet might be equipped, and in the end of 1609 he took to sea with 14 vessels and 15 companies of Spanish and Italian infantry. Further details about his cruise in the winter of 1609–10 are not known, but everything points to its having been an embarrassing failure. In addition the final cease-fire agreement with the Netherlands in 1609 had liberated the Spanish Atlantic fleet; the Spanish Admiral Fijardo in co-operation with the French fleet under Beaulieu directed a crushing blow against La Goletta already in June, before Sherley's fleet was ready, while in the latter's instructions of 4th October 1609 he was expressly forbidden to endanger his company by attacking strongly fortified points in North Africa or the Levant. His task was solely to clear the sea of pirates.[36]

The cruise of 1609–10 meant the end of Anthony Sherley's naval career and the end of his career as a project-maker in general. He was granted a pension of 3,000 ducats per annum, and this income was apparently incumbent on his remaining in Granada – a long way from the Court. But before then he had sent yet another interesting project into the world, which in subsequent years came to play an important part in the relations between Persia and Europe. He proposed diverting one of the most important commodities of intercontinental trade, Persian raw silk, from the usual trade routes through the Ottoman Empire to the route via Hormuz, Goa and Lisbon.

The first time Anthony Sherley presented this plan was in a memoran-

33. LINHARTOVA pp. 246, 294, 367.
34. Arch. Simancas, Estado, leg. 1171: "Relacion de lo que se trata con Serley desde el ano 1607 hasta el presente em que estamos de 1611", ff. 206 ff.
35. Ibid. f. 111 and passim.
36. The Viceroy's commission to Anthony Sherley, ibid. f. 186.

dum to Philip III dated 4th January 1607. With that mixture of foresight and phantasy so characteristic of his best ideas he emphasized herein that the Emperor's peace with Turkey would strain Spanish-Persian relations; as we already know he was proved right. He therefore recommended contacting his brother, who was still resident at the Persian Court, and attempting through him to win the Shah's friendship by offering to take over the export of his silk, so that in future it could not be a source of revenue for his enemies, the Turks. The project was discussed in a junta, which was in agreement with Sherley in so far as the risk of a breach with Persia was concerned, though on the other hand it thought that the connection could better be maintained through the ordinary channels – i.e. through the Augustinians – than through the younger Sherley. The thought of a diversion of the silk trade did not arouse any enthusiasm; according to the junta it would involve extra costs and no profit, but it would nevertheless appear advantageous to undertake these expenses if a guarantee that Persia would continue the war against Turkey was obtained at the same time. The junta could not recommend the Spanish taking any initiative in this matter. And this was the initial result; the King confirmed the junta's opinion.[37]

Anthony Sherley was reluctant to abandon a good idea, and so he tried the same year to get his project sponsored by unorthodox channels. Immediately after his arrival in Naples he acquainted the Viceroy, Benevento, with his project, and made sure that the latter would support his diversion plans. Sherley was nevertheless clever enough to realize that the matter contained political dynamite, and he therefore informed the King of this co-operation in a letter of 19th July 1607. The letter was placed before a junta, but the latter, playing for time, resolved to await the report from Benevento himself.[38] That such a report was actually received from Benevento, and what discussions it prompted if it existed, cannot be ascertained. It is certain that the matter went further, and that Spain too began to take some interest in it. In a Royal letter of 15th March to the Viceroy in Goa the project is referred to in detail. No names are mentioned ("it has been suggested to us") and the King stresses that he does not wish to take any decision in the matter before he has received additional information from Goa.[39]

But whereas, in the King's letter to the Viceroy, this project remained at a purely informative level, from Naples Sherley sought through Benevento to speed things on. As fate would have it, his proposal did not reach Persia until after Robert's appointment as Ambassador and departure for

37. Arch. Simancas, Estado, leg. 1171 ff. 7–15.
38. *Ibid.* f. 40.
39. *Documentos Remettidos* I p. 220.

Europe. Thus it was not Robert, but the Augustinian Gouvea, who conducted the first negotiations in Persia and Europe regarding the diversion project. In Aleppo in May 1608 Paulo Simon, who was on his way back from the Persian Court with the Shah's message to the Pope, met a messenger, presumably Domenico Stropene, who was on his way to Persia with letters from Anthony Sherley and Benevento to Robert Sherley and the King of Persia. Paulo Simon opened the letters to Robert Sherley "and wrote to the Fathers about how they should behave towards the King of Persia with regard to certain transactions the Viceroy bade the English negotiate."[40] There can scarcely be any doubt that the transactions referred to were the diversion of the silk trade, and that these were the letters that reached the Persian Court in the summer of 1608 while Gouvea was there. They were soon followed by several letters with a similar content; in June 1609 the otherwise unknown Englishman, Thomas Boyes, writes from Isfahan to Salisbury that since his (Boyes's) arrival in Persia Anthony Sherley has sent several letters to the Shah about diverting the silk trade to the Hormuz route.[41]

Apparently it was not until 1609 that the project was laid before its natural forum, the Council of Portugal; this occurred in conjunction with the consideration of Gouvea's report of 27th December 1608 from Isfahan. The Council remarked rather acidly on this occasion that it would have been nice to have known what Benevento had really offered Persia. In principle, however, the Council could agree to a diversion of the silk trade, and it recommended writing immediately to the Captain in Hormuz and ordering him to give the expected *kafila* from the Shah every concession. The fact that the silk, if everything had gone as planned, must have passed through Hormuz long ago and be ready for shipment in Goa, seems not to have worried the Council.[42]

The Augustinian Mission 1608

Abbas was really in a difficult position in 1608 as regards his foreign policy, despite the fact that he assured the Papal envoys of his ability to annihilate the Turks. It was the fighting on the Hungarian front and the revolts in Asia that had safeguarded him against the total force of the Ottoman Empire in the first years of the war. But after Sitva Torok there was no need for large Ottoman forces in the Balkans, and during 1607 and again in 1608 the Ottoman Empire under the Grand Vizier, Murad

40. *Chronicle* p. 140.
41. P. R. O. London, C. O. 77/1 no. 30.
42. Arch. Simancas, Secr. Prov., libr. 1479, f. 473.

Pasha, subjected the rebels in Asia to a number of crushing blows.[43] In these circumstances the Turks could not be expected to accept the conditions presented by Abbas's Ambassador in Constantinople in 1607. It is against this background we must see Abbas's reception of the European communications in 1608; if the outlook was not very promising it was important for Abbas to do as much as possible to procure the support of the Christian powers in the continued war against the Ottoman Empire.

The next European messenger presumably arrived at the Persian Court shortly after Paulo Simon's and Robert Sherley's departure; this was Anthony Sherley's previous interpreter, Michelangelo Coray, alias Fathulla,[44] who was sent by the Grand Duke of Tuscany to the Levant in 1607 in order to establish diplomatic contact with two of the Sultan's rebellious subjects, Janbulad Pasha in Aleppo and Fakhr ad-Din in the Lebanon.[45] Michelangelo succeeded in coming to an agreement with Janbulad Pasha, but shortly afterwards Aleppo fell (November 1607) and Michelangelo continued thereafter to Persia, where he must have arrived early in 1608.[46] It is presumably to this date we must refer the first of the two letters from Abbas to the Grand Duke of Tuscany, published by Pontecorvo, in which Abbas expresses his friendly feeling towards the Christians and calls attention to the concessions he has granted the Christian merchants.[47]

Some months later Abbas received a new Spanish-Portuguese envoy, once again an old acquaintance, the Augustinian, Gouvea. After the return of Lacerda it had been suggested from Goa that an Augustinian Mission should be maintained permanently at the Persian Court with the object of keeping the Shah orientated about the Portuguese points of view with regard to Hormuz, and of inciting the Persians to continue the fight against the Ottoman Empire. This plan was accepted in Spain and at the same time the necessary means were granted for the maintenance of the Mission,[48] but before this acceptance was received Gouvea had already left Goa in order to head the permanent Augustinian Mission in Isfahan – it is thus incorrect when he maintains in his account that the initiative in sending him as resident came from Lisbon.[49] Gouvea arrived in Isfahan

43. HAMMER IV pp. 397–413.
44. *Chronicle* p. 175 n. 2. CARALI p. 140 transcribes his signature on the agreement with Jambulad: Vasīlī ibn Yūhannā Quray.
45. CARALI I, p. 133. The same summer the Grand Duke's fleet attacked Cyprus, *ibid.* p. 143.
46. PONTECORVO p. 162.
47. PONTECORVO pp. 160–162.
48. *Documentos Remettidos* I pp. 169 ff.
49. GOUVEA f. 169. On Gouvea's appointment Goa was instructed from Lisbon merely to forward the letter from Philip III mentioned below in a suitable manner. *Documentos Remettidos* I p. 115.

at the end of June 1608. His initial reception was cool[50] – the Augustinians were still in disgrace, and the position around Hormuz was unsettled. The Shah left Isfahan without summoning him to an audience, and not until he sought out the Shah with the army was he received and able to present him with a letter from Philip III dated 17th January 1607. The letter did little to encourage the dialogue; it referred neither to the Emperor's armistice nor to planned Spanish actions against the Turks, but contained only congratulations on the numerous victories and praise of the reciprocal friendship. To this was added a complaint that this friendship apparently did not include their subjects, since the Khan of Shiraz had still not delivered Bahrein back to the King of Hormuz.[51] At an official audience some days later Gouvea presented the Shah with a gift from the Viceroy, accompanied by the appropriate ceremonial.

During this audience Abbas did not attempt to conceal what interested him most, since he requested Gouvea to travel back to Spain immediately accompanied by a Persian Ambassador in order to work for the league against Turkey.[52] At first Gouvea refused this request, saying that he was sent out as permanent resident in Isfahan, but when the question of the jurisdiction over the Armenians was broached, the Shah suggested, as he had suggested to the Carmelites, that a patriarch be sent out from Rome as supreme authority for all the Christians in Persia. Gouvea found this offer so advantageous that he decided to comply with the Shah's request and return to Europe. Abbas thereupon called his secretary, to whom he immediately dictated a letter to the King of Spain. The main points in this letter, as reported by Gouvea, were as follows: 1) the King of Spain was requested to send a Consul to Persia who could judge the resident Christians and Christians travelling through Persia according to their own laws, 2) the King was requested on the other hand to take steps to ensure that the Persian subjects were shown fitting respect when passing through Hormuz, 3) the King was requested to display great eagerness in his war against Turkey, 4) the King was requested to arrange for the dispatch of a prelate as spiritual head of all the Christian subjects of the Shah, and, 5) with regard to the proposals for diverting the silk trade (mentioned here for the first time in Gouvea's account), Abbas found the idea excellent, but only on condition that the King sent a person to Hormuz who could

50. *Chronicle* p. 166.
51. GOUVEA f. 176.
52. *Ibid.* f. 177. This, however, conflicts with his dispatch of 27/12 1608, in which he declared that he himself had taken the initiative of suggesting that he should return to Europe in company with a Persian Ambassador, Arch. Simancas, Secr. Prov., libr. 1579, f. 557. It is probable that the mystification is due to the fact that, on undertaking a mission to Europe, Gouvea was departing from the orders he had obtained in Goa.

protect the Persian merchants and their property. The formal draft of the letter was dated 11th November 1608, and Gouvea thereafter left the army in order to go to Isfahan accompanied by the designated Persian Ambassador, Janghiz Beg.[53]

Two new themes had been added to the old ones: the wish for a Spanish Consul in Persia and the plans for a diversion of the silk trade. While Gouvea was still with the King, Domenico Stropene had arrived with letters from Anthony Sherley and Benevento. Apparently the project did not immediately win Gouvea's warm support; at any rate he himself maintains that he straightway drew the King's attention to the fact that Benevento could not be authorized to act on behalf of the Spanish King in such a matter – as a Portuguese Gouvea had probably been somewhat taken aback by the Napolitan initiative. He cannot have been very much relieved by Stropene's information that it was Benevento's intention to send ships to Hormuz to fetch the silk himself.

There is no doubt, however, that Abbas immediately saw what possibilities the proposal opened up, because he reacted not only with the somewhat vague reference to the proposal in his letter, but also decided to make an immediate trial regarding the export possibilities along the suggested route, giving orders for the silk that lay in his warehouses to be sent to Europe via Hormuz together with the Ambassador. However, at this point some mystification arises. If we are to believe Gouvea, the Shah felt so embarrassed on learning that there were only 1600 man-i-shah in his warehouses that he told Gouvea and Janghiz Beg to forget all about the sale of the silk and instead to regard the silk as a modest gift to be presented to the Spanish King. In view of the fact that the gift was valued at 200,000 ducats in Madrid,[54] and that the matter developed into what the Spanish historian of the Carmelites has called "la malhadada historia de unas cargas de seda",[55] it is by no means uninteresting that Gouvea, amongst those persons who could have any knowledge of the matter, is the only one who insists on maintaining that the silk was a gift. It is not even until his relation from 1611 that he makes such a statement. In his dispatch from Isfahan of 27/12 1608 he says: "The Persian is the first to

53. GOUVEA ff. 177–183. This letter is only known in Gouvea's version, which cannot have been very far from the truth, however. The letter had been delivered to the King at the time when Gouvea in 1611 published his relation, and the presence of other Persian envoys in Spain has ensured fairly good chances for control.

54. *Calendar S. P. East Indies,* 1513/1616 p. 224. This estimate is probably too high though; officially it is stated that the value of the gift was 60,000 ducats, Arch. Simancas, Estado, leg. 494. Probably it is precisely this consignment Magalhães-Godinho has demonstrated in the Portuguese import from Asia in 1610 – 174 bales, MAGALHAES-GODINHO p. 708.

55. FLORENCIO del NINO JESUS, *En Persia* I p. 88.

send a load of silk; its value will be 400,000 cruzados, and he has told me that if everything turns out well he will not let as much as a single thread go via Aleppo, but everything will be sent via Hormuz." Nowhere is it suggested that the silk should be regarded as a present.[56] It also seems convincing when one of the Carmelites, Juan Tadeo, writes from Isfahan to one of the same Order in Hormuz in May 1609: "The King hurls a thousand words of abuse against the (Augustinian) Fathers and told the one who came out from the Emperor that, if this year our King does not make war on the Turks, they had better depart for their own country, for he will have no need of them. But although he says this, he is not likely to send them away till he gets the money from the silk which he sent with Fr. Antonio. God grant that the latter return with the Shah's money, or else they will be in difficulties and put in prison."[57]

Anthony Sherley's project had added a new interesting dimension to the relations between Persia and the European powers. But the project was confused from the very first by Gouvea's ambiguous attitude.

Robert Sherley in Rome and Spain

In 1607 the lack of fighting spirit among the Christian States and the report of the Peace of Sitva Torok had made Abbas abandon the hopes he had cherished regarding a co-operation with the Christian Princes. This reversal is marked by his negative attitude towards the Augustinians and the resumption of the aggressive policy towards the Portuguese in the Persian Gulf. During 1608 the picture changes once again. The reception of the Carmelite Mission, of the report of Anthony Sherley's appointment as Admiral of the Spanish Mediterranean fleet, of the Augustinian Mission in the summer of 1608 and, finally, of the proposals for a diversion of the silk trade must have given Abbas the impression that contact with Europe was still worth the trouble. Paulo Simon was sent back with a friendly answer to the Papal letter and during the same year yet another two Persian Ambassadors were sent to Europe: Robert Sherley and Janghiz Beg. However, in relation to the first embassies a slight alteration had occured in the emphasis of the Persian notes; it was now the possibility of co-ordinating the naval war in the Mediterranean with the Persian military campaign that took precedence. This was combined with an undoubtedly sincere interest on the part of the Shah in a diversion of the silk trade.

Paulo Simon was the first to bring the Shah's offer of co-operation, despite the Imperial-Turkish peace, to Europe. The Shah ordered the

56. Arch. Simancas, Secr. Prov., libr. 1479, f. 560.
57. *Chronicle* p. 169.

Armenians in Julfa to arrange for his return journey, which also took much shorter time than the outward journey.[58] He left Isfahan in the end of February 1608, disguised as a poor Armenian and, despite the unrest along the route, he reached Naples via Baghdad and Aleppo already on 20th July.[59] He immediately continued to Rome, where he reported to the Præpositus General of his Order and to the Pope, and delivered the Shah's letter.[60] He did not disguise the fact that he had gone pretty far in his promises to the Shah as far as the outlook for establishing cooperation between the Christian Princes was concerned. How the report was received in Rome we do not know; the risk such promises without actual political coverage involved must have been obvious, but more active participation on the part of Spain in the Levant was under all circumstances desirable from a Papal point of view – the problem was to convert the Spanish ministers to the same opinion. It was therefore decided to send Paulo Simon on from Rome to the Spanish Court with the task of working for "matters which in truth seem to be of decisive importance for Christendom and especially for the Spanish King."[61]

Paulo Simon arrived at the Spanish Court in the middle of November,[62] but apparently he did not succeed in getting his note dealt with by the Council of State until February 1609. In the memorandum he sent in he emphasized very strongly the seriousness of the situation in the Levant. The Shah already had an Ambassador in Constantinople to negotiate for peace and, on account of his anger over the treatment of the Persian subjects in Hormuz, there was an immediate danger that he might ally himself with the English or the Dutch in order to drive the Portuguese away from the Persian Gulf. – Here again we find the interconnection between the Turkish-Persian relations on the one hand and the Persian-Portuguese relations on the other hand. Peace between Persia and Turkey could mean an immediate threat to Hormuz. For Paulo Simon the conclusion is obvious. The danger could only be averted by a more resolute Spanish policy towards the Ottoman Empire, with which the Shah was engaged in a fight for life and death. He praises himself that during his talks with the Shah in the beginning of 1608 he once again has convinced the latter of the Spaniards' determination in the fight against the Turks, but he must at the same time admit that the advantage achieved by giving

58. *Chronicle* p. 130.
59. *Ibid.* pp. 135–140; Arch. Vaticano, Fondo Borghese II: 20.
60. The report in Arch. Vaticano, Fondo Borghese II: 20 ff. 130–142, summarized *ibid.* II: 24 ff. 250–56; cf. the extensive extracts in English translation in *Chronicle*. The Shah's letter in *Chronicle* pp. 131–133.
61. The Papal letter of recommendation in *Chronicle* p. 142.
62. In a memorandum of 12/3 1609 Paulo Simon states that he has been residing at the Spanish Court for four months, Arch. Simancas, Estado, leg. 493.

the Persians new hope could turn against the Spaniards, and especially against the Portuguese in Hormuz, if it were not followed up by action.[63]

Paulo Simon's memorandum was dealt with in the Council of State on 3rd February and 14th March.[64] There seems to have been full agreement about the matter's importance, but the shock was engulfed in the administrative bog. As far as the situation around Hormuz was concerned the matter was sent over to the Council of Portugal, who proposed that the Captains in Hormuz should be ordered to abide by the law regarding the treatment of the Shah's subjects and the private trade of the officials.[65] Apart from this not very constructive resolution Paulo Simon's note seems to have disappeared in the labyrinths of the Spanish administration before it was ever dealt with in principle. Neither in the *consultas* of the Council of State nor in the letters to Goa is there any trace of it. Presumably the top political leaders of the Spanish Empire have had some busy months in the beginning of 1609, and the relations with Persia have been overshadowed by the Dutch truce negotiations and the preparations for the expulsion of the Moriscos. After all, it would be sound policy to postpone a consideration of the Levant question until it was clear whether there was to be a truce in the Netherlands. At any rate Paulo Simon's mission proved to be fruitless. He never returned to Persia; perhaps he himself or his superiors feared that the Shah might call him to account for the promises he so rashly had made.

By the time the question of a truce in the Netherlands was settled the Persian policy had obtained a new advocate in Europe: Robert Sherley. Whereas we have shown that Anthony Sherley's right to the title of Ambassador was extremely doubtful there was no doubt about the authenticity of Robert Sherley's credentials. But this fact alone is not sufficient to explain the respect that surrounded him during his age-long residence and endless negotiations at several European Courts and the importance attached to his person and to his utterances. Part of the explanation is indicated above; there was a halo surrounding Robert Sherley, which was possibly to some extent the result of Anthony Sherley's deliberate public relations work. The idea of the representative and procurator of Christendom at the distant Oriental Court appealed both to the imagination and the latent feelings of guilt about the just war.

In addition Robert Sherley happened to stumble on a problem of far greater political relevance than the confrontation with the infidels, i.e. the clash between the Iberian and the North-West European powers regarding

63. Memorandum of 12/3 1609, Arch. Simancas, Estado, leg. 493.
64. Arch. Simancas, Estado, leg. 493.
65. Arch. Simancas, Secr. Prov., libr. 1479, f. 406.

European expansion. In the face of the structural confrontation accounted for in Part I, Robert Sherley's negotiations appear, to say the least, futile; those forces instrumental in causing a displacement in the European expansion from the Iberian to the North-West European nations were not to be restrained by adroit diplomacy. Nor does Robert Sherley's historical importance lie in the results he achieved, but in the fact that his career reflects the current attempts to comprehend and control the development that was under way. Uncertainty is the word that best characterizes in particular the Spanish-Portuguese politicians' attitude to the Persian question. In the midst of this uncertainty Robert Sherley could always be sure of a hearing when he appeared as the Shah's representative and confidential adviser. Also significant in this context is his dubious religion and his just as dubious nationality.

Robert Sherley left the Persian Court in February 1608 and took the route over the Caspian Sea, through Russia and Poland. He was received with great honours at Court, both in Moscow and Poland,[66] but there seems to have been no question of concrete negotiations. At the Imperial Court, which was the next stage of the journey, he acquired his title of Count, but there is no information about concrete negotiations here either.[67] A feeler thrown out in Venice gave negative results: the Republic had no wish to negotiate with a Persian Ambassador.[68] Robert Sherley continued thereafter to Florence, where he arrived in August 1609, a year and a half after his departure from Persia. He was warmly received by the Grand Duke, to whom he handed a letter from the Shah,[69] and from there at length we have some knowledge of the proposals he presented in the name of the Shah.

The most interesting points in the note Sherley handed over were a criticism of the trade of the Christian merchants with Turkey, terminating in an appeal to the Grand Duke to use his influence with the French King in order to precipitate a breach between France and Turkey, coupled with a request to Tuscany, as a member of the Holy League for which the Pope's representatives (the Carmelites) had held out prospects, to support the Persian offensive by attacking Turkey from the sea. The Grand Duke's answer was nothing short of banal. As regards exerting pressure on France the answer was evasive, but no doubt realistic: "The King of France is very great, and I cannot teach him in that way." He promised nevertheless

66. CHEW mentions (p. 303 n. 3), without reference, the existence of a Latin version of the Shah's letter to the King of Poland in the Vatican archives. It has not been possible to trace it. The original is reproduced by JOZEFOWICZ pl. 4.
67. CHEW pp. 304–305; PENROSE p. 174.
68. PAZ IV p. 644.
69. PONTECORVO p. 162.

to raise the question at an opportune moment. Concerning the League and the attack from the sea the Grand Duke had absolutely no reservations to make, but he had no concrete proposals either.[70] With this answer Robert Sherley left Florence and travelled on to Rome, where he arrived on 27th September 1609.[71]

It has already been mentioned that the letter the Shah sent to the Pope with Robert Sherley distinguished itself by its unusually factual contents. The note Robert Sherley handed the Pope on 4th October followed the same lines. The Shah's letter mentioned the possibility of a co-ordinated attack on Aleppo, and in Sherley's note this developed into a direct request to the Pope to use his influence in seeing that Spain made an immediate attack on Cyprus, which might serve as a basis for a conquest of Aleppo. This necessarily raises the question as to the extent of Robert's contact with his brother, Anthony, during this time. We have no proofs of such a contact, but at least it appears likely that an exchange of letters has taken place. In the summer and autumn of 1609, while Robert was moving from the Imperial Court via Tuscany to Rome, Anthony was busy fitting out his fleet in Palermo. We know that he set course for the Levant when his armada finally put to sea late in the autumn, but we also know that his instructions, dated the same day as Robert presented his note in Rome, expressly forbad him to launch any attacks against strongly fortified points.[72]

Apart from this detail Sherley's note to the Pope largely followed the same lines as the note to the Grand Duke of Tuscany; i.e. it was primarily a detailed account of the Shah's delight in receiving the Pope's promise to help promote a League of the Christian Princes against Turkey, and a request to supplement this by exerting diplomatic pressure on the Christian Princes who still maintained friendly relations with Turkey, and on the Christian merchants who traded in Ottoman territory. Finally Robert Sherley repeated the offer, that the Pope was welcome to send a Christian Archbishop to Three Churches.[73]

The Pope's letter in answer to the Shah's[74] referred to Robert Sherley's note – a strong indication that Robert himself did not think he had exceeded the authority the Shah had given him in his confidential instructions. The only exclusion, presumably on grounds of caution, is reference to a possible attack on Cyprus. The tone is cordial, if not effusive, but it

70. Pontecorvo pp. 165–168.
71. Chew p. 306.
72. Instructions from the Marquis of Villena, Viceroy of Sicily, to "conde Antonio Xerly, General de los navios de alto bordo del mar mediterraneo, 4/10 1609, Arch. Simancas, Estado, leg. 1171, f. 186.
73. Arch. Vaticano, Fondo Borghese, IV: 52 f. 2; cf. Chronicle, pp. 147–149.
74. Arch. Vaticano, Arm. 45 vol. V f. 49; cf. Chronicle p. 150 f.

still consists only of empty words. "We shall again perform the duties of Our pastoral care among Our sons the most dear Catholic Kings and Princes of the Christian commonwealth, and shall take pains to urge them with minds and arms united to shoulder a war as much glorious as necessary against our unconscionable enemies, the Turks, even as We have hitherto perpetually done." It would have been reassuring for the Shah – if the Papal admonitions had had any effect on the foreign political decisions taken at the European Courts. With regard to the appointment of an Archbishop the Pope merely declared that he would consider the matter carefully.

From Rome Robert Sherley continued to the Spanish Court, where he stayed from January 1610 until June 1611. The negotiations he carried on there have previously only been known through the dispatches of the English agent, Cottington, and other isolated letters.[75] This source paints a picture which is in several respects curious. The Spanish authorities showed no interest when Robert Sherley approached the Court around the turn of the year 1609–10. He also had to wait a long time for an audience, and when this eventually took place it was under uncomfortable conditions in the pleasure palace of Aranjuez. Sherley handed over his credentials and in his oration chiefly concerned himself with the necessity of a common policy with regard to the Turks. This aroused no enthusiasm: both the King and the Prime Minister, Lerma, treated him coldly; he is even reported to have had some heated exchanges with the latter. Already in the beginning of February he visited the English agent and informed him that he intended to leave Spain as soon as possible in order to proceed to England as Ambassador. On 31st March Cottington reported that Sherley had been in farewell audience, at which he had received a letter in answer to the Shah's together with 4,000 ducats (which it had been necessary to borrow) to cover his travelling expenses.[76]

With this the Spanish part of his embassy was apparently wound up, and according to programme he should have continued to England. But he did not go, he remained in Spain for over a year. From the Spanish side it was later on maintained that he had put forward fresh proposals after having been in farewell audience;[77] he himself seems to have said that his extended stay was due to Spanish initiative.[78] What lay behind this change in Sherley's plans, and what were the negotiations Sherley conducted during his long stay at the Spanish Court?

75. Both PENROSE (pp. 176–182) and CHEW (pp. 307–309) build on this material, which is published in SHIRLEY and in Calendar S. P. East Indies 1513/1616.
76. Cottington's dispatches in extract, PENROSE pp. 177–179.
77. Documentos Remettidos II p. 251; Calendar S. P. East Indies 1513/1616 p. 231.
78. Cottington, Madrid, to Salisbury, 9/5 1610, Calendar S. P. East Indies 1513/ 1616 p. 205.

The Spanish documents enable us to follow the negotiations at closer range. The main points in Cottington's accounts regarding the initial cool reception are confirmed. On 21st January the Council of State dealt with a note from Sherley in which he expressed his pleasure and gratitude regarding the treatment he had received at the Spanish Court, and requested that he might soon obtain his farewell audience so that he might proceed to England in order to present the Persian offers he unfortunately had had no opportunity of presenting in Spain.[79] The bait was well hooked, but the Council of State would not bite; his letter was merely acknowledged, and before 21st February a routine letter to the Shah was composed, which was intended to be given to Robert Sherley in answer to his credentials.[80] On 27th February a warrant for 4,000 ducats was issued to Robert Sherley together with an urgent request for payment, in view of the fact that he intended to leave Spain as soon as possible.[81]

Associated with the first phase of the negotiations is a note from Sherley and a Spanish answer, dated 13th February and 3rd March 1610 respectively.[82] This note was basically similar to the notes Sherley had presented in Tuscany and Rome, including the proposal for a Spanish attack on Cyprus. A new element of interest for the subsequent negotiations appears in this note for the first time, however, in connection with the question of the Christian merchants' trade in Turkey. In Tuscany and Rome Robert Sherley merely pointed out the evils of this traffic and proposed having it stopped by means of diplomatic pressure, but in Spain he went a step further. He maintained that the basis of European trade in the Ottoman Empire were the commodities transported from India via the Red Sea, and that the best weapon against this continued trade between Turkey and Europe would thus be a blockade of the Red Sea by means of an armada based in Socotra, co-ordinated with a Persian blockade of Turkey from the land side. Finally, this proposal was somewhat loosely combined with a proposal for opening up a Spanish-Portuguese trade with those commodities that would be cut off from their traditional export routes.

The Spanish reply of 3rd March was negative. With regard to an attack on Cyprus it was impossible to undertake such a task so long as Flanders and the Moriscos remained unsolved problems. Neither did the thought of a blockade appeal to the Spanish ministers. They merely replied

79. Arch. Simancas, Estado, leg. 494.
80. Arch. Simancas, Estado, leg. 2864, f. 88.
81. Arch. Simancas, leg. 2864 f. 2; cf. *consulta* of the Council of State of 25/2 1610, *ibid.* leg. 494.
82. Copia do papel que deu a S. Mg^d D. Roberto Shirley tocante ao embaxada . . . Madrid 16/2 1610, Torre do Tombo, Lissabon, Misc. Ms. do Convento da Graça de Lisboa, Cx. 6, tomo 2e, pp. 423–426; and Respuesta que se deu de parte de S. Mg^d a Don Roberto Sirley, 3/3 1610, *ibid.* pp. 443–444.

that the King's armadas had already been blockading the Red Sea for a number of years, but for the sake of the Shah they offered to place greater importance upon that blockade in future.

In the first phase of the negotiations the fight against Turkey was still the most important question; in Robert Sherley's note greatest emphasis was placed upon the attack on Cyprus, and the Spanish reply seemed solely to be dictated by the Spanish leaders' recognition of Spain's incapability of undertaking new obligations in the Eastern Mediterranean. It would scarcely be incorrect to regard the first round as a victory for Lerma and the pacifists in the Spanish Council of State. On 25th March the Papal nuncio, Caraffa, was informed of the answer to the Shah and reported the results of the negotiations to Rome.[83] His commentary was regretful: "I do not know whether this answer can satisfy the Ambassador; he has not concealed the fact that his King will not agree to further postponements. He has also declared that he intends to proceed to England, and that is something people here do not like to hear." On the other hand there was no wish to oppose Sherley's request too openly at the Spanish Court lest it might insult the King of England. On his part Caraffa adds that in accordance with his instructions he seeks to prevent Sherley travelling to England, and is backed up in this request by the English Jesuit, Creswell.

The little importance attached to the negotiations by the Spanish authorities at this point is also illustrated by the year's instructions to the Viceroy in Goa, dated 13th February 1610, concerning Hormuz and the relations with Persia.[84] The main impression to be gained from these instructions is that the Spanish were well aware of the Persian threat to the Portuguese position in the Persian Gulf, but that this threat was not considered to be of particular importance. It was reckoned that a modest increase in the local Portuguese defence forces would be sufficient to combat this threat. The number of effective soldiers in the garrison should be brought up to the prescribed 500, and a special admiral should be appointed over the Portuguese armada in the Gulf, the Captain of Hormuz remaining ultimately responsible, however. Bahrein was to be reconquered, if necessary by force; there was no need to fear the King of Persia, it was maintained, because he was dependent upon supplies arriving via Hormuz, whereas the Portuguese on their part could sell their goods by way of Basra in case of conflict. Rather self-contradictorily – but this was nothing unusual for the political instructions sent to *Estado da India* – reconciliation with Persia was recommended at the same time, both as regards the treatment of the Persian

83. Arch. Vaticano, Nunziature Spagna, 60 A, f. 57. Not until two months afterwards did he know the reply in full, *ibid*. ff. 100–101.
84. *Documentos Remettidos* I pp. 322 ff.

subjects in Hormuz and the payment of *mocarrerias,* which those locally responsible were authorized to defray. It is probable that this letter, as well as the attitude towards Robert Sherley in the beginning of 1610, was the result of the detailed discussions concerning the Hormuz question carried out in the Council of India and the Council of Portugal in October-November 1609,[85] since these discussions had resulted in similar recommendations. On the other hand there is nothing in the instructions to indicate that there actually was a Persian Ambassador in Spain on the date they were written.

The change of attitude on the part of Spain took place at the beginning of April. There is no evidence that Robert Sherley should have presented any new proposals at that time, as the Spaniards later maintained. It is probable that the turnabout was associated with two meetings in the Council of Portugal and the Council of State on 20th and 25th March respectively, at which two letters from the Augustinian prior in Isfahan, Diogo di Santa Anna, were up for discussion. Diogo had not shared the Carmelites' neutral attitude towards Robert Sherley; on the contrary, he insisted on portraying him as an important and dangerous man. Already on 13/1 1608, i.e. only a few days after Robert Sherley's appointment, he sent off the first warning to Spain. Robert Sherley was unreliable both in national and religious respects. He was not a good Catholic, he desired more than anything else to see the power of the Shah increase, both on land and sea, and he had himself taken the initiative of seeing that letters of recommendation were composed to the English King, not only for himself but also for a certain "capitano Pablo" (Powell) belonging to his company.[86] In a letter some weeks later Diogo was able to add further details to his first report, because, as he himself writes, Robert Sherley spoke very openly about his tasks. He had let it be known that he had important matters to lay before the King of England, and he maintained that he had been ordered to have the agents of the Spanish King, the Augustinians, called home.[87] Although he had no proof Diogo was certain that the confidential instructions to England were concerned with Hormuz.

85. Arch. Simancas, Secr. Prov., libr. 1479, ff. 544–553; *ibid.* Estado, leg. 436, f. 10.

86. Arch. Simancas, Estado, leg. 493.

87. When he was in Rome Paulo Simon, too, maintained that Robert Sherley had been ordered to petition the Pope to summon the Augustinians home from Persia, Arch. Vaticano, Fondo Borghese II: 24, f. 153, and in a letter from the Archbishop of Goa, dated 20–29/11 1608, it says: "The Augustinian friars are lepers in His Majesty's [Abbas's] eyes, and he has written to the Pope that he wishes to have his own friars [the Pope's] and not Spain's and Portugal's, because he does not want any lepers there", Arch. Simancas, Secr. Prov., libr. 1479, f. 447. In the letter Robert Sherley handed Paul V, however, this demand was only expressed as a request that the Pope would take special care when choosing the clerics who were sent to Persia. *Chronicle,* p. 148 f.

He deduced this from various indiscretions committed, amongst others, by Captain Powell, and from the curiosity the Shah had shown lately with regard to the defences of Hormuz. Finally he once again recommended caution, because Robert Sherley's dangerousness should not be under-estimated: "He also said he was willing to stake his life in the service of the King [the Shah], and he went to extremes in expressing his devotion to him ... he also said that he who cannot dissemble cannot rule." It would be naive, concluded Diogo, to place confidence in Robert Sherley as in a Christian; he was entirely the Shah's man.[88]

When the Council of State had received these letters from the Council of Portugal it resolved that the Ambassador should be treated with caution, and that extraordinary measures should be taken to strengthen Hormuz's state of defence.[89] It was a reasonable reaction to Diogo's warnings, not least considering the importance the Augustinian had placed on the risk of Persian-English co-operation against Hormuz. The curious thing is that these letters were not dealt with until two years after their dispatch, whereas Gouvea's dispatches, for instance, which were sent from Persia nearly a year later, had lain on the Council's table when the case of Hormuz came up for discussion in October and November 1609. We can discern an intrigue, without being able to see the whole picture, however. Diogo's strong tone of warning matched the tactics Robert had pursued from the very first with regard to his possible visit to England; already in Rome he had given the impression that the embassy to England was a necessity that could nevertheless be avoided if the reasons against it were sufficiently weighty, and he had obtained the promise of a separate Papal letter, which would excuse him to the Shah if, contrary to his instructions, he did not travel to England.[90] As Diogo's letter appeared just at that time, the possibility that the Council of Portugal or some of its members was responsible cannot be excluded. There was a not inconsiderable tension between Lerma and the majority of the Council of State on the one hand and the Council of Portugal on the other hand, brought about by the ambiguous wording of article 4 in the truce with the Netherlands of 9th April 1609. The Portuguese had stood firm in demanding the exclusion of the Netherlands from Asian trade. That Lerma was not too pleased about the situation appears from the fact that the Council of Portugal and the

---

88. Diogo di Santa Anna to the King, Arch. Simancas, Estado, leg. 493.
89. Arch. Simancas, Estado, leg. 436, ff. 39–40, 42. The letters are only summar-ized here, they may be found in full in Estado, leg. 493.
90. *Chronicle* pp. 149, 154–155. The letter was issued on 24/7 1610. The editor of *Chronicle* thus presumes that Robert Sherley paid another visit to Rome at this time. It appears from the nuncio's correspondence, however, that the latter was to hand Sherley the letter, – when it was certain that he was not going to England. Arch. Vaticano, Nunziature Spagna, 336, f. 158.

Council of India were still not informed as late as in August 1609 about the agreement's final form.[91]

Creswell seems at the same time to have continued his attempts to make Sherley more acceptable in the eyes of the Spanish-Portuguese authorities. He informed the Council of State on 31st March that in concert with the nuncio he had visited Robert and advised him to lock himself in his closet for some days in order to meditate upon his life with a general confession in view, such as his brother had done before him. Robert's answer was procrastinating – he did not think he had time just then.[92] It was not growing confidence that converted the Spanish-Portuguese authorities. On 10th April the Council of Portugal declared that Robert Sherley was as great a project-maker "tan inbencionero" as his brother – and vice versa.[93] But it was no longer advisable to treat Sherley with indifference; in the beginning of April the authorities decided to be rid of him by sending him straight back to Persia. On 10th April the Council of State decided to have Robert Sherley's wife, Teresa, brought over from London,[94] and on 14th April it was recommended to the King that he appointed an Ambassador who could accompany Robert Sherley back to Persia with an extraordinary armada already in the same autumn. The plan had nevertheless to be abandoned a few days afterwards for technical, or rather economic, reasons: it would not be possible to get the ships ready at that unusual time.[95]

An anonymous memorandum dated 23rd April 1610 exists concerning the Persian Ambassador, "Respuestas a las preguntas del Consejo de Estado."[96] The author of this memorandum is reticent about Sherley; after having investigated the letters Sherley brought with him and consulted the experts he does not feel convinced that Sherley is empowered to the same extent as the Persian Ambassadors previously received at the Spanish Court, but on the other hand he finds it sufficiently established that he has been sent out to solidify the friendship between Persia and the Christian Princes and that he finds great favour with the Shah. The author concludes that it would be advisable to negotiate with Sherley, not only in order to strengthen the friendly relations with the Shah, thereby counteracting the peace negotiations between Persia and the Ottoman Empire, but especially in order to prevent Robert Sherley from travelling to England.

91. Luz p. 296.
92. Arch. Simancas, Estado, leg. 494.
93. Arch. Simancas, Estado, leg. 436, f. 47.
94. Before his departure from Persia Robert Sherley had married the Circassian, Teresa, who afterwards accompanied him on all his journeys. However, she had left the embassy in Krakow and had travelled from there to London. Penrose p. 182.
95. Arch. Simancas, Estado, leg. 494.
96. B. N. Madrid, Ms. 8180, ff. 124–126.

It is probable that this memorandum lay before the Council of State on 27th April when the final decision was taken to resume negotiations with Robert Sherley. "It is only tricks he is negotiating" the Council of State declared blatantly, "but if we do not negotiate with him we merely risk his travelling back to England and obtaining support for his projects there."[97] Shortly afterwards the change in attitude towards Sherley was made public; Sherley's prolonged stay in Spain was reported by Cottington on 9th May[98] and by the nuncio on 25th May.[99] – The statements of both the Council of Portugal and the Council of State clearly indicate that they were agreed in their mistrust of Sherley. It was not the hope that the negotiations would lead to any practical results, but the fear that he might achieve results in England, that led to a resumption of the negotiations. It is probable that the Council of State had for once thought of taking advantage of its own legendary slowness. They had no intention of making greater offers than they had done in the first place, but they could win time by pretending that serious negotiations were under way – "usciendo della generalitá" as the nuncio put it.[100] This interpretation of the Council's motives is supported by the further course of the negotiations. The case was up for discussion in the Council of State repeatedly during the summer, but no decisions were made.

In September 1610 the situation was completely altered. A report came from Lisbon that the annual fleet had brought a new Persian Ambassador with it; this was Janghiz Beg, who had left Persia accompanied by Gouvea nearly a year after Robert Sherley. The Council of State's first reaction to this surfeit of Persian diplomats was to hand over the entire problem to the Portuguese authorities; Gouvea should remain in Lisbon and Robert Sherley was to contact him there.[101] Sherley protested against this insult: he was accredited to the King of Spain, not to the Viceroy in Lisbon, and he appealed to the nuncio for support.[102] Gouvea protested just as indignantly on behalf of Janghiz Beg,[103] and the Council of State had to give in and bring Janghiz Beg to the Court. Its hope was now at least to co-ordinate the negotiations with the two Ambassadors and if possible to get

97. Arch. Simancas, Estado, leg. 494.
98. *Calendar S. P. East Indies*, 1513/1616 p. 205.
99. Arch. Vaticano, Nunziature Spagna, 60 A f. 133.
100. *Ibid.*
101. *Consulta* of the Council of State 3/9 and 8/9 1610, Arch. Simancas, Estado, leg. 494.
102. Arch. Simancas, Estado, leg. 494; Arch. Vaticano, Nunziature Spagna 60 A, f. 260.
103. Presumably it was Lerma, who personally took the initiative of bringing Janghiz Beg to the Court, Arch. Simancas, Estado, leg. 436, f. 72.

them lodged in the same house. But of this there could be no question;[104] on behalf of Janghiz Beg Gouvea turned down every suggestion of co-operation with Robert Sherley, and Robert Sherley's tactics were now pri-marily to obtain his farewell audience before Janghiz Beg.[105] At the same time he resumed contact with Cottington, on this occasion with a material offer: the Shah, he declared, was willing to place two good harbours at the disposal of the East India Company and would offer them a trade worth many millions, without it being necessary to export silver from Europe. Apart from this he would exempt the English from customs and allow them consular jurisdiction. All that without demanding anything in return.[106]

The negotiations between Robert Sherley and the Spanish Council of State continued, however; they seemed first and foremost to have concerned the possibility of equipping an armada able to carry out an effective blockade of the Red Sea.[107] There is no doubt, however, that Robert Sher-ley was overshadowed by the new Persian Ambassador. In June 1611 the former obtained the definitive Spanish answer. It was quite surprising. It was not possible to promise him a Red Sea fleet, instead he was personally offered a post as observer with a Spanish Mediterranean fleet based on Naples, "that he should proceed to Naples where orders will be given to fit out a fleet against the Turks, and that His Majesty while he was in Naples would make him an allowance of 4,000 scudi per annum." This was pure bribery; Robert Sherley was to be removed by employing the same means as for his brother. But Robert Sherley was not satisfied with the offer; he felt insulted at having been offered such a small sum, and he declared himself made a fool of in Spain, and that he would now resume his interrupted journey and proceed to England. But the old threat no longer worked. In Spanish Court circles this was merely thought to be something he said in order to obtain his Red Sea fleet. But they would not make him another answer, because the King's ministers were quite clear

104. *Consulta* of the Council of State 22/1 1611, Arch. Simancas, Estado, leg. 494. Before this session an official communication had been received from Milan that yet another Persian Ambassador was on his way, namely Hogia Sefer (see above p. 105) A single voice, that of the Duke of Infantado, tried to cut through the complicated situation: "He said that he considers all these Am-bassadors to be swindlers and is sure that they buy their embassies". Cf. nun-cio, Caraffa, to Cardinal Borghese, 24/1 1611: "It seems as if so many Am-bassadors at one time causes uncertainty as regards which of them is to be believed." Bibl. Vaticano, Fondo Barberini, 8273, f. 76.

105. Arch. Simancas, Estado, leg. 494. It has certainly been an encouragement for Robert Sherley that Teresa arrived at the Spanish Court at that time, arch. Simancas, Estado, leg. 436, ff. 87, 90; their only child, their son Henry, was born in England at the beginning of November the same year, PENROSE p. 185.

106. *Calendar S. P. East Indies,* 1513/1616, p. 209, cf. PENROSE p. 280.

107. Bibl. Vaticano, Fondo Barberini, 8273, f. 180.

about the difficulties an organized war against Turkey in Asia could create.[108]

For Robert Sherley the first Spanish embassy ended in a failure. The offer of a post as observer in Naples was simply a manoeuvre to get him out of Persia politics – possibly that arrangement Anthony Sherley had suggested to Lerma as a sure way of preventing Robert from leaving the Spanish King's country.[109] Robert Sherley lost the game when Janghiz Beg (and Gouvea) came with instructions, which were not only more recent, but more comprehensive than his own. Thus his threat to travel to England lost its edge. In addition came the effect the rich gift of silk Janghiz Beg brought with him must have had on the two Ambassadors' relative prestige. Before 19th June 1611 Robert Sherley left the Spanish Court for England. Naturally, this step was much regretted at Court, but it was comforting to feel that the answer conveyed by Janghiz Beg, who left Madrid at the same time in order to travel home via Lisbon, would satisfy the Shah.[110]

Janghiz Beg and Gouvea in Spain

Already before the new embassy's arrival at Court it was known that it was to initiate negotiations about the diversion of the silk trade, and that the Ambassador had brought a quantity of silk with him. In the first instance nobody seemed to have expected the silk to be a present,[111] and, strangely enough, the Spanish documents are silent on this point. Thus we are unable to determine whether it was the gift that was instrumental in causing the friendly reception Janghiz Beg received at the Spanish Court, or whether there were other factors involved. At any rate Lerma expressed great satisfaction to the nuncio: he regarded the offers conveyed by Janghiz Beg as particularly extensive. He maintained that the Shah had offered to allow the re-instatement of the Catholic Church in all of his countries where it previously had been established, and would permit the erection of churches and the appointment to these areas of bishops from Rome.[112] However, this was probably a version of the Ambassador's instructions intended for Papal use; the negotiations led by Gouvea on behalf of Janghiz Beg were especially concerned with the silk trade – Anthony Sherley was at Court at that time, and he must have been extremely annoyed to see the Augustinian make use of his pet idea. As Gouvea

108. *Ibid.* f. 39.
109. *Calendar S. P. East Indies,* 1513/1616, p. 215 f., Ross p. 79 ff.
110. Bibl. Vaticano, Fondo Barberini, 8273, f. 56.
111. Arch. Vaticano, Nunziature Spagna, 60 A, f. 276.
112. Bibl. Vaticano, Fondo Barberini, 8273, ff. 85, 118; Arch. Vaticano, Nunziature Spagna, 336, ff. 201, 208, 233.

presented the project it appeared not only extremely favourable, but mere child's play to carry out. All one had to do was to inform the Shah that the road was clear, and make sure that his subjects obtained fair treatment in Hormuz. Ships would then be sent out twice a year to fetch the silk, freight and duties being determined according to silk prices in Venice. No investments other than the ships would be necessary, provided that the Persian merchants themselves were allowed to carry the silk to Europe on board the Portuguese vessels. By this simple means it would be possible at one and the same time to secure the Shah's unbreakable friendship, solve the problem of the security of Hormuz, deprive the Turks of considerable income from the transit duties and obtain an equally significant income for the Spanish-Portuguese Crown.[113]

The issue went from one Council to the next and found both supporters and opponents. Before a junta of the Council of Portugal and the Council of India in Lisbon in 1611 Gouvea supplemented the project with the proposal that a Spanish Consul to Persia should be chosen – at the same time recommending his brother for the office – and that a worthy prelate should be appointed as head of the Christians in Persia. The Council had no objection to the first of these proposals, provided that the Consul did not insist on payment. On the other hand the junta found a prelate to Persia unnecessary, since in their opinion there were no Christians in Persia, and "if there are no sheep, there is no need for a shepherd." All in all the junta was sceptical about Gouvea's project, but for the sake of friendship with the Shah it proposed sending two ships to Hormuz.[114]

The answer Janghiz Beg took home to the Shah is not known, but we can deduce what the results of the negotiations were from the King's letter to the Viceroy in Goa of 23/12 1611 and to the Shah of 23/12 1612.[115] Robert Sherley's proposal had been combined with that of Gouvea's, and the Persian suggestion interpreted as a proposal for the total blockade of Turkey by employing the following means: 1) The Persian export trade, i.e. first and foremost the export of raw silk, should be conveyed via Hormuz, 2) the Spaniards should carry out an effective blockade of the Red Sea, amongst other things by occupying Socotra, 3) the Spaniards should guarantee that the Persian merchants were well-treated in Hormuz. As far as points 1) and 3) were concerned, this was in accordance with the Shah's letter sent through Janghiz Beg, whereas regarding point 2), as intimated above, this is highly likely to have been Robert Sherley's own construction.

To these supposed Persian proposals the Spanish Government had found an answer that was at once positive towards the Shah and gratis for Spain.

113. Arch. Simancas, Estado, leg. 2864, ff. 89–91.
114. Arch. Simancas, Estado, leg. 494.
115. *Documentos Remettidos*, II, pp. 126–129, 277–278.

It was recommended that two ships should be sent to Hormuz from Goa in order to fetch the Persian goods and the Persian merchants. The merchants and their goods should thereafter be sent via Goa to Lisbon. They should be treated well in Hormuz, and they should not be charged customs, merely a registration duty of 5 larins per load of 2 bales. In Lisbon the merchants would be charged 7% in customs and 3% in consulage for both import and export; the silk would be valued at 20 reals per pound regardless of quality, and the customs on other commodities would be according to value. For the freight Hormuz-Lisbon the Persian merchants were to pay 100 reals per bale of silk and 600 reals per *tonelada* of other commodities.

The Council of State had thereby answered points 1) and 3) with a fully worked out programme for a redirection of the silk export to the route via Hormuz. Did the Spanish authorities imagine that this project could be carried out? This there is hardly any reason to doubt; the order to Goa to send two ships to Hormuz was clear enough. As far as the blockade of the Red Sea was concerned the aim was less clear. It was maintained in a somewhat insulting tone that the proposal was superfluous, the King having forbidden trade through the Red Sea long ago, but the Viceroy was urged to consider occupying Socotra in order to make a favourable impression on the Shah, and it was also suggested that the two ships to Hormuz should be accompanied by four galliots, which could cruise around the mouth of the Red Sea. If the plans for such a cruise were kept secret it might even be presumed to give a profit; it was some years since these waters had last been patrolled and there was reason to believe that there were many ships sailing there without *cartaze*.

Gouvea had reached yet another result before he left Lisbon in March 1612 together with Janghiz Beg: on 19th August 1611 the Pope had appointed him Bishop of Cyrene and Apostolic Visitor over all the Christians in Persia.[116] This appointment must naturally be seen in connection with the Shah's several times repeated offer to receive a Latin Archbishop to Persia, an offer that the Holy See at the moment preferred not to accept. It is understandable enough that the latter shrank from facing the dogmatic problems a union of the churches by this means would invariably raise. On the other hand it is surprising that the Holy See, after having determined to go half way and appoint a leading prelate to Persia, preferred to appoint an Augustinian rather than one of the Carmelites who were more closely attached to the Pope. It was the Carmelites' impression that the decision was due to Spanish pressure.[117] Della Valle made his own interpretation. He relates without comment that Philip III passed on the precious gift of silk Janghiz Beg har brought with him to the

---

116. *Hierarchia Catholica Medii et Recentioris Aevi IV*, p. 171.
117. *Chronicle*, p. 202.

Queen, who presented it in turn to the Augustinian Order. In direct continuation of this he remarks that shortly afterwards Gouvea was appointed Bishop of Cyrene, his income provided for by Portuguese India.[118]

Theoretically, the mission of Janghiz Beg accompanied by Gouvea was the most successful embassy hitherto sent from Persia to Europe. But nearly five years passed before the Ambassador was back in Persia. Before then the picture had altered; the offers that might have been welcome five years ago were now lacking in interest.

In Persia, 1608–13

It may be remembered that in 1608 Abbas had controlled his indignation over the Peace of Sitva Torok and decided once again to seek co-operation with the Christian Princes. Paulo Simon was sent back to Rome with a friendly reply to the Pope's letter and Robert Sherley and Janghiz Beg were sent to Europe as Ambassadors. Thereafter he had to sit patiently awaiting the results of his new move. Meanwhile the Turkish-Persian war continued, though for the time being without any big clashes. Under the command of the 90 year-old Murad Pasha the Turkish army concentrated in the first place on attacking the rebels in Asia, but it might be expected that after that task was accomplished Persia's turn would come. Abbas expected the attack already in 1609, but it was not until 1610, however, that Murad was able to advance upon Persian territory with a large army.[119]

It was not before 1613, however, that Abbas obtained an answer to the communication he must have regarded as being the most important: the appeal to Spain. But it is possible to ascertain in various ways that he cultivated friendship with the European powers by various means right up till 1611. He can scarcely have cherished any illusions regarding the sincerity of the Christian powers' protestations of friendship – he had at any rate been warned. In March 1609 he received a letter from the previous Ambassador at the Imperial Court, Zainal Khan, who had now throughout a number of years been trying to get home by various routes, and who on his wanderings had reached the Netherlands in the summer of 1608. The letter was extremely negative as regards the Christian Princes. Zainal – perhaps under Dutch influence – had reached the conclusion that the Christians in reality wished to see the Persians and the Turks destroy one another and the Islamic religion into the bargain.[120] As the publisher of the *Chronicle* remarks, this observation was possibly not very far off the mark.

118. della VALLE, *Delle conditioni* p. 71.
119. HAMMER IV pp. 397–436.
120. *Chronicle* p. 169.

To the Carmelites the situation in Persia at that time, in the spring of 1609, appeared disturbing. During the autumn and winter Abbas had manifested various signs of impatience and irritation regarding the Christian Missions. In addition there was the antagonism between the Carmelites and the Augustinians. When in the autumn the Carmelites had been turned out of the house that had been given them on their arrival, they were told that they could go and settle in with the Augustinians, but the Augustinians refused "for various reasons" to receive them.[121] It was no wonder that it proved to be difficult to assemble all the Christian nations in one crusade.

In the summer of 1609, however, the first answer to the letters Abbas had sent to Europe in 1608 arrived: the Pope's reply to the letter sent with Paulo Simon. Quite exceptionally, the postal communication, forwards and backwards, had only taken fourteen months. The Shah's interest in the contents of this reply was manifested by his impatience. The Carmelites were summoned to an audience the very next day after their arrival in Isfahan. They handed over the Pope's letter and Abbas immediately had it translated, but the contents were a disappointment. "Hardly had he translated a quarter of the letter when the Shah began to toss his head, saying that those were mere words. Then, breaking out very angrily, he began to complain bitterly of the Pope and the other Christian Princes, who for more than ten years past (he said) had given him words and mocked him with promises that they would declare war on the Sultan of Turkey, from whom in all that time they had not captured as much as a single kid. Then he bade the interpreter continue; but after a few more words he again got angry, saying that all those were empty words and lies and that they were deceiving him and the Christians did not want to fight the Turks, while he, without any acquaintance with artillery and his soldiers having no experience with arquebusses, had for so many years past waged war on the Turks and easily recovered all that had been filched from his predecessors: that never so long as he had breath would he cease to be a very bitter enemy of the Turks: just clothed like any poor soldier, and with a pair of rope shoes, to which he pointed as he spoke, he was then going off to the army, resolute to expose himself to any fatigues and dangers, and remain out in the wind and rain with a morsel of bread like the rest of his soldiers and in a tent. But the Christian sovereigns did not do that – to their exceeding shame they, intent on their pleasures, were daily suffering fresh hurts at the hand of the Turk, daily allowing him to rob them of some fresh country (citing Rhodes, Cyprus and the kingdom of Hungary). And, even if the Emperor had made peace, why did not the other princes declare war, without sending to tell him twaddle and lies so frequently?"[122]

121. *Ibid.* p. 167.
122. *Ibid.* p. 176.

This is Abbas in a scene of the kind he knew how to play so masterly, but his disappointment was scarcely theatrical, in fact he had only obtained twaddle and lies from the Christian Princes. The Carmelites immediately protested, and the conversation – if we are to believe the Carmelites – almost gave way to bickering, since they accused the Shah of having broken his promise by still not having given the Mission a site where they could build a church. After over an hour's discussion the Carmelites withdrew, heated in both senses, for the talks had taken place in the hottest mid-day sun outside the Shah's bath-house. After they had gone the agent of the Grand Duke, Michelangelo Coray, who was at that time in favour with Abbas, apparently succeeded in putting across the Pope's letter in a more favourable light. At any rate he was sent to the Carmelites with the task of bringing about a more conciliative atmosphere, but at the same time to order them to convey the Shah's words to the Pope "and put it plainly to the Pope that unless action were taken, and the Christian Princes made war upon the Sultan of Turkey, he (the Pope) should not afterwards complain that the King of Persia used harsh measures with Christians from Europe."[123] Shortly afterwards Abbas showed once more his willingness to co-operate by giving the Carmelites a new house.

On re-reading the Pope's letter[124] one is inclined to agree with Abbas – it was indeed nothing but words. Nor did he intend to answer the letter in the first place either, and it was not until some few months later that the Carmelites succeeded in obtaining a formal answer, which was immediately brought to Rome by one of the Carmelites, Vincent, where it arrived in January 1610. Only a dubious copy is known,[125] but if the preserved text is correct it proves that in the middle of 1609 Abbas still hoped to bring about a co-operation or a Christian offensive despite the disappointments of many years. In all probability this was the case, because in a single important point the wording of the letter is confirmed by a contemporary note. In 1609 Abbas promised that, if he should conquer Jerusalem it would be handed over to the Pope.[126]

The long drawn-out exchange of letters continued with a Papal letter of 22nd June 1610. "Would that the condition of the present times, altogether contrary to Our desire, did not prevent Us, or We would already indeed have shown Your Highness how much We long to assist Your victorious arms by attacking the common enemy from this side. But since We are unable to do anything else at least We do continually strive with Our

123. *Ibid.* p. 179.
124. *Ibid.* pp. 179–181.
125. *Chronicle* pp. 190–191. The editor does not reveal his source, which, judging from the context, may be assumed to be a version in a contemporary mission report.
126. Arch. Vaticano, Fondo Gonfalonieri, 22, f. 254.

fervent prayers to God to accomplish that, never relaxing zeal and diligence, whereby We may win over the minds of the Christian Princes, so that We may the more easily be able to push them on to so holy and so necessary a war."[127] A lot of good! The letter, which arrived in Isfahan with two Carmelites in May 1611, was probably never delivered. With that letter the exchange of letters begun by the Carmelite Mission in 1608 was concluded. It remained no more than words: the Pope could not in the long run maintain the illusion about the eagerness of the Christian Princes to go on a crusade, and the Shah had no use for the Pope's promises of prayer.

In the summer of 1610 the Turkish Grand Vizier had succeeded in putting down the rebels to such an extent that he was able to move towards Persia with a considerably army. The campaign and the concurrent negotiations are described quite differently in the Persian and the Turkish sources.[128] So much seems certain, however: neither of the two parties was interested in fighting a decisive battle;[129] on the contrary, they were negotiating with each other throughout the whole of the campaign. Towards the end of the year Murad Pasha withdrew to Turkish territory again after having received a Persian offer of an annual tribute of 200 loads of silk as compensation for the conquered provinces.[130]

The danger passed over in 1610, but there can be no doubt that Abbas's position became increasingly dangerous as the Ottoman Empire gained control over its internal crisis. It is in this light we must see his impatience over the procrastinating answers and the lack of activity on the European side and his impatience in repeating offers of co-operation. Two isolated moves regarding Venice and Russia respectively must also be seen in this connection. Connections with Venice were presumably resumed in 1609 when Abbas sent an Armenian merchant to Europe to salvage some goods that had been in the Republic's keeping ever since the outbreak of war in 1603. (see p. 104 f.) The Armenian merchant, Hogia Sefer, took a warm letter of recommendation with him to Venice from the Venetian Consul in

127. *Chronicle* p. 193.
128. HAMMER IV pp. 445–448; BELLAN pp. 192–196.
129. One of Abbas's utterances from the end of July or the beginning of August 1609 is a very good illustration of his tactics regarding the Turks; the Carmelite Vincent was to inform the Pope that "he [Abbas] was then going to march against the Turks, whom, if he were opposed by a small force, he would immediately cut to pieces, but that if the Turks should come against him with a large army he would immediately make all his people retreat and himself lay waste the countryside, allowing the enemy to penetrate many days' march into the interior until he had led them into a position where he could destroy them at his ease, as he intended to do without any doubt." *Chronicle* p. 188.
130. HAMMER IV p. 451 f.; BELLAN p. 195 f.

Aleppo, Sagredo, dated 2/9 1609,[131] and it was probably this contact that prompted the dispatch of a number of letters from Abbas to the Consul, in which Abbas expressed his gratitude for the services Sagredo had rendered the Persian subjects. In an undated letter, which the publisher refers to 1610,[132] Abbas actually appears to appoint Sagredo as Persian Consul: "And regard thus yourself as resident there, not only for the high and mighty Prince of Venice, but also for Us and Our Persian subjects." It is impossible to decide what importance Abbas attached to this appointment, whether it was just a compliment or whether there was a definite motive behind it, but apparently it had no practical effects. The consular dispatches from Aleppo from these years have not been preserved, and Sagredo's relation concerning the situation in Persia has also been lost,[133] but it may be established that in the preserved consular dispatches from Aleppo from 1613 and onwards there are no signs of the Venetian Consuls having undertaken special tasks on behalf of the Persian subjects.[134]

Just as isolated is a still more comprehensive letter from Abbas to Sagredo in 1611, in which Abbas appoints the Consul as his "procuratore generale" in Venice, and a letter from Abbas to the Venetian merchants in general "honorata turba di mercanti venetiani" from the same year, in which he orders them to have no fear in coming to Persia to trade.[135] As mentioned, it is impossible to determine what realities lay behind these communications, but we may safely conclude nevertheless that Abbas was still interested in finding allies in Turkey's rear.

This at any rate is the motive behind the last Persian attempt in this series to bring about co-operation with the Christians: the dispatch of the Carmelite, Juan Tadeo, in the beginning of 1611. Juan Tadeo was appointed to Moscow, Poland and the Pope. In Moscow he was to negotiate about extended trade over the Caspian Sea and to discuss the re-establishment of some fortified points on the Persian-Russian border, which the Turks had demolished. In Poland he was to present a general offer of friendship and urge co-operation against the Ottoman Empire. In Rome he was to urge the Pope to use his authority over the Christian Princes, especially over the Polish King, in order to promote an offensive war. At the same time he was to repeat the request for the Pope to send out a prelate who was to take up residence in Echmiadzin and have supreme jurisdiction over all the Christians in Persia. In return the Shah promised to have three churches built in Isfahan, including one for the use of the prelate from

131. FAVARO pp. 399–401.
132. BERCHET, Persia p. 253, cf. p. XVII.
133. FAVARO p. 411, n. 1.
134. A. d. S. Venezia, Senato, Dispacci Console, Soria I.
135. BERCHET, Persia p. 255.

Rome, and two palaces – one for the prelate and another for the European Ambassadors. The Carmelites themselves commented: "The King does this for reasons of state in order with this demonstration to show his kindness towards the Franks, the Pope and the Christian Princes."[136] These offers and proposals never reached their destination, however. Juan Tadeo was retained in Astrakhan for three years;[137] when in 1614 he finally obtained permission to travel he sensibly gave up trying to carry out his out-dated mission and returned to Isfahan.[138]

In 1611–12 the sources are silent as regards diplomatic contact between Persia and the Christian Princes. The skirmishes continued on the Persian-Turkish frontier, but on the other hand the negotiations were not interrupted. Finally, around the turn of the year 1612–13, the Sultan recognized a peace treaty in accordance with the Persian offer of 1610; the Persian conquests were recognized against payment of an annual tribute of silk.[139] Abbas must have known this in the beginning of 1613; for the time being he could feel safe from the threat of a Turkish war of revenge. But the Shah's interest in maintaining friendly relations with Spain and the Christians was diminished thereby.

The Crisis of Confidence 1613–15, Gombroon's Fall

Gouvea and Janghiz Beg left Lisbon in March 1612 and arrived in Goa in the autumn of the same year. Both in Goa and in Hormuz Gouvea negotiated with the local Portuguese authorities on the basis of the result of the negotiations already carried out in Europe concerning the redirection of the Persian silk export through Hormuz. However, it is unmistakable that he tried to take advantage of these negotiations in order to strengthen his own position with regard to the Persian Armenians. Early in 1613 it was carried in the Viceroy's Council in Goa that the special customs charges for non-Christians should be waived in Hormuz as far as the Armenians were concerned. The Armenians should be able to document their status, however, and it was this requirement Gouvea sought to utilize to his own advantage, since in order to be eligible for customs exemption the Armenians were required to possess a certificate from the Bishop of Cyrene (Gouvea) or, in his absence, from the Spanish Ambassador, or should there be none at Court, from the Augustinian prior in Isfahan.[140]

136. Arch. Congregazione de Propaganda Fide, Scritture Originale, Congregazioni generali, vol. 209, f. 173.
137. FLORENCIO del NINO JESUS, En Persia I, pp. 77–80.
138. Chronicle p. 194.
139. HAMMER IV pp. 459–460; BELLAN p. 211.
140. BOCARRO pp. 82–83.

Already in Goa it was proposed to make a distinction regarding customs exemption between "Catholic" Armenians – presumably Armenians recognizing Gouvea as their pastor – and other Armenians, but Bocarro is not quite clear on this point. With the corresponding negotiations in Hormuz some months later, in April 1613, there is no doubt, however. Gouvea tried to narrow the definition of an Armenian to a uniate Armenian who came under his jurisdiction, a definition which would mean that the schismatic Armenians would be worse off than the Muslims. To the relief of the Carmelites this was nevertheless thwarted by the Captain of Hormuz, who stated that the Royal order concerning the abolishment of customs did not contain such a distinction.[141]

While Gouvea confidently sought to realize the plans for diversion in Goa and Hormuz, Janghiz Beg had travelled to the Shah in advance. He reached the Court early in the spring of 1613. When he was received by the Shah and was about to kiss the latter's foot, as was the custom, he was greeted by a kick. Some days later he was executed and all his possessions confiscated.[142] Abbas had indicated a change in his foreign policy.

The official reasons for Janghiz Beg's harsh reception were that he had worn mourning at the funeral of the Spanish Queen and that he had treated members of his embassy so badly that several of them had let themselves be baptized and had remained in Europe.[143] This sounds a poor reason for such a drastic step, and contemporaries were more inclined to think that the real reason was the Shah's anger over the silk he had sent with Janghiz Beg in order to investigate the possibility of sales via Hormuz having been given instead to the Spanish King without the latter having sent a return gift of similar value. This cannot have been the sole cause, however, since Abbas could not yet have been certain about this – Janghiz Beg had been executed before Cyrene's return. Most likely it was a gesture calculated to make an impression on the Turkish Ambassador who was at the Persian Court at that very moment bearing the Sultan's offer of peace.[144]

On the other hand Abbas appeared more amiable when he received Cyrene in audience in June 1613, but immediately the present was brought

141. Vincent, Ormuz, to Benignus, Isfahan, 16/4 1613, *Chronicle* p. 205.
142. *Chronicle* p. 203.
143. *Don Juan* p. 310, n. 7.
144. Belchior dos Anjos' report and memorandum of January 1614, Arch. Simancas, Estado, leg. 495. Cf. the Shah's gesture at the reception of the Imperial envoy, Tectander, in 1603. A distinguished Turkish prisoner was brought into the room during the audience and Abbas himself cut the Turk's head of, expressing the wish that the Christians would treat the Turks in a like manner, TECTANDER pp. 57–58.

in he appeared suspicious. He wanted to know which was payment for the silk and which was the gift from the Spanish King. Cyrene tried to get over the embarrassing situation by maintaining that the spices he brought with him from Hormuz were payment for the silk, whereas diverse jewels and curiosities were the gift. Abbas was not to be satisfied with this explanation, however; he immediately had the spices valued and his advisers came to the result that they could not be worth more than 30,000 ducats, whereas the silk, if it had been sold in Aleppo, would have fetched 106,000 ducats.[145] When the account was made op the Shah told Cyrene that he must pay both the value of the silk and the accumulated interest on the capital since it was exported. Cyrene tried to maintain that the silk had been given to the Ambassador as a present for the Spanish King, but if we are to believe the Carmelites, he had none the less to agree to write home to Spain that the silk had never been intended as a gift, its dispatch should be regarded as an ordinary business transaction in accordance with the proposals put forward by the Spaniards.[146]

That Gouvea was in disgrace over the delivery of the gift is confirmed by both the Augustinians and the Carmelites; nevertheless Abbas tried once again in the summer of 1613 to approach the Spanish King through the Augustinians. In July, Belchior dos Anjos, who had followed the Court for six years, was summoned before the Shah. Abbas told him straight out that he now intended to receive the Turkish offer of peace if he did not obtain help from the Christian Princes. In order to make a last attempt to bring about co-operation he would send Belchior to Spain, however, with a letter to the King and verbal instructions with regard to what the Shah would offer in return for the Christian support against the Ottoman Empire. He would support the King of Spain against his enemies. He would place his Christian subjects under a prelate to be appointed by the King

145. Arch. Simancas, Estado, leg. 495. The Carmelite, Redempt, maintained that the spices were only worth 15,000 ducats, *Chronicle* pp. 205–206; Bocarro states in purchase value in Goa 15,000 xerafims. (p. 175).

146. *Chronicle* p. 206. Such a declaration on the part of Gouvea has naturally not been found; on the whole the Spanish documents are strikingly taciturn with regard to the large present. If it was included in Belchior's instruction, that he should complain that the silk was given to the King and not sold, he has preferred not to mention it on his arrival in Spain. He stressed in his report of January 1614 that the Shah felt insulted because the gift that was sent him in return was not as valuable as the silk, and this was what had cost Janghiz Beg his life, even if the official reasons were different and more idealistic, but he does not intimate that the silk was never meant to be a present. Arch. Simancas, Estado, leg. 495. Five years afterwards, in his memorandum of 1619, however, he had changed his mind. At that time Cyrene was out of the running, and Belchior has not seen any reason to conceal the true facts of the case. Belchior's memorandum in Luz p. 589.

of Spain or his successors. Finally, the Shah said he had received an English offer to take over the export of silk that usually went through Aleppo, but that he had rejected this offer for the sake of his friendship with the King of Spain. He concluded (in Belchior's version) with the words cited above: "He says that there can be two reasons for Kings to be friends, either on account of belief, if they both profess to the same faith, or for reason of state, and that the first of these reasons cannot be applied to Your Majesty and himself, because there is such great difference in belief, and that if the other reason was not present either, there was no basis for friendship."[147] The letter Belchior carried to the King was both less cordial and less concrete than the previous ones. Cyrene's arrival in Isfahan was reported in brief, Janghiz Beg was not mentioned at all, nor were the actual points of negotiation between the two powers. The project concerning the diversion of the silk trade was not touched upon.[148] After the careful planning it once more receded into the background in 1613. Not even the Viceroy seems to have abided by his part of the agreement; there is no mention of sending ships to Hormuz with the silk export in view.

No matter whether this letter, as maintained by Belchior, was a last warning on the part of Abbas or was merely a courtesy gesture acknowledding to the Spanish authorities the reception of Gouvea, the atmosphere in Isfahan soon became noticeably chillier for the Christians. This was first apparent in the treatment of the Armenians. The Shah's attitude at this point is not easy to make out – probably also because we become acquainted with it almost exclusively through the Christian envoys. On the one hand he had totally rejected the proposals for union put forward in 1607,[149] but on the other hand he had repeatedly expressed his wish for the posting of a Latin prelate to Echmiadzin,[150] and now finally offered the Spanish King the right to appoint such a prelate. Gouvea's appointment as Bishop of Cyrene and Apostolic Visitor in Persia would seem to accommodate the wish the Shah himself had expressed, at any rate partially, and Gouvea's negotiations in Goa and Hormuz in 1612–13 indicate that he himself was bent on establishing himself as the special protector of the uniate Armenians. But when, in Isfahan, the news of his appointment was received from Hormuz in the beginning of

147. Arch. Simancas, Estado, leg. 495.
148. *Ibid.*
149. GOUVEA ff. 167–169; *Chronicle*, p. 101.
150. Thus in 1608 through the Carmelites, *Chronicle* p. 206, through Robert Sherley *ibid.* p. 150, and through Janghiz Beg, GOUVEA f. 181. The offer was repeated on several occasions, finally through Juan Tadeo on the latter's unsuccessful mission in 1611. FLORENCIO del NINO JESUS, *En Persia* I pp. 73–75; Arch. Congregazione de Propaganda Fide, Scritture Originale, Congregazioni Generali vol. 209, f. 173.

1613, it aroused terror among the Armenians who hastened to assure the Shah that they had had nothing to do with it.[151] According to the Carmelites the direct cause of Abbas's more rigorous policy towards the Armenians in 1613 was Cyrene's tactless behaviour – he is supposed amongst other things to have described the Armenians, as "my subjects" in the presence of the Shah.[152] The matter was more complicated than that, however, amongst other reasons because there was also an outstanding account to settle between the Shah and the Armenians, the former having advanced them a loan in connection with the enforced removal of population in 1604–05.[153] But first and foremost it seems feasible to connect the persecution of the Armenians begun in 1613 with the execution of Janghiz Beg and the attack on Gombroon the following year, i.e. as an indication of a change in Persian foreign policy and a strengthening of the Orthodox party at Court.

At any rate during September a number of sanctions were taken against the Armenians in New Julfa outside Isfahan. The Christian missionaries, the Carmelites and the Augustinians, tried to mediate and offered the Armenian nation a loan that would enable it to pay back half of the debt to Abbas,[154] but their interfering rather seems to have increased the antipathy towards the Armenians, and on the 3rd of October, at a meeting of Carmelites and Augustinians, Cyrene suggested withdrawing both the Christian Missions in Isfahan. Cyrene's proposal was not accepted, however, and he decided to travel to Hormuz immediately himself,[155] while the remaining Augustinians left Europe for Baghdad shortly afterwards. The Carmelites also left Isfahan, though one of them remained behind in the town. Early in 1614 he, too, made up his mind to leave, but before he reached Hormuz he turned back on an order from Cyrene.[156]

The persecution of the Armenians soon stopped and those who had

---

151. *Chronicle* pp. 205–206.
152. *Ibid.* p. 206.
153. Brosset I pp. 341–342; *Chronicle* p. 207.
154. Brosset p. 343 f.
155. Cyrene (Gouvea) had thereby outplayed his role in the Persian negotiations; subsequently we only catch isolated glimpses of him. In October 1618 he travelled without permission from Goa to Hormuz, *Assentos* I pp. 8–9; In 1619 it is reported that he stayed in Baghdad on his way back to Europe with a new volume of his Persian relation: "It is said that he deals with many subjects, and that he writes the exact opposite of what he wrote in the first one." Della Valle *Persia* II: 2 p. 20.
156. *Chronicle* pp. 209–210. Cyrene gave the Portuguese authorities a somewhat different version of the events. He maintained that the whole thing had been a trick to get the Carmelites to abandon the Persian Mission, but that his plan had failed because they would not comply with his orders. *Documentos Remettidos* II p. 408.

been forcibly converted obtained the opportunity of returning to the Christian faith.[157] The whole episode would have been entirely lacking in interest if it had not formed the prelude to the serious events of 1614: the Persian attack and conquest of the last Portuguese bridgehead on the Persian coast: Gombroon. In 1613 it was still maintained that the Shah, by his personal intervention, had prevented a new Persian-Portuguese confrontation in the Persian Gulf,[158] but several episodes in the end of 1613 and beginning of 1614 increased the tension. Gouvea explained away his flight from Isfahan by saying that a Spanish-Portuguese Ambassador of great distinction was on his way from Goa. It was an unfortunate stratagem considering the prestige attached to the reception of Ambassadors in Persia, and the significance the reception of an Ambassador might actually have in the strained situation that existed in 1613. Several distinguished Persians felt they had been fooled when the promised Ambassador did not turn up, amongst these Allah Verdi Khan's son and successor as Khan of Shiraz, Imam Quli Khan.[159] Finally some of the Arab merchants from one of the smaller ports on the Persian Gulf (in the Portuguese version – pirates) were treated roughly by the Captain of Hormuz, Luis da Gama, when, around the turn of the year 1613–14, they were seized in the neighbourhood of Hormuz without *cartaze*. This action was regarded on the part of Persia as a decisive challenge. During the spring and summer of 1614 several caravans on their way through Persia to Hormuz were stopped, in August Imam Quli Khan moved southwards with an army and on 29th September he began the siege of Gombroon with the connivance of the Shah. [160]

For several years it had been recommended in Lisbon and Madrid that the defence works around Gombroon and the fortress itself should be prepared for the expected or feared Persian attack, but despite all recommendations the defences seem to have been ill prepared.[161] The garrison consisted of 80 Portuguese and an unknown number of native soldiers; Hormuz dared not send reinforcements lest the modest forces of the main fortress – hardly more than 300 men – should be depleted. The Captain in Hormuz maintained later that the fortress had ample supplies and could

157. BROSSET I 347.
158. *Chronicle* p. 212.
159. *Chronicle* p. 209.
160. *Ibid.* p. 212; FIGUEROA II p. 135; *Documentos Remettidos* III, p. 366, BOCARRO pp. 346–348; "Instrumento da fortaleza do Comorão" (examination of witnesses in connection with the court martial of the commander, Andre de Coadros) Torre do Tombo, Lisboa, Misc. Ms. 1109, ff. 58–89.
161. *Documentos Remettidos* II pp. 142, 147; III pp. 173, 360. Ironically enough the last order concerning the improvement of Gombroon's defence is dated 27th January 1616, more than a year after the fall of the fortress.

resist a year's siege, but already on 21st December Gombroon capitulated.[162]

The Khan of Shiraz did not attempt to follow up this victory, although with Gombroon and Qishm in his possession he should have had quite good possibilities of starving, or rather thirsting, Hormuz out. That, together with the pretty humane treatment the Christian prisoners received, suggests that the Persians were not interested in a final settlement, but on the contrary wished to limit the conflict. It is in accordance with the procedure the Persians had employed in the two previous clashes in the Persian Gulf, and has its tactical explanation in the Persian lack of a fleet. But to this must be added the concurrent development of the Turkish-Persian relations. In October 1614 the Turkish Grand Vizier, Nasuf Pasha, was executed. To a larger degree than the Sultan he had stood for the Persian-Turkish peace, and it is even maintained that he had imported a consignment of silk, which he had presented to the Sultan in order to conceal the uncomfortable fact that the promised tribute of silk from Abbas had not arrived.[163] The change of personnel at the Sublime Porte meant the resumption of war against Persia. Although the new Grand Vizier did not leave Constantinople for the East until May 1615, it is probable that already in the months around the conquest of Gombroon Abbas was prepared for a resumption of the war against the Turks. The logical consequence was a resumption of the negotiations with the Portuguese in Hormuz. It was also on Persian initiative that negotiations between the Persians and the Portuguese were begun shortly after the fall of Gombroon, with the Carmelites as mediators. The Persians were willing to bury the hatchet, but on the other hand they offered not the slightest compensation for Gombroon, which they maintained had been a Persian possession right from olden times.[164]

At this critical moment Robert Sherley turned up again at the Persian Court. He returned in order to report on his appointments to the European Princes after well over seven years' absence.

Robert Sherley 1611–15

It will be necessary at this point to jump several years back in order to follow the movements of Robert Sherley after 1611, when he had left the Spanish Court in anger. As mentioned, Robert Sherley had also been appointed to the English Court and had made use of this in order to apply

162. See above, n. 160.
163. BELLAN p. 221; HAMMER IV p. 474.
164. BOCARRO p. 511.

pressure on the Spanish authorities. Also during his stay in Spain he had on several occasions sought to obtain a promise through the English resident that he would be received as Ambassador if he travelled to England, but it is not known whether he ever obtained such a guarantee.[165] At any rate, when in the summer of 1611 he left Spain without having been in official farewell audience, he decided first of all to try his luck in the Netherlands. This was arranged through a merchant, la Faille, who on 1st July 1611 presented the States General with a very vague offer on Sherley's behalf concerning the Persian trade, stressing that the matter must be treated with the greatest discretion otherwise Sherley's life would be in danger. The Dutch spent less time on Sherley's offer than the Spaniards. The case was first sent over to a committee under the *Heeren XVII* and finished by the States General already three days later, on 4th July. Although Sherley's move seems to have obtained some support on the part of the stadtholder, the States General resolved not to continue the negotiations on the grounds that neither person aroused their confidence (hebbende beyde verscreven persoonen suspect), and that a contact with Persia would constitute a risk for the Levant trade.[166]

Undaunted, Sherley, whose Persian embassy up to now had cost the Spanish Crown possibly 30,000 ducats,[167] possibly 40,000,[168] proceeded to England, where the first evidence of his presence is a "warrant for payment of allowances", dated 13th October 1611.[169] From the Spanish side everything possible was done to counteract Sherley. Shortly after his departure from Spain it was asserted that information had come to hand which not only raised doubts concerning his diplomatic status, but justified the bringing of a criminal charge against him. On 7th July, on Lerma's initiative, orders for his arrest were issued, but it was already too late, since he had left the country.[170] At the English Court the remonstrances the Spanish Ambassador uttered concerning his person rather won than lost him sup-

165. *Calendar S. P. East Indies* 1513/1616 *passim*.
166. DUNLOP pp. 1–4 and pp. LXII–LXIII, in which, referring to the Dutch chronicler, van Meteren, it is revealed that Sherley himself visited the Netherlands in July 1611. Also FIGUEROA II p. 128 maintains that Sherley visited the Netherlands in between his stay in Spain and in England. PENROSE (p. 182) expresses doubts concerning Figueroa's statement, but apparently without grounds – apart from the fact that such a visit was embarrassing from a national point of view.
167. FIGUEROA II p. 127.
168. *Calendar S. P. East Indies*, 1513/1616 p. 210.
169. *Ibid.* p. 227. The total bill for 472 days' stay amounted to £ 2,854 13 sh. 4 d. PENROSE app. F p. 273.
170. It concerned complaints raised by the Armenian agent for the Shah, Hogia Sefer, and the Venetian merchant, Gradenigo. Arch. Simancas, Estado, leg. 494.

port, at least in certain circles. At any rate the English agent in Madrid with some right pointed out that if Sherley had fooled the English King he had also fooled the Emperor, who had made him a Count, and the Pope, who had made him a Chamberlain.[171]

Sherley was received as Ambassador in England and treated accordingly. In particular he seems to have won over the Crown Prince, Prince Henry, since the latter was willing to be godfather to the son Teresa bore him in the autumn of 1611.[172] But the actual negotiations went pretty badly. Sherley had now entirely adopted his brother's idea of a diversion of the Persian silk export to the route via the Persian Gulf, but the Levant Company naturally fought the project with tooth and nail – very naturally, since its putting into effect would mean that the Company lost its most important import commodity.[173] Not even the East India Company, which had after all a natural interest in the project, was willing to be involved in the plans.[174] Unfortunately Robert Sherley's first stay in London is coincident with a gap in the Court minutes, so that we are debarred from following the negotiations in detail, but it seems clear enough that Sherley attempted to apply pressure, partly by appealing to the fear of the Spanish intentions[175] and partly, with the King's and Henry's help, by preparing an expedition to Asia without regard to the East India Company's Charter.[176] An agreement exists between Robert Sherley and a Sir Henry Thynne concerning the chartering of a ship to Persian ports;[177] similarly, a Royal commission of 31/4 1612 allowing Sir Henry Thynne to employ martial law during his impending expedition to Persia;[178] and finally, even a farewell sonnet to a gentleman in Sir Henry Thynne's company.[179] Chew concluded from this that the *Expedition* – the ship that carried Robert Sherley back to Asia – was not a Company ship, but belonged to Sir Henry

171. Sir John Digby to Salisbury, 19/1 1612, *Calendar S. P. East Indies* 1513/1616 p. 233.
172. CHEW p. 314.
173. WOOD p. 48; cf. "Breve Relacion de la Justificacion que da el Conde Roberto Sherley a la Mag^d Catholica de Espana y a sus ministros sobre las cosas que falsamente algunos han levantado", Bibl. Nac., Madrid, Ms. 8180, f. 129. In this account, which originates from Robert Sherley's second stay in Spain around 1619, he denies having negotiated with the Netherlands about the silk trade; he admits having negotiated in England, but maintains that these were halted by protests from the Levant merchants.
174. Robert Sherley to Salisbury, 7/11 1611, *Calendar S. P. East Indies*, 1513/1616, p. 231.
175. *Ibid.* p. 231, 233.
176. *Ibid.* p. 235, 242; PENROSE p. 187.
177. SHIRLEY p. 81.
178. *Calendar S. P. East Indies*, 1513/1616, p. 236.
179. CHEW p. 318, n. 3.

Thynne.[180] But Sir Henry never departed; in a communication of December 1614 he complained to the Company's Directors that the Company had forestalled the journey to Asia he should have undertaken for Prince Henry.[181] The journey of the *Expedition* is reckoned as the Company's twelfth "separate voyage";[182] the Company may have forestalled the sending of a ship without regard to the Company's privileges, but in return they had to undertake to ship Robert Sherley back to Persia.[183]

Robert Sherley's journey home to the Shah was fantastic. Scarcely in any other period of his life did he demonstrate more convincingly his incredible ability to cope with even the most hopeless situations. The Portuguese authorities in Asia were instructed to prevent at any price his slipping back to Persia.[184] The Captain of the *Expedition* tried to put him ashore on the coast of Baluchistan, but this attempt failed on account of the hostile attitude of the local population.[185] Instead he went ashore at Diul Sind on the mouth of the Indus, where the Portuguese agents tried to kill him, amongst other ways, by blowing up his house. Sherley and his faithful Teresa nevertheless managed to reach the Court of the Grand Mogul in Agra, where Jahangir generously compensated him for the real or alleged losses he had suffered as a result af attacks on the part of the officials of the Mogul Empire. Thus he did not need to return home empty-handed to the Shah.[186]

Between Lahore and Isfahan Robert Sherley met another of the brilliant young men of the time: the learned traveller, Thomas Coryat. Coryat, who has himself described the historical meeting on the distant caravan trail, was not least satisfied to learn that Sherley had both his books in his travelling library – it was the only opportunity he had of seeing them in print – as well as for the forty shillings Teresa contributed to his little travelling purse; but he also informs us that Sherley brought two elephants

180. *Ibid.* p. 318.
181. *Calendar S. P. East Indies*, 1513/1616 p. 347. Cf. the Royal commission to the *Expedition's* Captain, Christopher Newport, dated 6/1 1613. *First Letter Book* pp. 442–445.
182. CHAUDHURI p. 226.
183. In the spring of 1612 it was believed in Spain that Sherley had been successful, and that four ships were on their way to Persia. This rumour – due no doubt to the mixing up of the reports of Sherley's and Thynne's plans and the information about the dispatch of the East India Company's 10th separate voyage, which was instructed to call at Surat – was forwarded to Goa, *Documentos Remettidos* II, p. 251. It is accepted as fact by LUZ, who thereby comes to overestimate the effects of Robert Sherley's negotiations in England.
184. BOCARRO p. 201.
185. PURCHAS IV pp. 194–198.
186. PENROSE pp. 193–194.

and eight antilopes with him, which he intended to present to the Shah.[187]

Gombroon had fallen in December 1614, but when Sherley arrived at the Persian Court in the summer of 1615 negotiations had been opened up, as mentioned, between the Persians and the Portuguese. Abbas had decided to send an Ambassador to Goa and possibly on to Europe to negotiate for a settlement of the conflict. A distinguished Persian was appointed for this task, and the Augustinian, Belchior dos Anjos, who had returned to Persia, and who had played an important role in the provisional negotiations, was chosen to accompany him.[188] The circumstances under which this original plan was altered in favour of the appointment of Robert Sherley as Persian Ambassador, accompanied, not by an Augustinian, but by the Carmelite, Redempt, are uncertain, since there are two quite different versions of the events following Sherley's arrival in Persia. All the sources are agreed that Robert Sherley was kindly received by Abbas, not so much on account of the diplomatic results he had achieved on his lengthy journey, because they were almost non-existent, but on account of the gifts he brought with him, and the amount of news he could relate from the wide world for the ever inquisitive Shah. That he was soon dispatched on a new journey was due, according to Figueroa, the Spanish Ambassador to Persia, to an intrigue between the Carmelites and Robert Sherley, supported by the Captain in Hormuz, Luis da Gama, who, by dispatching a Carmelite agent to Spain, hoped to be able to conceal his responsibility for the outbreak of war and the loss of Gombroon, whereas an Augustinian would on the contrary have betrayed him unmercifully.[189] But if we are to believe the Carmelite, Redempt, it was only by tooth and nail that Abbas succeeded in persuading Sherley to set out on a new journey so shortly after his return home.[190] Belchior is silent in his account regarding the detailed circumstances surrounding the change of plans,[191] but on the other hand he was himself under suspicion for having mismanaged the negotiations with the Shah in order to achieve the status of official representative for Spain-Portugal.[192] The Carmelite, Redempt, is undisputably in the best position to know, but he is much too eager in

187. PURCHAS IV pp. 471–472.
188. Belchior, Isfahan, to Philip III, 30/11 1615, Arch. Simancas, Estado, leg. 437 f. 215; FIGUEROA II p. 133; *Chronicle* p. 214.
189. Figueroa, Goa, to Philip III, 26/3 1616, Arch. Simancas, Estado, leg. 495; cf. FIGUEROA II pp. 143–144. The background to the co-operation between the Carmelites and Luis da Gama lay in the rivalry with the Augustinians, who tried to hinder the erection of a Carmelite monastery in Hormuz. *Chronicle* and *Documentos Remettidos passim*.
190. *Chronicle* p. 215.
191. Arch. Simancas, Estado, leg. 437, ff. 213–216.
192. "Relacion de la embaxada que hiço en Persia Dom Garcia de Silva y Figueroa," *Documentação Ultramarina Portuguesa* I, p. 180.

his account to prove that the idea was the Shah's – in fact he protests a knowledge of the Shah's plans, even before the latter had spoken of them. With the available source material the question is unsolvable, but although one is reluctant to accuse the venerable Carmelite of untrustworthiness, it is difficult to imagine that Sherley should have remained passive in this situation, just as the replacement of an Augustinian by a Carmelite companion for the Ambassador can scarcely have been an accident.

With what tasks did Abbas entrust Robert Sherley, now that he sent him out as Ambassador for the second time? Considering he conducted comprehensive negotiations both in Spain and England throughout the following years, it is a pity that none of his credentials seems to have been preserved. The closest we can come to an authoritative account of the purpose of his dispatch is a summary of his credentials in the *consultas* of the Spanish Council of State, in which three points are emphasized. Firstly, the conquest of Gombroon, which is justified by pointing out that the area was formerly Persian territory, and that the Portuguese in the fort annoyed the Persian merchants. The expedition undertaken was solely aimed at destroying the fort, but the Portuguese prisoners taken were treated like guests and sent back together with Robert Sherley. Secondly, the plans for blockading the Red Sea are mentioned. The Shah declared that, as far as that was concerned, the King of Spain must do as he pleased. Thirdly, Abbas requested once again that the Captains in Hormuz should be ordered to treat the Persian merchants with more consideration.[193]

During his negotiations in Europe Robert Sherley far exceeded these three points, but it is difficult to decide whether he was thereby acting entirely on his own initaitive or carrying out the verbal instructions of the Shah. There were rumours of secret instructions of this nature in Persia even before Sherley had left the country. Belchior maintained that on his return Robert Sherley had promised Abbas to procure a Dutch fleet with which to blockade the Red Sea and to build a fort on Socotra, on condition the Shah would advance 200,000 cruzados worth of silk, to be delivered in Aleppo. After this initial investment the fleet could maintain itself and even send a profit to Persia with the aid of the prizes they would capture from the Shah's enemies.[194] It is easy to recognize the Sherley family in this plan. Belchior also maintains that Sherley's secret instructions ordered him to negotiate with Spain concerning a peace or a truce around Hormuz, a Spanish blockade of the Red Sea with the aid of a fleet of ten ships and a fort on Socotra and the dispatch of a Mediterranean armada against

193. Arch. Simancas, Estado, leg. 437, f. 57.
194. Belchior, Isfahan, to Philip III, 30/11 1615, Arch. Simancas, Estado, leg. 437, f. 214; Luz p. 341.

Turkey as big as the one His Majesty had once sent against England.[195] Figueroa, who was still in Goa at this time, adds to this that Robert Sherley was authorized to negotiate about a redirection of the silk trade.[196]

There is a certain agreement between these rumours and the policy Sherley himself conducted in Europe, but it does not prove anything with regard to the Shah's intentions, however, because Sherley himself had presumably been the source of the rumours. Belchior dos Anjos asserts that the talks between Abbas and Sherley were surrounded with the greatest secrecy. Abbas himself can scarcely have been responsible for the leakages.

Of course Sherley had instantly to weigh up his relations with the Portuguese, to whom he was now sent out as Ambassador shortly after they had tried to get rid of him by every possible means. As a precaution he sent Redempt to Hormuz in advance to learn something of the general attitude towards his person and his errand before he ventured into Portuguese territory himself.[197] He had no grounds for anxiety, however; he was not only received with the honours befitting an Ambassador,[198] but even with great warmth.[199] The change in the Portuguese attitude towards Sherley both in Hormuz and in Goa is so striking that it can scarcely be put down to respect for the Ambassador's diplomatic status or gratitude over the fact that he brought with him the prisoners taken by the Persians at the fall of Gombroon. Figueroa was indignant: he thought more fuss was being made of this gypsy baron "conde de gitanos" than of himself, and he was in no doubt as to the explanation. After two years' stay in Goa he saw *Estado da India* as one great Portuguese plot against the Spanish King. Luiz da Gama himself had been guilty of the attack on Gombroon in 1614 and of the poor state of the fort's defences. Sherley's good reception was due to a secret agreement that Sherley was to save the situation for da Gama at the Spanish Court.[200]

Sherley left Persia too late to be able to travel to Portugal with the spring fleet in 1615 and thus had to spend nearly a year in Goa. It must have been during this stay that he carved his name in a tree at the port of Santa Clara: DNUS ROBERTUS SCHURLEIUS LEGATUS REGIS PERSARUM[201] Figueroa was convinced that he exploited Portuguese hospitality in order to conspire secretly with the English in Surat.[202] There

195. Arch. Simancas, Estado, leg. 437, f. 215.
196. Arch. Simancas, Estado, leg. 495.
197. *Chronicle* p. 218.
198. Bocarro p. 514.
199. Figueroa II p. 144; *Chronicle* p. 219.
200. Figueroa II pp. 143–144.
201. Bocarro p. 35 n. 2.
202. Figueroa *loc cit.* above n. 200.

is not the least sign of such a contact in the English sources, however; on the other hand, the English regarded Sherley with equal suspicion. The English Ambassador at the Court of the Grand Mogul, Sir Thomas Roe, felt certain that Sherley's real task was to negotiate about a monopoly contract comprising the whole of the Persian silk production and, with his usual pessimism, he was convinced that the Spanish King was prepared to accept his offer. Thomas Roe was in no doubt that Robert Sherley was an arrant papist who was only doing the Spanish King's bidding.[203]

With Sherley's interpreter in Isfahan, Robbins, as source, Roe was also convinced that Sherley had made peace with the Portuguese in Goa on behalf of the Shah.[204] This seems to have been a false rumour. In Goa Sherley presented a letter from the Shah rejecting the Portuguese protests about the conquest of Gombroon on the grounds that it was old Persian territory.[205] A formal truce is not mentioned in the Portuguese sources; probably, as previously, an actual cease-fire in Goa has been considered sufficient and the formal clarification of the question has been left to the authorities in Spain.

203. Sir Thomas Roe to East India Co., 14/2 1616, Roe pp. 111–112.
204. Ibid. pp. 312–313.
205. Bocarro p. 514 f.

Chapter VII: The Loss of Hormuz

During the years following 1615 the confusion enveloping the Persian policy gradually acquires some symmetry. There was a Spanish Ambassador at the Persian Court from 1617 onwards and, from the same year, a Persian Ambassador at the Spanish Court. This should have created the basis for a constant communication that would be able to clear up at any rate the most glaring misunderstandings between Persia and the Portuguese-Spanish monarchy.

It did not succeed. Sherley and Figueroa were both worthy representatives of the diplomatic corps, but neither Sherley's wealth of ideas nor Figueroa's loyalty were adequate for the complicated task of formulating the interests common to Spain and Persia. During the same years Spain-Portugal also tried to strengthen its military position in the Persian Gulf, but time was running short. In December 1616 the first English Company ship visited Persia. The English initiative in Persia began as a side-issue – an idea conceived, not by the people ultimately responsible for the Company's policy, but by those of its servants posted in India; at the time it must have seemed a trifle compared with the year-long considerations in the Spanish-Portuguese Government offices and the persistent attempts to secure Persia's friendship and Hormuz's safety. But the presence of the English Company in Persia undermined Portugal's very position in the Persian Gulf. Already for some years English and Dutch trade had seriously affected the income of the Portuguese Empire; with the presence of an alien European naval force off Persia the strategical position on which Portuguese power had depended for more than a hundred years disappeared.

Sherley's Second Spanish Embassy, 1617-22

It has been said that Sherley achieved nothing at all during his nearly five-year long stay at the Spanish Court on his second journey to Europe, from September 1617 to March 1622. "Sherley waited in vain for a reply to his propositions ..." "Robert simply did not get anywhere."[1] Robert

---

1. PENROSE pp. 204–206.

obtained a reply and got astonishingly far, but the diplomatic victory was won in a dreamland, in a world of make-believe that lay as far from the political realities in the Persian Gulf as from the economic and organizational capacity of the implicated parties.

Considering Sherley had terminated his previous embassy by leaving Spain without a farewell audience and with a warrant for his arrest on his heels, it is not surprising that he experienced some difficulty in gaining a hearing at the Spanish Court on his arrival. His brother, Anthony Sherley, was no help. Shortly after the news of Robert's arrival in Lisbon was known, i.e. in October 1617, Anthony Sherley sent the Council of State a memorandum that was a knife in the back of his little brother. If Anthony's advice had been taken with the last embassy, it said, Robert would never have travelled to England. And now that he had returned, he should be neutralized by detaining him in Lisbon; he should not be given the opportunity of going to the Court, where he would be able to contact the English Ambassador. The Council of State thought well of this proposal and resolved that Robert should be detained in Lisbon pending his speediest possible return to Persia.[2] It made absolutely no difference that the Council of State received an important report by special post from Hormuz in the end of October; an English ship had touched at the Persian port of Jask in December 1616, and the English were now negotiating with the Shah regarding a contract to buy Persian silk. The decision to avoid negotiations with Robert Sherley was maintained, but the Council of State was aware of the dangers of the situation: "If this (the English trade) is put into practice it will be the destruction of Hormuz."[3]

There can be no doubt that Robert was dissatisfied about being kept away from Court in this manner, but for the time being the Council of State was adamant; as late as May 1618 one of the Council members said that to recognize Robert Sherley as Ambassador at the Court would be indecent.[4] Thus for the time being Robert was obliged to set to work indirectly through the Portuguese authorities, to whom he presented his credentials and his proposals. We can form an idea of his initial move in connection with the Council of Portugal's handling of the matter on 17/3 1618.[5] The credentials are referred to above, and to these Robert added a note with the following contents: the Shah was satisfied with the proposal to blockade the Red Sea and offered to contribute to the blockade of Turkey by diverting the silk exports through Hormuz. He declared himself willing to negotiate regarding three possibilities: either the silk

2. Arch. Simancas, Estado, leg. 437, ff. 127–128.
3. Ibid. f. 130.
4. Ibid. f. 67.
5. Ibid. ff. 57–58.

could be conveyed to Hormuz, where it would then be bought by Spanish-Portuguese merchants, or it could be taken over by the Spanish King at his own expense in Hormuz, or the Spanish King could suffice with placing ships at its disposal, the silk being transported to Lisbon at Persian expense and sold there.

The Council of Portugal declared in its *consulta* that above all it was wise to humour Sherley in order to prevent his continuing to England. As regards Gombroon the Council of Portugal was irreconcilable; the Shah's reason for taking Gombroon, on the grounds that it was really Persian territory unlawfully fortified by the Portuguese, was rejected. It therefore desired clarification as to whether Robert Sherley was entitled to negotiate on that point, because both Gombroon and Bahrein must be restored.

As far as the blockade of the Red Sea was concerned the Council of Portugal had just as many misgivings as when the question had been debated during Sherley's first visit to Spain. This point is interesting because it reveals what lay behind the pretended blockade of the Red Sea. This, emphasized the Council of Portugal, was not only a matter concerning the Turks and other hostile nations; on the contrary, an effective blockade would first and foremost hit the friends of *Estado da India,* who sailed the Red Sea regularly by virtue of Portuguese *cartazes.* An effective blockade would contain within it the risk that both friends and enemies might join in forming an anti-Portuguese coalition, as had happened before. In addition the Council envisaged such a blockade as being first and foremost an advantage to the Persians, who would consequently be able to exert more pressure on Hormuz. If the blockade of the Red Sea was to be tightened, it would be necessary to ensure that it did not affect friendly nations.

Regarding the redirection of the silk trade the Council of Portugal recalled the fact that it was an old project, referring to the King's order of 30/10 1611 in respect of which the Viceroy was ordered to send two ships from Goa to Hormuz to convey the Persian silk to Europe.[6] The order had not been put into practice because there was not at that time any available tonnage in Goa. But now the suggestion had been put forward once again the Council wished to emphasize that the precondition for its realization must be a close bond of friendship between Spain/Portugal and Persia, otherwise there would be a constant risk of a Persian-English attack on Hormuz. And this precondition, friendly relations, could not be said to be fulfilled until Gombroon and Bahrein were restored. If this precondition was fulfilled the Council of Portugal would agree to accept the

6. See above, p. 285 cf. *Documentos Remettidos* II pp. 126–129, 277–278.

proposal in its third version, since in this way a considerable guarantee for the Shah's friendly policy would be procured, quite apart from the stimulating effect of the silk trade on Hormuz and the Royal customs revenue.

The Council of State received this *consulta* together with one (amongst many) of Anthony Sherley's memorandums, which, well wrapped up and with very few concrete arguments likewise recommended the redirection of the silk trade and the closing of the Red Sea. On the basis of this advice the Council of State decided to follow the Council of Portugal's recommendation.[7] During the further negotiations with Robert Sherley, however, it transpired that he was not authorized to negotiate about Bahrein, but only about Gombroon. On the Spanish side the demand for the restoration of the two places was considered a precondition for realistic negotiations concerning the remaining proposals; consequently it was decided to transfer the negotiations to Persia. Figueroa, the Spanish Ambassador at the Persian Court, was instructed through the Captain of Hormuz to negotiate regarding the plans put forward by Sherley, but with the surrender of Bahrein and Gombroon as the primary and indispensable precondition.[8]

Thus at this point, in May 1618, the Spanish Government decided to conduct the negotiations through Figueroa, thereby putting Sherley out of the running. Even Sherley's threat to travel to England seems at this juncture to have lost its effect; in June the Council of State still declared that there was no longer any reason to detain Sherley.[9] In the beginning of August mail arrived from Persia, however: dispatches from Figueroa and from Belchior dos Anjos containing serious news. The reports of the English initiative in Persia were confirmed; the English merchant, Connock, had been received at the Persian Court in the summer of 1617 and secured comprehensive trade privileges for the English Company, and a consignment of English goods had been landed in Jask.[10]

Following the reception of this information the whole of the Spanish-Portuguese policy as regards Persia was taken up for renewed consideration. On 8th August the Council of State declared that the case was so important that it could best be dealt with in a joint session with representatives of the Council of Portugal. The problem this junta was to

---

7. Arch. Simancas, Estado, leg. 437, ff. 59–60.
8. "Noticias de las guerras . . ." B. N Madrid, Ms. 2352. This anonymous manuscript is very informative as regards the negotations carried on, and its information, in so far as it can be checked with the aid of the acts of the Council of State, is reliable.
9. Arch. Simancas, Estado, leg. 437, f. 72.
10. *Ibid*. ff. 75–76.

consider was, how could Hormuz best be safeguarded against a possible English attack.[11]

The junta subdivided the question into three: firstly, should the Shah's offer of friendship as presented by Robert Sherley be accepted, and if the answer was in the affirmative, in which form? Secondly, what could be done to prevent Sherley making contact with Spain's enemies? Thirdly, was it desirable or necessary to send military reinforcements to the Captain in Hormuz immediately? As far as the first point was concerned the junta found it desirable, both in respect of the threat to Hormuz and of the possibility of weakening Turkey, to accept the Shah's offer of a redirection of the silk trade. Twelve vessels per annum should be sent to Hormuz from Goa in order to fetch the Persian silk, while the further transport from Goa should be carried out by the ordinary annual fleet to Lisbon. In return for the silk the Shah might even be offered payment in the form of pepper and other spices. On the other hand the junta found it advisable to abandon the idea of an effective blockade of the Red Sea; the venture was impossible. The demand for the return of Gombroon and Bahrein was to be maintained, but the junta was nevertheless so disturbed by the news from Persia that it advised postponing the demand should the Shah still refuse to consider it. It was decided that two members of the Government – one from the Council of State and one from the Council of Portugal – were to negotiate on this basis with Robert Sherley through his companion, the Carmelite, Redempt.

Regarding the second point the junta did not cherish any illusions concerning the reliability of the Persian Ambassador; they regarded both Robert Sherley and his brother with the greatest mistrust. It was still thought advisable to keep him away from the Court and to send him home as soon as possible with the Spanish offer.

As regards the third point the junta was agreed that it was no longer advisable to expect that Hormuz would be able to defend itself solely with the aid of its own resources. Two galleons were being made ready to be sent to Malacca; instead it was thought advisable to send them together with a third one to Hormuz under the command of the Portuguese Ruy Freire de Andrada.[12]

During the following months the negotiations were conducted in all earnestness, and on November 20th the Venetian Ambassador, Pietro Gritti, reported the many difficulties attached to the project: the high

11. *Ibid.* ff. 79–82. It is interesting that, exactly at this time, P. Joseph arrived at the Spanish Court as an unofficial Ambassador for the Duke of Never's proposed crusade. FAGNIEZ I p. 162. There was no longer any thought to connect the crusade policy and the question of Hormuz.
12. Arch. Simancas, Estado, leg. 437, f. 82.

customs rates in Lisbon, the interests of the Spanish silk producers, the necessity of discovering a form of payment for the silk that was not detrimental to other Portuguese interests in Asia, the fear that the Persian merchants would not be sufficiently interested and the lack of tonnage. For the time being the case was transferred to the Council of Portugal in Lisbon pending the arrival of news from the Spanish Ambassador in Persia.[13]

During the autumn and winter agreement was reached regarding a draft treaty, but Robert Sherley would not commit himself finally before the draft had been submitted to the Shah – his instructions did not permit it, he insisted. The draft was therefore sent overland to Persia by direct messenger and also with Redempt, who left Lisbon with Ruy Freire's fleet in March 1619. Redempt was ordered in his instructions first of all to present the letters entrusted him, including Figueroa's instructions, to the Captain in Hormuz, and thereafter – after the Captain had considered the matter – to contact Figueroa in Persia.[14]

There is no reason for going into much detail as regards the abortive draft treaty; it was never ratified and is only interesting as an expression of the Spanish-Portuguese Governments's intentions and appraisal of the situation. It is more important to note that, as in 1611, there was now a serious and even more meticulous attempt to put into effect the redirection of the Persian silk trade. Evidence for this is provided not least by the extremely detailed rules regarding customs exemption for Persian subjects in Hormuz, Goa and Lisbon. Furthermore, the King of Spain declared it was his intention to supplement this attempt to harm the Ottoman Empire by hitting at the transit trade with the dispatch of a fleet to blockade the Red Sea. As already mentioned this blockade was probably first and foremost Sherley's idea and it did not interest Abbas very much. Neither were the Portuguese authorities interested in an effective blockade, but no doubt they misjudged Abbas's wishes, because the King of Spain furthermore stated that he expected the Shah would return this gesture of friendship by the restoration of Gombroon, that he would banish all alien European ships, merchants and agents, and that he would demonstrate his appreciation of the Spanish King's magnanimity by restoring Bahrein as well. In the confidential instructions to Figueroa the Spanish conditions were listed in order of importance: "And as far as the banishment of Englishmen and other foreigners from Europe and the return of Gombroon is concerned, these things must under all circumstances be put into effect before the trade agreement comes into force." On the other

13. A. d. S. Venezia, Senato, Dispacci Spagna, filza 50, disp. 48.
14. B. N. Madrid, Ms. 2352 f. 485; *Chronicle* pp. 224–225 (Redempt's instructions).

310

hand Figueroa might give in as regards the question of Bahrein's return provided he saw to it that the question remained open.[15]

The junta's proposal to accept the Persian possession of Gombroon for the time being was thus abandoned, and the Council of State determined to give its restitution precedence, thus with certainty rendering the realization of the treaty impossible. To the demand for the return of Gombroon a further demand was added for the banishment of the English. With these conditions the Council of State was quite out of touch with the actual state of affairs. The draft treaty contained no advantages for the Shah, neither were there any guarantees for the threatened Hormuz. The draft is no unrealistic that this circumstance in itself reveals something essential about the situation of the Spanish leaders during those years. Lack of information and mental habits from a hundred years of Spanish gunboat diplomacy had rendered them unfit to take action when truly vital interests were threatened.

The draft treaty of March 1619 was probably the closest Robert Sherley ever got to a result in the whole of his long life as a diplomat. The fate awaiting the draft treaty when it reached Persia will be discussed below. For the time being Sherley awaited the Shah's reply in Spain. Concerning his life during the following years there is only little information. In August 1620 the Council of State was informed that Figueroa had left Persia, and it was said that it was on time Sherley, too, was given his farewell audience and sent back to Persia with the next departing fleet.[16] This apparently did not suit Robert Sherley, since he did not leave Spain until 1622, when he set off for Rome via Tuscany.[17]

Lack of information and little sense of reality were partly responsible for the impracticable form of the draft treaty of 1619, but in addition to this the Spanish Government tried at the same time to solve the question of Hormuz's safety by another and more direct method: the dispatch of a strong armada to the Persian Gulf. This possibility had already been suggested in connection with the re-appraisal of the Persian policy in August 1618, and the idea was put into practice with unusual efficiency with the dispatch of five galleons under the experienced and popular Ruy Freire de Andrada the following spring, April 1619.[18]

The plan was particularly subtle in that it was hoped by that means to

15. B. N. Madrid, Ms. 2352 f. 485; the draft treaty and Figueroa's instructions dated 14/3 1619 in Torre do Tombo, Lisbon, Documentos Remettidos, livro 12, ff. 148–150.
16. Arch. Simancas, Estado, leg. 437, ff. 2–3; he received a pension from the Spanish Crown of 1500 ducats per month until the summer of 1619; thereafter it was cut down to 1000 ducats, *ibid*. ff. 23, 52, 53.
17. PENROSE, p. 206.
18. BOXER, *Commentaries*, p. 2.

be able to strengthen the military position in the Persian Gulf without arousing the Shah's suspicion. Figueroa was instructed to give the Shah the impression that the armada was sent solely in connection with the blockade of the Red Sea, which he had requested for so many years through his Ambassador, Robert Sherley, and with the redirection of the silk trade.[19] Ruy Freire's instructions, however, listed the tasks in quite a different order of importance. His primary task was to trace and destroy any foreign European ships that tried to establish trade connections with Persia; his second task was to patrol the Hormuz Straits and the mouth of the Red Sea, not with regard to an effective blockade, but in order to seize ships sailing with forbidden goods or ships not in possession of Portuguese *cartaze*.[20] As yet there was nothing in these instructions that would jeopardize the maintenance of friendly connections with Persia, but after the instructions were completed, on 15th January 1619, another order was added to them, which, if complied with, must inevitably lead to an open breach between Persia and the Portuguese. Ruy Freire was ordered to establish a fortress on the island of Qishm, which the Persians had held since 1614.[21] It was Ruy Freire's attempt to carry out this order in 1621 against the advice of the local authorities that led to the breach with Persia and to a fatal weakening of the Portuguese forces before the decisive English-Persian attack the following year.[22]

Figueroa in Persia

The decision to dispatch a distinguished Ambassador with an impressive gift to the Shah of Persia was already made in connection with Janghiz Beg's and Gouvea's stay at the Spanish Court in 1611. Janghiz Beg's valuable present naturally demanded one in return, and the proposals put forward: Robert Sherley's project for closing the Red Sea and the redirection of the silk trade demanded careful negotiations. But the Spanish governmental machinery operated slowly. Gouvea and Janghiz Beg left Lisbon with the spring fleet of 1612 without being accompanied by a Spanish diplomat. The official reason was that it had not been possible to find a suitable person in such a short time; Gouvea was therefore ordered to function as representative for the Spanish King and, in that capacity, to hand over a letter to the Shah and inform him that a proper Ambassador

19. B. N. Madrid, Ms. 2352, ff. 485–486.
20. Ruy Freire's instructions in BOXER, *Commentaries*, app. I pp. 211–218.
21. Arch. Simancas, Estado, leg. 437, ff. 35–36; BOXER, *Commentaries*, pp. XVII–XXVIII, 31–34; CORDEIRO pp. 47–48.
22. See below, p. 339 f.

was on the way.[23] Just as instrumental in causing the delay as the choice of a person was the chronic lack of money. On 9th March 1612, i.e. a few weeks before the spring fleet embarked from Lisbon, the Council of State discovered that there were only 20,000 ducats available in Lisbon to purchase a present for the Shah, whereas the corresponding gift received was valued at 60,000 ducats.[24]

In 1612 Don Garcia de Silva y Figueroa was appointed Ambassador to Persia, but in December it was reported in Spain that peace negotiations were in operation between Persia and Turkey, and that peace would probably soon be concluded. The Council of State hesitated, but resolved in January 1613 that Figueroa should nevertheless be dispatched with the fleet due to set sail in the spring of 1613.[25] Whether it was owing to eleventh hour uneasiness about the unclarified situation in the Levant or some other circumstance, Figueroa did not manage to set off that time either. His instructions are dated 9th August 1613,[26] and his departure took place with the spring fleet of 1614.[27]

Valuable time was lost by this disastrous inefficiency; Janghiz Beg had lost his head and Gouvea had made a sudden departure from Persia even before Figueroa left Europe. But there was probably more behind the delay than lack of money and tardiness. The sources provide us merely with hints; in the summer of 1611 the dispatch of two joint Ambassadors was discussed in all seriousness – a Portuguese and a Castilian.[28] The project must pretty soon have been abandoned, but when some years later, in 1614, the Council of Portugal was consulted about Figueroa's embassy following the receipt of new information from Asia, the Council replied coldly that it was not prepared to make a pronouncement in a case about which it was so badly informed – "His Majesty must have the case considered by the authority who has instructed the Ambassador" – i.e. the Council of State.[29] These references are sufficient to indicate the problem's existence; Figueroa was a Castilian and instructed by the Council of State, but it was the Portuguese authorities who were to procure transport for him and find the money for the present for the Shah. There is no doubt that the problem became important following Figueroa's arrival in Goa, but it is probable that it had already delayed his departure from Lisbon.

23. *Documentos Remettidos* II, pp. 222–223.
24. Arch. Simancas, Estado, leg. 494.
25. Arch. Simancas, Estado, leg. 494, *consulta* 15/12 1612, and leg. 495, *consulta* 21/1 1613.
26. Luz p. 343.
27. Figueroa II p. 1.
28. Arch. Simancas, Estado, leg. 494.
29. Arch. Simancas, Estado, leg. 436, f. 181.

The Spanish-Portuguese Crown meticulously fulfilled its obligations as regards not appointing Castilians to offices in the Portuguese colonies,[30] but of course the agreement could not be binding where the appointment of an Ambassador was concerned. The formalities were in order regarding Figueroa's appointment, but it did not prevent his being regarded as a foreigner and treated with ill-concealed hostility after his arrival in Goa at the end of 1614.[31] Figueroa had to wait another two and a half years before he could get further than Goa. It is difficult to see this as anything other than the result of a Portuguese policy of obstruction.

In addition to this antagonism towards the Castilian – one might almost say it was on grounds of principle – the Persian question was placed rather low in order of importance in Goa at the time of Figueroa's arrival. The Portuguese had plenty of worries; apart from the continual clashes with the Netherlands they were at war with the Grand Mogul whose army was besieging Damao. On Figueroa's arrival the most pressing task was to fit out a fleet that could attack the English ships expected at Surat in the beginning of 1615. For the Portuguese it was not only a question of avenging their defeat in the Battle of Swally Hole in 1612 and placing obstacles in the way of the still quite modest English trade with the Indian coast – there was far more at stake. A victory over the English was necessary in order to prove to the Indian Princes and merchants that it was still the Portuguese who commanded the Indian Ocean. On this status depended both the issue of *cartazes* and the customs dues in the ports under Portuguese control.[32] The amount of importance placed upon this encounter in Goa appears from the size of the armada fitted out: 6 galleons, 2 ships, 2 galleys and 60 frigates manned by 2,700 men apart from the sailors themselves, and armed with 134 guns,[33] and by the fact that the armada was personally commanded by the Viceroy. That, following these preparations, the fleet had to withdraw before seriously harming the English when the victuals were all eaten up, was almost a worse defeat than a decisive battle.

To this came the uncertainty with regard to the developments in Persia. A few days after Figueroa's arrival the Persian siege of Gombroon was

30. Pyrard de Laval maintains that there was only one Castilian in Goa during his stay there in 1608–10, PYRARD de LAVAL II p. 21.
31. See especially "Relacion de la embaxada que hiço en Persia Don Garcia de Silva y Figueroa"", *Documentação Ultramarina Portuguesa* I pp. 177–195. The author of this anonymous relation can presumably be identified as Figueroa's secretary, Saulisante, see pp. 194–195 concerning the author's return journey. cf. FIGUEROA II p. 473.
32. BOCARRO pp. 336–338.
33. The examination of Domingo Francisco, a Portuguese prisoner, PURCHAS IV, p. 263.

reported in Goa,[34] and in December 1614 the Portuguese fortress fell. Under these circumstances Figueroa could not continue to Persia without new instructions from Spain, but he wished to travel as quickly as possible to Hormuz, from where he would be able to take over the management of the cease-fire negotiations. However, the Viceroy could not accommodate Figueroa's wish for a quick passage to Hormuz; he maintained he could neither procure the means for the gift Figueroa was to hand over nor find a suitable ship to carry him to Hormuz. The situation remained a dead-lock until eventually Figueroa received revised instructions in October 1616, at the same time as the Viceroy was enjoined from Spain to see that Figueroa proceded to Persia immediately. The tug-of-war for money and passage continued, but in March 1617 Figueroa eventually set sail with a merchant vessel from Bassein.[35]

From the Portuguese side originates a different version of the background to Figueroa's delay in Goa. Bocarro maintains that it was entirely the Ambassador's own reluctance to continue the journey that kept him in Goa, since he had heard in 1614 that the Persians had attacked Gombroon, and he seeks to substantiate this statement by printing a correspondence between Figueroa and the Arcbishop of Goa, who functioned as Governor during the Viceroy's absence with the armada off Surat in the beginning of 1615.[36] The documentation is not convincing, however; it applies to the situation in February 1615, but is misleading as far as the overall picture is concerned. Figueroa undoubtedly described the essence of the problem when he wrote: "In spite of this embassy having been dispatched and instructed by the Council of State, it is the Council of Portugal and the officials in India who have to provide the money and all the necessities ..."[37] Figueroa's delay was a result of the Spanish-Portuguese Empire's complicated and ambiguous distribution of authority.

Figueroa's original instructions were issued on 9th August 1613. He was ordered herein to urge the Shah to continue the war against Turkey by holding out the prospects of strengthened Spanish forces in the Mediterranean – the Spanish authorities had apparently decided to ignore the rumours of a peace between Persia and Turkey. He was furthermore authorized to negotiate about the proposal to redirect the silk trade, which had been presented by Janghiz Beg through Gouvea. If he was satisfied with the results achieved, he was not compelled to insist on the return of

34. FIGUEROA I p. 219.
35. *Ibid.* p. 223.
36. BOCARRO pp. 372–374. The Portuguese point of view also appears in *Documentos Remettidos* III p. 336.
37. FIGUEROA I p. 222.

Bahrein. Finally he was ordered to co-operate with Gouvea and to consult him regarding all important decisions.[38]

They were very moderate and quite realistic instructions, but it should be noted that they were elaborated before the loss of Gombroon. In the first instance, however, the reports of this loss do not seem to have altered the attitude of the Spanish authorities. Everything suggests that all the authorities, including the Viceroy in Goa and the Council of Portugal in Lisbon, tried to play down the loss of Gombroon to the King and the Council of State; in May 1616 the Council of Portugal declared it was a minor fortress, the demolition of which had already been considered.[39] Not until Figueroa's dispatches, sent in the period 3rd May 1615 to 1st February 1616, arrived in October 1616 did the seriousness of the situation dawn upon the Council of State, and in his letter to the he Viceroy of 21st March 1617 the King emphasized that there could be no question of making peace, let alone of entering into any co-operation with Persia before Gombroon was restored.[40] We do not know what correspondence Figueroa received at the time, but there cannot be any doubt that before his arrival in Persia he had received similar orders: no peace before Gombroon was restored.

On 12th October 1617 Figueroa eventually landed in Persia and could begin his embassy after more than four years' delay. He was in no hurry to reach the Court, however. He spent the winter of 1617–18 in Shiraz so as not to expose himself to the severe winter in Isfahan and because the Shah was in any case resident in Farabad, to which he maintained it was not possible to travel during the winter. He was received during his stay by Imam Quli Khan, but there is no sign of there having been any political negotiations between them. In the spring of 1618 he left Shiraz, on 15th June he arrived in Kazvin, where the Shah was now staying, and a few days later he was received in audience.

The man the Spaniards had appointed to represent them at the Court of the Shah was of quite a different calibre than the Sherley brothers. He was not only intelligent, but also scholarly; that appears in all clarity from his own account of the embassy. He was honest (about that all are in agreement), he was modest and bore himself with dignity, but he was also devoid of humour and had none of the qualities that could win over the inquisitive and impulsive Abbas. He was born in 1551 and, according to the

38. Luz p. 343.
39. Arch. Simancas, Estado, leg. 437, f. 163.
40. Arch. Simancas, Estado, leg. 437 f. 203; *Documentos Remittidos* IV p. 151. Figueroa complains time and time again that the mail between himself and Spain was delayed, and he blamed the Viceroy in Goa, the Captain in Hormuz and the Augustinians in Persia in turn for keeping back his mail on purpose. The extraordinarily long time it took to reach its destination might well suggest there was some truth in it.

concepts of the time, was thus an old man,[41] and when he refused a hospitable offer of female company it was even rumoured that he was over eighty years old and had visited Persia already in Tahmasp's time.[42] His beard was white and he had no teeth, says della Valle.[43] In short, he was a fitting representative for Lerma's administration.

But his task was hopeless, and his instructions quite unconnected with reality. He was to press for the return of Gombroon as condition for an agreement, a condition he himself had been active in having inserted in his instructions, but he had nothing to offer in exchange other than empty promises and equally empty threats. Spain-Portugal's prestige was reduced in Persian eyes. Despite many years of promises they had accomplished nothing in the fight against the power they maintained was the arch-enemy of Christendom, and Portuguese power in the Persian Gulf had turned out to be a paper dragon unable to protect either Bahrein or Gombroon. Abbas's attitude prior to Figueroa's arrival appears clearly from his conversation with della Valle in April 1618. As so often before he expressed his impatience over the Spanish promises to co-operate against the Ottoman Empire. Della Valle referred evasively to the corsair war in the Mediterranean and to the many obligations placed on such an extensive Empire as the Spanish. But Abbas felt only contempt for that kind of prevarication. It only went to show, he said, that the King of Spain did not understand how to make war; he ought to assemble his troops in one place and strike his enemies a decisive blow, one by one, as he himself had done in Persia. It was his own strategy Abbas placed at the disposal of Philip III. And he had yet another piece of advice for the Spanish King: he ought to place himself at the head of his army – generals were not to be trusted.[44]

Abbas's negative attitude in 1617 is all the more remarkable because his foreign policy was in a critical situation that very year. The unstable political conditions in Constantinople, where during these years not only Grand Viziers, but also Sultans, followed each other in rapid succession, had after the resumption of war been his best defence, but he was now threatened with a massive attack. The change of personnel in 1614 had, as expected, brought a fresh outbreak of the war with it, but so far, in 1615, it had only amounted to skirmishes in Georgia. In 1616 Mehmed Pasha invaded Persia with a considerable army; via Erzurum and Kars, in September he reached as far as Erivan, which he put under siege. Once again Abbas saved himself by means of his defensive strategy. He sent no reinforcements to the besieged town, but instructed his troops to raid the enemy's supply lines while he waited for time to work to his advantage.

41. *Boletin de la Real Academia de Historia*, t. 102, p. 494 ff.
42. FIGUEROA II pp. 48–49.
43. Della VALLE, *Persia* II:2 p. 234.
44. Della VALLE, *Persia* II:2 pp. 259–261.

By November Mehmed Pasha had had enough; he could not stay encamped in front of the town all through the winter, but, on the other hand, he did not dare start a retreat with hostile forces around him. He sent an envoy to Abbas to negotiate, but even before the negotiations were concluded he spread the news among his troops that peace had been declared and began the retreat.[45]

The retreat from Erivan cost Mehmed Pasha his post as Grand Vizier and Halil Pasha was appointed in his stead.[46] The latter immediately began to assemble a new army, and by the end of 1617 he was ready to march off from Diyarbekir. The death of Ahmed I in November 1617 gave Abbas a few more months' respite, however. Ahmed's successor, Mustapha I, wished to end the war, and among his first governmental actions was the dispatch of the Persian Ambassador, Quazim Beg, who had virtually been held prisoner by the Turks since 1614. Already in February 1618 the peace-loving Sultan was deposed, however, and under Osman II the aggressive policy towards Persia was resumed. Halil started preparing for war again and began the advance on Persia in the spring of 1618.[47]

Thus on Figueroa's arrival Abbas found the political situation very threatening, and the summer was marked by hectic political and military activity, which we can follow at close hand, thanks to della Valle, who was present at the public audiences and who, by virtue of his personal connections, was especially well-informed. A few days before Figueroa arrived at the Court in Kazvin a Turkish envoy had been received, and although the military operations continued during the following months the negotiations between the Ottomans and the Persians remained in fact unbroken during the summer campaign. In July the Persian army was gathered in Sultaniyeh, from whence in the beginning of August the advance towards Tabriz had begun, while Abbas himself took up residence in the holy city of his dynasty, Ardebil, where he prepared for an evacuation of the family relics, maintaining contact at the same time with the Turkish Grand Vizier with the help of Turkish and Persian envoys. The Turkish army continued its advance, however, and on 25th August the Shah was informed that the enemy was close to Tabriz, on 30th that Tabriz had been evacuated by the Persians and on 4th September that the Turks had occupied Tabriz.[48]

But a week later the scene changed to the Persians' advantage. A large Ottoman contingent was attacked by the main Persian forces while advancing in the direction of Kazvin, and suffered a bitter defeat. The attack,

45. BELLAN pp. 227–229.
46. HAMMER IV p. 447.
47. BELLAN pp. 234–235; HAMMER IV p. 499.
48. Della VALLE, *Persia* II:2 pp. 348–417 contains a very detailed account of the summer's political and military events.

at least officially, was against the orders of the Shah, which were to avoid major battles, but it seems to have convinced Halil Pasha of the impossibility of spending the winter on Persian soil. Once again there was an exchange of envoys between the Shah and the Grand Vizier, and during the following weeks the parties reached agreement. The Turkish army was to retreat along the road by which it had come, although the Shah was to send them supplies to help them through the ravaged provinces. The actual frontiers, i.e. Abbas's conquests, were recognized, but the question of tribute was apparently left open. A considerable gift of silk was sent immediately from Persia to Constantinople, but in the ratification of the so-called Peace of Sarab, which was received in Persia in 1620, the question of tribute was unmentioned.[49]

Those were the political events that took place the summer Figueroa arrived at the Persian Court; one might think they provided great diplomatic possibilities for an envoy from one of Turkey's arch-enemies. It is doubtful, however, whether Figueroa was at all clear about the import of the events that went on around him. Before Abbas left Kazvin at the end of July in order to attach himself to the army in Sultaniyeh Figueroa had three separate chances of winning Abbas over to the Spanish-Portuguese point of view, but it is obvious that the parties misunderstood each other. The Shah spoke of his victories and asked to hear of effective Spanish actions against the Turks; Figueroa handed over a memorandum about the corsair war in the Mediterranean – about which Abbas was tired of hearing – and demanded the restoration of the Persian conquests in the Gulf.[50] There was no common ground for wishes and offers, and Figueroa would not or could not exceed his instructions. He was certainly right in feeling that his most important function in Abbas's eyes was to give the Turkish envoy the impression that the Spanish King was angling for his friendship.[51]

After these first conversations Figueroa abandoned all hope of seeing any results of his mission.[52] To Abbas's annoyance he refused to accom-

---

49. Della VALLE, *Persia* II:2 422–435; BELLAN pp. 239–40; HAMMER IV, p. 499.
50. Apart from Figueroa's own account of the audiences in Kazvin and the above (n. 31) mentioned "Relacion de la embaxada", the conversations are summarized in "Embaixada de Don Gracia de Silva y Figueroa enviada por Don Filippe III, B. N. Lisboa, Ms. F. G. 580, and by della Valle.
51. FIGUEROA II pp. 119–120.
52. Although the English cannot yet have had the opportunity of demonstrating their potential, it may have contributed to the Shah's negative attitude that they had already landed a cargo of money and goods and thus opened up the possibility of an alternative to the trade connection via Hormuz. On the road between Gombroon and Shiraz Figueroa was passed by the English agent, Connock, who deliberately avoided a meeting, however, possibly because he wished to avoid a dispute about his diplomatic status. *Calendar S. P. East Indies* 1617/21 p. 157.

pany him to the army and asked for a farewell audience so that he might reach Goa before the embarkation of the European fleet the following spring, 1619, but he was put off on the excuse that the Shah was occupied with the summer campaign and the negotiations with Turkey. In addition Figueroa had a suspicion that there was a wish to detain him until it was known how Robert Sherley had been received in Spain.[53]

However, it is probable that Figueroa overestimated the Shah's interest in his Ambassador at the Spanish Court. While the Shah was again resident in Kazvin in October 1618 Robert Sherley's report arrived about the negotiations in Spain up till May the same year. Apparently Sherley had not taken a Persian secretary with him and did not trust his own ability to write the language, because the report was composed in "Frankish" and addressed to Juan Tadeo, who was entrusted with translating and forwarding the dispatches. When Juan Tadeo brought this news to the Shah he showed very little interest; the matter could wait until the following spring, since he was on his way to Mazanderan where, according to custom, he would spend the winter months.[54] Shortly afterwards, in November 1618, Figueroa received the Royal letter of May 1618 concerning Robert Sherley's negotiations. As previously mentioned, Figueroa was instructed in that letter to continue the negotiations with the Shah concerning a redirection of the silk trade on the basis sketched by Sherley, the return of Bahrein and Gombroon nevertheless remaining the absolute condition for an agreement. With the summer's discussions in Kazvin fresh in his memory, Figueroa did not for one moment believe in the possibilities of the project, and did not wish to inconvenience himself by taking it to the Shah in his winter residence on the Caspian Sea; instead he sent the Augustinian prior, Belchior dos Anjos, who could only confirm that Figueroa's pessimism was justified. The Shah would not even discuss the project with Belchior, but merely let him know through his secretary that he neither had any use for a fleet in the Red Sea nor for a redirection of the silk trade, because he had made peace with Turkey and intended in the future to export the silk through the usual channels.[55]

The summer of 1619 provided Figueroa with new possibilities for direct contact with the Shah after the latter had moved to Isfahan in June, but

53. FIGUEROA II p. 340.
54. Della VALLE, Persia II:2 pp. 460–461.
55. FIGUEROA pp. 359–360; della VALLE, Persia II:1 p. 472. Figueroa sent Belchior to Spain with this answer. At the Spanish Court the latter tried to represent the result of the note as less negative. He had of course to admit that the Shah's reaction on that occasion had been discouraging, but on the other hand he declared that he still had the impression that the Shah, in his heart, still wished to redirect the silk export from Turkey to the Persian Gulf. Belchior dos Anjos's memorandum of Sept. – Oct. 1619, printed by Luz pp. 588–590.

the parties still had nothing to say to each other. The Shah liked showing Figueroa off as a strange animal in the menagerie to the foreign Ambassadors at the Persian Court, which at that time included Indian, Turkish, Russian and English envoys,[56] but when Figueroa once again tried to raise the question of the return of the Persian conquests in the Gulf Abbas turned his back and went away without answering.[57]

At an informal farewell audience on the *meidan*, the square in Isfahan, on 2nd August 1619 Figueroa finally obtained the opportunity of presenting a more detailed account of the Spanish-Portuguese points of view. The audience was characteristic for Abbas and merits further description. It was nine o'clock in the evening. Figueroa was told beforehand that the Shah was expected on the *meidan*, and had consequently set off for the square accompanied by the two priors from the Augustinian and Carmelite monasteries. The Shah arrived somewhat later, like Figueroa on horseback and surrounded by a big train of servants, courtiers and torch-bearers. As soon as he saw Figueroa he turned his horse towards him, shouting : "Hispania, Hispania." And when he reached the Ambassador he asked: "What is it you want on behalf of my brother, the King of Spain?"

Figueroa had by then written off all hope of being heard and consequently answered with a short reference to the conversations of the previous summer in Kazvin and to the note through Belchior in Farabad, but to Figueroa's surprise Abbas now wished to have more detailed information. On Abbas's orders his followers and the surrounding crowd withdrew to the edges of the square leaving an open space around them. The Shah himself sat down on the ground, bidding his "first secretary", Sara Koja, the Carmelite prior, Juan Tadeo, and the interpreter, Domingo Rodriguez from Hormuz, take their seats with the Ambassador at the somewhat unorthodox conference table. Six paces behind the Shah the guardian of the harem, Yusuf Aga, took up position with bow, arrows and scimitar.

Figueroa now plunged into a more detailed account of his mission. In accordance with his instructions he raised the first question about the common war against Turkey. Abbas instantly rejected every thought about a resumption of the war in definite terms: "breve y vulgar". He had made peace with his neighbour and would not declare war again until the Christians attacked their common enemy. Significantly enough he recalled once more with bitterness – thirteen years after – how the Christian Princes had left him in the lurch when the Emperor made peace in Sitva Torok without informing him beforehand.

56. On one occasion, amongst those present at a reception, were the Ambassadors from the Grand Mogul and Turkey, a brother of the Caliph of Mecca (sic), who was to mediate between Persia and Turkey, a Tartar prince and three envoys from Moscow. B. N. Lisboa, Ms. F. G. 580, f. 75.
57. FIGUEROA II, p. 396.

Rather undiplomatically, though also in accordance with his instructions, Figueroa then put forward the two conditions for an agreement with regard to a blockade of the Red Sea and a redirection of the silk trade – undiplomatically, because he thereby cut himself off from placing the Spanish proposals in a more attractive light. The conditions, as mentioned above, were the return of the Persian conquests and a promise that the Shah would not permit the English or any other foreigners to trade in Persia. The Shah's answer was naturally in the negative: with regard to the conquests in the Gulf, this time he produced a new reason, maintaining that the King of Hormuz, from whom Bahrein and Gombroon had formally been wrested, was a Sunnite. With regard to the second point, the expulsion of the English and other foreigners, Figueroa obtained no answer at all, although he repeated the question several times. For Figueroa, the only positive thing about the conversation was that the Shah for the first time had heard him right to the end without protesting.

The talks concluded with Figueroa requesting on his own behalf to be given a farewell audience, while on behalf of the two Orders he asked for permission to extend the buildings they already had in Isfahan. The Shah could give a reassuring answer to these requests, and when he rose to his feet after the talks were over, Abbas helped the stiff-legged Ambassador up and embraced him cordially in farewell. Figueroa has certainly felt even more lost than ever.[58]

In the meantime, in the winter of 1618/19, serious negotiations had taken place as mentioned between Robert Sherley and the Spanish ministers, negotiations that ended in the dispatch of Ruy Freire's fleet with a draft treaty in March 1619. The draft treaty was at the same time sent to Figueroa overland; it did not arrive before his farewell audience, but caught up with him between Isfahan and Gombroon in September 1619. This draft maintained the demand for the return of Gombroon, although it permitted Figueroa to show flexibility with regard to Bahrein, and repeated the demand for the expulsion of Englishmen and other alien Europeans. It is not surprising therefore that Figueroa regarded it as unnecessary to turn back and resume the negotiations on this basis; the Shah would not return the conquests and at the moment he was not at all interested in the plans for blockade and redirection. So he decided to continue his homeward journey, sending the papers to Juan Tadeo in Isfahan and authorizing the latter to continue the negotiations.[59]

58. This unusual conversation was reported by two of those present, Figueroa, FIGUEROA II pp. 407–411, and Juan Tadeo, *Chronicle* pp. 242–244. Several onlookers witnessed the audience at a distance, *Documentação Ultramarina Portuguesa* I, pp. 190–191; B. N. Lisboa, Ms. F. G. 580, f. 77; della VALLE *Persia* II:2 pp. 43–45.

59. FIGUEROA II pp. 418–421; *Chronicle* p. 243.

Thus it was Juan Tadeo who came to present Robert Sherley's draft treaty to the Shah. On 13th September he handed over the letters: one from the King of Spain, one from Robert Sherley and one from Figueroa, all of them dealing with the project concerning the blockade of the Red Sea and the redirection of the silk trade about which Robert Sherley had negotiated in Spain. The Shah handed him back the letters and asked to have them translated for the following day, but his immediate reaction to the Carmelite's verbal summary of the contents of the letters was unambiguous: the silk was to go to the highest bidder. Shortly afterwards he summoned the Carmelites, the English and the Armenians to a public auction concerning the silk export.[60]

Not until 4th October did he ask to have the translations of the letters read. His reaction to the big project of Sherley's was negative. Concerning the redirection of the silk trade he is reported to have amused himself audibly over the Spanish conditions – "si rideva di tante conditione."[61] He was not interested in the blockade of the Red Sea, and the still once more repeated demand for the return of the conquests in the Gulf made him so furious that he tore up Figueroa's letter. Characteristically enough, at the same time he smoothed everything over by declaring himself willing to continue the discussions with Redempt when he came, and shortly afterwards he gave orders that an Ambassador should be sent to Spain in reply to Figueroa's embassy.[62]

The breach was not final, but Figueroa's embassy had contributed as little as Sherley's towards an understanding between Spain-Portugal and Persia. On the contrary, it had chased away every illusion concerning common interests.

British Beginnings

It is described elsewhere how Robert Sherley had in vain sought to interest the East India Company in the redirection of the Persian silk export already during his stay in England in 1611–12. The Company had no appetite for

60. Della VALLE, *Persia* II:2 pp. 63–67.
61. *Ibid.* p. 68.
62. *Ibid.* p. 69, cf. Barker et al. to E. I. Co. 16/10 1619, *Calendar S. P. East Indies* 1617/21 p. 305 and *Documentação Ultramarina Portuguesa* I p. 194. The Ambassador mentioned should have accompanied Figueroa, but was not ready at the latter's departure from Isfahan, which undoubtedly should be considered an insult. The fate of this last embassy was significant. In 1624 it was reported in Goa that the Ambassador, Qara Sultan, had died on the journey to Europe, whereas his secretary had been taken prisoner by Algerian pirates shortly before his arrival in Lisbon. Della VALLE, *India* p. 435.

the experiment; it managed to thwart any attempt being made outside the jurisdiction of the Court of Committees, and the Court had certainly been well satisfied when it escaped with having to ship Robert Sherley home at the Company's expense. Although the sources are few it is obvious that Robert had obtained no commission from the Company before his departure. When Sherley met Kerridge, the English agent at the Court of the Grand Mogul and subsequent leader of the English factory in Surat, in Ajmer in 1614 he once more urged the English to take the initiative in the Persian trade and threatened to summon the Dutch, "who (as he saith) have been very importunate on him for it." That, at any rate as far as the official Dutch attitude was concerned, was somewhat of an exaggeration.[63]

The English initiative regarding trade with Persia did not originate in London, but in the factory in the North-West Indian port of Surat, which was established in 1612. One of the features of this town that had strongly attracted the English was the apparently very promising outlook for the sale of English cloth, and the factors had immediately sent home orders that made the Court of Committees stake their money on this traditional English export commodity to an unusual extent in the shippings of 1614 and 1615.[64] But the market was quickly saturated, the stock of unsold cloth was considerable already in 1614, and greater consignments were expected with the next fleet according to the orders sent home.[65] This was the situation when an English merchant, Richard Steele, arrived in Surat from Aleppo after a journey along the caravan routes through Persia.[66] He spoke exuberantly about the possibilities of trade in Persia; like Sherley he emphasized the silk trade, but also produced information which was most welcome in the present situation, that the possibilities for selling English cloth were very considerable in Persia.[67] Since further information had been received in Surat in August 1614 about the Persian-Portuguese conflict concerning Gombroon, there was serious talk of making a sales drive at the Persian market should the next fleet from England carry large consignments of cloth.[68]

It was decided, however, to start with a general reconnaissance of the market, and Steele was sent back to Persia accompanied by one of the factory's own servants – Crowther. The two envoys were instructed to investigate the possibilities for trade and also to contact Robert Sherley with a view to obtaining the Shah's permission to open up trade with Persia. Having accomplished these tasks they were to separate and make for

63. Aldworth & Biddulph, Surat, to E. I. Co., 19/8 1614, *Letters Received* II, p. 99.
64. CHAUDHURI pp. 15–16.
65. Aldworth & Biddulph, Surat, to E. I. Co., 19/8 1614, *Letters Received* II p. 97.
66. *loc. cit.* p. 98.
67. *Ibid.* cf. *Letters Received* II, p. 170.
68. *Ibid.* p. 99.

London and Surat respectively, in order to report their results and observations.[69]

Thereupon the matter was allowed to rest pending the arrival of the two envoys' reports. These were sent by messenger from Persia at the end of 1615, and came into the hands of the English Ambassador at the Mogul Court, Sir Thomas Roe, in February 1616. Steele and Crowther had arrived in Isfahan via Kandahar in September 1615. On their arrival they found Robert Sherley on the eve of his departure to Hormuz as the Shah's Ambassador. For very good reasons Sherley was none too pleased to see his countrymen; his situation was delicate already, and he had no wish to be suspected of additional intrigue. On the other hand he had to think of his future; a point-blank rejection of the English merchants might give rise to difficulties if his path should ever lead him to England again.[70] So, undiscovered by the Carmelites, he succeeded in establishing a secret contact between the Englishman and the Grand Vizier, which resulted in the issue of a firman, three identical copies of which were sent to England, Surat and to the Governor of the Persian port of Jask. This firman contained very little: the officials were urged to receive the Englishmen well and, if they should visit Jask or any other port, to escort them to their destination in the country and to defend them against other "franks", i.e. the Portuguese.[71] It was referring to this firman when Roe said: "It is of no consequence, for who would doubt that he would refuse us leave to trade?"[72] This was rather a severe judgement, however, which undoubtedly reflects Roe's irritation over the factors' initiative; the Spanish-Portuguese authorities at least hoped it would be possible to persuade the Shah to refuse the Englishmen entrance.

The report from Steele and Crowther was addressed to Edwardes and Aldworth, the two merchants at the head of affairs in India, at the time of their departure, but by the time Roe received the letter one of them had returned home to England and the other was dead, and Roe took advantage of this fact not only by opening the letter, but also by dealing with the matter immediately without consulting the new leaders in Surat. This action was instrumental in causing a conflict between the Ambassador and the factory that in several respects is significant. It was not only a question of competence, as to whether the opening up of trade with Persia was ultimately a political or a commercial question, but the entirely dif-

---

69. Consultations, Surat, *Letters Received* II, pp. 153–154, 170–171, 208–211, Steele's and Crowther's instructions, dated 2/1 1615, *ibid.* pp. 279–280.
70. Robert Sherley and Teresa had left their son, Henry, with Robert's family in England. PENROSE p. 200.
71. Steele's & Crowther's report, PURCHAS IV pp. 276 ff.; the firman, *ibid.* pp. 266–268.
72. ROE p. 112.

fering views of the Persian question presented by the Ambassador and the factors are revealing.

In 1615 Roe had still expressed great interest for the possibilities in Persia, and had even suggested to the Court of Committees that he himself should be sent to Persia, where he might be of greater service than at the Mogul Court.[73] But on receiving Steele's and Crowther's report in February 1616 his attitude was negative. In the meantime the report of Sherley's appointment as Ambassador to the Spanish Court had arrived. Roe believed in the reports that Sherley was empowered to offer Spain-Portugal the monopoly of the Persian silk export, and he does not seem to have doubted the feasibility of this project or that the Spanish Government would be eager to embrace such a fantastic offer. This, in spite of the fact that he invariably describes Robert Sherley in contemptuous phrases as a charlatan and a project-maker. Roe's judgement was that of the diplomat, the English diplomat under *pax hispanica*; he overestimated the Spanish-Portuguese Empire's dangerousness and potential. The English leaders in Surat apparently did not even take the risk of such a development into consideration. Where the diplomat saw a ghost, they saw a chance of getting rid of some of their cloth at a good price.

In accordance with his points of view Roe answered Steele's and Crowther's report by writing a letter to the Shah in which he gravely warned him against the crafty Spaniards and suggested that Abbas establish a protected free port in South Persia. At the same time he informed the Court of Committees that the Persian trade had no value if it was not "royally undertaken"; the English must prove that they were able to take on the total Persian silk export. Finally, he advised the factors in Surat not to take any further steps in the matter.[74]

The Surat factors had no mind to follow Roe's advice, however. They were indignant about the Ambassador having interfered in what they regarded as being a purely business matter lying beyond his powers. From a commercial point of view the report gave good reasons for optimism, and they still had to see to the excessive stocks of English cloth. After consulting the commanders of the fleet from England it was thus decided in the autumn of 1616 to send a small consignment of English goods, predominantly cloth, to Jask.[75] The initiative consequently originated exclusively from the English merchants in Surat in concert with the commanders of the fleet. To be sure, the factory received with the very same fleet the Court's permission to dispatch Steele and Crowther, and in the Court's

73. Roe to E. I. Co. 24/11 1615, ROE pp. 75–76.
74. ROE pp. 111–115.
75. Consultations, Surat, *Letters Received* IV p. 194; Connock's commission, *ibid.* pp. 220–224; cf. ROE pp. LXII–LXIII.

letter (according to the report of the consultation that initiated the dispatch of the expedition) one could read that it was "encouraging them for the future", but the reference is so vague that one might be justified in concluding that the Court had not given any orders or express authority for the Persian initiative.[76]

The first English expedition to Persia touched at Jask in December 1616. A cargo was landed to the value of £6,333 of which £550 was in cash – not a tremendous investment.[77] The leader of the English expedition, Connock, who, as secretary to the Ambassador in Constantinople, had had previous experience as regards Levant trade and politics,[78] was an exuberant person. It is said of him that he was "very forward, and in my conscience had rather hazard your ship, goods and men than be disappointed of his employment."[79] Thus, to distinguish between the hopes and the facts in the enthusiastic letters he sent to the Court during the next year is difficult, and the possibility of controlling the letters by comparing them with those of others taking part in the expedition is limited by the fact that the English merchants soon divided themselves into two parties around Connock and the next-in-command, Barker, respectively, who maligned and irritated one another as best they could.

Connock's commission and the consultations preceding the embarkation of the expedition from Surat anticipated a procedure the main features of which were as follows: Connock, as soon as the goods were unloaded and safely stored, was to go to the Court in order to procure a more detailed firman: "conditions of peace and privileges for trade." Thereafter he was to attend to the sale of the imported goods and invest the proceeds in the return goods for England, first and foremost silk. There was no suggestion herein of highflown plans for a redirection of the Persian silk export, let alone a monopoly on the export of Persian silk. The factors in Surat in all modesty saw a possibility of doing some good business, because the war had made it difficult to supply English cloth to Persia through Turkey, and because there was a stock of cloth in Surat that was difficult to sell.[80]

But if Connock had originally intended to stick to these moderate instructions, it was at any rate not long before he was seized by the Persian disease of project-making. The infection can be traced back to the old bacteria-carrier, Robert Sherley, even though, paradoxically enough, it was transferred through the prosaic Sir Thomas Roe, whose above mention-

76. Consultation, Swally Road, 2/10 1616, *Letters Received* IV pp. 189 ff.
77. Connock & Barker, Jask, to E. I. Co., 19/1 1617, *Letters Received* V pp. 56–60; cf. *ibid.* p. 60 ff., pp. 65–66.
78. P. R. O. London, S. P. 105/110 f. 63.
79. Thomas Doughty, Surat, to E. I. Co., 26/2 1617, *Letters Received* V, p. 102.
80. *loc. cit.* above n. 75.

ed letters of February 1617 Connock opened on his arrival in Isfahan.[81] In April 1617 Connock, too, was convinced that it was Sherley's task to negotiate in Spain concerning a monopoly on the export of Persian silk, and like Roe he regarded it as probable that Spain could and would accept the offer, such that "as well we as the French, Hollanders and Italians, shall be forced of them to re-buy if not request for ready moneys, wherewith they may yearly supply and support this silken trade, the only richest yet known in the world."[82] But Connock, unlike Roe, did not give up in advance in the face of the Spanish-Portuguese Empire; he thought the chance of the English lay in daring action. Referring to the stronger English ships and to the English experience in trading with Persian silk from Aleppo, the Shah was to be persuaded to grant the monopoly to the English Company, and he asked the Court to grant him the authority to carry out this plan as soon as possible. Connock was of course merchant enough to realize that a business, which he himself valued at an annual turnover of one million pounds sterling with a purchase price of 6s. per lb. of 16 oz., far exceeded the capacity of the Company, but he held out the prospects to the Company that the Shah would be personally willing to finance the export, either by entering the business himself or by advancing the silk on credit. He does not reveal the basis of these magnificent hopes, and his ideas concerning the ability of great Princes seem to have been somewhat naive: "Now that this may be effected is not without great hope, since we see that with princes large sums and great undertakings that promise either honour or benefit (as this doth both) are as soon performed and trivially accounted of as by poor men and poorer thoughts they are accounted to be great or even hideous."[83] But the possibility that he really had received an offer of credit cannot be excluded. In a strange, exited letter to one of the other English factors in Persia he intimates something of this nature, even though he expresses himself with as much mystery and histrionics as the villain in a Jacobite melodrama: "Hear me, if you are your own and country's friend. I am here proffered by the King's lieutenant one hundred thousand pounds sterling worth of silk, to be paid for in one year or two in goods and money. Of this I pray you no words."[84]

In July 1617 Connock visited the Shah himself, who was with his army on the Turkish border, 25 days' march from Isfahan. Also present at the discussions was an Augustinian, most probably Belchior dos Anjos, but if we are to believe Connock, he had no difficulty in persuading the Shah of the injustice in the accusations of piracy the Portuguese directed against

81. *Letters Received* V p. 188 n. 2.
82. Connock, Isfahan, to E. I. Co. 2/4 1617, *Letters Received* V p. 189.
83. *Ibid* p. 191.
84. Connock, Isfahan, to Pley, Shiraz, 10/4 1617, *Letters Received* V p. 198.

the English, and that it was the Portuguese alone who were responsible for the clashes between the two nations' ships. At the ceremonial handing over of the presents on 3rd August 1617, three weeks after Connock's arrival at the camp, the Shah – still according to Connock – seemed particularly interested in Connock's proposal; he promised to deliver 3,000 bales of silk on credit, 500 of them already in the first year.[85]

Connock seems in good faith to have believed in his triumph. He already had visions of a total redirection of the Persian silk trade and of London as the world market for Persian silk. Already the day after the audience he sent the offer by messenger via Aleppo to London, urging the Court most earnestly not to let this unique chance slip through their fingers.

A gap in the correspondence debars us from following Connock's further negotiations, but we know the formal result: that firman which up to 1629 constituted the legal basis for the English nation in Persia.[86] If this firman is compared with other Persian or Turkish privileges it is conspicuous that they were extraordinarily wide concessions the Shah was willing to grant the English in 1617. By comparing, for instance, the firman issued to the English in 1629, after Abbas's death, it may be ascertained that not least the religious concessions were more extensive in the firman of 1617.[87] In 1617, unlimited freedom is granted to build churches and hold services (article 8); the Ambassador may imprison and repatriate English renegades (article 10); the English themselves may choose and lay out a burial ground (article 18). In 1629 the religious concessions are less comprehensive: the English are allowed general freedom of conscience, but renegades are to be allowed to settle in Persia and live there in peace (article 14), and with regard to burial it merely says that the English may undertake burials in those places where other Christians are buried. The jurisdictional rights, too, were more comprehensive in 1617 than in 1629.

85. Connock et al., the Court, to E. I. Co., 4/8 1617, *Letters Received* VI pp. 31 ff. The letter was sent through the consul in Aleppo, who was ordered in the covering letter to forward it as soon as possible and without thought to the costs, "For I let know they are of high importance, such as to like purpose never passed from Aleppo." One must hope that the consul did not become curious, because the letter to the Court of Committees also contained an exhortation not to let the trade with Turkey interfere with the Persian project.
86. Foster was of the opinion that no copy of the firman of 1617 had been preserved, and printed instead the firman of 1629, which he presumed to be identical in contents and form. *Letters Received* VI p. 293 n. 1. However, the firman is preserved in the Dutch material in several mutually corroborating versions (French, Italian and Dutch). DUNLOP pp. 675 ff., van DAM II:3, pp. 328–331.
87. The Dutch text in Dunlop is compared here with the 1629 firman in *Letters Received* VI pp. 293 ff.

In 1617 the English were allowed criminal jurisdiction in mixed cases, and the Ambassador's house was granted extra-territorial rights and the right of asylum, whereas in 1629 that right was reduced to the right to be represented along with Persian judges in more important cases.

But just as important as the granting of the extensive concessions in 1617 is the fact that there were many wishes on the part of the English that Abbas had been unwilling to accommodate. In the Dutch version of the 1617 firman two articles are listed about which it is briefly noted that they were rejected by the Shah. One was a minor point: the right in general to buy back Christian slaves; but the other was very important: the monopoly of the Persian silk export. Neither was the proposal that had made Connock dizzy with expectation – the offer of credit with regard to the silk export – mentioned in the firman. Finally there seems to have been a certain lack of clarity – perhaps deliberate on Connock's part – with regard to the Englishmen's customs obligations. The Dutch version says: "That the English should not pay any dues or customs like the Franks must do in Constantinople and in Aleppo, but that the goods or capitals which they import or export should be exempt from every customs, but that they shall merely pay *rahdaris* (a special duty charged for the payment of "highway police"), since that is a very old custom."[88] In two letters from Connock's successors, Barker[89] and Monox,[90] both from April 1618, it is nevertheless maintained that the firman did not contain any promises of customs exemption, even if Connock had given the impression by a fallacious translation of the firman in the copy that was sent home in the autumn of 1617. On the contrary, a custom of 10% on all imports and exports was expressly reckoned with. However, the Shah – when and in which form is not revealed – had later proclaimed that it was contrary to his intentions and that the English should be exempted from customs.[91] It is undeniable that, unlike the Dutch, the English were not at any time expected to pay customs.

Thus the firman did not correspond to Connock's hopes and not at all to the prospects he had held out to the Company in his letter of 4th August 1617, but it was in all modesty a good result in accordance with the first point in his instructions: he had procured "conditions of peace and privileges for trade." Also the remaining tasks in the instructions – the sale of the imported goods and purchase of return goods – were carried out. The imported goods were sold to the Royal factor, Lala Beg, the latter being ordered by the Shah to take over the Company's goods at market prices

88. DUNLOP p. 675.
89. Barker to Roe, April 1618, C. R. O. London, O. C. 792.
90. Monox, Isfahan, to E. I. Co., 18/4 1618, C. R. O. London, O. C. 586:2.
91. *Letters Received* VI p. 293 n. 1.

against payment in raw silk. Should there be any disagreement about the correct price, private merchants were to mediate between Lala Beg and the English. This order was rather unfavourable for the English, however; at any rate they had the impression that the private merchants did not dare to oppose the powerful Royal factor.[92] For the goods Connock received a consignment of silk consisting of 71 bales, i.e. roughly corresponding to the value of the goods the English had imported. With this consignment, Connock travelled in the end of 1617 with a caravan from Isfahan towards Jask in order to meet the English ship expected from Surat. It proved impossible to ship the goods, however; before the caravan reached the coast it was arrested on the orders of Lala Beg. At the same time Connock was informed that the English ship to Jask had not brought any new capital, but instructions from the Court of Committees and Roe, which demanded new negotiations with the Shah before any new investments were made in Persia.[93] A few days afterwards Connock suddenly died. Whether it was sorrow and exhaustion that deprived the sanguine Connock of his life,[94] or whether he had been poisoned, as the rumour went,[95] cannot be determined. Connock became the first of a number of English agents in Persia who died after an uncannily short time in office.

The English initiative in Persia got off to a false start. It was begun on a limited scale by the factors in Surat. Roe opposed it because he perceived the widespread political complications that might result from the Persian trade, but it was precisely this point of view that had made Connock so ambitious and so eager to persuade the Court of Committees to think likewise. At the end of 1617 neither the more modest nor the more comprehensive project seemed to have any possibilities. The thought of an economic partnership with the Shah seemed to have been pure phantasy, and not even the year's return cargo had got as far as being shipped.

The Loss of Hormuz

In the meantime the Court of Committees in London had had the opportunity of considering the plans for trading with Persia, partly on the basis of Steele's and Crowther's report and partly on that of Roe's letters of 1615, in which he had still been in favour of Persian trade and even offered to travel to Persia himself.[96] Unfortunately we do not know the details of

---

92. Pettus, Isfahan, to E. I. Co., 27/9 1618, C. R. O. London, O. C. 699.
93. *Loc. cit.* above n. 90; cf. *Letters Received* VI p. 284.
94. *Letters Received* VI p. XVI.
95. della VALLE, *Persia* II:1 p. 300.
96. Roe to E. I. Co., 24/11 1615, ROE pp. 72 ff.; Richard Steele to E. I. Co. *First Letter Book* pp. 457 ff.

the Court's deliberations in this connection because of an interruption in the series of Court Minutes, but we are able to ascertain from other evidence that the Court was now interested in the Persian trade. In January 1617 the Governor laid Roe's letter before the Privy Council, who urged the Company to proceed with the matter,[97] and in the following month a complimentary letter from James I to Abbas was completed and obtained through Winwood.[98]

Most likely because the project was regarded as politically complicated the Court not only took the unusual step to communicate its considerations to the Privy Council, but it also decided to deprive the factors in Surat of the ultimate responsibility for the Persian trade and transfer it to the Ambassador at the Court of the Grand Mogul, Sir Thomas Roe. The Court's view of the matter was communicated to him in detailed instructions that must have been completed early in 1617, i.e. before the Court was aware of the initiative the factors had taken when they had sent Connock to Persia some months previously.[99] Already at that time the Court was contemplating a redirection of the silk trade, and had thus eventually – probably through Roe – been taken in by Sherley's project. It nevertheless called for circumspection; two phases in the establishment of the trade were foreseen: a meticulous collection of information about the Persian silk trade, followed by direct negotiations with Abbas. The Company declared itself willing to buy up to 8,000 bales of 180 lb. per annum, but it set up formidable conditions, such as fixed customs rates, fixed prices on both import and export goods, (the tariff the Court was willing to accept was enclosed) and the establishment of a protected port to serve as a place of exchange for the Persian and European goods.

The instructions of the Court of Committees reached India at the end of 1617. It was a personal triumph for Roe, who had opposed the appointment of Connock in 1616 and been indignant over the factors in Surat having acted without consulting him. He celebrated his taking over responsibility by ordering that no further capital should be supplied to the factory in Persia before the conditions demanded by the Company in its instructions had been fulfilled.[100] Instead he drew up a commission for the management of the Persian factory authorizing it to negotiate on his behalf within the limits set by the instructions of the Court. To the letter from the Court he added his own detailed instructions for the Persian business. These papers became the Persian factory's only "import" in 1617/18.[101]

97. *Letters Received* VI p. XV.
98. ROE p. 503 f. and p. 503 n. 1.
99. *First Letter Book* p. 455 ff.
100. Roe, Mandu, to the factors, Surat, 8/10 1617, ROE p. 398 ff.
101. Commission and instructions printed in *Letters Received* VI pp. 107–113.

In accordance with these orders Barker, who succeeded Connock as agent, went to the Court in Kazvin in the summer of 1618, i.e. at the same time as Figueroa arrived at Court. The negotiations were carried on with great discretion; Figueroa remained ignorant of their subject-matter, which is not so surprising perhaps, but even the otherwise so well-informed della Valle was unable to procure reliable information. Not that there was much to boast about. Customs exemption, which had possibly been granted the English in the firman of 1617, was ratified, but this was the only of the Court's wishes that could be fulfilled. Abbas was willing to buy the whole of the English import of goods, but this was to be at market price – he would not bind himself to the Company's tariff. As to the wish for a fortified port, possibly Jask, the Shah entirely dismissed this.[102] Thus the results in Persia 1618 were not encouraging for the English, but on the other hand the factors in Surat had in the meantime succeeded in convincing Roe of the opportuneness of proceeding with the plans for the Persian trade, even if the results of the negotations were not yet available, and with the ship from Surat 1618/19 the Persian factory eventually received a considerable working capital.[103] However, as time was to show, the path for a regular trade was not opened thereby. That very year, 1619, Abbas determined to take decisive action regarding the silk trade.

Since Anthony Sherley's first proposal in 1608 Abbas had been showered with communications from Europe concerning a redirection of the Persian silk trade; as late as January 1619 he had received while in Farabad the Spanish Government's offer as negotiated with Robert Sherley and forwarded by Figueroa through Belchior dos Anjos. His answer had been negative: the basis for his earlier interest for the plan no longer existed, he had made peace with Turkey and decided in future to let the silk export follow the traditional routes. But naturally it was unavoidable that he himself or people in his entourage had gradually become aware of the possibilities the situation contained for an increase in the Crown revenue. The roads had been closed during the campaign of 1618, and if we are to believe della Valle, in January or February 1619 Abbas let an Armenian delegation know that there could be no question of reopening the export because the peace with Turkey was only feigned. During the talks, to the indignation of the others, one of the minor Armenian merchants made an offer of an export duty of five tomans per load on condition the routes were opened. Abbas jumped at this offer and said that if this was the case he would recommend the immediate opening up of the export.[104]

---

102. Pettus, Isfahan, to E. I. Co., 30/11 1618, C. R. O. London, O. C. 699; cf. *Calendar S. P. East Indies* 1617/21, p. 198.
103. *English Factories* 1618/21 p. 55.
104. Della VALLE, *Persia* II:1 pp. 465–466.

From here to a Royal monopoly trade in Persia's most important export commodity was not very far. Already in 1619 Abbas took the consequences and "caused it to be published that all silks made throughout his whole dominion shall be brought into his treasury and there to receive money for the same . . ."[105]

In September Abbas proceeded to fix the price under the new monopoly. In 1617 the English in Isfahan had paid Lala Beg a price that presumably lay somewhat above the market price, 250–270 shahi per man-i shah,[106] i.e. 45–48.6 tomans per load. Shortly after receiving Sherley's final draft treaty through Juan Tadeo in September 1619 Abbas decided to put the silk up for auction; the English, the Carmelites, with Juan Tadeo at their head, and the Armenians were called to a public divan. Juan immediately declared that he was not authorized to participate in the bidding, however; he might only act according to the instructions given him by Figueroa. The Armenians on their part hesitated to make the first bid, but they eventually bid a price that undoubtedly lay somewhat above the ordinary market price, i.e. 50 tomans per load of 36 man-i shah. The English, on the contrary, would not bid higher than 43.2 tomans per load.[107]

At an audience some days later Abbas tried to press the English to take just a small consignment at the price offered by the Armenians, but they refused, insisting that the Armenians' price was conditioned by deferred payment until the proceeds of the sale were brought back from Aleppo, whereas it was demanded of the English that they paid cash. When the King denied this to be the case the English replied that in that event the Armenians would be trading at a loss, and insisted that they themselves could not possibly contemplate making any purchases whatsoever at that price. Privately the English thought that the Armenian offer was not a true offer, but a show staged in order to entice them to bid higher. They therefore reckoned that a buyers' strike would automatically bring down the price again, and the decision to refrain from making any purchases in the current year was confirmed by a Council meeting in Isfahan on 24th September.[108]

It is probable that the factors also banked on the Royal monopoly not being put into force immediately; at any rate they made sure of obtaining permission to buy privately. But "the King's minde was too well knowne and published", and so nobody dared to offer them silk at a lower price than the King demanded. The silk that had entered the King's stocks with

105. Barker et al., Isfahan, to E. I. Co., C. R. O. London, O. C. 815. Della Valle assigns the introduction of the monopoly to September, *Persia* II:2 p. 67.
106. Barker to Roe, April 1618, C. R. O. London, O. C. 792.
107. Barker et al., Isfahan, to E. I. Co. 16/10 1619, C. R. O. London, O. C. 815; della VALLE, *Persia* II:2 p. 66 f.
108. C. R. O. London, O. C. 717.

a view to selling it to the English he sent to Venice.[109] This is presumably the consignment described in 1621 in Venice as being in the merchant, Sassuar's keeping.[110]

The monopoly proved to be effective, and the price increase seriously intended. With the fleet of 1619/20 the English factory again received a considerable capital, including 138,000 piastres in cash.[111] Normally an import of that size should have strengthened the bargaining power of the English – in previous years the Persians had been quick enough to point out that the English import chiefly consisted of English goods with a limited demand in Persia – but the fear of being left with so much on their hands turned the buyers' strike against the English themselves. In May 1620 it was decided to make a last attempt to bring down the silk price by sending Monox, who had succeeded Barker as agent that same year, to the Court. But the English had by then already realized the weakness of their position. They knew their only possibility of procuring returns was to buy the Shah's silk, and they knew that the Shah could perfectly well get rid of his silk without the help of the English Company. They therefore decided to make some purchases of silk immediately, irrespective of whether they succeeded in forcing the price down or not. On the other hand they hoped that some of the loss they incurred because of the high price would be offset by the Shah offering them credit, possibly on the security of the stock of unsold goods that lay in the factory.[112]

They did not succeed in getting the price down, nor in obtaining credit, and Abbas did not keep his previous promise to buy the whole of the English import of goods. The English nevertheless made considerable purchases in accordance with their decision, but although the Persians thereby dictated their own conditions the English felt that in actual fact they did not care whether the English bought or not.[113] This situation continued the following year, during which the English were once again able to control a considerable capital, a large proportion of it in ready cash. Immediately after the arrival of the 1620/21 fleet they requested that 500–600 bales of that year's harvest might be reserved for them, which must undeniably have weakened their attempts to force the prices down. But the factors felt, certainly correctly, that they had struck the wrong time to open up trade: the Shah was not interested in the export route towards the south so long as the route through Turkey remained open.[114]

109. *Loc. cit.* above n. 107.
110. BERCHET, *Persia*, p. 214.
111. Bell, Shiraz, to Monox, Isfahan, 8/5 1620, C. R. O. London, O. C. 864.
112. Consultations, Isfahan, 10/5 1620, C. R. O. London, O. C. 865.
113. Monox et al., Isfahan, to. E. I. Co., 30/9 1621, C. R. O. London, Factory Records, Persia I, p. 66.
114. B. M. London, Egerton Ms. 2123 f. 26.

The Shah's negative attitude is so much the more remarkable because in the years following 1619 the relations between the Persians and the Portuguese steadily worsened, whereas in January 1621 the English on their part had the chance of proving that they could be a valuable ally in the Persian Gulf. As mentioned above, in connection with its revision of the Persian policy in August 1618 the Spanish Government had decided to send an armada to the Red Sea and the Persian Gulf (see above, p. 311). The armada of five galleons left Lisbon in April 1619; the dispatch had been carried through with unusual efficiency, but the voyage was delayed by bad weather, and it was not until June 1620 that the armada dropped anchor off Hormuz. The wording of the armada's instructions was ambiguous. It could have been regarded as Spain's answer to Robert Sherley's proposal on behalf of the Shah to blockade the Red Sea in connection with a redirection of the silk trade, but there is scarcely any doubt that its primary task was to safeguard Hormuz against a Persian attack and against the English naval forces.

The events immediately before the arrival of the fleet had done nothing to strengthen the bonds of friendship between the Portuguese and the Persians. In the autumn of 1619 it was rumoured in Isfahan that Abbas had sworn to reconquer Hormuz,[115] and in the following spring a minor force under the Khan of Shiraz attacked some Arab tribes who were regarded as vassals of the King of Hormuz.[116] Redempt, Robert Sherley's Carmelite companion, might have been able to reopen the negotiations; in October 1619 Abbas had still declared himself willing to resume the talks with him as mediator, but he had died before Ruy Freire's fleet reached Hormuz.

Apparently in the summer of 1620 there was a certain amount of disagreement among the Portuguese leaders in Hormuz as to the best course to take after having obtained with the fine galleons a real instrument of power. In the event of the death or absence of both Redempt and Figueroa they were instructed by the Spanish King to send a prominent man, possibly the *veedor de fazenda,* from Hormuz to the Shah as Ambassador, in order to continue the negotiations commenced by Sherley. In view of the fact that the relations between the Khan of Shiraz's people and Hormuz's vassals was already that of open conflict, and the contents of Sherley's draft treaty had already been laid before the Shah and been met with total rejection, even ridicule, the leaders in Hormuz did not feel themselves bound by the instructions. Ruy Freire was eager for an immediate confrontation and he manifested his intentions immediately on his arrival by denying his crew shore leave. The Captain of Hormuz and the

---

115. Della VALLE, *Persia* II:1 pp. 238–239; C. R. O. London, O. C. 815.
116. FIGUEROA II pp. 465–467; della VALLE, *Persia* II:2 pp. 116, 142.

veedor, on the other hand, were eager for a resumption of the negotiations, no matter, as della Valle remarks, whether this was because they were better informed about local conditions, or whether it was because they foresaw personal economic losses should the trade be broken off within their particular time of office.[117]

The Portuguese leaders in Hormuz obtained the advice of the experienced Fathers, both the Carmelites and the Augustinians in Isfahan. For once they were in agreement in sizing up the situation: further negotiations with the Shah would be hopeless and the dispatch of an Ambassador would only complicate the issue because he would get into difficulties if it came to an open breach. The Augustinians even went so far as to declare that they would register a formal protest should an envoy be sent from Hormuz to Persia.[118] Thus Ruy Freire obtained support in his intransigent policy, but before the conflict had developed any further, he himself changed his mind, presumably after receiving new information from Spain.[119] An English fleet could be expected in Jask in the winter of 1620/21 and Ruy Freire decided once and for all to demonstrate the realities behind the Portuguese demand for the control of these waters by blockading the Persian coast and driving away the English fleet.[120]

With this a temporary lessening of tension in the Persian-Portuguese relations set in. The Portuguese let it be widely known that their armada was only directed against the English, and that the Persians had nothing to fear from the reinforcement of the Portuguese forces in the Persian Gulf. Abbas on his part let it be known that he would not take any final decision with regard to the Portuguese before he had seen the outcome of the expected encounter between the English and the Portuguese. And della Valle comments: "I am in no doubt that the question of peace or war between the Portuguese and the Persians greatly depends on what happens between the Portuguese and the English this year."[121]

The background for the Portuguese decision was undoubtedly their consciousness of a momentary naval superiority off the Persian coast, but it turned out that they had underestimated the strength of the English Company ships. From November on Ruy Freire cruised off Jask with five ships and more than a thousand men; in the end of December the English fleet of four ships arrived, Ruy Freire tried to cut off the English from the coast,

117. Della VALLE, *Persia* II:2 pp. 141–142.
118. *Ibid.* pp. 149–150, 154–155.
119. BOXER, *Commentaries* p. 17; *Relations* pp. 66–67.
120. BOXER, *Commentaries*, pp. 16–17. At this point there was a half-hearted attempt on the part of the Portuguese to establish contact with Abbas again, the Carmelites from Hormuz being ordered to visit the Shah. The plan was abandoned, however, on account of the Shah's absence. Della VALLE, *Persia* II:2 pp. 155–156, 158–164; Arch. Vaticano, Fondo Gonfalonieri 65, f. 11.
121. Della VALLE, *Persia* II:2 pp. 194–195.

but after one day's hard fight he had to withdraw. The next day the English ships succeeded in reaching Jask, where they hurriedly landed the goods for the Persian factory and took the returns on board. Ruy Freire did not give up, however, although he had suffered severe losses during the first encounter. A fresh attack when the English left Jask and set sail for Surat did not prove more fortunate for the Portuguese than the first one, however. Once again it was Ruy Freire who suffered the greatest losses, whereas the English were able to continue the voyage to India unhindered.[122] The defeat off Jask was characteristic of the misfortunes that struck the Spanish-Portuguese Empire on all fronts during those years. Ruy Freire's fleet was a galleon fleet, equipped solely with military opperations in view. His opponent, Andrew Shilling, had one ship less at his disposal and his ships were essentially trading vessels, though equipped for defence. The Portuguese did not lack initiative or personal courage, but the figures covering the losses reveal a glaring incongruity between the tactical potentials of the two fleets. The Portuguese losses were 160, the English, 8.[123]

The English victory naturally attracted attention in Persia, in March 1621 the opinion in Isfahan was that Abbas would take the consequences and launch an attack against Hormuz. In his report of March 1621 Monox emphasized Hormuz's potential value for the English Company, but he mentions nothing to the effect that negotiations might already be going on. At any rate Abbas showed no signs of being impressed by the English when, in the summer of 1621, they were received in special audience in order to hand over a handsome present. Amongst other things the gift comprised a coach, which the Shah rejected, declaring that he was not a stone to be dragged from place to place in a cart, because he on his part preferred to go about on horseback as long as he lived. And, he added, his subjects were of the same mind.[124] The only part of the present Abbas accepted was a mirror and two dogs.[125] The English naturally wished to seize this opportunity in order to talk business, especially regarding the

122. BOXER, *Commentaries,* pp. 21–30; Richard Swan's account, *ibid.* pp. 250–254; *English Factories* 1618/21 pp. 200–225; CORDEIRO pp. 27–40; della VALLE, *Persia* II:2 pp. 200–202.
123. The difference between the Portuguese and the North-West European ships was undoubtedly of a technical nature, but the technique was closely connected with the function of the ships and to the whole economic and social structure of the society concerned. See, for instance BOXER, *Portuguese Empire,* pp. 299–300.
124. *Chronicle* p. 255.
125. Monox et al., Isfahan, to E. I. Co. 15/6 1621, C. R. O., London, Factory Records Surat, 102, f. 246. When, some years afterwards, there was a question of closing down the factory, there was a coach amongst the items that proved to be difficult to turn into cash. Barker et al., Isfahan, to E. I. Co. 30/5–28/8 1624, C. R. O., London, O. C. 1159.

silk price, but the Shah let them understand through one of his men that he regarded business to be an unsuitable topic of conversation because of the presence of the Carmelites. Instead, on Abbas's initiative, the discussion concerned the number of nails in the Cross as well as the Catholic contra the Protestant version of the Testaments. The Shah also took the opportunity of comparing the English trustworthiness with that of the Spanish King, who had promised to go to war with Turkey several times, but had never kept his promise.[126]

The audience in 1621 is characteristic of Abbas's diplomacy; we are fairly safe in assuming that he had arranged for the Carmelites to be present, and, had he no wish to discuss the silk trade, this was surely deliberate; the English had won a victory, but he had no intention of throwing himself into their arms as a consequence; the possibility of a military alliance was left unmentioned. Nevertheless, within the very same month the tension in the Persian Gulf was succeeded by open conflict.

Following the defeat off Jask Ruy Freire proceeded to the next item in his instructions: the fortification of Qishm. In view of the fact that the Portuguese forces were absolutely not in a suitable condition to undertake large-scale operations, the authorities in Hormuz presumably had not only reckoned with reinforcements from Goa,[127] but had hoped that the fortifications of Qishm would not be regarded by the Persians as giving cause for war. But it is doubtful whether the relief from Goa got through, and it is obvious that the fortification of Qishm was regarded by Abbas as a gross provocation. The first reports about the Portuguese move reached Isfahan on one of the last days of June. The Shah's secretary told the English factory's interpreter in confidence that the Shah was pleased to obtain a *casus belli* in this way; he now intended to drive the Portuguese out of Hormuz, and when it was done he would give the English Gombroon. Monox found the offer favourable; he thought the Company would thereby be in a position to control the trade between India and Persia, but he also pointed out that it would demand the full force of six small ships of 100 tons and 4 big ships in order to undertake protection.[128] Although this is a question of a confidential report the secretary's information regarding the Shah's intentions seems to indicate that the plans at this point have been clear, because the goal described – that Hormuz should be de-

---

126. The audience described in *Chronicle* pp. 252–253; Arch. Vaticano, Fondo Gonfalonieri 65, ff. 12–17; Monox et al., Isfahan, to E. I. Co., 15/6 1621 C. R. O. London, Factory Records, Surat, 102, f. 246; in the last mentioned the Carmelites' interference elicited the English correspondent's deeply felt comment: "Ell diavolo leva los frailes for hindrance of our busines . . ."

127. Immediately after the defeat at Jask was reported in Goa it was decided to send two galleons to strengthen Ruy Freire's squadrons, *Assentos* I pp. 120–122.

128. Monox et al., Isfahan, to E. I. Co., 15/6 1621, C. R. O. Factory Records, Surat, 102, ff. 251–252.

molished and the trade moved to Gombroon – comes to correspond very well with the events of the subsequent years.

Abbas made yet another attempt to solve the problem by negotiation, however. In June he summoned the Augustinians and informed them that he regarded the fortification of Qishm to be a hostile action, and he therefore wished one of the Augustinians to travel to Hormuz immediately to ask whether the leaders there wanted peace or war. The Augustinians willingly fulfilled his wish and dispatched a man, but he was secretly instructed to advise the leaders in Hormuz to choose war.[129]

The leaders in Hormuz were as frivolous as the Augustinians in Isfahan. In September the Augustinian returned with an answer that was as good as a declaration of war. The Portuguese in Hormuz let the Shah know that they did not desire war, but only intended to safeguard the water supply from Qishm for the island and the town. But even before the Shah received that answer his soldiers were on the way towards the Persian Gulf. He himself was preparing for a campaign against the Indian border fortress of Kandahar, so he ordered the Khan of Shiraz to place himself at the head of the campaign against Hormuz. On 20th October the Viceroy and Council in Goa were informed about the war; 10,000 men were said to be on their way towards the coast, and in Hormuz everything was lacking for the defence of the fortress: guns, ammunition and, above all, soldiers. In Goa the leaders were immediately aware of the dangers of the situation: a big English fleet was expected to touch at Persia during the winter and Persian-English co-operation was foreseen. Although there was a shortage of men and weapons in Goa, too, an armada consisting of ten small vessels was fitted out and sent to Hormuz under Simão de Melo, in time to take part in the defence.[130]

The crucial point in this conflict from a military angle was the control of the sea. Some few years before the fall of Hormuz the Portuguese still regarded it as impregnable, but this was based on their experience of the inferiority of the traditional enemies, both with regard to guns and ships. But the battle at Jask had revealed that there was now another force in the Gulf, superior to the Portuguese on both these counts. Ruy Freire ran an incredible risk when he began the fortification of Qishm and refused the last offer of negotiation, although he acted in accordance with his instructions and with the advice he received from the Augustinians in Isfahan. The danger of a coalition between the two powers, who would be able to wipe out his modest forces with the greatest of ease, was so obvious that his action must be characterized as either a gigantic misjudgement or a histrionic gesture.

It cannot be determined with certainty when the first negotiations con-

129. Della VALLE, *Persia*, II:2 pp. 241–242.
130. *Assentos* I, p. 123.

cerning a military co-operation between the English and the Persians took place, but there is no reference in the sources to any concrete discussions before November 1621, when the annual English return cargo was being transported from Isfahan to the coast.[131] The Persian proposal was accompanied by pressure, at any rate that was what the English leaders themselves maintained; if they did not agree to co-operate they would be prevented from conveying their goods to the coast. Monox at first played for time: he could not take any final decision before he had contacted the ships and the question had been discussed in the ship's council, but he did not conceal the fact that he himself would support the proposal. Perhaps the rumours of these negotiations reached Hormuz. At any rate Ruy Freire tried at the last moment to avert the threatened danger by reopening the negotiations, informing the Khan of Shiraz in the beginning of December that he did not think old friends should go to war about a drop of water; he offered to pay all the expenses the Persians had so far incurred in connection with the campaign on conditions the troops were withdrawn. Whether in addition he offered to give up Qishm does not appear.[132] But the proposal was rejected without hesitation by the Khan.[133]

As soon as Monox was informed of the English fleet's arrival at Jask – this year no less than seven ships – he travelled to the coast to lay the Persian proposal before the ship's council. The latter decided to accept the proposal, supporting itself partly on the commanders' commission from Surat, which, in reaction to Ruy Freire's attack the previous year, allowed them to take the offensive if they saw therein their best defence, and partly on the emergency that had arisen as a result of the Persian threat to arrest the annual returns. On 18th January Monox, together with Bell, who was to succeed him as agent, visited the Khan in Minab with the positive answer of the ship's council and the draft of an agreement, and already the following day they received the Khan's acceptance of the agreement with a few modifications, which they immediately brought to the fleet.[134]

The articles agreed upon are preserved in two versions, which differ from one another in essential points. Both versions, however, stipulated that

---

131. The silence of the sources, however, constitutes no proof of Monox not having made a promise at an earlier date; since such a promise would clearly lie beyond his powers, he would under no circumstances have mentioned it in his correspondence with Surat or England. Already in September 1621 the Carmelites describe the English as the Persians' allies, *Chronicle* p. 258, but the first certain information of the English-Persian discussions concerning military co-operation is from 3rd December, della VALLE *Persia* II:2 p. 335.
132. Della VALLE *Persia* II:2 pp. 339–340.
133. *Ibid.* p. 345.
134. Monox's account of the negotiations in "History at large of the taking of Ormuz Castle", printed in BOXER, *Commentaries*, pp. 256–257; Blyth et al., Gombroon Road, to Surat 7/2 1622, *English Factories* 1622/23, p. 31 ff; della VALLE, *Persia* II:2, pp. 346, 364.

the profit from the conquest and future customs receipts should be divided
equally between the contracting parties; the Shah's, the Khan's and the
Company's goods should in the future be exempted from customs, but on
all other goods, including those on board the ships of the contracting
parties, customs should be paid. The expenses for the English ships' ammunition and victuals should, as long as the campaign lasted, be shared
equally. If necessary the English promised to allow the English ships to
remain in the Persian Gulf after the fall of Hormuz in order to help
repulse any possible Portuguese counter-attacks. The disagreements first
and foremost concerned the very important matter as to who was to have
the fortress when it was wrested from the Portuguese. The lack of clarity
can scarcely be an accident; presumably either the Khan deceived the English or Monox wished to give the impression of a more favourable situation
than actually existed.[135]

135. The preserved versions are 1) a copy sent from Surat to Java, now in C. R. O.
London, Factory Records, Java III:1 p. 301, printed in *English Factories* 1622/
23 pp. 13 ff., 2) A copy in C. R. O. Factory Records, Persia, 1, p. 104. The
publisher of *English Factories* preferred the Java version; since, however, the
Persian Factory Records version must have been entered in the volume in
January 1622, it must represent the basis on which the English thought they
were fighting. Monox's report to the Court of Committees, which was presumably compiled during his return journey or after his return home, refers to the
agreement in accordance with the Java version. BoxER, *Commentaries*, p. 257.
The two versions of the decisions regarding the fortress's future are as follows:

Java	*Persia*
That if it please God that	God granting that wee may
Jeroone be conquered,	over come the castle,
that a governour of ours	that halfe Englishe, halfe
and an other governour of	Persians shall remain therin;
the Englishe remaine in the	
castle,	
and shall joyntly ayde and	the one to doe nothing
asist on the other in all	without mutuall consent of
accurrances and accidents,	the other,
smale or great; and without	
consent on both sides ought	
nott to be performed.	
And unles I for the said	till such time as I shall
Company sake doe make re-	wright unto the Kinge to
quest unto His Majestic that	deliver it into the hands
the castle be delivered to	of the English.
the English; and if His	
Majestic grant my request and	
give them the castle, accord-	
inge to His Hightnes command it	
shalbe delivered unto them;	
elce nott.	

Before the English could go into action there was still a minor difficulty to overcome. Whereas the commanding officers were fully agreed, or at least decided without great discussion, to form a military alliance with the Persians against the Portuguese, the crew of the *London* showed rather less fighting spirit. They maintained that they were not employed to fight, and some were so ingenious as to suggest that an attack on the fortress of a friendly nation would constitute "a breach of the peace." A mixture of threats and promises soon converted the stubborn ones, however.[136]

The critical mass was thereby present. Faced with a superior number of Persian soldiers on the one hand and English ships on the other, the Portuguese were lost. The allies first of all turned against the fortress at Qishm, where Ruy Freire, whose galleons had not been able to be made ready for battle and were drawn in under Hormuz's guns, had already been besieged by the Persians throughout several months. The bombardment of the fortress from the sea side by the English fleet decided the matter in a few days: on 11th February Ruy Freire surrendered with 400 Portuguese soldiers.[137] A couple of weeks afterwards the Persian army went on shore at Hormuz where the town was taken without a fight. The fortress was more difficult to overthrow, although its defences were far from being in the best condition, but on May 1st it had to give in after a tough fight. The Portuguese had lost "the key to *Estado da India.*"[138]

Della Valle maintained that the English, as a result of their insufficient knowledge of the language and the unreliability of their interpreters, had been hoodwinked by the Khan of Shiraz. According to della Valle the Khan had promised them half of the fortress in Hormuz, but when they had the firman translated they discovered that it was the town, not the fortress, they had obtained half of. Della VALLE, *Persia*, II:2 p. 515–516. Also significant in this connection is the disappearance of the original. Already in 1623 the factors in Isfahan complained that the ships' "commanders" had removed it, creating great difficulties with the Persian authorities who wished to see the Persian original. Bell et al., Isfahan, to E. I. Co. 15/10 1623, C. R. O. London, O. C. 1120.

136. BOXER, *Commentaries* pp. 257–258.
137. *Assentos* I p. 130.
138. *Assentos* I p. 120, n. 4.

Part III: After Hormuz

Part III continues the account of the sequence of events following the fall of Hormuz. The losers' final attempt to regain the losses and their first steps towards an adaptation to the new situation. The victors' attempts to profit from the victory and their costly experiences while adapting to the new situation. And, finally, the beginning of a new balance is sketched; the Companies find their place in the Asian trade pattern and they contribute new and vital features, but they do not yet succeed in overthrowing it.

The traditional historical approach used in Part II is maintained, but the breach of continuity caused by the fall of Hormuz is reflected by the fact that the atmosphere of unreality and the inability to control development that characterized the events preceding the fall of Hormuz are now, despite all difficulties of communication and misunderstandings, replaced by greater coincidence between the intentions of the institutions involved and the sequence of events.

Chapter VIII: The Losers

Hormuz perished as if it had been blasted away by a volcanic eruption. The Portuguese downfall in 1622 was not a defeat of the kind that can be rectified by the next confrontation; the superior position of the Portuguese in the Persian Gulf was irrevocably lost. It was some years before the Portuguese acknowledged the disaster, and throughout the 1620s they still fought in order to regain what was lost. But at the same time they began to adapt themselves to the new state of affairs, and a Portuguese controlled trade route via Masqat and Basra was soon under development.

There was yet another loser – Robert Sherley. With the fall of Hormuz the events had overtaken his projects and his diplomacy; some of his ideas were adopted by the Companies, but his own last exertions were entirely without practical relevance.

The Demolishment of a Town

In 1624 the *bewindhebbers* of the Dutch Company warned Visnich, their agent in Persia, against Abbas: do not depend upon his friendship, "for we know, . . . that His Majesty is a very shrewd monarch, who is mostly concerned with his own country and his own subjects."[1] The English had experienced this after the fall of Hormuz; Abbas did not let reason of state be affected by gratitude. In January 1623, eight months after the fall of the fortress, della Valle embarked in Gombroon in the English Company ship, the *Whale*. Della Valle was always entertaining, and the Captain, Woodcock, who had himself taken part in the siege, enjoyed his company. One evening, when he had drunk more than he was accustomed to, he disclosed the English plans in the Persian Gulf to the Italian. The English would demand half of the town of Hormuz from the Shah, half of the customs receipts and the right to man the fortress. In return they would rebuild and colonize Hormuz and constantly keep four ships in the Persian Gulf, which could keep up the war against the Portuguese in Masqat. It is possible that Woodcock's confidences were only boasts and local armchair

---

1. *Bewindhebbers*, Amsterdam, to Visnich, Isfahan, Dec. 1624, DUNLOP p. 126.

politics, but it is significant that the figure of four ships turns up again here as it did in Monox's first estimate (see p. 339). Della Valle took the plans seriously, but he found them quite impracticable. He had already found out that the English had been hoodwinked when they made an agreement with the Khan preceding the attack, and he was convinced that Abbas would never hand over Hormuz to another European power.[2]

Unfortunately we have very little information about the negotiations carried on between the English and the Persians in the year following Hormuz's fall, but the little there is, and not least the final result, confirms della Valle's view. Abbas did not intend to let go of all the advantages won, by handing over Hormuz to another European power, and the English were not in a situation that enabled them to exert any pressure. The fleet of 1622/23 had not brought any supplies to the Persian factory, but an order to stop all investments in Persian silk until a more favourable agreement had been reached with the Shah. The order was made out in London long before the news of the English-Persian attack on Hormuz had reached there, and it naturally meant a serious setback for the English immediately following upon their political triumph. There is an almost baroque incongruity between the loss of Hormuz and the conquest of Hormuz seen with English eyes. The Portuguese lost one of the buttresses of their Empire, the English won a symbolic share of the customs receipts in Gombroon.

The Persian gained the decisive advantage of the victory by simply destroying Hormuz. They could not hold the island themselves because they possessed no fleet able to safeguard communications; Hormuz was maintained as a garrison, but the commercial and military centre was transferred to the mainland immediately after the conquest. It was not necessary to forbid the merchants to return to the town. The Portuguese still possessed the mastery of the seas in those waters, apart from the months when the Company ships lay off Gombroon, but the Persians had the fortress. Between the Persian fortress and the Portuguese sea the town was lost.

Della Valle visited Hormuz in December 1622;[3] his description of the deserted town is illuminating. The houses lay already in ruins, the streets torn up by treasure-hunters, but the fortress had been repaired and the moat, which had been neglected under the Portuguese, had been enlarged and deepened. There were 200 men in the fortress under a commander who had moved into the house previously inhabited by the vassal King of Hormuz, but the trade was gone and the merchants were gone and the streets of the town were empty. Everything that could be carried away had been

2. Della VALLE, *India* pp. 8–10.
3. Della VALLE, *Persia* II:2 pp. 524–534.

removed, "tutti i legni, tutti i ferri, e porte, e finestre, e travi ... Resta hora la Citta' senza gente, e con le case totalmente destrutte." The following year the English merchant, Kerridge, visited Hormuz. "Ormuz is become a ruyned heape, though the castle fortefyed;"[4] was his comment.

The Portuguese Attempt at Revenge

The news of the fall of Hormuz spread over the whole of Europe in the last months of 1622 and made a sensation overall. Hormuz was perhaps the most well-known of the Portuguese fortresses in Asia, and so the loss of this fortress to an alliance of merchants and infidels was not only a tactical defeat, but meant a serious loss of prestige for the Spanish Crown. In addition Europe as well as Asia knew that marriage negotiations were taking place between London and Madrid.[5] Hormuz would be capable of upsetting the balance between the Hapsburg and the Protestant powers.

This did not happen. But the fact that the Spanish reaction to the English Company's attack on a lawful Portuguese possession in time of peace and in alliance with the infidels was comparatively moderate must be seen against a European background. Spanish diplomacy had been successful in isolating James I from the natural allies of his son-in-law, the Palsgrave, and former King of Bohemia; the Spanish Council did not wish to jeopardize this advantage in order to defend the Portuguese interests in the Persian Gulf.

Here there was a strong contrast between Madrid and Lisbon, between the interests of the Council of State and the Council of Portugal. Portugal accepted these conditions and attempted instead to procure Castilian aid in the form of money, ships and particularly guns.[6] But during 1623 the stream of disturbing news from all parts of the Portuguese Empire increased, and in October the Council of State received an unusually terse consulta from the Council of Portugal, which thereby trespassed upon the preserves of the Council of State – foreign policy. As things had turned out, maintained the Council of Portugal, there were only three possible solutions to the problems of Estado da India. It was necessary either to make peace or to declare a truce with the Netherlands, to seek co-operation with England in connection with the marriage negotiations, or to create a fleet strong enough to defend the Empire wherever it might be attacked.

4. Kerridge a/b the Jonas, Swally Road, to E. I. Co., 15/11 1624, English Factories 1624/29 p. 37.
5. Della VALLE, India pp. 278–279.
6. Documentação Ultramarina Portuguesa II pp. 356–358, 364–366.

The comments in the Council of State were no less acrimonious. It is especially interesting to encounter here the assertion put forward by Pedro de Toledo, that it was the Council of Portugal that had exerted most pressure when it was decided in 1621 to resume the war against the Netherlands: "... When it was a question of breaking off the truce with the Netherlands it was the Council of Portugal that was the most eager, reasoning that if the Netherlands were not attacked from the land they [the Netherlands] would be free to use all their forces in the overseas areas." The Council of State was agreed that Portugal's difficulties did not provide any grounds for resuming the negotiations with the Netherlands. On the other hand the members were willing to consider conjoining this question to the English marriage negotiations; it stands to reason, however, that the English *entente* was so precious at that time as to render it unlikely that any greater results would be expected in that way. The only possibility remaining was that of returning force with force, and the Council of State referred in this respect to the help already offered on the part of Castile, or which was under preparation.[7]

Negotiations or fighting, those were the alternatives. The Council of State chose to fight, but had neither the will nor the ability to reserve the necessary resources. In the 16th century *Estado da India*, militarily speaking, had been based on small, heavily manned vessels with a few guns that were very effective against the Asian merchant ships or in raids on the Asian coastal towns. Since the beginning of the 17th century the North-West European Companies' big, heavily armed ships in Asian waters had altered the situation for the Portuguese as regards tactics and military technique. Apart from single galleons and carracks on the routes between Africa, India and the Far East the only high sea ships in *Estado da India* had been the three to five carracks that constituted the annual *carreira da India*. In particularly dangerous situations this fleet had been supplemented with war galleons sent out from Portugal;[8] this had also taken place in order to counter the North-West European Companies in Asia, but the Portuguese had not succeeded in developing a type of ship suitable for both war and trade like the Dutch and English ships, in the last resort because it conflicted with the social and economic constitution of the Empire. Under these conditions the dispatch of fighting ships to Asia placed an excessive burden upon the Portuguese finances. Since, moreover, the life-time for the big wooden ships was short in tropical waters, *Estado da India* did not at any time succeed in building up a navy comparable with the Companies' annual fleets to Asia.

7. *Ibid.* pp. 505–506.
8. Thus in 1601, 1605, 1608, 1619, FARIA y SOUSA VI pp. 505–511.

The dispatch of Ruy Freire's fleet in 1619 was an example of this dilemma; it was a strong and specialized armada, but its performance was not worth the cost; it had not been able to beat the English fleet off Jask, and at the siege of Qishm and Hormuz it was already too worn to be of service.[9] Deservedly or undeservedly Ruy Freire never again obtained the command of a high-sea ship, but the attempts to create a Portuguese navy in the Indian Ocean were resumed under another capable leader when Nuno Alvares Botelho was dispatched in command of a galleon fleet in March 1624. Botelho's next-in-command was João Pereira de Corte Real, whose unconventional attack on the four-decked carracks actually affected the composition of this fleet which consisted of six galleons and two three-decked carracks.[10] The outward voyage of this fleet was a fine achievement according to the standards of the time, not least in the light of the bad results of the previous years; less than six months after embarkation from Lisbon Botelho dropped anchor off Goa with the whole of his fleet intact.[11]

But before we follow Botelho's fleet it is necessary to go back to the time immediately after the fall of Hormuz in order to see what *Estado da India* had done to recover or revenge the loss. The chief role in the Portuguese policy as regards Persia during these years was still played by Ruy Freire. For him the fall of Hormuz had been a personal tragedy. He had had command of that armada which, with an unambiguous show of force, was to obtain compensation for the results of two decades' disintegration of the Portuguese position in the Persian Gulf, and he was to win over the Shah with a mixture of threats and offers and drive away the English competitors. But in the battle of Jask in the beginning of 1621 he had had to withdraw with far greater losses than the English and without carrying out the blockade of the Persian coast that had been the strategic aim of the action. His next step – the construction of the superfluous fortress on Qishm – became the direct cause of the Persian attack, and the defences of Qishm had tied up his strength and important resources at a time when it was necessary to use all available energy to improve the defences of Hormuz. During the siege his galleon fleet was

9. After the fall of Qishm and the capture of Ruy Freire together with some of his men, the galleon captains maintained that they had neither crew nor ammunition enough to get the ships into fighting condition. Later the Council of Portugal sharply criticized their attitude, but there is little reason to doubt that the immediate resources were insufficient. CORDEIRO pp. 117–118; *Documentação Ultramarina Portuguesa* II pp. 330–333 and 350.
10. BOXER, *Corte Real*, pp. 394–397.
11. "A summary and very trustworthy Narrative of what happened to the Armada of the Captain-General Nuno Alvares Botelho ...", printed in BOXER, Commentaries App. VI, pp. 231–232; della VALLE, *India* pp. 437–438.

destroyed without ever having been in action, and he himself was taken prisoner by the English when Qishm fell.

Ruy Freire was a true representative of the Portuguese military tradition, however. He was conveyed to Surat on board the English ship, the *Lion*, but succeeding in escaping, and in Bassein the very same spring he fitted out a galliot with 50 men, in which he returned to the Persian Gulf. This extraordinary feat proved to be in vain, however. In Masqat, which he visited in order to obtain information about the latest developments, he had the luck to meet a relief fleet from Goa consisting of fourteen vessels under Constantin de Sa, but even before the two commanders had left Masqat the boats arrived with the survivors from Hormuz. The fortress had fallen.[12]

Ruy Freire now decided to return to Goa – in order to become an Augustinian friar, says his biographer.[13] It would not have been surprising if he had felt a trifle weary of this world, but more likely his intention was to procure a broader basis of power than the one ship that was then under his command. In Goa he was charged with the surrender of Qishm, but even before the verdict was brought a new Viceroy arrived in Goa,[14] and in April 1623 Ruy Freire was sent back to the Persian Gulf with a fleet of 5–6 small vessels and the title of Admiral over the Red Sea and the Straits of Hormuz.[15]

In the winter of 1622/23 the Khan of Shiraz had tried to follow up the previous year's success with an attack on Masqat. Troops were moved to the coast, but the English, according to orders from Surat, denied him their support, pointing out that in their opinion the Persians had broken the agreement of the previous year as far as the partition of the fortress of Hormuz was concerned.[16] The Khan tried nevertheless to carry out the attack with the support of Arab allies, but this attacking force was rapidly driven away after the arrival of Ruy Freire, and Ruy Freire was thereafter able to take the offensive, first with an attack on a number of coastal towns that had offered to support the Persians although – according to the Portuguese – they were vassals of the King of Hormuz, and thereafter with a siege of Hormuz.[17] Since no reinforcements reached him from Goa, however, he had to raise the siege when the Company fleet, now both

12. Boxer, *Commentaries* pp. 174–178; Cordeiro pp. 160–164.
13. Boxer, *Commentaries*, p. 178.
14. This was Francisco da Gama, who, during the outward voyage of 1622, was attacked by the English-Dutch "fleet of defence" outside Mozambique and forced to winter off the African coast. This meant that during the whole of 1622 Goa received no reinforcements from Europe. Mac Leod I pp. 277 f.
15. Boxer, *Commentaries*, p. 181; della Valle *India* p. 158; *Assentos* I p. 164.
16. Barker et al., Gombroon, to Surat, 24/1 1623, *English Factories* 1622/23 p. 186.
17. Boxer, *Commentaries*, p. 183 ff.

English and Dutch, arrived at the end of the year.[18] He sent some of his ships to Basra and one to the Red Sea, which latter provoked criticism in Goa, where it was maintained that he was thereby neglecting his original task – the blockade of the Straits of Hormuz.[19] After the embarkation of the Company fleet he resumed the siege of Hormuz and continued his raids on the Persian coastal towns during the whole of 1624 while he was awaiting reinforcements.

Reinforcements were on the way. In the spring of 1624 the Viceroy had considered placing himself in command of a relief fleet, but the plan was abandoned, most likely because it was impossible to muster sufficient forces.[20] In September 1624, as mentioned, Botelho's galleon fleet arrived at Goa, but before it could go into action supplies had to be taken on board, and there were also repairs to be undertaken after the outward voyage. These preparations took such a long time that Botelho left Goa too late to be able to cut off the English-Dutch fleet on its way from Surat to Persia. When Botelho eventually reached Hormuz in February 1625 Ruy Freire had already had to raise the siege of Hormuz for the second time some weeks previously, when the combined English-Dutch fleet arrived. The rumour about Botelho's preparations had reached Surat, and the English and the Dutch factories had therefore sent all available ships to Persia in convoy; with eight big and two smaller ships the allied fleet was almost equal to Botelho's eight galleons assisted by Ruy Freire's rowed vessels.

Botelho began the attack already the day after his arrival, on 11th February 1625. The battle was one of the biggest sea battles ever fought in Asian waters during that period. The Portuguese chronicler maintains that the Persians inland appeared quite stupified to see the mouths of Hell open like that,[21] whereas the English commander, Weddell, reports in more concrete terms that the English agent and the Persian Governor of Gombroon watched the fight from the roof of their houses, and that they counted 16–17,000 shots.[22]

After two days' fight the fleets withdrew to some distance from one another; they had inflicted considerable damage on one another, but none

---

18. Della VALLE, *India*, pp. 397–398; DUNLOP p. 45; "Relacion de lo que avisan Nuno Alvarez Botelho ... y Ruy Freire de Andrade", *Documentação Ultramarina Portuguesa*, II p. 541.

19. *Assentos* I pp. 192–193; it should be noted that the dissatisfaction in Goa only applied to the dispatch of a ship to the Red Sea; so far as Basra was concerned the Viceroy's Council agreed that it was necessary to ensure that it, too, did not become Persian.

20. *Assentos* I p. 192 and *passim*.

21. BOXER, *Commentaries*, p. 235.

22. Weddell, off Cape Comorin, to E. I. Co., 27/4 1625, *English Factories* 1624/29 p. 81.

of the ships had suffered total shipwreck. The Company ships anchored under cover of Gombroon's guns – ironically enough it was the same guns which, after the fall of Hormuz, had been carried over to the mainland, that were now directed against the Portuguese –[23] while Botelho dropped anchor by the neighbouring island of Lareka. The majority in the Portuguese ship's council were for an immediate withdrawal to the Arabian coast; the ships were severely damaged after the fight; they had only few supplies with them and lacked water. Botelho rejected this advice, however, though he could scarcely have believed just then that he would have greater luck in the next encounter. Presumably he has feared that a withdrawal at that time might have tempted the Persians and the commanders of the Company fleets to a combined action against Masqat.[24] Thus the Portuguese fleet remained lying off Lareka until, in the end of February, the Company fleet left Gombroon and took part in a final indecisive encounter before it set sail for Masqat in order to repair the damage and take in supplies. The number of losses gives an idea of how hard the fight had been. The official Portuguese report estimates its own losses as 130 killed,[25] whereas the official English and Dutch figures were 29[26] and 45, respectively, in all, 74 killed.[27] The difference between these figures still reflects a considerable dissimilarity in technique and tactics, but is nevertheless far more favourable to the Portuguese than after the battle of Jask four years previously.

Masqat proved to be unsuitable as a base for repairs; two of the most heavily damaged ships had therefore to be taken out of the fleet and sent to Goa, while in return Botelho was reinforced with a galleon from India. Already on 24th August 1625 Botelho set course for the Indian west coast in order to lie in wait for the Company ships expected to reach Surat with the new monsoon. It was early in the year to venture into these waters, especially in view of the damaged condition of the ships – too early, it turned out, because on the way the fleet was struck by a storm and three of the seven ships were lost.

With the remaining four ships Botelho continued to Surat, where a superior Company fleet lay at anchor in the natural harbour of Swally Road, which he could not enter. He sent one of his captains to Surat with a challenge to the English and Dutch commanders to leave the sheltered roadstead and come out to meet him, singly or altogether.[28] The challenge was not accepted, but Botelho maintained the blockade of Surat and Swally

23. Della VALLE, *Persia* II:2 pp. 468–469.
24. BOXER, *Commentaries* p. 242.
25. *Documentação Ultramarina Portuguesa* II p. 541.
26. *English Factories* 1624/29 p. 50.
27. DUNLOP p. 152.
28. The challenge printed in BOXER, *Commentaries*, app. VIII, p. 248 f.

Road, until in October he sighted three ships which turned out to be the annual English fleet to Surat. During a short encounter he drove the three ships to flight; two of them were forced to winter at the Comores, whereas the third, the *Lion*, escaped under dramatic circumstances after having been boarded by Botelho's people.[29] Severely damaged, the *Lion* managed to reach the Straits of Hormuz, but before it came under cover of Gombroon's guns, it was attacked and set on fire by Ruy Freire's fleet of rowed vessels. Ruy Freire had an old score to settle with that ship, because it was on board the *Lion* in 1622 that he was carried to Surat as prisoner of the English. He had all the surviving members of the crew executed exepting the ship's cook, to whom he thereby repaid the services he had offered him during his confinement.

With this encounter Botelho's galleon *armada* had in fact outplayed its role; to be sure, during the years that followed he continued to cruise in the Indian waters, to the inconvenience of the Companies who were thereby forced to sail in convoy, but he never again succeeded in isolating a fleet that laid itself open to a successful attack.

The Portuguese Without Hormuz

The re-conquest of Hormuz continued to be given priority in the Viceroys' instructions,[30] but as far as we know the Portuguese made no attempts after 1624 to reconquer the island and its fortress. In the years following the fall of Hormuz the Portuguese learnt to live without it. A new route between the Portuguese controlled parts of the Indian coast and the Middle East was opened up via Masqat and Basra and later supplemented by Kung on the Persian side of the Gulf.

It is interesting that this possibility had already been foreseen shortly after Hormuz's fall became known in Europe. In a memorandum to the King, dated 10th February 1623, João Corte Real maintained that Hormuz had in fact outlived its function before the fall. When Albuquerque occupied the island it was the centre of a kingdom comprising the coastland on both sides of the Persian Gulf, and thus there were no difficulties in procuring supplies for the island. But with Persia's conquest of the coastline this basis was removed. Since it would be impossible to reconquer Hormuz's old possessions, Masqat, which had a fertile hinterland, was a far safer base for controlling navigation in the Persian Gulf than Hor-

---

29. The *Lion* was boarded by the Portuguese, but the crew dropped anchor and thereby brought the ship to such a sudden standstill that the ropes that bound it to the attacking Portuguese ships broke. Thereupon the *Lion* made off under cover of darkness. The Portuguese who were on board were disposed of by blowing up part of the deck. *English Factories* 1624/29 p. XV.

30. Boxer, *Commentaries*, p. LI.

muz. Hormuz, concluded Corte Real, was not worth reconquering. Should the Persians relinquish the island after having destroyed the fortress it would not even be worth while establishing it again. If, on the other hand, the Persians chose to preserve and strengthen the fortress it would be wise to drive them away from it, but only in order to destroy the defences. Masqat was the natural stronghold for the Portuguese trade on the Persian Gulf and for the levying of the Royal customs dues. According to Corte Real, to divert the trade to the route Masqat-Basra, thereby avoiding Persian territory, would even lead to an increase in the Portuguese customs receipts.[31]

Basra, like the remainder of Iraq, had been under Turkish suzerainty since the middle of the 16th century, but the Ottoman control over the distant town had never been secure, and before 1615 a local leader, Afrasiyab, had made himself practically independent of the Porte, even if he still formally acknowledged the Sultan as his overlord.[32] Officially the Portuguese ships had of course been forbidden to touch at Basra, but this ban had to a large extent been evaded, also by the ships belonging to the Captains of Hormuz. Thus contact remained from previous times, and within a few years trade connections between Basra and the Portuguese base in Masqat were extended and strengthened. The first to enter into direct negotiations with the Pasha in Basra were the missionaries. On 30th April 1623, i.e. less than one year after the fall of Hormuz, the first Carmelite arrived in Basra. He was sent out from Isfahan, and it is significant that a strong motive behind his appointment was the hope of obtaining alms for the Isfahan Mission as compensation for the decrease in income the Carmelites had suffered with the loss of their house in Hormuz.[33] The monk dispatched, Basil de S. Francisco, nevertheless found that he had arrived too early: there was not a single "Frank" in the town and no Portuguese ships in the harbour. During the subsequent negotiations with the Pasha, however, he obtained the support of a ship's captain, whose nationality is not disclosed, and who, because he possessed no *cartaze,* had been pursued by the Portuguese armada in the Persian Gulf. As far as one can judge the mysterious person was a Portuguese smuggler, a *pimenteiro* resident in Basra. When Basil requested permission to open a church in Basra and celebrate Mass the Pasha proved to be very accommodating; in return he wished Basil to try and seek the Viceroy's permission for Portuguese ships to call at Basra. Whether the Carmelite acted as mediator, or whether negotiations had al-

31. "Discursos sobre los medios que se deven tomar para la redificacion del comercio de Ormuz ..." *Documentação Ultramarina Portuguesa* II pp. 450–457.
32. LONGRIGG pp. 99–101.
33. GOLLANCZ pp. 329–330; *Chronicle* p. 274.

354

ready taken place before his arrival, is not apparent, but the latter is the most probable, because already in June 1623 the first Augustinian friar arrived in Basra, and in August 1623 the presence of nine Portuguese ships was reported in the harbour, "something which has never been seen before, and the Pasha was therefore delighted, because it was a great honour for the town, and many goods arrived by that route."[34]

The Pasha's desire for friendship with the Portuguese was not only for economic reasons, because precisely in 1623, after many years of peace, Basra was involved in the Persian-Turkish conflict. Since 1618 there had been peace between the two great Islamic powers, but the war flamed up again in the end of 1622 when the Pasha of Baghdad revolted and called for Persian aid against a Turkish punitive expedition. In November 1623, the year after the conquest of Hormuz and Kandahar, Abbas was able to move into the third of the gateways to his kingdom, Baghdad.[35] The Pasha of Basra stayed out of this conflict, but with the fall of Baghdad he was put into a very dangerous position. From Baghdad the Persians controlled central Iraq and the middle section of the rivers. Basra's only connecting route with the Ottoman Empire was now the great desert route – the direct caravan route from Basra to Aleppo – and the Pasha had to reckon with the fact that the Persians would soon turn against him, both in fear of a combined attack on Baghdad from the north and the south and of co-operation between Basra and the Portuguese. In 1623 the Khan of Shiraz requested the Pasha to close his harbour to the Portuguese; the Pasha placed the demand before the Portuguese *feitor* and asked for military assistance; the *feitor* communicated this wish to Ruy Freire, who immediately complied with it, sending a Portuguese squadron of five vessels to the aid of the Ottoman town in January 1624.[36] Presumably quite shortly after the arrival of the Portuguese relief vessels the Persians attacked Basra under the command of the Khan of Shiraz.[37] The attack was repeated the following winter, but thanks not least to the Portuguese relief vessels the attackers were repulsed.[38]

34. *Chronicle* pp. 1125–1127.
35. It is characteristic of the uncertainty surrounding even the most important events in the Middle East in this period that the various accounts diverge greatly with regard to the details surrounding the fall of Baghdad in 1623. See Longrigg pp. 52–57; Huart pp. 48–58; Hammer V pp. 4–15; Bellan p. 268. The last mentioned is alone in dating the conquest of Baghdad as late as January 1624. The news of the town's fall reached Smyrna after 24th January, but before 5th March 1624, Arch. Chambre de Commerce, Marseille J. 1565.
36. *Chronicle* p. 1127; *Assentos* I' pp. 192, 194–95.
37. Barker et al., Isfahan, to E. I. Co., C. R. O. London, O. C. 1159, *English Factories 1624/29* p. 22.
38. *Chronicle* p. 1127; Dunlop p. 55; Boxer, *Commentaries* pp. 204–205; della Valle, *Ritorno* pp. 556–573.

The news of Basra's new role soon got about; in May 1624 the English factors reported from Persia that the Portuguese had obtained permission to build several monasteries and a fortress (this latter was an exaggeration, however) in Basra, which was now their most important market;[39] the following year the Dutch Vice-Consul wrote from Aleppo that trade in Basra had flourished enormously after the Portuguese had begun to visit the port.[40] In August 1623 nine Portuguese ships had called there, presumably the first official Portuguese sailing; in February 1624 seven Portuguese ships called at Basra apart from the five Ruy Freire had sent in aid. In connection with the Khan's attack on the town in the end of 1624 no less than twenty Portuguese vessels are mentioned, including five warships, and in April 1625 there were twelve Portuguese ships in the harbour, whose salute of guns was instrumental in making the inauguration of the Carmelite church a festive occasion.[41] In 1625 Abbas tried to hit the new line of communication by persuading his allies among the Bedhuins to block the great desert route, but the Bedhuins preferred to take substantial though not prohibitive dues from the caravans passing through their territory. A big caravan, which left Basra on 11/5 1625, arrived in Aleppo on 12/8.[42] In May 1626 a caravan was expected in Aleppo from Basra with "goods of the kind that were previously brought from Hormuz via Persia.[43]

In January 1625 the Khan of Shiraz sent a very urgent request to the English for support in his attack on Basra. The English rejected the request pointing to the fact that it concerned Turkey; they were authorized to help the Persians against the Portuguese, but not against the Ottoman Empire, and not even when the Persians insisted that the English aid was in fact only to be used against the Portuguese ships in Shatt-al-Arab did they give in. Furthermore, in the same year they refused to let a fleet remain in the Straits of Hormuz after the Company ships had sailed in defence against Ruy Freire and Botelho.[44] At this juncture the Persians probably regarded their previous allies with a great deal of scepsis and looked uneasily upon the re-establishment of the Portuguese position in the Persian Gulf. It has been maintained by some historians that agreement

39. Barker et al., Isfahan, to E. I. Co., 30/5 1624, C. R. O. London, O. C. 1159.
40. DUNLOP p. 148
41. *Chronicle* pp. 1127–1130.
42. della VALLE, *Ritorno* pp. 578–80, 626.
43. DUNLOP p. 192.
44. Consultations, Gombroon, C. R. O. London, O. C. 1173, *English Factories* 1624/ 29 pp. 42–45. The next year the English factors in Persia also received a warning from the Consul in Aleppo against interfering in the Basra conflict. The Consul had been summoned to the Pasha and ordered to send them such a warning. Consul Kirkham, Aleppo, to Isfahan, 5/11 1625, C. R. O. Factory Records, Persia I, p. 189.

was reached between Ruy Freire and the Persians already the same year;[45] whether or not this was the case is difficult to determine, because the chronology in Ruy Freire's *Commentaries,* which are our main source, is on this point hopelssly confused.[46] It is probable, however, that a *rapprochement* took place, because at the end of the year the Portuguese squadron was withdrawn from Basra.

Late in 1628 the Khan of Shiraz attacked Basra once again. This time the Pasha had no Portuguese ships to support him, and in the beginning of 1629 the report of Basra's fall was celebrated with a salute of guns in Gombroon, but this proved to be over-hasty. Presumably it was the report of Abbas's death, which reached the armies of the Khan in January 1629, that became the town's salvation. The Pasha had proved before then, however, that it would be no easy task to take Basra, since he had ordered the dikes to be broken so that the surroundings of the town were submerged.[47]

Perhaps because Abbas was now dead, a final regulation of Persian-Portuguese relations was obtained in the agreement of 1630. This agreement is known to us in a Dutch version sent to the *bewindhebbers* in Amsterdam by the Dutch agent in Persia, del Court, in December 1630. The parties to the agreement were the Captain of Masqat, Ruy Freire, and the Khan of Shiraz. Judging by the Dutch translation and del Court's remarks it was in the form of a one-sided Portuguese declaration issued by Ruy Freire, though ratified by the Khan. It mainly contained a Portuguese promise to grant Kung the monopoly of the Portuguese controlled trade with the Persian Gulf and Arabia, at the cost of a number of specified ports. In return for that monopoly the customs in Kung was to be shared equally between the Khan and the Portuguese. This corresponded with the existing agreement, at least on paper, between the English and the Persians in Gombroon. To the monopoly agreement were conjoined some detailed conditions regarding the collection and administration of the customs and regarding jurisdiction in Kung. Finally, the agreement contained guarantees for a number of specified Persian coastal towns and their shipping.[48]

If the Persians had hoped to throttle Basra with this agreement and

45. WILSON p. 154, BOXER *Relations* pp. 127–128.
46. BOXER, *Commentaries* pp. 198–203.
47. LONGRIGG p. 104, *Chronicle* p. 285; BOCARRO, *Livro do Estado* p. 92.
48. DUNLOP pp. 683–686, cf. del Court, Isfahan, to *Bewindhebbers*, Amsterdam, 20/12 1630, *ibid.* p. 356. The agreement is also mentioned in Heynes et al., Gombroon, to E. I. Co. C. R. O. London, O. C. 1347, where it is linked together with the mention of a request from the Khan to the English and the Dutch to leave the Portuguese in the Persian Gulf in peace and with the mention of a new Persian attack on Basra in the winter of 1630/31.

transfer all of the transit trade to Gombroon and Kung, they did not succeed, because the Portuguese guarantees with regard to ships calling at Basra were not complied with. On the contrary, from 1630 activity in Basra seems to have been on the increase. In August 1630 the most considerable fleet of Portuguese trading ships hitherto arrived in Basra – 25 vessels;[49] in the autumn of 1631 25 Portuguese ships in Basra are likewise mentioned.[50] In 1633 there was friction between the Portuguese and the authorities in Basra, but the difficulties were smoothed over the very same year, and in December the Carmelites once more reported that the town was prospering greatly as the result of the Portuguese ships calling there.[51] In 1635 it is even compared with Constantinople as far as wealth and population is concerned.[52] Concurrently with this the Portuguese continued to call at Kung. *Circa* 1635 it is reported that the town possessed 200 Arabian and Persian houses, but that it was additionally populated by a number of Arabs in tents and huts.[53] Philippus a Santissima Trinitate, who passed through Kung in 1631 and again in 1640, maintained that within that period the town had grown from an insignificant fishing hamlet to an important town.[54] Finally, the Portuguese also traded with other ports in the Persian Gulf, such as el Katif.[55]

There is very little information about the Portuguese trade on the Persian Gulf, but the little there is indicates a surprisingly vigorous trade carried on by the Portuguese directly or from the Portuguese controlled towns. The downfall of *Estado da India* did not necessarily mean the downfall of Portuguese trade on the whole. In one respect, however, there was a decisive difference before and after 1622: the Portuguese were no longer the only naval power in the Persian Gulf. As tax-gatherers they had to compete with other institutions; the peddling merchants had the choice between the Portuguese controlled routes and the route that was controlled by the Company ships and the Persian Gombroon.

Sherley's Last Journey

In March 1622 Sherley was graciously granted a farewell audience at the Spanish Court. He was in Rome in August of the same year, but thereafter we lose track of him until more than a year later, in December 1623,

49. *Chronicle* p. 1135.
50. Philippus a SS^ma Trinitate p. 51.
51. *Chronicle* p. 1135.
52. *Ibid.*
53. Bocarro, *Livro do Estado*, p. 88.
54. Philippus a SS^ma Trinitate p. 52 cf. p. 443.
55. *Ibid.* p. 85; Bocarro, *Livro do Estado* p. 93.

when he turns up in London, "as if fallen down from Heaven", and on 28th January 1624 James I received him in audience.[56] He translated his credentials himself, as there were no other Persian-speaking persons present, and presented thereafter on behalf of the Shah a grandiose project concerning military and economic co-operation. In return for an English delivery of galleys Sherley declared himself willing on behalf of the Shah, unconditionally, to provide 20–25,000 men who were to aid in English military actions everywhere in Asia. As far as economic co-operation was concerned the Shah requested through Robert Sherley permission to freight his silk on board the English East India Company's ships with the view to a total redirection of the Persian silk export.[57]

It was pure invention. Sherley had been away from Persia for over eight years, and there is nothing to suggest he had received instructions of that nature from Abbas since he took his leave. We may here safely conclude *e silentio*, because there is no doubt that Sherley would have been sure to advertize the arrival of any letter from the Shah or his ministers. But Sherley mastered the art of selling real estate on the moon, and James I believed in the project. On 30th January the project was sent through Conway to the Levant Company and the East India Company for comment, the Courts of Committees at the same time being reminded that they were expected to contribute to the Ambassador's keep.[58] Thereby began a game of pretence that lasted more than three years. The Companies' attitude was clear from the very first: they did not wish to have anything to do with Sherley, they trusted neither him nor his projects. But Sherley had won the support of influential people at Court, and most of important of all – James I was interested. The matter was thereby raised from the practical to the political level; confederates and opponents had other than practical considerations in mind when they took sides.

The answer of the Levant Company stated briefly and to the point that the project could only damage their trade, and was therefore nothing for them.[59] The East India Company's reply is not known, but its contents may be deduced from the Court Minute of 3rd February 1624. The sins of

56. PENROSE pp. 205–206; Chamberlain, London, to Carleton, 17/1 1624, *Calendar S. P. East Indies* 1622/24 p. 233. It is probable that in the intervening period he tried to travel back to Persia through Russia, but that the Russian authorities prevented this. *Calendar S. P. East Indies* 1625/29 p. 71 and 1622/24 p. 242.

57. PENROSE p. 207; *Calendar S. P. East Indies* 1622/24 pp. 243–244, cf. P. R. O. London, C. O. 77/3 no. 33: Sherley to Conway 24/8 1624.

58. Robert Sherley was always an expensive guest; the Companies seem to have got out of paying his keep, however; he was allowed £ 30, a week by the King, this sum being increased afterwards to £ 40, back-dated to the time of his welcome audience. *Calendar S. P. East Indies* 1622/24 pp. 258, 322.

59. Levant Co. to. Conway, 4/2 1624, *Calendar S. P. East Indies* 1622/24 p. 243.

the past were not forgotten; the Court recalled how Sherley on his first journey to Europe had not arrived in England until after he had tried in vain to sell his project in Spain and in the Netherlands, and neither had it been forgotten that the Company had incurred great expenses and obtained no advantages from the first embassy. In addition the Court doubted whether Robert Sherley really was accredited to the English Court on this occasion, and at any rate knew with certainty that they themselves were considerably better informed about the immediate situation in Persia through their factors than Robert Sherley.[60]

The details of this precarious diplomatic dance of the following period cannot be discerned and are scarcely of any particular interest. The most conspicuous feature is the parties' endeavours to procure influential allies. It is scarcely lacking in significance that at the meeting of 3rd February mentioned above the Court decided to open negotiations with Buckingham regarding the prize money he demanded in connection with the conquest of Hormuz. Sherley on his part, before the problem was eventually dealt with in the presence of the King in 1624, had made contact with Steele, who with his greater knowledge of Persian trade conditions could lend some respectability to Sherley's projects.[61] James handed over the matter to the Privy Council, where it rested for several months while Secretary Conway and Sir John Coke, who were apparently regarded to be those members of the Council especially authorized to deal with the matter, were beleaguered with applications from Robert Sherley. From August we have a fresh reply from the East India Company to a question from the Privy Council. It is a downright rejection. The Court of Committees found that it would be both rash and stupid to place warships at the disposal of the Shah. In the Court's opinion Sherley's conception of the extent of the Persian silk production was exaggerated and, judging from their experience, they were sure that Abbas had no intention of letting them buy the silk on credit.[62]

However, in December 1624 a project began to take shape behind the backs of the Committees. James I decided to set up a Company with the nobility and anyone else willing to go into partnership with him in order to put into effect the total redirection of the Persian silk trade in co-operation with the Persian Shah. Two Royal ships had already been chosen for this purpose.[63] That it was not just a question of a manoeuvre the purpose of which was to blackmail the Company seems to appear from the fact that at about the same time various courtiers contacted a circle of prom-

60. Court Minute 3/2 1624, *ibid.* pp. 243–244.
61. *Ibid.* pp. 323, 445.
62. P. R. O. London, C. O. 77/3 no. 35.
63. *Calendar S. P. East Indies* 1622/24 pp. 462, 466.

inent men from the City, amongst these the Grand Old Man of the East India trade, Sir Thomas Smith, who for reasons unknown had had to retire from his post as Governor of the Company in the summer of 1621.[64] During negotiations connected with this Sherley slung around promises on behalf of the Shah. The Shah would deliver silk at the coast for two piastres per lb. of 24 oz., all other export routes would be closed and what the English would not buy the Shah would send to Europe himself on the English ships, paying £30 per ton in freight, etc.[65] In February the plans had reached the stage when orders had been given to make four small ships of the Royal navy ready to sail to Persia.

The turning-point followed shortly afterwards; the decisive event seems to have been the arrival of fresh letters from Persia, which were dealt with at a Court meeting on 18th March.[66] The Court of Committees were now able to inform the King and the Admiral that the English Company's factors had threatened to close down the Persian factory, and that they had now succeeded in this manner in obtaining better conditions for themselves. At the same Court Meeting it was already noted with some satisfaction that those who had once been keen on Sherley's Persian project were now crestfallen and placed more trust in the Company than in the wily birds who, in their own interest, had gone so far as to offer the French the monopoly of the Persian silk trade. There is no evidence of such a move, but it would be just like Sherley.

Although the details remain obscure there is no doubt that before the end of March 1625 the Company's victory over the projected Royal Persian silk trade was total. On 4th April Steele presented himself to the Court with a letter of recommendation from Conway in order to seek employment in the service of the Company; it cannot be more obvious: the Persian project must already have been shelved.[67] But Sherley would not have been Sherley if he had thereby given up. In May followed his next move: the Company was requested through the Privy Council to take over the proposal for alliance, lock, stock and barrel, on their own account, including the galleys, the Persian soldiers and the redirection of the Persian silk trade in co-operation with the Shah. Conway, who to a marked extent supported Sherley, exerted strong pressure on the Company, but the Court's negative answer, which could be accompanied that time by a promise that

64. *Calendar S. P. East Indies* 1622/24, pp. 465, 475; 1625/29, p. 17; P. R. O. London, C. O. 77/3 no. 58.
65. P. R. O. London, C. O. 77/3 nos. 60–61.
66. Court Minute 18/3 1625, *Calendar S. P. East Indies* 1625/29 p. 41.
67. *Ibid.* p. 48. PENROSE (p. 212) thinks that it was James I's death 27/3 1625, that wrecked the project. Whether the King's increasing weakness had played a part is left open; according to the sequence of events his death cannot have been decisive.

considerable sums would be invested in Persia during the next shipping season 1625/26, convinced the Privy Council of the pointlessness of pursuing Sherley's project after the Company had clearly manifested its intention of extending the Persian trade according to its own judgement.[68]

Robert Sherley continued to pester Conway with letters, but his demands were now more modest: he merely desired free transport to Persia and then – of course – the money still left on his warrant.[69] But before these applications had been dealt with the situation took an unpleasant turn for Sherley. In the beginning of February 1626 another Persian Ambassador, Naqd Ali Beg, arrived in England. The Company had more or less openly refused to recognize Robert Sherley's Ambassadorial rank, but immediately made haste to show that it intended to regard Naqd Ali Beg as such, if for no other reason than to accentuate the distance between him and Robert Sherley. The Court declared itself willing to pay his expenses and took steps to procure him a suitable residence in London.[70]

Shortly afterwards Robert Sherley paid a visit to Naqd Ali Beg, taking with him what he alleged were his credentials. This strange meeting is described briefly in a letter from Chamberlain to Carleton and in more detail by the chronicler, Finett.[71] Sherley handed over his letter to Naqd Ali Beg, who, to the consternation of those present, returned this gesture by tearing up the letter and slapping Sherley's face. During the subsequent tumult the Ambassador's son also hit Sherley on the nose a couple of times. When the courtiers in attendance had eventually called the diplomats to order and upbraided Naqd Ali Beg for his unseemly behaviour, the latter excused himself by saying that he could not control his rage towards a man who had dared to forge the Shah's handwriting (presumably the seal) and spread the rumour that his wife was the niece of the Shah.

Sherley had taken cover behind some of those present; he now tried to reply to Naqd Ali Beg's accusations, but with a lack of conviction that, combined with his humiliating beating, merely served to weaken his prestige. Chamberlain reports that the majority of the courtiers present took Sherley's part, but Charles I received Naqd Ali Beg in audience shortly afterwards and decided at the same time to send Sherley back to Persia together with a personal envoy from the English King, so that the uncertainty regarding his status could be cleared up.[72]

The Court of Committees was anything but enthusiastic about this Royal

68. Court Minute 30/5 1626, *Calendar S. P. East Indies*, 1625/29 p. 71 f.
69. *Calendar S. P. East Indies* 1625/29 p. 119.
70. *Ibid.* p. 162.
71. Chamberlain, London, to Carleton, 7/3 1626, *Calendar S. P. East Indies* 1625/29, p. 170. Finett in PENROSE pp. 214 ff.
72. Court Minute 3/3 1626, *Calendar S. P. East Indies* 1625/29 p. 169, cf. undated "Instructions for a letter to the king of Persia", *ibid.* p. 170 f.

decision although, to be sure, the embarkation season was at hand, the annual fleet to India was due to sail in a few weeks' time and the plan thus had the advantage that the embarrassing Ambassadors could be got rid of in a thrice. On the other hand, the Court was certainly justified in fearing that, after the latest events, it had even less reason to trust Sherley's devoted feelings for his mother country and the English East India Company. In addition, the transport of the three Ambassadors, Robert Sherley, Naqd Ali Beg and Sir Dodmore Cotton, was naturally to be at the East India Company's expense, and strong pressure was laid on the Company to take care of Robert Sherley's petty debts, a mere £2,000, before the Ambassadors' departure.[73]

However, the Company succeeded in obtaining a guarantee that the English Ambassador would not be authorized to interfere in the concerns of the Company in Persia, before the three Ambassadors set off for the three ships waiting in the Downs. What happened afterwards is uncertain; the only sure thing is that the dramatic events in March 1626 ended in a farce-like anticlimax. When the three diplomats reached the Downs together with their train the fleet had sailed, with the exception of the *Expedition* that was destined for Java. It is difficult to believe this was an accident. The Company was interested in preventing Sherley's and Cotton's departure, Sherley was interested in preventing Naqd Ali Beg's departure and possibly himself wished to avoid meeting the Shah; Naqd Ali Beg's subsequent fate might indicate that he thought on the same lines. Several of the implicated persons might be said to have an interest in sabotaging the programme. Naqd Ali Beg returned immediately to London, Sherley and Cotton made a last attempt – or undertook a final demonstration – by going on board the *Expedition* and demanding to be sailed to Persia. The Company naturally refused the request: the *Expedition* was fitted out for a voyage to Java, it was to sail to Java or stay where it was. After a month's stay on the anchored ship the company returned to London, where Sherley was soon busy sending new appeals to the Privy Council.[74]

Nothing spectacular happened during the Ambassadors' prolonged stay in London 1626–27. Sherley once again tried to raise money for a ship that could sail to Asia under his own command; the Company declared itself willing on the highly significant condition that he must guarantee that he would not undertake any piracy in Asian waters. It was easy for the Company to be tolerant, however, since Sherley did not succeed in raising the necessary capital.[75] Presumably it was after this fiasco that Sherley offered to enter the Company's service. The Court's answer was an in-

73. *Ibid.* p. 173.
74. *Calendar S. P. East Indies* 1625/29 pp. 186–196; PENROSE pp. 220–221.
75. *Calendar S. P. East Indies* 1625/29 p. 280 f.

sulting reference to the fact that the Company already employed sufficient competent people.[76] Sherley's farewell salute before the three Ambassadors eventually left England in March 1627 was a petition, presented in the name of Teresa, in which the Privy Council was requested to order the Captains of the Fleet to make sure that "the barbarous heathen", who called himself Ambassador, i.e. Naqd Ali Beg, was not allowed to go ashore during the voyage at the same time as Sherley, so that the latter's person should not be exposed to molestation.[77] At the same time the Company had its own difficulties with "the barbarous heathen", who wished to have "that lewd strumpet" whom he had met and lived with in London accompany him on board.[78] However, the Company was unwilling to go thus far in its eagerness to please the Persian envoy; on the other hand, he was supplied with better quarters and victuals than Sherley and Cotton.[79]

The tragic end of the three Ambassadors is well-known. The first to succumb was Naqd Ali Beg, who died the day the fleet dropped anchor off Surat, on November 30th 1627. Herbert maintains it was suicide – he had not eaten anything but opium for four days; the motive was to have been his fear of the fate awaiting him on his arrival in Persia.[80] However, Herbert's version of the Persian Ambassador's end is not confirmed by contemporary English letters from Surat; moreover, Herbert, who belonged to Cotton's company, could scarcely have been on the same ship as Naqd Ali Beg, and, furthermore, he was undoubtedly fascinated by Robert Sherley.

From Surat the ships sailed shortly afterwards to Gombroon, where the Ambassadors were formally received by the local Governor. The voyage then continued to Shiraz, where in the beginning of 1628 the English were received by the Khan at a formal banquet. From this banquet we obtain an irresistible glimpse of that Sherley who, penniless and self-confident, had frequented the European and Asian Courts for twenty years: "... in a cup of pure gold (Sir Robert Sherley) drank his Grace's health, and then put it in his pocket; paying him home with this compliment; That after so meane a person as himselfe had breath'd in it, it was impiety to offer it to him ..."[81] By the end of May 1628 the Ambassadors reached the Shah's winter residence in Ashraf on the Caspian Sea, where they were received in audience. From this, thanks to Herbert, we obtain the last view of Abbas, who died six months later. Abbas received them surrounded by

76. *Ibid.* p. 320.
77. *Ibid.* p. 327.
78. Court Minute 2/3 1626, *Calendar S. P. East Indies* 1625/29 p. 328.
79. *Ibid.* p. 233.
80. HERBERT pp. 34–35.
81. *Ibid.* p. 138.

tremendous pomp and riches, but, in contrast to his courtiers, he himself was quite simply clad in a red robe. After the handing over of the credentials Cotton made known his errand through an interpreter: he had come to congratulate the Shah on his victory over the Turks, to negotiate with the Shah regarding the silk trade and to clear Sir Robert Sherley's name of the accusations Naqd Ali Beg had heaped upon him.

Abbas rose and gave his answer standing. He expressed his thanks for the congratulations, at the same time repeating his wish that the Christian Princes would unite in order to slay the common foe. Regarding the silk he promised then and there to deliver 10,000 bales in Gombroon every January; as payment he would accept cloth. As for Sherley, he declared that the latter had been in his service for a long time, and that he had served him better than any Persian. Naqd Ali Beg's accusations he merely brushed aside; his suicide was sufficient proof of his fear of returning home, and – had he ventured to do so – the Shah would have ordered him to be cut into pieces and burnt on the market-square together with the stinking excrements of dogs.[82]

It was a very encouraging audience for Sherley, but after that reception the light of mercy was abruptly extinguished. The English were not received in audience again, none of the prominent people at Court paid them a visit, and Robert Sherley was not called to the Shah to report on his mission. After the Court was removed to Kazvin some months later Cotton attempted through Muhammad Ali Beg, who is referred to as Prime Minister, to establish contact anew. Muhammad Ali Beg received him very coldly and, according to Herbert, declared amongst other things that all Sherley's missions to the Christian Princes were fabrications. When Cotton protested, referring to Sherley's credentials, Muhammad asked leave to borrow them until the next day, to which Cotton agreed. Three days later Cotton was again called to the Prime Minister, who informed him that he had shown the Shah the letter, but that the latter had denied its authenticity and immediately burnt it. Herbert, however, thought that in truth Muhammad had been bribed, without disclosing who the culprit might have been. That he is referring to the Company's agent, however, there is scarcely any doubt.[83]

Thus Herbert. But the version of the same events we encounter in the report of the English Company's agent, Burt, is perhaps more reliable. According to Burt, Cotton raised two questions: whether Sherley was indeed Ambassador, and whether he was in fact authorized to negotiate about the dispatch of galleys for the use of the Persian Shah. Muhammad answered both these questions in the negative: the letters Sherley had ob-

82. *Ibid.* pp. 170–171.
83. *Ibid.* 202.

365

tained from Persia were only intended to be letters of recommendation to the Christian Princes, and Persia was not at all interested in obtaining galleys, since there were no sailors to man them.[84]

Sherley's credentials have been lost and it has not been possible to find any copy or translation. We are thus debarred from reaching any solution to the problem of the authenticity of Sherley's last mission to England, but it appears probable that he himself believed in it. His confidence on presenting the document to Naqd Ali Beg and the fact that he finally returned to Persia points in that direction. We may assume that he had been accredited to the English Court already on his departure from Persia, but that he had kept this fact hidden during all his long stay in Spain. But there is also another possibility. Sherley is unlikely to have been very proficient at Persian; the letter he presented as credentials in good faith may have been a pass or a letter of recommendation like the one issued to his brother on the latter's departure from Persia. Be that as it may, Burt's statement that Sherley was not authorized to negotiate concerning an agreement for military and economic co-operation was undoubtedly correct.

Shortly after Muhammad's rejection of Cotton's final note Robert Sherley died. "He was the greatest traveller of his time, and no man had eaten more salt than he, none had more relisht the mutabilities of Fortune. He had a heart as free as any man; his patience was more Philosophicall than his Intellect, having small acquaintance with the muses ..."[85] For once Herbert's flowery style came into its own in Sherley's epitaph. It is only regrettable that Robert did not employ the tedious months of the last sea voyage in dictating his memoirs to the young Herbert.

84. Burt et al., Isfahan, to E. I. Co. C. R. O. London, O. C. 1282.
85. HERBERT p. 203. The leader of the embassy, Sir Dodmore Cotton, died a few days later; the chaplain, Gooch, assumed the leadership, and returned for England shortly afterwards, having taken formal leave of the proper authorities.

Chapter IX: The Attempt at Redirection
of the Silk Trade

Silk was the dream commodity of the project-makers; at the beginning of the 17th century silk was for Asian trade what gold and silver had been for the *conquistadors*. The men who were at the head of the Dutch and English East India Companies were not project-makers or dreamers, nor were they *conquistadors*. But Eldorado had in fact developed into Potosi's world of reality, and the Persian raw silk, after all, was the second biggest European import from Asia. In the first two decades of the 17th century the North-West European Companies had definitively succeeded in diverting the pepper and spice trade from the caravan routes to the ocean route, so it was natural to attempt the redirection of the Persian silk trade too.

The attempt turned out impossible to realize; the Persian trade acquired quite a different place among the activities of the Companies than what was originally envisaged. But in the years following the fall of Hormuz, when the Dutch Company, too, established trade connections with Persia, it was the attempt at redirection that dominated the North-West European endeavours in Persia and the Companies' evaluation of the Persian trade.

The Companies and the Persian Silk Trade

From the very first the English East India Company's attitude towards the Persian silk trade was characterized by uncertainty; the investments in Persia took place spasmodically, and their rhythm to a large degree reflects the planning difficulties resulting from the long distances. The English investments were pursued by misfortune; they arrived almost without fail at the wrong times and failed to show up when they were most needed.

It has already been mentioned that the first to take the initiative respecting trade with Persia was the factory in Surat; Robert Sherley had been unable to tempt the Court of Committees during his first stay in London as Ambassador. The Court recognized the mission of Steele and Crowther in 1615, but had not yet been able to come to any conclusion regarding the results of their reconnaissance when, in the end of 1616, the Surat factors sent the first proper trading expedition to Persia under the leadership of Connock; and while Connock was already at the Persian Court the Company in London had only got to the stage of elaborating instructions for the opening up of trade. This lack of co-ordination was not without unfortunate results because it meant that the factors in Persia only had quite small means at their disposal during the first years, and thus were unable to make much impression on the Shah in the years when Persia and Turkey were still at war.

Finally, at the Court meeting on 14th May 1618 – a few months before Persia and Turkey concluded the so-called Peace of Sarab – Connock's sanguine letter of 4th August 1617, in which he accounted for his reception in Persia and his negotiations with the Shah, was discussed. Connock's letter was greeted with enthusiasm by the Court, which immediately decided to proceed with the purchase of 500 cloths for Persia and to seek Royal confirmation of Connock's self-assumed title of agent. The Court took Connock's optimistic hopes that the Shah would provide 2–3,000 bales of silk per annum on credit quite seriously, but it also took care that the next departing fleet to Surat and Persia brought ample stocks with it, including not less than £50,000 in goods and money for Persia.[1] These big investments were maintained in the two following embarkation seasons; with the fleet of 1619/20 the Court decided to send no less than 250,000 piastres to Persia, even if it meant having to seek an increase in the legal limit for the annual export of bullion.[2] Because of a gap in the Court Minutes during the subsequent year we cannot follow the discussions in London, but the reception in Persia in January 1622 of 148,000 piastres, 201 bales of cloth and 2 bales of kersey[3] shows that the Court's interest in the Persian project was unabated.

But thereafter the tide turned. During the following four years English investments in Persian trade were insignificant; in 1625/26 the interest flared up again, it being decided in March 1625 to send 2,000 cloths and 40–50 tons of tin to Persia with the next fleet.[4] Thereafter followed another two years without investments in Persia, but, with the establishment of the Persian voyages from 1628/29, three years of considerable investments in Persia followed, predominantly in the form of cloth and tin.[5]

This uneven policy of investment was extremely badly timed. The opportunities offered by the Persian-Turkish war were lost during the first few years of caution, and the first three years with considerable investments coincided with one of the rare periods of peace in which the

1. Court Minute 19/5 1618, cf. 9/11 1619, *Calendar S. P. East Indies* 1617/21 pp. 167, 318.
2. Court Minute 9/11 1619, *ibid.* p. 318.
3. C. R. O. London, Factory Records Persia I p. 87.
4. Court Minute 26/3 1625, *Calendar S. P. East Indies* 1625/29 p. 44.
5. CHAUDHURI p. 221.

Shah did not place any great importance on the attempts at diversion. The decision to suspend the export to Persia was taken shortly after the fall of Hormuz and the resumption of the Persian-Turkish war. The English factors thus lacked the means with which to exploit the possibilities in the years immediately following the fall of the town, and idly had to watch while the Dutch obtained full advantage of the good prices for Asian goods resulting from the dislocation of trade after the fall of Hormuz, and of the Shah's renewed interest in the plans for redirection. When the export to Persia from England was finally taken up again to its full extent at the end of the 1620s it coincided with Abbas's death and the lack of efficiency of the Royal monopoly trade that followed thereafter.

It could not have been more unfortunate, and thus it was not surprising that the decisions of the Court suffered sharp criticism on the part of the generality. At a General Court in March 1625 the Court of Committees was accused of having sabotaged Persian trade since 1621, it being asserted that the Court had allowed concern for the Levant trade to take precedence over concern for the East Indian trade because so many Levant merchants had a seat in the Court.[6] The Court rejected the accusations, but one of the ordinary shareholders, Anthony Wither, was not to be put off by the Court's reply and lodged a complaint with the Privy Council. In May the Governor had to appear before the Council and defend the Court against Wither's accusation.[7]

Wither asserted that the Levant merchants in the Court had sabotaged the Persian trade by spreading disparaging rumours about its economic possibilities, by having the ships touch at Surat on the outward voyage to Persia and by delaying the sale of the Company's import of silk until their own silk had come home from Turkey. Wither concluded that if the Persian trade was to be carried on by the Company with advantage, it ought not at any rate to be under the direction of a Court of Committees in which, apart from the Governor, 15 of its members were Levant merchants.

In his reply the Governor did not try to deny the dominating position of the Levant merchants in the Court – that would also have been difficult – but he maintained that this dominance was by no means detrimental, but to the great advantage of the trade. He even thought he could show that there had been fewer Levant merchants in the Court at the time when the trade was stagnating than in the preceding years in which Persian trade was conducted with great vigour and in 1625 when trade with Persian silk was being resumed once more on a large scale. The only reason for these four years of stagnation was the unsatisfactory conditions in Persia, which it

6. General Court 30/3 1625, *Calendar S. P. East Indies* 1625/29 p. 25.
7. Court Minute 11/5 1625, *ibid.* p. 66.

had finally – thanks not least to the caution of the previous years – been possible to improve.[8] The accusation of having kept the Company's silk out of the market was also rejected most firmly.[9]

The Company's arguments convinced the Privy Council, but what are the rest of us to think? The Persian silk trade was not popular among the members of the Levant Company when the possibility had first turned up – that at least can be established. In 1618, presumably at the same time as he forwarded Connock's letter of August 1617 on to London, the Consul in Aleppo informed the Levant Company of the local reaction to the reports about Connock's negotiations with the Shah. The Pasha and the *defterdar* were quite clear that the project was sure to have a detrimental effect on the customs receipts in Aleppo, and the Venetians and the French saw their chance to set the Ottoman officials and the English by the ears.[10] The matter was discussed at a General Court in the Levant Company on 16th November 1618; it was decided to forbid the Consul or any other member of the nation to forward the East India Company's letters, but first and foremost for fear of political complications – in London it was rumoured that Connock had offered to supply the Shah with guns.[11] The Consul was instructed, moreover, to spread the news "that it is a new begon businesse by other merchants and not like to take effect,

8. P. R. O. London, C. O. 77/3 nos. 85–86. Wither's statement about the predominance of Levant merchants in the Court was not exaggerated. In the years 1622/23–1634/35 60 persons had a seat in the Court apart from the Governor, Deputy and Treasurer. Of these, at least 29 may be identified as Levant merchants, and they were, furthermore, the most active in both Companies. In each separate year the proportion of Levant merchants in the 24-strong Court of the East India Company was:

1622/23	8	1627/28	15	1632/33	14
1623/24	11	1628/29	15	1633/34	15
1624/25	14	1629/30	15	1634/35	16
1625/26	16	1630/31	16		
1626/27	16	1631/32	12		

Finally it should be noted that throughout the whole period the Governor, Deputy and Treasurer were all Levant merchants. The Court members are identified with the aid of *Calendar S. P. East Indies*, the Levant merchants from RABB p. 233 ff. There are no striking fluctuations in the representation of the Levant merchants – on the contrary, one might say there was a striking constancy.

9. P. R. O. London, C. O. 77/3 no. 87.

10. P. R. O. London, S. P. 105/110 f. 108.

11. P. R. O. London, 105/148 f. 18. The order was registered officially at a meeting of the English nation in Aleppo 1/2 1619, P. R. O. London, S. P. 110/54 f. 21, but must have been withdrawn before 1623: "Your conveying of letters for the East India Company we both like and allow", Levant Co. to the Consul, Aleppo, 3/10 1623, P. R. O. London S. P. 105/110, f. 163.

which for our part we sincerely believe, it will faile over a while when experience hath taught, and barrenness of that trade for profitt hath setled some mens' judgements ..."[12]

But despite this outspoken displeasure there is no certain evidence that the Court of Committees allowed itself to be dictated by the Levant interests. On the basis of Connock's letter it was decided to take up the Persian trade immediately from the embarkation season of 1618/19. When the continuation of the trade was up for discussion the following year the Court had more detailed information at its disposal. The English Ambassador at the Mogul Court, Sir Thomas Roe, had returned home in September 1619; after his initial opposition he was now completely converted to the Persian project. In addition the information about price and market conditions, which the factors had sent home from Persia during 1618, had arrived. On the basis of the available information a rough calculation had been made, which revealed that a profit of 70–90% might be expected, at any rate not less than 50%, provided the journey could be undertaken within sixteen months.[13] Under these circumstances nobody in the Court seems to have objected to the trade's continuation.

The Court of Committees realized of course that it would be unable to manage the complete redirection of the Persian silk trade quite alone. On the other hand it undoubtedly knew that the risk of unforeseen price fluctuations would be considerable so long as the route through the Levant also remained open. The hope of being able to get the Shah to finance the diversion failed. It is presumably in this light we must see the proposals the English Company made the Dutch Company in 1620 and 1621 regarding co-operation according to article 5 of the defence treaty, i.e. a cartel based on a quota agreement.[14]

The proposal for co-operation was rejected or ignored on the part of the Dutch, but the final reason for the decision in 1621 to suspend the Persian trade indefinitely was the Shah's price increase in 1619, coupled with the negative result of the factors' buyers' strike the following year. The information concerning these matters was at the disposal of the Court when the Persian trade was up for discussion in October 1621. There was general agreement in the Court that it did not pay to continue the trade under the present conditions; the terms of trade left too small a profit margin if the expenses for personnel and transport were taken into account. It was decided not to send any supplies to Persia in the coming

---

12. Levant Co. to the Consul Chapman, Aleppo, 29/11 1618, P. R. O. London, S. P. 105/110 f. 108.
13. Court Minute 9/11 1619, *Calendar S. P. East Indies* 1617/21 p. 318.
14. *Bewindhebbers*, Amsterdam, to Gov. Gen. 24/3 1620 and the same to the same 4/3 1621, DUNLOP pp. 6, 11.

season in order to seek improved conditions through negotiations with the Shah. If these were not obtained the factory should be closed down. – There is, however, a slight indication during these discussions that the Court considered the Persian trade as being linked with the Levant trade, it being urged that only Levant merchants would be able to help the Company to dispose of the considerable amounts of cotton material and indigo expected from Surat: "If God bless us with the two ships upon their way, there will be so many calicoes and so much indigo as will make a glut except the Turkey merchants ship them away, and therefore the Company may well refrain one year's trading there [in Persia], and in that time either they shall procure conditions such as may encourage them, or else resolve to fall off."[15] The final decision was taken on 23rd January 1622 – by then the English ships already lay off Hormuz. Trade was to be suspended for a year in the hope that this might make the Persians more willing to negotiate.[16]

As described elsewhere it was not the Company's demonstration, but the resumption of the war against Turkey that in 1624 made the Persians grant the Company better conditions, principally fixed prices for cloth and tin. The report of this development was sent home in O.C. 1165 of 26th August 1624, and there is scarcely any doubt that it was this letter the Court referred to in March 1625, when it declared that the prices now paid for English goods were satisfactory. A few days later it was decided to send 2,000 cloths and 40–50 tons of tin to Persia in the following season.[17] Once again developments in Persia had determined the Court's decision. On the other hand the suspension of Persian investments that occurred during the next two years is confusing; from the information available it is difficult to make out the determining factor behind the Company's decisions. For the season 1626/27 it is probable, however, that political considerations had been decisive in connection with the Company's poor liquidity. On 13th December 1626, during the negotiations between the Privy Council and the Court, it was revealed that the Court intended to suspend trade with Persia and call the factors home.[18] It is a curious revelation, because the report of the Court meetings from the previous months does not even hint at such an important decision having been taken. At a General Court on 19th December the Governor confirmed the

15. Court Minute 19/10 1621, *Calendar S. P. East Indies* 1617/21 p. 471.
16. Court Minute 23/1 1622, *Calendar S. P. East Indies* 1622/24 p. 6. In a marginal note in the Court Minutes it was emphasized that the Court did not intend by this decision to give up trading completely, but the intention was merely to demonstrate a little cautiousness until better conditions for trading were obtained.
17. Court Minute 26/3 1625, *Calendar S. P. East Indies* 1625/29 p. 44.
18. Court Minute 13/12 1626, *ibid.* p. 280.

decision not to make any investments in the Persian factory. On the other hand there is no mention on this occasion of the Court's intention to close down the factory; the reason given for the suspension of investments is simply "the many Ambassadors bound thither."[19] This may be the whole explanation; the decision did not provoke any comments at the General Court. In that event the statement to the Privy Council, that it was the Company's intention to abandon the Persian trade entirely, had been part of the political intrigue surrounding Robert Sherley. That the Court discussed the Persian trade the following February and March without even mentioning the fact that the closing down of the factory had been under discussion also points towards this.[20]

The reason why the season 1627/28 is also characterized by lack of investments in the Persian trade is most likely due to concern over the Company's liquidity. The Company was in serious difficulties at this time; in 1627/28 only one ship could be sent to Surat with goods and money amounting to £60–70,000, of which £36,000 was originally intended for Persia.[21] It never got there, however;[22] the President in Surat may have kept back the supplies for use in his own factory, which was heavily in debt, but it cannot be ruled out that the money may also have remained in Surat on the Court's orders, because there was a faster return on investments in Surat than in Persia.

In 1628 the Company was in the most serious crisis it had been in so far; repeated attempts to obtain new capital for the ill-fated Second Joint Stock or for a new joint stock failed.[23] Not until the last months of the year was a new capital raised by returning to the system of separate voyages that had been the rule until 1612. Hopes were first and foremost attached to Persia, especially because the accounts received gave reason to hope for a rapid and remunerative turnover of the capital sent out, but also because trade with Persia could more easily be kept separate from the business that was still carried on by the languishing Second Joint Stock. In addition the *William* returned home in December 1628 with the silk that was the outcome of the investments of 1625/26 – the richest cargo that had hitherto been shipped from Asia to England. Its value was estimated as £170,000.[24] In the following two years two further "Persian Voyages" were organized, but an attempt to organize a fourth voyage in 1631 failed. The Company still regarded the Persian trade to be the most remunerative branch of the Company's activities, however, and with the shareholders' permission in-

19. *Ibid.* p. 280.
20. Court Minutes 28/2 1627 and 5/3 1627, *ibid.* pp. 326–27, 329.
21. Court Minute 1/2 1628 and General Court 30/5 1628, *ibid.* pp. 458, 506.
22. Swanley's instructions, Surat; 12/12 1628, C. R. O. London, O. C. 1286.
23. CHAUDHURI pp. 220–221.
24. *Calendar S. P. East Indies* 1625/29 p. 588.

vestments in Persia continued on behalf of Second Joint Stock in the following two seasons, although to a reduced extent.[25] Not until 1633 did the information obtained from Persia begin to give cause for worry; it was by then obvious that the Royal trade did not operate with the same reliability as under Abbas. The expectations of an annual sale of 5000 cloths and 100 tons of tin had not been fulfilled, so there were considerable stocks of English goods in Persia and at the same time the European silk price was falling.[26] The same objections were raised against the trade the following year, and it was decided to wind up the silk trade, although this was to be done gradually on account of the considerable capital already tied up in Persia.[27] The following years' development did not provide any reason to alter this decision: the difficulties in Persia continued as well as the slump in European silk prices. In 1639 the Court gave orders to close down the factory in Isfahan; the order was not carried out (see below, p. 390), but marks the Court's definitive abandonment of the great diversion project.[28]

The Dutch were later than the English in seeing the possibilities of the Persian trade, but when it was finally opened up, the Dutch trade with Persia was carried on with far greater regularity and energy than the English. The attention of the *Heeren XVII* was directed towards Persia in the years after 1620 from several quarters. It was mentioned above that the English Company proposed that the Dutch should enter into a cartel arrangement for the Persian silk trade, so that it would be possible to gain control over the whole of the Persian silk export. Van d. Broecke, the leader of the Dutch factory in Surat, was also extremely interested in the Persian trade – the fact that the English had something the Dutch did not have was in itself a challenge – and in several letters he urged the Directors of the Dutch Company to take up trade connection with Persia.[29] The curiosity of the *Heeren XVII* was aroused, and in 1621 the Governor General was ordered to procure detailed information about the possibilities of trade in Persia, particularly the silk trade, through the factory in Surat,

25. Court Minute 27/5 1631, *Calendar S. P. East Indies* 1630/34 p. 163.
26. Court Minute 6/3 1633 *Calendar S. P. East Indies* 1630/34 p. 372; cf. E. I. Co. to the factory in Persia, in spring 1633: "silk is here brought to a very low rate by reason of great quantities continually brought into Aleppo and other parts of Turkey from there into Europe notwithstanding your advice that silk was very scarce and deare in Persia perceiving whereof the King could not perform with us for the delivery of his silk according to his contract. And that the transportation of all silk into Turkey was at that time prohibited upon great penalties wherin by the way we have cause to blame your light credulity . . ." C. R. O. London, Factory Records Persia I p. 367.
27. Court Minute 9/7 1634, *Calendar S. P. East Indies* 1630/34 p. 553.
28. Merry, Isfahan, to E. I. Co. 3–12/12 1639 C. R. O. London, O. C. 1723.
29. Terpstra p. 146.

and, without further authorization, possibly to direct some of the ships sent to Surat further on to Persia.[30]

In the beginning of 1622 Coen, in compliance with the Company's instructions ordered Hubert Visnich, a former Levant merchant, to travel overland from India to Persia in order to investigate the possibilities for trade and make some trial purchases of silk. Visnich chose the road via Surat, but before he had left the Dutch factory the reports came in of the Persian-English victory at Hormuz. Under these circumstances there was far less risk attached to letting a single ship undertake a voyage to Persia than previously; so instead of letting Visnich travel to Persia overland it was decided to dispatch a ship to Mocha and Hormuz with a cargo that was sufficient to establish a factory. The fall of Hormuz had smoothed the path for the Dutch initiative.[31]

From the very first there were differences and similarities between the Dutch and the English factories in Persia. As opposed to the English the Dutch factory was primarily supplied with Asian goods from Batavia and only to a limited extent with European goods and ready money, but – like the English factory – its function was that of buying, of making investments with regard to returns to Europe. In the end of 1625 the first consignment of Persian silk was received in the Netherlands, and it was at once advantageously disposed of on the market. Middelburg's *bewindhebbers* were particularly enthusiastic about the new return goods; they pointed out to the Governor General that silk was a commodity that might even rival pepper as the foundation of the trade,[32] while Amsterdam's *bewindhebbers* declared themselves able to sell 6–800 bales a year of the quality received at a good profit, provided the payment could chiefly be in goods and without too much use of ready money.[33] Satisfaction with the Persian silk as a return commodity persisted in the Netherlands in the following years; in 1628 the annual demand was put up to 1200 bales, and the fact that Visnich had promised to deliver some ready money along with the imported goods in payment for the silk was accepted.[34]

In the beginning of the 1630s the Company's interest in the Persian silk apparently declined, probably in connection with the difficulties the Persian trade encountered after Abbas's death and with the slump in silk on the European market.[35] However, in 1635 the Company decided to make a special effort concerning the Persian trade. In a letter of 13th September 1635 to Batavia the *bewindhebbers* of Amsterdam gave the starting signal

30. DUNLOP p. 11.
31. TERPSTRA pp. 147–148.
32. *Bewindhebbers,* Middelburg, to Gov. Gen., Batavia, 8/12 1625, DUNLOP p. 172.
33. *Bewindhebbers,* Amsterdam, to Surat, 29/8 1626, *ibid.* p. 202.
34. *Bewindhebbers,* Amsterdam, to Persia 27/11 1628, DUNLOP p. 266.
35. DUNLOP p. 411.

for an all out attempt at diversion. The objective was now nothing less than the monopoly in Persian silk. The *bewindhebbers* would not only try to oust the English from the Persian market, but also to oust the transport through the Levant. The Company's representatives in Persia were authorized to buy silk practically regardless of the cost and with no upper limit, as it was assumed that the silk that was not bought by the Company would reach Europe in some way or other just the same. Thus, should the investments not be immediately remunerative, they could on the other hand be expected to damage the competitors, and thereby procure more elbowroom for the Dutch in the silk trade. The purchases in Persia were to continue regardless of price increases, to the point where the other nations dropped out and refrained from investing in silk.[36]

It was a gigantic corner in silk the Court of Directors was aiming at, and a remarkable example of the Company's conscious endeavour to establish its own quasi-monopoly in areas where it did not have any control over price determination. The order suited Overschie, the energetic leader of the Persian factory, very well. He hurled himself into the most extensive purchase of silk ever undertaken, regardless of the expense and regardless of the risk he ran of incurring problems over customs. The hope of procuring the control over the European imports of Persian silk for the Company failed, however. Overschie himself thought he had succeeded in buying practically all the silk that was exported from Persia,[37] but in 1638, after three years' big purchases, the Company maintained that at the most half of the silk that reached the Netherlands from Persia was exported by the VOC.[38] This was certainly an exaggeration, but the monopoly was out of reach and the profit became steadily less during the frantic purchases, which were even partly financed by 20% loans contracted in Persia. Already in November 1636 it was established that ready money was not to be sent to Persia and that no loans were to be raised; the purchases were to be financed solely with the help of the proceeds from the sale of the goods.[39]

This did not mean that the attempt at diversion immediately ceased, since considerable quantities of Persian silk were still sent to the Netherlands in the years following, but it did mean an abandonment of the attempts at monopolization, and it became the first stage in the development of the Dutch factory in Persia from a purchasing factory to a sales factory and supplier of ready money to other Dutch offices in Asia.

36. *Bewindhebbers*, Amsterdam, to Batavia, 13/9 1635, *ibid.* pp. 540–541.
37. DUNLOP p. 618.
38. DUNLOP p. 657.
39. *Ibid.* p. 597.

Silk Purchases in Persia

It has been established above that the Persian Shah traditionally engaged himself in the export of raw silk, but that there is nothing to suggest that the bulk of the Persian silk or any considerable amount of it was exported on the Shah's account before 1619. Previous to the establishment of the Companies there was no Royal export monopoly, as has been presumed by some historians.[40]

During the course of 1619, however, there came a change in the Shah's silk trade policy; as described above Abbas decided to monopolize the silk trade, commanding that all silk should in future be sold to the Royal treasury. At the same time, or shortly afterwards, he established his silk price at a more or less feigned auction at 50 tomans per load, a price that undoubtedly lay above the previous market price.

Whether the Royal monopoly became effective immediately we cannot determine, but it was nevertheless effective in so far that the English, when in 1619–20 they declared a 'buyers' strike in order to force down the Shah's price, had found it impossible to procure silk for export on the free market.[41] In the following years the Shah's agent, Lala Beg, was the English factors' only important business contact; he took over the greatest part of the English import and delivered practically all the silk the English exported.[42] The system that was built up around the Persian deliveries of silk to the East India Company in the years preceding the fall of Hormuz gives the impression of being rather a moderate adaptation of the traditional Royal interest in the silk trade, and the quite considerable amounts of silk demanded by the English were delivered without great difficulties and delays. The deliveries were agreed upon in connection with the audiences with the Shah, although the details, including the prices of the English import goods, were arranged with Lala Beg. The silk was packed in Gilan, to which the English might send one or more representatives to supervise the sorting and packing. Thereafter it was conveyed at the Shah's

---

40. Thus TERPSTRA p. 137; van LEUR p. 187.
41. ". . . the King's minde was too well knowne and published", Barker et al. to E. I. Co. 16/10 1619, C. R. O. London, O. C. 815.
42. It is possible that in 1619–20 Barker had still hoped to be able to undertake purchases and sales in the open market; his successors at any rate accuse him of having neglected Lala Beg, about which they say, "He is the heifer we must plough withall if we will do any good in this country." Monox et al., Isfahan, to Surat, 3/3 1620, C. R. O. London, O. C. 835. Some months later, in June 1620, it was decided at a Council meeting in Isfahan to reserve the whole year's import of cloth and tin for the King, "to work the King our Merchant for those two commodities which must be the substantiall pillars of our trade", Jeffries et al. Isfahan, to Monox at the Court, 12/6 1620, C. R. O. London, O. C. 873.

expense to Kazvin, where repacking took place. From Kazvin the English had to pay for the further transport themselves, although they were exempted from road-tax on the way.[43] Some instructions to one of the factors who was sent to Gilan in 1622 to supervise the packing of the silk shows how dependent the English were upon the Royal officials as far as purchases of silk were concerned. He carried with him a consignment of English goods, which he might sell on the way or in Gilan; the proceeds were to be used to procure more silk, but still through the official channels by buying from the Vizier of the province, Orslan Beg.[44]

Thus Abbas entirely succeeded in taking the lead in the business connections with the Company. The English could not purchase silk in the free market, and furthermore found it difficult to find buyers for their imports other than the Royal factor; both as regards imports and exports they were bound to the conditions dictated by the Shah or his agent. Naturally the Company's agents tried every year to get the conditions improved, but in vain. The seemingly obvious possibility of linking the question of the silk price together with that of miliary co-operation against the Portuguese does not seem to have occurred to the Company merchants, and when Hormuz had fallen it was too late. If the Shah really was so eager to divert the silk from Turkish territory as the project-makers maintained, he concealed it very well. The English had the impression that he was quite indifferent as to whether they purchased his silk or not, so long as the route through Turkey remained open and the Armenians were willing to buy.[45] There is no reason to doubt the correctness of this judgement. Throughout the years Abbas had received numerous European offers of help against the Turks and offers to buy his silk. The only time he had actually been able to make a trial his silk had been converted into a present for the Spanish King as soon as it was out of his sight. From 1619 there was eventually a possibility for a large-scale redirection of the silk trade, but he was at peace with Turkey at that time and had no interest in the alternative route, except in so far as it could ensure him a good bargain.

The greatest chance of the English thus lay in a Persian foreign policy that to an increasing extent obstructed the caravan trade and made Persia dependent upon trade through the Persian Gulf. Shortly after the fall of Hormuz Abbas himself moved into Kandahar, the frontier fortress confronting the Mogul Empire.[46] At the same time the English factory prepared itself for decisive negotiations concerning trade conditions. The fleet of

43. B. M. London, Egerton 2123 f. 41; della VALLE, *Persia* II:2 pp. 146–147.
44. Instructions from the Council, Isfahan, to Johnson, 25/3 1622, C. R. O. London, Factory Records, Persia I pp. 123–124.
45. Monox et al., Isfahan, to E. I. Co., 30/9 1621, C. R. O. London, Factory Records, Persia I p. 66.
46. BELLAN p. 259.

1622/23 from Surat to Persia had brought no supplies to the factory, but merely an order to close it down if no better conditions for trade could be obtained than what the Shah had hitherto offered. While the English were preparing these negotiations the increasing tension around Baghdad in 1623 operated to their advantage, but before the tension had developed into open conflict their threats to close down the factory and abandon the silk purchases lost their weight. In June 1623 the first Dutch trading expedition arrived in Persia and a Dutch factory was established. With this the short-lived key position of the English as the only European nation in Persia came to an end. Future negotiations had to be carried out fully realizing that the Dutch could take over what the English might reject.

That the Shah was aware of this state of affairs and intent on acting accordingly there can be no doubt. When in August 1623 Abbas arrived back in Isfahan from a journey to the easterly parts of the kingdom, the English agent called on him immediately with a new letter from James I and with the instructions ordering him to close down the factory if he could not obtain better conditions for the trade. Abbas was worried about the developments around Baghdad at this time, and everyone expected a resumption of the Persian-Turkish war. Nevertheless he did not even allow the English to make their wishes known. He limited the conversation to polite questions regarding the health of the English King and a not very tactful interrogation concerning the Dutch, about whose arrival in Gombroon he had been informed shortly before. Nor did the subsequent negotiations with the Shah's agents result in any concessions in relation to the previous years' trade conditions.[47]

In the winter of 1623/24 Abbas conquered Baghdad; the war was resumed once more after six years of peace and the caravan traffic from Persia towards the West thereby rendered difficult. Already in January 1624 it was maintained that the Armenian silk exporters stayed at home on account of the uncertain conditions.[48] When in 1624 there was yet another reversal in Abbas's silk trade policy, this time with greater concessions to the European merchants and with more widespread consequences for the Persian silk export than in 1619, it must undoubtedly be seen in this light.

The first sign of a change in attitude towards the Companies was in the beginning of 1624, when a new Royal factor, Mullaim Beg, offered to reduce the silk prices to 45 tomans per load.[49] The offer was withdrawn

47. Bell et al., Isfahan, to E. I. Co., C. R. O. London, O. C. 1120.
48. ibid.
49. Visnich to v. d. Broecke, Surat, 18/1 1624, the same to Bewindhebbers, Amsterdam. 19/1 1624, DUNLOP pp. 39, 42; likewise in Barker et al., Isfahan, to E. I. Co. 28/8 1624. C. R. O. London, O. C. 1159, where in a marginal note it says: "But it was either misunderstood or resented for he would not performe it as afterward appeareth."

some months later, however, on the order of Abbas himself.[50] The Shah had apparently been obstinate regarding the price fixed in 1619 – this was not to be touched – but the treasurer must have needed the money or import goods, because during the course of 1624 the Persians conceded other points under the pressure of both the English and the Dutch factors. Both nations were allowed a discount of two bales in every hundred, what in reality amounted to reducing the price to 49 tomans per load. At the same time a definite promise was given that in future it would not be necessary to fetch the silk in Gilan, it would be brought to Isfahan and put on sale there. Finally, agreements were made with the Royal factor concerning what were considered to be favourable prices for the import goods. According to the English factors the price determined upon would thus yield a profit of 60% on the imported cloth.[51]

A final important development in the Persian monopoly trade occurred when, in April 1626, the Dutch concluded a three year contract fixing both quantities of goods and prices. Formally speaking, the contract was drawn up between Mullaim Beg and the Company, but it was confirmed with the seal of the Shah. The contract comprised annual Dutch deliveries to the value of 40,000 tomans, at the Dutch conversion rate, 1,600,000 fl. A quarter of the Dutch deliveries were to be in the form of ready money, the remainder goods within the limits agreed upon. Among the goods pepper was by far the most important item with 60,000 man-i shah at 40 shahi, to the total value of 12,000 tomans or 480,000 fl. It was an enormous quantity, about 750,000 lb. On the whole it was Asian goods that dominated the import agreed upon in the Dutch contract; apart from tin, which could be both European and South-East Asian in origin, the only European goods on the list were small lots of cloth and kersey, to the total value of 2,600 tomans. The return commodity for the Dutch deliveries was to be silk, half legia and half ardasse, and the price, if paid in goods, was to be 48 tomans per load, whereas the part that was to be paid in cash was reckoned at 45 tomans per load.[52]

The Dutch contract made the English curious; the competitors tried to keep their terms secret, but the English nevertheless managed to obtain a copy through one of Mullaim Beg's people. The English factors assured the Company Court that it was not so satisfactory as the conditions they had achieved in 1624 – a statement that must certainly be taken with a grain of salt, because they reported at the same time that they had immediately sent agents to the Royal camp at Baghdad in order to obtain the same

50. Visnich, Isfahan, to Gov. Gen., Batavia, 24/7 1624, DUNLOP p. 54.
51. Visnich, Isfahan, to Bewindhebbers, Amsterdam, 2/9 1624, DUNLOP p. 64 f.; Barker et al., Isfahan, to E. I. Co. 28/8 1624, C. R. O. London, O. C. 1159.
52. DUNLOP pp. 184–186.

terms as the Dutch.[53] It is unlikely, however, that these negotiations led to any result. From 1622/23 until Abbas's death the English factory in Persia only obtained appreciable supplies in one single year, 1626/27. This import was transferred to Mullaim Beg, but the question of fixing the prices was postponed until the Shah came to Isfahan. Thus there can scarcely have been any English-Persian contract in 1627.[54] On the other hand, the contract between Mullaim Beg and Visnich formed the basis of the Dutch-Persian trade during the remainder of Abbas's reign.

The organization of the silk trade in the 1620s must be regarded as one of Abbas's great organizational achievements. He did not succeed in putting into effect the intended ban on export through Turkey, and the export merchants still made direct purchases in the production areas. When purchases other than from the Royal treasury were made, however, 12 tomans per load had to be paid in duty on the silk bought for export and 4 toman per load on the silk bought for processing in Persia.[55] On the other hand, the Royal trade consisted of more than just the deliveries to the Companies; the Armenian exporters also bought silk from the Royal stocks at 50 tomans per load, says one source,[56] at ten tomans profit to the King, says another.[57] Whatever was not sold at once was stored in the treasuries. In the last year of Abbas's life, 1,600 bales of silk were conveyed to Isfahan. Of these the Dutch acquired 910 bales, the English, 100, while part of the rest was sold to the Armenian merchants with a view to export via Baghdad and Aleppo.[58]

But the system did not outlive Abbas, and it began to crack up already during his lifetime. Nationalizing the peddling trade was no easy matter. The difficulties began to show up particularly after 1626, when the three-year contract described above was signed between Mullaim Beg and the

53. Barker et al., Isfahan, to E. I. Co., 14/6 1626, C. R. O. London, O. C. 1228.
54. Gibson, Gombroon, to Surat, C. R. O. London, Factory Records, Surat 102, p. 492.
55. Burt, the Shah's camp, to E. I. Co., 6/10 1630, C. R. O. London, O. C. 1317: ". . . the old King extracting on every load of silk bought by whomsoever, although manufactured in his own country 4 tomans, and transported 8 . . .". Presumably it must be read as 8 tomans over and above the 4, cf. Visnich, Isfahan, to *Bewindhebbers*, Amsterdam, 17/8 1626, DUNLOP p. 197: "op t'in-coopen van de syde wort ongeloofelycke naeu geletth dat door nimandt als door t'volck van den Coninck vercoft wordt, ofte dat voor Sijn Ma^t den tol van 12 tomannen per carge wordt betaelt by den cooper." In the same letter Visnich maintains that the local officials had tightened their hold on the producers by paying an advance on the silk harvest.
56. DUNLOP p. 196 f.
57. Heynes et al., Isfahan, to E. I. Co. 26/9 1631, C. R. O. London, O. C. 1378. This letter together with the two letters quoted in note 55 is the most detailed account of the silk trade organization under Abbas.
58. Visnich, Isfahan, to *Bewindhebbers*, Amsterdam, 1/11 1628, DUNLOP p. 255.

Dutch. As mentioned, the contract comprised annual deliveries to the value of 40,000 tomans or 1,600,000 fl. – a gigantic sum. Of this 12,000 tomans worth was to be in pepper and 10,000 tomans in ready money. But whereas the Dutch complied with the contract regarding the quantities delivered, they did not do so as regards the import's composition; thus the first deliveries in 1626/27 did not contain any ready money at all. Mullaim Beg was in a very uncomfortable position; he had entered into a business that comprised a considerable part of the Persian foreign trade, but he did not obtain any influence over the import's composition. He himself did not determine this, nor did his immediate Dutch business contact, Visnich, but it was determined by the Governor General and Council in Batavia.

During the friction that soon arose in connection with the contract the Dutch maintained that the agreement did not guarantee the Dutch deliveries, but only the Persian purchases. It cannot be denied that the preserved Dutch version of the contract can only be read in that sense: "... dat ... Mollaimbeyck gehouden sal wesen gedurende den tijdt van drie jaren ingaende anno 1627 – byaldien met onse schepen mochten arriveren, deselleve te ontvangeen ten pryse als volcht..."[59] Without any knowledge of the Persian version of the agreement we cannot determine whether Mullaim Beg really entered into such a one-sided agreement with his eyes open, but it is certain that, as long as the contract lasted, he vigorously protested against the Dutch version.

On one single point the Company admitted that it was guilty of a breach of contract, namely in the question of payment in ready money. In the Dutch version of the agreement the passage quoted above continued: "... midst dat altijdt de coopmanschappen met en derde contandt, 't sy goudt ofte sillever, sullen geacompagneert wesen." But liquidity was always the Companies' weak point, and in Batavia it did not take long to make a small calculation. The return goods bought for cash in Surat gave 300% profit in Europe, whereas silk bought with cash in Persia gave only 75% profit. Coen concluded that it would be worth paying even considerable bribes in order to avoid sending the promised quantity of cash to Persia.[60]

That the bewindhebbers in Amsterdam thought less cynically and promised Visnich that he should have the cash he was obliged to deliver under the contract did not help –[61] it was Batavia's policy that was carried out in practice. With his annual journeys to the Court Visnich procured delivery orders for the silk at the prices agreed upon in 1626 without regard to Mullaim Beg's more and more embittered protests about the com-

59. DUNLOP p. 184.
60. Coen, Batavia, to Visnich, Isfahan, 18/7 1628, DUNLOP p. 236.
61. Bewindhebbers, Amsterdam, to "the director" in Persia, 27/11 1628, DUNLOP p. 265.

position of the import and especially about the lack of ready money. Mullaim was left in the lurch; he saw his warehouses crammed with goods he had no possibility to get rid of, and which he could in no circumstances sell without a loss. Already before the beginning of the contract trade Visnich had pointed out that the sales possibilities in the country were limited. The war cut off the transit trade with Turkey, and the country's own consumption was too small to empty the stocks that had been accumulated at the King's expense.

The fall in the price of pepper illustrates the situation which the too eager exploitation of the contract created. The agreed price was 40 shahi per man-i shah, which was reckoned to be a good price already at the time the contract was signed. The Company willingly delivered at that price; in both the second and the third year of the contract the deliveries were over half a million Dutch pounds. Since the Persian market was at the same time supplied with pepper by other routes, and the possibilities for export were limited on account of the war, the market reacted with a big fall in prices: in 1628/29 pepper in Gombroon was quoted at 17–18 shahi per man-i shah, or less than half of Mullaim Beg's contract price.[62]

Visnich countered Mullaim Beg's protests by means of his connections at Court, but it is not surprising that the relationship between the Dutch and the Persian agent became embittered. On the other hand from 1627 a *rapprochement* took place between Mullaim Beg and the English. In 1628 the English achieved a contract that secured them the same prices on the import goods as the Dutch, with the exception of cloth, which was fixed at 38 shahi per covad as against the Dutch 40 shahi per covad. On the other hand it was understood that cloth was to become the most important item in the English contract. At the same time Mullaim Beg sent a letter to the English Company's Court through the English factors, in which the English agent, Burt, was highly praised, it being said amongst other things that the respect shown Sir Dodmore Cotton's embassy in Persia had been out of respect for Burt.[63] A still more convincing sign that Mullaim Beg now wished a closer co-operation with the English was his offer, partly put into effect, to deliver to the English a consignment of silk on credit.[64] It was that *rapprochement* which formed the basis of the Company's Persian voyages after Abbas's death and of the close co-operation between Mullaim Beg and the English factors during these years. But if Mullaim had hoped to gain on the swings what he had invested in the roundabouts he was disappointed. The contract with the English became just as catastrophic as the contract with the Dutch. To be sure the English delivered cash to

62. Visnich, Gombroon, to Coen, Batavia, 28/2 1629, DUNLOP p. 286.
63. C. R. O. London, Factory Records, Persia I pp. 323–324.
64. Burt et al., Isfahan, to E. I. Co., C. R. O. London, O. C. 1282.

the extent they had committed themselves, but their deliveries of goods according to the contract consisted almost exclusively of cloth and tin,[65] and the same thing happened with the English goods as had happened with the pepper – the large supplies were followed by a slump.

It seems surprising that Mullaim should not be able to utilize his position on the market and his political backing in order to stop the price fall; other importers, primarily the Companies, would undoubtedly have supported such a strategy. But Mullaim's "strategy" led to the opposite result. The spices that were imported through the Dutch were distributed on credit to the retailers round about in the Persian towns on the condition they paid a bisteg per toman per day, i.e. 1/500 of the price.[66] The English imports were thrown on the market in a way which was even more detrimental to price stability, being used as payment for the soldiers. The soldiers obtained cloth valued at 42 shahi per covad and tin at 70 shahi per man-i shah – a very liberal valuation. They then had to try to exchange the goods for money in the bazaars, but the year after the first big English deliveries it was already reported that the market was oversaturated and prices had fallen to 24 shahi per covad for cloth and 40 shahi per man-i shah for tin.[67] Moreover, according to the Persians, the English cloth was coarse and had been damaged by transport; the poor soldiers ran after the English in the street to curse them for the poor quality of the cloth distributed. The factors were inclined to agree with them; they thought that the cloth which was invoiced at £10 and £11 per piece must have been bought for £5.[68]

The unfortunate business transactions cost Mullaim Beg his office and possibly more than that. In 1632 the Dutch agent writes about him: "The

65. In 1629/30 tin and cloth to the value of 17,430 tomans was delivered and 5,000 tomans in cash, C. R. O. London, O. C. 1389. In 1630/31 cloth, kersey and perpetuanos to the value of 12,740 tomans was delivered, and tin to the value of 6,514 tomans as well as 10,670 tomans in cash, *ibid*. O. C. 1646.

66. Visnich, Isfahan, to *Bewindhebbers*, Amsterdam, 17/8 1626, DUNLOP p. 199. The price development is very well illustrated by comparing the contract prices in 1626 with the prices paid (presumably the market prices), Isfahan, 1630 (DUNLOP pp. 185, 356–357).

	1626	*1630*
Pepper	40 shahi per man-i-shah	21 shahi per man-i-shah
Tin	70 shahi per man-i-shah	56 shahi per man-i-shah
Mace	130 shahi per man-i-shah	170 shahi per man-i-shah
Cloves	240 shahi per man-i-shah	180 shahi per man-i-shah
Nutmeg	100 shahi per man-i-shah	100 shahi per man-i-shah
Cloth	40 shahi per covad	33 shahi per covad

67. Heynes et al., Isfahan, to E. I. Co., 26/9 1631. C. R. O. London, O. C. 1378. Also spices were distributed to the soldiers, DUNLOP pp. 391–392.

68. Enclosure, Heynes, Isfahan, to E. I. Co. 26/9 1631. C. R. O. London, O. C. 1380.

King's factor, Mullaim Beg, is quite in disgrace with His Majesty, who daily relieves him of his dignities and offices and hands them over to others; he relieves him, too, of all businesses and assigns every day such great sums for him to pay that he, before half a year is gone, will be quite impoverished and exhausted, and there is no doubt that according to the custom of this land he will lose his head when it is not possible to squeeze any more out of him."[69] Mullaim Beg may have deserved his ruin, considering his colossal misjudgements of the capability of the market to absorb the great quantities of imports from the Companies, but his problem illustrates strikingly the conditions of the pedlar market. There was no merchant to attend to the functions of "the second hand"; the Royal factor traded like a gigantic pedlar, not like a capitalist who could influence the price formation by virtue of his share in the market.

It is probable that Abbas had managed to institute the silk monopoly in the 1620s counter to strong interests. The complaints of the Armenians are referred to repeatedly in the Company letters,[70] but also in the silk-producing provinces there must have been persons or groups who saw their income greatly reduced by the Shah's trade policy. The reaction following Abbas's death at any rate suggests this because, within a year, the system built up during his reign had collapsed.

Abbas died in January 1629. The rumour reached Isfahan on 23rd January and immediately turned the town upside down. The shopkeepers shut up their stalls and people buried their valuables for safe-keeping. The town authorities immediately issued an order that the stalls should be kept open, however, and a couple of bandits who had tried to take advantage of the unstable situation were publicly executed. Safi's arrival in the town on 29th completely restored the calm. During the next few days he received those of his subjects who might want to kiss his foot and present him with valuable gifts.[71]

For many years the Company merchants had feared that Abbas's death would mean a breakdown of the law and order that had hitherto characterized the Persian towns and roads, but their fear proved to be unfounded. For a short period the Dutch had to move out of their house in Isfahan in order to make room for some old, blind princes who had come to Court in connection with the new King's accession. In the meantime the Dutch moved in with the French Capuchin Mission, though with extreme reluctance on the part of the Capuchins.[72] Safi was soon tired of his family, however;

---

69. DUNLOP p. 394.
70. See, for example, Visnich, Isfahan, to *Bewindhebbers*, Amsterdam, 17/8 1626, DUNLOP p. 196 ff.
71. Antonio Stick, Isfahan, to Visnich, Gombroon, 3/2 1629, DUNLOP pp. 283–285.
72. Gabriel de Paris, Isfahan, to Pacifique de Provence, no date B. N. Paris, Fonds Français 16167 f. 319.

the princes were transferred to a castle outside Kazvin and the Dutch were able to take over their house again.

This was a minor inconvenience, however. What was really at stake in connection with the accession of the new King was the whole of the Royal silk trade that had been built up under Abbas. So long as Abbas was alive there had never been problems about the deliveries of the silk, but from 1629 onwards the question as to whether the Persians complied with the contract became big and recurrent. The English were the longest to keep up trade connections with the Shah's people, possibly first and foremost because their import of cloth and tin could not be sold to others, and so they were the ones to suffer the most under the changed conditions. The course of the Dutch was more varied; they alternated between contract trade and purchase on the free market and thus did not become so dependent upon the instability of the Persian administration after the death of Abbas.

The reaction against Abbas made itself felt already a few months after his death, when a revolt broke out in the province that had delivered the main part of the silk to Isfahan in previous years – Gilan. The rebels attacked amongst others the silk towns of Lahijan and Resht, which they then plundered; the revolt was suppressed the same year, but the very people sent to defend law and order also encroached into the silk stocks: "Who were the greater thieves, the faction or the King's forces, is yet disputable."[73] Not until well into 1630 were the areas under revolt fully pacified.[74] The immediate effect of the revolt upon the silk trade was that the stocks of raw silk that had apparently been quite considerable were abruptly thrown on the market and the majority of it conveyed to Aleppo. The silk harvest of 1629 and 1630 suffered during the disturbances; in February 1630 still no deliveries from the 1629 harvest of silk had arrived in Isfahan.[75] But coincident with these events a liberalization of the Persian silk trade was put into effect. All the restrictions on the silk trade, both purchases and export, were removed, and both the duty on silk bought on the free market and the export duty fell away.[76] Abbas's silk monopoly was thereby abandoned; this did not mean an abandonment of the Royal silk trade, however, but only that in future the Royal trade existed side by side with the private, presumably a situation corresponding to the situation before 1619.

There is no point in going into detail here concerning all the complicated negotiations and business transactions between the Royal officials and

73. Burt, the King's camp, to E. I. Co., 6/10 1630, C. R. O. London, O. C. 1317.
74. RABINO di BORGOMALE, *Guilan* pp. 461, 463.
75. Burt, the King's camp, to E. I. Co., 6/10 1630, C. R. O. London, O. C. 1317.
76. *Ibid;* Visnich, Isfahan, to *Bewindhebbers,* Amsterdam, 26/9 1629, DUNLOP p. 305.

the Companies after the death of Abbas, but it will be sufficient to take up some points capable of illustrating how the system functioned, or rather, malfunctioned. It is conspicuous, although the European sources only give a fragmentary picture of internal Persian politics, that the first years after the accession of the new King were marked by comprehensive changes of personnel in the Persian administration. Nobody had been allowed to dominate under Abbas – he had been his own Prime Minister many years before Louis XIV had the same idea – but two of the men who had co-operated intimately with the Shah for a number of years, and who are most frequently emphasized in the European sources, left the Court during the summer of 1629. One of these was the Khan of Shiraz, Allah Verdi Khan's son, Imam Quli Khan, who left at the end of July officially for the sake of his health, but, according to the Dutch Ambassador, Jan Smidt, first and foremost because he could not get on with the new Shah's favourites. Shortly afterwards the Companies lost another of their permanent contacts at Court, Muhammad Ali Beg, who in the last year of Abbas's reign was often described as Prime Minister. He was got rid of by appointing him Extraordinary Ambassador to the Grand Mogul. Indicative of the situation at this time were undoubtedly Mullaim Beg's complaints to Jan Smidt: it was impossible to get matters attended to at Court; the people of experience who had previously taken the decisions did not dare to promote the affairs of foreigners or any private petitions at all in the Council, because the King's favourites were always ready to cast suspicion on them and accuse them of corruption.[77]

The English none the less succeeded in concluding a new contract with Mullaim Beg in August 1629. The prices agreed upon for the English import goods were certainly not impressive, but on the other hand the price of silk was less than what it had been previously, i.e. 37 tomans per load, a price fall that undoubtedly reflects the liberalization of the silk trade and the abandoning of the export duties.[78] The English fulfilled their part of the contract with the imported goods in 1629/30, but the weaknesses of the new administration were revealed when the equivalent value of silk was to be delivered. In July 1630 the English agent had still only received 90 small bales in Isfahan, and was thus obliged to visit the King's camp in order to acquire an effective delivery order. This proved to be difficult, because in the meantime those people who in 1629 had helped the English to arrange the contract – with the help of considerable bribes – had fallen into disgrace. Their servants had admitted under torture that bribes had been taken, and on comparing the English

77. Jan Smidt's *Reisverhaal*, DUNLOP pp. 746–747.
78. C. R. O. London, Factory Records, Persia I p. 327.

contract of 1629 with the agreements from the time of Abbas the new circles at Court had ascertained that the new agreement was far more advantageous to the English. The English agent nevertheless comforted himself with the fact that the newcomers, according to report, were no less corrupt than those they had replaced. But unmistakably it was not only unwillingness that prevented the Persians from complying with their part of the contract. The revolt in Gilan had wiped out the Royal stocks and caused a decrease in the 1629 silk harvest. In addition the organizational part of the Royal trade no longer functioned. Apparently the new leaders had no idea how much silk the Shah really had at his disposal; at any rate, before having the delivery orders made out they felt obliged to investigate in Gilan and Mazanderan how much silk there was in the Royal warehouses and how much was entered annually on the Shah's account.[79]

In 1630 the English agent, Burt, succeeded with the help of liberal bribes in obtaining delivery orders and a new contract for the next two years.[80] A fair result – if only the delivery orders had been effective and the contract abided with, but the same difficulties occurred the following year and the following and the following. The regular rhythm of deliveries that had characterized the time of Abbas was gone. The cause was stated precisely in an English letter in 1638: "It is not with this King as with the former, he had the whole trade of the silks in his own hands and by that meanes had his warehouses still stored to deliver out in seasonable times. This King will first contract and then send to buy silk."[81]

As far as one can judge the Persian administration achieved somewhat greater stability after the intrigues following the accession had come to an end and Safi, between August and October 1634, had effected a purge of the old guard from the time of Abbas by executing, amongst others, the Grand Vizier, the chief guardian of the harem and Imam Quli Khan and his three sons and had appointed a new Grand Vizier, Mirza Taqi.[82] But the change in the system was scarcely an advantage to the English, because Mirza Taqi was no friend of the English factors, who not long before had tried to have him sentenced for dishonesty in the delivery of silk while he was Vizier in Gilan.[83] The English factory in Persia was further handicapped by the unusually high mortality rate among the factors in

79. Burt, the King's camp, to Isfahan, 17/8 1630; the same to E. I. Co. 6/10 1630, C. R. O. London, O. C. 1310 and 1317.
80. Burt, the King's camp, to E. I. Co., 6/10 1630, C. R. O. London, O. C. 1317.
81. Merry et al., Isfahan, to E I. Co., 25/9–12/11 1638, C. R. O. London, O. C. 1648.
82. Overschie to *Bewindhebbers*, Amsterdam, 8/5 1635, DUNLOP pp. 423–424.
83. Gibson et al., Isfahan, to E. I. Co., 28–30/9 1633, C. R. O. London, O. C. 1514.

Persia,[84] and during the 1630s the business got into hopeless disorder. In 1638 an arduous attempt was made to settle the account between the Company and the Shah during lengthy negotiations with Mirza Taqi. According to the English statement at that time deliveries of 86 loads of silk in return for English goods and money delivered in 1629/30 were still outstanding as well as 143 loads of silk for goods and money delivered in 1631–33. The last item was recognized by the Persians, whereas they denied knowledge of the older demand.[85]

During these years the contract had been a nuisance for both parties. The English tin and cloth was delivered punctually, but the fall in prices had made the business rather disadvantageous for the Shah. On the other hand the English had been kept waiting for years to obtain the silk in return for their deliveries. The resulting loss of interest was more than sufficient to swallow up any profit there might have been. At best cloth and tin bought in London in 1630, for instance, would only be in Persia in the winter of 1631/32; the proceeds could be invested the following winter and the silk be in London late in 1633. Provided there was an immediate sale against cash the loss of interest on the original investment would be 25–30%, but this was at best. If the fleets were delayed, or if the Shah had to be given credit for some years, as happened in the 1630s, the loss of interest rose to heights that extinguished anything in the way of profit on the Persian silk.

Besides that of settling accounts with the Shah the English factory had yet another difficult problem in 1638. Despite the contract deliveries and many years of retail sale there were still large quantities of cloth and tin in stock. Thus the result of the negotiations with Mirza Taqi was that the English agent, in order to get rid of the remaining stocks and retrieve his debts, signed a new contract regardless of the fact that the instructions of the Surat Presidency expressly forbade him to take such a step.[86] Mirza Taqi took over the rest of the English stocks of cloth and

84. With the aid of *Calendar S. P. East Indies* 69 Company employees in Persia may be identified up to and including 1634. Of these 35 are known to have died in Persia, 10 were still alive in 1634 and 6 are known to have returned to England. The fate of the last 18 is unknown; this is chiefly a matter of subordinate personnel who are only mentioned on an isolated or a few occasions in the letters from Persia, and there is no reason to believe that the percentages as regards mortality should be any different than in the case of those whose fate is known. Of the 35 deceased, 22 died within the first two years after their arrival in Persia. The factory had 9 leaders within these 18 years, of which only one returned home alive, whereas one, Gibson, was still alive in Persia in 1634.

85. Merry et al., Isfahan, to E. I. Co., 30/8–25/9 1638, C. R. O. London, O. C. 1646.

86. Fremlin, Gombroon, to Honeywood, Isfahan, 4/1 1638, C. R. O. London, O. C. 1612.

tin on the part of the King, but the English agent was obliged in addition to deliver a sum in ready money. Finally a bribe of 200 tomans had to be given to the Grand Vizier, who maintained that the contract he had entered into would cost the Shah at least 2,000. However, the Englishman was cautious enough to pay the little gift in the form of bonds that would not fall due for payment until the silk had been delivered.[87]

Thus in 1639 the factory continued its usual practice of trying to procure the silk from the Royal stocks with the help of delivery orders – and met with the same difficulties in getting the delivery orders put into effect. The Company in London, however, shared the Surat Presidency's view of the prospects of the Persian trade. In December 1639 the English in Persia received an order from London of 30th March 1639 stating that the factory in Isfahan was to be closed down; the English trade was to be centred around Gombroon, i.e. concentrated on the sale of Asian and European commodities for cash, whereas the silk trade was to be abandoned. A few months later the factory reported that in the previous season 227 loads of silk had been received, and that only 29$\frac{1}{2}$ loads remained of the King's debt. To this should be added the claim for the remainder of the goods that had been paid for in 1629/30 but not yet delivered; these had to be given up as lost, however, since the receipts for the English deliveries had disappeared.[88]

The Company's orders to close down the factory in Isfahan were complied with as slowly as possible – probably they conflicted with the private investments of the factors. In December 1641 the agent, Merry, received a repeat of the Company's orders to close down the Isfahan factory; this time the order was complied with, in so far as Merry left Persia and travelled to Surat. The intention therafter was to maintain only the factory in Gombroon, but in concert with the Surat Presidency it was nevertheless decided to retain an office in Isfahan with a view to the sale of cloth.[89] There was no longer any question of purchasing silk in large amounts; it happened occasionally during the following decades that the English bought Persian silk, but on the whole Merry's contract of 1638 marked the conclusion of the English Company's participation in the attempt to redirect the Persian silk trade. The connections with Persia were maintained,

87. Merry et al., Isfahan, to E. I. Co., 25/9–12/11 1638, C. R. O. London, O. C. 1648.
88. Merry et al., Isfahan, to E. I. Co., 3–12/12 1639, 28/2 1640, C. R. O. London, O. C. 1723.
89. Merry, Isfahan and Gombroon, to E. I. Co., 1/12 1641–20/4 1642, C. R. O. London, O. C. 1783.

but only as regards the freight trade, the collection of the English share of the customs receipts in Gombroon and cash sales.[90]

As mentioned the Dutch followed a somewhat different course than that of the English in the years following Abbas's death; they did not stake their money on contract trade alone, but began to undertake big purchases of silk on the free market. This possibility had been ruled out as long as Abbas was alive, but the liberalization of the silk trade after 1629 altered this situation, and during the contract negotiations both the English and the Dutch were told that, if they were unsatisfied with the conditions offered, they might buy the silk from private merchants.[91]

The Dutch did not entirely sever trade connections with the Royal officials during the following years, but they had the same experience as the English: there was now very little correspondence between promises and practice in the Persian administration. Out of 465 bales of silk paid for in advance in 1632, only 189 were delivered at the agreed time.[92] On the other hand the Dutch agents still had the impression that trade would not be possible on a large scale without trading with the King. Overschie, who took over the management of the Dutch factory in the beginning of 1633, travelled to the Court in Kazvin shortly after his arrival in order to draw up a new contract.[93] But two years later Overschie had changed his mind. He now maintained that it was not absolutely necessary to transport the goods inland from Gombroon so that they might be handed over to the Royal factor or sold in small lots; there existed the third possibility, that they could be sold for cash in Gombroon immediately after the unloading of the ships. With ready money in hand the silk could now be procured wherever the bargain was the best. This practice had already been tried out to a limited extent concurrent with the contract trade and had produced a good result, but Overschie realized that it contained certain elements of risk. The Governor in Isfahan had raised the question of the duty on the silk the Dutch had bought from private merchants and in Gombroon, too, the customs official had begun to mention the fact that export duty ought to be paid on the silk that was bought from private merchants. Overschie hoped he would be able to avoid paying customs by referring to the Company's privileges in Persia, but he also thought that, even if this customs duty was enforced, it would

90. *English Factories passim.*
91. Del Court, Isfahan, to *Bewindhebbers,* Amsterdam, 20/2 1630, DUNLOP p. 353; Heynes et al., Isfahan to E. I. Co., 26/9 1631, C. R. O. London, O. C. 1378.
92. DUNLOP p. 411.
93. Overschie, Kazvin, to Gov. Gen. Batavia, 30/6 1633, DUNLOP pp. 425 ff.

be a more favourable procedure for the Company, because the loss of interest incurred as a result of the protracted Royal deliveries would thereby be avoided.[94]

Regardless of this conclusion Overschie nevertheless entered into a new contract the same year, but this proved to be just as disappointing as the previous ones,[95] and the following year Overschie decided to stick entirely to the free market. He bought part of the silk in Isfahan, at the same time attempting a new procedure, in that he sent an Armenian merchant to Gilan with orders to purchase silk for 2,600 tomans on behalf of the Dutch.[96] The severing of business connections with the Royal officials, however, led to renewed pressure regarding the customs payment, and in 1637 Overschie felt obliged to conclude a new contract with Mirza Taqi concerning the delivery of 200 loads of silk.[97] But concurrently with this Overschie undertook far greater purchases from private merchants – these were the years in which the *Heeren XVII* had given him *carte blanche* in his attempts to create a corner in Persian silk – and 1637/38, which was Overschie's last season in Persia, became the peak of the Dutch silk export. As in the previous year some of the silk was bought through an Armenian agent in Gilan, partly with the Company's own means, but also with the means procured by raising a loan with the Armenian merchants in Isfahan at 20% interest per annum.[98] On his departure from Persia in the beginning of 1638 Overschie took with him a cargo of silk of not less than 1,620 bales, of which 1,186 were bought from private merchants. At the same time he triumphantly declared that, apart from the debts outstanding right from the time of Visnich, there were now only 45 bales remaining on the King's account.[99]

But it was precisely this season when Mirza Taqi put into effect his threat to charge customs on the silk bought privately. A considerable sum was involved: 13½ % of the 1,186 bales was estimated at 4,006 tomans, i.e. well over 160,000 fl. It was Overschie's successor, van Oostende, who had to settle the matter; Overschie travelled to Batavia with his "glorious" cargo. But before his departure he urged his successor to threaten to close

94. Overschie, Gombroon, to Gov. Gen. Batavia, 15/3 1635, DUNLOP pp. 523 ff.
95. Overschie, Isfahan, to *Bewindhebbers*, Amsterdam, 15/12 1635, DUNLOP pp. 546 ff.
96. Overschie, Gombroon, to *Bewindhebbers*, Amsterdam, 15/5 1636, DUNLOP pp. 590 ff.
97. Overschie, Isfahan, to *Bewindhebbers*, Amsterdam, 15/6 1637, DUNLOP pp. 621 ff.
98. Overschie, Isfahan, to *Bewindhebbers*, Amsterdam, 25/7 1637, DUNLOP pp. 630 ff.
99. Overschie, Gombroon, to Pietersen, Surat, 19/1 1638, DUNLOP p. 639.

down the factory entirely if the money was not paid back and the customs charges abandoned. At the same time he urged him to avoid buying from private merchants and to draw up a contract with Mirza Taqi.[100]

In accordance with these instructions van Oostende initiated negotiations with the Grand Vizier, who felt unable, however, to deliver more than 200 loads. He therefore allowed the Dutch, over and above this delivery, to export up to 50 loads of silk purchased from private merchants.[101] The following year, however, it was decided in Batavia entirely to forbid the purchase of silk from private merchants. But the motive for this was not only fear of the Persian customs charges; in the meantime the orders for Persian silk for the Netherlands had been reduced and the plans for monopolization abandoned. In addition, owing to Overschie's final exertions, the Persian factory had incurred a considerable debt and it was desirable to settle this as quickly as possible by means of the proceeds from the sale of the Company's imports. Thus the silk purchases should until further notice be limited to the consignments that were forced on the Dutch by the Grand Vizier.[102]

Van Oostende ignored this order, however. For the embarkation season of 1640/41 he contracted for 300 loads with the additional right to export duty-free up to 100 loads bought from private merchants. In practice purchases became even greater, since the year's export was 900 bales. Van Oostende himself maintained that the contract was forced on him, and that he had bought the silk privately in order to counteract the losses the contract had inflicted on the Company, but those in Batavia were more inclined to connect the big purchases with the fact that van Oostende was to leave that season, and that he, like his predecessor, wished to do so with a "glorious" cargo.[103]

After van Oostende's departure the ban on the purchase of silk from private merchants was maintained, and the Company's silk export from Persia was limited to the consignments forced on it by the Grand Vizier. Despite the short-lived war in 1645 and the subsequent negotiations this policy was maintained during the rest of the century.[104] The Dutch Company, too, had abandoned the attempt to divert the Persian silk export to the Cape route; the silk conveyed by that route during the following

100. Overschie, Gombroon, to Adriaensz: et al., 15/2 1638; van Oostende to *Bewindhebbers*, Amsterdam, 10/8 1638, DUNLOP pp. 642 f., 654.

101. van Oostende, Isfahan, to *Bewindhebbers*, Amsterdam, 10/8 1638, DUNLOP p. 654 ff.

102. *Generale Missiven* II, 30/11 1640, pp. 112–114.

103. *Ibid.*, 12/12 1641, pp. 141–143.

104. GLAMANN, pp. 119 ff.

decades was only bought because it was cheaper than paying customs in Gombroon. Gombroon had obtained another function in the Dutch network of factories in Asia; it had become a sales factory and an exporter of silver. The turning-point was 1643/44. In this season 250,000 fl. in cash were transferred from Gombroon to Surat, and in the following season the opinion in Batavia was that it would prove possible to transfer approximately 550,000 fl.[105]

How Much?

A determination of the extent of the silk trade that was redirected is not in itself very interesting, but it is necessary if we are to relate the Persian silk trade to the total activities of the Companies and to the Levant trade. No homogeneous material exists from this period that permits a reliable determination of the extent of the silk trade, but from the scattered material available, primarily the letters from Persia, it is possible to compile an almost complete series for both the Dutch and the English silk export. Obviously statistical material of this nature is not reliable, the information contained in the letters served only as a supplement or summary of information contained in bills of lading and accounts that are now lost, and thus did not aim at completeness or exactitude. In addition, in the letters the entries generally appear as the number of bales, which, true enough, may usually be regarded as of a fixed size, though not invariably. The purchases were usually made in loads of 2 bales of 18 man-i shah and regard to the camel load made it necessary to maintain the standard size of the bales, but as a result of wastage and tare the average net contents of the bales of silk are likely to have been somewhat less than 18 man-i shah.[106] Thus, with these reservations, the material cannot be used for a detailed analysis of the market trends over the short period, but on the other hand it is entirely valid as an expression of the extent of the attempt at redirection.

105. *Generale Missiven* II, 23/12 1644, pp. 247–248.
106. Silk is very sensitive to the humidity of the atmosphere, a fact that caused a lot trouble at the weighing. Even if the sellers had not, as is in some cases maintained, "watered" the silk before weighing, there was always a certain amount of wastage between the damp Gilan and the hot and dry Gombroon that was not regained on the journey home. Tare was fixed in Persia at 1/3 man-i shah per bale, or about 2 %. English invoices 1620/21, B. M. London, Egerton, 2123 f. 12; 1639/40, C. R. O., London, O. C. 1764; Dutch invoice 1627/28, Dunlop p. 226. Concerning tare and wastage see also "Amsterdamsch rapport omtrent perzische zijde" Dunlop pp. 638–639.

Table 19. *Company exports of silk from Persia 1618/19 – 1645/46, bales of approximately 100 kg.*[107]

Year	E. I. Co.	VOC	In all
1618/1619	71	0	71
1619/1620	0	0	0
1620/1621	523	0	523
1621/1622	772	0	772
1622/1623	820	0	820
1623/1624	0	0	0
1624/1625	160	512	672
1625/1626	105	352	457
1626/1627	60	602	662
1627/1628	938	350	1288
1628/1629	93	910	1003
1629/1630	186	279	465
1630/1631	790	0	790
1631/1632	350	750	1100
1632/1633	224	193	417
1633/1634	110	784	894
1634/1635	371	870	1241
1635/1636	?	744	?
1636/1637	373	500	873
1637/1638	253	1620	1873
1638/1639	342	484	826
1639/1640	527	593	1120
1640/1641	43	900	943
1641/1642	–	470	470
1642/1643	–	487	487
1643/1644	–	527	527
1644/1645	–	?	?
1645/1646	–	52	52

Reckoned at 100 kg. per bale[108] the average annual silk export in the 1620s was a little less than 70,000 kg., while in the 1630s it was well over 100,000 kg. Only in one single year did the Companies' export of

107. See below, Ch. IX app. p. 396 f.
108. "I have caused a man-i-shah to be tryed and find it just the waight of 210 Rials of eight", C. R. O., London, O. C. 1317. If, as may be assumed, new and good piastres have been used for this experiment it gives us an equivalent of approximately 5,750 grm. per man-i shah. Cf. DUNLOP p. 799.

silk from Persia approach 200,000 kg. The total European import of silk from the Levant before the attempt at redirection occurred has been estimated above (p. 162) at approximately 200,000 kg. Thus the attempt at redirection never at any time reached such an extent as to constitute a real threat to the Levant markets. On the other hand there is no doubt that in these two decades the silk must have played a considerable part in the Companies' returns. In the middle of the 1620s the silk was quoted in Amsterdam at 10.20–10.80 fl. per pond, in 1634 at 9 fl. per pond;[109] judging from these prices the average import of Persian silk in the 1620s would have had a sales value of approximately 1¹/₂ million fl., in the 1630s of almost 2 million fl. We possess no data from this period respecting the total sales of the Companies, but we can compare the value of the silk returns with the sales value of the Companies' pepper import, which has been estimated above (p. 156) at a maximum of 4 million lbs. per annum. In the 1620s and the 1630s the Dutch Company's pepper prices, as far as they are known to us, were never below 0.60 fl. per pond and only exceptionally over 1 fl. per pond;[110] thus the sales value of the Companies' annual pepper import must have been between 2 and 3.5 million fl. Undoubtedly pepper was the Companies' most important return commodity in this period, but the comparison shows that in these years the Persian silk played a considerable part in the Companies' returns, and in some years it may have surpassed pepper as the most important return commodity.

The comparison also serves to illustrate the flexibility and mobility of the Dutch Company's investment policy, which Glamann has drawn attention to. The attempt at redirection coincided with a period in which the satisfactory disposal of the pepper on the European market was connected with obvious difficulties. It is scarcely accidental that the Dutch Company's abandonment of the attempt at redirection coincided, not only with falling prices of raw silk,[111] but also with rising prices of pepper.[112]

Appendix: Sources, Table 19.

England

1618/19: *English Factories* 1618/21 p. 77.
1620/21: B. M. London, Egerton 2123 f. 12.
1621/22: C. R. O. London, Factory Records, Persia I pp. 101–103.
1622/23: *English Factories* 1622/23 p. 180; C. R. O. London, Factory Records, Surat 102, p. 298.

---

109. GLAMANN p. 117.
110. *Ibid.* pp. 76–79; cf. CHAUDHURI pp. 148–150 and ff.
111. GLAMANN p. 117; CHAUDHURI p. 205 f.
112. GLAMANN pp. 78–79.

1624/25: DUNLOP p. 139; C. R. O. London, O. C. 1165. The approximately 100 bales the Ambassador carried with him to England is included in the export.

1625/26: C. R. O. London, Factory Records, Persia I p. 181.

1626/27: C. R. O. London, O. C. 1228.

1627/28: DUNLOP pp. 269, 276 f.

1628/29: C. R. O. London, O. C. 1293.

1629/30: C. R. O. London, O. C. 1311.

1630/31: C. R. O. London, O. C. 1347.

1631/32: C. R. O. London, O. C. 1423 (somewhat doubtful: "Our silke ready to be laden this year for England is not above 350 bales").

1632/33: DUNLOP pp. 421.

1633/34: DUNLOP p. 470.

1634/35: DUNLOP p. 528.

1636/37: DUNLOP p. 612; C. R. O. London, O. C. 1602.

1637/38: DUNLOP p. 653; C. R. O. London, O. C. 1623, 1641.

1638/39: English Factories 1637/41 p. 195.

1639/40: C. R. O. London, O. C. 1764.

1640/41: C. R. O. London, O. C. 1774, 1787.

The Netherlands

1624/25: DUNLOP p. 65, 131, v. d. BROECKE II p. 305. The approximately 100 bales the Ambassador carried with him to the Netherlands is included in the export.

1625/26: DUNLOP p. 173.

1626/27: DUNLOP p. 213, C. R. O. London, O. C. 1228.

1627/28: DUNLOP p. 226.

1628/29: DUNLOP pp. 255, 280 f.

1629/30: DUNLOP pp. 317, 329.

1630/31: DUNLOP p. 371.

1631/32: C. R. O. London, O. C. 1442. This estimate seems somewhat low, however, see DUNLOP p. 371.

1632/33: DUNLOP p. 420.

1633/34: DUNLOP pp. 467–469, 517–518, 472.

1634/35: DUNLOP pp. 518, 523, 527.

1635/36: DUNLOP p. 569.

1636/37: DUNLOP pp. 611, 612, 615.

1637/38: DUNLOP p. 640.

1638/39: Generale Missiven II p. 32.

1639/40: Generale Missiven II p. 112.

1640/41: Generale Missiven II p. 141.

1641/42: Generale Missiven II p. 163.

1642/43: Generale Missiven II p. 204.

1643/44: Generale Missiven II p. 247.

1645/46: Generale Missiven II p. 293.

Chapter X: Instead of Hormuz

The fall of Hormuz signified first and foremost the collapse of a redistributive system – a specialized system for the protection and exploitation of the transcontinental stream of goods. Thus the fall of the fortress plus the taking over by the Companies of the larger part of the European-Asian trade constitutes a whole.

The expansion of the Company trade in the first decades of the 17th century undoubtedly reduced the transit trade through the Persian Gulf, but it did not stop it. Neither was the fall of Hormuz able to stop the transit trade to the densely populated areas in the Safavid and Ottoman Empires. It was with this smaller, though far from negligible, transit trade that the Persian trade acquired its greatest international significance after the fall of Hormuz. During the first years after the fall of Hormuz the Companies were blinded by the silk; it was not until later that they became aware of the potentialities of the transit trade, and only the Dutch were able to exploit these potentialities to the full. Nevertheless during the 1620s and the 1630s the Companies found their place in the old Asian trade. The Company trade became integrated with the peddling trade.

The Rise of Bandar Abbas

Hormuz was dismantled, and the little fortress on the mainland, Gombroon, which the Persians had taken already in 1614, changed its name to Bandar Abbas, or the Port of Abbas.¹ As a Portuguese bridgehead Gombroon had been a very modest establishment. The English merchant, Newbery, who passed by in 1583, found only a Portuguese garrison of 7–8 men.² Only for a few months of the year was it the scene of a certain amount of activity in connection with the arrival and departure of the

---

1. The new name is met for the first time in a letter from the Khan of Shiraz to the English General Weddell in the monsoon of 1624/25, *English Factories* 1624/29 p. 83, but it was a long time before the new name caught on; in the whole of the period dealt with here Gombroon was the name most frequently used.
2. Purchas VIII p. 460.

caravans; it could not achieve any importance as a trading centre so long as the Portuguese possessed both Hormuz and that naval power which enabled them to force all ships to touch at their port. In 1617, according to Figueroa, the town consisted of 200 houses; the inhabitants were "moros de la tierra ... gente pobre."[3] But already della Valle, who passed through Gombroon in the monsoon of 1622/23 following the fall of Hormuz, noted Gombroon's cosmopolitan character; probably many merchants from Hormuz had moved across to the mainland. Della Valle did not otherwise think much of the town; the streets were few and narrow, the bazaars badly supplied, and there were only three small ships from Basra in the harbour. In an informal conversation with della Valle the Governor in Bandar Abbas voiced his anxiety about the financial situation. The garrisons on Hormuz and Qishm and in Bandar Abbas were expensive to maintain; if the roads were not soon opened and the merchants began to come to the town it would be necessary to relinquish the conquests. But for the time being the Persians were busy strengthening the fortress of Bandar Abbas, amongst other things with the guns that were taken in Hormuz and from Ruy Freire's galleons.[4]

Five years later Bandar Abbas was already on its way to becoming a port of international status. The English traveller, Herbert, describes Bandar Abbas as "rising daily out of the ruines of late and glorious (now most wretched) Ormuz." The town now had over 1,000 houses, and a bazaar had recently been erected, which provided shelter for the stalls and public houses. In Herbert's description there is the unmistakable smell of a harbour town; he dwells on the plentiful supplies of good wine from Shiraz, arrak, fresh fruits and sherbet and describes the many coffeehouses whose wares he characterizes, however, as "more wholesome than toothsome."[5] And from about the same time originates Boothby's description: "Gombroon, when I first knew it, had but eighteen houses in it; and now it is a great City or Town as most in England, it may compare for commerce of trade, that there is not the like place of trade in all Asia..."[6]

It was not the climate that should entice the merchants to Bandar Abbas; that was no better than in Hormuz, if anything slightly worse. The heat was unbearable all the year round and rose in the summer months to a level that drove all the inhabitants who could afford it inland and up into the mountains. It was possible for ships from the west, from Mocha or Europe, to call at Bandar Abbas in the summer months; obviously the

3. FIGUEROA I p. 272.
4. Della VALLE, *Persia* II:2 pp. 466–69, 523.
5. HERBERT p. 121.
6. BOOTHBY pp. 43–44.

Companies tried to exploit this possibility, but it was a plan that always met with inveterate resistance from the resident factors. Nobody wished to remain by the coast except in the winter months when the shipping from India arrived. In 1631 two Englishmen and a Dutchman remained in Bandar Abbas after the spring fleet was sent to Surat, but before June all three of them were dead. The same year some Armenians and Moorish merchants remained in the town because there was a shortage of camels to transport the goods inland, but 40 of them died.[7]

However, although it was only able to exist for a few months every year, Bandar Abbas had some advantages over its competitors, Jask and Kung. From both these towns the roads inland were difficult to negotiate and in parts unsafe. Kung had the additional disadvantage that big ships could only navigate the shallow waters around Hormuz with difficulty.[8] But the most important reason for Bandar Abbas's success in the years following Hormuz's fall was undoubtedly its security, i.e. low and predictable protection costs for the pedlars. The route from Bandar Abbas inland benefited greatly from the law and order characterizing the main Persian communication lines. In addition the shipping route from India to Bandar Abbas had become safer and cheaper than before. The customs duties that used to be paid in Hormuz were now paid in Gombroon, but we do not hear of extortions on the part of the Persian officials like those that previously had characterized the Portuguese system in Hormuz. The Companies possessed the mastery of the seas in the Indian Ocean and in the Persian Gulf, but they did not try to exploit their dominant position by demanding tribute.

One of the most interesting features of the new situation was the co-operation between the pedlars and the Companies: the Companies transported the pedlars' goods on their ships as freight goods. Already in 1622, during the siege of Hormuz, a Persian merchant embarked with all his goods on an English ship making for Surat. According to an agreement with the factors in Persia he was on his arrival in Surat to pay freight according to the usual tariff between Hormuz and Goa – 12 larins per camel load.[9] In a letter written a few days after the fall of Hormuz, Monox, the English agent in Persia, recommended pursuing this practice; the Company was not by itself able to fill the vacuum that had arisen after the Portuguese defeat.[10]

7. Heynes et al., Isfahan, to E. I. Co., 26/9 1631, *Calendar S. P. East Indies* 1630/34 p. 196.
8. TAVERNIER I p. 622.
9. Bell et al., Kuhistak, to Surat, 24/1 1622, C. R. O. London, Factory Records, Persia I, p. 101.
10. Monox et al., Hormuz, to Surat, 27/4 1622, *English Factories* 1622/23 pp. 77–78.

The idea was followed up. During the following winter, 1622/23, the English fleet from Surat to Bandar Abbas carried goods on which 3,321 larins and 868 piastres was paid in freight, whereas 5,217 larins was paid on the return journey.[11] In 1623/24 the freight from Surat to Bandar Abbas fetched 174 tomans; on the other hand the return journey to Surat was less remunerative, because the Dutch had already turned up as competitors in the freight trade this season.[12] The following year there seems to have been less interest in the freight trade, presumably resulting from the fear of Botelho's squadrons. In 1625/26 the English refused to carry freight goods from Surat on account of the Portuguese threat, but they maintain that the same year the Dutch earned £2–3,000 on the freight to Bandar Abbas.[13]

During the following years the route became considerably busier.[14] In 1626/27 the English Company ships carried goods for Indian merchants that fetched 22,000 Indian mahmudis in freight. In 1627/28 they carried nearly 300 passengers and goods for 20,000 Indian mahmudis. This was somewhat less than the previous year, but according to the reports of the English, this was due to their Dutch competitors having been the first to set sail from Surat.[15] The extent of the Dutch freight on this voyage is not known, but in the same monsoon the Dutch earned approximately 10,000 fl. on the return freight to Surat.[16]

There is no reason to believe that the freight charges contained any element of tribute, partly because the two Companies were competing with each other and partly because, should the Companies show themselves unwilling to carry freight, pressure was brought to bear on them by the Indian merchants and Indian authorities. This became very apparent in 1628/29. In the autumn of 1628 the English had originally thought of sending no less than seven ships to Bandar Abbas, but later they transferred one of the ships to the return fleet and began loading it for the journey to England. In the beginning of December, however, it was discovered that there was not room for all the goods awaiting shipment on board the ships to Bandar Abbas. On that occasion the President of

11. Barker et al., Gombroon, to Surat 24/1 1623, *English Factories* 1622/23 p. 186.
12. Barker et al., Isfahan, to E. I. Co., 30/5 1624, *English Factories* 1624/29 p. 21; van den Broecke, Surat, to *Bewindhebbers*, Amsterdam, 12/3 1624, Dunlop p. 44.
13. Kerridge et al., Surat, commission and instructions to Weddell 14/11 1625, *English Factories* 1624/29 pp. 108, 110.
14. Kerridge et al., Surat, to E. I. Co. 29/11 1626, *English Factories* 1624/29 p. 161.
15. The same to the same, 4/1 1628, *ibid.* p. 207.
16. Journal, Dirck van der Lee, 14/2 1629, Dunlop p. 233.

the English factory received a deputation from the merchants in Surat; it was the two prominent banyans, Virji Vora and Hari Vaisya, who, on behalf of their colleagues and themselves, politely requested that more tonnage be transferred to the Persian fleet. They were so considerate as to emphasize that they would not accompany their request with force, they merely wished most respectfully to insist that no Company goods should be exported from Surat before they had recovered their loans to the factory – at that time amounting to about £30,000. The English were sufficiently impressed by this argument that, already the next day at a Council meeting, they decided to transfer yet another English ship to the Persian fleet. In all, the freight on the outward journey in 1628/29 fetched about £3,400.[17]

In the same monsoon a corresponding pressure was brought to bear on the Dutch. Jan Smidt, the Dutch Ambassador in Persia, was quite indignant: "... they do not at all realize what profit and advancement their country and its inhabitants achieve with our extensive trade, on the contrary they brazenly assert that it is *us* who are quite dependent upon their trade and cannot manage without it." The Dutch were threatened with expulsion from Surat if they could not procure sufficient tonnage for all the merchants whose goods they had carried to Surat in the previous year. If what Jan Smidt reported was really true, the humility of the Dutch is much to be admired, because, rather than risk expulsion, they gave in. Some of the goods on the Dutch ships were unloaded in order to make room for more freight goods.[18] When the Dutch ships sailed from Surat they were so tightly packed with goods that it was almost impossible to get at the guns.[19] The English had had to hire space for 100 lasts on an Indian ship in order to find room for all their customers.[20] The total fleet which left Swally Road on one of the last days of the year consisted of 12 English and Dutch ships and 11 junks from the ports in Gujarat.[21] On the return journey from Bandar Abbas to Surat the Dutch fleet carried 800 chests and bales and 215 passangers.[22]

It is probable that the pressure exerted on the freight trade in 1628 reflected the tendency of the peddling trade to seek a substitute when other routes were blocked, because in these same years the route via Masqat

17. Consultation, Surat, 8/12 1628, *English Factories* 1624/29 p. 300; Wyld et al., Surat, to E. I. Co., 21/12 1628, *ibid.* p. 306.
18. Jan Smidt, Surat, to Gov. Gen., Batavia, 25/12 1628 – 3/1 1629, DUNLOP pp. 282–283.
19. van den BROECKE II p. 351.
20. Instructions, Surat, to Richard Predys, 12/12 1628, *English Factories* 1624/29 p. 301.
21. *Ibid.* p. 312.
22. DUNLOP p. 282.

and Basra and the Red Sea route were beset with difficulties.[23] Already in 1629/30 the pressure put on the freight trade to Bandar Abbas declined. To be sure the English earned the same in freight as in the previous year – 64,000 Indian mahmudis – but on four ships only, of which only two were fully loaded with freight goods.[24] Perhaps more room was suddenly obtained on the ships due to a stricter control on the private trade of the Company employees having been put into force,[25] but probably an equally important factor was that in the previous year the market in Bandar Abbas had shown signs of over-saturation and there was some talk of shortage of money and falling prices of Indian goods as compared to the previous years.[26]

In 1630/31 the English freight trade to Gombroon fetched only 22,000 Indian mahmudis. It was suggested at the time that the reason for this recession was that the Grand Mogul's war against Deccan had halted the supplies of cotton materials from that quarter.[27] The English ships were not quite empty, however. Concerning the *Royal James* we know that on the outward journey to Bandar Abbas it carried 100 passengers with 589 bales and on the return journey to Surat, 70 passengers with 800 bales.[28] The information that the Deccan materials had already begun to follow the route to Persia via Surat before the war is interesting, however. Surat was not the natural port of embarkation for these goods; it is very probable that this trade route was an innovation that reflected the wish of the pedlars to avoid the South Indian ports, which were still predominant-

---

23. Revolts broke out in the Yemen in October 1626. In 1626/27 trade was still normal in Mocha; the Indian merchants sold their wares to the merchants from Cairo, but lived in constant fear of an Arab attack and buried their money every time a forthcoming offensive was rumoured. This uncertainty obtained effects in the following season. Two Dutch and an English ship called at Mocha together with some Indian junks, but they found no market for their goods; neither ships nor caravans came from Egypt and most of the goods had to be returned unsold to India. Knightley to E. I. Co., Oct. 1629, *English Factories* 1624/29 p. 347 ff; Wyld et al., Surat, to E. I. Co., 21/12 1628, *ibid.* p. 304. – In the winter of 1627/28 Basra was blockaded by a hostile Beduin chief, and in February 1628 it was reported from Basra that the town had not been visited by as many Portuguese ships as in the previous season, *Chronicle* p. 1134.
24. Heynes et al., Gombroon, to E. I. Co., 20/2 1630, *English Factories* 1630/33 p. 2.
25. Wyld et al., Surat, to E. I. Co., 13/4 1630, *English Factories* 1630/34 p. 26.
26. Visnich, Gombroon, to Gov. Gen., Batavia, 28/2 1629, DUNLOP p. 288.
27. Heynes et al., Gombroon, to E. I. Co., 17/3 1631, *English Factories* 1630/33 p. 141.
28. Barry, a/b *Royal James* to E. I. Co., 22/3 1631, *English Factories* 1630/33 p. 143.

ly under Portuguese control, by using instead the more economic route via Surat.[29] The war closed this route, but provided the impetus for a plan for a new route to Bandar Abbas, i.e. from Masulipatam on the Coromandel coast. It was the English who put this plan into practice in 1632. Two ships were sent from Surat to Masulipatam, where they took 130 passengers with 4–500 bales on board. The passengers paid 20 piastres each for the journey plus 16% of the custom house valuation in freight charges; altogether this fetched 8,000 piastres.[30]

Unfortunately the preserved material does not allow the reconstruction of a full series able to show the development of the freight trade, but the examples given are sufficient to show the part played by the Company ships in the development of Bandar Abbas into an international peddling market. We can conclude the series of examples with the freight trade of 1638/39 as seen through the Dutch general missives. From Surat to Persia 40,800 fl. was earned in freight on the Dutch ships. From Bandar Abbas the Dutch ships sailed to various destinations: on the voyage to the Coromandel coast they carried freight for 12,164 larins, to Dabhol, 16,620 larins, and to Surat, 29,131 larins. Altogether the freight that monsoon fetched 69,757 fl. Naturally the Council in Batavia was pleased with these earnings, but not at all pleased with the way in which the money was earned. The Company ships' own passengers might occasionally be unpleasant competitors when the ships reached their destinations. The greatest wish was to forbid the freight trade entirely, but since the English were engaged in this trade there was nothing else to do but carry on with it.[31] But there is already a question as to whether a rejection of the freight would have been sufficient to reduce Asian competition; in 1638/39 besides the Company ships there were no less than 40 Asian ships at Bandar Abbas.

29. Cf. above ch. IV n. 160. It is impossible from the available information to decide how much the internal Indian trade routes were effected by the Portuguese defeat, which must automatically have removed the optimum security from the Portuguese controlled harbours to Surat, but it is remarkable that in 1629 in Diu there were complaints that merchants no longer came to the town; everyone traded in Surat, and in time Diu's *alfandega* did not yield enough to cover the ordinary expenses. *Assentos* I pp. 233–234.
30. Slade, a/b *Mary*, Gombroon, to E. I. Co., 12/10 1632, *English Factories* 1630/33 pp. 236–237.
31. *Generale Missiven* II p. 34.

The Companies and the "Early Asian Trade"

Bandar Abbas was not only the scene of competition between the Companies and the pedlars, but also a place where they traded with one another. From 1641/42 we have an unusually detailed description of the English trade in Bandar Abbas.[32] 322 English cloths, which presumably should have been put on sale in Isfahan, unexpectedly found a group of buyers who offered 32 shahis per covad. It was not a very high price, but since a report had been received in Bandar Abbas that prices in Isfahan were as low as 29 shahis per covad after the King had paid the soldiers their wages in cloth and the soldiers in turn had sold the cloth in the bazaars, the English accepted the offer. But the business was not concluded thereby. First of all agreement had to be reached as to which covad should be used. The buyers insisted on its being the Bandar Abbas covad, whereas the English wished to measure with the Isfahan covad, which was of course the shortest. When after a long discussion it was agreed to use the Isfahan covad the buyers would not accept the English measuring rod and another one had to be procured from the *shahbandar*, which the latter maintained was correct. This time the English gave in, even though they thought the *shahbandar*'s rod was an inch longer than the one they usually used in Isfahan. The cloth in one of the bales was now measured up; it happened to contain three of the longest pieces of 31³/₄, 32¹/₄ and 32 covads, respectively. On this basis the parties now agreed to reckon all the cloth at 32 covads per piece, and the buyers departed with the cloth in order to divide it among themselves. But they were soon back again. When they were distributing the cloth none of the pieces had been found to measure as much as 31¹/₂ covads, and some were only 31 covads. The buyers were furious and refused to pay. The *shahbandar*'s scribe was sent for; obtaining 2¹/₂ covads in payment he mediated between the parties and determined that the tarc, which had in the first case been fixed at ¹/₄ covad per bale of 3 pieces, was to be increased to 1 covad per bale. By then the buyers were satisfied, and what the English thought of the result may be judged from the English factor's account of the transaction: "This agreement we are glad of, and is much better than to have the clothes opened and measured, whereby their defects in spotts and wormeatings would have been discovered, and consequently tare must have been allowed for those, as well as want in measure ... We wish the buyers a better pennyworth than we believe they have, that it may incourage them and others to buy your cloth att this markett hereafter ..."

32. Merry, Isfahan and Gombroon, to E. I. Co., 1/12 1641–20/4 1642, C. R. O. London, O. C. 1783.

The description of the year's business continues: "Your cargazoone of coast goods came in such a seasonable time before the arriveall of any jounkes with clothing that they are all vended to a competent profitt, near about 30% towards charges and interest, all of which sorts of goods are fallen now 15 or 20% since arriveall of one extraordinary great jouncke from thence, and store of clothing from other places ... The cargazoone from Surat also is sold ... the pepper at 26 larins pr man Surat, the clothing for the most part from 50 to 70% advance towards charges and interest ... Agra indigo at 100 larins per man Surat ..." The Sirkej indigo is sent on to Basra in the hope of a better market there ... "Sinda goods are of late meanly requested yet all we received we sold to some profitt to witt nearest 25% towards charges and interest ... Though the greatest quantity of your goods was quickly sold yet a great part of them remaineth yet untold out and consequently a great part of the money Unreceived, merchants having even to this time been so intent on buying of goods that they have had little time either to tell or pay for what they have bought." – The proceeds from the sales are transferred to Surat in ready money or are used to honour the bills of exchange drawn by the factory in Surat on the factories in Bandar Abbas and Isfahan.[33]

The market described in this report is the peddling market. We recognize a number of the characteristic features, primarily the sudden price fluctuations and the poor transparency of the market. There is no "second hand" to even out a momentary discrepancy between supply and demand in a market in which all business has to be concluded before the monsoon veers and the climate becomes dangerous.

As far as the continuity in the Asian trade pattern is concerned we must agree with van Leur's conclusion, that the North-West European Companies did not before the middle of the 17th century endow the traditional trade with any important new features except as regards the few instances where they had aquired political power.[33] But against van Leur we must add that the Companies constituted an important new element in the traditional trade. The Companies did not transform the early Asian trade, but they were not transformed themselves either; they were as profit-making institutions distinct from and superior to the pedlars and the redistributive enterprizes.

In 1619 Coen had presented his famous programme for the Dutch trade in Asia. "Our wishes we have often repeated before: many ships, good warships, good return ships, medium-sized ships for the intra-Asian trade, ordinary ships, flutes and small sloops and a great many frigates. Once we obtain them we can not only procure gold for the Coromandel Coast, but also rials for the pepper trade and silver for the trade with China,

33. van LEUR pp. 189, 221–222, 226–27.

without it being necessary to send the bullion from home, but the supplies from the Netherlands must on no account be stopped immediately, because first such plentiful supplies and so many ships must be sent that the intra-Asian trade is well-founded."

Coen continued with a passage that justly has become famous: "Piece goods from Gujarat we can barter for pepper and gold on the coast of Sumatra, rials and cottons from the coast for pepper in Bantam, sandalwood, pepper and rials we can barter for Chinese goods and Chinese gold; we can extract silver from Japan with Chinese goods, piece goods from the Coromandel coast in exchange for spices, other goods and gold from China, piece goods from Surat for spices, other goods and rials, rials from Arabia for spices and various other trifles – one thing leads to the other. And all of it can be done without any money from the Netherlands and with ships alone. We have the most important spices already. What is missing then? Nothing else but ships and a little water to prime the pump. Is there any other country in the world with more ships than the Netherlands? Is there a shortage of water with which to prime the pump? (By this I mean sufficient money so that the rich Asian trade may be established). Hence, gentlemen and good administrators, there is nothing to prevent the Company from acquiring the richest trade in the world."[34]

Coen's project does not in spirit sound very different from that of the project-makers; his vision was just as far removed from the bilateral, restricted trade that had been the aim of the voorcompagnieën and the English separate voyages as from the redistributive policy that had formed the basis of Estado da India. But Coen's project was practicable. Coen and many other North-West European merchants with him had observed the rich Asian peddling trade; his aim became to centralize and co-ordinate it by means of ships and a capital that was not to be returned immediately, but to circulate permanently in Asia.

The project succeeded; in the 17th century the multilateral, co-ordinated trade based on Dutch capital in Asia became reality. Already in 1635 the Dutch factory in Persia's order list to Batavia resembles a catalogue of the richest products from the whole of Asia. There are spices, nutmeg, mace and cloves from the spice islands, pepper from Java and Sumatra, cinnamon from Ceylon and cardamom from the west coast of India, preserved ginger from China and dried ginger from India. There is sugar, white powdered sugar and candy sugar; in 1635 sugar from China and Taiwan was most sought after, but sugar from Bengal soon proved to be just as profitable on the Persian market. There are dyes, indigo, sapanwood and alum. There are metals, tin from England and Achin and copper

34. Coen to Heeren XVII, 5/8 1619, Coen I pp. 485–486.

from Japan (some years later a successful attempt was made to place Hungarian copper on the Persian market). There is porcelain from China, camphor and benzoin from Achin and Siam. There is gum lac (several qualities are expressly mentioned), lac from Ahmadabad and lac from Pegu, there is sandalwood and there are cheap "coarse" goods from India, such as rice, cotton and tobacco. The list does not yet include cotton materials, but the next preserved order from 1637 includes these, too.[35]

An order list does not constitute evidence for the trade that actually took place, but for the sales that were imagined as being possible to realize; the Dutch factories in Persia certainly obtained the articles they had ordered just as little as any other factory. It was not only a question of misunderstandings or indifference, it was also a question of co-ordinating all the Dutch Company's interests in Asia and Europe. The clearest impression of that totality of which the factories formed a part may be obtained from the general missives from Batavia. The general missive was a complete annual report which could be supplemented if it proved possible to bring the development up to date, but which in principle was to cover the year's results and the planning for the coming year. Like an enormous radar screen the glance of the observers searched the entire horizon round from their post in Batavia. The political situation and market trends, from Japan to Arabia, were registered and compared, the collected data relating to the Company's own trade was summarized in a few figures: profit and loss in the separate factories and in Asia as a whole, the returns and arrivals in relation to *Patria*, the stock and cash in the various factories and the item that was eventually called "t'indisch fons" – the circulating capital at the disposal of Batavia when the account was closed.[36]

A good illustration of the integration of the Persian factory within the whole is provided by the general missive of the 18th December 1639, in which questions especially concerned with Persia comprise eight of the edition's 82 pages.[37] In the monsoon of 1638/39 eight Dutch ships touched at Bandar Abbas. Two came directly from Batavia, with a cargo presumably of spices, pepper and East Asian goods, the invoice value of which was 214,262 fl. One of them came from Vingurla, with a cargo presumably of pepper valued at 28,607 fl.. Four ships came from Surat

35. DUNLOP pp. 541, 617.
36. For the use of *fons*, see, for instance, van Diemen et al., general missive 9/12 1637, *Generale Missiven* I p. 655: "welckers incoop (of return goods) ons Indisch fons in de dertich tonnen sal verminderen ..." or van Diemen et al., general missive 18/12 1639, *Generale Missiven* II p. 37: "Om't Indisch capitael te stercken ende fons te maecken ... is soo grooten parthije peper ... affgesteecken."
37. Van Diemen et al., general missive 18/12 1639, *Generale Missiven* II, pp. 7–89, Persia dealt with pp. 30–38.

with a cargo invoiced at 217,167 fl.. Two of them had been loaded in India, whereas the two others had touched at Surat on their way from Taiwan with a cargo consisting chiefly of sugar; part of their cargo had been unloaded in Surat and part in Bandar Abbas. The eighth came from Mocha, where it had called on its way from Batavia; in Bandar Abbas it unloaded the rest of its cargo of sugar, some sapanwood and some of the coffee from Mocha. The invoice value of this cargo was 36,278 fl.. Thus altogether goods to the value of 496,000 fl. were transported to Persia. Over and above this 40,800 fl. was earned in freight between Surat and Bandar Abbas. At Bandar Abbas five of the ships had taken on freight goods on foreign account; three of them were bound for Surat, one for the Coromandel coast and one for Dabhol. The destination of the three last ships after they left Bandar Abbas is not mentioned, presumably they sailed direct to Batavia.

The plans for the monsoon of 1639/40 are then stated. Three ships are sent from Batavia to Bandar Abbas via Surat already in August, with a cargo for Bandar Abbas consisting of 3,648 piculs (about 450,000 pond) of pepper, nutmeg and cloves, 64 chests of cloth, 24 bales of cotton material, 778½ piculs of preserved ginger, gum lac, cardamom, long pepper, cassia, benzoin, sapanwood, sandalwood, etc., with an invoice value of altogether 220,424 fl.. In October one more ship was sent to Bandar Abbas from Batavia which was to touch at Ceylon on its way; it carried a cargo to Persia valued at 46,268 fl., including tin and sulphur from Achin. Furthermore Batavia had instructed the factory on Taiwan to send three ships to Surat and Bandar Abbas, at which latter place they were to take on a cargo of 12,000 piculs of candy and powdered sugar, 548,000 pieces of porcelain sorted with the Persian market in view, half of the copper that was expected from Japan in exchange for tin, 300 piculs zinc, 30 piculs radix china and 1,000 pond tea. Finally Taiwan was to send a sloop carrying Chinese gold to the Coromandel coast, where it was to take on a cargo of Bengal sugar for Persia. On the other hand in Agra and Gujarat no investments were planned as regards Persia for the current monsoon owing to lack of capital in Surat.

Not until December 1639 had it been possible to undertake the final calculation of the proceeds from the goods supplied to the Persian factory in the monsoon of 1637/38. At the end of the previous year a profit of 250,000 fl. had been provisionally forecast, but after the account was closed it could be stated that the net profit was 349,339 fl. after having subtracted 33,065 for expenses incurred in Persia. For the supplies of 1638/39 the accounts were not yet concluded; provisionally a net profit of 260,000 fl. was forecast.

Persia was only one of the Dutch factories in Asia; the total Dutch capital circulating in Asia at that time was as much as 8–10 million fl.. Nevertheless the Dutch Company's annual investments in Persia alone were up at a level that corresponded to or exceeded the Portuguese investments in the pepper trade in the best times of *Estado da India*. Or an even more striking comparison: the proceeds from the goods the Company supplied to Persia via Bandar Abbas could be compared with the Crown's gross revenue from the Portuguese custom house in Hormuz.

Any discussion as to whether the achievements reached by the middle of the 17th century were great or small is futile; even in a European context a permanent, well-consolidated trading company that, over and above its buildings and ships, had a trading capital of 4–5 million piastres at its disposal would be a factor to be reckoned with. By virtue of its size alone and its communications network it would necessarily influence the supply, demand and price formation on the relevant markets. On the other hand, as far as one can judge, there was a long way to go before the Companies (and here this applies only to the Dutch Company) secured that same quasimonopolistic position on the Asian markets as they had acquired in Europe so far as Asian goods were concerned. In the intra-Asian trade the peddling trade continued side by side with the Company trade. In 1638/39 there were 40 Asian ships in Bandar Abbas apart from the goods that were carried as freight on board the Company ships.

How did the peddling trade manage to survive? Batavia asked itself precisely this question in 1639. The problem was particularly conspicuous in two respects. Firstly, the attempt to redirect the Persian silk had gone by the board and silk was still conveyed to the Levant, although the Company's employees could not understand how this trade was able to survive if the merchants bought silk in Persia under the same conditions as the Company and sold it in Europe at the Company's prices. A similar problem was encountered in connection with the import of Indian cottons into Persia. As far as one could judge, 25–30,000 camel loads of cotton materials were imported annually by Persia from India. Inspired by this observation the Company had for some years attempted to trade with this article, but the results had been disappointing. In 1638/39 cotton material worth nearly 200,000 fl. was sold in Persia, some at a 4–5⁰/₀ loss and some with 10–40⁰/₀ profit, but only the material from Bengal and Coromandel had brought in a profit of 60–70⁰/₀. The result was not satisfactory. "You, gentlemen, and all who have managed the Company's business here, know that such trade, especially where textiles are concerned, is worthless unless 60–70⁰/₀ profit can be made over and above the purchase price and the direct costs ... Costs, high wages, bad management and whatever else is concealed therein (which are all part of the Company's costs) reduce a profit of 60–70⁰/₀ so much that when the account is closed there is nothing left, especially when the trade cannot be carried on with our own means."

In Batavia two possible solutions were given to the mystery of the pedlars' competitive ability. One was that the pedlars bought and sold with greater shrewdness than the Company employees. The other possibility was that the pedlars actually were satisfied with such a modest profit. "It is possible that the Moors carry on their business with considerable capital and travel forwards and backwards themselves ... and use no more than if they had stayed at home, and therefore are satisfied with 10, 12 or 15% profit; if this is the case we cannot compete with them."[38]

Both explanations were probably correct. Gradually, as the Dutch merchants' knowledge of the goods increased, the results of the export of cotton material from India to Persia were so satisfactory that it was maintained and expanded. But the reverse side of the explanation is worth noting. The Companies constituted a more effective form of organization, but they were not in every respect superior to the pedlars. The general costs were high, and the advantages the Company possessed – the internalization of the protection costs and greater control of the market – were not of decisive importance on every route or on every market. The 60–70% the Company had to have before a transaction could pay still left room in the 17th century for the Armenian Hovhannes and all the nameless pedlars of the early Asian trade.

38. *Ibid* pp. 32–33.

Conclusion

In the introduction the question was raised as to why the Companies were able to carry out the reorientation of the intercontinental trade, whereas the Portuguese had been forced to abandon the project. The problem was simplified and rendered more precise by focussing attention upon Hormuz and by employing two different methods of approach. Firstly, did the Companies as institutions show features of innovation that secured their superiority in relation to the older institutions? Secondly, did the plans and actions of the persons involved contain any features that might explain the fall of Hormuz?

It is the first of these two hypotheses that has proved to be the most fruitful. Without doubt the Companies represent an example of an institutional innovation, an instance of progress, if you like, in the sense of an institution that makes it possible to procure economic goods with a more economic use of scarce resources. The comparative investigation was concentrated on protection and market conditions; in both these fields the gap between the Company and the pedlar is considerable. The Companies internalized the protection costs that constituted such a considerable item among the pedlar's expenses, and eliminated the extra element of risk the peddling market involved on account of the non-transparency and short-term price fluctuations of the market. The distinction between the Companies and the redistributive institutions is less clear-cut; especially as far as the Dutch Company is concerned that organization whose primary function was to produce violence for the protection of the trade was also able to become the primary instrument for creating income, and thus the commercial activity, under cover of armed protection, could turn into the demanding of tribute, while on the other hand the redistributive organizations, especially Portugal, were actively engaged in trade. It must be stressed, however, that there was a fundamental difference between the institutions, which, like the Companies in the beginning of the 17th century, kept an eye on the market also as regards the practice of violence and whose ultimate measure of success was economic profit or loss, and those institutions, which, in their production of protection, collection of tribute and possible market policy, maintained the redistributive aim and merely remained passive when subjected to the influence of the market.

The designation "structural crisis", in the sense of a confrontation between fundamentally different institutional complexes, thus appears justified, and the central problems of the book – the redirection of the trade routes and the fall of Hormuz, appear already to be solved with the help of the comparative investigation in the first part. The investigation of events in the second part shows that this solution is alien to the sources, in the sense that only few of the persons involved suspected and none of them was able to survey such a correlation of facts as the one presented. Of especial interest in this connection is the Spanish-Portuguese policy, because it may clearly be ascertained that the Persian problem and Hormuz's strategic situation were the objects of careful consideration for several years previous to the fall of the town and that considerable resources were set aside for a diplomatic or military solution to the problem, while at the same time it may be ascertained that these considerations and proposals for solving the problem did not have very much contact with reality and only affected the sequence of events superficially. The one who came closest to understanding this correlation was in fact the visionary, Anthony Sherley. The idea he put forward, the redirection of the Persian silk export, was practicable within a Persian and global context – the Companies proved this in the 1620s and 1630s – but it had no place within the socio-economic structure of Estado da India, as may be shown by the intrigues surrounding the Persian envoys and the slow and halfhearted manner in which the negotiations concerning the proposal for redirection as well as its realization were carried on. The Council of State accomplished what could be accomplished within the system by dispatching Figueroa and Ruy Freire, but the possible was not sufficient. The Companies rode the storm that raged against the Spanish-Portuguese Empire. Perhaps nothing illustrates the situation so strikingly as the ironic contrast between the Spanish-Portuguese authorities' year-long deliberations regarding the defence of Hormuz, and the parenthetical decision on a local level, which secured for the Persians the aid of the English fleet that destroyed the walls of Hormuz.

The fall of Hormuz was as definitive as the fall of a town can be: it never rose again. With the information available we can only catch a faint glimpse of the fate of the Portuguese trade in the years following the fall of Hormuz; we know it found new routes, and in all probability it continued to prosper within the institutional framework of the early Asian trade. The peddling trade survived at any rate in Hormuz's successor, Bandar Abbas, and the pedlars won the first round in the fight over the trade in Asian raw silk that was fought out in the 1620s and 1630s. It gives occasion for determining more precisely the limits that for the moment were set for the scope of the Companies. With their high overheads they were not in all cases able to compete; their immediate victory concerned the goods especially burdened by protection costs and which followed routes so long and difficult to survey that the market was to a high degree non-transparent.

Economic history knows nothing of leaps and revolutions, therefore the impracticable discussions about "Wirtschaftstil" or "stages of development" so easily get out of hand. We know that every period must be analysed according to its own conditions, but periods are not "pure". A precise definition of a style or a stage captures an abstract moment in the stream of reality, whereas fidelity to the idea of all things' transitoriness deprives us of the possibility of sharpening our analytical tools.

The confrontation around Hormuz offers a rare, if not unique, opportunity in an empirical investigation of relating two styles or stages in a concrete historical moment.

414

Appendix

Currency and Weights

"One of the minor difficulties attendant on the study of the commercial records of our period is the diversity of units employed by the writers."[1] Moreland's words are a nice piece of understatement, in fact the multitude of units employed may cause the researcher infinite trouble. The difficulties are greatest, however, so far as currency is concerned, while units of weight present greater stability and practically always may be identified with a fair amount of certainty.

Weights

There is no difficulty in determining the equivalents of the English *pound avoir-du-pois*, the Dutch *pond* and the *small pounds of Venice*[2] *and Marseilles*.[3] It should be noted, however, that silk ordinarily was sold in England by the *great pound* of 24 oz.

In Portugal and in Estado da India a number of units of weight were in use. The only important one in the present context, however, is the peso pequeno of the Casa da India, a hundredweight, *quintal*, of 112 pounds, *arrateis*. This was considered equal to the English hundredweight,[4] to 166 libbre sottile of Venice[5] or to 101^1/$_2$ Dutch ponds,[6] i.e. 50.802, 49.966 and 50.141 kg. respectively.

In Persia the most important unit of weight was the *man-i shah*, equalling 2 *man-i Tabriz*. The man-i shah was considered equal to 12^1/$_2$ lb. av.[7] or 11^1/$_2$ Dutch ponds,[8] i.e. 5.662 and 5.681 kg. respectively. An interesting corrective to the conventional conversions is offered by the experiment carried out by the English factor, who found that the weight of the man-i shah

1. MORELAND, *Aurangzeb* p. 329.
2. BERENGO p. 357.
3. BERGASSE & RAMBERT pp. 302–303.
4. LANE p. 31, n. 27.
5. dall'OLMO pp. 24–25.
6. KELLENBENZ, *Poivre* p. 21.
7. Pettus, Isfahan, to E.I.C.O., 27/9 1618, C.R.O., London, O.C. 699.
8. TERPSTA p. 294.

equalled 210 piastres,[9] i.e. 5.773 kg., assuming that the coins had the standard gross weight of 27.493 grammes. Conventionally the *bale* in Persia was reckoned at 18 man-i shah, the *load* at 2 bales or 36 man-i shah.

In Aleppo the *rotolo* was considered equal to 6 lb. $9^3/_5$ oz. Venetian weight[10] or 3 English great pounds,[11] i.e. 1.984 and 2.040 kg. respectively. The *Aleppo quintal* of 100 rotolos was considered equal to $5^1/_3$ quintal of Marseilles or 4 English cw.,[12] i.e. 207.2 and 203.2 kg. respectively.

The *kantar forfori* employed in the spice trade in Alexandria may be considered equivalent to 45 kg.[13]

For the sake of convenience, but without any pretension to metrological exactitude, the equivalents may be summarized in a table of conversion into the metric system.

Table 20. *Metric equivalents of the most current units of weight.*

	kg
Engl. lb. av.	0.452
– great lb.	0.680
– cw	50.802
Dutch pond	0.494
Venetian pound	0.301
Marseilles pound	0.388
– quintal	38.800
Casa da India arratel	0.447
– quintal	50.000
Persian man-i Tabriz	2.838
– man-i shah	5.675
– bale	102.150
– load	204.300
Aleppo rotolo	2.000
– quintal	200.000
Alexandria kantar forfori	45.000

Currency

Determining the equivalents of units of payment is much more hazardous than determining the equivalents of units of weight. Firstly, because the unit referred to may be either a specific coin or a unit of account. Where a speci-

9. "I have caused a man shah to be tryed and find it just the waight of 210 pieces of eight." Burt, at the Persian army, to E.I.Co., 6/10 1630, C.R.O., London, O.C. 1317.
10. BERENGO p. 357.
11. SANDERSON p. 290.
12. *Ibid.*
13. HINZ p. 25.

fic coin is referred to a rough conversion may always be made, assuming that its silver content or its rate of exchange in relation to a known coin may be established. Where, on the other hand, it is a question of money of account, it may be difficult or even impossible to fix a rate of conversion, because the price of silver or specific coins as expressed in money of account might undergo violent fluctuations. As a principal rule the equivalent of a unit of account must be established in relation to the specific quotation, preferably on the basis of evidence from the source of information in question itself.

Secondly, it must be taken into account that coins of gold and silver in intercontinental trade must in certain respects be considered a commodity; precious metals *were* more valuable in terms of commodities in Asia than in Europe. The distortion this circumstance may cause may be compared to the distortions created by 19th century historians when they tried to convert the coins of former times into *Reichsmark* or *francs*. Where distant areas are concerned, conversions into grammes of silver does not represent exact equivalents but only numerical relations, disregarding the actual buying power of the units in question. It follows that any conversion involving distant areas must be taken with caution and considered in its context. A table of conversion of the coins and units of account referred to in this book would give the impression of an exactitude that cannot be established. I have preferred rough conversions into the most current of the international trade coins of the time, the Spanish *piastre (peso de a ocho, rial of eight, stuk van achten)*. The piastre was coined in the 16th and 17th centuries with great stability with a silver content only slightly below the prescribed 25.57 grammes of pure silver.[14]

England and the Netherlands enjoyed relatively stable monetary conditions in this period, the Dutch *guilder* (fl.) corresponding to 10–11 grammes of pure silver,[15] the English *crown* was coined with a content of 27.527 grammes of pure silver after 1604[16] and the *shilling* with a content of 5.75 grammes of pure silver after 1601.[17] Of course the rates of exchange in terms of piastres fluctuated; roughly, however, the piastre may be considered equivalent to $2^1/_2$ fl. and $4^1/_2$ sh.

The Portuguese *cruzado* was originally a gold coin; it had disappeared from circulation by the middle of the 16th century, but was perpetuated as a unit of account, one cruzado being equal to 400 reis. The *xerafim*, which became the most current unit of account in Estado da India, was originally an Egyptian gold coin. As a unit of account it was equivalent to 300 reis. The pardao was originally a Persian unit of account, equal to 5 larins. In Estado da India pardao was used in various combinations to designate more than

14. Friedrich von Schrötter, *Wörterbuch der Münzkunde* s.v. *Peso*.
15. Posthumus p. CIX.
16. Schrötter, *op.cit.* s.v. *Crown*.
17. *Ibid.* s.v. *Schilling*.

one unit of account. When pardao is mentioned alone, however, it may gene- rally be taken to represent one xerafim or 300 reis.

The basal unit of account in Portugal and Estado da India was thus the *real* (pl. *reis*), which was linked to silver through various coins of larger denomination. At the beginning of the 16th century 2340 reis were coined from one mark silver (229.5 grammes) in Portugal. The real was devaluated on more than on occasion, however, and from 1588–1641 2800 reis corre- sponded to one mark silver. The relation between the real and the mark sil- ver in Estado da India differed, however, from the relation fixed in Por- tugal, the light coins coined in Goa from the second half of the 16th century having an appreciably lower silver content than the small coins coined in Portugal. *Circa* 1580 one mark silver thus corresponded to 4398 reis in Goa. The discrepancy between the real of Portugal and the real of Estado da India may be explained as an attempt on the part of the authorities in Goa to stop the outflow of good coins from Goa by offering the importer of silver coins better value in terms of money of account, but it may also be considered an expression of the fact referred to above: silver coin was worth more in Asia than in Europe.[18]

Conversions of Portuguese units into piastres. Where the unit may be linked to the Portuguese reis, the rate of conversion may be established as corresponding roughly to the official rate of exchange, i.e. one cruzado equivalent to 10 Castilian *reals* or 1$^{1}/_{4}$ piastre. In Asia the rate of conversion must be established in every single case, taking into account not only the fluctuations in the silver content of the coins, but also the seasonal fluctua- tions in the rates of exchange.

The Persian system of money of account was distinguished by an unusual simplicity. Without regard to changes in the rates of exchange or debase- ments the relation between the Persian units were fixed in the period under review:

1 toman	10.000	dirham
1 azar	1.000	–
1 abasi	200	–
1 mahmudi	100	–
1 shahi	50	–
1 bisteg	20	–
1 kasbek	5	–

Information about the value of Persian coins is very scant in the 16th century, but in the letters of the Venetian merchant, Andrea Berengo, from

18. The Portuguese and Luso-Indian coinage has been treated exhaustively in MAGALHAES-GODINHO *passim*. Important sources are LINSCHOTEN I pp. 161–162, SASSETTI p. 345, Barret in HAKLUYT pp. 18–20, PYRARD de LAVAL II pp. 68–69.

Aleppo in 1555 we have some evidence enabling us to make a rough calculation of the value of the shahi. No silk arrived from Persia that year, and Berengo informs us that this was because the Shah himself had bought 500 loads of silk for export to India, and that he had only paid the merchants half the accustomed price "because he has made the money the half of what they were worth in spite of the protests of the people, i.e. his coins are called saie they are worth here 18 soldi a piece, and he has made two out of one and give them out as good coin."[19] In another context Berengo states that the new shahi is equal to $2^1/_4$ maidin of Aleppo.[20] On the basis of the Berengo letters we may further establish the silver content of the Aleppo maidin at 0.943 grammes.[21] Assuming the silver content to be the same as in Venetian coin the gross weight of the *shahi* may be calculated at 4.473 grammes before the "crying down" and 2.236 grammes after the "crying down".

This calculation would be too roundabout to be trusted, if it were not supported by the numismatic evidence. In the period 1538/38 – 1593/94, however, all known Persian silver coins, apart from a few lighter ones, weigh either 2.30 or 4.60 grammes approximately.[22] As a less pure alloy than the one found in the very fine Venetian coins might be expected, this confirms the calculation based upon Berengo's information. Of course this does not disprove the "crying down" of 1555, as the coins carried no inscription to indicate their denomination, a 50 % devaluation in terms of money of account would leave no trace in the numismatic material.

From the 1560's we have some scattered evidence to support the assumption that the shahi was identical with the preserved coins of 2.30 grammes. In 1566 one shahi is considered equal to 6 English pence, in 1568 1 piastre is considered equal to 10 shahi.[23]

Fernand Braudel states that a Persian devaluation had taken place before the Turkish devaluation of 1584.[24] I myself have found no evidence in support of this statement, but there can be no doubt that a debasement did take place not later than 1593/94 and possibly before, because from that year the series of coins of 2.30 and 4.60 grammes (i.e. approximately $1/_2$ and 1 mizqal) was parallelled by another series of coins of 3.84, 7.68 and eventually 1.92 grammes, i.e. based upon a unit of weight corresponding to $5/_6$ mizqal.[25] The

19. BERENGO p. 78.
20. *Ibid.* p. 126.
21. *Ibid.* p. 77 cf. p. 355.
22. Rabino di Borgomale, *Coins, Medals and Seals of the Shahs of Iran 1500–1941*, pp. 30–34.
23. D. Morgan & C. H. Coote (ed.s) *Early Voyages and Travels to Russia and Persia.* Hakluyt Society, First Ser., vol. xx pp. 369, 401.
24. BRAUDEL II p. 477.
25. RABINO di BORGOMALE, *op.cit.* pp. 30–34 jf. p. 7.

existence of the two parallel series raises two problems: which of the two is referred to in the records of the Companies, and how could the two series of coins co-exist?

From the beginning of Company trading to Persia we have ample information concerning the rates of exchange between piastres and shahi. Thus in 1620 the English contracted with the mint-master in Shiraz to deliver Persian coin at the rate of 13.3 shahi a piastre. When the Royal factor Lalabeg heard about this contract, he declared that it would cost the man his head, for Abbas had ordered that nobody should pay more than 13.1 shahi for a piastre.[26] We are not informed if the contract had fatal consequences for the mint-master, but probably the transaction caused him some trouble, for still in 1622 he had not settled his account with the Company.[27] Anyhow, the rate of exchange he had contracted for was not only above the official rate of exchange, but also above the rate of exchange of the free market, which with minor fluctuations became 13.1 shahi a piastre.[28] If the content of silver was the same in the Persian shahi as in the piastre this rate of exchange would correspond to a gross weight of 2.09 grammes per shahi. As no doubt a seignorage was claimed, the coins encountered by the Companies were in all probability the lighter of the two series, the one based upon a unit of weight of $5/6$ mizqal. There is no reference to the heavier coin in the Company records, but a stray reference seems to indicate that this series circulated in Khurasan.[29]

The Persian coin was stable throughout most of the 17th century. Tavernier still calculates with 13 shahi per piastre, but in the last decades of the century a certain depreciation seems to have taken place.[30] On the basis of the calculations in the accounts of the Armenian merchant Hovhannes Kachikian has estimated the toman *circa* 1686 at 306.4 grammes of silver, corresponding to 1.53 grammes of silver per shahi.[31]

The *larin*, the famous trade coin of peculiar shape and very pure alloy, originated in Lar and deviated from the Persian system of units of account. It weighed a little more than 5 grammes,[32] in 1619 it is stated that the usual

26. B.M., London, Egerton 2123 f. 36.
27. C. R. O., London, Factory Records, Persia I p. 17, pp. 160–161.
28. Consultations Lar 16/1 1619, C. R. O., London, O. C. 717; Barker et al., Isfahan, to E. I. Co. 19/5 1626, O. C. 1228; Gibson et al., Gombroon, to E. I. Co. 22/3 1632, O. C. 1425.
29. Heinrich von Poser, *Lebens- und Todesgeschichte*, Jena 1675. von Poser travelled in 1621 from Isfahan over Kandahar to Lahore. Under 15th of August 1621 he states, that the coin in Khurasan was different from what he had encountered in Isfahan "here the pay twelve kasbek for a shahi".
30. Rabino di Borgomale, *op. cit.* pp. 38–39.
31. KHACHIKIAN p. 267.
32. MAGALHAES-GODINHO pp. 301–302.

rate of exchange in Persia is 4¹/₂ larin per piastre, but that this is a disadvantageous rate involving a loss of 1.85 shahi per piastre.[33]

Conversions of Persian units into piatres. Between the possible devaluation of the shahi in 1555 and the depreciation in the last decades of the 17th century two periods may be distinguished: in the first period the shahi was one mizqal, in the second period ⁵/₆ of a mizqal. Assuming the fineness to be unchanged, this corresponded to a little less than 11 and a little more than 13 shahi per piastre respedtively. When the debasement took place cannot be established, but according to the numismatic evidence it cannot have been later than 1593/94. The rate of exchange of the larin may be put at 4¹/₂–5 larin per piastre.

The Turkish coinage presents the greatest problems. The economic difficulties of the Ottoman Empire were reflected in violent fluctuations in the rates of the ordinary coins. Apparently no coins of large denominations were coined in the Ottoman Empire in this period, the demand for large coins being satisfied through the import of European gold and silver coins. The Turkish coins were of small denomination: *aspres* in Constantinople and *maidins* (3 aspres = 2 maidins) and *shahis* (1 shahi = 5 maidins) in Syria and Egypt. These units at the same time served as units of account, 60 aspres or 40 maidins until 1584 being equivalent to 1 ducat or *veneziano*. When in the last decades of the 16th century the silver content of the small coins was reduced, it gave rise to great confusion, the "black market" price of foreign coins in terms of aspres or maidins being above the official rate of exchange. At the same time the use of the terms "ducat" and "veneziano", both in the sense of money of account, linked to the debased aspre, and in the sense of real money makes it even more difficult to fix the correct rate of conversion. The problem, however, in many cases solves itself through the fact that European coin was used af means of payment. Where Turkish coin or units of account linked to Turkish coin is used, however, it will always be necessary to establish the actual rate of exchange, preferably on the basis of the source of information concerned. In the merchants' letter books from Aleppo, for example, we find that European silver coins were bought by weight by the mint at varying prices in terms of maidins – the rate of exchange was so to speak kept floating – and thus the actual rate of exchange may be determined by means of the mint price.[34]

From the last years of the sixteenth century the ducat as unit of account was fixed at 120 aspres or 80 maidins; at the same time merchants begin to use the piastre as unit of account, being fixed at 54 maidins or 80

33. Consultations, Isfahan, 14/6 1619, C. R. O., London, O. C. 717.
34. BERENGO pp. 77, 95; HERMITE pp. 51, 60, 63, 72; B. M., London, Sloane 867 f. 30, 64.

aspres. While the relation between the real ducat and the ducat as money of account was unrealistic even at this rate, the correspondence between the real piastre and the piastre as unit of account appears to have been closer.[35]

The *rupee,* the standard silver coin of the Mogul Empire, weighed approximately 11¹/₃ grammes. The conventional rate of conversion in the English Company records was 2¹/₄, later 2¹/₂ sh., while the Dutch Company fixed the rupee at 24 st. i.e. a littele less than 1¹/₄ fl. The Gujarat *mahmudi* (not to be confused with the Persian coin of the same name) was still coined half a century after the Mogul conquest. The weight of the mahmudi was approximately 4.7 grammes, the usual rate of exchange being 5 mahmudis for 2 rupees.[36] Slightly exaggerating its value, the piastre may thus be equalled to 2 rupees or 5 mahmudis.

35. Vuk Vinaver, „Der Venezianische Goldzechin in der Republik Ragusa", *Bolletino dell'Istituto de Storia della societa e dello stato Veneziano* IV, 1962 pp. 140–144.
36. MORELAND, *Aurangzeb* pp. 329–331.

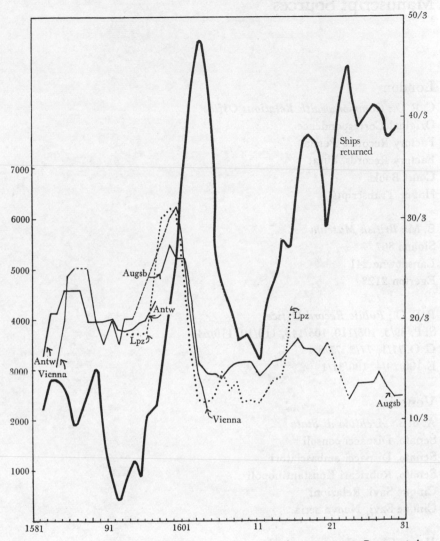

Ships returned from Asia 1581–1630. 3 Year moving averages. Pepper prices 1581–1630, grm.s of fine silver per 1,000 kg.s. Augsburg, Leipzig, Vienna and Antwerp. Sources: ELSASS, PRIBRAM, van der WEE.

Manuscript Sources

London
C. R. O.; *Commonwealth Relations Office*
Original Correspondence
Factory Records, Persia
Factory Records, Surat
Court Books
Hague Transcripts

B. M.: *British Museum*
Sloane 867
Lansdowne 241
Egerton 2123

P. R. O.; *Public Record Office*
S. P. 89/3, 105/110, 105/148, 110/10, 110/54
C. O. 77/1, 77/2, 77/3
E 190/29/4. 190/31/1

Venezia
A. d. S.: *Archivio di Stato*
Senato, Dispacci consoli
Senato, Dispacci ambasciatori
Senato, Rubricari Konstantinopoli
Cinque Savi, Relazioni
Cinque Savi, Nuova seria

Museo Civico-Correr
Cicogna 2698, 3036/6–10
P. D. 988, 1480, 2339 xi

Paris
B. N.: *Bibliothèque Nationale*
Fonds Portugais 1, 36
Fonds Français 16161, 16167

Archive du Ministère des Affaires Étrangères
Correspondance Politique, Turquie

Marseilles

Archive de la Chambre de Commerce
J. 889, 890, 891, 921, 922, 969, 1565, 1729

Roma

Archivio, Congregazione de Propaganda Fide
Scritture Originale, Congregazioni Generali, vol 209

The Vatican

Arch. Vaticano: *Archivio Segreto Vaticano*
Principe 54
Fondo Borghese I: 965; II: 20, 24, 68, 152; III: 106 e; IV: 52.
Fondo Gonfalonieri 22, 65
Nunziature Spagna 60 a, 333
Armarium 45

Bibl. Vaticano: *Biblioteca Apostolica Vaticana*
Fondo Barberini 8273

Madrid

B. N. *Biblioteca Nacional*
Ms. 2352, 8180

Simancas

Arch. Simancas: *Archivo general de Simancas*
Estado, legajos 435, 436, 481, 494, 495, 493, 618, 707, 972, 1171, 1352, 1856, 2864.
Secretarias Provinciales, libros 1479, 1551

Lisboa

Torre do Tombo: *Arquivo Nacional da Torre do Tombo*
Corpo Chronologico
Documentos Remettidos
Misc. Ms. 1104, 1109, 1113
Misc. Ms. do Convento da Graça de Lisboa, Cx. 6, tomo 2 e.

Arquivo Historico Ultramarino
Papeis avulsos, India

B. N. *Biblioteca Nacional*
Fundo Geral 580

Printed Sources and Modern Works

Ackerlee: – H. W. Ackerlee, 'Amsterdamer Börsenpreislisten 1624–26', *Economisch-Historisch Jaarboek*, XIII (1927).

Ain-i Akbari: – H. Blochmann (ed.), *The Ain-i Akbari*. 3 vols. 1873–1907.

Alexandre de Rhodes: – *Divers voyages et missions du P. Alexandre de Rhodes*. Paris 1653.

Alexandrowicz: – C. H. Alexandrowicz, *An Introduction to the History of the Law of Nations in the East Indies*. Oxford 1967.

Allen: – W. E. D. Allen, *Problems of Turkish Power in the Sixteenth Century*. London 1963.

Archivo Portuguez-Orinetal: – J. H. da Cunha Rivara (ed.), *Archivo Portuguez-Oriental*, 7 vols. Nova Goa 1857–65.

Arup: – Erik Arup, *Studier i engelsk og tysk handelshistorie*. København 1907.

Assentos: – P. S. S. Pissurlencar (ed.), *Assentos do Conselho do Estado*, 2 vols. Bastora 1953–54.

Atti: – *Atti del X Congresso Internazionale di Scienze Storiche, 1955*. Roma 1957.

Babinger: – Franz Babinger, *Sherleiana I, Sir Anthony Sherley's persische Botschaftsreise 1599–1601*. Berlin 1932.

Babinger, *Sherleiana II:* – Franz Babinger, *Sherleiana II, Sir Anthony Sherley's marokkanische Sendung 1605–1606*. Berlin 1932.

Barassin: – J. Barassin, 'Compagnies de navigation et expéditions françaises dans l'Océan Indien au XVIIe siècle', *Océan Indien et Méditerranée*. Paris 1964.

Barbiche: – Bernard Barbiche (ed.), *Correspondance du Nonce en France Innocenzo del Bufalo 1601–1604*. Acta Nuntiaturae Gallicae, t. 4. Rom-Paris 1964.

Barozzi: – N. Barozzi & G. Berchet (ed.), *Le relazioni dagli ambasciatori Veneziani*, seria V: Turchia.

Bayani: – K. Bayani, *Les relations de l'Iran avec l'Europe occidentale a l'époque Safavide*. Paris 1937.

Bellan: – Lucien-Louis Bellan, *Chah' Abbas I*. Paris 1932.

Berchet, *Nuovi Documenti:* – G. Berchet (ed.), *La Repubblica di Venezia e la Persia, Nuovi Documenti e Regesti*. Venezia 1866.

Berchet, *Persia:* – G. Berchet (ed.), *La Repubblica de Venezia e la Persia*. Torino 1865.

Berchet, *Siria:* – G. Berchet (ed.), *Relazioni dei consoli veneti nella Siria*. Torino 1866.

Berengo: – Ugo Tucci (ed.), *Lettres d'un marchand vénetien Andrea Berengo, 1553–1556*. Paris 1957.

Bergasse & Rambert: – Louis Bergasse & G. Rambert, *Histoire du commerce de Marseille de 1599–1660, de 1660 a 1789*. Paris 1954.

Bocarro: – Antonio Bocarro, *Decada 13 da Historia da India*. Collecção de monumentos ineditos para a historia das conquistas dos portuguezes, 1ª serie, t.VI. Lisboa 1876.

Bocarro, *Livro do Estado:* – Antonio Bocarro, *Livro do Estado da India Oriental*. Arquivo Portugues Oriental, Nova Edição, tomo IV, vol. II:1. Bastora 1937.

Boothby: – Richard Boothby, *A Brief Discovery or Description of the Most Famous Island of Madagascar*. London 1646.

Boxer, *Commentaries:* – C. R. Boxer (ed.), *Commentaries of Ruy Freyre de Andrada*. London 1930.

Boxer, *Corte Real:* – C. R. Boxer, 'Admiral João Pereira Corte Real and the Construction of Portuguese East-Indiamen in the Early Seventeenth Century', *The Mariner's Mirror*, 26 (1940).

Boxer, *Empire:* – C. R. Boxer, *The Dutch Seaborne Empire, 1600–1800*. London 1965.

Boxer, *Portuguese Empire:* – C. R. Boxer, *The Portuguese Seaborne Empire, 1415–1825*. London 1969.

Boxer, *Society:* – C. R. Boxer, *Portuguese Society in the Tropics*. Madison and Milwaukee 1965.

van Brakel: – S. van Brakel, *De hollandsche handelscompagnieën der zeventiende eeuw*. s'Gravenhage 1908.

Braudel: – Fernand Braudel, *La Méditerranée et le monde méditerranéen à l'époque de Philippe II*, 2. éd. Paris 1966

Braudel, *Réalités économiques:* – Fernand Braudel. *Réalités économiques et prises de conscience*, Annales E. S. C., 12 (1957).

Braudel & Romano: – Fernand Braudel & R. Romano, *Navires et marchandises à l'entrée du port de Livourne*, 1547–1611. Paris 1951.

Braun: – H. Braun, *Geschichte Irans seit 1500*. Handbuch der Orientalistik, ed. B. Spuler, 1. Abt. 6. Bd. 3. Abschn. Leiden 1959.

Brockelmann: – Carl Brockelmann, *Geschichte der islamischen Völker und Staaten*, 2. Aufl. München-Berlin 1943.

van den Broecke: – W. Ph. Coolhaas (ed.), *Pieter van den Broecke in Azië*. Werken uitgegeven door de Linschoten Vereeniging, LXIII–LXIV. s'Gravenhage 1962–63.

Brosset: – M. Brosset (ed.), *Collection d'historiens arméniens*. St Petersborg 1874.

Bugnon: – Didier Bugnon, *Relation exacte concernant les caravanes ou cortèges des marchands d'Asie*. Nancy 1707.

Busse:– Heribert Busse, *Untersuchungen zum islamischen Kanzleiwesen*. Kairo 1959.

Calendar S. P. East Indies: – *Calendar of State Papers, Colonial Series, East Indies*, 5 vols. London 1862–92.

Calendar S. P. Venetian: – *Calendar of State Papers, Foreign Series, Venice*, vol. XI–XII. London 1897–1905.

Carali: – P. Paolo Carali, *Fakhr ad-Dīn, principe del Libano, e la Corte di Toscana, 1605–1635*. Reale Accademia d'Italia Studi e Documenti, t. 5. Roma 1936.

Carré: – *The Travels of the Abbé Carré in India and the Near East 1672–74*. Hakluyt Society, Sec. Ser., vol. 95 & 97. London 1947.

Chaudhuri: – K. N. Chaudhuri, *The English East India Company*. London 1965.

Chaunu, *Galion:* – Pierre Chaunu, 'Le galion de Manille, grandeur et décadence d'une route de la soie', *Annales E.S.C.*, 6 (1951).

Chaunu, *Séville:* – Pierre Chaunu, *Séville et l'Atlantique*, 12 vols. Paris 1957–60.

Chew: – Samuel C. Chew, *The Crescent and the Rose*. New York 1965.

Chronicle: – *A Chronicle of the Carmelites in Persia and the Papal Mission of the 17th and 18 th Centures*. London 1939.

Cipolla: – Carlo M. Cipolla, 'The Economic Decline of Italy', Brian Pullan (ed.), *Crisis and Change in the Venetian Economy*. London 1968.

Clark: – G. N. Clark & W. J. M. van Eysinga, *The Colonial Conferences between England and the Netherlands in 1613 and 1615*, part II. Bibliotheca Visseriana XVII. Leyden 1951.

Coen: – H. T. Colenbrander & W. Ph. Coolhaas (ed. s), *Jan Pietersz. Coen, Bescheiden omtrent zijn bedrijf in Indië*, 8 vols. Haag 1919–1953.

Collier & Billoud: – Raymond Collier & Joseph Billoud, *Histoire de commerce de Marseille, 1480–1599.* Paris 1951.

Cordeiro: – Luciano Cordeiro, *Como se perdeu Ormuz.* Lisboa 1896.

Court Minutes: – Ethel Bruce Sainsbury (ed.), *A Calendar of the Court Minutes of the East India Company.* London 1906.

Coverte: – Robert Coverte, *A True and almost Incredible Report of an Englishman . . .* London 1612.

Cunaeus: – A. Hotz (ed.), *Journal der Reis van der Gezant der O. I. Compagnie J. Cunaeus . . . door Cornelius Speelman.* Amsterdam 1908.

van Dam: – F. W. Stapel (ed.), Pieter van Dam, *Beschryvinge van de Oostindische Compagnie.* Rijksgeschiedkundige Publikatiën, Bd. 63, 68, 74, 76, 83, 87. s'Gravenhage 1927–43.

Danvers: – F. C. Danvers, *The Portuguese in India,* 2. vols. London 1894.

Davis: – Ralph Davis, 'Influences de l'Angleterre sur le déclin de Venise au XVIIe siècle', *Aspetti e cause della decadenza economica veneziana nel secolo XVII.* Venezia-Roma 1961.

Delacroix: – S. Delacroix (ed.), *Histoire universelle des missions catholiques,* t. III. Paris 1957.

Dermigny: – L. Dermigny, *La Chine et l'Occident,* 4 vols. Paris 1964.

van Dillen: – J. G. van Dillen, *Het oudste aandeelhoudersregister van de Kamer Amsterdam der Oost-Indische Compagnie.* s'Gravenhage 1958.

Dobel: – Friedrich Dobel, 'Über einen Pfefferhandel der Fugger und Welser, 1586–91', *Zeitschrift des Historischen Vereins für Schwaben und Neuburg,* 13. Jahrg. (1886).

Documentação Ultramarina Portuguesa: – *Documentação Ultramarina Portuguesa,* 3 vols. Lisboa 1960–63.

Documentos Remettidos: – *Documentos Remettidos da India ou Livros das Monsões,* 4 vols. Lisboa 1880–1893.

Dunlop: – H. Dunlop (ed.), *Bronnen tot de geschiedenis der Oostindische Compagnie in Perzië.* Rijksgeschiedkundige Publikatiën, bd. 72, s'Gravenhage 1930.

Early Travels: – *Early Voyages and Travels to Russia and Persia.* Hakluyt Society, First Ser., vol. 72. 1886.

Elliott: – J. H. Elliott, *The Revolt of the Catalans, a Study in the Decline of Spain, 1598–1640.* Cambridge 1963.

Elsas: – M. J. Elsas, *Umriss einer Geschichte der Preise und Löhne in Deutschland.* Leyden 1936–49.

English Factories: – William Foster (ed.), *The English Factories in India.* London 1906.

Eysinga: – G. N. Clark & W. J. M. van Eysinga, *The Colonial Conferences between England and the Netherlands in 1613 and 1615,* part I. Bibliotheca Visseriana XV. Leyden 1940.

Fagniez: – Gustave Fagniez, *Le père Joseph et Richelieu.* Paris 1894.

Falcão: – Luiz de Figueiredo Falcão, *Livro em que se contém toda a fazenda e real patrimonio . . . anno de MDCVII.* Lisboa 1859.

Faria e Sousa: – Manuel de Faria e Sousa, *Asia Portuguesa,* 6 vols. Porto 1947.

Faroughy: – Abbas Faroughy, *Histoire du Royaume de Hormuz depuis son origine jusqu'à son incorporation dans l'Empire Persan des Séfévids en 1622.* (Dact.) Bruxelles 1949.

Favaro: – Antonio Favaro, 'Giovanfrancesco Sagredo e la vita scientifica in Venezia al principio del XVII secolo', *Nuovo Archivio Veneto,* Nuova serie, t. IV. (1902).

Ferreira: – Godofredo Ferreira, *Relacão da viagem de um correio do vice-rei das*

Indias Orientais a sua magestade expedido de Goa no primeiro de janeiro 1608. Lisboa 1953.

Feynes de Monfart: – Henri Feynes de Monfart, *An Exact and Curious Survey of the East Indies even to Canton.* London 1615.

Figueroa: – *Comentarios de D. Garcia de Silva y Figueroa de la embajada que del parte del Rey de Espana Don Felipe III hizo al Rey Xa Abas de Persia,* 2 vols. Madrid 1903.

First Letter Book: – Sir George Birdwood (ed.), *The First Letter Book of the East India Company, 1600–1619.* London 1893.

Fitzler: – M. A. Hedwig Fitzler, 'Der Anteil der Deutschen an der Kolonialpolitik Philipps II von Spanien in Asien', *Vierteljahrschrift für Sozial- und Wirtschaftsgeschichte,* 28 (1935).

Florencio del Niño Jesus, *A Persia.*

Florencio del Niño Jesus, *En Persia.*

Foster: – William Foster, *England's Quest for Eastern Trade.* London 1933.

Foster, *Early Travels:* – William Foster (ed.), *Early Travels in India 1583–1619.* Oxford 1921.

Gaspar de S. Bernardino: – Aug. Reis Machado (ed.), *Fr. Gaspar de S. Bernardino, Itinerario da India por terra.* Lisboa 1953.

Gédouyn: – A. Boppe (ed.), *Journal et correspondance de Gédouyn „le Turc",* *Consul de France à Alep 1623–25.* Paris 1909.

Generale Missiven: – W. Ph. Coolhaas (ed.), *Generale Missiven van Gouverneurs-Generaal en raden aan Heeren XVII der vereenigde Oostindische Compagnie,* 2 vols. Rijksgeschiedkundige Publikatiën, bd. 104, 112. s'Gravenhage 1960–64.

Glamann: – Kristof Glamann, *Dutch-Asiatic Trade 1620–1740.* København-Haag 1958.

van Goens: – 'Rapport van van Goens', *Bijdragen tot de taal- land- en volkenkunde van Nederlandsch Indië,* IV (1856).

Gollancz: – Sir Hermann Gollancz (ed.), *Chronicle of Events between the years 1623 and 1733 Relating to the Settlement of the Order of Carmelites in Mesopotamia.* Oxford 1927.

Gouvea: – Antonio de Gouvea, *Relaçam em que se trata as guerras e grandes victorias que alcançou o grãde Rey da Persia Xá Abbas ...* Lisboa 1611.

Grant: – Christina Phelps Grant, *The Syrian Desert.* London 1937.

Greenlee: – W. B. Greenlee (ed.), *The Voyage of Pedro Alvares Cabral to Brazil and India.* Hakluyt Society, Sec. Ser., vol. 81. London 1938.

Haebler: – Konrad Haebler, 'Konrad Rott und die Thüringische Geselschaft', *Neues Archiv für sächsische Geschichte und Altertumskunde,* Bd. 16 (1895).

Haebler, *Fuggerschen Handlung:* – Konrad Haebler, *Die Geschichte der Fuggerschen Handlung in Spanien.* Zeitschrift für Sozial- und Wirtschaftsgeschichte, Ergänzungsheft, Sozialgeschichtliche Forschungen I. Weimar 1897.

Hakluyt: – Richard Hakluyt, *The Principal Navigations, Voyages, Traffiques and Discoveries of the English Nation,* 12 vols. Hakluyt Society, Extra Ser. Glasgow 1905–1907.

Hamilton: – Earl J. Hamilton 'The Role of Monopoly in the Overseas Expansion and Colonial Trade of Europe before 1800', *The American Economic Review, Papers and Proceedings,* 38 (1948).

Hammer: – Joseph von Hammer, *Geschichte des Osmanischen Reiches,* Bd. 4–6. Pest 1829.

Hammond: – L. D. Hammond (ed.), *Travellers in Disguise.* Cambridge Mass. 1963

Hartung & Mousnier: – Fritz Hartung & Roland Mousnier, 'Quelques problèmes concernant la monarchie absolue', *Relazioni del X Congresso Internazionale di Scienze Storiche*, IV. Firenze 1955.

Hazan: – Aziza Hazan, 'En Inde aux XVIe et XVIIe siècles: Trésors américains, monnaie d'argent et prix dans l'empire mogol', *Annales E. S. C.*, 24, 1969.

Heckscher: – Eli F. Heckscher, *Merkantilismen*. 2 vols. Stockholm 1953.

Heeringa: – K. Heeringa (ed.), *Bronnen tot de geschiedenis van den levantschen handel*, I. Rijksgeschiedkundige Publikatiën, bd. 9, s'Gravenhage 1910.

Herbert: – Thomas Herbert, *Some Yeares Travels into divers Parts of Asia and Afrique*, rev. ed. London 1638.

Hermite: – Micheline Baulant (ed.), *Lettres de négociants marseillais, les Frères Hermite 1570–1612*. Paris 1953.

Heyd, *Documents:* – Uriel Heyd, *Ottoman Documents on Palestine, 1552–1615*. Oxford 1960.

Hicks: – John Hicks, *A Theory of Economic History*. Oxford 1969.

Hierarchia Catholica Medii et Recentioris Aevi IV.

Hinz: – Walther Hinz, *Islamische Masse und Gewichte*. Handbuch der Orientalistik, ed. B. Spuler. Ergänzungsband 1, Heft 1. Leiden 1955.

Holt: – P. M. Holt, *Egypt and the Fertile Crescent 1516–1922, a Political History* London 1966.

Horst: – W. A. Horst, 'De peperhandel van de vereenigde Oostindische Compagnie', *Bijdragen voor Vaderlandsche Geschiedenis en Oudheidkunde*, 8 (1941).

Huart: – Clément Huart, *Histoire de Bagdad dans les temps modernes*. Paris 1901.

Hurstfield: – J. Hurstfield, 'Political Corruption in Modern England', *History*, 52 (1967).

Inalcik: – Halil Inalcik, 'Capital Formation in the Ottoman Empire', *Journal of Economic History*, XXIX (1969).

Ismail: – Adel Ismail, *Histoire du Liban du XVIIe siècle à nos jours, I, Le Liban au temps de Fakhr-ed-Din II (1593–1633)*. Paris 1955.

Jourdain: – William Foster (ed.), *The Journal of John Jourdain* Hakluyt Society, Sec. Ser., vol. 16. London 1905.

Jozefowicz: Zofia Jozefowicz, 'Z dziejów stosunkow polsko-perskich', *Przeglad Orientalistyczny*, 1962.

Don Juan: – G. Le Strange (ed.), *Don Juan of Persia*. London 1926.

Kellenbenz, *Le front hispano-portugais:* – Hermann Kellenbenz, 'Le front hispano-portugais contre l'Inde et le rôle d'une agence de renseignements au service de marchands allemands et flamands', *Océan Indien et Méditerranée*. Paris 1964.

Kellenbenz, *Poivre:* – Hermann Kellenbenz, 'Les frères Fugger et le marché international du poivre autour de 1600', *Annales E. S. C.*, 11 (1956).

Khachikian: – Lvon Khachikian 'Le registre d'un marchand arménien en Perse, en Inde et au Tibet (1682–1693)', *Annales E. S. C.*, 22 (1967).

van Klaveren, *Fiskalismus:* – Jacob van Klaveren, 'Fiskalismus, Merkantilismus, Korruption. Drei Aspekte der Finanz- und Wirtschaftspolitik des Ancien Regime', *Vierteljahrschrift für Sozial- und Wirtschaftsgeschichte*, 47 (1960).

van Klaveren, *Korruption:* – Jacob van Klaveren, 'Die historische Ercheinung der Korruption in ihrer Zusammenhang mit der Staats- und Gesellschaftsstruktur betrachtet', *Vierteljahrschrift für Sozial- und Wirtschaftsgischichte*, 44–45 (1957–58).

Klein: – P. W. Klein, *De Trippen en de 17e eeuw*. Assen 1965.

Klerk de Reus: – G. C. Klerk de Reus, *Geschichtlicher Überblick der administrativen, rechtlichen und finanziellen Entwicklung der Niederländisch-Oostindischen Compagnie*. Verhandelingen van het Bataviaasch Genootschap van Kunsten en Wetenschapen, XLVII. Batavia-Haag 1894.

Kogabeg: – W. F. Behrnauer (ed.), 'Kogabegs Abhandlung über den Vervall des osmanischen Staatsgebäudes seit Sultan Suleiman dem Grossen', *Zeitschrift der Deutschen morgenländischen Gesellschaft,* XV (1861).

van der Kooy: – T. P. van der Kooy, *Hollands Stapelmarkt en haar verval.* Amsterdam 1931.

Lach: – Donald F. Lach, *Asia in the Making of Europe,* I. Chicago-London 1965.

Lambert: – *Relation du sieur Cæsar Lambert de Marseille de ce qu'il a veu de plus remarcable au Caire, Alexandrie ... és années 1627, 1628 & 1632.* Relations véritables et curieuses de l'isle de Madagascar. Paris 1651.

Lane: – Frederick C. Lane, *Venice and History.* Baltimore 1966.

Lannoy & van der Linden: – Charles de Lannoy & Herman van der Linden, *Histoire de l'expansion coloniale des peuples européens,* 2 vols. Bruxelles 1907–11.

Lawes or Standing Orders: – *The Lawes or Standing Orders of the East India Company.* London 1621.

Leeuwenson: – P. A. Leupe (ed.), *Joannes Leeuwenson, Daghregister van de Landreijs ... beginnende A° 1674.* 1862.

Letters Received: – *Letters Received by the East India Company from its Servants in the East.* Ed. William Foster, 6 vols. London 1902.

van Leur: – J. C. van Leur, *Indonesian Trade and Society.* Haag-Bandung 1955.

Lewis: – Bernard Lewis, 'Some Reflections on the Decline of the Ottoman Empire', *Studia Islamica,* IX (1958).

Linhartova: – Milena Linhartova (ed.), *Epistulae et acta nuntiarum apostolicarum apud Imperatorem 1592–1608,* t. IV 1607–1611, pars 1. Prag 1932.

Linschoten: – H. Kern / H. Terpstra (ed.s), *Jan Huygen van Linschoten, Itinerario, Voyage ofte Schipvaert.* Werken uitgegeven door de Linschoten Vereeniging, 57, 58, 60. s'Gravenhage 1955–57.

Lithgow: – Willam Lithgow, *A most Delectable and True Discourse of an Admired and Painefull Peregrination.* London 1614.

Longrigg: – Stephen H. Longrigg, *Four Centuries of Modern Iraq.* Oxford 1925.

da Luz: – F. P. Mendes da Luz, *O conselho da India.* Lisboa 1952.

Mac Leod: – N. Mac Leod, *De Oost-indische Compagnie als Zeemogendheid in Azië,* 2 vols. Rijswijk 1927.

Magalhães-Godinho: – Vitorino Magalhães-Godinho, *L'économie de l'empire portugais aux XVe et XVIe siècles.* Paris 1969.

Magalhães-Gordinho, *Crises:* – Vitorino Magalhācs- Godinho, *Crises et changements géographiques et structuraux au XVIe siecle.* s. d.

Magalhães-Godinho, *Descobrimentos:* – Vitorino Magalhães-Godinho, *Os descobrimentos e a economia mundial.* Lisboa 1963.

Manrique: – C. Eckford Luard (ed.), *Travels of Fray Sebastian Manrique 1629–43.* Hakluyt Society, Sec. Ser., 59, 61. Oxford 1927.

Mansvelt: – W. M. F. Mansvelt, *Rechtsvorm en geldelijk beheer bij de Oost-indische Compagnie.* Amsterdam 1922.

Masselman: – George Masselman, *The Gradle of Colonialism.* New Haven-London 1963.

Masson: – Paul Masson, *Histoire du commerce francais dans le Levant au XVIIe siècle.* Paris 1896.

McCulloch: – J. R. McCulloch (ed.), *Early English Tracts on Commerce.* Cambridge 1954.

Meilink-Roelofsz: – M. A. P. Meilink-Roelofsz, *Asian Trade and European Influence in the Indonesian Archipelago between 1500 and about 1630.* Haag 1962.

Meilink-Roelofsz, *Aspects:* – M. A. P. Mcilink-Roelofsz, 'Aspects of Dutch Colonial Development in Asia in the Seventeenth Century', J. S. Bromley & E. H. Kossmann (ed. s), *Britain and the Netherlands in Europe and Asia.* London-New York 1968.

Meyer: – A. O. Meyer (ed.), *Die Prager Nuntiatur des Giovanni Stefano Ferreri und die Wiener Nuntiatur des Giacomo Serra, 1603–1606.* Nuntiaturberichte aus Deutschland, Abt. IV, Bd. 3. Berlin 1913.

Millard: – A. M. Millard, *Analyses of Port Books Recording Merchandises Imported into the Port of London . . . between 1588 and 1640.* Unpublished thesis, University of London.

Minorsky: – V. Minorsky (ed.), *Tadhkirat al-Muluk, a Manual of Safavid Administration.* E. J. W. Gibb Memorial Series, New Ser., XVI. London 1943.

Mocquet: – Jean Mocquet, *Voyages en Afrique, Asie, Indes Orientales et Occidentales.* Rouen 1665.

Moreland, *Aurangzeb:* – W. H. Moreland, *From Akbar to Aurangzeb.* London 1923.

Mousnier: – Roland Mousnier, *Les XVIe et XVIIe siècles.* Histoire générale des civilisations IV. Paris 1961.

Mun: – Thomas Mun, *A Discourse of Trade from England into the East Indies.* London 1621. See Mc. Culloch.

Nuovo Ramusio: – Olga Pinto (ed.), *Viaggi di C. Federici e G. Balbi alle Indie Orientale.* Il Nuovo Ramusio IV. Roma 1962.

North & Thomas: – Douglass C. North & Robert Paul Thomas 'An Economic Theory of the Growth of the Western World', *Econ. Hist. Rev.* Sec. Ser., XXIII (1970).

dall'Olmo: – *Informazione di G. dall'Olmo, Console Veneto in Lisbona (1584 18. maggio).* Venezia 1869.

Olsen: – Gunnar Olsen, *Dansk Ostindien 1616–1732.* Johannes Brøndsted (ed.), Vore gamle tropekolonier, Bd. 5. København 1967.

Opkomst: – J. K. J. de Jonge (ed.), *De opkomst van het Nederlandsch gezag in Oost-Indië.* 11 vols. Haag-Amsterdam 1862–83.

Pacifique de Provins: – *Le voyage de Perse fait par le R. P. Pacifique de Provins.* Paris 1645.

Palombini: – Barbara von Palombini, *Bündniswerben abendländischer Mächte um Persien 1453–1600.* Freiburger Islamstudien I. Wiesbaden 1968.

Parker: – John Parker, *Books to build an Empire.* Amsterdam 1965.

Pasdermadjian: – H. Pasdermadjian, *Historie de l'Arménie depuis les origines jusqu'au Traité de Lausanne.* Paris 1949.

Pastor: – Ludwig von Pastor, *Geschichte der Päpste seit dem Ausgang des Mittelalters,* XI–XII. Freiburg im Breisgau 1927.

Paz: – Julian Paz, *Archivo General de Simancas, Catalogo IV. Secretaria de Estado, Capitulaciones con Francia y negociaciones diplomaticas de los embajadores de España en aquella corte.* Madrid 1914.

Pelsaert: – W. H. Moreland & P. Geyl (ed. s), *Jahangir's India, the Remonstrantie of Francisco Pelsaert.* Cambridge 1925.

Penrose: – Boies Penrose, *The Sherleian Odyssey.* Taunton 1938.

Peschel: – O. Peschel, 'Die Handelgeschichte des Rooten Meeres', *Deutsche Vierteljahrschrift,* III (1855).

Peso Politico: – Xavier-A. Flores (ed.), *Le „Peso politico de todo el mundo" d'Anthony Sherley.* Paris 1963.

Philippus a SSma Trinitate: – Philippus a SSma Trinitate, *Orientalische Reisebeschreibung.* Frankfurt 1671.

Pigafetta: – Filippo Pigafetta, *Lettere inedite.* Nozze Sacardo – di Veco. 1855.

Plakaatboek: – J. A. van der Chijs (ed.), *Nederlandsch-Indisch Plakaatboek,* I–II. Batavia-Haag 1885–86.

432

Polanyi: – Karl Polanyi, Conrad M. Arensberg & Harry W. Pearson (eds.), *Trade and Market in the Early Empires*. Glencoe Illinois 1957.

Pontecorvo: – Virgilio Pontecorvo, 'Relazioni tra la scià 'Abbas e i granduchi di Toscana Ferdinando I e Cosimo II', *Atti della Accademia Nazionale dei Lincei*, Ser. 8, vol. IV. Roma 1949.

Posthumus: – N. W. Posthumus, *Nederlandsche Prijsgeschiedenis*, deel I. Leiden 1943.

Pribram: – A. F. Pribram, *Materialien zur Geschichte der Preise und Löhne in Österreich*. Wien 1938.

Purchas: – Samuel Purchas, *Hakluytus Posthumus or Purchas His Pilgrimes*, 20 vols. Hakluyt Society, Extra Ser. Glasgow 1905–1907.

Pyrard de Laval: – Albert Gray & H. C. P. Bell (eds.), *The Voyage of François Pyrard of Laval*. Hakluyt Society, First Ser., vol. 76, 77 & 80. London 1887–90.

Rabb: – Theodore K. Rabb, *Enterprise and Empire, Merchant and Gentry Investment in the Expansion of England 1575–1630*. Cambridge Mass. 1967.

Rabino di Borgomale; *Guilan:* – H. L. Rabino di Borgomale, *Les provinces caspiennes de la Perse, le Guilan*. Revue du monde musulman, XXXII. Paris 1917.

Rauwolf: – Leonhart Rauwolf, *Aigentliche Beschreibung der Raiss* ... Laugingen 1582.

Ravenstein: – E. G. Ravenstein (ed.), *A Journal of the First Voyage of Vasco da Gama 1497–1499*. Hakulyt Society First Ser., vol. 99. London 1898.

Riemersma: – Jelle C. Riemersma, 'Government Influence on Company Organization in Holland and England (1550–1650)', *Journal of Economic History*, Supplement X. (1950).

Roe: – William Foster (ed.), *The Embassy of Sir Thomas Roe to India, 1615–19*. London 1926.

Roemer: – H. R. Roemer, 'Die Safawiden. Ein orientalischer Bundesgenosse des Abendlandes im Türkenkampf', *Saeculum*, 4 (1953).

Ross: – E. Denison Ross, *Sir Anthony Sherley and his Persian Adventure*. London 1933.

Sanderson: – William Foster (ed.), *The Travels of John Sanderson in the Levant*. Hakluyt Society, Sec. Ser., vol. 47. London 1931.

Sassetti: – *Lettere edite ed inedite di Filippo Sassetti*. Ettore Marcucci (ed.). 1855.

Schurz: – W. L. Schurz, *The Manila Galeon*. New York 1959.

Scott: – William R. Scott, *The Constitution and Finance of English, Scottish and Irish Joint Stock Companies*, 3 vols. Cambridge 1910–12.

Sella: – Domenico Sella, *Commerci e industrie a Venezia nel secolo XVII*. Venezia-Roma 1961.

Sella, *Woollen Industry:* – Domenico Sella, 'The Rise and Fall of the Venetian Woollen Industry', Brian Pullan (ed.), *Crisis and Change in the Venetian Economy*. London 1968.

Sherley: – Anthony Sherley, *His Relation of his Travel into Persia*. London 1613.

Shirley: – E. P. Shirley, *The Sherley Brothers*. Chiswicke 1848.

Silva: – J. Gentil da Silva, *Alguns elementos para a historia do comercio da India de Portugal existentes na Biblioteca Nacional de Madrid*. Lisboa 1951.

Silva, *Contratos:* – J. Gentil da Silva, *Contratos da trazida de drogas no seculo XVI*. Lisboa 1949.

Silva, *Lettres de Lisbonne:* – J. Gentil da Silva, *Marchandises et finances, Lettres de Lisbonne 1563–1578*. 2 vols. Paris 1959–61.

Siyassi: – Ali Akbar Siyassi, *La Perse au contact de l'Occident*. Paris 1931.

Solis: – Duarte Gomes Solis, *Alegacion en favor de la compania de la India Oriental*. Moses Bensabat Amzalak (ed.). Lisboa 1955.

Steensgaard, *Consuls and Nations:* – Niels Steensgaard, 'Consuls and Nations in the Levant from 1570 to 1650', Scandinavian Economic History Review, XV (1967).

Steensgaard, *European Shipping:* – Niels Steensgaard, 'European Shipping to Asia 1497–1700', *Scandinavian Economic History Review*, XVIII (1970).

Steensgaard, *Freight Costs:* – Niels Steensgaard, 'Freight Costs in the English East India Trade 1601–1657', *Scandinavian Economic History Review*, XIII (1965).

Stevens: – Henry Stenvens (ed.), *The Dawn of British Trade to the East Indies as Recorded in the Court Minutes of the East India Company 1599–1603.* 2d imp. London 1967.

Stripling: – G. W. F. Stripling, *The Ottoman Turks and the Arabs 1511–74.* Illinois Studies in the Social Sciences, vol. XXVI no. 4. Urbana 1942.

Sykes: – Percy M Sykes, *A History of Persia.* 3d ed. 2 vols. London 1930.

Tavernier: – Jean-Baptiste Tavernier, *Les six voyages.* 2 vols. Paris 1682.

Tectander: – Georg Tectander von der Jabel, *Kurtze und wahrhafftige Beschreibung der Reiss von Prag aus . . . bis an den königlichen Hoff in Persien.* Leipzig 1608.

Tenenti: – Alberto Tenenti, *Venezia e i corsari.* Bari 1961.

Terpstra: – H. Terpstra, *De opkomst der Westerkwartieren van de Oost-Indische Compagnie.* Haag 1918.

Terpstra, *Voorcompagnieën:* – H. Terpstra, 'De nederlandsche voorcompagnieën', *Geschiedenis van Nederlandsch Indië*, II. Amsterdam 1938.

Texeira: – W. F. Sinclair & D. Ferguson (ed.), *The Travels of Pedro Texeira.* Hakluyt Society, Sec. Ser., vol. 9. London 1902.

Valentijn: – Fr. Valentijn, *Oud en Nieuw Oost-Indien,* t. I. Dordrecht-Amsterdam 1724.

della Valle, *Conditioni:* – Pietro della Valle, *Delle conditioni di Abbas Re di Persia.* Venezia 1628.

della Valle, *India:* – Edward Grey (ed.), *The Travels of Pietro della Valle in India.* Hakluyt Society, First Ser., vol. 84–85 London 1892.

della Valle, *Persia:* – Pietro della Valle, *Viaggi,* 2 vols. Roma 1650–1658.

della Valle, *Ritorno:* – Pietro della Valle, *Viaggi . . . parte terza cioé l'India, co'l ritorno alla Patria.* Venezia 1663.

Vasquez de Prada: – V. Vasquez de Prada, *Lettres marchandes d'Anvers,* I. Paris 1960.

Vecchietti: – Ugo Tucci (ed.), 'Una relazione di G. B. Vecchietti sulla Persia', *Oriente Moderno*, 35 (1955).

Wätjen: – H. Wätjen, *Die Niederländer im Mittelmeergebiet zur Zeit ihrer höchsten Machtstellung.* Abhandlungen zur Verkehrs und Seegeschichte, Bd. 2. Berlin 1909.

van der Wee: – Herman van der Wee, *The Growth of the Antwerp Market and the European Economy.* 1963.

Wicki: – J. Wicki (ed.), *Documenta Indica.* 7 vols. Roma 1948–62.

Willan: – T. S. Willan, 'Some Aspects of English Trade with the Levant in the Sixteenth Century', *English Historical Review*, 70 (1955).

Wilson: – A. Wilson, *The Persian Gulf.* London 1928.

Wood: – Alfred C. Wood, *A History of the Levant Company.* London 1964.

Zeller: – Gaston Zeller, 'Une légende qui a la vie dure, les capitulations de 1535', *Revue d'histoire moderne et contemporaine*, II (1955).

Index of names and places

435

437